Writing Baseball

THE SOUTHERN ILLINOIS UNIVERSITY PRESS SERIES

Other Books in the Writing Baseball Series

THE NATIONAL GAME

Series Editor's Note

Unlike Albert G. Spalding's *America's National Game*, which was written as a story of baseball's beginnings and not as a history of baseball, Alfred H. Spink's *The National Game* was published as "a faithful and accurate history of baseball, a history extending from the very time the game was played up to the present moment." Spink's *The National Game*, which first appeared in 1910, a year before the publication of Spalding's book, was also meant to be the first total baseball book, both history and encyclopedia "with an addenda each year, so that the happenings of the game from its commencement up to the ever present period may be chronicled and kept close at hand."

For our Writing Baseball series, we have reprinted the second and enlarged edition of *The National Game*, published in 1911. The second edition, expanded by over fifty pages, not only updates and increases the hundreds of biographical sketches and the nearly two hundred photographs present in the first edition, but it also adds a number of new stories and items including *How to Play Baseball*, a booklet that contains essays attributed to such baseball luminaries as Cy Young, Napoleon Lajoie, Hugh Jennings, and Fred Clarke. In our reprint, we add a foreword by Steven P. Gietschier of *The Sporting News* and, as an aid to readers, a new index prepared by Skip McAfee of the Society for American Baseball Research. Other than these additions and a few minor alterations, we have preserved the original state of the book, including any possible historical inaccuracies.

Often reprinted, Spalding's story of baseball continues to entertain and influence our understanding of early baseball history, but Spink's *The National Game*, despite its extensive documentation, its richly drawn sketches of the pioneers of baseball, and its amazing gallery of photographs, has become so rare that even *The Sporting News* library lacks a copy of the second edition. While Spink's hope for an ever expanding publication of *The National Game* proved vain after the 1911 edition, the book merits, because of its value as a history of baseball, a better fate than that of a rare find for baseball collectors. It also deserves recognition as perhaps the first real attempt at a standard history of baseball.

—Richard Peterson

THE
SECOND EDITION
NATIONAL
GAME

Alfred H. Spink

With a Foreword by Steven P. Gietschier

Southern Illinois University Press
Carbondale and Edwardsville

Series editor's note and foreword copyright © 2000 by the Board of Trustees,
    Southern Illinois University
First edition published 1910 by The National Game Publishing Co.
Second edition published 1911
Writing Baseball series edition published 2000 by Southern Illinois University Press
Printed in the United States of America
03 02 01 00   4 3 2 1

The publisher gratefully acknowledges the cooperation of the University of Illinois at
Urbana-Champaign Libraries and the St. Louis Mercantile Library at the University of
Missouri-St. Louis in providing the text of *The National Game* that was used for the
present edition.

Library of Congress Cataloging-in-Publication Data

Spink, Alfred H. (Alfred Henry), b. 1853.
    The national game / by Alfred H. Spink.
        p. cm. — (Writing baseball)
    Originally published: 2nd ed. St. Louis, Mo. : National Game Pub. Co., 1911.
    Includes index.
    1. Baseball—United States—History—19th century.
    2. Baseball—United States—History—20th century. I. Title. II. Series.
    GV863.A1 S743 2000
    796.357'0973—dc21
    ISBN 0-8093-2304-4 (paper : alk. paper)   99-046257

The paper used in this publication meets the minimum requirements of American
National Standard for Information Sciences—Permanence of Paper for Printed Library
Materials, ANSI Z39.48-1992. ∞

Writing Baseball Series Editor: Richard Peterson

DEDICATION

I dedicate this book to the professional base ball players of America, to the silent army, to the force that is in the field to-day, and to the legions that are to follow in years to come.

I want this book to live forever, so that the names of those who helped to build up and make base ball the greatest of outdoor sports may never be forgotten.

It is my sincere wish that this history of the National Game shall be continued for all time, with an addenda each year, so that the happenings of the game from its commencement up to the ever present period may be chronicled and kept close at hand.

Alfred H. Spink.

THE NATIONAL GAME

PRICE, $1.50

A HISTORY of baseball, America's leading out-door sport, from the time it was first played up to the present day, with illustrations and biographical sketches of the great players who helped to bring the game into the prominence it now enjoys.

BY

ALFRED H. SPINK

The National Game Publishing Company

312 CHESTNUT STREET
SAINT LOUIS, MISSOURI

CONTENTS

Photographs following

CHARLES A. COMISKEY.
President and Owner of the Chicago White Stockings.

BANCROFT B. JOHNSON.
President of the American League.

ALFRED J. REACH.
President of the A. J. Reach Company of Philadelphia.

A. G. SPALDING.
Head of the A. G. Spalding & Bros. Sporting Goods Company.

C. H. EBBETS.
President Brooklyn National League Club.

HORACE S. FOGEL.
President of the Philadelphia National League Club.

THOMAS J. LYNCH.
President of the National League.

AUGUST HERRMANN.
President of the Cincinnati National League Club.

XIII

WILLIAM MACDONALD SPINK.
St. Louis' first real baseball editor.

W. M. RANKIN.
Dean of New York Baseball Writers.

JOHN A. HEYDLER.
Secretary-Treasurer of the National League.

ROBERT McROY.
Secretary of the American League.

GEORGE TEBEAU.
President Kansas City American Association Club.

CHARLES S. HAVENOR.
President Milwaukee American Association Club.

CHRISTOPHER MATHEWSON
New York Nationals

CHARLES WEBB MURPHY.
President Chicago National League Club.

ADRIAN C. ANSON.
The old commander of the Chicago White Stockings.

XXIII.

HARRY DAVIS.
Commander of the present World's Champion Athletics of Philadelphia.

XXIV.

JACK BARRY.
The Famous Shortstop of the World's Champion Athletics of Philadelphia.
XXV.

JAMES E. SULLIVAN.
President American Sports Publishing Company.

T. M. CHIVINGTON.
President American Association.

HENRY CHADWICK.
The Father of Baseball.

HARRY PULLIAM.
Late President of the National League.

WILLIAM SULLIVAN.
The Great Catcher of the Chicago White Sox.

XXX.

FRED TENNEY.
Manager Boston National League Team.

JOHN C. CHAPMAN.
Famous as Left Fielder of the Atlantics of Brooklyn.

XXXII.

M. E. CANTILLON.
President Minneapolis Club of the American Association.

GEORGE MUNSON.
For Years Secretary of the St. Louis Browns

JACK RYAN.
St. Louis' Champion Baseball Fan.

EDWARD SCHOENBORN.
President Columbus Club of the American Association. From a Recent Photo by Baker of Columbus, Ohio.

WILLIAM GRAYSON, JR.
(President of the Louisville Club of the American Association.

W. R. ARMOUR,
President Toledo Club of the American Association.

W. H. WATKINS.
President of the Indianapolis Club of the American Association.

ROBERT LEE HEDGES.
President St. Louis American League Club.

M. S. ROBISON.
Late President St. Louis National League Club.

T. P. SULLIVAN.
One of the Real Builders of Baseball. From a Very Recent Photograph of the
Veteran Manager.

GEORGE WRIGHT.
Famous Shortfielder of the Cincinnati Reds of 1869, As He Looks Today.

E. A. STEININGER.
President St. Louis National League Club in 1911.

XLIV

THOMAS C. NOYES.
President Washington American League Club, 1911.

JOHN T. BRUSH.
President and Owner of the New York National League Club.

JOHN J. McGRAW.
Manager New York National League Club.

CHARLES SOMERS.
President Cleveland American League Club.

THOMAS J. LOFTUS.
Captain of the St. Louis Reds in the Sixties.

BARNEY DREYFUS.
President Pittsburg National League Club.

FRED CLARKE.
Manager of the Pittsburg National League Club in 1911.

TYRUS COBB.
The Greatest Player in the American League in 1911.

JOHN P. (HANS) WAGNER.
The Greatest Player in the National League in 1911.

JOHN McNEARY.
Who Owned and Managed the St. Louis Reds in the Seventies.

FRANK McNEARY.
Who With His Brothers Thomas and John Owned The St. Louis Reds in The
Eighties.

JOHN E. BRUCE.
Secretary The National Commission in 1911.

CHRIS VON DER AHE.
President of the St. Louis Browns When They Were Called Four Time Winners.

JOHN I. TAYLOR.
President Boston American League Club, 1911.

WALTER JOHNSON.
The Great Pitcher of the Washington American League Club in 1911.

BEN MULFORD.
The Cincinnati Base Ball Writer Who Has Done Much For Base Ball.

ALFRED H. SPINK.
Author of The National Game and Founder of the Sporting News, Now the
Greatest Baseball Paper.

FOREWORD

Steven P. Gietschier

About the time Union soldiers were introducing the game they called Base Ball to the Confederate South, the Spink family immigrated to the United States from Canada. William Spink, at one time a Quebec legislator, and his wife, Frances Woodbury Spink, together with their eight children, settled on the west side of Chicago. The elder Spink boys, Frederick, William, and Alfred—Charles was but a baby—brought with them a Canadian enthusiasm for cricket, but they soon became devoted to the game already dubbed the National Pastime. As they grew older, the Spinks played on one of Chicago's prominent amateur teams, the Mutuals, named after the famous New York nine bankrolled by Boss Tweed. Frederick Spink became a businessman and later served as adjutant general under Illinois governor John Peter Altgeld, but his three brothers parlayed their youthful interest in baseball into colorful and varied careers.

The second Spink son, known as Billy, had become a telegraph operator while still a teenager in Quebec. He carried this expertise from Chicago to St. Louis, working for Western Union, but lost his job when the telegraphers union of which he was secretary went on strike. Vowing never again to work for the company that dismissed him, Billy entered the newspaper business, where he could use his telegraphic skills, first in Cincinnati and then back in St. Louis for the *Globe-Democrat*. According to his brother Al, who boasted of his sibling's accomplishments in *The National Game*, Billy persuaded his editor to introduce sports coverage to the *Globe-Democrat*, coverage that he often wrote himself. "'Billy' Spink was, in fact," wrote Al, "the best all around sporting writer of his day, if not the best all around sporting editor that ever lived."

Alfred Henry Spink, the third son, joined his older brother in St. Louis and became a journalist too, probably with Billy's encouragement. He worked for the *St. Louis Post* about the time Joseph Pulitzer was merging it with the *Dispatch* and later became sports editor of the *Missouri Republican* and then of the *St. Louis Chronicle*. The brothers used their positions to promote amateur and professional baseball and worked to restore the game's image after the city's National League club was tainted by a gambling scandal. For financial support when funds ran low, Al turned to a German immigrant saloonkeeper, Chris Von der Ahe, the man generally credited with making the connection between baseball and beer. Von der Ahe became "Der Poss Bresident" of the St. Louis Browns, a team that entered a new major league, the American Association, when it began play in 1882.

Al served the Browns as secretary and press agent and was at least partially responsible for hiring the players who won four straight Association pennants starting in 1885. Despite this success, a year after the Browns' first pennant win Al left the team to start a weekly newspaper devoted entirely to sports. Perhaps he was motivated by his friend Pulitzer's assertion that "given a good business manager and an editor who can really write, any newspaper should fast become a good paying institution." Or perhaps he was encouraged that there was only one other national sports publication extant, *The Sporting Life*, and that in faraway Philadelphia. At any rate, *The Sporting News*, eight pages long, hit the streets for the first time on St. Patrick's Day, 1886.

The Sporting News was an immediate success, so much so that Al soon summoned his youngest brother, Charles Claude Spink, to abandon a homesteading venture in South Dakota for an offer of fifty dollars a week as business manager. As the story is told, Charles arrived in St. Louis with ten dollars in his pocket. Al promptly borrowed the money and bought his brother dinner with it. Charles was not the great baseball fan that Al was, but he certainly was a business manager to fit Pulitzer's mold. He skillfully solicited advertising, mailed each edition to all sections of the country, and sent unsold copies to newsdealers as samples. Moreover, he got several minor leagues to name *The Sporting News* as their "official organ," thereby cementing its place, even at a young age, in the baseball establishment.

In 1890, *The Sporting News* took an editorial position supporting the Players League, a one-season effort to wrest control of the professional game from the owners, and fell on economic hard times when the league collapsed. Simultaneously, Al was losing interest in his creation and turning his attention from baseball to his other love, the theater. He wrote and produced a play, *The Derby Winner*, that required a cast of forty-two persons (including Tod Sloan, later a famous jockey) and six horses. A moderate hit in St. Louis, the play flopped monumentally on the road. Al was wiped out financially, and Charles bought up *Sporting News* stock that Al had pledged as collateral for loans he could not repay. Al then tried homesteading in the Dakotas with his nephew Ernest Lanigan, later a prominent baseball statistician, and when he returned to the family business, he did so as an employee.

Al wrote about horse racing and boxing and baseball. He lampooned his old boss, Von der Ahe, now the owner of the National League Cardinals, for turning his ballpark, Sportsman's Park, into a Coney Island–like sideshow complete with rides, a Wild West show, an all-girl band, and betting pools. Von der Ahe was driven from the game, and Al, no doubt resentful and jealous of his brother, left *The Sporting News* around the turn of the century. He operated two race tracks in St. Louis for a while and then liquidated these interests to found the *St. Louis World*, a generally unprofitable newspaper that lasted about a decade. He turned to writing books, publishing the first edition of *The National Game* in 1910 and the three-volume

Spink Sport Stories: 1000 Big and Little Ones in 1921.

Al sued his brother over the loss of his *Sporting News* stock in 1913, but the suit was never tried. The brothers reconciled, fortunately, for Charles died suddenly at age fifty-one on April 22, 1914, after attending the home opener of the St. Louis Terriers in the upstart Federal League. Control of *The Sporting News* passed to Charles's son, J. G. Taylor Spink, who prevailed upon his uncle to write a moving tribute to his late brother. Uncle and nephew remained in contact, Al once writing Taylor a letter strewn with pithy advice and signing it "Dad." Al Spink died in Chicago on May 27, 1928. His eulogy was delivered by Judge Kenesaw Mountain Landis, the commissioner of baseball.

August 1999

THE NATIONAL GAME
Second and Enlarged and Revised Edition.
September, 1911.

When in October, 1910, the first edition of The National Game made its appearance it marked the initial endeavor to present a faithful and accurate history of baseball, a history extending from the very time the game was first played up to the present moment

The book met with a tremendous sale. In no time all of the first edition was exhausted

Its publishers were so elated at the wonderful demand for the book that work was immediately started on a new and revised edition.

It is this book that is presented in the accompanying pages.

Before referring to the new book it may be well at this time to refer to the original volume, to the things that helped make the real demand for it and that really led to the getting out of this second and revised edition.

The first lift the book received was at the December meeting of the major leagues in New York City in December, 1911.

At the American League meeting held at that time at the Hotel Walcott in New York City, the author of this book was called before the gathering, advised that his work was appreciated and a magnificent order for several hundred copies of the book was given him.

President Johnson of the American League, President Comiskey of the Chicago White Sox, President Hedges of the St. Louis Browns, President Taylor of the Boston Reds, President Somers of the Cleveland Naps, President Shibe of the World's Champion Athletics of Philadelphia, President Navin of the Detroit Tigers, President Farrell of the New York Highlanders and Manager James R. McAleer, who was there representing the Washington American League Club, all personally congratulated the author of The National Game on his work and showed a desire to make the book a permanent fixture in the literature of baseball by their kindly words and a substantial financial offering.

Their great kindness and liberality was the first real recognition the book received and assured its future.

At the Hotel Breslin where the National League men were in session the author of this book received a warm reception at the hands of President Thomas J. Lynch, Secretary John A. Heydler and other members of the National League.

Big-hearted Garry Herrmann, the brainy president of the Cincinnati National League Club, and president of the National Commission, congratulated the author of The National Game personally on the great work he had done for baseball and added to this congratulation an order for one hundred copies of the book.

Mr. Herrmann called attention to the fact that this book contained a complete history of the National League and paid honest and faithful and accurate tribute to each of its members.

As though to vie with the members of the American League in paying honorable tribute and extending the great hand of good=fellowship and kindness to the author of this work, the presidents of the clubs of the American Association at their meeting held at the Hotel Congress at Chicago outdid themselves in this direction.

There was present at this meeting representatives of the eight clubs of the American Association as follows:

Milwaukee—President Charles S. Havenor and Manager Barrett.
St. Paul—President George E. Lennon and Manager Mike Kelly.
Minneapolis—President M. E. Cantillon and Manager Joe Cantillon.
Louisville—President William Grayson and Manager Del Howard.
Kansas City—President George Tebeau.
Columbus—President E. M. Schoenborn and Secretary Bobby Quinn.
Toledo—President William Armour and Secretary George Wild.
Indianapolis—President W. H. Watkins.
And Thomas M. Chivington, President of the American Association.

Each and every one of the above gentlemen congratulated the author of The National Game on the work he had done for baseball and like the American League, every one of the American Association presidents sub=scribed for hundreds of copies of the book. Their splendid recognition of this work added to the previous action of the American League officials and Garry Herrmann, of the National League was an additional incentive to make this book the permanent and lasting volume it is today.

It also proved that the American Association is composed of men having some real sentiment and love of the sport in them as well as the brain and intelligence to soon place their organization in a position where it will be looked on as the peer of any baseball league in America.

The National Game, being a complete history of baseball, the only real history of the game ever written, will from this time forward be recognized as the only standard work of this character and it is, therefore, only right and proper that all acts of the men who helped build it up and pre-serve its pages should be recorded.

One of the first kindnesses shown the author of this work was at the meeting of the National Association of Baseball Clubs, held at Hotel Congress in Chicago on November 16, 1910.

President Sexton then and there announced that a resolution had been drawn up thanking the press for the excellent manner in which the meeting had been reported. The resolution was as follows:

"Whereas, baseball has been recognized as the national sport in which both old and young may engage, and which furnishes more wholesome entertainment to the American people than all other sports combined and,

"Whereas, the members of the press generally and special writers have educated the public up to a proper appreciation of the sport; therefore be it

"Resolved, That our thanks be extended to the members of the daily press and to the special writers who contribute thereto (to name them all would be impossible), and that our thanks and indorsements be extended to the Sporting News and the Sporting Life and to Mr. A. H. Spink for having written his book entitled 'The National Game' which is heartily recommended to the baseball loving public as the standard authority on baseball."

At other meetings of other baseball associations, too numerous to mention compliments like the above were paid the author of this book.

In length of service, in long and arduous endeavor, in connection with the writing up and reporting of professional baseball games, the author of this book will admit of but one genuine rival, and that is William M. Rankin, for years associated with Henry Chadwick, "the Father of the Game." Having had access to the records of Mr. Chadwick and being for nearly half a century associated with the first and then the later corps of professional baseball players, Mr. Rankin has had far greater opportunity than I to follow the game's progress and to keep an accurate record of its doings.

When this book was first issued, therefore, one of the first copies of it was forwarded to Mr. Rankin, and on receipt of it he sent a letter of which this is a facsimile:

THE NEW YORK CLIPPER

Established 1855

The Frank Queen Pub. Co., Ltd.
Albert J. Borie,
Editorial and Business Manager.

**THE OLDEST
AMERICAN
THEATRICAL
JOURNAL**

47 West 28th Street

New York Feb. 1, 1911

My dear Al

Acknowledge the receipt of an advance copy of your history of baseball, and will say that it is the best and most complete one that has ever been issued. It is so good that one wonders why any of the preceding ones was ever written, for they appear to have been a mere waste of energy, as none of them contain such an amount of valuable information as is to be found in your book. Your work has been so correctly and tastefully executed that it should appeal to and be appreciated by every one in any way interested in our great national game of baseball, and no one who admires the game should be without a copy of it. You have covered the field so thoroughly that there doesn't appear to be a feature that can complain of being slighted. You have imparted tone and quality and better still the realism necessary to leave nothing to the imagination. And it is free of that method so peculiar to the fakir, which is a blessing to all who deplore such means of deceiving the people, whether "It is only a simple little good-natured game" or a lie, pure and simple. It's the same. I am.

Yours very truly,

W. M. Rankin

Later I wrote to Mr. Rankin and asked him to go over the book carefully, for I figured that his keen eye would detect many inaccuracies not visible to one not so well informed. Pursuant to my request, therefore, Mr. Rankin went over the book carefully from end to end, made many corrections and additions and also sent in a story of his own, giving sketches of the men he had known in his time as writers of baseball. To Mr. Rankin therefore, I am indebted in a great measure for the labor of revising this book, and especially for the kindly and generous spirit he has shown towards this work; a spirit that I think should come from all who love the game for its own sake and who are not wholly absorbed in the money-making end of it.

The National Game having been written and revised by the two oldest writers of baseball living, it is now fairly and squarely entitled to a place in every bonafide library in America and this includes all the school libraries of this country, for the curriculum of no place of education can possibly be complete without a knowledge of a game recognized by every great college and school in the land as the National Game of America.

But the book, besides being recognized by the leading baseball associations as the standard work on baseball, has been pronounced by veterans and other prominent baseball presidents and officials, the only history of baseball ever published. From letters received from baseball men the country over congratulating me on my work in writing and circulating this book I clip the following:

Ban B. Johnson, the brainy, live and up-to-date president of the American League and considered the most powerful and influential man connected with baseball—Please accept my sincere thanks for the handsomely bound copy of "The National Game," your latest and best contribution to baseball literature. I found its early chapters so interesting and instructive that I feel safe in asserting that you have written the standard history of America's most attractive and popular pastime. The American League at its annual meeting held in New York on December 14, 1911, by a unanimous vote endorsed "The National Game," the history of baseball prepared by you as the standard work on baseball and in recognition of the quality of your work, all the club presidents subscribed for a liberal number of the books. I also subscribed for one hundred copies. With kindest regards and best wishes, etc.

T. J. Lynch, president of the National League of Professional Baseball Clubs—Many thanks for the copy of "The National Game," which you sent me. I trust your book will prove a great success. Please accept my thanks for your kind words of endorsement.

Charles A. Comiskey, president and owner of the Chicago White Sox—The baseball world will ever be indebted to you for "The National Game," the only real and complete history of baseball ever written. The task must have been a great one, and for your reward you deserve the unstinted thanks of all interested in the building up of the greatest of all games. The American League is with you to a man.

Charles W. Murphy, president Chicago National League Club—I have a copy of your book, "The National Game," and wish to thank you very much for your kindness in sending it to me. At the same time I want to express my appreciation of your work, in acknowledging receipt of the book and to say that you have done a mighty good thing for baseball in the preparation of this volume.

A. J. Reach, president of the A. J. Reach Sporting Goods Company of Philadelphia—"The National Game" is the best history of baseball ever published. No baseball man's library is complete without it.

Charles H. Ebbets, president Brooklyn National League Club—Permit me to thank you for the copy of "The National Game," which I found awaiting me with your kindest and best wishes upon my return from the World's Series. From a hasty glance through its pages I imagine that it fills a long-felt want for the baseball fans of this country. I expect to read it from cover to cover during the winter months.

George Wright, president of the Wright & Ditson Sporting Goods Company of Boston and shortfielder and captain of the Cincinnati Reds in 1869—"The National Game" is the best book on baseball from its early days to date that has been published.

James E. Sullivan, president of the American Sports Company—I want to congratulate you on "The National Game." It is the best book ever; no question about it. It is the standard work on baseball. The book is a good one, and I congratulate you on it. It shows work and a knowledge of the game that few men possess.

T. P. Sullivan—You have written the only real history of baseball ever published. You have given the actual facts in connection with the game; you have given credit where credit was due. The book will live long after you and stand as a monument to the hard and honest work you did to build up the game in its early days and when it needed just such friends as you. I hope the rich and influential baseball men will join the rest in making your book the success it deserves to be.

David J. Davis, sporting editor Pittsburg Dispatch—Permit me to congratulate you on the success which has attended your efforts to give people of this great and glorious land a complete, and at the same time, unburdensome, handbook of baseball. I have gone through your volume with care, and I am free to confess that never before have I encountered such a complete work of this kind. The sporting writers, as well as the fans of the United States, owe you unstinted thanks. While there have been many other efforts along the same line, I know that there has never before been anything produced which even approached your work in point of completeness and lucidity of detail.

Jacob C. Morse, editor Boston Baseball Magazine—I want to thank you very cordially for your kindness in sending me the copy of "The National Game." It is all right and I congratulate you with all my heart for your success in giving to the baseball world the most interesting work of its kind ever written. It is a work that everybody will want to read from beginning to end. The illustrations are A1 and add a great deal to the excellence of the publication. You ought to meet with unqualified success with the work, and you may be assured that I will boost it for all I am worth in this section.

A hundred other letters just like these have been received but space forbids mention of them.

In this second edition of the book will be found many lines not in the first book, notably the story of the Baseball Writers Association of America, written by William G. Weart, baseball editor of the Philadelphia Evening Telegraph; a story of "Baseball Writers Prominent in Their Day," by W. M. Rankin, the veteran baseball editor of the New York Clipper; an interview with Charles A. Comiskey, president and owner of the Chicago American League Club, who compares the World's Champion teams of twenty-five years ago to the World's Champion teams of the present day; a story of the fun of the game including the poems, "Casey at the Bat" and "Casey's Revenge;" a story about the great umpires of the past and present and a great deal of other interesting baseball matter, nearly all of which will be found on the last pages of this book.

ALFRED H. SPINK.

THE NATIONAL GAME

THE NATIONAL GAME.

A HISTORY OF BASEBALL, AMERICA'S LEADING OUTDOOR SPORT.

BY ALFRED H. SPINK.

October, 1910.

* * *

Walking along Broadway in St. Louis one day in the summer of 1907, a friend stopped to ask me:

"Have you a history of baseball?

"Has such a book ever been written?

"If one has, won't you get me a copy?"

The next day I wrote to Henry Chadwick, then the dean of New York's corps of baseball writers. I had known Mr. Chadwick for many years. If a history of the National Game had ever been written surely he would know of it.

"If you or Al Wright (another veteran baseball writer of New York City) have ever written a history of the National Game, send me a copy of the book or tell me where I can get it," I wrote to Mr. Chadwick. He replied:

"A history of the National Game has yet to be written. No one here has gotten up anything of that sort and all the old records of the game left by Al Wright have disappeared from the Clipper office.

"If a history of the National Game is to be written, covering its life from the beginning up to the present period it is up to you to write it.

"I know of no one else capable of the task. When I say this I mean that no one can write a history of the game except one who has followed it from its first real beginning, who is familiar with the battles it has had and who understands all its curves and tangents.

"The task, too, will have to be accomplished by a writer able to weave a consecutive and detailed story and who is capable of telling it interestingly and intelligently. I therefore with all of these ideas at hand see no one so fit for the task as you and in making this statement I consider not only your ability as a writer but the active and aggressive part you have taken in building up minor and major leagues and helping the game in every way to increase its areas and become the greatest and most widely known outdoor sport in the world. Having played the game as well as written about it, you are doubly equipped for the great task. Myself and the entire fraternity of baseball writers I am sure will, if you set to work, do all in their power to help you make the work an interesting one and one that will go down in the history of the ages as the only standard work of its kind in existence."

It was this letter that spurred me on to the task of performing this work, i. e., writing a history of the National Game and preserving a record of its earliest days, a record which should be kept if only to tell of the splendid and honorable work of the pioneers of the game who laid the foundation for the great baseball edifice which to-day rears its head so proudly in all corners of the land.

Henry Chadwick, the father of the game, died on April 20, 1908. I had always looked to him to do the work which I am trying to do here, but he having failed I will try in my poor way to gather up the lost threads and place them together.

And out of this flotsam and jetsom I hope to weave a history that while perhaps lacking here and there in unity and certain detail will be found to cover all the great

1

THE NATIONAL GAME.

happenings of the game since it was first played up to the present moment.

THE COMMENCEMENT.

I will not spend much time in referring to the birth of baseball.

The first record we have of it being played was in the New England States in 1830, which would make the game nearly eighty years old.

The game played in New England at this time much resembled the old game of "town ball" played in England more than a century ago.

THE FIRST DIAMOND.

The players used a square field instead of a diamond as now. The ball weighed but three ounces and was thrown to the bat. The bases were four wooden posts standing four feet high.

The batsman stood in a space four feet square, located between the first and fourth base posts, the field of play forming a square with sixty-foot sides. The thrower—the pitcher now—stood in a space thirty-five feet from the batsman's position. A base runner, while running to the base, if hit by a thrown ball was out.

The sides were made up of from ten to fourteen players. The rule of play was one out all out. The score was 100 tallies up, the side first scoring 100 runs being the winner.

This in fact was the style of baseball played in New England eighty years ago.

THEN CAME PHILADELPHIA'S CLAIM.

Like the people of New England, the Philadelphia folks claim to have been the first to have played baseball in this country.

According to the people of the Quaker City, baseball is now only seventy-six years old and the first games in this country were played in Philadelphia in 1833 by the Olympics of Philadelphia which, according to these same claimants, was the first baseball club ever organized in this country.

The Olympics of Philadelphia played about the same game as was played in 1830 by the New England clubs and the sport was known there as in New England as "town ball."

In this "town ball" game the runner was out when touched or when the ball reached a base ahead of him.

The game at this time consisted of twenty-one counts or aces, but at the conclusion an equal number of hands had to be played.

Every baseball score of a completed game had a "21" in it, for instead of playing nine innings, as they do to-day, the rule was that the team which had scored 21 runs when both sides had had an equal number of innings, was the winner.

THEN THE KNICKERBOCKER.

This town ball game was in vogue until 1845, when the old Knickerbocker Baseball Club of New York modified the rules of play and formulated a new game entirely, which, for several years, was known as "The New York Game" in contradistinction to "town ball," then known as the Massachusetts game.

The Knickerbocker Club changed the form of the town ball square field to that of the diamond field; and introduced base bags in the place of posts; they also enlarged the size of the ball to six and a quarter ounces in weight and ten inches in circumference and added two and a half ounces of rubber to the composition of the ball.

They also prohibited throwing the ball to the bat, and substituted the square pitch, and they made nine innings a full game. They also allowed a catch of a fair ball on the bound to put the batsman out.

THE FIRST MATCH GAME.

The first regular match game of baseball, under the above rules, of which there is any record was played in New York City on June 19th, 1846, the Knickerbocker and New York clubs being the contestants. The latter won by 23 to 1 in four hands or innings.

So little interest was then taken in the game that it was not until five years later that another match game was played June 3, 1851, being the day on which the Knickerbockers of New York defeated the Washingtons in an eight-inning game by 21 to 11.

The rules which governed the playing of the clubs at this early period differed somewhat from those now in force, but they covered really all the main points of the game as it is now played.

The main distinction was in the liberty given to the players, for the pitcher could move as he liked provided he did not overstep his boundary line, which was forty-five feet from the batsman and the batsman was required only to stand back of his six-foot line crossing the home base.

On the other hand the pitcher could send the ball in only by a square pitch or toss.

These crude rules governed the New York game up to the time of the organization of the first National Association in 1857 just a little over fifty years ago.

Baseball of that period was played under an authorized code of rules. The association rules, though far superior to the old Knickerbocker Club rules, were nevertheless crude and incomplete.

The ball played with was too heavy and large and also too elastic. The pitching gave every chance to the batsman. The pitcher was forced to deliver fair balls to the bat, while the batsman could refuse to strike at good balls. In a game at Bedford in the early sixties, between the Atlantics and Mutuals, Al Smith of the Atlantics pitched

THE NATIONAL GAME.

over fifty balls to McKeever before a strike was called.

The advance of the game from the time it was played in this crude way up to the present time is a most interesting story.

It has come up from an originally crude form and unorganized state to a scientific perfection which seemingly leaves room for little further improvement, and to a basis of business methods which insures to it a lasting existence as an organized sport.

THE FIRST REAL NINE.

The first regularly recognized baseball club was the Knickerbocker of New York which was formed in the autumn of 1845.

At least it was that club which first used basemen in fielding out runners instead of hitting the latter with the thrown ball.

The Knickerbockers were followed by many other clubs in and around New York. In 1857 and 1860 clubs were organized at Boston and Philadelphia, and the game lost its local nature,

In 1857 the numerous clubs, which by this time had sprung up in New York, Brooklyn and in the vicinity thereabout "got together" and adopted a system of rules to govern their play.

For some years the Knickerbockers had the game almost to themselves, but in 1852 the Gotham Club took the field.

Two years later the Eagle and Empire clubs came into existence. These four clubs were the only ones playing regularly around New York until the Putnams and Baltics joined them in 1856.

THE FIRST BASEBALL CONVENTION.

Then other clubs formed so rapidly around New York City that a call for a convention to formulate a code of playing rules was sent out.

This convention—the first of its kind—met at Smith's Hall, 426 Broome street, New York, January 22, 1857.

At this convention the following clubs were represented by three delegates each: Knickerbocker, Gotham, Eagle, Empire, Putnam, Baltic, Excelsior, Atlantic, Harmony, Harlem, Eckford, Bedford, Nassau, Continental, Union and Olympic.

Here were taken the first steps to draft a regular set of rules for the playing of the game and here the National Association of Baseball Players was formed.

THE FIRST REGULAR ORGANIZATION.

It was the first regular baseball organization ever put together, but it accomplished many great things.

Then and there the diamond, whose shape in all these years has never changed, was drawn and a set of rules was drafted to govern the playing on the diamond and the ground surrounding it.

With the adoption of the regular set of rules baseball teams of some prominence sprang up all over the country.

On March 10th, following, (1858) the second convention was held in New York City, at which the number of clubs represented was twenty-five, or nine more than had sent delegates to the first meeting in New York.

At this convention a committee was appointed to draw up a constitution and by-laws, and "The National Association of Baseball Players" was organized.

THE FIRST ANNUAL MEETING.

The second annual meeting of this association was held at Cooper Institute, New York, on March 9, 1859. The first president of the new organization was W. H. Van Cott, a relative of one who was later the presiding officer of the New York Club.

In those first rules of baseball playing the regulation thickness of the bat (not to exceed two and one-half inches in diameter) was established, and it has never been changed to this day.

But, whereas the present rules prescribe the bat's length to be forty-two inches, these original rules permitted it to be of any length to suit the batsman.

The ball of these days, as stipulated, was required to weigh not less than five and a half nor more than five and three-fourths ounces. The maximum and minimum weights have since been reduced to five and five and a quarter ounces.

At this time the batsman was out if the ball was caught, either on the fly or first bound. Afterward the bound catch was abolished, except as to foul balls, and finally even the foul bound was stricken out of the rules.

THE FIRST IMPORTANT SERIES.

The first important event which started the present game into popularity under the rules formulated at the convention of 1858 was the series of picked-nine contests at the Fashion race course at Flushing, Long Island, in 1858, in which the New York nine came off victorious in two games out of the three played.

It was the first gate-money series of matches known to baseball history, and a crowd of about 25,000 people witnessed the first contest.

The next important event was the tour of the Excelsior Club of Brooklyn, in July, 1860, when they defeated all opposing nines through Western New York, and afterward in Pennsylvania and Maryland. That year of 1860 was the most eventful one in the history of the National Association, for during 1860 clubs multiplied by the hundred.

THE NATIONAL GAME.

FIRST SERIES FOR CHAMPIONSHIP.

The first series of home and home games for a real championship took place in 1858 and 1859.

At this time the Elysian Field at Hoboken, N. J., directly opposite New York City was the great playing ground and here the first championship games took place in 1858 and 1859.

Here the Eagle, Gotham, Empire and Knickerbocker clubs played their games and played so well that rivalry sprang up over the way at Brooklyn where the Atlantic and Eckford teams were organized. Challenges were sent back and forth and a series of games was arranged in which the Atlantics came out first best.

The Civil War materially affected the game in and around New York during 1861, 1862 and 1863.

In 1862 the Atlantics and Eckfords of Brooklyn furnished the bulk of the sport and the latter wrested the championship from their rivals.

THE CHAMPION ECKFORDS.

The Eckford champion team was made up of: Beach, c.; Sprague, p.; Al Reach, 1b.; Jimmy Wood, 2b; Ed. Duffy, 3b; Devyr, ss, and Manalt, Josh Snyder and Swandell in the outfield.

The Atlantics' champion nine at the time included: Pearce, c.; Pratt, p.; Start, 1b.; Crane, 2b.; C. Smith, 3b.; Galvin, ss. and Chapman, p.; O'Brien and S. Smith in the outfield.

The Atlantics went through the seasons of 1864 and 1865 without sustaining a single defeat.

In 1863 the Eckfords had gone through the season without losing a game, but after that their best players went to other teams and the Atlantics were looked on as the champions until their great series in the Fall of 1866 with the Athletics of Philadelphia.

ATLANTICS MEET ATHLETICS.

The first of these great games took place in Philadelphia on October 1, 1866. It was estimated that 30,000 persons saw this game from the inside and outside of the enclosed grounds.

Inside the enclosure after the first inning the crowd was packed so closely that it was impossible for the fielders to do anything. So after one inning both teams consented to a postponement and the game was played on October 22, 1866, with the Athletics winning by the decisive score of 31 to 12.

The Athletic team on this occasion included Dockney, c.; McBride, p.; Berkenstock, Reach and Pike, on the bases; Wilkins, ss. and Sensenderfer, Fisler and Kleinfelder in the outfield.

Their victory over the Atlantics gave the Athletics the championship or, rather they claimed it after the first game; for on account of a bitter controversy over a division of the gate receipts a second game was not played during the season of 1866.

The Athletics therefore held the championship in 1866, 1867 and 1868 and in that time they presented changes in their ranks; Dockney, Berkenstock and Pike giving way to Radcliffe, Cuthbert and Berry in 1867 and Shaefer taking Kleinfelder's place in 1868.

FIRST PRIZES FOR PLAYERS.

In 1868 the series of games for the gold ball, presented by Mr. Frank Queen of the New York Clipper, was won by the Athletics and gold medals offered by the same gentleman to the players having excelled in their respective positions of catcher, pitcher, first base, second base and center field, went to McBride, Radcliffe, Fisler, Reach and Sensenderfer, all of the Athletics.

Other medals from the same source that year went to Waterman, Hatfield, Johnson and George Wright of the Cincinnati Club, they having excelled at third base, left field, right field and shortstop.

From the date of the first convention in New York the game grew rapidly in popularity. But the great Civil War which broke out in 1860 put a serious check on the sport, though through all the excitement of the four years which followed, a few clubs kept playing, and perpetuated the game.

THE CONVENTION OF 1865.

As soon as the war was ended, baseball took a new lease of life and at the convention which assembled in New York City on December 13, 1865, thirty clubs sent delegates and six other applicants for membership were favorably received.

Of the new members were the Empires of St. Louis, Mo.; the Lookouts of Chattanooga, Tenn.; the Louisvilles of Louisville, Ky.; three clubs from Washington and organizations in Boston and Philadelphia.

Thus it will be seen the game was reaching out, and had not only crossed the Allegheny Mountains, but had got beyond the Mississippi River, and had invaded the still bloody battlefields below the Mason and Dixon line.

The Excelsior Club of Brooklyn, was the first to send a team on a tour. This occurred in 1860. The team started out visiting towns in New York State, Pennsylvania and Maryland, playing local teams as they went, and arousing such enthusiasm everywhere as would certainly have had a most widespread effect had not the civil strife between the North and South checked it.

During this tour the Excelsiors visited Boston, where their style of playing was much admired, and was called "The New York Game" to distinguish it from "The Massachu-

4

THE NATIONAL GAME.

setts Game," as played in New England previous to this trip. The result was that the New York system of play was adopted thereafter by the New England clubs.

At this time in many places it was considered a disgrace to take money in payment for playing the game. So great was the prejudice against anything of this sort that in 1865 James E. Roder, of the Empire Club of New York, was expelled by that organization for accepting money for playing in one of its games. This incident sounds ludicrous in these days of high salaried players and managers.

THE FIRST TRANS-ALLEGHENY TOUR.

It remained for the Nationals, of Washington, in 1867, to make the first trans-Allegheny tour.

This celebrated club had for its president at that time, Arthur Pue Gorman, for years the distinguished Maryland member of the United States Senate.

This club made this first trip at its own expense and played games at Columbus, Cincinnati, Louisville, Indianapolis, St. Louis and Chicago, and up to the arrival of the Nationals in Chicago, victory perched on their banner in every game. In Chicago, however, the Nationals sustained their only defeat, and that was at the hands of the Forest City Club of Rockford, of which club young A. G. Spalding was pitcher.

When the National Club first proposed to send a club to the far Western cities, the Eastern public for a time regarded it as a joke. Nothing of such a Quixotic nature had ever been suggested in baseball.

But when the proposed trip became a reality wonder turned to admiration, and the progress and triumphs of the team through the West were noted daily by the press of the East.

The National Club paid every dollar of the expenses of this trip without benefitting by receipts from the games en route, as at that period the game had not reached a money-producing basis.

In every city the Nationals were received with generous hospitality and their tour was one continual fete and feast.

They came as far West as St. Louis and Chicago, and succeeded in leaving in their trail such enthusiasm over the sport that clubs sprang up in their footsteps like mushrooms after a warm rain in May.

THE FOREST CITYS OF ROCKFORD.

The managers of the Forest City Club, of Rockford, Ill., were the first to pay regular salaries to their players.

All other baseball teams, up to August 10, 1865, when the Forest Citys of Rockford were organized, were playing then and for several subsequent years on the co-operative plan.

And the noteworthy thing about the Forest City of Rockford was their being the first club to defeat the famous Nationals of Washington, with George Wright as their leader.

That defeat was administered July 25, 1867.

The game of that day should have been between the Excelsiors of Chicago and the Nationals.

The Excelsiors, however, declined the issue and the Forest City team met the Nationals in their place.

The Forest Citys, then called the "Country Boys" by the people of Chicago, on this occasion defeated the Nationals by 29 to 23, quite a modest score.

The Forest City Baseball Club was organized August 10th, 1865. The club numbered about 150 members, the playing members being boys who grew to manhood in Rockford, having received liberal educations and every one of them being engaged in business, filling stations of profit and honor, having only the hours of evening after their day's work was done to practice.

The following were the names of the players:

George E. King, Albert G. Spalding, Robert E. Addy, Alfred Barker, Ross C. Barnes, Fred C. Cone, G. Stires, Ballard Osborne, Frank Trumbull, Lee Cheney and Scott Hastings.

FOREST CITY'S RECORD—1865.

The scores of the Forest Citys against their opponents were:

	F.C. O.		F.C. O.
Empire, Freeport, Aug. 30	21 to 50	Shaffer, Freeport, Oct. 20	31 to 23
Atlantic, Chicago, Sept. 19	29 to 26		

Total played, three; won one, lost two.
The games played in 1866 were:

	F.C. O.		F.C. O.
Mystic, Belvidere, May 13	123 to 8	Empire, Freeport, July, (forfeited)	0 to 9
Shaffer, Freeport, June 27	37 to 23	Minnising, Rockford, July 15	50 to 11
Cream City, Milwaukee, June 4	33 to 14	Cream City, Milwaukee, Aug. 21	24 to 10
Clipper, Rochelle, July 4	39 to 16	Badger, Beloit, Sept. 26	42 to 8

Total played, 8; won seven; lost one.
Games played in 1867:

	F.C. O		F O.
Phoenix, Belvidere, May 8	56 to 0	Nationals, Washington (in Chicago).	
Byron, Byron, May 18	20 to 4	July 25	2 to 23
Excelsior, Chicago, June 20	41 to 45	Bloomington, Bloomington, Sept. 5	60 to 57
Phoenix, Belvidere, July 2	24 to 16	Star, Marengo, Oct. 4	63 to 9
Excelsior, Chicago, July 4	5 to 28		

Total played, eight games; won five, lost three.
Games played in 1868:

THE NATIONAL GAME.

	F.C. O.		F.C. O.
Byron, Byron, May 21	43 to 25	Buckeye, Cincinnati, July 23	11 to 19
Harvard, Harvard, June 3	73 to 7	Union, St. Louis, July 25, (forfeited)..	9 to 0
Excelsior, Chicago, June 12	20 to 18	Union, Morrisania, Aug. 11	17 to 23
Athletics, Philadelphia, June 18	13 to 94	Excelsior, Dubuque, Aug. 20	75 to 5
Atlantics, Brooklyn, June 24	29 to 31	Atlantic, Chicago, Sept. 4	31 to 14
Excelsior, Chicago, July 4	36 to 27	Atlantic, Chicago, Sept. 22	29 to 14
Capital City, Madison, July 9	28 to 9	Bloomington, Bloomington, Sept. 24	21 to 14
Capital City, Madison, July 16	43 to 12	Bloomington, Bloomington, Oct. 29	20 to 12
Mutual, Janesville, July 17	88 to 6		

Total played, seventeen games; won thirteen, lost four.

THEN CAME THE CINCINNATI "REDS."

Out of this trip of the Nationals sprang the famous Cincinnati Red Stockings, destined to make a record never before nor afterwards excelled.

The Nationals found in Cincinnati a very fertile field for their missionary work. There were at this time in the Queen City two local teams in the field, between whom much rivalry existed—the Cincinnatis and the Buckeyes.

After the Nationals left Cincinnati for Louisville, St. Louis, Chicago and other cities. this rivalry between the Buckeyes and Cincinnatis increased, and ended in the organization of the first professional team that ever took the field.

The Buckeyes paved the way by importing several players from the East to whom they were compelled to pay salaries. The Cincinnatis had among their club members some very wealthy and baseball loving men who foresaw that the local fight would settle down to a question of the survival of the fittest, or of the victor, so when they took up the fight in earnest they did not go half way.

A bunch of professionals were brought on by them from the East, among whom were the Wright brothers, George and Harry, and John Hatfield, the long distance thrower. The result was the extinction of the Buckeyes in one of the most exciting series of games ever played.

The "Red Stockings," as the Cincinnatis were called, because they wore red stockings as part of their uniform, were victorious and the Buckeyes disbanded in despair, leaving the local field to their successful rivals.

THE FIRST REAL PROFESSIONAL TEAM.

In 1869 the Cincinnatis put their entire nine under salaries. So they might be called the first real professional team. In 1868 four of the Cincinnati players were compensated for their work, but the Cincinnati Reds of 1869 was a professional team from stem to stern and a comparison of the salaries paid then and now will prove interesting. The Cincinnati Reds of 1869 included these players who drew the salaries named:

Harry Wright, captain	$1,200	Charles Gould, first base	$ 800
George Wright, shortstop	1,400	Douglas Allison, catcher	800
Asa Brainard, pitcher	1,100	Andrew J. Leonard, left field	800
Fred Waterman, third base	1,000	Calvin McVey, right field	800
Charles Sweasy, second base	800	Richard Hurley, substitute	800

The season lasted eight months, from March 15 to November 15, so it will be seen that most of the players drew $100 a month for the term of their contracts—an absurdly small sum, according to modern standards.

In fact it will be noted that it was not an extravagant proposition to get a team in these days. The entire salary list of the ten players who composed the Cincinnati Reds of '69 amounted to only $9,300, or less than the Cincinnati Club paid its non-playing manager alone in 1907.

At this period a nine and a team were almost identical inasmuch as few clubs carried more than nine players. The pitcher and catcher were expected to fill their places regularly, the same as the other members of the nine.

THE FIRST REAL AMERICAN TOUR.

The success of this salaried nine was so decided—hundreds of spectators willingly paying to see their games—that a tour of the North, West, East and South was decided on. This tour was included in the marvelous record made by the Red Stockings which will immortalize their names as long as baseball is played or talked about. The club began a series of victories at the beginning of 1869 and never suffered a defeat until the middle of June, 1870.

In this time they traveled from the Mississippi to the Atlantic, and from the Gulf to the Lakes—playing in all sixty-nine games without suffering a single defeat.

Before the season of 1870 was well under way, the whole United States was watching the work of the Cincinnatis.

In some cities the bulletin boards were surrounded each day of a game by thousands of people who stood watching the returns by telegraph as they were posted by innings.

Every city which could boast of a club was eagerly seeking a chance to take a tilt at the invincible conquerors, for it was agreed that defeat must come to them some time, and the club which would secure the honor of administering the first defeat would become almost as famous as the Red Stockings themselves.

So pretty much the same spirit pervaded the various clubs of the land in their desire to play the Cincinnati team as animated people in the olden days who spent money for one chance in ten thousand to draw a capital prize in the Louisiana Lottery.

THE FIRST TEAM OF BASEBALL PLAYERS TO EVER MAKE A TRIP AWAY FROM HOME ON THEIR OWN ACCOUNT, AND WHICH TRIP THEY MADE IN 1865.

THE FOREST CITYS OF ROCKFORD in 1869.

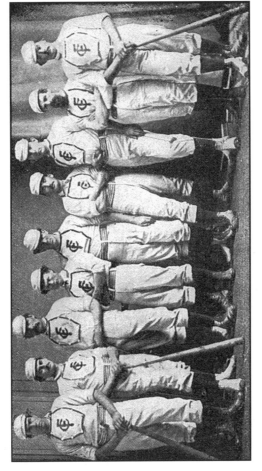

THE FOREST CITYS OF ROCKFORD IN 1869.

Reading from left to right: Foley, 3b; Barnes, ss.; Barker, lf.; Cone, 1b.; Addy, c.; Spalding, p; King, rf.; Hastings, 2b.

The Forest Citys of Rockford were the greatest baseball team in the early sixties and a description of their first tour is given elsewhere in these columns. The portrait above contains the faces and figures of several players who later became famous in the professional world. First and foremost of these men is A. G. Spalding, one of the leaders now in baseball, and who for many a year was the king pitcher; Ross Barnes, in his day, the ablest infielder in America, and most scientific batsman; Scott Hastings, for years one of the top notch catchers, and Bob Addy, known long in the professional field as a fine infielder.

THE NATIONAL GAME.

THE FIRST DEFEAT FOR THE REDS.

To the Atlantics of Brooklyn fell the glory of checking the Red Stockings' victorious career.

The event occurred on the Atlantics' grounds in Brooklyn on June 14, 1870, in the presence of a multitude of spectators. Zettlein and Brainard were the pitchers; nine innings were played and the score had ended in a tie amid great excitement.

The two captains, Harry Wright and Robert Ferguson, came together for a conference, and had about agreed to call the game a draw when President Champion, who was traveling with the Red Stockings, ordered Captain Wright to play it out. So the Cincinnatis went to bat for their tenth inning and made two runs. In the minds of the spectators this settled the game and the cry went up, "They can't be beaten."

Nevertheless Captain Robert Ferguson would not give up, and he led his men to bat for their last chance. An error gave one batsman a base; then "Joe" Start sent the ball over Right Fielder "Cal" McVey's head into the crowd. The spectators tried to keep McVey away from the ball, but he broke through. Then one of the spectators threw the ball back into the field, whence it was returned to the diamond in time to keep Start on third base.

FERGUSON'S WINNING HIT.

Captain Ferguson came along at this point with a hit, which sent Start home and again tied the score, leaving him (Ferguson) at second. There were two out when Hall went to bat to win the game. He sent a ground ball toward Shortstop George Wright. Ferguson, by jumping over the ball, succeeded in "blinding" Wright, and the ball got partially away from the latter.

Meanwhile the captain of the Atlantics kept on toward the plate, intent on scoring the run which should end the wonderful series of victories of the Red Stockings. He did score, but by an error of Charley Sweasy, who muffed the ball, which was fielded in by Wright in time enough to cut off Ferguson had it been held.

Thus in a moment ended the year and a half of unprecedented and unbroken triumphs of the Cincinnatis, and the news within half an hour after that run was scored had been telegraphed to almost every city, town and hamlet in the United States.

The officers of the Cincinnati Club of 1869 were: Aaron B. Champion, president; Thos. G. Smith, vice president; Edward E. Townley; treasurer, and John P. Joyce, secretary.

THE TOUR OF THE REDS IN 1869.

The Cincinnati Reds reported in Cincinnati early in April, 1869, and played a number of practice games with local and neighboring teams.

It was soon decided to visit the Eastern cities, and a challenge was issued to all the ball teams of the country for match games with the Reds.

The Eastern trip began in May, and the Reds visited every city where they could get a game, including St. Louis, Cleveland, Buffalo, Rochester, Troy, Albany, Springfield, Boston, New York, Brooklyn, Philadelphia, Baltimore, Washington, Wheeling and other places.

Their tour was one triumphant march, and they returned home on July 1, 1869, unbeaten. The progress of the team through the East had been watched with the most in' se interest by Cincinnati enthusiasts, who welcomed the club with open arms on its return.

FIRST TRIP TO THE COAST.

During July and August the Reds played a long series of games at home, meeting and defeating all comers. In September they took a trip to the Pacific Coast ,where their appearance created great excitement, and they were hailed as the champions of the country.

The playing season of 1869 lasted from April 17, when the Reds won from a picked nine by a score of 24 to 15, until November 5, when they defeated the famous Mutuals, of New York, 17 to 8. During the entire season the Reds did not suffer defeat, playing sixty-five games with the leading teams of the country.

Their largest score was 103 to 8, in a game against the Buckeyes of Cincinnati. And they scored double figures in every game played except the great contest with the New York Mutuals on June 15. which they won 4 to 2, a remarkably close score at that time.

One game played by the Reds that year is recorded as a tie game, but it was really a victory for the Reds and was so declared by the umpire.

In the fifth inning of a contest with the Haymakers of Troy, N. Y., the latter club kicked on a decision of the umpire and refused to continue. The score at the time was 17 to 17, which has caused the impression that this was a drawn game, but the contest was awarded to the Reds by the umpire. This was the only game not decisively won by the Reds in 1869.

THE REDS OF 1870.

The Cincinnati Reds entered the field in 1870 with the same players as in the preceding year, and started out in the same victorious manner They won twenty-seven straight games before suffering defeat in their hard-fought contest on the Capitoline grounds, Brooklyn, at the hands of the Atlantics, by a score of 8 to 7.

The team played seventy-five games that season, winning sixty-eight and losing only six, a record that would have made the club famous had it not been eclipsed by the wonderful performance of '69.

Cincinnati was the pioneer in professional baseball, and the Reds of '68, '69 and '70,

THE NATIONAL GAME.

by their sensational playing on their various tours, gave the game a tremendous impetus all over the country. Teams were organized in every city and the game put on a purely professional basis.

This caused a sudden raise in salaries, owing to the competition for playing talent, and the Cincinnati Club found itself unable to retain its stars, who went to other teams in 1871, most of them going to Boston, where George, the most famous of the Wright brothers, not only played sensational ball, but established himself there later in the sporting goods business, where he is living and prosperous to this day.

Of course, no other professional team will ever go through an entire season without being defeated, and this record, though made nearly forty years ago, is still pointed to with pride and serves as an inspiration to the people and players of Cincinnati.

THE WONDERFUL RECORD OF THE CINCINNATI REDS.

The scores of the games played by the Cincinnati Reds, the first professional team, during their famous tour in 1869, were as follows:

		Reds.	Op'ts.				Reds.	Op'ts.
April 17	Picked nine	24	15		July 22	Keystone, Philadelphia	71	15
April 24	Picked nine	50	7		July 24	Forest City, Rockford	15	14
May 4	Great Western, Cincinnati	45	9		July 28	Empire, St. Louis	15	0
May 10	Kekionga, Ft. Wayne	86	8		July 30	Cream City, Milwaukee	85	7
May 15	Antioch, Yellow Springs	41	7		July 31	Forest City, Rockford	53	32
May 10	Kekionga, Ft. Wayne	86	8		Aug. 2	Forest City, Rockford	28	7
May 29	Great Western, Mansfield	35	5		Aug. 4	Central City, Syracuse	37	9
June 1	Independents, Mansfield	48	14		Aug. 5	Central City, Syracuse	36	22
June 2	Forest City, Cleveland	25	6		Aug. 6	Forest City, Cleveland	43	27
June 3	Niagara, Buffalo	42	6		Aug. 11	Riversides, Portsmouth	40	0
June 4	Alerts, Rochester	18	9		Aug. 16	Eckfords, Brooklyn	45	18
June 7	Haymakers, Troy	37	31		Aug. 23	Southerns, New Orleans	35	3
June 8	Nationals, Albany	49	8		Aug. 27	Haymakers, Troy	17	17
June 9	Mutuals, Springfield	80	5		Aug. 31	Buckeyes,	103	8
June 10	Lowells, Boston	29	9		Sept. 9	Olympics, Pittsburg	54	2
June 11	Tri-Mountain, Boston	40	12		Sept. 10	Alerts, Rochester	32	19
June 12	Harvards, Boston	30	11		Sept. 15	Unions, St. Louis	70	9
June 15	Mutuals, New York	4	2		Sept. 16	Empires, St. Louis	31	9
June 16	Atlantics, New York	32	10		Sept. 26	Eagles, San Francisco	35	4
June 17	Eckfords, Brooklyn	24	5		Sept. 27	Eagles, San Francisco	58	4
June 18	Irvingtons, New Jersey	20	4		Sept. 29	Pacifics, San Francisco	66	4
June 19	Olympics, Philadelphia	22	11		Sept. 30	Pacifics, San Francisco	54	5
June 21	Athletics, Philadelpih	27	18		Oct. 1	Atlantics, San Francisco	76	5
June 22	Keystone, Philadelphia	45	30		Oct. 11	Omahas, Omaha, Neb.	65	1
June 24	Marylands, Baltimore	47	7		Oct. 12	Otoes, Omaha	56	3
June 25	Nationals, Washington	24	8		Oct. 13	Occidentals, Quincy, Ill.	51	7
June 28	Olympics, Washington	16	5		Oct. 15	Marions, Marion, In1	63	4
June 30	Baltics, Wheeling	44	0		Oct. 18	Athletics, Philadelphia	17	12
July 1	Picked nine	53	11		Oct. 24	Louisvilles, Louisville	59	8
July 3	Olympics, Washington	25	14		Oct. 24	Cedar Hill, Ohio	40	10
July 5	Olympics, Washington	25	14		Nov. 4	Eagles, Covington	40	10
July 10	Forest City, Rockford	34	13		Nov. 5	Mutuals, New York	17	8
July 13	Olympics, Washington	19						

THEN CAME THE CHICAGO WHITE STOCKINGS.

This tour of the Cincinnati Reds awakened interest in baseball the country over and professional teams were organized in many of the larger cities with but one end in view and that to even up scores with the great players of Cincinnati.

In 1870 all of the Chicago people banded together for the purpose of organizing a team that would annihilate the Cincinnati Reds and out of their efforts came the Chicago White Stockings of 1870—a team of players selected from many of the best teams in America.

This team included Craver and Mart King, catchers; Meyerle and Pinkham, pitchers; McAtee, first base; Wood, second base; Meyerle or Pinkham, third; Hodes, short field; Treacy, left field; Cuthbert, center, and Flynn, right.

As though in contrast and in opposition to the red-stockinged players who hailed from the Queen City the Chicago baseball promoters christened their team the "White Stockings," a name that has clung to a team hailing from that city ever since.

This original Chicago White Stocking team the people of Chicago put in the field for the express purpose of defeating the Cincinnati Reds and although the Atlantics of Brooklyn forestalled the Chicagos in their creditable endeavor, the White Stockings proved to be the first club to beat the Red Stockings twice in succession. This double defeat from the Chicago foe, coming so close after the sudden ending of the Red Stockings' Brooklyn defeat, acted in the nature of a death blow.

The Cincinnati followers of the great club suddenly descended from their high pinnacle of enthusiasm to the lowest depths of dissatisfaction.

The result was that at the end of the season such poor support was given to the team that the club disbanded in the Fall, and four of the great nine—the Wright brothers, Gould and McVey—went to Boston to play in 1871 and most of the other players became members of the Olympics of Washington, and four years and a half thereafter Cincinnati was not represented by a professional team.

THE CAPITOLINE GROUNDS IN 1870.

The tour of the Cincinnati Reds in 1869 and the visit of the Chicago White Stockings and other teams to the East in 1870 aroused great interest in the game in that direction.

9

THE NATIONAL GAME.

In 1870 when I visited New York I found that baseball had taken a firm hold there.

The Capitoline grounds over in Brooklyn, which were then the leading baseball grounds in that vicinity, were enclosed by a high fence and, in diagonal corners stands and diamonds were built so that two crowds could be accommodated and two games be played in the one enclosure at one and the same moment.

And so it happened that on one occasion the baseball people of Brooklyn and New York were able in these Capitoline grounds to witness at one and the same time a two-ringed circus, as it were, the famous Atlantics and Eckfords of Brooklyn playing in the one corner and the Stars of Brooklyn, claiming to be the best non-professional team in America, and the Fordham College nine appearing in the other.

TWO GAMES ON ONE FIELD.

The grounds were as level as a billiard table, the diamonds in superb shape and the field of such great dimensions that one set of outfielders in no way interfered with the other.

Perhaps it was, the impetus given the game on these same Capitoline grounds that led to its subsequent rapid growth in all directions, for from this field came players who did as much as any others to make the game the popular idol it is to-day.

First of all from these grounds came "Candy" Cummings, the famous pitcher of the Stars of Brooklyn, who according to the veteran players of that day (and all of whom spoke from experience) was the first to pitch a curve ball.

From these grounds too came Martin of the Eckfords who was the first successful pitcher when it came to slow delivery and head work.

Here was graduated Pinkham of the Atlantics of Brooklyn, the first of the speedy left-handed pitchers.

From these grounds came Zettlein of the Atlantics of Brooklyn ,the first of the great speed merchants, no man of his day being able to compete with him in this direction.

The first attempt to steal a base by sliding head first for the bag was made on these grounds during the summer of 1865. The honor belongs to Eddie Cuthbert, then a member of the Keystone Club of Philadelphia. It was during the progress of a game between the Keystones and the Atlantics of Brooklyn that Cuthbert surprised the spectators by trying to steal second base by diving headlong for the bag. His first attempt was successful, but on a second trial he was caught in the act and retired.

THE FIRST GREAT CATCHER.

From the Capitoline field out into the open came Ferguson, one of the first to catch the ball up close to the bat and from here came Mills and Hicks, premier catchers of their day.

It was on this field that we have the first record of any catcher wearing a mask and this honor is given to Tyng, then famous as the catcher of the Harvard College Club.

From the Capitoline grounds too came Dickey Pearce, the short fielder of the Atlantics of Brooklyn, the first player of his day to drop a fly ball in order to make a double play—an act that gives to him the honor of being the father of the double play.

Here Dickey Pearce, too, invented the bunt and the fair foul hit which followed it and which was subsequently legislated out of existence.

Here John C. Chapman of the Atlantics, "Young Jack," as he was then called, often surprised the natives by his wonderful running one-hand catches and earned the name of "Death to Flying Things."

From the Atlantics too came a great lot of speedy runners, notably Smith, Start, Crane, Chapman, Ferguson, Pike, Pearce and Hall.

From the Unions and partly from these grounds were graduated Martin, Austin, Shelly, Aiken, Smith and Pabor.

To these grounds, too, often came the Nationals of Washington, with such clever players as George Wright, Berthrong, Norton, Parker, Gibney, Fox and others, all of whom were noted for their fleetness of foot and speed as base runners.

THE FIRST GREAT INFIELDERS.

Many later famous infielders came from the Capitoline grounds, notably, Joe Start, known as "Old Reliable," famous for years as the first baseman of the Atlantics of Brooklyn.

Here too were graduated many famous second basemen, notably, John Burdock who was the second baseman of the Atlantics of Brooklyn and in later years the guardian of that bag for the Boston National League champions.

Jimmy Wood, second baseman of the Eckfords of Brooklyn and subsequently famous as the commander of the original Chicago White Stockings, won his first great fame on the Capitoline field and many other later famous second base players came from this same ground.

The Capitoline grounds being unusually roomy gave the outfielders the opportunity to cover much territory and to extend themselves to the limit and so from them was partly graduated many famous outfielders, notably Al Gedney of the Eckfords. Fred Treacy of the Chicago White Stockings, Tom York of the Atlantics, Andy Leonard of the Bostons, Lipman Pike of the Atlantics, Edgar Cuthbert of the Athletics and later of the Chicago White Stockings, Dave Eggler of the Mutuals, Jack Remsen of the Atlantics and many others.

The boom in the game which was started so well by the Cincinnati Reds and the Chicago White Stockings in 1869 resulted in the organization of many crack clubs in the East and West. These were made up of the great players who had come into prominence during the famous tour of the Cincinnati Reds in 1869.

THE NATIONAL GAME.

THE GREAT PLAYERS OF 1870.

The great players of 1870 were then scattered among different clubs, all of whom played for a division of the gate receipts in their respective cities with the exception of the Cincinnatis, who were a regular salaried nine. The others called themselves either semi-professional or co-operative teams. The full list of players playing on these best-known teams of 1870 was as follows:

ATHLETICS OF PHILADELPHIA.
Malone, c.
McBride, p.
Fisler, 1b.
Reach, 2b.
Pratt, 3b.
Radcliffe, ss.
Bechtel, lf.
Sensenderfer, cf.
Berry, rf.

RED STOCKINGS OF CINCINNATI.
D. Allison, c.
Brainard, p.
Gould, 1b.
Sweasy, 2b.
Waterman, 3b.
G. Wright, ss.
Leonard, lf.
H. Wright, cf.
McVey, rf.

FOREST CITYS, ROCKFORD.
Hastings, c.
A. G. Spalding, p.
Doyle, 1b.
Addy, 2b.
Foley, 3b.
Barnes, ss.
Cone, lf.
Simmons, cf.
Stires, rf.

HAYMAKERS OF TROY, N. Y.
McGeary, c.
McMullin, p.
Fisher, 1b
Dick, 2b.
Bellan, 3b.
Flowers, ss.
S. King, lf.
Yorke, rf.
Foran, rf.

ATLANTICS OF BROOKLYN.
Ferguson, c.
Zettlein, p.
Start, 1b.
Pike, 2b.
Smith, 3b.
Pearce, ss.
Chapman, lf.
George Hall, cf.
McDonald, rf.

WHITE STOCKINGS OF CHICAGO.
M. King, c.
Pinkham, p.
McAtee, 1b
Wood, 2b.
Meyerle, 3b.
Hodes, ss.
Treacy, lf.
Cuthbert, cf.
Flynn, rf.

ECKFORDS OF BROOKLYN.
Jewett, c.
McDermott, p.
Allison, 1b.
R. Hunt, 2b.
Duffy, 3b.
Jas. Snyder, ss.
Connigan, lf.
J. Snyder, cf.
Malone, rf.

FOREST CITYS OF CLEVELAND.
J. White, c.
Pratt, p.
Carleton, 1b.
Kimbal, 2b.
Sutton, 3b.
Ward, ss.
Heubell, lf.
Allison, cf.
Ed. White, rf.

MUTUALS OF NEW YORK.
C. Mills, c.
Wolters, p.
E. Mills, 1b.
Swandell, 2b.
Nelson, 3b.
Hatfield, ss.
Patterson, lf.
Martin, rf.
Eggler, cf.

THE PURIFYING OF THE SPORT.

It was the life put into the game by the teams of 1870 that led to the organization in 1871 of the first "Professional Association." It was called the National Association.

This organization was managed mostly by the players and it was during its first five years of life that the game fell into disrepute and into the hands of the gamblers.

In fact, in 1875 the game fell into a state of demoralization which threatened its existence and its popularity among respectable people.

In 1875 competition among the professional clubs ran so high that bribery, contract breaking, dishonest playing, poolroom manipulation and desertion of players became so public that the highly respectable element of patrons began to drop out of the attendance until the crowds which attended the games were composed almost exclusively of men who went to the grounds to bet money on the results. The money was bet openly during the progress of the games.

So notorious was this practice that one section of the grounds of the Atlantic Club in Brooklyn became known as the "Gold Board." There on every afternoon of a game scores of men would gather, and at times their "Puts" and "Calls" would rival a scene on the floor of the Stock Exchange.

THE NATIONAL LEAGUE'S ENTREE.

This evil was so fast driving the decent element away from the game that in the Spring of 1876 a meeting was called of the principal professional clubs at Louisville, Ky., to take steps to rescue the game from the fatal clutch of the gambler.

At this meeting was organized the National League which accomplished the purpose proposed, and snatched baseball from the utter ruin into which it was so fast drifting.

The National League has lived, flourished and grown stronger every season in the years which have followed.

THE LEAGUE'S FIRST PRESIDENTS.

At New York, in March. 1876, ex-Governor Bulkeley of Connecticut, then the head of the Hartford Club, was elected the league's first president.

In the following year he was succeeded by William A. Hulbert of Chicago, whose ideas put the National League on its feet, and to whose memory lovers of the great game owe so much.

Standing side by side with Mr. Hulbert in those early days of the league was A. G. Mills, then a prominent lawyer of the Lake city, now a successful business man of New York and a prominent active worker in amateur athletics, and aiding them both was Charles Fowle of St. Louis, head of the League Club of the Mound City and a thorough gentleman and sportsman.

When in 1882 Mr. Hulbert died, his friend. A G. Mills stepped into his place at the head of the League and of professional baseball playing in the United States, where he.

THE NATIONAL GAME.

carried out the strong policy which the deceased executive had so well established.

Mr. Mills held the position until the winter of 1884, when the league, by reinstating contract jumpers, McCormick, Briody, Dunlap and Glasscock, who had been expelled during the previous playing season, offended Mr. Mills' ideas of discipline and he resigned.

The man who had been secretary from the very beginning of the league, N. E. Young of Washington, succeeded Mr. Mills to the presidency, and remained in that office until 1902, when he resigned and his place was taken by Harry C. Pulliam. The latter was in turn succeeded by the present incumbent, Thomas J. Lynch.

THE WAR ON THE GAMBLERS.

The National League from its inception waged a relentless war against the gamblers and against all forms or practices which could cast a reflection on the respectability of the game.

Open betting in any part of a league ground was forbidden and any club which failed to expel from its ground any spectator caught in the act of betting on a game in progress rendered itself liable to expulsion; players who should bet or would "jump" a contract must be expelled or blacklisted, and rendered forever ineligible to play for any club a member of the National League, or which had any desire to play against any National League Club.

These regulations were so strictly enforced that one after another the evils which were sapping the life of the game were eradicated and the National League soon came to stand for all that was honest, fair and commendable in public sports.

Poolrooms were denied reports from ball grounds, and the games became so "square" that in less than two years after the League was formed scarcely a poolroom in the United States could be found where pools were sold on the result of the games.

THE PUNISHMENT OF THE DISHONEST PLAYERS.

That which forever rooted out dishonest baseball playing and which did more than any other one act to make the game so popular in succeeding years was the blacklisting in December, 1877, of four of the most prominent ball players of the League, namely, Devlin, Hall, Nichols and Craver of the Louisville Club.

Thus it happened that the first great punishment under the new penal laws enacted at the Louisville meeting was meted out to offenders of the team representing that city.

When the Louisville team left on their final trip through the East that season (1877) they were looked upon as having the championship as good as won. By their playing they had shown themselves to be far the strongest team in the league, and from that point to the end they could lose more than half of their games and still win the pennant.

THE HARTFORD SCANDAL.

The Hartfords at that time were playing on the old Mutual Club grounds in Brooklyn, and thither the Louisvilles went first for six games.

The Hartfords up to this time had been mere "practice material" for the Louisvilles, but on the day of the latter's first game of the trip in Brooklyn the poolrooms in Hoboken laid heavily on the Hartfords in the game for that afternoon, and the Louisvilles were badly beaten. The game had been lost by errors of Craver, Hall and Nichols.

On the day of the second game the Hoboken poolrooms once more laid heavy odds against the Louisvilles, and again the Louisvilles lost through errors by Devlin, Hall and Nichols. This bad work continued and when the Louisvilles returned from the East they had won only two games out of twelve played. The result was that they lost the championship by a margin of three games.

The Louisville directors were certain that there had been crooked work, but they had no absolute proof. Nichols and Hall were suspected. Hall had recommended Nichols to the club in mid-season when the regular third baseman was laid up with boils.

When the team got to Brooklyn, Hall asked Manager Chapman to put Nichols on the team, because the latter was a Brooklyn boy and would have a great many friends among the spectators.

THE EXPOSURE.

When the team returned to Louisville they found that rumors of the dishonesty of certain of the players had preceded them.

Thereupon Devlin, the pitcher (and perhaps the greatest pitcher who ever handled a ball) called upon President Charles E. Chase to deny his guilt. Chase made Devlin believe he had more knowledge than he really had, and gave Devlin till eight o'clock that night to make a full confession.

Hall saw Devlin go into Chase's office and leave it. Fearing Devlin might confess, Hall went to Chase to feel his ground. Then Chase saw his opportunity, and by working one against the other Chase got a full confession from each. Devlin accused Hall of leading him into it, and Hall laid his downfall on Nichols. Nichols remained silent and took his punishment without a word.

The entire team were summoned before the directors and each was asked to give a written order on the Western Union Telegraph Company's office at Louisville for duplicates of all telegrams received and sent out by him during the season.

The only member of the team to refuse was Captain Craver, and he was promptly expelled.

A search of the telegraph company's files turned up evidence of the players' guilt beyond question. So Hall, Nichols, Craver and Devlin were expelled, and from that day none of the four blacklisted men have been able to play in a single professional game.

THE CINCINNATI REDS OF 1869.

THE FIRST REAL TEAM OF PAID PROFESSIONALS AND THE ONE THAT WENT THROUGH THEIR FIRST SEASON WITHOUT SUSTAINING A SINGLE DEFEAT.

THE CINCINNATI RED STOCKINGS OF 1869.
Top row reading from left to right: Calvin A. McVey, rf.; Charles H. Gould, 1b.; Harry Wright, captain and cf.; George Wright, ss.; Fred Waterman, 3b.
Bottom row reading from left to right: Andrew F. Leonard, lf.; Douglas Allison, c.; Asa Brainard, p.; Charles Sweasy, 2b.

Elsewhere in this book will be found a story of the Cincinnati Red Stockings of 1869, the team that went through that whole season without sustaining a single defeat. The above portrait gives one an idea of the appearance of that team when on the field. It will be noticed that all the players are of athletic build, that each and every one of the lot is well uniformed and that while this was really the first professional team, the players appeared to be in fine form physically and to be well dressed and disciplined.

This was one of the first teams, too, to wear the baseball uniform that is in evidence to-day on every regular baseball team. The one figure that looms up prominently in the picture, the figure that

appears full to the brim of quickness and strength, is that of George Wright, who was then and who remained for years afterwards the king of short fielders. The picture next to him is that of his brother, Harry Wright, for many a day after 1869 one of the most prominent and successful of major league managers.

This portrait of the Cincinnati Reds of 1869 is from the original photograph of that team, taken by M. B. Brady in Washington at the time the Reds played the Nationals there in 1869. A cut of this photograph first appeared in Colliers Weekly and I am indebted to that periodical which a year ago published some great stories of the old-time professional baseball players.

THE NATIONAL GAME.

DEVLIN'S PLEAS UNHEEDED.

Devlin pleaded for pardon at every league meeting till he died, but the league had no pardon for this offense. The result was to purify the game to that extent that in subsequent years not a breath of suspicion has been raised against the honesty of any player's work on the ball field.

For the sake of one hundred dollars—all the money Devlin got for the sale of these few games—he lost the ability to earn many thousands of dollars in later years and died absolutely in want. His fate and the fate of the three survivors of the quartet has been a lesson no ball player has ever forgotten.

In 1882 the American Association of Baseball Clubs was formed and became, in a business sense, antagonistic to the National League. The two organizations for the first season opposed each other in the signing of players, and the result was a double encouragement to contract-jumping.

THE FIRST OF THE NATIONAL AGREEMENT.

This slight encouragement to an evil which was once more entering the game caused some uneasiness among those who had the future of the sport "at heart," and the result was a conference committee made up of delegates from the National League, American Association and Northwestern League, who met in the latter part of 1882 and adopted what was called a tripartite agreement which was extended so as to include all reputable organizations of baseball clubs which might desire membership benefits under its provisions, and the name was changed to the National Agreement.

The instrument itself provided for a National Board, which should act as an executive to enforce the National Agreement law.

The object of the National Agreement which has been the supreme baseball law since 1883, is to furnish a central government for all professional baseball clubs and players, and to settle disputes which may arise between two associations or leagues, or between clubs of different organizations.

It is based on the principles of the reserve rule, a privilege which it grants to and enforces for every club which is a membership participant under its provision.

The National Agreement in its eleven years of existence has done more to establish baseball permanently than any other idea which has been brought into the game since the sport was professionally introduced. It was conceived and drafted by A. G. Mills, who was the first chairman of the National Board.

THE FIRST OF RESERVE RULE.

The reserve rule was first adopted by the National League about 1880.

It gave each league club the right at the end of every playing season to name five of its players with whom such club alone would have the right to negotiate for their services for the following season.

Of course, there being no National Agreement or central power, such reservation was respected only by National Agreement clubs and the newly organized American Association of 1882 made war on the league's reserve list, which more than any other cause led up to the conference of the fall of that year.

When the National Agreement was formed and adopted this reserve rule was incorporated and the number of reservations accorded to each club was increased to eleven. The number was afterwards raised to a figure which practically meant the entire team.

The object of the rule was to preserve teams intact from year to year after they had been brought up to a degree of efficiency worth preservation, and to make impossible the destructive practices of tempting good players by offers of fabulous salaries to desert cities where they had made reputations and friends. It also kept salaries within money-making bounds and checked the tendency among the players to gradually demand such sums for their services as could not be taken in at the gate.

THE FIRST REBELLION OF PLAYERS.

In 1884 the Union Association was organized and the first revolt of the players took place. It disbanded after its first year.

In 1890 the second revolt of the players against the reserve rule and other things developed and the Brotherhood or Players' League came into existence. Like the Union Association, the Players' League lasted but one season.

In 1891 the American Association took exception to the decision in the National Board in a dispute over the players, Bierbauer and Stovey, and withdrew from the National Agreement compact. Another struggle followed and again the National Agreement forces won.

THE PASSING OF THE AMERICAN ASSOCIATION.

In the winter of that year a peace conference was held at Indianapolis, which resulted in the National League buying out four of the American Association clubs and taking the other four into partnership, thus wiping out all opposition and combining the major league teams under the one banner.

The next ripple on the sea of organized baseball came in 1900 when the American League managers invaded National League territory.

The Cincinnati Peace Compact which ended this war between the National League and American League was signed in Cincinnati on January 10, 1903, by:

Harry C. Pulliam, B. B. Johnson, Aug. Herrmann, Charles A. Comiskey, James A. Hart, Charles W. Somers, Frank DeHass Robison and H. J. Killilea.

THE NATIONAL GAME.

At this meeting it was also agreed that the circuits of each league should consist of the following cities: American League—Boston, New York, Philadelphia, Washington, Cleveland, Detroit, Chicago and St. Louis; National League—Boston, New York, Brooklyn, Philadelphia, Pittsburg, Chicago, St. Louis and Cincinnati. Neither circuit, it was agreed, should be changed without the consent of the majority of the clubs of each league. It was further provided that there should be no consolidation in any city where two clubs exist; nor should any club transfer or release its players for the purpose of injuring or weakening the league of which it is a member.

The National Agreement for the government of professional baseball was entered into between the National and American leagues and the National Association, at Cincinnati, Ohio, September 11, 1903, and it was changed somewhat and revised on January 1, 1908.

THE NATIONAL ASSOCIATION.

A COMPLETE AND OFFICIAL LIST OF THE CLUBS AND OFFICIALS OF THE PROFESSIONAL ASSOCIATIONS WHO ARE NOW WORKING UNDER THE BANNER OF THE NATIONAL AGREEMENT AND WHO ARE LOYAL TO ITS CAUSE.

This National Agreement took under its banner the clubs of the National League, the American League and the National Association.

I have already told of the teams and officers composing the National and American leagues. Just to show the great scope and power of this National Association I give below a complete list of the clubs and the officials at the head of them:

President, M. H. Sexton, Rock Island, Ill.; Secretary, J. H. Farrell, Box 214, Auburn, New York.

Board of Arbitration—John H. Farrell, chairman; W. M. Kavanaugh, J. Cal Ewing, T. H. Murnane, D. M. Shively, Jas. H. O'Rourke, Dr. F. R. Carson, N. L. O'Neill.

LEAGUE MEMBERS.

American Association—T. M. Chivington, president, Chicago, Ill.
Pacific Coast League—Thomas F. Graham, president; W. D. Long, secretary, San Francisco.
Eastern League—Edward Barrow, Toronto, Canada.
Southern Association—W. M. Kavanaugh, president, Little Rock, Ark.
Western League—N. L. O'Neill, president, Chicago.
New York League—J. H. Farrell, president,
Northwestern League—W. H. Lucas, president Tacoma, Wash.
Connecticut League—W. J. Tracey, president, Bristol, Auburn, N. Y.
Indiana-Illinois-Iowa League—A. R. Tearney, president, Chicago, Ill.
New England League—T. H. Murnane, president, Boston, Mass.
Texas League—W. P. Allen, president, Austin, Texas.
Central League—Dr. F. R. Carson, president, South Bend, Ind.
Tri-State League—C. F. Carpenter, president, Altoona, Pa.
Western Association—J. H. Shaw, president, Enid, Okla.
South Atlantic League—W. R. Joyner, president, Atlanta, Ga.
Central Association—M. E. Justice, president, Keokuk, Ia.
Virginia League—Jake Wells, president, Richmond, Va.
Western Canada League—C. J. Eckstrom, president, Lethbridge, Alta.; J. H. Lamb, secretary, Winnipeg.
Southern Michigan Association—J. S. Jackson, president, Detroit, Mich.
Wisconsin-Illinois League—Chas. F. Moll, president, Milwaukee, Wis.
Carolina Association—J. H. Wearn, president, Charlotte, N. C.
Eastern Carolina League—R. T. Gowan, secretary, Raleigh, N. C.
Arkansas State League—R. M. Rider, president, Helena, Ark.
Illinois and Missouri League—A. E. Blain, president, Canton, Ill.
Ohio State League—R. W. Read, president, Columbus, Ohio.
Kansas State League—P. H. Hostutler, president, Hutchinson, Kan.
Minnesota-Wisconsin League—J. A. Elliott, president, La Crosse, Wis.
Blue Grass League—Dr. W. C. Ussery, president, Paris, Ky.
Central Kansas League—H. Cramer, president, Ada, Kan.
Virginia Valley League—John C. Bond, president, Charleston, W. Va.
Nebraska State League—Henry Sievers, president, Grand Island, Neb.
Northeast Arkansas League—J. R. Bertig, president, Paragould, Ark.
Missouri-Iowa-Nebraska-Kansas League—T. A. Wilson, president, Clarinda, Ia.
Southwest Texas League—B. S. Dickinson, president, Austin, Tex.
Central California League—W. W. Brackett, secretary, San Francisco, Cal.
Southern California Trolley League—J. P. McCormick, president, Los Angeles, Cal.
Cotton States League—A. C. Crowder, president, Jackson, Miss.
Ohio and Pennsylvania League—J. H. Maxwell, president, East Liverpool, Ohio.
Washington State League—W. R. MacFarlane, president, Aberdeen, Wash.
Kentucky-Indiana-Tennessee League—C. A. Gosnell, president, Vincennes, Ind.
Indiana-Michigan League—Robert E. Proctor, president, Elkhart, Ind.
Michigan State League—E. W. Dickerson, president, Grand Rapids, Mich.
Southeastern League—A. Gaines, president, Knoxville, Tenn.
Eastern Kansas League—Dr. J. C. Grindle, president, Seneca, Kan.

THE NATIONAL GAME.

San Joaquin Valley League—J. N. Young, president, Visalia, Cal.
Northern Indiana League—C W. Halderman, president, Marion, Ind.

AMERICAN ASSOCIATION.

Club.	President.	Manager.
Columbus.	E. M. Schoenborn	Wm. Friel.
Indianapolis.	W. H. Watkins.	Chas. C. Carr.
Toledo.	W. R. Armour.	H. Hinchman.
Louisville.	W. Grayson, Jr.	Del Howard.
Milwaukee.	C. S Havenor.	J. J. McCloskey.
Kansas City.	George Tebeau.	D. C. Shay.
St. Paul.	Geo. E. Lennon.	M. J Kelley.
Minneapolis	M. E. Cantillon.	Joe Cantillon.

SOUTHERN ASSOCIATION.

Club.	President.	Manager.
Atlanta.	J W.Heisman.	O. Jordan.
Birmingham.	R. H. Baugh.	C. Molesworth.
Chattanooga.	O. B. Andrews.	John Dobbs.
Memphis.	F. P. Coleman.	Chas. Babb.
Montgomery.	E. B. Joseph.	Ed. Greminger.
Mobile.	C. Z. Colsson.	George Reed.
Nashville.	F. E. Kuhn.	W. Bernhard.
New Orleans.	Charles Frank.	Chas. Frank.

NEW YORK STATE LEAGUE.

Club.	President.	Manager.
Elmira.	F. L. Breese.	M. O'Neill.
Wilkesbarre.	W. J. Clymer.	W. J. Clymer.
Scranton.	E. J. Coleman.	Monte Cross.
Binghamton.	J. J. Warner.	Harry Lumley.
Syracuse.	G. N. Kuntzsch.	E. M. Ashenback.
Utica.	H. W. Roberts.	C. L. Dooley.
Troy.	J. W. Fleming.	James Kennedy.
Albany.	C. M. Wincheste	W. J. Clarke.

CENTRAL LEAGUE.

Club.	President.	Manager.
Wheeling.	B. F. Perkins.	Wm. C. Phillips.
Zanesville.	W. E. Hemick.	R. Montgomery.
Ft. Wayne.	C. H. Varnell.	James Burke.
Grand Rapids.	Bert. Annis.	G. Craven
Terre Haute.	Louis D. Smith.	Geo. Groeschow.
South Bend.	L. Wills (Sec.)	Ed. Wheeler.
Evansville.	Angus A. Grant.	Angus A. Grant.
Dayton.	Elmer Redelle.	C. Punch Knoll.

CONNECTICUT LEAGUE.

Club.	President.	Manager.
Waterbury.	H. R. Durant.	M. J. Finn.
New Haven.	G. M. Cameron.	W. M. Carrick.
Hartford.	J. H. Clarkin.	Thos. J. Connery
New Britain.	W. W. Hanna.	Joseph Connor.
Springfield.	J. A. Zeller.	J. A. Zeller.
Holyoke.	Fred Winkler.	C. Foster.
Northampton.	Gilbert Edwards.	William Luby.
Bridgeport.	H. E. McCann.	H. E. McCann.

VIRGINIA LEAGUE.

Club.	President.	Manager.
Roanoke.	C. R. Williams.	F. Shaughnessy.
Norfolk.	A. C. Omohundro	Winn Clark.
Richmond.	W. B. Bradley.	J. J. Lawler.
Danville.	Jno. W. Boswell.	Stephen Griffin.
Petersburg.	F. Thos. Briggs.	Robert Stafford.
Lynchburg.	J. M. McLaughlin	Walter J. Smith.

SOUTH ATLANTIC LEAGUE.

Club.	President.	Manager.
Augusta.	A. H. DeVaughn	Frank Norcum.
Columbia.	Wm. Banks.	F. Cavender.
Columbus.	H. A. Williams.	James Fox.
Jacksonville.	W. E. Gullett.	E. P. Lauzon.
Macon.	N. J. Ethridge.	Perry Lipe.
Savannah.	M. A. O'Byrne.	G. H. Magoon.

SOUTHWEST TEXAS LEAGUE.

Club.	President.	Manager.
Bay City.	Allen Stinnett.	E. Haralson.
Beeville.	J. C. Dougherty.	H. S. Longley.
Brownsville.	H. G. Dubose.	S. H. Bell.
Corpus Christi.	Walter Timon.	H. R. Sutherland
Laredo.	Dr. J. T. Halsell.	George R. Page.
Victoria.	J. A. Malone.	John Burke.

EASTERN LEAGUE.

Club.	President.	Manager.
Baltimore.	John Dunn.	John Dunn.
Buffalo.	J. J. Stein.	Wm. A Smith.
Jersey City.	Geo. W. Henry.	John P. Ryan.
Montreal.	S. E. Lichts'n.	Ed. Barrow.
Newark.	Jos. McGinnity.	Jos. McGinnity.
Providence.	T. J. Crowley.	Jas. J. Collins.
Rochester.	C. T. Chapin.	John Ganzel.
Toronto.	J. J. McCafferty.	Jos. J. Kelley.

WESTERN LEAGUE.

Club.	President.	Manager.
Denver.	J. C. McGill.	J. C. Hendricks.
Des Moines.	John Higgins.	George Davis.
Lincoln.	D. C. Despain.	James Sullivan.
Omaha.	W. A. Rourke.	W. A. Rourke.
St. Joseph.	John Holland.	John Holland.
Sioux City.	T. Fairweather.	Jay Towne.
Topeka.	R. G. Cooley.	R. G. Cooley.
Wichita.	Frank Isbell.	Frank Isbell.

PACIFIC COAST LEAGUE.

Club.	President.	Manager.
Los Angeles.	W. H. Berry.	FrankE. Dillon.
Oakland.	E. N. Walter.	H. Wolverton.
Portland.	W. W. McCredie	W. H. McCredie
San Francisco.	F. M. Ish.	D. W. Long.
Sacramento.	W. L. Curtin.	Chas. Graham.
Vernon.	Edward Maier.	W. L. Hogan.

TRI-STATE LEAGUE.

Club.	President.	Manager.
Altoona.	W. H. McEld'n'y	H. D. Ramsey.
Harrisburg.	W. H. Baker.	A. Selbach.
Johnstown.	G. K. Kline.	Bert Coun.
Lancaster.	John H. Meyers.	M. Hogan.
Reading.	Benj. E. Jones.	H. L. Barton.
Trenton, N. J.	James H. Letts.	G. W. Heckert.
Williamsport.	F. C. Bowman.	W. P. Coughlin.
York, Pa.	H. Keister Free.	C. Wiegard.

ILLINOIS-IOWA-INDIANA LEAGUE.

Club.	President.	Manager.
Waterloo.	P. J. Martin.	Frank Boyle.
Davenport.	Richard Lane.	P. Holycross.
Rock Island.	W. H. Reck.	John Tighe.
Peoria.	D. Drohan.	David Drohan.
Bloomington.	E. Howland.	Joe Keenan.
Danville.	J. Boyle.	J. A. McCarthy.
Springfield.	R. F. Kinsella.	Richard Smith.
Dubuque.	Theo. Scharle.	Huntley Hines.

NORTHWESTERN LEAGUE.

Club.	President.	Manager.
Seattle.	D. E. Dugdale.	Frank Weed.
Spokane.	Jos. P. Cohn.	Jos. P. Cohn.
Tacoma.	E. E. Quinn.	C. O. Blanks'p.
Vancouver.	R. P. Brown.	R. P. Brown.

TEXAS LEAGUE.

Club.	President.	Manager.
Dallas.	Joseph Gardner.	Jimmy Maloney.
Ft. Worth.	Walter Morris.	Walter Morris.
Galveston.	Ben C. Doherty.	Frank Donnelly.
Houston.	Otto Sens.	Hunter Hill.
Oklahoma City.	R. E. Moist.	Dr. J. Andrews.
San Antonio.	Morris Block.	George Leidy.
Shreveport.	W. T. Crawford.	Dale Gear.
Waco.	W. R. Davidson.	Brooks Gordon.

SOUTHERN MICHIGAN ASSOCIATION.

Club.	President.	Manager.
Saginaw.	A. S. Burkart.	F. Wessells.
Flint.	A. J. Wildauger.	Edward Herr.
Jackson.	Charles Sarvis.	Bo Slear.
Kalamazoo.	J. W. Ryder.	Charles Wagner.
Bay City.	W. J. Lambert.	Leon C. Foye.
Lansing.	J. A. Morrissey.	J. A. Morrissey.
Battle Creek.	T. C. Morgan.	Wm. Earl.
Adrian.	F. T. Reed.	Carl Vandegrift.

Since the signing of the Cincinnati Peace Compact the game, which during the bick-erings of 1890 and 1891 received a great backset, has been steadily regaining its mighty hold on the people, which it attained in 1888 and 1889. Last season the clubs of the two leading leagues all made money.

This season sees the great sport established in all directions on a paying basis and extending its influence throughout the United States.

It has required just such wars as the professional game experienced in 1884, 1890 and 1900, to give the organized sport a permanency which can not be destroyed. These struggles have done for honest baseball and the National Agreement what the Revolution and the War of the Rebellion have done for the United States and the Constitution—namely, made both stronger, more lasting and all the dearer to the heart of every true American.

To-day more millions are spent yearly for baseball than belonged to the richest men in the United States at the time the game was getting its start.

Last season in the minor leagues, 5000 players signed contracts, this year the number will reach 6000, with a salary list for the season of $2,900,000, while $650,000 more goes to this for the payment of players in the National and American leagues. This makes a total of $3,550,000. Members of the outlaw leagues and independent clubs bring the total up to the huge figure of $4,000,000. Traveling expenses, making due allowance for hotel bills and grading the sum according to the caliber of the leagues, shows that the movement of the various clubs takes about $750,000 yearly.

The cost of playing fields sends the total soaring higher still, whether the club owns or rents its grounds. Not less than $2,000,000, either in rental or in the interest tied where grounds are owned, goes out yearly for places on which the nation's game shall be played.

For umpires $180,000 would not be excessive. Controlling bodies, the National Commission and the National Association of Baseball Clubs, have expenses that amount to $75,000. The managers take about $300,000 for work they do, and training trips, which each year increase in cost, mean another $150,000. Baseballs and other equipment put a final $100,000 on the sum, making the grand total of $6,295,000 spent every year by owners of large clubs. Baseball is conducted at a profit, and this expenditure means that at the gate the American public must have paid in not less than $7,000,000 in a single year.

These are figures obtainable and capable of proof, but no way offers to get at the cost of Uncle Sam's amateur baseball. There never were so many amateur players as now. Thousands of men and boys play the game for love to one who did so in the old times. Every town and hamlet has its clubs, and in many of them the players spend their own money for expenses.

THE NATIONAL LEAGUE.

A. G. SPALDING TELLS IN AN INTERESTING WAY OF HOW THE SENIOR BASE-BALL ORGANIZATION OF AMERICA WAS PLANNED AND BUILT UP.

Organized 1876. Thos. J. Lynch, president; Jno. A. Heydler, secretary.
Headquarters—St. James Building, New York.
St. Louis—President, M. S. Robison; manager, R. Bresnahan.
New York—President, Jno. T. Brush; manager, J. J. McGraw.
Chicago—President, Chas. W. Murphy; manager, Frank Chance.
Cincinnati—President, Aug. Herrmann; manager, Clarke Griffith.
Philadelphia—President, Horace S. Fogel; manager, Chas. Dooin.
Brooklyn—President, C. H. Ebbets; manager, Wm. Dahlen.
Boston—President, John C. S. Dovey; manager, Fred Lake.
Pittsburg—President, Barney Dreyfus; manager, Fred Clarke.

Standing of Clubs in 1909.

	W.	L.	Pct.		W.	L.	Pct.
Pittsburg	110	42	.724	Philadelphia	74	79	.484
Chicago	104	49	.620	Brooklyn	55	98	.359
New York	92	61	.601	St. Louis	54	98	.355
Cincinnati	77	76	.504	Boston	45	108	.294

Game Forfeited—By Philadelphia to New York, at New York, Oct. 4, 1909 (second game).

Winners in Previous Races.

	Pct.		Pct.
1910—Chicago	.676	1892—Boston	.650
1909—Pittsburg	.743	1891—Boston	.630
1908—Chicago	.643	1890—Brooklyn	.667
1907—Chicago	.704	1889—New York	.659
1906—Chicago	.765	1888—New York	.641
1905—New York	.688	1887—Detroit	.637
1904—New York	.693	1886—Chicago	.726
1903—Pittsburg	.650	1885—Chicago	.770
1902—Pittsburg	.741	1884—Providence	.750
1901—Pittsburg	.647	1883—Boston	.643
1900—Brooklyn	.603	1882—Chicago	.655
1899—Brooklyn	.682	1881—Chicago	.667
1898—Boston	.685	1880—Chicago	.798
1897—Boston	.705	1879—Providence	.702
1896—Baltimore	.698	1878—Boston	.683
1895—Baltimore	.669	1877—Boston	.646
1894—Baltimore	.695	1876—Chicago	.788
1893—Boston	.667		

THE NATIONAL GAME.

Leading Batsmen in Previous Races.

	G.	Pct.		G.	Pct.
1910—Crandall, New York	43	.342	1891—Hamilton, Philadelphia	138	.338
1909—Wagner, Pittsburg	137	.339	1890—Glascock, New York	124	.336
1908—Wagner, Pittsburg	151	.354	1889—Brothers, Boston	126	.373
1907—Wagner, Pittsburg	142	.350	1888—Anson, Chicago	134	.342
1906—Wagner, Pittsburg	140	.339	1887—Anson, Chicago	122	.421
1905—Seymour, Cincinnati	149	.377	1886—Kelly, Chicago	118	.388
1904—Wagner, Pittsburg	132	.340	1885—Connor, New York	110	.371
1903—Wagner, Pittsburg	129	.355	1884—O'Rourke, Buffalo	104	.350
1902—Beaumont, Pittsburg	131	.357	1883—Brothers, Buffalo	97	.371
1901—Burkett, St. Louis	142	.382	1882—Brothers, Buffalo	84	.367
1900—Wagner, Pittsburg	134	.380	1881—Anson, Chicago	84	.399
1899—Ed Delahanty, Philadelphia	145	.408	1880—Gore, New York	75	.365
1898—Keeler, Baltimore	128	.379	1879—Anson, Chicago	50	.407
1897—Keeler, Baltimore	128	.432	1878—Dalrymple, Milwaukee	60	.356
1896—Burkett, Cleveland	133	.410	1877—White, Boston	48	.385
1895—Burkett, Cleveland	132	.423	1876—Barnes Chicago	66	.403
1894—Duffy, Boston	124	.438	1875—		
1893—Stenzel, Pittsburg	51	.409			
1892—Brothers, Brooklyn	152	.335			

Mr. A. G. Spalding recently told in an interview of just how the National League came into being.

After reciting the story of the building up of professional baseball from 1869 on, Mr. Spalding, dating his career from that time, said:

"The Boston nine won the National championship four years in succession, from 1872 to 1875 and in the latter year they did not lose a game on their own grounds. The team appeared almost invincible. Other cities were becoming disheartened and were dropping out, and professional baseball began to be looked upon as a sort of local Boston affair.

"Chicago was able to win the championship for only one year—1876—when it came back to Boston again for two years. The places of the four seceders were filled by John Morrill, Tom Bond, Tim Murnane and 'Jim' White.

"As one of the results of this so-called secession movement of the big four from Boston to Chicago in 1876 the present National League was organized. This in reality marked another epoch in professional baseball and it came about in this way: The constitution of the original National Association of Professional Baseball Players provided the extreme penalty of expulsion to any player who signed a contract with any other club, except the one he was then playing with, before the playing season was over. The succeeding Big Four violated the clause in the old constitution and did sign with the Chicago Club in 1875, and consequently were liable to expulsion. An effort was made to keep the action a secret, but the secret lasted just ten days, and I believe that is longer than any other baseball secret was ever kept. You can not keep anything secret in baseball.

"That great organizer, William A. Hulbert, was president of the Chicago Club in 1876 and was largely responsible for the leaving of the big four from Boston. In the fall of 1875, when the newspapers were full of threats that the Boston big four would be expelled from the association for violating the constitution by signing with Chicago, planning the overthrow of this old association and the organization of the present National League.

"To appreciate the importance of this movement, the demoralized condition of the game at that period should be considered, for the game in several large cities, especially in New York and Philadelphia, was largely under the domination of the gambling element. I do not mean by this that the club officials were gamblers, but some of those officials were of the opinion that professional baseball, like horse racing, must have the extraneous aid of betting in order to attract the public.

"After deciding on the name of the new organization, we worked out the new league constitution, section by section, having in mind only one thing—to raise the standard of the game in every possible way, and without much regard to the then existing customs and methods of operating professional clubs. Pool selling and all forms of gambling were prohibited, liquor selling on the grounds was abolished and contract jumping penalized.

"Mr. Hulbert and myself were quite proud of the final draft. We were both confident that the new departure would be favorably received by the better class of club officials, players and public generally. The feeling was strong against Mr. Hulbert on account of the action of the Chicago Club in enticing the big four from their allegiance to the Boston Club. The newspapers were full of all sorts of threats as to the drastic action that would probably be taken at the next annual meeting of the old association in March, 1876.

"The more these threats were circulated the more determined Hulbert became that the new regime should be put into effect, in order, as he often said, to save professional baseball from annihilation as a sport. First it was deemed wise to feel the four western clubs, which resulted in a secret meeting in Louisville in 1878, at which the St. Louis, Cincinnati and Louisville clubs pledged their support to the new league. At this secret conference Mr. Hulbert and Mr. Fowle of St. Louis were appointed a special committee to confer with the officials of the four Eastern clubs—Boston, Hartford, New York and Philadelphia—and if possible bring them into the new league. The presidents of the four Eastern clubs met the Western committee at the Grand Central Hotel, New York, February 2, 1876, and before that conference ended the new National League was born."

18

THE CHICAGO WHITE STOCKINGS.

THE TEAM WHICH WON NATIONAL LEAGUE CHAMPIONSHIPS FOR MANY YEARS IN SUCCESSION AND WHICH WILL GO DOWN IN HISTORY AS THE HEROIC LEGION OF BASEBALL.

THE CHICAGO WHITE STOCKINGS OF THE EIGHTIES.

Top row, reading from left to right: George Gore, lf.; Frank Flint, c.; Adrian C. Anson, 1b.; James McCormick, p.; Michael J. Kelly, rf. and change c.; Fred Pfeffer, 2b.

Bottom row, reading from left to right: Edward Williamson, ss.; Abner Dalrymple, lf.; Thomas Burns, 3b.; John G. Clarkson, p.; William Sunday, rf. and substitute.

For years the Chicago White Stockings were known as the heroic legion of baseball. Adrian C. Anson, their leader, was one of the famous figures in baseball, guiding them through National and Worlds Championships. In magnificent appearance on the field; in great skill as fielders; in great strength as batsmen, this team has never had an equal.

THE NATIONAL GAME.

CHAMPIONSHIP WINNERS.

The following is a list of the clubs winning the championship in the leading baseball leagues of America, since 1870, when the National Association of Professional Baseball Players took the field, up to the present day:

NATIONAL ASSOCIATION.

Year.	Club.	W.	L.	Pct.	Manager.
1871	Athletics-Philadelphia	22	7	.759	Hicks Hayhurst.
1872	Boston	39	8	.830	Harry Wright.
1873	Boston	43	16	.729	Harry Wright.
1874	Boston	43	17	.717	Harry Wright.
1875	Boston	71	8	.899	Harry Wright.

NATIONAL LEAGUE.

Year.	Club.	W.	L.	Pct.	Manager.
1876	Chicago	52	14	.788	A. G. Spalding.
1877	Boston	31	17	.646	Harry Wright.
1878	Boston	41	19	.683	Harry Wright.
1879	Providence	59	25	.702	George Wright.
1880	Chicago	67	17	.798	A. C. Anson.
1881	Chicago	56	28	.667	A. C. Anson.
1882	Chicago	55	29	.655	A. C. Anson.
1883	Boston	63	35	.643	John F. Morrill.
1884	Providence	84	28	.750	F. C. Bancroft.
1885	Chicago	87	25	.770	A. C. Anson.
1886	Chicago	90	34	.726	A. C. Anson.
1887	Detroit	79	45	.637	W. H. Watkins.
1888	New York	84	47	.641	James Mutrie.
1889	New York	83	43	.659	James Mutrie.
1890	Brooklyn	86	43	.667	Wm McGunnigle.
1891	Boston	87	51	.620	F. G. Selee.
1892	Boston	102	48	.680	F. G. Selee.
1893	Boston	86	43	.667	F. G. Selee.
1894	Baltimore	89	39	.695	Edward Hanlon.
1895	Baltimore	87	43	.669	Edward Hanlon.
1896	Baltimore	90	39	.698	Edward Hanlon.
1897	Boston	93	39	.705	F. G. Selee.
1898	Boston	102	47	.685	F. G. Selee.
1899	Brooklyn	101	47	.682	Edward Hanlon.
1900	Brooklyn	82	54	.603	Edward Hanlon.
1901	Pittsburg	90	49	.647	Fred Clarke.
1902	Pittsburg	103	36	.741	Fred Clarke.
1903	Pittsburg	91	49	.650	Fred Clarke.
1904	New York	106	47	.693	John J. McGraw.
1905	New York	105	48	.668	John J. McGraw.
1906	Chicago	117	35	.705	Frank Chance.
1907	Chicago	107	45	.704	Frank Chance.
1908	Chicago	99	55	.643	Frank Chance.
1909	Pittsburg	110	42	.724	Fred Clarke.
1910	**Chicago**	104	50	.676	Frank Chance.

AMERICAN LEAGUE.

Year.	Club.	W.	L.	Pct.	Manager.
1900	Chicago	82	53	.607	C. A. Comiskey.
1901	Chicago	83	53	.610	Clark Griffith.
1902	Athletics-Philadelphia	83	53	.610	Connie Mack.
1903	Boston	91	47	.659	James Collins.
1904	Boston	95	59	.617	James Collins.
1905	Athletics-Philadelphia	92	56	.621	Connie Mack.
1906	Chicago	80	56	.614	Fielder Jones.
1907	Detroit	92	58	.613	Hugh Jennings.
1908	Detroit	90	63	.558	Hugh Jennings.
1909	Detroit	98	54	.645	Hugh Jennings.
1910	Athletics	102	48	.680	Connie Mack.

AMERICAN ASSOCIATION.

Year.	Club.	W.	L.	Pct.	Manager.
1882	Cincinnati	55	25	.680	Justus Thorner.
1883	Athletics	66	32	.670	Lew Simmons.
1884	Metropolitan	75	32	.700	James Mutrie.
1885	St. Louis	79	38	.705	C. A. Comiskey.
1886	St. Louis	93	46	.669	C. A. Comiskey.
1887	St. Louis	95	40	.704	C. A. Comiskey.
1888	St. Louis	92	43	.611	C. A. Comiskey.
1889	Brooklyn	93	44	.679	J. McGunnigle.
1890	Louisville	88	44	.667	John C. Chapman.

UNION ASSOCIATION.

Year.	Club.	W.	L.	Pct.	Manager.
1884	St. Louis	91	16	.850	T. P. Sullivan.

THE NATIONAL GAME.

THE LEAGUE ORGANIZED.

The National League was organized in New York City at a meeting held there on February 2, 1876.

There were delegates present at this meeting representing the Athletics of Philadelphia, the Boston, Chicago, Cincinnati, Hartford, Louisville, Mutual of New York, and St. Louis clubs. At the close of the season the Mutual and Athletic clubs were expelled from the league for their failure to complete their season.

THE INTERNATIONAL ASSOCIATION.

THE FIRST REAL COMPETITOR OF THE NATIONAL LEAGUE FOR BASEBALL HONORS AND ITS EARLY AND LATE CAREER.

On February 20, 1877, at Pittsburg, a second prominent baseball league was formed.

It was called the International Association of Baseball Clubs and its roster included the Tecumsehs of London, Canada; the Maple Leafs of Guelph, Canada; the Alleghenys of Pittsburg; the Live Oaks of Lynn, Mass.; the Buckeyes of Columbus, Ohio; the Rochesters of Rochester, N. Y., and the Manchester, N. H. teams.

The Tecumsehs won the championship of the International Association in 1877, their playing team including Goldsmith, pitcher; Powers, catcher; G. W. Bradley, Doescher and Dineen on the bases; Somerville, shortstop, and Hornung, Magner and Knowdell in the outfield. Reid and Spence were the substitutes.

THE FIRST AMERICAN ASSOCIATION.

THE FIRST REAL COMPETITOR OF THE NATIONAL LEAGUE FOR BASEBALL HONORS.

It was the success scored by the co-operative St. Louis Browns in 1881 that led to the first American Association taking the field in 1882.

The Browns playing on the co-operative plan had induced other teams to come to St. Louis in 1881 and they played games on a percentage basis. Many of these games were played on Sundays and were largely attended.

Billy Barnie, a famous ex-National League catcher, brought a team here he called the Atlantics of Brooklyn and the same season of 1881 O. P. Caylor brought a nine from Cincinnati which he called the Cincinnati Reds.

Horace B. Phillips at about the same time got a team together in Philadelphia, which he called the Athletics and he brought that nine here in the 1881 season and by the aid of their magic name they too drew out a fine attendance.

The success scored by Barnie, Phillips and Caylor and their teams led to a conference and the result was a meeting at Cincinnati in the fall of 1881 which led to the organization of a six-club league called the American Association.

Its roster included St. Louis, Cincinnati and Louisville in the West, and Pittsburg, Baltimore and Philadelphia in the East.

The men who organized this league were Denny McKnight and Horace B. Phillips of Pittsburg; Billy Barnie of Baltimore; Charles Mason, Lew Simmons and Billy Sharsig of Philadelphia; Aaron Stern, Louis Kramer, Louis Herancourt and O. P. Caylor of Cincinnati; Chris Von Der Ahe, W. W. Judy and A. H. Spink of St. Louis, and J. W. Reccius and John Botto of Louisville.

The first championship in the American Association in 1882, its first season, was captured by the Cincinnati Reds of which team Charles Fulmer was the manager and Charles N. Snyder the field captain. The playing team included Snyder and Phil Powers, catchers; William H. White and Henry McCormick, pitchers; Dan Stearns and Harry Luff, first basemen; John A. McPhee, second base; W. W. Carpenter, third base; Charles Fulmer, shortstop; Joe Sommer, left field; James Macullar, center, and Harry Wheeler, right.

To win the American Association pennant that year Cincinnati had only to win fifty-four games and lose twenty-six.

This by the way was the only real championship baseball team Cincinnati ever could boast of and it played two games in the Fall of 1882 with the Chicago White Stockings who had won the National League pennant that year. These were really the first two games ever played for a world's championship, but they amounted to nothing, as Chicago captured one game and Cincinnati the other.

In 1883 the Athletics of Philadelphia captured the American Association pennant and the people of the Quaker City nearly went daft in consequence. The race that year had been a wonderful one and the pennant was taken from the St. Louis Browns by the following wonderfully close score:

Competitors.	Games Won.	Games Lost.
Athletics	66	32
St. Louis Browns	65	32

So close was the race that it was not until the Athletics had beaten the Louisvilles at Louisville in a ten-inning game by a score of 7 to 6, that the real question was decided.

The team which won this 1883 American Association flag for the Athletics was made up of:

Catchers, O'Brien and Rowen; pitchers, Bobby Matthews, George Washington Bradley, Carey and Jones; first base, Stovey; second base, Stricker; third base, Bradley; shortstop, Carey; left field, Birchall; center field, Blackiston; right field, Knight and Crowley.

THE NATIONAL GAME.

In 1884 the American Association increased its membership to twelve clubs and the St. Louis Browns, the team of which we make prominent mention later on in this work, went on and landed the pennant four times in succession.

In 1889 the American Association came near going to the wall. The St. Louis, Philadelphia, Louisville and Columbus clubs wanted Zach Phelps of Louisville for their president. The others wanted L. C. Krauthoff of Kansas City. There was a deadlock for two days and numerous ballots were taken. Finding they could not win the owners of the Brooklyn and Cincinnati clubs withdrew and joined forces with the National League. Kansas City joined the Western Association and Baltimore the Atlantic Association. The clubs remaining elected Mr. Phelps president of the association and added Syracuse, Rochester, Toledo and Brooklyn to their circuit. The season was an unprofitable one, the Brooklyns and Athletics disbanding in mid-season owing to poor patronage.

Louisville captured the pennant this season of 1890 and the Athletics finished last. In 1891 Boston captured the American Association pennant and it was the last play of that kind the National League absorbing all that was left of the Association the following year.

THE AMERICAN LEAGUE.

AN INTERESTING STORY OF HOW THIS BASEBALL ORGANIZATION HAPPENED TO COME INTO LIFE AND BEING.

Organized 1900. Byron Bancroft Johnson, president; Robert B. McRoy, secretary.
Headquarters—Fisher Building, Chicago, Illinois.
St. Louis—President, Robt. L. Hedges; manager, Jack O'Connor.
Chicago—President, C. A. Comiskey; manager, Hugh Duffy.
Philadelphia—President, Ben F. Shibe; manager, Connie Mack.
Detroit—President, F. J. Navin; manager, Hugh Jennings.
Boston—President, Jno. I. Taylor; manager, Pat Donovan.
Cleveland—President, Jno. Killfoyl; manager, James McGuire.
Washington—President, Thos. C. Noyes; manager, Jas. R. McAleer.
New York—President, Frank J. Farrell; manager, Geo. T. Stallings.

Standing of Clubs in 1909.

	W.	L.	Pct.		W.	L.	Pct.
Detroit	98	54	.645	New York	74	77	.490
Philadelphia	95	58	.621	Cleveland	71	82	.464
Boston	88	63	.583	St. Louis	61	89	.407
Chicago	78	74	.513	Washington	42	110	.277

Winners in Previous Races.

	Pct.		Pct.
1909—Detroit	.645	1904—Boston	.617
1908—Detroit	.588	1903—Boston	.659
1907—Detroit	.615	1902—Athletics	.610
1906—Chicago	.616	1901—Chicago	.610
1905—Athletics	.621	1900—Chicago	.607

Leading Batsmen in Previous Races.

	Hits.	Pct.		Hits.	Pct.
1909—Cobb, Detroit	116	.377	1904—Lajoie, Cleveland	140	.381
1908—Cobb, Detroit	150	.324	1903—Lajoie, Cleveland	126	.255
1907—Cobb, Detroit	150	.350	1902—Ed Delahanty, Washington	123	.376
1906—Stone, St. Louis	154	.358	1901—Lajoie, Cleveland	131	.422
1905—Lajoie, Cleveland	65	.328	1900—Sam Dungan, Kansas City	117	.337

I think I may fairly lay claim to being the first to suggest the formation of the American League which is now a genuine rival of the National League.

It was in the Fall of 1898 while engaged as sporting editor of the St. Louis Post-Dispatch that I called attention to the fact that interest in baseball was on the decline and that something ought to be done to put new life and energy into the sport.

I said then that what was needed to arouse new life and new and added interest was a rival association to the National League.

I said this because the Fall seasons in baseball at this time were absolutely devoid of interest and the conditions were in marked contrast to those which existed when the champion clubs of the National League and American Association battled with each other each fall for a world's championship.

There was considerable opposition, however, to my suggestion. This came mostly from men who held National League franchises and who had a monopoly of the baseball patronage in the leading cities.

I pointed out to these gentlemen that an opposition league would not injure their business but that on the contrary it would add new life to the game and that in cities where there would be rival teams in the field these teams could play a series with each other in the Spring and Fall, the receipts from which would more than offset any losses likely to follow from the appearance of competition.

I also called attention to the fact that a rival association would awaken interest in

THE NATIONAL GAME.

the game in new places, bring out additional patronage and prove in the end of great benefit to all concerned.

To bring about the organization of a new league, I wrote letters to well-known baseball men throughout the country asking them to help me put the new association in the field.

I also wrote to many leading sporting writers and asked them to join me in the proposed venture. I had no interest in the matter, save to awaken and put new life into the sport.

I regret to say that I met with small encouragement in all directions. Most of the Eastern sporting writers made fun of the proposed league.

THE OPPOSITION TO THE ENTERPRISE.

The leading sporting writers of New York, Boston and Chicago all belabored the proposed enterprise.

Among those who favorably recognized my efforts to reorganize an opposition association to the National League was T. P. Sullivan, a man of shrewd mind and long experience in the organizing of baseball associations and one who perhaps has excelled all other managers in this direction for it was mainly through his efforts that the first American Association was thoroughly organized and that the Union Association, the first Texas League, and other baseball associations were formed.

Sullivan in 1898 was so favorably impressed with my suggestion to organize an association in opposition to the National League that he came here in the summer of 1898 from Chicago and volunteered to help place the new baseball body in the field.

I introduced him to the promoters of the St. Louis end of the proposed association, Mr. George D. Schaefer, being then the leader, and then and there Mr. Sullivan was engaged to scout the country in search of cities for the new body. It was mainly through his efforts that the first meeting for the organization of the American League was held at Chicago in the fall of 1898.

FIRST MEETING OF AMERICAN LEAGUE.

This meeting, to avoid notoriety and the criticism of an unfriendly press, was held at an obscure hotel in Chicago.

It was the first meeting ever held for the purpose of placing the American League in the field and as a result of the work of Mr. Sullivan and myself there was a fair attendance. In fact the attendance exceeded our most sanguine expectations and gave us great hope for the future.

I had the honor of calling this meeting to order and as near as I can remember there were present: Frank Hough, sporting editor of the Philadelphia Press; Francis C. Richter, editor of the Sporting Life of Philadelphia; Thomas J. Navin of Detroit; Charles S. Havenor and H. D. Quinn of Milwaukee; T. P. Sullivan, Chris Von Der Ahe, Thomas L. Harlan, George D. Schaefer, George P. Heckel and myself of St. Louis, and A. C. Anson of Chicago.

At this meeting I showed letters from John J. McGraw of Baltimore and William Barnie of Brooklyn, promising to help us place teams in New York and Brooklyn in the event of the league being organized.

While the meeting was in progress baseball reporters of Chicago and Ban Johnson, Charles A. Comiskey and Thomas J. Loftus, all then members of the Western Association, were on the lookout for us.

These latter three gentlemen knew that the organization of the American League would prove a hard blow to their Western Association inasmuch as it would oppose one of its members, the Milwaukee, and perhaps deprive it of many of its players.

When Johnson, Comiskey and Loftus, all old and dear friends of mine, discovered our meeting place, instead of barring their entrance, we invited them to join us in putting the new league on a proper footing.

Pointing to South Chicago where we contemplated building a ground and placing a team, I said to Comiskey:

"You're a Chicago boy, you belong down there and not out in St. Paul."

"Yes, and I'm willing to go right down there now and join you gentlemen in the furthering of this enterprise, but I have partners in the Western Association not situated as I am and I do not think it would be fair for me to quit them at this time," said Comiskey.

Loftus and Johnson assumed a friendly air, but like Comiskey, were not then ready to join the new body.

After a brief stay in Chicago our little party disbanded, but another meeting to be held at the Great Northern Hotel in Chicago was arranged for and there, late in the Fall of 1898 the second meeting for the organization of the New American League was again called to order.

THE SECOND MEETING OF THE AMERICAN.

This time John J. McGraw of Baltimore was there in person and with him from the East came Frank Hough and Francis C. Richter.

The West was again represented by the same parties as had appeared at the initial meeting.

McGraw reported that Freedman and Sullivan had a mortgage on New York City and that no one would be permitted to place a club in the metropolis in opposition to the New York Giants, the club which then represented the National League in the greatest baseball city.

At about the same moment Anson reported that his original Chicago backers had

23

THE NATIONAL GAME.

gone back on him. With (New York and Chicago both out of the question, the meeting again adjourned without attempting to complete an organization to take the field in 1899.

Never wavering and never giving up the hope that I would still see the American League in the field in the summer of 1899, I still worked incessantly to bring about the organization of the American. I even wrote to Ban Johnson and other of the Western Association leaders like Comiskey and Loftus and tried to secure their co-operation in the building up of the new enterprise.

A LETTER FROM BAN JOHNSON.

For a while Johnson acted as though he would come over to the movement and on the date named I received the following letter from him:

"Chicago, Ill., Aug. 28th, 1899.

"Mr. A. H. Spink, St. Louis, Mo.

"My Dear Al.—I delayed replying to your letter for the reason that I expected to meet Loftus at Milwaukee yesterday. I have not seen him since his trip to the Northwest. I went to Milwaukee, but Tom was not there. He went over to Dubuque on Friday night, and for some reason did not return for the Sunday game. I presume it will be three or four days before I will have a chance to see him as he will be very much occupied in looking after his business in Dubuque.

"It is just as well the meeting should be postponed. Sullivan was here Saturday and told me he had written you relative to the matter. I will try and arrange to run over to St. Louis for a day. As our season is drawing to a close I am full of business in adjusting accounts for the year With kind regards, I am,

"Yours sincerely,

"B. B. JOHNSON."

It will be noticed that as late as August, 1899, Johnson had not yet determined to help reorganize the American League, of which he is now the head.

It will be noticed by his letter too that he was friendly and that he, Loftus and Sullivan were at least considering a proposition that had been laughed at in many quarters the year before.

THE MEETING IN NEW YORK.

Not hearing definitely, up to this time, from Johnson and his friends, in November, 1899, with George D. Schaefer and Chris Von Der Ahe of St. Louis, Charles S. Havenor and H. D. Quinn of Milwaukee, and T. P. Sullivan of Chicago, I journeyed to New York to attend a meeting which was held in Tom O'Rourke's Hotel, on Broadway in that city on November 3, 1899.

There were present at this meeting John J. McGraw, who represented Baltimore; Frank Hough and Francis C. Richter, who were there in the interest of Philadelphia; Tim Murnane who came from Boston and who had been with me in the Union Association and Brotherhood movements; Jacob Morse of the Boston Herald, an enthusiast for the new league, and William Barnie of Brooklyn.

This little crowd in the face of adverse newspaper and other criticism were brave and willing to go ahead.

But again no real headway was made and again the New York baseball writers almost to a man laughed at our endeavors and declared that no team would ever on this earth be placed in New York in opposition to Freedman and his Giants.

But the seeds sown at Chicago and New York during the winter of 1898 and 1899 took root and from them came the meeting on January 29, 1900, at Chicago ,when the American League was launched.

The appearance of this opposition rival to the National League did for the game just what I predicted it would do.

In places where interest had been on the wane there was an immediate revival and following the appearance of the new organization came the series in each succeeding Fall for the world's championship, contests which brought out record-breaking crowds and drew new admirers to the game from all directions.

The appearance of the new league in fact was of such great benefit to the game that those who were the first to discourage its building up were later the very first to admit the good it did and to welcome and help foster its various club members.

The first cities in the American League were Indianapolis, Milwaukee, Cleveland, Kansas City, Detroit, Buffalo, Cleveland and Minneapolis.

In 1901 Washington, Baltimore, Boston and Philadelphia took the places of Indianapolis, Kansas City, Buffalo and Minneapolis.

In 1902 St. Louis took the place of Milwaukee and in 1903 Baltimore retired from the Eastern end to make room for New York.

This left the circuit with St. Louis, Chicago, Cleveland and Detroit forming the Western wing and Washington, Philadelphia, New York and Boston, the Eastern, and so it remains to-day.

The American League in fact today ranks right alongside its old and once powerful rival, the National League. It has built magnificent baseball parks at Philadelphia, Chicago, Cleveland and St. Louis and is planning to build other magnificent grounds, notably in New York City to be the home of the New York Highlanders. This latter ground in fact will perhaps be the most costly and magnificent ever built.

GEORGE BAKER.

George Baker, a St. Louis boy, was perhaps the greatest catcher in the Union Association. He played on the St. Louis Union team under Dunlap, and on that team caught the terrific pitching of Sweeny, Boyle, Healy and Taylor.

The teams which were playing in the American League in its 1902 season while the war was still on between the National and American leagues and which took part in the opening games on April 23, 1902, were as follows:

ST. LOUIS.	CLEVELAND.	DETROIT.	CHICAGO.
Burkett, lf.	Pickering, lf.	Barrett, cf.	Strong, 3b.
Heidrick, cf.	McCarthy, cf.	Holmes, lf.	Jones, cf.
Jones, rf.	Harney, rf.	Casey, 3b.	Green, lf.
Anderson, 1b.	Shreck, c.	Harley, lf.	Davis, ss.
Wallace, ss.	Bonner, 3b.	Elberfield, ss.	Mertes, rf.
Padden, 2b.	Bradley, ss.	Gleason, 2b.	Daly, 2b.
McCormick, 3b.	Gochnauer, 2b.	Dillon, 1b.	Isbell, 1b.
Sugden, c.	Bemis, 1b.	McGuire, c.	Sullivan, p.
Maloney, c.	Moore, p.	Siever, p.	Patterson, p.
Donahue, p.	Hemphill, lf.		
BALTIMORE.	PHILADEPHIA.	BOSTON.	WASHINGTON.
Gilbert, ss.	Hartzell, lf.	Parent, ss.	Ryan, rf.
Sheckard, cf.	Fultz, 2b.	Stahl, cf.	Keister, cf.
Kelly, 1b.	Davis, 1b.	Collins, 3b.	Wolverton, 3b.
Seymour, rf.	L. Cross, 3b.	Freeman, rf.	Delehanty, lf.
Williams, 2b.	Flick, rf.	Hickman, lf.	Coughlin, 2b.
Selbach, lf.	Seybold, cf.	Lachance, 1b.	Carey, 1b.
McGann, 1b.	M. Cross, ss.	Ferris, 2b.	Ely, ss.
Robison, c.	Powers, c.	Criger, c.	Drill, c.
Hughes, p.	Plank, p.	Young, p.	Carrick, p.

It will be noticed by the above list that by this time the old league had been drawn on heavily for players.

THE UNION ASSOCIATION.

THE ORGANIZATION WHICH WAS STARTED IN 1884 TO DELIVER THE PROFESSIONAL PLAYERS FROM BONDAGE.

I have always been the friend of the professional baseball players and I must admit that each time they set up in business for themselves I went with them.

In the Fall of 1883 I became associated with Henry V. Lucas in the getting up of the Union Association of baseball teams.

These efforts resulted in the first revolt and attack on the National Agreement and reserve rule which came in 1884, when the Union Association was regularly organized.

Very few of the old players could be tempted to desert the League and American Association, however, and after a year of very expensive experiment the backers of the Union Association surrendered and withdrew from the field, counting their losses at nearly a quarter of a million.

Soon after the Union Association was talked of Mr .Lucas enlisted the services of T. P. Sullivan of Dubuque to assist him not only in the selection of a team of players, but in the organization of the new league.

Sullivan in the interest of the new organization visited Boston, Philadelphia, Washington and Altoona in the East, and St. Louis, Chicago, Cincinnati and Kansas City in the West, and helped put teams in all of these cities.

The St. Louis Unions were backed by Henry V. Lucas, a young St. Louis millionaire who was practically the backer and organizer of the whole outfit, for whenever funds were needed in any direction to bolster up a club or to keep it in line, Mr. Lucas was the one angel who appeared with the thing needed and always at the right time and place.

The team which he selected the first year to represent St. Louis in the Union Association included Dolan, Baker and Brennan, catchers; Taylor, Hodnett, Healy and Kirby, pitchers; Quinn, first base; Dunlap, second base; Whitehead, shortstop; Jack Gleason, third base; George Schaefer, right field, and Dave Rowe, center field.

I have said I was always with the ball players in their fights for independence and while I first went with them in the old Union days, I also hooked up with the boys in the Brotherhood of 1890.

I call to mind in the Union days a few great thoroughbreds who were with us from the time the first gun was fired in 1883 until the association was gobbled up by the National League, two years later.

Among these fine fellows were Tim Murnane, who captained and played at right field for the Boston Unions; Tom Pratt and his lieutenant, Catcher Clements, who piloted the Philadelphia Unions; Mike Scanlon who put Washington into the Union Association and kept it in there until the finish; Fred Dunlap, perhaps the greatest second baseman that ever lived; Joe Quinn, George Schaefer and Dave Rowe, all great players; Justus Thorner and Frank Wright of Cincinnati; Dan O'Leary, who was the captain and manager of the Cincinnati Unions and many other thoroughbreds just like him.

But the greatest figure of all in the Union Association was Henry V .Lucas, who by the splendid battle he made in 1883 and 1884 for the players, became known as "The Napoleon of Baseball."

Mr. Lucas was one of the Lucas heirs of St. Louis. His father at one time owned half the town and when he died Henry V. Lucas was left over a million as his share of the great Lucas fortune.

Henry V. had always been a great lover of the National Game and he was an everyday attendant at the games played at Sportsman's Park by the St. Louis Browns from 1882 until 1883 when Mr. Lucas' sympathies went out to the players.

He had heard their story that they were being abused and he set out to organize a baseball league that would deliver the players out of bondage. He called his league the Union Association and he treated his players as they had never been treated before.

They were given carte blanche as to salaries; were allowed to come and go as they pleased and to discipline themselves as they saw fit.

But kind and liberal as was Mr. Lucas' way of doing things, the plan failed to work successfully and after a disastrous career which lasted only through the season of 1884 the Union Association was laid away on the shelf and never afterwards resurrected.

The batting order of the teams which made up the Union Association in the initial games of that organization played in April, 1884, was as follows:

ST. LOUIS.	ALTOONS.	CINCINNATI.	CHICAGO.
Dunlap, 2b.	Leary, lf.	Harbridge, cf.	Elleck, rf.
Shaffer, rf.	Smith, ss.	Hawes, rf.	Krieg, c.
Dickerson, lf.	Murphy, lf.	O'Leary, lf.	Hengle, 3b.
J. Gleason, 3b.	Brown, cf.	Powell, 1b.	Householder, lf.
Rowe, cf.	Harris, 1b.	Bradley, p.	Foley, 3b.
Taylor, p.	Koons, 3b.	Burns, p.	Shoeneck, 1b.
Baker, c.	Moore, rf.	McLaughlin, ss.	Mathias, .
Whitehead, ss.	Noftsker, c.	Swartz, c.	Tony, cf.
Quinn, 1b.	Dougherty, 2b.	Jones, 2b.	Daily, p.
		Barber, 3b.	

KEYSTONES OF PHILADELPHIA.	BALTIMORE.	BOSTON.	NATIONALS OF WASHINGTON.
Kenzie, cf.	Say, ss.	Murnane, 1b.	Baker, c.
Hoover, 2b.	Fuselbach, c.	O'Brien, 2b.	Wise, p.
Geer, ss.	Robinson, 3b.	Brown, c.	Evers, 2b.
Luff, lf.	J. Sweeney, rf.	Hackett, ss.	Moore, ss.
McCormick, 3b.	Levis, 1b.	Bond, p.	Voss, 1b.
Meyerle, 1b.	W. J. Sweeney, p.	Crane, lf.	McKenna, rf.
Pattison, rf.	Seery, lf.	Slattery, cf.	Cregan, cf.
Blakely, p.	O'Brien, cf.	Daniels, rf.	Leahan, 3b.
Gillen, c.	Phelan, 2b.	Riley, 3b.	Musz, lf.
	Stanley, cf.		

This list shows all the clubs that played with the Union Association during its only year and the games played and won by each:

Teams.	Games Won	Games Played	Teams.	Games Won	Games Played
St. Louis	97	118	Milwaukee	8	12
Cincinnati	70	113	Altoona	6	25
Baltimore	57	100	Pittsburg	6	16
Boston	56	105	St. Paul	2	7
Nationals	48	111	Wilmington	2	18
Chicago	34	74		—	—
Keystone	22	68		423	846
Kansas City	17	79			

After playing twenty-five games Altoona dropped out of the Union Association and Kansas City was substituted. It was the latter's maiden attempt at professional baseball and the game which took place in Kansas City on June 7, 1884, between the Kansas City Unions and the Chicago Unions was the first real professional game ever played in Kansas City. For that reason we give the full score:

CHICAGO.	R.	B.H.	P.O.	E.	KANSAS CITY	R.	B.H.	P.O.	E.
Ellick, rf	1	1	0	2	Wheeler, lf	1	1	2	1
Shoeneck, 1b	3	3	3	1	Cross, 3b	1	2	0	5
Cross, lf	0	1	1	0	Hickman, p	0	1	0	1
McLaughlin, 2b	1	0	5	5	Berry, 2b	1	1	6	1
Krieg, c	0	1	11	1	Shaffer, rf	1	2	2	1
Mathias, ss	0	0	1	1	Alexander, c	0	0	9	3
Beggs, cf	0	0	4	0	Fisher, ss	0	0	0	1
Householder, 3b	0	1	0	1	Connors, cf	0	0	3	0
Horan, p	1	0	0	0	Chatterton, 1b	1	0	12	0
	—	—	—	—		—	—	—	—
	6	5	35	11		5	7	34	13

Innings.

Kansas City ....1 0 0 0 0 1 2 0 0 0 0 1—5
Chicago ....1 0 0 0 0 2 1 0 0 0 0 2—6

Two-base hits—Berry 1. Three-base hits—McLaughlin 1, Shaffer 1. Double plays—Chatterton, Berry, Beggs and McLaughlin. Time of game—Two hours and fifteen minutes.

FIRST MAJOR LEAGUE GAME IN KANSAS CITY.

This was the first game in which the Kansas City players had ever played together as well as the first major league game ever played in Kansas City. It took twelve innings to decide the battle and Chicago won by a single tally. One-armed Daly, the Chicago's crack pitcher, was ill and did not play in this game and changes all around in the team were made on this account.

No official score was kept of this game for the reason that no one in Kansas City at that time knew how to keep a regular tabulated score and the score above is the best that can be given under the circumstances.

The St. Louis Unions, the leaders in the Union Association, greatly overmatched the other clubs.

THE NATIONAL GAME.

In four games, for example, played with Altoona, the St. Louis team averaged fourteen and a quarter runs to the game, while the Altoonas made but twelve runs in the four games or not as many as the St. Louis had made in a single game.

In so far as the St. Louis end of it was concerned the Union Association, however, ended its only season in a blaze of glory.

On Sunday, October 19, 1884, the St. Louis and the Boston Union teams closed their season at Union Park at Cass and Jefferson avenues in the City of St. Louis before a crowd that numbered over 10,000 persons.

At Sportsman's Park, the home of the Browns, two amateur teams appeared and though a free gate was on parade only a few hundred spectators were present.

On the other hand, over 10,000 persons assembled at Union Park to see the St. Louis and Boston Unions play and also to see an athletic tournament which consisted of a 135-yard foot race between Joseph A. Murphy, E. W. Saunders and Taylor Lingo, which Murphy won, and an attempt on the part of Edward Crane of the Boston Unions to beat John Hatfield's record at throwing a baseball. Hatfield's record was 133 yards, 1 foot and 7 inches. Crane set out to beat it. A strong breeze was blowing almost due East so that Crane, who was throwing from the Southeast to the Northwest, had to throw almost three-quarters against the wind. It was claimed that at Cincinnati a few days previous Crane had thrown a baseball 135 yards and 7 inches. On this Sunday, October 19, 1884, the best he could do was 134 yards and 5 inches.

As Messrs. Lucas and Murnane had backed Crane to the extent of $50 that he would throw better than 135 yards, they lost their bet by seven inches.

The Athletic exercises and the game ended the career of the Union Association in St. Louis and the country over, for in the following winter, peace was restored. Mr. Lucas put his team into the National League and the Union Association was forgotten. But during its existence it was a most popular establishment in St. Louis and had all the other teams in the Union Association been as self-supporting as the St. Louis Unions that organization would have remained a fixture in the baseball world.

On October 24 and 25, 1884, the St. Louis Unions played games at Union Park with the Louisvilles of the American Association. The Louisvilles had Browning, c.f.; Wolf, r.f.; Sweeney, c.; Gerhardt, 2b.; Cline, l.f.; Sullivan, 3b.; Andrews, 1b.; Reccius, p., and McLaughlin, s.s. In the game of October 24 the Louisville won by 7 to 2 and friends of the American Association laughed at the Union players and asserted they were not in the same class with their opponents. On October 25, however, the St. Louis Unions had the laugh on the other side for that day they beat the Louisvilles by 15 to 1 and scored 19 hits to their opponents' 2. A third game was to have been played on October 26 but rain interfered. These were the last games ever played by the St. Louis Unions and ended their sensational career.

The complete record of the eight clubs which took part in the majority of the games played in the Union Association during 1884, the only season of its existence, was as follows:

Union Association Record in 1884.

Club.	W.	L.	Pct.	Club.	W.	L.	Pct.
St. Louis	91	16	.850	Pittsburg	40	40	.500
Cincinnati	68	35	.660	National	47	66	.416
Baltimore	56	48	.538	Keystone	21	46	.313
Boston	58	51	.532	Kansas City	14	63	.182

THE PLAYERS' LEAGUE.

A LIST OF THE BOYS WHO JOINED THE BROTHERHOOD IN 1890 AND TOOK PART IN THE MOST IMPORTANT FIGHT EVER MADE ON THE NATIONAL AGREEMENT.

The most desperate war made on the National Agreement was that instituted in 1890 when the Players' League, or the Brotherhood as it was best known, went in business for itself.

That year the Brotherhood of Baseball Players of the National League secured rich backers, fitted up grounds and waged a desperate war against what they denounced as the injustice of the reserve rule.

The consequence was that salaries advanced nearly 100 per cent and hundreds of thousands of dollars were lost in the fight.

The Brotherhood League had the advantage of favorite players, but the National League had the best of the battle in leaders and experienced generals.

The plans for the organization of the Brotherhood of Baseball Players which took the field in 1890 were, I believe, worked out by Charley Crane, who had played at second base for the Cincinnati Unions and other professional teams.

While I was the secretary and official scorer of the St. Louis Unions in 1884 I found in the secretary's office of that club a lot of memoranda which Crane had written and which looked like the constitution and by-laws of a baseball league, resembling very much those used later by the founders of the Brotherhood of Professional Baseball Players when they perfected their organization in 1890.

It was said later that John M. Ward, E. R. Hanlon and other players conceived the idea of the Players' League during the tour of the Spalding baseball party on their trip around the world, and the season of 1889 was given up to getting the players into line and forming stock companies.

The Players' League or the Brotherhood of Baseball Players, as it was best known, lasted but the one season—1890.

Nearly every great player in America, however, went to it.

Among those who joined in the revolt were big-hearted fellows like "Mike" Kelly, Charles Comiskey, Jim Galvin, Ned Hanlon, Cliff Carroll, Tip O'Neill, Fred Pfeffer,

28

Roger Connor, Jim O'Rourke, Buck Ewing, Tim Keefe, Harry Stovey, Dan Brouthers, Joe Quinn, Billy Nash, Arthur Irwin, Emmet Seery, John M. Ward, Jack Rowe,. Jim McAleer, Jack Brennan and other famous players whose names at this time were a household word in the baseball arena and who were really the pick of the playing talent of that day.

The first championship games of the Brotherhood of the Players' League as the organization was then best known were played on April 19, 1890. At Chicago the Chicagos won over the Pittsburgs by 10 to 2 and the batting order was:

PITTSBURG.	CHICAGO.
Hanlon, cf.	Latham, 3b.
Visner, 1f.	Duffy, cf.
Carroll, c.	O'Neill, lf.
Beckley, 1b.	Comiskey, 1b.
Fields, lf.	Pfeffer, 2b.
Keuhne, 3b.	Farrell, rf.
Robinson, 2b.	Bastian, ss.
Corcoran, ss.	Boyle, c.
Galvin, p.	King, p.

At Philadelphia, New York lost to the local Players' League team. The score was 12 to 11 and the batting order was as follows:

NEW YORK.	PHILADELPHIA.
Richardson, 2b.	Griffin, lf.
Gore, cf.	Shindle, ss.
Connor, 1b.	Fogarty, cf.
O'Rourke, lf	Wood, rf.
Ewing, c.	Pickett, 2b.
Slattery, rf.	Mulvey, 3b
Hatfield, ss.	Farrar, 1b.
Whitney, 2b.	Buffington, p.
Keefe, p.	Cross, c.

At Boston that team was victorious over the Brooklyn Players' League team by 3 to 2. The batting order of the teams was:

BOSTON.	BROOKLYN.
Richardson, lf.	Seery, lf.
Stovey, rf.	Bauer, 2b.
Kelly, c.	Andrews, cf.
Nash, 3b.	Ward, ss.
Brouthers, 1b.	Orr, 1b.
Quinn, 2b	McGeary, rf.
Johnston, cf.	Joyce, 3b.
Irwin, ss.	Daly, c.
Kilroy, p.	Van Haltren, p.

At Buffalo the home team defeated the Clevelands by the awful score of 23 to 2 and the batting order was:

BUFFALO.	CLEVELAND.
Irwin, 3b.	Stricker, 2b.
Hoy, cf.	Delehanty, ss.
Rowe, ss.	Browning, lf.
Wise, 2b.	Twitchell, rf.
Carney, 1b.	Tebeau, 3b.
Beecher, lf.	Larkin, 1b.
Rainey, rf.	McAleer, cf.
Mack, c.	Gruber, p.
Haddock, p.	Brennan, c.

The above list shows just which of the players broke away from the old baseball associations and set out to establish an independent league of their own. Their names will go down in history as those of a lot of brave fellows who believed in standing by one another and who lost out in the battle not because their hearts were not in the right place.

Their battle resulted in a most exciting year's fight, in which it is estimated that a million dollars and more was lost by the fighting leagues, the Brotherhood revolt failed, and the National League, under the banner of the National Agreement and reserve rule, remained in possession of the field.

But the fight had some good results for it led to a much better understanding between owners of clubs and players and a respect for the latter's rights that had been conspicuous for its absence in certain places previous to the rebellion.

John M. Ward, the president of the Brotherhood, said at the time that that organization was really formed on account of the passage by the National League in 1885 of an arbitrary $2,000 salary limit rule.

In 1887 the Brotherhood endeavored to amend the old form of contract asking the officers of the National League to strike out the $2,000 clause.

The League officials, Ward claimed, promised to strike out the offensive figures at their next annual meeting in 1888.

With this agreement the players signed up for the following season, but when the National League officials, according to Ward, went back on their agreement and in the Fall of 1888 enacted a classification law which completely ignored the requests of the players, then the latter concluded to strike out for themselves and the result was the organization of the Brotherhood or Players' League. At a meeting of the Brotherhood held in New York on November 4, 1889, a public declaration of intention to withdraw from the National League was issued.

Two days later, November 6, 1889, at the Fifth Avenue Hotel in New York City, the Players' League was organized or rather the first steps for its organization were taken.

Legal obstacles were in the way and prevented the real organization at this first meeting, but by December 16, 1889, they were removed and the Players' League was launched with Boston, Brooklyn, New York and Philadelphia in its Eastern circuit and Buffalo, Pittsburg, Cleveland and Chicago in its Western wing.

The Bostons won the Players' League's only pennant in 1890 with a team that included Kelly, Murphy and Swett, catchers; Radbourne, A. Gumbert, Daley, Kilroy and Madden, pitchers; Brouthers, Quinn and Nash on the bases; Arthur Irwin, shortstop, and H. Richardson, T. Brown and Harry Stovey in the outfield.

The war between the Players' League managers and those of the National League was a costly and bitter one. The courts were often applied to for injunctions by both sides.

Conflicting schedules were arranged and all things done to make the rival paths thorny.

At the end of the season of 1890 the Players' League bought the Cincinnati Club of the National League.

This left the latter organization with but six clubs for its Pittsburg Club was all but dead. When matters reached this stage the National League men consented to a conference which ended in secret meetings afterwards between the capitalists of both leagues with the result that the rival clubs in New York City, Pittsburg and Chicago were consolidated and this virtually brought the career of the Players' League to a close and caused its disbandment.

THE PRESENT AMERICAN ASSOCIATION.

A BODY THAT PROMISES TO SOON TAKE RANK WITH THE TWO LEADING MAJOR LEAGUES.

When the American League was getting ready to invade Chicago and St .Louis in the West and New York and Boston in the East, the Western Association men saw their opportunity.

They organized in the winter of 1901-1902 the flourishing body that is now so well known as the American Association.

This body opened its initial season in the spring of 1902, its roster then including Columbus, Milwaukee, Toledo, St. Paul, Minneapolis, Kansas City, Indianapolis and Louisville. This circuit has never been changed and all of its clubs have been wonderfully prosperous.

The American Association operated as an independent body in 1902 and 1903 and in those years it had to face opposition at Milwaukee and Kansas City. It beat out its rivals in the end and now holds full sway of that once disputed territory. In 1903 after it had won its fight the American Association managers joined forces with those having at heart organized baseball and are now in good standing with the parent body.

Thomas J. Hickey of Chicago was the first president of the present American Association. He held the reins in 1902.

In 1903 J. Ed Grillo, a well-known baseball writer, took the place of Mr. Hickey, and in 1905 Mr. Grillo gave way to Joseph D. O'Brien of Milwaukee, who was succeeded by Thomas Chivington, the present very efficient head of the American Association, who promises to hold that high office for an indefinite period.

With the best schedule in its history, with Sunday ball all over the circuit, and with more evenly matched teams than ever before, the American Association is now in the high tide of its prosperity.

With the Western teams materially strengthened, and the teams in the Eastern cities of the circuit retaining their form of 1909, the race for the pennant in 1910 was an interesting one and at the end Minneapolis landed in front.

The American Association was organized in the winter of 1901-1902, and opened its first season in the Spring of 1902, with teams in Columbus, Milwaukee, Toledo, St. Paul, Minneapolis, Kansas City, Indianapolis and Louisville. The circuit has remained unchanged to this date, and bids fair to remain the same for many seasons to come.

The association operated as an independent organization in 1902. It was paralleled in two cities, Milwaukee and Kansas City, in 1902 and 1903, by the Western League, and a bitter struggle for supremacy developed. At the close of the latter year, however, the Western League was forced to capitulate, and withdrew from the two association cities, the Western League forming a six-club circuit, which continued until the present season.

The original American Association circuit included Omaha, but early in 1902, before the season opened, the owners of the Omaha franchise deserted to the Western League. This defection of the Omaha people forced the American Association promoters to cast about for an eighth city to complete the circuit. This was no easy task.

Baseball at this time did not appeal to men with money, or to the players as it does to-day, and the prospect for financial reward for those who took an active part in promoting the sport was not so alluring as it is now. Baseball franchises practically went begging in the early days.

Finally, however, George Tebeau, who held the association franchise in Kansas City, where he was opposed by the Western League, consented to take the Louisville franchise. It was a great risk, and many of the wise acres shook their heads and gloomily prophe-

JOE CANTILLON.

PRESIDENT OF THE MINNEAPOLIS CLUB, CHAMPIONS OF THE AMERICAN ASSOCIATION IN THE 1910 SEASON.

JOSEPH CANTILLON.

The above is a likeness of Joseph Cantillon, who with his famous brother, Mike Cantillon, is the owner of the Minneapolis Club, the 1910 champions of the American Association. The fact that Joe Cantillon, after having experienced anything but success while looking after the destinies of Noyes' Senators, at Washington, "came right back" and in the first year of management handed the thousands of enthusiasts of baseball in the north a top-liner, has caused his thousands of friends and admirers in the American League cities to give vent to much joy. Cantillon is one of the real, live, lovable characters in baseball. After quitting the game as a player he took up umpiring. He was without a doubt one of the best judges of balls and strikes the American League fans ever saw. Cantillon's popularity with the ball players, and fans as well, always won for him easy sailing. When he took hold of the Washington Club a few years ago, affairs in the Capital City from a baseball standpoint, were anything but lovely. It was just as the noted baseball wit, Charlie Dryden, so cleverly put it: First in War, First in Peace, but Last in the American League. Cantillon gathered together a band of mighty nice looking ball players, but he was never able to line up a strong pitching staff. At that during the few years while he was looking after the National's interests, the club made money. His pleasant manner, winning ways and "ginger" made his band of players popular drawing cards. Cantillon to-day stands high among the big men of baseball. Comiskey, John I. Taylor, Ban Johnson, Garry Hermann and every athlete who plays the game, has a good word for genial Joe Cantillon.

sied disaster. Mr. Tebeau has been severely criticised in Louisville, Kansas City and elsewhere for holding two franchises in the association, but his critics forget that he was game enough to take a chance and risk what little money he had saved to make the prosperous association of to-day a possibility. Mr. Tebeau devoted his baseball ability and energy to developing his two association clubs, and what success he to-day enjoys he has honestly earned and is entitled to. Let those who criticise Tebeau but review the early struggles of the association, when he fought against odds and risked his savings in the struggle for existence, and it will be evident that he is deserving of tne reward of his efforts and foresight.

When the American Association was organized in 1902, Thomas J. Hickey of Chicago, now of Minneapolis, was selected as president. Mr. Hickey was in office until the close of the season of 1903, when J. Ed Grillo of Cincinnati, now sporting editor of the Washington Post, was appointed, holding the office until January, 1905.

Joseph D. O'Brien of Milwaukee was elevated to the presidency in 1905, and unanimously re-elected in 1906, and again in 1907 for a three-year term, with a substantial increase in salary. Mr. O'Brien's term expired in 1909 and in the 1910 season Thomas Chivington was elected to the place filled so well by Mr. O'Brien.

When Mr. O'Brien assumed the reins of government in 1905, the association was beset with factionalism. There seemed little chance of bringing the warring parties together, but Mr. O'Brien took up the herculean task, and with his suave diplomacy and executive ability he soon began to get order out of chaos. As late as 1906 the factions in the organization fought for supremacy, the only issue upon which the conflicting interests could agree being the retention of Mr. O'Brien as chief executive. Since 1906, however, peace has prevailed and to-day factionalism is unknown, the various club owners standing shoulder to shoulder, in harmony, and all working for the best interests and advancement of the association and the good of baseball in general.

In the Fall of 1903, after it had won its fight against the Western League in Kansas City and Milwaukee, the American Association entered organized baseball, and from that time its advance has been continually forward. To-day the association represents an investment of from $600,000 to $750,000 in grounds and improvements. The poorest franchise in the association to-day probably could not be purchased for $100,000. This statement best illustrates the marvelous advancement of the American Association as an organization.

The equipment in the various plants is on a par with those of the major league. The Toledo Club, owned by W. R. Armour, has recently invested $100,000 in new grounds and stands, which were ready about July 1. At Indianapolis where the franchise is owned by W. H. Watkins and others, the grandstands have recently been remodeled to accommodate fully 20,000 persons.

Columbus furnishes a splendid example of the baseball possibilities in the American Association. The franchise now is owned by a syndicate with E. M. Schoenborn at the head, that gentleman having been chosen president to succeed Thomas J. Brice, who died last year.

The Columbus Club was one of the first to own its grounds and plant. Nearly $100,000 was invested in the park at the start of the association, and this amount was repaid back out of the profits of the club within a little over two years. The Columbus Park is one of the most modern in the circuit. Public telephones are installed at easily accessible places, and all other conveniences for patrons are at hand. An idea of the popularity of the league there may be gained from the fact that though Columbus is the smallest city in the circuit its patronage classes with the best.

C. S. Havenor, president of the Milwaukee Baseball Club owns outright both the franchise and the grounds. The Milwaukee park is unusually large, and will serve the purpose of the owner for all time, no matter how great the increase in attendance.

The St. Paul franchise is owned by George E. Lennon, a prominent merchant and one who is identified with the largest business interests of that city.

The Minneapolis franchise is in the hands of M. E. Cantillon and his brother, Joseph Cantillon, late manager of the Washington American League team.

The Kansas City property is controlled by George Tebeau.

The Louisville Club is now owned by William Grayson, formerly of St. Louis.

The American Association is fortunate in possessing as officials men who are practical both in a business way and in baseball.

TRIPS ABROAD OF AMERICAN TEAMS.

HOW THE BOSTON AND ATHLETIC TEAMS WENT TO ENGLAND AND HOW SPALDING'S ALL AMERICA AND CHICAGO TEAMS MADE A TRIP AROUND THE WORLD.

On several occasions professional American baseball teams have gone abroad in search of fortune and fame.

The first of these trips was made in the summer of 1874. On July 16 of that year the players of the Boston Club of Boston and the Athletic Club of Philadelphia left the latter city on the steamship Ohio and arrived in Liverpool, England, on July 27, just a week later.

The Athletic contingent was made up of thirty-eight persons, including players McBride, Clapp, Anson, McGeary, Sutton, Batten, Gedney, McMullen, Murnane, Fisler and Sensenderfer. Al Reach was the only one of the Athletic team not on hand, business keeping him at home.

The Boston party included George Wright, Harry Wright, Spalding, Barnes, Schaefer, McVey, Leonard, O'Rourke, Hall and Beals.

Jim White, the Bostons' regular catcher, declined the trip and his place was taken by Kent of the Harvard College team.

Sam Wright, a younger brother of George and Harry was drafted to take part in the cricket games, he being an experienced cricketer.

THE NATIONAL GAME.

It was A. G. Spalding who suggested this trip and who made the arrangements which were carried out on the other side.

Fourteen games were played, all of an exhibition character at London, Liverpool, Manchester and Sheffield in England and at Dublin in Ireland.

Of the fourteen games played the Bostons won eight to the Athletics six. The teams in these games were made up in this way:

Boston	Positions.	Athletic.
Jas. White	Catcher	John E. Clapp.
A. G. Spalding	Pitcher	Jas. D. McBride.
Jas. O'Rourke	First Base	West D. Fisher.
Ross C. Barnes	Second Base	Jos. Battin.
Henry Shafer	Third Base	Edw. B. Sutton.
Geo. Wright	Shortstop	M. H. McGeary.
A. J. Leonard	Left Field	A. W. Gedney.
Harry Wright	Center Field	J. F. McMullen.
Cal. C. McVey	Right Field	A. C. Anson.
Geo. W. Hall	Substitute	
Thos. L. Beals	Substitute	J. P. Sensenderfer.
Sam Wright, Jr	Substitute	Tim Murnane.

CRICKET MIXED WITH BASEBALL.

Cricket was sandwiched in between the baseball games and as two days were usually required to finish a cricket match the American players spent a pleasant six weeks abroad, varying the monotony when not playing baseball and cricket by trips at sightseeing.

At cricket, to the great surprise of the English and Irish people, the American players won all seven games played in opposition to the English and Irish elevens.

The Americans on this trip met with some curious experiences.

At Chatsworth Palace, one of the show places of England, Spalding of the Bostons and Fisler of the Athletics were suddenly drenched on a clear day by standing under a weeping willow when someone in the secret touched a hidden spring.

The teams left Queenstown, Ireland, for home on August 27, 1874, and after a stormy voyage arrived in Philadelphia on September 9, 1874.

It was the success scored on this initial trip of American players to England that led to other enterprises of the same sort.

THE FIRST TRIP TO HAVANA.

The next trip abroad of an American team was that taken in 1879, when Frank C. Bancroft of Cincinnati took a lot of American players to Havana, Cuba, the team being made up of Foley and Nichols, pitchers; Bennett and Bushong, catchers; Sullivan, first base; A. Whitney, third base; A. Irwin, shortstop; Wood, left, and Knight, outer field. The positions of second base and center field were filled by the change catcher and pitcher. This trip to Havana was a financial failure.

But it did not deter others from making the same experiment, for in 1886 teams representing the Athletic and Philadelphia clubs were taken to Havana by Lew Simmons and J. P. Scott of Philadelphia, but this trip, owing to bull-fight opposition, like the trip of Bancroft's men, was also a failure financially.

THE GREAT WORLD TOUR.

It was the success scored by the Boston and Athletic teams in 1874 during their visit to England and Ireland that perhaps induced A. G. Spalding to plan for another foreign tour, one that would eclipse all its predecessors in length of voyage and in the magnitude of its undertaking. It was in the late summer of 1888 that Spalding made known his plans to send two professional teams on a tour around the world.

This greatest trip ever made by American professional baseball players took place in 1888-1889, when Spalding completed all arrangements for the all around the world tour of teams which he called the Chicago and the All Americans.

These teams which made up the twenty players in the party of 1888 were as follows: Chicago—A. C. Anson, captain and first baseman; N. F. Pfeffer, second baseman; Thomas Burns, third baseman; E. N. Williamson, shortstop; M. Sullivan, left fielder; James Ryan, center fielder; R. Pettit, right fielder; Thomas P. Daly, catcher; J. K. Tener and M. Baldwin, pitchers.

All Americans—J. M. Ward, captain and shortstop; G. A. Wood, first baseman; H. C. Long, second baseman; H. Manning, third baseman; J. Fogarty, left fielder; E. Hanlon, center fielder; J. C. Earl, right fielder; F. H. Carroll, catcher; John Healy and F. N. Crane, pitchers. Earl also acted as change catcher.

The All Americans team included players from the League Clubs of New York, Philadelphia, Detroit, Pittsburg and Indianapolis, and from the American Association Clubs of Cincinnati and Kansas City. Mr. Spalding stood at the head of the tourist party, with Mr. Leigh S. Lynch as his business manager and H. H. Simpson as assistant; Mr. J. K. Tener being the treasurer and cashier.

The tourists also included George Wright, who went to coach the Americans when they met the foreigners at cricket; Harry C. Palmer, sporting editor of the Chicago Tribune; Si Goodfriend, sporting editor of the New York World; James C. Kennedy, sporting editor of the New York Times, and others.

They stopped first at Honolulu where they were entertained by the King of the Sandwich Islands. From there they went to Auckland, New Zealand, and thence to Sydney, N. S. W., where they arrived on December 14, 1888.

THE NATIONAL GAME.

FIRST GAMES IN AUSTRALIA.

The tourists played their first game at Auckland on December 10, and then visited Sydney, Melbourne, Adelaide and Ballarat, and returning to Melbourne left Australia for Europe on January 5, 1889, playing in Colombo on January 26, at the Egyptian Pyramids at Ghiza on February 8, at Naples, February 19 and at Rome and Florence on February 23 and 25, the party reaching Paris—they did not stop at Vienna or Berlin —on March 3.

The two nines played a series of games at Naples, Rome, Florence, Paris, London, Bristol, Manchester, Liverpool, Birmingham, Glasgow, Belfast and Dublin.

They sailed for home March 28, 1889, on the steamship Adriatic and arrived at New York City on April 6, a week later.

The teams were given a very warm reception on their return home. Banquets were tendered them at New York, Philadelphia and Chicago.

The tour might be said to have ended when on April 20, 1889, the Chicago and All American team played their fifty-third and last game at Chicago.

Out of these fifty-three games played on the tour the All Americans won twenty-eight to the Chicagos' twenty-two. Three of the games resulted in a tie.

THE LAST GREAT TRIP ABROAD.

Probably no trip save the round-the-world tour of the Chicago and All-American teams in the latter eighties had such a beneficial effect on baseball, made more converts to the great National game, and proved more interesting than the tour of the Reach All-American team through Japan, China, the Philippines and the Hawaiian Islands during the winter of 1908 and 1909.

With a line-up comprising a number of big league stars, together with a number of first-class ball players from the Pacific Coast, the Reach team played before great crowds, introducing the game in some spots where it had never touched, revived it in others and gave the soldier boys in the far-off Philippine Islands a chance to see a real American team in action.

The trip began on November 3, 1908, when the players sailed from San Francisco under the management of Mike Fisher, the well-known baseball man. Fisher had with him the following players:

Jim Delehanty of Washington, Pat Flaherty of Boston Nationals, Bill Burns of Washington, Jack Bliss of St. Louis Nationals, Jack Graney of Cleveland, Heitmuller, drafted by Philadelphia Americans; Nick Williams of San Francisco; Dansig of Pacific Coast League; Hildebrand of San Francisco; Devereaux of Oakland; Curtis and Harry McArdle of San Francisco.

The Americans played four games at Tokio, winning them all and in the presence of major league city crowds. When they met the Tokio University Club 6,000 Japanese rooters turned out on a bitter cold day to cheer their favorites, who had beaten all comers during the season. The grounds were jammed and it was unfortunate that the seating capacity was not larger. It was only recently that the Japanese enclosed their baseball fields at all.

AMERICANS VERSUS CHINESE.

The Chinese witnessed some exceptionally good games during the stay of the Americans there, as on several occasions the surplus Americans played with the native teams and once a team from the American fleet which was at that time in Chinese waters combined with the extra Reach players and had a fine game.

After a stay in Japan and a number of other good games, the tourists moved on to Manila where they arrived on Christmas Day. The first game in Uncle Sam's possessions was played with Lieutenant Johnson's Twenty-eighth Infantry team and resulted in a victory for the Reach team by the score of 2 to 1 in eleven innings. Two days later the Reach combination received a defeat at the hands of Lieutenant Johnson's team, the first beating for the Americans on the trip. The games in the Philippines attracted big crowds and everywhere there was an evidence of a boom in baseball. The soldiers brushed up their nines and there was great rivalry for the honor of playing against Mike Fisher's nine.

The players finally left Manila on January 5th and sailed for Honolulu. Here the Americans again found a host of fans of their own nationality ready to greet them and the games were played with more dash and greater spirit than in the Oriental countries.

The date for the arrival of the team in Honolulu was January 30, 1909, and in San Francisco, on February 15, giving the players time to scatter to their homes before joining their teams for Southern training.

Other tours abroad of American teams have taken place since, but none to compare with the all-around tour planned and carried out so successfully by Mr. Spalding.

There have also been many great trips made by professional baseball clubs in America, notably the two long training trips to the Pacific Coast made in 1908 and 1910 by Comiskey and his White Stockings, and the notable tour to San Francisco in the eighties of the Chicago White Stockings and the St. Louis Browns of that day.

As this book goes to press other long training trips like those made by the teams above named are now being planned, but there will perhaps never be another trip of professional baseball players to compare with the All Around The World of Spalding's All Americans.

That tour spread the name and fame of the National Game to all corners of the world, spread it so well that now there are baseball teams in existence in nearly all the cities visited and this is notably the case in England, Ireland, Scotland and Australia.

THE NATIONAL GAME.

BASEBALL IN THE CITIES.

TABLE SHOWING POSITIONS OCCUPIED BY TEAMS FOR THE PAST THIRTY-FOUR YEARS IN THE NATIONAL LEAGUE AND THE OLD PROFESSIONAL ASSOCIATION, INCLUDING THE GAMES OF 1909.

Team.	1	2	3	4	5	6	7	8	9	10	11	12	Won.	Lost.	Pct.
Providence	2	3	2	1	0	0	0	0	0	0	0	9	434	276	.611
Hartford	0	0	2	0	0	0	0	0	0	0	0	0	71	47	.602
Baltimore	3	2	0	1	0	0	0	0	0	0	0	1	644	447	.590
Chicago	9	6	5	4	3	2	1	2	2	0	0	0	2,409	1,747	.579
New York	4	4	5	2	2	2	3	3	1	1	0	0	2,057	1,621	.559
Pittsburg	4	5	1	1	1	4	3	4	0	0	0	0	1,769	1,470	.546
Boston	8	4	2	5	5	5	3	2	0	0	0	0	2,191	1,976	.526
Philadelphia	0	2	7	9	1	2	3	3	0	1	0	0	1,852	1,852	.500
Detroit	1	1	0	1	1	2	1	1	0	0	0	0	426	437	.494
Brooklyn	3	1	2	0	5	6	1	1	0	2	0	0	1,392	1,481	.488
Cincinnati	0	1	3	5	4	4	3	4	0	1	0	0	1,558	1,655	.485
Buffalo	0	0	3	1	1	0	2	0	0	0	0	0	312	333	.484
Cleveland	0	3	2	1	4	2	4	0	0	0	0	1	977	1,061	.479
Troy	0	0	0	1	1	0	1	1	0	0	0	0	134	191	.412
Louisville	0	1	0	0	1	0	0	0	3	0	2	3	477	740	.392
St. Louis	0	1	0	2	3	2	2	4	1	1	3	2	1,123	1,794	.385
Indianapolis	0	0	0	0	1	0	2	1	0	0	0	0	170	285	.374
Worcester	0	0	0	0	1	0	0	2	0	0	0	0	90	159	.361
Washington	0	0	0	0	0	0	2	3	1	2	3	1	573	1,034	.357
Syracuse	0	0	0	0	0	0	1	0	0	0	0	0	15	27	.357
Milwaukee	0	0	0	0	0	1	0	0	0	0	0	0	15	45	.250
Kansas City	0	0	0	0	0	0	1	0	0	0	0	0	30	91	.247

No history of the National Game would be complete without full reference to its building up in cities that have in their day owned major league clubs.

It would be impossible to cover all the cities where baseball is played now by professional teams, and so I will only give a history of the game in those cities which in their day have built up and helped maintain clubs in the various major leagues.

Cleveland and Washington are the only leading league cities that have never had pennant winning teams, but they are included in this list for obvious reasons.

In fact my summing up of baseball in the cities will cover some places whose teams' have won pennants as well as others whose teams have not been so fortunate. The pennant winning towns mentioned and the number of flags won by nines representing them as well as Cleveland and Washington, the non-winning cities, are as follows:

CHICAGO—Ten in National League, three in American League; total twelve.

BOSTON—Eight in National League, two in American League, one in Players' League, one in American Association; total twelve.

NEW YORK—Four in National League, one in American Association; total five.

ST. LOUIS—Four in American Association, one in Union Association; total five.

BROOKLYN—Three in National League, one in American Association; total four.

DETROIT—Three in American League, one in National League; total four.

PITTSBURG—Four in National League; total four.

BALTIMORE—Three in National League; total three.

PHILADELPHIA—Three in American League, one in American Assn; total four

PROVIDENCE—Two in National League; total two.

CINCINNATI—One in American Association; total one.

LOUISVILLE—One in American Association; total one.

INDIANAPOLIS—One in International Association, one in American Association.

THE GAME IN ST. LOUIS.

BY COMMON CONSENT BASEBALL DID NOT AMOUNT TO MUCH IN ST. LOUIS UNTIL THE EMPIRES WERE ORGANIZED IN 1860.

The following is the record made by the clubs which have represented St. Louis in the various baseball associations of which she has been a member from 1875 when the

THE NATIONAL GAME.

St. Louis Club was a member of the old Professional Association up to the present day:

Professional Association.

Year. Position.	W.	L.	Pct.
1875—Fourth	39	39	.426

National League.

Year. Position	W.	L.	Pct.
1876—Second	45	19	.703
1877—Fourth	19	29	.369

American Association.

Year. Position.	W.	L.	Pct.	Year. Position.	W.	L.	Pct.
1882—Fifth	36	35	.450	1887—First	95	40	.701
1883—Second	65	33	.660	1888—First	92	43	.681
1884—Eleventh	67	40	.626	1889—Second	93	44	.619
1885—First	79	33	.708	1890—Third	78	58	.574
1886—First	93	40	.669	1891—Second	85	52	.620

Union Association.

Year. Position.	W.	L.	Pct.
1884—First	91	16	.850

National League.

Year. Position	W.	L.	Pct	Year. Position.	W.	L.	Pct.
1885—Eighth	36	72	.233	1901—Fourth	76	64	.543
1886—Sixth	79	43	.352	1902—Sixth	56	78	.418
1892—Eleventh	57	75	.432	1903—Eighth	43	94	.304
1894—Ninth	56	76	.424	1904—Fifth	75	79	.422
1895—Eleventh	39	92	.298	1905—Sixth	58	96	.347
1896—Eleventh	40	90	.308	1906—Seventh	52	98	.347
1897—Twelfth	29	102	.229	1907—Eighth	52	101	.337
1898—Twelfth	39	111	.260	1908—Eighth	49	105	.318
1899—Fifth	83	66	.557	1909—Seventh	54	98	.355
1900—Sixth	65	75	.464				

American League.

Year. Position,	W.	L.	Pct	Year. Position.	W.	L.	Pct.
1902—Second	78	58	.574	1906—Fifth	76	73	.510
1903—Sixth	65	74	.468	1907—Sixth	69	83	.451
1904—Sixth	65	87	.428	1908—Fourth	83	69	.546
1905—Eighth	54	99	.354	1909—Seventh	61	89	.407

In writing of the games building up in these cities I have told the story with the aid of such facts and figures as I have been able to secure from all directions. I will not claim that the record is either complete or that there are no errors in it. I have simply covered the field as best I could and if there are mistakes ,they will be corrected if pointed out and when the second edition of this work is published.

It has been hard work keeping up the record for the reason that in the early days of the game there was little material to build from.

Some idea of the little interest taken in the National Game, even up to 1871, may be gleaned from the fact that on July 4 of that year the only games of importance played in America were four in number.

At Chicago on that day the Chicago White Stockings defeated the Forest Citys of Rockford by a score of 17 to 13. At Cincinnati the Boston Reds beat the Olympics of Washington by 7 to 3. At the Capitoline Grounds in Brooklyn the Eckfords defeated the Mutuals 7 to 0 and at Philadelphia the Athletics got away with the Forest Citys of Cleveland by 22 to 9. These eight clubs were about the only professional teams in America in this (1871) year and they had in their ranks nearly all the real players that were worth having.

As late as 1878 there were but sixty-seven professional players named in the list of averages given out for publication by the National League.

With this lack of material I have done the best I could in building up a story of the game through these early years and up to this time in cities where the game found its first friends and where it is flourishing so well now.

According to the early historians of the game the first actual baseball "match game" that ever took place in St. Louis was that played on July 8, 1860, on the old Fair Grounds.

The "Cyclones" and the "Morning Stars" were the competitors. No official score of the game was published so that it can not positively be stated just which club won.

St. Louis' first baseball grounds were located in this way:

The field opposite the Rock Church on Grand avenue, where the Empires and Unions played their earliest games.

The Stocks Park, just off Easton, near Vandeventer avenue.

The Elephant and "Saw Log" Grounds on the river front, open field east of Broadway and north of North Market street, where the Elephant and "Saw Log" teams played their games in the early seventies.

The open field just south of Lafayette Park where the Rowenas and Varieties played their games.

The Gamble Lawn Grounds near the old Rock Springs on the ground now occupied by the Terminal Railroad Association.

The Empires and Unions played some of their games on these grounds.

In 1871 August Solari built what were known later as the Grand Avenue Grounds which were located on the open field now occupied by Sportsman's Park.

In 1875 William L. Cassidy, Josh Rothschild and other baseball enthusiasts and live-

THE ST. LOUIS BROWNS OF 1875.

THE FIRST NINE TO EVER REPRESENT THE MOUND CITY IN A MAJOR LEAGUE ORGANIZATION.

THE ST. LOUIS BROWNS OF 1875.

Top row reading from left to right: Joseph Blong, right field and change pitcher; George Washington Bradley, pitcher; John Clapp, catcher; Richard Pearce, short fielder.

Bottom row reading from left to right: Joseph Battin, third base; George Seward, substitute and change catcher; John C. Chapman, right field; Lipman Pike, right; Edgar Cuthbert, center; Michael McGeary, second base; Denny Mack, short fielder and general utility man.

The above is a likeness of the first team to ever represent St. Louis in an out and out professional organization. This team had in it many famous players, notably Edgar Cuthbert, who was the champion base runner and center fielder of that year; Dickey Pearce, then considered the greatest of short fielders; George Washington Bradley, the speediest pitcher of that time; Mike McGeary, then considered the king of second basemen; John Clapp, the sturdiest and best receiver of that year; John C. Chapman, the best of the right fielders of his time; Lipman Pike, the champion right fielder from the Athletics of Brooklyn; Tommy Miller, one of the best of the early professional catchers; Joe Batten, the crack third baseman around Philadelphia; Joe Blong, then the speediest and best of the St. Louis pitchers and George Seward, famous then and long afterward as one of the best of the early catchers.

THE NATIONAL GAME.

stock dealers built the Stocks Park which was located near the car sheds in the vicinity of Easton and Vandeventer avenues.

James Galvin, St. Louis' first great pitcher, and the Gleason boys, Jack and Billy, went with the Stocks in their first and only year.

To this day there is a controversy on in St. Louis as to who it was that introduced baseball to these parts. As high an authority as Shepard Barclay, Esq., late judge of the Supreme Court of Missouri, gives the credit of that sort of thing to Jere Fruin, St. Louis veteran contractor and now the head of the Fruin-Colnon Construction Company of St. Louis.

"It was in the early fifties," said Judge Barclay, recently, "that Mr. Fruin brought the game to St. Louis. I was a little fellow at the time and with other boys I played all sorts of games on a field located right where Lafayette Park is now. I remember while playing there one day Jere Fruin, a great tall boy came among us. He was a stranger who had come from somewhere in the East and on our field he laid out a diamond and showed us how to play the modern game of baseball. He built us a diamond much the same as the diamond in use to-day, and in fact, showed us just how to play the game. That was really the introduction of the game to St. Louis."

John W. O'Connell, head of the John W. O'Connell Painting Company of St. Louis, and J. D. Fitzgibbon, the well-known St. Louis builder, take issue with Judge Barclay. They say the first game was brought here by men who had played baseball in the East, but that the first game ever played here took place in what was then Northwest St. Louis and on the ground now occupied by Carr Square Park.

Fitzgibbon and O'Connell were members of the Empire Club which was organized in 1860 and by general all-round consent baseball in St. Louis did not amount to much until that year.

Up to that time indeed games were played on the prairie in North, South and West St. Louis by the boys of the town, who gave no heed to club organization or anything of that sort.

THE EMPIRE CLUB ORGANIZED.

There was considerable comment, therefore, when on April 16, 1860, fifty years ago, the Empire Baseball Club was organized under a regular set of rules and by-laws.

Later the St. Louis Unions and the St. Louis Red Stockings came into the field of organized baseball, working under local rules and regulations.

By general consent, therefore, the first baseball games of prominence ever played in St. Louis were those between the Empire, Union and Red Stocking nines. Those were the first games in fact that brought about genuine rivalry between both the players and patrons.

The Empire Club was a finely-formed aggregation. It had in its ranks many wide-awake business men as well as some of the most influential mechanics and tradesmen. It had for its officers the most popular men in the community—men selected for their great heart, wide acquaintance and numerous following.

In 1864 and from 1870 to 1873, Henry Clay Sexton, for years St. Louis' most popular chief of the fire department, was the club's president. No man at this time had so large a following among all classes as "Old Clay."

For captains they had men like James Yule, Jerry Fruin, Adam Wirth, J. W. Shockey, J. D. Fitzgibbon and James J. Spaulding, now Judge Spaulding.

The Empires played only with home nines until 1865, and though pitted against players who were then considered very strong they were generally victorious, and won the title of "Champions of the State." On the Fourth of July, 1865, at Freeport, Illinois, was played the first "Fly" game in the West and it was won by the Empires by a score of 27 to 20, their opponents being the "Empires of Freeport." On September 20, following, the same clubs again met at Dubuque, Iowa, with a similar result; score, 12 to 5. The following day they defeated the Dubuque Club 16 to 14, and brought home a silver ball presented them by the Agricultural Association. In 1866 the play ground was changed to near the Pacific Railroad machine shop, and during that season they played some hard fought games with home clubs, still retaining the championship, and also participated in a grand tournament at Bloomington, Ill., where they defeated the Pacifics of Chicago, 22 to 11, and in turn were defeated by the Excelsiors of Chicago, 21 to 10. The players of the Empire Club received five out of the nine individual prizes awarded, and refused to contend for the second club prize, as they considered they had been unjustly treated in the Excelsior game for the first prize. In 1867 they succeeded in obtaining permanent grounds at the Baseball Park, which was then located on the grounds occupied in 1910 by the St. Louis Browns and known as Sportsman's Park, and where many interesting games occurred, especially the games running through several seasons with their old-time rivals, the Union Club, who in the year 1867 wrested the championship from the Empires and retained it until the following year. The number of games played with home clubs by the Empires was so very large as to preclude more than a general reference to them; but those with foreign clubs are condensed in the following, which will prove of value for reference and of interest to many:

1867—April 16, with Lone Star at Alma, Ill.; Alma, 28; Empire, 90.
July 23, with National of Washington, at St. Louis; Nationals, 53; Empire, 26.
1868—June 29, with Atlantic of Brooklyn, at St. Louis; Atlantic, 53; Empire, 15.
July 10, with Athletic of Philadelphia, at St. Louis; Athletic, 63; Empire, 6.
July 8, with Buckeye of Cincinnati, at St. Louis; Buckeye, 44; Empire, 9.
August 15, with Union of Morrisiania; Union, 36; Empire, 11; at St. Louis.
September 9, with Lone Star of Alma, at St. Louis; Star, 53; Empire, 14.
September 15, with Kaw Valley of Lawrence, at St. Louis; Kaw Valley, 12; Empire, 20.
1869—July 4, with Lone Star of Alma, at St. Louis; Star, 38; Empire, 49.
July 27—Buckeye, at Cincinnati; Buckeye, 14; Empire, 27.
July 29—Kentucky, at Louisville; Kentucky, 28; Empire, 30.
July 30—Eagle, at Louisville; Eagle, 24; Empire, 35.

THE NATIONAL GAME.

Aug. 16—Southern of New Orleans, at St. Louis; Southern, 23; Empire, 10.
August 19—Old Capital of Vandalia at St. Louis; Old Capital, 16; Empire, 65.
August 31—Forest City of Rockford at St. Louis; Forest City, 70; Empire, 6.
September 16—Cincinnati at St. Louis; Cincinnati, 34; Empire, 14.
1870—April 30, White Sox of Chicago at St. Louis; White Sox, 36; Empire, 8.
June 28—Lone Star; Alma, 23; Empire, 43.
July 3—Garden City at St. Louis, 39; Empire, 17.
July 24—Lone Star of New Orleans, 29; Empire, 16; at St. Louis.
August 18—Shabbona of Ottawa, 18; Empire, 32; at St. Louis.
September 29—Cincinnati, 7; Empire, 5; at St. Louis.
October 25—White Sox of Chicago, 46; Empire, 10; at St. Louis.
1871—April 23—White Sox of Chicago, 34; Empires, 8; at St. Louis.
June 5—Clinton; Iowa, 7; Empire, 16; at St. Louis.
July 30—Lone Star of New Orleans, 7; Empire, 6; at St. Louis.
September 20—Southern of New Orleans, 7; Empire, 16; at New Orleans.
September 21—R. E. Lee of New Orleans, 5; Empire, 29; at New Orleans.
September 22—Crescent of New Orleans, 10; Empires, 19; at New Orleans.
September 23—Lone Star of New Orleans, 16; Empires, 13; at New Orleans.
1872—July 14, R. E. Lee, 6; Empire, 16; at St. Louis.
July 21—Lone Star of New Orleans, 17; Empire, 13; at St. Louis.
July 22—R. E. Lee, 7; Empire, 14; at St. Louis.
July 28—Lone Star of New Orleans, 10; Empire, 21; at St. Louis.
July 29—Riverside of Evansville, 12; Empire, 22; at St. Louis.
August 11—Riverside of Evansville, tie at 13; at St. Louis.
August 15—Riverside of Evansville, 5; Empire, 31; at St. Louis.
August 30—Western, 7; Empire, 50; at Keokuk.
August 31—Occidental, 18; Empire, 26; at Quincy.

Many of the clubs which the Empires met were professionals and this fact should be borne in mind in comparing the scores. The Empire Club in its 1872 year had a membership of one hundred and twenty-five, honorary and active, and meetings were held weekly in a finely furnished hall at the corner of Sixth and Morgan streets.

The Empire nine in 1872, twelve years after its organization included Seward, catcher; Schempler, pitcher; Klein, first base; Spaulding, second base; Oran, third base; Barron, shortstop; Siedekum, left field; Wirth, center field, and Murray, right field.

The Empire Club was organized in 1860 at a meeting held in the office of Justice Hequemberg on the south side of Vine, between Second and Third streets.

There were present at that meeting, B. J. Higgins, J. W. O'Connell, John F. Walton, Dan'l Coyle, P. J. Cooney, H. G. D. Barklage, J. C. Adams, James Utley, P. H. Tobin, Jacob Ruppenthal, J. Schenck, James Fitzgerald, Thos. Cappell, Jacob Hollenbeck, J. Kinwiddy and Wm. Henley, who after adopting the constitution and by-laws of the "Knickerbocker" Club, elected the following officers: President, Jos. Kinwiddy; secretary, J. Hollenback; treasurer, H. G. D. Barklage. These were succeeded by B. G. Higgins, president; J. F. Walton, secretary, and H. D. Barklage, treasurer, the latter for nearly ten years filling that position uninterruptedly. Under their administration the club was gotten into good working order and played with varying fortunes against the other clubs of that day and among their opponents were the Morning Star, the Laclede, the Cyclone, the Commercial and Union clubs. At first the games were played at Lafayette Park, but the superior advantage of the Gamble street lawn ground soon became apparent, and the club played there for several years. The following list comprised the officers of the Empire Club, for each year, the name of the treasurer being omitted for the reason that it was the same each year, as stated above:

EMPIRES' FIRST GREAT TOUR.

Years.	President.	Vice-President.	Secretary.
1861.	L. P. Fuller.	P. Naylor.	J. W. Williams.
1862.	L. P. Fuller.	P. J. Cooney.	James Reynolds.
1863.	L. P. Fuller.	J. F. Walton.	J W. Williams.
1864.	H. C. Sexton.	J. F. Walton.	Wm. Thorn.
1865.	J. F. Walton.	P. J. Cooney.	Wm. Thorn.
1866.	L. P. Fuller.	W. S. Parr.	F. H. Tobias.
1867.	L. P. Fuller.	W. S. Parr.	W. McGeary.
1868.	W. S. Parr.	J W. O'Connell.	H. J. Jones.
1869.	L. P. Fuller.	J. W. O'Connell.	C. H. Stevens.
1870.	H. C. Sexton.	W. S. Parr.	C. H. Stevens.
1871.	H. C. Sexton.	W. S. Parr.	C. H. Stevens.
1872.	H. C. Sexton.	J. H. Farrar.	C. H. Stevens.
1873.	H. C. Sexton.	J. H. Farrar.	C. H. Stevens.

Year.	Field Captains.	Year.	Field Captains.
1861.	James Yule and John O'Connell.	1868.	Adam Wirth and James Yule.
1862.	James Yule and John Quinn.	1869.	J. W. Shockey and James Barron.
1863.	James Yule and John Barrett.	1870.	James D. Fitzgibbon and H. Little.
1864.	Jerry Fruin and John Quinn.	1871.	J. Spaulding and W. D. Gorman.
1865.	Jerry Fruin and John Quinn.	1872.	J. Spaulding and A. Wirth.
1866.	Jerry Fruin and John Quinn.	1874.	J. Spaulding and W. S. Parr.
1867.	Jerry Fruin and John Quinn.		

THE CHAMPION EMPIRES.

The first Empire nine to make an extensive tour, the one that won the championship belt in 1868 and 1869 was made up of John W .O'Connell, catcher; James D. Fitzgibbon, pitcher; Adam Wirth, first base; James J. Spaulding, second base; Jake Murray, third base; James Barron, short field; John Shockey, left field; Tom Walsh ,center field, and Charles Stevens and John Heep, right field.

In 1869 the Cincinnati Reds came to St. Louis and beat the Empires by scores of 15 to 0 and 31 to 9. The following year with James Fitzgibbon pitching for the Empires, the latter would have won the game but for a dropped thrown ball which Fitzgibbon had thrown easily to first. The error netted Cincinnati three runs and decided the game in their favor by 7 to 5.

On August 14, 1874, the Empires met the Bostons, and just to show who were playing on those two teams that far back I append the full score:

BOSTON.	1B.	R.	P.	EMPIRE.	1B.	R.	P.
Wright, Geo. ss	0	2	4	Spaulding, 2b	0	1	4
Barnes, 2b	3	3	3	Wirth, cf	1	0	3
Spalding, p	2	2	3	Seward, c	1	0	5
Leonard, lf	1	1	5	Oran, 3b	1	0	3
White, c	4	3	4	Klein, 1b	1	0	3
O'Rourke, 1b	4	2	2	Siedekum, lf	1	0	3
Addy, rf	1	4	1	Murray, rf	2	1	2
Schafer, 3b	0	2	4	Schimper, p	2	2	2
Manning, cf	3	3	3	Barron, ss	1	0	4
Total	18	22	27	Total	10	4	27

Runs in each inning.   1 2 3 4 5 6 7 8 9

Boston ....3 2 1 2 4 1 6 0 3—22
Empire ....0 0 1 0 0 0 3 0 0— 4

James Spaulding, now Judge James J. Spaulding of St. Louis, started this game off for the Empires with a three base hit to left field.

OLD VERSUS NEW EMPIRES.

On the Grand avenue grounds in the season of 1876 teams called the "New" and "Old" Empires took part in a game. We publish the score entire to show the men that made up the Empire team at its commencement sixteen years before and the men who were still playing with it in its 1876 year. We also publish a brief story of the game as follows:

The much-talked of baseball contest, between the present Empire nine and the veterans of the organization, came off in the presence of a large number of spectators yesterday afternoon.

It was thought that the veterans would be able to give their more youthful opponents a good tussle, but the game showed that baseball players may be classed among the things that do not become the better for age. Among the old ones who showed up were nine members who had been in the first nine of the club at one time or another, and to these were added H. Clay Sexton, their president, and an eleventh man. Much merriment was indulged in by all hands, Mr. Sexton leading in the fun and astonishing the spectators by his ability as a base ballist. In the first inning the Empires made fourteen runs and gave the old 'uns two, one of them being donated to Mr. Sexton as a mark of respect to his official standing in the club. Fifteen more runs were scored by the champions in the next six innings, while their opponents were whitewashed six times in succession. The next two innings yielded the contestants ten and seven runs respectively, and the game closed. The Empires played a careless and evidently purposeless game, the only redeeming feature of it being two handsome double plays by Oran, Spaulding and Kline, and Barron, Spaulding and Kline. Seward injured his thumb in the fore part of the game, and went to short field, Barron replacing him behind the bat. Shockey showed that his hands had not lost their cunning by capturing five flies in left field. Tobias caught a neat liner at short.

NEW EMPIRES.	O.	R.	"OL 'UNS."	O.	R.
Barron, ss	4	3	Sexton, p	2	2
Spaulding, 2b	4	3	Duffy, c	2	2
Wirth, cf	2	5	Barrett, cf	4	0
Seward, c	3	5	Yule, rf	2	2
Oran, 3b	2	6	Shockey, lf	2	1
Kline, 1b	3	4	O'Connell, 1b	3	1
Siedekum, lf	4	4	Tobias, ss	3	0
Murray, rf	2	5	Murphy, 3b	2	0
Schimper, p	3	4	Conroy, rs.	2	0
			Robinson, rf	3	0
	27	39	Jerry Fruin, 2b	2	1
				27	9

1 2 3 4 5 6 7 8 9
Empires ....14 3 1 8 2 1 0 9 1—39
Veterans ....2 0 0 0 0 0 0 2 5— 9

JERRY FRUIN'S LAST GAME.

This was perhaps the last St. Louis game that Jerry Fruin ever took part in and the big contractor had lots of fun out of it.

Mr. Fruin had joined the Empires in 1864. He came to them fresh from the Charter Oak Club of Brooklyn, having in his day played on the same grounds in that city with some of the later famous professional players. Mr. Fruin played actively with the Empires at second base until 1867 and then he gave up the position to his brother Dick who covered that point in the first game in which the Empires faced the Unions.

In 1868, four years after Mr. Fruin had joined the Empires, James D. Fitzgibbon came to St Louis from the Charter Oak Club of Hartford, Conn. Mr. Fitzgibbon, like Mr. Fruin, is now a wealthy contractor in St. Louis.

In 1867 while Mr. Fitzgibbon was a member of the Charter Oaks he went with his team to the Capitoline grounds in Brooklyn to meet the Excelsiors of that city. The Charter Oaks in that game faced the pitching of Cummings who had Jewell for his catcher. The Charter Oaks could not hit the pitching of Cummings at all but were not surprised when later they discovered that they had been trying to hit the pitching of Arthur Cummings, the first man in America to use the curve ball and the real inventor of that sort of thing.

Father Chadwick was on the ground that day and commented on the wonderful work of Cummings.

Mr. Fitzgibbon is now an old man but wonderfully alive and active. Two years ago he visited Hartford and while there asked about the Bunce brothers, Henry and Fred, who had played on the Charter Oaks with him. He found they had become bank presidents. Calling on one of the brothers, the president of the Phoenix Bank at Hartford, Mr. Fitzgibbon was recognized instantly, called by name and given a hearty reception by a fellow player who had seen him but twice in forty years.

The St. Louis Reds who came into the field with the Unions in the late sixties had a playing nine which included Packie Dillon, catcher and captain; Danny Morgan, pitcher; Joe Blong, first base; Zack Mulhall, second base; Trick McSorley, third base; Arthur Redmond, shortstop; Packie Dillon, left field; Andy Blong, center field, and George Bradley, right field.

On July 4, 1874, two games of baseball were played at the rival parks. These games were between the St. Louis Reds and a team of prairie players brought from Chicago and called the Chicago Whites, and the Empires and the Rowenas. The first game was played at the Compton avenue and the other at the Grand avenue grounds, which was still the Empires home park. I give the scores of these games just to show who were playing on the crack home teams at this time.

At Grand Avenue (now Sportsman's Park).

EMPIRE.	R.	O.	ROWENA.	R.	O.
Spaulding, 2b	3	3	Murray, 1b	0	5
Gorman, lf	1	2	Wilkens, ss	2	3
Murray, rf	2	4	H. Sikings, 2b.	0	5
McCall, p	2	3	Cunningham, lf	3	1
Dean, 3b	2	4	W. Sikings, r.f.	1	2
Wirth, cf	2	4	Maher, p	0	3
Barron, ss	3	3	Reinhardt, 3b	0	3
Houtz, 1b	3	3	Savage, c	0	3
Seward, c	3	1	Rossman, cf	0	2
	21	27		6	27

Runs earned—Empires, 7; Rowenas, 3. Base hits—Empires, 20; Rowenas, 13. First base on errors—Empires, 6; Rowenas, 3. Passed balls—Seward, 0; Savage, 2. Time of game—Two hours and twelve minutes. Umpire—E. W. Thompson.

At Compton Avenue Park.

ST. LOUIS REDS.	R.	B.	P.	A	CHICAGO WHITES.	R.	B.	P.	A.
P. Dillon, c	1	1	8	1	W. Lapham, 1b	2	1	8	0
J. Blong, 1b	2	2	1	1	White, ss	1	2	1	4
Morgan, p	2	1	1	1	Boardman, lf	1	1	0	0
A. Blong, cf.	3	1	0	1	Dorgan, 2b	0	0	3	0
Bradley, rf.	3	1	0	1	Lawlor, c	1	0	9	0
Redmond, ss.	3	3	2	1	Coffman, 3b	1	1	0	0
McSorley, 3b.	3	2	0	1	J. O'Day, cf	2	1	2	0
J. Dillon, lf	1	0	1	4	Tabor, rf	0	0	0	0
Mulhall, 2b	3	3	14	1	M. Brenock, p	3	4	4	1
	21	14	27	12		11	10	27	5

St. Louis ....0 1 7 3 0 1 0 7 2—21
Chicago ....0 0 1 0 0 2 0 8 0—11

Earned runs—Reds, 4; Chicago, 2. Passed balls—Dillon, 5; Lawler, 9. Wild pitches—Brenock, 5. Umpire—John Kelly of the Liberty Club of Springfield, Ill. Official scorer—William M. Spink.

It will be noticed by the scores that the best scored game was that played at Compton Avenue Park. At that time "Billy" Spink was scoring for the Reds down there.

It was just after this game that the St. Louis Reds went to Chicago and met with the most exciting incident in their career. They had played several games in the Lake City and their manager, Andy Blong, had been given a large amount of money as the Reds share of the gate receipts. On the train in which they left Chicago, several three-card monte men got hold of Blong and relieved him of all the money he had in his possession.

When he informed the players of his loss they took possession of the car in which the monte men had been operating, one part of the team going to one end of the car and the other part to the other. Flourishing their baseball clubs they promised to beat the monte men to death unless they at once returned the money they had stolen from Blong. The monte men, glad to escape with their lives, gave up willingly and the St.

THE NATIONAL GAME.

Louis boys came home with money in their pockets and much richer in experience than when they started.

THE UNIONS AND THE REDS.

The success in St. Louis of the Empires in the sixties led to the organization of other baseball teams.

In the early sixties the Union and the Red Stocking teams came into the field. The Union had for their playing team Charles H. Turner, catcher; R. J. Lucas, pitcher; Henry Carr and Henry Berning, first base; E. C. Meacham, second base; Charles Cabanne, third base; Eugene Greenleaf, shortstop; Asa Smith, left field; Walter Wolf, center field, and Archie Easton, right field.

It will be noticed by the above list that the Union team was made up of the silk stocking element of that day and the name Union was taken because the players of the teams were all men who had stood by the Union during the Civil War. Their very name at that time aroused feeling and animosity and added to the rivalry that already existed between the then leading local baseball teams. The Unions almost immediately became a rival of the Empires. The Unions at once engaged the Grand avenue grounds to play on for four days of the week, the Empires securing the ground for the other three days, including Sunday.

The first great games between the Unions and the Empires took place in 1868, the Unions winning the best two out of three that year and the local championship.

In 1869 the Empires turned the tables on their opponents winning both of the only two games played. The Empire team of 1869 was unchanged from that of the few years previous except that Tom Oran, an Indian catcher, had taken the place of John W. O'Connell, who had retired as the Empires catcher on account of broken fingers.

THE ST. LOUIS TEAMS OF 1875

HOW THE WORK OF THE REDS, THE EMPIRES, THE STOCKS AND THE ELEPHANTS LED TO THE MOUND CITY GETTING HER FIRST REAL PROFESSIONAL NINE.

By 1875 baseball had become epidemic in St. Louis and clubs were playing in all parts of the city.

Each end of the town now claimed to have the best playing team and rivalry reached a high point.

Before the season was well under way, five prominent nines appeared in the arena, all claiming the local championship.

These were the Empires, the St. Louis Reds, the Unions, the Elephants and the Stocks.

The Reds played in inclosed grounds on Compton avenue, adjoining the Missouri Pacific Railroad tracks.

The Empires and Unions took up their home in the Grand avenue grounds, which occupied the field now known as Sportsman's Park.

The Stocks built a ground on the prairie just south of what is now the United Railways sheds on Easton and Vandeventer avenues.

The Elephants played their games on a ground east of Broadway and near North Market street.

In these teams were players who later became famous in the baseball world, the full playing roster being as follows:

THE ST. LOUIS TEAMS OF 1874.

ELEPHANTS.	EMPIRES.
Flint, c.	Seward, c.
Welch, p.	Schimpert, p.
Carpenter, 1b.	Klein, 1b.
Loftus, 2b.	Spaulding, 2b.
Murray, 3b.	Oran, 3b.
McCormick, ss.	Barron, ss
Ryan, lf.	Siedekum, lf.
Magner, cf.	Worth, cf.
James, rf.	Murray, rf.

ST. LOUIS REDS.	UNIONS.	STOCKS.
Sulivan, c.	Turner, c.	Ring, c.
P. Dillon, c.	Lucas, p.	Maher, p.
Morgan, p.	Carr, 1b.	Carpenter, 1b.
McSorley, p.	Berning, 1b	Simpson, 2b.
Collins, p.	Meacham, 2b.	J. Gleason, 3b.
J. Blong, 1b.	Cabanne, 3b.	W. Gleason, ss.
Zack Mulhall, 2b.	Greenleaf, ss.	O'Reilly, lf.
McSorley 3b.	Smith, lf.	Fry, cf.
Redmond, ss.	Wolf, cf.	Johnson, rf.
J. Dillon, lf.	Easton, rf.	
T. Oran, cf.		
A. Blong, M'g'r.		

The above four teams created so much enthusiasm that in the fall of 1874 steps were taken to put a professional team in the field, and, in fact, from the boom given the game

JOHN McSORLEY.
The above is a likeness of John McSorley, better known as "Trick" McSorley, and who in his day captained and played nearly every position on the St. Louis Reds. In the regular list there is a full sketch of McSorley.

by these teams in 1874 came the St. Louis Browns of 1875, the first nine to represent St. Louis in a regularly organized association.

THE ST. LOUIS BROWNS OF 1875.

A STORY OF THE FIRST TEAM THAT EVER REPRESENTED THE MOUND CITY IN A REGULAR BASEBALL ASSOCIATION

It was perhaps the impetus given the game by the trips of the Cincinnati Reds and the Chicago White Stockings to the East that led to the establishment early in the seventies of professional teams in all the large cities in the East and West.

At New York the Mutuals came into existence, and across in Brooklyn the Atlantics, the Eckfords and other teams were organized on a professional basis.

At about the same time the Athletics of Philadelphia, the Eclipse of Louisville, the Browns of St. Louis, the White Stockings of Chicago, the Forest Citys of Cleveland and other professional teams took the field.

The first out and out professional baseball game played in St. Louis was in the summer of 1875.

During the fall and winter preceding a number of St. Louis gentlemen organized a corporation to put a professional baseball club in the Mound City. The officers of the first St. Louis baseball corporation were J. B. C. Lucas, president; Chas. A. Fowle, secretary, and Charles H. Turner, treasurer. The directors were C. Orrick Bishop, Jos. P. Carr and Nat Hazard.

In the fall and winter of 1874 and 1875 these gentlemen got together and secured a charter in the National League for the season of 1875, and selected a playing team which included: Catchers, Thomas Miller and W. Cordell; pitchers, George W. Bradley and Charles Waitt; first base, Dehlman; second base, Joseph Battin; third base, William Hague; shortstop, Dickey Pearce; left field, Edgar Cuthbert; center field, Lipman Pike; right field, John C. Chapman, and George Seward, substitute. Mason Graffan was the manager of this nine.

The St. Louis team of 1876 included John Clapp and H. McGinley, catchers; George Washington Bradley and Joe Blong, pitchers; Herman Dehlman, first base; Mike Mc-Geary, second base; Joe Battin, third base; Dickey Pearce and Denny Mack, short fielders; Edgar Cuthbert, left field; Lipman Pike, center field, and Joe Blong, right field.

The St. Louis team of 1877 included John Clapp, catcher; Tricky Nichols, pitcher; Arthur Croft, first base; Mike McGeary, second base; Joe Battin, third base; David Force, shortstop; Mike Dorgan, left field; Jack Remsen, center, and Joe Blong, right.

In the Browns' first season they were beaten for the championship by the Bostons, the Hartfords and the Athletics.

In their second season the Browns were beaten out by only the Chicagos and Hartfords.

ST. LOUIS AND THE NATIONAL LEAGUE.

In the fall and winter of 1875-76 Charles Fowle and Orrick C. Bishop, now a famous St. Louis judge and attorney co-operating with William Hulbert and A. G. Spalding of Chicago set about the movement which led to the organization of the National League. These four gentlemen decided on a plan for putting a league club in eight cities, each having a population of not less than 150,000. The cities agreed on to form the league were St. Louis, Chicago, Cincinnati, and Louisville, for the Western circuit, and Boston, Hartford, Brooklyn and Philadelphia for the Eastern division.

Messrs. Fowle and Bishop were the representatives of the St. Louis Club at the initial meeting of the National League at Louisville in 1876 and it was Judge Bishop who that year wrote the constitution of the National League which stands practically unchanged to-day and who formulated the first players' contracts and drew up the first regular baseball schedule.

It was during the Fall of 1877 that Messrs. Fowle and Turner of the St. Louis Club determined to place a team in St. Louis in the 1878 season which would prove a world beater. They secured contracts with Snyder and Craver, catchers; Devlin and Nichols, pitchers, and Hall, outfielder, of the Louisville Club; Johnny Peters, shortstop of the Chicago Club and other great players, and it was thought the combination would prove invincible. But soon after the signing of the Louisville players by the St. Louis management, Devlin, Hall, Craver and Nichols were all blacklisted for reasons stated elsewhere in this work, and the gentlemen at the head of the St. Louis Club were so disgusted over the discovery of the crookedness of the players they had engaged that they washed their hands of the whole business and on December, 1877, the St. Louis Club resigned its membership in the National League. All of this shows how it came that St. Louis had no real professional team in the field in 1878.

During this dull year in baseball the time of all was devoted to the amateur and semi-professional teams.

GREATEST GAME EVER PLAYED IN ST. LOUIS.

It was the St. Louis Browns and the Stars of Syracuse, New York, that played a game on the Grand avenue grounds, now Sportsman's Park, that must take rank with the best in the history of the national sport. It took place on Tuesday, May 1, 1877. Fifteen innings were played and not a run had been scored on either side when darkness compelled the umpire to call the game. During the progress of this remarkable contest only one man reached first base.

. The Browns' batting list on this occasion was headed by Dorgan and he was followed by Clapp, McGeary, Battin, Force, Remsen, Croft, Blong and Nichols.

The Stars' list had Higham at the top with Geer, McKinnon, Mansell, Clinton, Hotaling, Farrell, McCormick and Carpenter, following in the order named. The batteries were Clapp, catcher, and Nichols, pitcher, for St. Louis, and Higham, catcher, and Mc-Cormick, pitcher, for Syracuse

The score made in this game was a wonderful one for many reasons. First of all the game was played with a lively ball and while the hitting was terriffic, the fielding was simply magnificent. Below I give the full score of the wonderful contest, the most wonderful ever played on a St. Louis field:

ST. LOUIS	AB.	R.	H.	O.	A.	E	SYRACUSE.	AB.	R.	H.	O.	A.	E.
Dorgan, lf	6	0	0	1	0	0	Higham, c	6	0	1	17	1	3
Clapp, c	5	0	1	19	2	1	Geer, ss	5	0	0	3	3	0
McGeary, 2b	5	0	1	4	4	0	McKinnon, 1b	6	0	0	8	1	0
Battin, 3b	6	0	0	2	3	0	Mansell, lf	5	0	1	5	0	0
Force, ss	6	0	2	0	4	0	Clinton, rf	5	0	0	0	1	1
Remsen, cf	6	0	2	5	0	0	Hotaling, cf	5	0	0	4	1	0
Croft, 1b	6	0	2	21	0	0	Farrell, 2b	5	0	0	4	2	0
Joe Blong, rf	5	0	0	2	1	0	McCormack, p	5	0	0	1	0	0
Nichols, p	5	0	0	0	3	3	Carpenter, 3b	5	0	0	2	0	0
Totals	50	0	8	45	17	4	Totals	47	0	2	44*	9	4

Club.	1	2	3	4	5	6	7	8	9	10	11	12	13	14	15	
St. Louis	0	0	0	0	0	0	0	0	0	0	0	0	0	0	0—	0
Syracuse	0	0	0	0	0	0	0	0	0	0	0	0	0	0	0—	0

Two-base hits—Higham. Total bases on hits—Syracuse, 2; St. Louis, 8. Total left on bases—Syracuse, 2; St. Louis, 5. Double plays—Hotaling and Higham; Blong and Croft. Struck out—By McCormack, 5; by Nichols, 5. Total battery errors—On Higham, 3 stolen bases; on Clapp, 1 stolen base, 1 foul tip missed; on Nichols, 3 men to base on balls. Total fielding errors—Clinton, 1 overthrow to first base. Time of game—Two hours and forty minutes. Umpire—George Seward. Scorer—W. M. Spink.

Still another great game was that played at Sportsman's Park, June 5, 1875, between the St. Louis Browns and the Boston Reds and we give the full score just to show who were playing on these teams at this time:

ST. LOUIS.	R.	H.	O.	A.	E.	BOSTON.	R.	H.	O.	A.	E.
Cuthbert lf	2	3	2	0	0	Geo. Wright, ss	1	1	1	2	0
Pearce, ss	1	2	1	3	1	Barnes, 2b	1	2	4	4	1
Pike, cf	0	0	2	0	0	O'Rourke. 3b	1	1	0	1	1
Chapman, rf	1	2	2	0	0	Leonard, lf	1	1	3	0	0
Hague, 3b	0	2	1	1	0	McVey, c	0	0	6	0	3
Bradley, p	0	0	2	2	1	Spalding, p	0	2	3	0	1
Battin, 2b	0	0	3	3	0	Franklin, 1b	0	0	6	1	0
Dehlman, 1b	0	0	10	1	0	Manning, rf	0	0	1	1	2
Miller, c	1	1	4	2		Beals, cf	0	1	3	0	0
Totals	5	10	27	12	4	Totals	4	8	27	9	8

Club.	1	2	3	4	5	6	7	8	9	
St. Louis	1	0	0	1	2	0	0	1	0—	5
Boston	4	0	0	0	0	0	0	0	0—	4

Earned runs—St. Louis, 2; Boston, 1. Passed balls—McVey, 2. Bases on errors—St. Louis, 2; Boston, 2. Left on bases; St. Louis, 4; Boston, 3. Times at bat—St. Louis, 37; Boston, 34.

FIRST MISSOURI STATE ASSOCIATION.

It was during 1878 that a State Association was formed and I give the names and addresses of its secretaries to show just who were interested in baseball in St. Louis at this time.

M. E. Dempsey, secretary Flyaway Baseball Club, 1523 Monroe street.

E. Leclaire, secretary Anchor Baseball Club, care A. M. Leslie & Co., Fifth and Locust.

Wm. Turner, Peerless Baseball Club, 316 North Second street.

O. Moseal, Aetna Baseball Club, Anna and DeKalb street.

Chas. P. Eberle. Future Baseball Club, 740 South Second street.

I. Rolfes, Black Stocking Baseball Club, care Padberg & Bros., corner Eighth and Carroll.

Wm. J. Fletcher, Hartford Baseball Club, 300 N. Canal street.

J. Cunningham, Willow Baseball Club, 2930 Pine street.

David L. Reid, Empire Baseball Club, 207 North Fifth street.

Elb. H. Grere, Haymaker Baseball Club, 2031 Carr street.

J. C. Finigan, Atlantic Baseball Club; 1506 Franklin avenue.

Ed. McGroarty, Benton's Baseball Club, 1001 North Main street.

F. T. Hogan, Athletic Baseball Club, 1513 Austin street.

P. A. Peterson, Alert Baseball Club, 1008 Chestnut street.

Lawrence Cass, Liberty Baseball Club, 1712 North Tenth street.

Albert Gredel, Eckford Baseball Club, 2104 Franklin avenue.

ST. LOUIS' FIRST AMATEUR ASSOCIATION.

The same year an amateur baseball association, local to St. Louis, was perfected by a meeting of representatives from eight well-known amateur clubs. This association, which was intended to succeed the state organization was founded on principles almost similar to the professional league, and shut out all the amateur clubs of this city excepting the eight whose representatives met together on this particular evening.

The meeting was held at Smith's Hall, corner of Twenty-second street and Frank-lin avenue, and was called to order by Mr. Frank Julian of the Haymakers, who acted as temporary chairman, Mr. E. H. Greves performing the duties of secretary.

A previous meeting had been held, and the plans of the organization made out and decided on. Only eight clubs were admitted to membership, and the Atlantics, Athletics, Willows, Grand Avenues, Fly Aways, Alerts, Empires and Haymakers were the ones selected. Representatives from these clubs were on hand and the following names were submitted to represent their respective clubs in the association during the year: Atlantic, J. I. Mathews, E. W. Zeigler; Willows, D. Woods, C. F. Seiner; Grand Avenue, A. Solari, E. W. Leslie; Flyaway, M. Dempsey, H. Genner; Athletic, E. T. Hogan, C. D. Thornburg; Empire, H. Barklage, John H. Farrar; Haymakers, F. Julian, E. H. Greves.

The above teams played games throughout the 1878 season and that was the only baseball St. Louis could boast of that particular year. We give below a score of the game played this year (1878) by the Athletics of St. Louis against the Madisons of Edwardsville, Ill., just to show how the game was being played then and of the advance being made in the scoring of the game:

ATHLETIC.	R.	1B.	TB.	PO.	A.	MADISON.	R.	1B.	TB.	PO.	A.
Hogan, 1b	2	2	2	8	0	W. Williams, 2b	0	2	2	4	
League, 2b	3	2	2	2	1	Jones, ss	2	3	3	2	4
Levis, p	4	3	5	1	5	Wendel, p	1	1	1	2	5
Barnidge, c	4	5	7	6	2	H. Williams, 1b	1	3	6	9	0
Cunningham, lf	2	3	3	1	0	F. Smith, cf	0	0	0	2	0
Peters, 3b	5	5	7	3	2	Vanderoot,m	1	1	1	2	0
Helmer, cf	2	3	5	3	0	W. Smith, c	0	0	0	5	0
Marr, rf	7	2	4	2	1	Crossner, 3c	0	0	0	0	1
Farrelly, ss	3	4	3	1	1	Parker, lf	0	0	0	1	1
Totals	32	29	39	27	21	Totals	5	10	13	27	14

Innings.   1 2 3 4 5 6 7 8 9

Athletics ....4 3 4 7 4 3 1 4 2—32

Madison ....1 0 0 0 1 3 0 0 0—5

Umpire—M. M. Besnor of Edwardsville.

THE ST. LOUIS BROWNS OF 1879-80.

THE SEASON WHEN A TEAM OF CO-OPERATIVE PLAYERS WAS THE ONLY THING MISSOURI'S LEADING CITY COULD BOAST OF.

At this time my brother William Spink was the sporting editor of the Globe-Democrat and I held that sort of a position on the then Missouri Republican, now the St. Louis Republic. After the failure to land a professional team in St. Louis in 1878 we did our best and worked together to replace the game here on a substantial footing.

But the baseball-loving public, disgusted at the way they had lost the splendid team they had hoped for, would have none of it.

Out of the remnant of the old St. Louis professional team we organized a nine that included holdover veterans like Dickey Pearce, Edgar Cuthbert, Lipman Pike, Mike Mc-Geary, Joe Blong, Arthur Croft, Charles Houtz, Tom Sullivan, Packie Dillon, Danny Morgan and others.

This team played games on Sundays sometimes at Grand Avenue Park, now Sports-man's, and sometimes at the Reds' Park on Compton avenue, to what Shakespeare would have termed a beggarly array of empty benches. One day in the summer of 1878 we went to the pains of bringing the Indianapolis Browns here, a team that had won the championship of the International Association and that included in its ranks such fa-mous players as the "only" Flint and the "only" Nolan.

But this team and our picked nine of professionals did not take in enough money at the gate at its initial game to pay the street car fares of the twelve players on the Mound City bob-tailed cars from the park back to their hotel quarters downtown.

The season of 1879 was as unfruitful of results as that of the season which preceded it. A picked up team of left-over professionals was again organized, called the St. Louis Browns and it stood ready to play any team of players that happened on Sundays to drop into Grand Avenue Park. During the close of the season of 1879 the game showed signs of returning life, and with my brother William, I again set out to recon-struct the old edifice and bring it back to its own.

SPORTSMAN'S PARK AND CLUB ASSOCIATION.

Together we brought about the meeting which at the close of the season of 1880 led to the organization of the Sportsman's Park and Club Association, an organization effected for the purpose of fitting up Grand Avenue Park for baseball purposes. This organization included Christ Von Der Ahe, president; John W. Peckington, vice president; W. W. Judy, treasurer, and A. H. Spink, secretary.

The Grand Avenue Park, which at this time contained a weather beaten grand-stand and a lot of rotten benches, was torn away and in its place was erected a new covered stand and an open "bleachers."

Sitting out in the field early in the spring of 1881 before the new grandstand was completed, I organized the St. Louis Browns of that year, Edgar Cuthbert, the only one of the old professionals still remaining in the city assisting me in the selection of a nine which included George Baker and George Seward, catchers; George McGinnis, pitcher; Edward Gault, first base; Hugh McDonald and Dan Morgan, second base; Jack Gleason, third base; William Gleason, short field; Harry McCaffrey center field; Edgar Cuthbert, left field, and John T. Magner, right field.

It was agreed as we all sat there on the green sward that we would work together to build up the sport and each player promised to be prompt at each game, to do his level best at all times and to take for his pay just as small a percentage of the gate receipts as the general welfare of the park and its owners would allow.

On Sunday, May 22, 1881, these grounds were really opened with an exhibition game between the newly organized St. Louis Browns and the St. Louis Reds. The Reds won by 2 to 1 and the batting order which shows who the players were at this time was as follows:

REDS.	BROWNS.
McCaffery, ss.	J. Gleason, 3b.
Cunningham, lf.	W. Gleason, ss.
Morgan, 2b.	McSorley, cf.
Gault, 1b.	Seward, rf.
Houtz, cf.	Gault, 1b.
Decker, c.	Baker, c.
Schenk, rf.	Magner, lf.
Hogan, p.	McDonald, 2b.
Oberbeck, 3b.	McGinnis, p.

Of the players named above who took part in this game twenty-eight years ago, Croft and Schenk are the only Reds not now among the living. Of the Browns only Seward, Gault and McDonald have passed away.

Despite the good attendance at this opening game between the Reds and Browns the outlook seemed cold and bleak, for St. Louis stood badly then in the eyes of the outside baseball world.

THE WORK OF UPBUILDING.

The blacklisting of the Louisville players, Devlin, Hall, Nichols and Craver, all of whom were to have played here in 1877, had given this city a black eye in baseball circles the country over. Somehow St. Louisans were considered to blame in a great measure for the guilt of these players. The fact that all of them had been guilty of crooked practices and that all of them the year of their guilt had been engaged to play here the following season, was used as proof that we had known of their double dealing.

It is needless to say that these charges were uncalled for and frivolous for the men at the head of the St. Louis National League Club in 1876 and 1877 were all thorough gentlemen and sportsmen, and incapable of double dealing of the sort suggested.

But at the time we organized the team of 1881 seated out there in the field we were helpless to dispel the cruel illusion which had surrounded and barred us from the National League, the only baseball association then in existence. We were out in the cold as it were—a ball team on our hands, but with no other team to play with.

We had a fine nine of willing players, but there were no opposition teams in sight. It was up to me to fill the breach. I looked in all directions for ammunition. There was at this time, as I have already stated, but one regular baseball association in existence. That was the National League and the owners of its clubs had no use for us.

While wondering how I could start the ball rolling I wrote to O. P. Caylor, then sporting editor of the Cincinnati Enquirer and I suggested to him the idea of picking up all that was left in Cincinnati of the old professional players, forming them into a nine, christening them the Cincinnati Reds and bringing them here to play three games on a Saturday, Sunday and Monday with my reconstructed St. Louis Browns.

At this time Cincinnati, like St. Louis, was off the baseball map, but Mr. Caylor, accepting my suggestion, quickly got together a team of semi-professionals, called it the Cincinnati Reds and brought it here to help open the reconstructed St. Louis baseball grounds which my brother William had named Sportsman's Park.

The names St. Louis Browns and Cincinnati Reds proved magic in so far as reawakening interest in the game in this city was concerned, the largest crowds that had ever attended baseball games up to this time in St. Louis came out to see the contests and our nine beating the other out of its boots, we began to see daylight and to again hope for better things.

The first game of this series between our newly organized Browns and the Cincinnati Reds the game which was really the opening contest on the newly fitted up Sportsman's Park, took place on May 22, 1881.

It was played with a lively ball which accounts for the big score which we give in full for the reason that it was the first real game of consequence played in St. Louis in 1881, between the local professionals and a team of outside players. The full score was:

ST. LOUIS.	AB.	R.	BH.	PO.	A.	E.	CINCINNATI.	AB.	R.	BH.	PO.	A.	E.
Morgan, 3b	6	1	2	2	2	1	Merney, 3b	5	1	2	0	2	0
McSorley, ss.	6	2	2	6	2	0	Reilly, 1b	5	2	2	12	0	1
Seward, cf	4	2	0	4	0	0	Pearce, ss.	5	3	2	0	7	2
McGinnis, cf., p.	5	2	2	6	14	1	Carey, cf	5	0	2	0	0	3
Baker, rf., c.	4	3	4	14	2	0	Ellick, 2b	5	0	1	2	3	1
McDonald, 2b.	5	2	2	4	0	3	Mitchell, p., lf	5	1	2	1	6	3
Magner, lf	5	1	2	0	0	1	Archibald, c., rf	5	1	1	3	0	0
Bowles, ss., cf.	5	1	1	3	1	0	Bauer, c.	5	0	1	5	0	2
Gault, 1b.	5	1	1	4	1	1	Shall, lf., p	5	0	1	4	4	0
Totals	45	15	16	27	22	7	Totals	45	8	14	27	22	11

Earned runs—Cincinnati, 2; St. Louis, 6. Two-base hits—Archibald, 1; Morgan, 1; McGinnis, 1; Baker, 1. Three-base hits—Reilly, 1; Carey, 1. Home runs—Reilly, 1; Magner, 1; Carey, 1. Time of game—Three hours and thirty-five minutes. Umpire—Charles Levis. Official scorer—A. H. Spink.

I had Caylor organize other teams and bring other nines from Cincinnati and then I imported prairie nines from Chicago. The work of getting these teams here was strenuous to say the least.

The home players at this time were in receipt of sixty per cent of the gate receipts. Out of the remaining forty per cent the expenses of advertising the games, the general expenses of the park and the expense of bringing the visiting players here had to be paid.

The nines that came from Chicago were paid nothing for their work above their expenses. These latter included only railroad fares (the sleeping car being unknown to the baseball player at this time), lodging at a second rate hotel and a bus ride to and from the baseball grounds. The players, it will be seen, came all the way from Chicago just for the fun of playing.

There was of course no discipline, no order, no anything, each player coming and going as he pleased. Sometimes a team would arrive from Chicago with only seven or eight men and then I would discover that the missing one or two were the very men we needed most; a pitcher or a catcher. I recall one Sunday when a Chicago team called the Eckfords arrived here. It was minus a battery.

The captain, however, had brought on uniforms for the missing pair and suggested that I find men to fill them. En route to the grounds I picked up two youngsters I found playing on a lot in North St. Louis, one Kid Baldwin, famous afterwards as the catcher of the Cincinnati Club, and the other Henry Overbeck, who was subsequently well known in minor league circles as a pitcher. These players proved a find for the Eckfords who were that day voted the best team Chicago had sent down here; those rendering the verdict being ignorant of the fact that the best two players on the Eckford team were the St. Louis boys, Baldwin and Overbeck.

THE ST. LOUIS BROWNS OF 1882 TO 1901.

THE TEAM WHICH CAPTURED AMERICAN ASSOCIATION AND WORLD'S CHAMPIONSHIP FLAGS AND WHICH FOR A LONG WHILE WAS INVINCIBLE.

It was while these co-operative Browns were playing these prairie teams that Ted Sullivan came in here with a team which he called the Dubuque "Rabbits" and which hailed from the city of that name in Iowa. On this team was a player, now perhaps the foremost figure in the whole baseball world.

He was a tall, lanky sort of a lad with a serious face. His home position was at first base and his name was Charles A. Comiskey. He had learned to play baseball on the prairies which surrounded Chicago, had gone to Dubuque from Chicago to act as train "butcher" for the Western News Company and while in Dubuque had become a member of Ted Sullivan's Dubuque "Rabbits."

On this same team with Comiskey were Tom Loftus, one of the best fellows ever prominently identified with the game, and later manager of the Cleveland and other league teams.

The Dubuque Rabbits of which Ted Sullivan was the manager, came into the Grand avenue grounds on the afternoon of July 16, 1881.

It was the first time Comiskey had ever played baseball in a regular enclosure. Ted Sullivan appeared as the pitcher for Dubuque in this famous game, but after six innings, on account of the fearful heat, he retired. His place was taken by Morrison. When Sullivan quit the score stood 2 to 1 in favor of the Browns, but after his departure St. Louis had a walkover and won by this score:

ST. LOUIS.	AB.	R.	BH.	PO.	A.	E.
J. Gleason, 3b.	5	1	1	1	3	3
W. Gleason, ss.	5	1	1	0	6	0
McCaffery, cf.	5	2	2	2	0	0
Seward, c.	5	1	3	9	1	1
Morgan, rf.	5	1	1	1	1	0
McGinnis, p.	5	1	1	0	0	0
Magner, lf.	5	1	1	2	0	0
McDonald, 2b.	4	1	0	2	0	0
Gault, 1b.	4	0	2	10	0	1
Totals	43	9	12	27	11	5

DUBUQUE.	AB.	R.	BH.	PO.	A.	E.
Sullivan, p., ss.	4	1	0	2	4	0
Loftus, 2b.	4	0	1	3	3	0
Comiskey, 1b.	4	0	1	12	0	0
Ross, c.	4	0	0	2	0	0
Burns, 3b.	4	0	0	0	2	1
Lear, rf.	4	0	0	2	0	0
Morrison, ss., p.	4	0	0	0	2	3
Keys, lf.	4	0	0	2	0	0
Phelan, cf.	4	0	0	1	0	1
Totals	36	1	2	24	11	5

Earned runs—Browns, 8; Dubuque, 0. Two-base hits—McGinnis, Gault, W. Gleason and Comiskey. Base on balls—Sullivan and Magner. Umpire—Charles Levis. Official scorer—A. H. Spink.

COMISKEY'S FIRST ENGAGEMENT.

It was on this field and just before this game that I had an introduction to Comiskey which led to me writing him a letter the following winter, and offering him a position as first baseman of the St. Louis Browns, a position which he not only accepted, but which he filled with wonderful success from 1882 to 1899 inclusive.

Other teams beside the Dubuques, the Cincinnati Reds and the Chicago prairie teams came to St. Louis and the games drew such crowds, especially on Sundays, that soon news of the prosperity wave reached the East.

Near the close of the season of 1881, I arranged games between the co-operative Browns of that year and crack Eastern teams.

I brought the Akron, Ohio, team here, a nine which included Charles Morton Ed Swartwood, Sam Wise and other players who later became famous in the baseball world.

Later I wrote to Horace B. Phillips, then managing the Athletics of Philadelphia; and to William Barnie, then operating the Atlantics of Brooklyn. Both the Athletics and the Atlantics were free lances outside of the pale of the National League and were

THE ST. LOUIS BROWNS OF 1882.—Reading from left to right: Edgar Cuthbert, William Gleason, Charles Morton, Oscar Walker, Charles Comiskey, Jack Gleason, Daisy Dorr, Harry McCaffery, Tom Sullivan, Joe Crotty, Edward Brown and George McGinnis. This was the team from which came the "Four Time Winners," the nine which won the American Association pennant four times in succession and which under leadership of Comiskey, twice captured world's honors.

willing to come all the way to St. Louis to meet the St. Louis Browns for a division of the gate receipts.

They arrived here late in the fall of 1881 and the series was such a successful one from a playing and gate receipt standpoint that Phillips, Barnie, McKnight of Pittsburg, Caylor of Cincinnati, Von Der Ahe of St. Louis, and others set out to organize the American Association, which appeared in the field in 1882.

The players of the 1882 team, St. Louis' first representative in the American Association, were Tom Sullivan, George Ward and Joe Crotty, catchers; George McGinnis, W. Shappert and Daisy Dorr, pitchers; Charles A. Comiskey, first base; William Smiley, second base; Jim Davis, third base; William Gleason, shortstop; Eddie Cuthbert, left field; Oscar Walker, center field; one of the catchers, right field; and Edward Brown, substitute.

The first game played by these St. Louis Browns, the team organized by Von Der Ahe to represent this city in the American Association, took place at Sportsman's Park, on April 2, 1882, the Standards, a crack local team, to the great mortification of the Browns and their friends, beating them by the following score:

BROWNS.	AB.	R.	BH.	P.	A.	E.	STANDARDS.	AB.	R.	BH.	P	A.	E.
W. Gleason, ss.	5	0	1	0	0	0	Morgan, 3b.	4	1	1	2	0	0
Walker, cf.	4	0	1	0	0	0	Simpson, 2b.	4	1	0	2	0	0
Comiskey, 1b.	4	1	1	9	0	0	Decker, c.	4	1	1	2	1	3
Davis, 3b.	4	1	1	1	0	2	Cunningham, l.f.	4	0	0	8	1	0
Smiley, 2b.	4	0	0	1	3	0	Wagner, ss.	4	0	2	3	4	0
Seward, c.	4	0	0	13	0	3	Croft, 1b	4	0	0	5	2	0
McGinnis, p.	4	0	0	0	2	1	Hogan, p	4	0	0	1	10	0
Cuthbert, lf.	4	0	2	0	0	1	Dillon, rf	4	1	1	1	0	0
Shappert, rf.	4	0	1	0	0	0	Houtz, c.	3	0	0	3	0	0
Totals	37	2	7	24	5	7	Totals	35	4	5	27	18	3

Innings.	1	2	3	4	5	6	7	8	9
Browns	2	0	0	0	0	0	0	0	0— 2
Standards	1	0	2	0	0	0	0	1	0— 4

Earned runs—None. Total bases—Browns, 8; Standards, 3. Umpire—Dave Ring. Time—One hour and thirty-five minutes.

I was at this time president of the Standard Club and was greatly pleased at their victory for the Standards were made up mostly of local players while the Browns were now an out and out professional team, the country having been scoured by Cuthbert for good players.

He had gotten Walker, Smiley and Shappert from the Atlantics of Brooklyn. Comiskey, as already stated, came from Dubuque, and Will Gleason, Jim Davis, Seward and McGinnis were St. Louis players who had some reputation abroad as well as at home, having previously played with outside semi-professional teams.

That the team was of the right sort was proven on April 9, 1882, a week after its initial game when it walloped the life out of the Standard, its opponent of the week before, and established itself as a fit representative of St. Louis, in the newly organized American Association.

THE BROWNS OF 1883.

From this crude organization came the St. Louis Browns of 1883, a playing team put together with great skill by T. P. Sullivan, who was selected that year to manage the nine.

Sullivan had gone into Boston and had captured Tom Deasley, the great catcher of the Boston League team From Chicago he brought Hugh Nicol, the wonderful little right fielder.

The full St. Louis team in 1883 was made up of Tom Deasley, Tom Dolan and Tom Sullivan, catchers; Tony Mullane, Charles Hodnett, George McGinnis and Henry Oberbeck, pitchers; Charles A. Comiskey, first base; George Strief, second base; Walter A. Latham, third base; William Gleason, shortstop; Eddie Cuthbert, left field; Oberbeck or Mullane, center and Hugh Nicol, right.

It was from this team which was put together by Ted Sullivan in 1882 that came the St. Louis Browns, the nine that was later known as the four-time winners, that captured the American Association pennant in 1885, 1886, 1887 and 1888, and that won the Worlds Championship in 1885 and 1886. It was Comiskey who led this nine from 1884 on through its most successful years. This team was the wonder of the baseball world for many a day. The players were not stalwart looking but rather slight and slim waisted and when they met heavy nines like Chicago and Detroit they suffered on the field in comparison. But the players of the team played wonderful and speedy ball and that they knew how to win games and had the pluck and skill to capture a majority of the contests was proven by the record at the end of each season.

THE ST. LOUIS UNIONS.

Up to 1884 Von Der Ahe and his St. Louis Browns held sole possession of the local field of professional baseball. In the 1884 year, however, the St. Louis Union team under the leadership of Henry V. Lucas, its president, T. P. Sullivan, its manager, and Fred Dunlap, its field captain, stepped into the arena and remained in it during that year.

FIRST UNION GAME IN ST. LOUIS.

The first championship game played by the St. Louis Union team in the Union grounds at Jefferson and Cass avenues took place on April 20, 1884. It was a Sunday afternoon and a cold, drizzling rain was falling, but the teams went six innings before the game was called and nearly ten thousand persons sat through the rain to see it.

On this occasion the St. Louis Union team's opponent was the Chicago Unions and the occasion being a red letter one in the history of the game in St. Louis, I give the score in full just to show who the players were then and how they played:

ST. LOUIS UNIONS	AB.	R.	BH.	PO.	A.	E.	CHICAGO.	AB.	R.	BH.	PO.	A.	E.
Dunlap, 2b.	2	3	2	2	3	0	Ellick, rf.	3	0	1	0	0	0
Shaffer, rf.	3	1	2	1	0	0	Kreig, c.	2	0	2	10	3	0
Dickerson, lf.	3	0	0	0	1	0	Hengle, 2b.	2	1	0	1	2	0
J. Gleason, 3b.	3	1	2	2	1	0	Householder, lf.	3	0	1	0	0	0
Rowe, cf.	3	1	1	2	0	0	Foley, 3b	3	0	0	1	1	0
Taylor, 1b.	3	0	1	5	0	0	Shoeneck, 1b.	3	0	1	6	1	0
Whitehead, ss.	3	1	0	0	0	1	Mathias, ss.	3	0	0	0	2	0
Brennan, c.	3	0	0	5	3	1	Cady, cf.	2	1	0	0	0	2
Hodnett, p.	3	0	0	0	4	0	Daly, p.	1	0	1	0	9	2
Totals	26	7	8	17	12	2	Totals	22	2	6	18	18	4

	Innings.	1	2	3	4	5	6
St. Louis		1	0	0	2	2	2— 7
Chicago		0	0	0	1	1	0— 2

Earned runs—St. Louis, 2. Two-base hits—Dunlap, 1; Kreig, 1. Left on bases—St. Louis, 3; Chicago, 4. Wild pitches—Hodnett, 1. Base on balls—Off Hodnett, 3; off Daly, 4. Passed ball—Kreig, 2. Wild pitches—Hodnett, 1. Time of game—One hour and thirty minutes. Umpire—M. H. Hooper. Scorer—A. H. Spink.

It was the nine that played in this game that won the first championship for St. Louis. A year or two later championship pennants became common things in St. Louis, for then it was that Comiskey was planning to put a championship team in the American Association.

THE BROWNS OF 1884.

It was in 1884 that Comiskey took full charge of the St. Louis team filling the dual position of captain and first baseman.

The St. Louis Browns of 1884 were made up of Tom Deasley and Tom Dolan, catchers; William Widmer and George McGinnis, pitchers; Charles A. Comiskey, first base; George Strief and Joe Quest, second base; Walter A. Latham, third base; William Gleason, shortstop; Tip O'Neill, left field; Fred Lewis and Harry Wheeler, center, and Hugh Nicol, right.

There were few changes in the above team in 1884 and in 1885 Comiskey put together the combination subsequently known as "The Four Time Winners," for they captured the American Association pennant in 1885, 1886, 1887 and 1888, and the Worlds Championship in 1885 and 1886. This nine included Bushong, Boyle, Milligan and Dolan, catchers; Hudson, Chamberlain, Devlin and King, pitchers; Comiskey, first base; Robinson, second base; Latham, third base; White and Will Gleason, shortstops; O'Neill, left field; Lyons, center; McCarthy, right, and Joe Herr, substitute.

It was during the life of this nine that Von Der Ahe was at the height of his fame as a baseball president.

Its career lasted until 1890 when the American Association disbanded and Von Der Ahe and his team joined the National League.

This team's success lay mostly in the wonderful energy, skill and intelligence of its commander. Comiskey, above any other baseball general, had the knack of winning games down to a science. At a glance he could see the weak spot of the opposition and at a word his men were ready to scale that spot and run over it. He taught his players always to play for the game and not for individual batting or fielding record. He could forgive one of his men quickly for missing an opportunity, but he had no forgiveness for the fielder who shirked a hard hit ball or who failed to sacrifice when a sacrifice was needed.

He taught his men, too, how to play for the batsman, and at his signal his fielders played in close or in deep field just as they were ordered.

"No game is lost until the last man is out," was an old saying of his, and following this line, Comiskey's men often pulled a game out of the fire when it appeared lost beyond redemption.

In the baseball world this team was known for many a day as "The Four Time Winner," and their captain as "The Noblest Roman of the National Baseball Field."

This name indeed clung to the team and players until 1889 when Comiskey left to join forces with the Chicago Brotherhood Club. In 1890 the famous St. Louis Browns were scattered to the four winds and their departure was the commencement of the breaking up of the great fortune of Chris Von Der Ahe, who had been the president of the corporation owning and controlling the St. Louis Browns during the halcyon days of their career from 1882 until 1890 when Comiskey left them to join the Brotherhood and other of the famous players went elsewhere.

ST. LOUIS JOINS NATIONAL LEAGUE.

The St. Louis Browns were in the American Association from 1882 until 1892 but after the disastrous Brotherhood year of 1890 Von Der Ahe moved his nine into the National League. From 1892 to 1897 inclusive, six years in all, Von Der Ahe was the president of the St. Louis Browns during their National League membership. They were for him, unlucky years, ill fortune pursuing the St. Louis president in many ways.

In 1898 Von Der Ahe was forced out of the presidency of the St. Louis Club and B. S. Muckenfuss, his former secretary, was installed in that office. This was the National League's first move in its effort to put Von Der Ahe beyond the pale of organized baseball, and in the Fall of 1878 after he had served the people of St. Louis in the baseball line for a period of seventeen years he was deprived of his National League franchise which was sold to the Robison brothers of Cleveland, Frank De Haas Robison and Stanley Robison.

Ever since, the team has been in the possession of these gentlemen. During its first few years in the National League the team which the Robisons now own and which represents St. Louis in the National League, changed the color of its stockings from brown to cardinal and the team dropping the name of St. Louis Browns is known now and has been known since the change as the St. Louis Cardinals.

When in 1901 St. Louis entered the American League the present St. Louis Browns took the field and have held the old name ever since.

The most interesting season for Von Der Ahe and his team was that in which the St. Louis Maroons playing in Union Park at Jefferson and Cass avenue were opposed to them. That was the season of 1885. During that year the Browns and Maroons played a most interesting series of games. We give one of the scores below just to show the sort of baseball Comiskey, Dunlap, Glasscock and the other famous players were playing in those days. It will be noticed that of the twenty-seven men put out by the Maroons, Dunlap had no less than thirteen scalps to his credit:

BROWNS.	AB.	R.	1B.	TB.	P.	A.	E.	MAROONS.	AB.	R.	1B.	TB.	P.	A.	E.
Gleason, ss.	4	0	0	0	2	2	0	Glasscock, ss.	4	0	0	0	2	4	1
Welch, cf.	3	0	0	0	0	0	0	Dunlap, 2b.	3	0	0	0	3	5	0
O'Neill, lf.	2	0	0	0	1	0	0	Seery, lf.	3	1	1	1	0	0	0
Comiskey, 1b.	4	0	0	0	12	1	0	McKinnon, 1b.	3	0	1	2	11	3	0
Robinson, 2b.	4	0	0	0	1	2	0	Howard, cf.	3	0	0	0	0	0	0
Latham, 3b.	2	0	1	1	0	3	1	Cahill, rf.	3	0	0	0	2	0	0
Nicol, rf.	3	1	1	2	1	0	0	Denny, 3b.	3	0	1	2	0	0	0
Foutz, p.	3	0	1	2	3	2	3	Dolan, c.	3	0	0	0	2	4	0
Bushong, c.	3	0	1	1	4	2	1	Sweeny, p.	2	1	1	2	1	1	0
Totals	28	1	4	6	24	12	5	Totals	27	2	4	7	27	17	1

Innings.   1 2 3 4 5 6 7 8 9
Browns .... 0 0 0 1 0 0 0 0— 1
Maroons .... 0 0 0 0 0 2 0 0 0— 2

Runs earned—Browns, 1; Maroons, 2. Two-base hits—McKinnon, Denny, Sweeny, Nicol and Foutz. Total bases on hits—Browns, 6; Maroons, 7. Sacrifice hits—Glasscock. Left on bases—Browns, 3; Maroons, 0. Struck out—by Foutz, 4; by Sweeny, 2. Double plays— McKinnon, Dunlap, Glasscock, 1; Foutz, Robinson and Comiskey, 1. Bases on called balls—None. Stolen bases—Latham, 3; Denny, 1; Dunlap, 1; Nicol, 1. Wild pitches —Foutz, 2. Time—Two hours. Umpire—Kelly.

In 1884, the year before this game was played, the St. Louis Unions were playing at Union Park in opposition to the Browns. Only in those two years did the Browns have real opposition during the Von Der Ahe regime.

THE PASSING OF VON DER AHE.

The fortunes of Von Der Ahe began to wane in 1898. The season before he had a rough row to hoe. His 1898 season also opened most disastrously. While on April 16, 1898, the St. Louis and Chicago clubs were playing a game in League Park at Vandeventer avenue and Natural Bridge road, a fire broke out in the stands. It spread with fearful rapidity and half an hour after its start there was not a stick left of the grandstand, bleachers or fences. In the scramble to escape from the stands many persons were injured. The result was a great loss to Von Der Ahe, for after the fire many damage suits were filed against him. So great were his losses that on August 10, 1898, his club was forced into the hands of a receiver. Soon after he lost his hold on his park, club and franchise and in the winter of 1898-1899 the Robisons came in and took possession. They brought with them the great Cleveland Club which had won fourth place in the twelve-club race in 1898. This Cleveland team, afterwards known as the St. Louis Cardinals, was made up of O'Connor, Zimmer, Sugden and Criger, catchers; Young, Powell, Cuppy, Hughey, Sudhoff and Wilson, pitchers; Tebeau, first base; Childs, second base; Cross, third base; McKeon, shortstop, and Burkett, McAleer and Heidrick in the out field.

THE ST. LOUIS BASEBALL LEAGUE.

On March 8, 1889, a strong local organization was founded.

Joe Flood was the president of this organization; Ed Joy, vice president; James Bell, treasurer, and Robert Dimmick, secretary.

It was known as the St. Louis Baseball League and was composed of five teams, which will readily be remembered by old-time fans, those who are familiar with baseball in the days of Charles Comiskey.

The St. Louis Baseball League was the result of Von Der Ahe's four-time champion Browns. The continued victories of Comiskey's team made professional or semi-professional baseball, as it was called, possible in those days. Out of the professional baseball players the league was evolved. And though the league had a meteoric career, lasting one season, many players who afterwards gained national prominence were in it given their start to fame and glory, likewise money, on the diamond.

The St. Louis Reds, the Sultan Bitters, the Jolly Nine, the Home Comforts and the Dimmicks were the teams that took the field when play was called in the Spring of 1889. When the league closed its season and career the Home Comforts were the semi-professional champions of St. Louis and Theodore Breitenstein had attained prominence as a pitcher.

THE NATIONAL GAME.

For it was Breitenstein who pitched the Home Comforts to the championship after one of the keenest struggles that ever marked a league race.

The Home Comforts and the Sultan Bitters closed the twenty-two game schedule with an equal number of victories. Unlike the present day magnates, who would have arranged a series of games to determine supremacy, the Sultans and Comforts agreed to hang the championship on one game.

Theodore Breitenstein, as pitcher, and Frank Meek as his battery mate, were the hope of the Home Comforts. The Sultans rested their chances with Pitcher "Curley" Maloney and Catcher Schultz.

The game was played on the Kensington Garden grounds and the Comforts were the winners by a score of 3 to 2. That game marked the passing of semi-professional leagues in St. Louis, and it was not until eight years ago that another league was formed to take its place.

Among the league players in 1889 were many who afterwards went higher and became national figures. Breitenstein was foremost among them. Then there was Catcher Billy Kleiber, Pitcher Tommy Gillan, Johnny Schultz, "Curley" Maloney, who is still in harness in Dallas, Tex.; Frank Meek, who afterwards caught for the St. Louis Browns; Pitcher Frank Figgemeier, Frank Pears and Paddy Betz.

Though there were five teams in the league, but four were regularly scheduled. Two games were played weekly, one at Kensington Park, at Union and Page avenues, and the other at the St. Louis amateur grounds, at Missouri and Russell avenues. A general admission of 15 cents was charged, and Joe Flood, president of the league, is authority for the information that 20,000 people witnessed a single game.

Two of the four officers of the league are living. Mr. Flood, who was president, lives in St. Louis, as does James Bell, the treasurer. Ed Joy, vice president, and Robert Dimmick, treasurer, have since died.

COMING OF PRESENT ST. LOUIS BROWNS.

The National League team which the Robinsons had brought here from Cleveland in 1899 had full and complete possession of the professional field of baseball in St. Louis from 1899 until the appearance in the Mound City in 1902 of the St. Louis Browns, now representing St. Louis in the American League.

When the American League came into St. Louis in 1902 the present Sportsman's Park was refitted and the St. Louis Browns, the representatives of that organization, took the field and have remained in it ever since.

This new team and grounds are really the creatures of President Robert Lee Hedges of the St. Louis American League team now known as the St. Louis Browns, the name taken by the nine on its entry into St. Louis in 1902.

Failing to secure the necessary backing here, President Johnson went to Cincinnati for capital, there he met Mr. Hedges and unfolded the proposition to him. Mr. Hedges took the chance and the result was the rebuilding of old Sportsman's Park and its reestablishment as a baseball ground. Under the Hedge's management, Sportsman's Park, the present home of the St. Louis Browns, the American League representative was thrown open to the public on April 23, 1902.

This opening of this 1902 season and with it the reopening of Sportsman's Park as a major league ground and with it the introduction to St. Louis of the American League proved a most auspicious occasion.

The attendance was over eight thousand and all the most prominent city officials and baseball patrons were in attendance. The opening game was between the St. Louis and Cleveland Clubs and I give the full score below, just to show who the players were that took part in this opening game in the old and historic baseball grounds:

ST. LOUIS.	AB.	R.	BH.	PO.	A.	E.	CLEVELAND.	AB.	R.	BH.	PO.	A.	E.
Burkett, lf.	3	1	2	3	0	1	Pickering, lf.	5	0	2	1	0	0
Heidrick, cf.	4	0	0	2	0	0	McCarthy, cf.	4	0	2	1	0	2
Jones, rf.	3	1	2	0	0	0	Harvey, rf.	4	1	2	1	0	0
Anderson, 1b.	4	1	1	8	2	1	Schreckenghost, c.	4	0	1	7	2	1
Wallace, ss.	3	1	1	2	3	0	*Bonner, 3b.	4	1	1	6	2	0
Padden, 2b.	3	0	1	4	2	0	Bradley, ss.	4	0	0	0	2	0
McCormick, 3b.	3	0	0	2	1	1	Gochnour, 2b.	3	0	2	3	3	0
Sugden, c.	0	1	0	3	1	0	Bemis, 1b.	4	0	0	5	3	0
Maloney, c.	2	0	2	1	1	0	Moore, p.	1	0	1	0	0	0
Donahue, p.	2	0	0	1	4	0	**Hemphill,	1	0	1	0	0	0
	—	—	—	—	—	—		—	—	—	—	—	—
Totals	27	5	9	*26	14	3	Totals	34	2	12	*24	12	3

**Hemphill batted for Moore.
*Bonner out on bunted third strike.

Innings.	1	2	3	4	5	6	7	8	9	
St. Louis	0	0	5	0	0	0	0	0	0—	5
Cleveland	0	0	0	0	0	2	0	0	0—	2

Earned runs—St. Louis, 1; Cleveland, 2. Two-base hits—Jones. Home run—Wallace. Double play—Anderson and Wallace. Struck out—By Donahue, 3; by Moore, 4. Umpire—Robert Carruthers. Time of game—One hour and forty-five minutes.

This opening game was preceded by a bitter war in the courts in which the American League men were bitterly opposed by their National League rivals. The American League managers ignored the National League's reserve list and took players from the latter organization, right and left. The National League sought by injunction in the courts to prevent Burkett, Heidrick, Wallace, Sugden and Donahue from playing with the St. Louis Browns, but failed. As a result the latter team retained its strength throughout the season and remained intact until the winter of 1902 and 1903, when peace between the two major baseball leagues was declared.

THE NATIONAL GAME.

The new grounds and the new St. Louis Browns from 1902 prospered so wonderfully that in the winter of 1908-1909 Mr. Hedges dismantled the old park, increased the ground space and built for St. Louis the finest baseball park in this part of the country. At the same time he got together a team that promised to land the American League pennant in the 1909 season. That it was not successful was through no fault of Mr. Hedges who gave his manager free rein and supplied him with all the resources that capital and liberality had to give.

This brings us up to the present time in the history of baseball in St. Louis, the Mound City in this year (1910) being equipped with two great baseball grounds and two promising professional teams, one the St. Louis Browns of the American League under the management of the veteran catcher, Jack O'Connor, and the other the St. Louis Cardinals under the management of the famous catcher and player, Roger Bresnahan.

These teams at the start of the 1910 season were made up in this way:

St. Louis Cardinals, members of the National League: Pitchers—Willis, Corridon, Sallee, Lush, Backman, Harmon, Geyer, Higgins, Reiger and Johnson. Catchers—Bresnahan, Phelps, Bliss and Kelly. Infielders—Koney, Huggins, Hulswitt, Barbeau, Mowery, Betcher and Hauser. Outfielders—Ellis, Oakes, Evans and O'Hara.

St. Louis Browns, members of the American League: Pitchers—Powell, Pelty, Howell, Bailey, Waddell, Kinsella, Stremmel and Graham. Catchers—Allen, Killefer and Stephens. Infielders—Newnam, Abstein, Griggs, Hartzell, Wallace, Truesdale and Hetling. Outfielders—Stone, Hoffman, Schweitzer, Demmitt, Fisher and Criss.

THE GAME IN NEW YORK.

WILL RANKIN CLAIMS THE GREAT SPORT REALLY HAD ITS ORIGIN ON MANHATTAN ISLAND.

It seems like carrying coal to Newcastle, this attempt of mine to write up a history of the game in New York. For far abler men than me have written of the game's early history in that section, notably, Henry Chadwick, Al Wright and William M. Rankin.

The latter has recently been at work writing of the game's early history in New York and Boston and in a letter which Mr. Rankin wrote me on March 13, 1909, he claimed that baseball really had its origin on Manhattan Island and that the first real games played there were those taken part in by the old and famous Knickerbocker Club in 1853. In his letter to me on March 13, 1909, Mr. Rankin said:

"There are undisputed facts to show that baseball had its origin right here on Manhattan Island.

"All the old newspapers which began in 1853 to print baseball, speak about it as being the old Knickerbocker Club's game and nothing of an authenticated nature has ever been produced to refute this.

"Many years ago there was a game played in Great Britain which was known as rounders and several writers of English origin have claimed that the game of their boyhood was imported to this country, modified and improved until brought to its present state of perfection. Another writer, with a very imaginative mind that carries him back to the dark ages, says that baseball belongs to prehistoric times, and claims that the Egyptians were ball players, but he is candid enough to admit that they left no printed books, manuscript or anything else to prove his assertion, other than a lot of figures that might be utilized for any purpose.

"The latest of all the fakes was the one with the Coopertown flavor in which one Abner Graves of Denver, Colo., declared that the late General Doubleday was 'its designer and christener.' He said he was a 'kidlet' and was on the ground when General Doubleday turned the trick in 1839. What a pity for him he did not select some other year so that his air bubble could not have been pricked so easily. The records at West Point, N. Y., and the War Department at Washington, D. C., were the means of exposing his fake.

"Baseball is purely an American game and owes its origin to Mr. Alexander J. Cartwright, who also suggested the organization of a club to play his new game. This bit of information came from Mr. Duncan F. Curry, the first president of the old Knickerbocker Club, and is practically corroborated by Mr. Charles A. Peverelly, who wrote the first history of baseball that there is any record of.

"It was in the summer of 1877 that Mr. Curry said:

"Well do I remember the afternoon when Alex Cartwright came up to the ball field with a new scheme for playing ball. The sun shone beautifully, never do I remember noting its beams fall with a more sweet and mellow radiance than on that particular Spring day. For several years it had been our habit to casually assemble on a plot of ground that is now known as Twenty-seventh street and Fourth avenue, where the Harlem Railroad Depot afterward stood. We would take our bats and balls with us and play any sort of a game. We had no name in particular for it. Sometimes we batted the ball to one another or sometimes played one o'cat.

"On this afternoon I have already mentioned, Cartwright came to the field—the march of improvement had driven us further north and we located on a piece of property on the slope of Murray Hill, between the railroad cut and Third avenue—with his plans drawn up on a paper. He had arranged for two nines, the ins and outs.

"That is, while one set of players were taking their turn at bat the other side was placed in their respective positions on the field. He had laid out a diamond-shaped field, with canvas bags filled with sand or sawdust for bases at three of the points and an iron plate for the home base. He had arranged for a catcher, a pitcher, three basemen, a short fielder, and three outfielders. His plan met with much good natured derision, but he was so persistent in having us try his new game that we finally consented more to humor him than with any thought of it becoming a reality.

"At that time none of us had any experience in that style of play and as there were no rules for playing the game, we had to do the best we could under the circumstances, aided by Cartwright's judgment. The man who could pitch the speediest ball with the most accuracy was the one selected to do the pitching. But I am getting ahead of my

HAL CHASE.
Manager and Captain New York American League Team.

story. When we saw what a great game Cartwright had given us, and as his suggestion for forming a club to play it met with our approval, we set about to organize a club.

"A meeting was held on September 23, 1845, when the club was fully organized, and the following officers elected: Duncan F. Curry, president; Wm. R. Wheaton, vice president, and Wm. H. Tucker, secretary and treasurer. These officers were requested to draft a constitution and by-laws and a set of rules for governing the game.

"At a special meeting held June 5, 1846, Messrs. Curry, Adams and Tucker were selected as a committee to arrange for a match game, or a series of home and home games, with the New York Club. It was finally agreed to play the first game on June 19, at Elysian Fields, Hoboken, N. Y.

"Well do I remember that game," continued Mr. Curry, "the first regular game of baseball ever played hereabouts, and the New Yorks won it by a score of 23 to 1.

"An awful beating you would say at our own game, but, you see, the majority of the New York Club's players were cricketers, and clever ones at that game, and their batting was the feature of their work. The chief trouble was that we had held our opponents too cheaply and few of us had practiced any prior to the contest, thinking that we knew more about the game than they did. It was not without misgivings that some of the members looked forward to this match, but we pooh poohed at their apprehensions, and would not believe it possible that we could lose. When the day finally came, the weather was everything that could be desired, but intensely warm, yet there was quite a gathering of friends of the two clubs present to witness the match. The pitcher of the New York nine was a cricket bowler of some note, and while one could use only the straight arm delivery he could pitch an awfully speedy ball. The game was in a crude state. No balls were called on the pitcher and that was a great advantage to him, and when he did get them over the plate they came in so fast our batsmen could not see them."

While Mr. Rankin, the highest authority on that subject, claims that baseball really had its origin on Manhattan Island, one thing is certain and that is that the first game of baseball in which the tabulated score was printed took place in New York City July 5, 1853, and was published in the New York Clipper, July 16, 1853. The game was between the Knickerbocker and Gotham teams and resulted in a score of 21 to 12. In those days runs were not recorded. Instead of runs, "aces" they were called, and when one side scored 21 "aces" they had won the game, regardless of the number of innings played. This was the score:

GOTHAM.	O.	R.	KNICKERBOCKERS.	O.	R.
Vail	1	3	Brotherson	0	4
W. H. Faucet	2	2	Dick	1	4
Thos. Faucet	2	2	Adams	2	3
Pinckney	0	3	Niebuhr	2	2
Cudlip	2	1	Dupignac	4	1
Winslow, Jr.	4	0	Tyron	3	2
Winslow, Sr.	2	0	Parison	1	2
Lalor	2	1	Tucker	3	1
Wadsworth	3	0	Waller	1	2
	18	12		18	21

Then, too, the first extra inning game there is any record of also took place on Manhattan Island. This was the game played in New York City on October 26, 1854, and was between the Knickerbockers and the Gothams. The game lasted 12 innings and was called with the score tied. The following was the score:

GOTHAM.	R.	KNICKERBOCKER.	R.
Van Cott	2	DeBest	2
Demlit	0	Gurry	3
Salzman	3	Dupignac	2
Sheridan	2	Winslow	1
Cudlip	1	Adams	1
Ewen	0	Dick	0
Jackson	1	Wadsworth	1
MacFarlane	1	Davis	1
Vail	2	Kissam	1
	12		12

Knickbockers	1 2 1 0 2 3 0 2 0 0 0 1—12
Gothams	2 0 2 2 0 0 2 1 0 2 0 1—12
Innings.	1 2 3 4 5 6 7 8 9 10 11 12

As neither team scored the necessary 21 aces before darkness the game was called. It will be noted that in the first nine innings the score stood Knickerbockers 11, Gotham, 9. Van Cott and Vail was the battery for Gotham, while Dick and De Best officiated for the Knickerbockers.

When baseball was first introduced by the Knickerbocker Baseball Club of New York in 1845, the ball used was of home make, an uneven and rather crude affair and constructed with strips of old rubber shoes as a base, wound with old stocking yarn and covered with cowhide.

In 1865, when the game became nationalized by the returning soldiers from the Civil War, a small factory in New York commenced the manufacture of baseballs as a regular article of merchandise.

In 1868 the late Frank Queen, proprietor and editor of the New York Clipper, offered a series of special prizes to be contested for by all the leading clubs of the country; a gold ball being offered for the champion club and a gold badge to the player in each of the nine positions who had the best batting average.

After considerable jockeying by certain clubs the Athletics of Philadelphia were awarded the ball in 1869, after defeating the Mutuals of New York twice.

The gold medals were awarded to McBride, Radcliffe, Fisler, Reach and Sensenderfer of the Athletics; Waterman, Hatfield and Johnson of the Cincinnati Reds, and George Wright of the Unions of Morrisania, N. Y.

Mr. Queen in 1861 offered a silver ball to the victors of a picked nine game between New York and Brooklyn players. Brooklyn won and the ball can still be seen in that city.

After the first games of the Knickerbockers, came others and with them the organization of the first actual baseball association referred to in the early part of this work.

In New York after the Knickerbockers came the Gotham, Eagle, Empire, Baltic, Mutual, Harlem, Active, Marion, Wayne, Champion, Young America, Manhattan and Metropolitan teams.

In the fifties and sixties after the commencement in New York came the establishment over in Brooklyn of the Atlantic, Eckford, Putnam, Star, Excelsior, Charter Oak, Enterprise, Resolute, Niagara, Green Point, Continental, Clinton, Pacific, Hiawatha, Osceola and many other teams.

UNIONS AND ATLANTICS.

And while great teams were growing up in New York and Brooklyn in the sixties, there was building a few miles out from New York a team that became famous as the Unions of Morrisania.

When in the early seventies the first real professional association was organized, these teams of New York, Brooklyn and Morrisania were drawn on heavily for players. And at this time there was not a professional nine in America but that had one or more players hailing from these three grounds.

From the historic Atlantics of Brooklyn, who in the seventies were playing their games on the Capitoline grounds in Brooklyn were drawn such later famous players as Dickey Pearce, the first of the great short fielders; Robert Ferguson, the great catcher and second and third baseman who spent his last years umpiring in the National League; Joe Start, the first of the really great first basemen, so good a player that in the eighties he held his own while covering the initial bag for the Champion Providence team; Charles D. Smith, in his day prince of third basemen; John C. Chapman, the fielder who in later years held his own with the best in the National League; Lipman Pike, great then and later as a fielder and hard-hitting left-handed batsman. George Zettlein, the speediest pitcher in the sixties and early seventies; Charley Mills, the great first baseman, and George Hall and Dan McDonald, great outfielders.

From the Eckfords came Al Reach, later the second baseman of the Champion Athletics of Philadelphia; Al Gedney, who in his day had no superior as a left fielder; Jimmy Wood, the second baseman, who later played at second and captained the first Chicago White Stockings; Ed Pinkham, the greatest left-handed pitcher of his time; Tom Devyr, Edward Duffy and Jack Nelson, all great short fielders in their time, and David Eggler and Martin Swandell, who held their own on the baseball stage for many a day.

From the Eckfords, too, came Alphonse Martin, known as "Phonnie" or "Old Slow Ball," the first pitcher to ever try that sort of thing on the batsman.

From the Stars of Brooklyn came Arthur Cummings, known in the baseball world as "Candy" Cummings, the first to pitch a curved ball, and admitted by all to be the father of that sort of pitching.

From the Stars, too, came Frank Norton and Fraley Rogers, noted players of their day.

From the other Brooklyn teams came such later prominent players as Asa Brainard, Herman Doescher, Wm. Barnie, Herman Dehlman, William West, Joseph Roche, Al Metcalf, Teddy Larkin, Thos. Bond, Eddy Booth, John G. Dailey, John Valentine and many others.

From the Knickerbockers and the Unions of Morrisania, came the Wright brothers, George and Harry, and from the other teams which played in and around New York in the sixties and seventies came such later noted players as John Hatfield, David Force, Fred Waterman, Dick Highman, Dave Birdsall and Charley Pabor. The last two were the great battery of the Unions of Morrisania, Birdsall, without gloves or mask, catching the speedy, left-handed pitching of Pabor.

Other later noted players who were graduated from these early New York teams were Frank Fleet, Al H. Nichols, Frank Hankinson, Edward McGlynn, John Kelly, Harry Spence, Phil Powers, W. H. and Mel Buchanan, Rooney Sweeny, Johnny Troy, Gil Hatfield and many others.

The Atlantics of Brooklyn, the most famous of all the old time teams, who won their greatest glory by being the first nine to administer a defeat to the up to that time invincible Cincinnati Red Stockings, were organized in the Spring of 1854. It was not, however, until August 16, 1855, that they played their first practice game and their first actual contest took place on October 21, 1855. Their opponents in this, their first match game, were the Harmonys of Brooklyn, the Atlantics winning by a score of 24 to 22.

The original Atlantic team, the nine which took part in this initial game, was made up of C. Sniffin, p.; W. P. Whitson, c.; T. Powers, 1b.; T. Hamilton, 2b.; J. Loper, 3b.; W. Babcock, ss.; W. Bliss, r.f.

The Harmonys were: G. Phelps, p.; L. Berger, c.; R. Boerum, 1b.; J. Ireland, 2b.; J. Price, 3b.; A. W. Robbins, ss.; J. McKay, r.f.; J. Layton, l.f. and P. Backman, c.f.

This team of the Atlantics and the nine named as the Harmonys were bitter rivals

THE NATIONAL GAME.

until 1856, when the teams were consolidated and a nine was formed which went far to give the Atlantics the fame and renown they enjoyed in later years

In 1856 too, the Eckfords of Brooklyn, afterwards known the baseball world over, and the Unions of Morrisania came into being and they battled early and often with the Atlantics for leading honors.

It was in this year (1856) too that Dickey Pearce joined the Atlantics as their short fielder, a position he filled even after the Atlantics' great victory over the Cincinnati Reds in 1870.

It was on January 22, 1857, that the first baseball convention was held in Smith's Hotel, at 426 Broome street, New York, the meeting being held for the purpose of revising the rules. Just to show what clubs were then in the field I give the names of those represented at this first great baseball meeting:

Knickerbocker—D. L. Adams, Wm. H. Grinelle and L. F. Wadsworth.
Gotham—Wm. H. Van Cott, R. H. Cudlip and Geo. H. Franklin.
Eagle—W. W. Armfield, A. J. Bixby and John W. Mott.
Empire—R. H. Thorn, Walter Scott and Thomas Leavy.
Atlantic—C. Sniffin, W. V. Babcock and Thomas Tassie.
Putnam—Theodore E. Jackson, James W. Smith and Edward A. Walton.
Excelsior—James Rogers, P. R. Chadwick and James W .Andrews.
Baltic—Philip Weeks, Robert Cornell and Dr. Charles W. Cooper.
Harmony—R. Justin. Jr., G. M. Phelps and Frank D. Carr.
Eckford—Charles M. Welling, Francis Pidgeon and James M. Gray.
Harlem—E. H. Brown, John L. Riker and C. M. Van Voorhis.
Bedford—John Constant, Chas. Osborn and Thomas Bagot.
Nassau—William P. Howell, J. R. Rosenquest and Eph Miller.
Continental—John Silsby, Nath. B. Law and James B. Brown.

The delegates shortly after the convention was called to order elected the following officers: President, D. L. Adams of the Knickerbocker Club; vice presidents, Reuben H. Cudlip, Gotham; John W. Mott, Eagle; secretary, James W. Andrews, Excelsior; assistant secretary, Walter Scott, Empire; treasurer, E. H. Brown, Harlem.

On February 3, 1857, the committee on rules appointed at the first convention, reported and gave out a set of rules that were adopted. These rules were far different to those in existence now. The bases were four in number, thirty yards apart and there were many other arrangements far different from those in vogue at the present time. But from these crude rules came others revised early and often until the late sixties when the game had grown to be a great deal like the game of to-day and when the Atlantics of Brooklyn were considered by many to be the greatest team in America.

A SKETCH OF THE ATLANTICS.

The Atlantic team of 1869-1870 was made up of Ferguson, catcher; Zettlein, pitcher; Start, first base; Pike, second base; Smith, third base; Pearce, shortstop; Chapman, left field; Hall, center, and McDonald, right.

Not one of the original team of 1854 remained on this nine. The speed, the march of progress and other things had forced the originals one by one to retire and give way to the speediest and best players then to be found.

I had a close acquaintance with many of these great Atlantic players and especially with Dickey Pearce, Jack Chapman and Lipman Pike with whom I was later associated in the St. Louis Browns of 1875 and so I believe I can write intelligently of their ability as men and players.

Pearce was a short, stocky built man who won his first real honors on the baseball field while covering short field for the Atlantics of Brooklyn. He was with that team when they gave the Cincinnati Red Stockings of 1869 the first beating they ever received and Pearce had much to do with the Atlantics' victory on that occasion. Pearce was a remarkable player in every sense of the word. There was no man playing ball who was cooler, or showed more judgment in critical positions of a close contest than Pearce. His judgment was sound and his knowledge of strategy was up to the highest point. He was generally considered a model representative of ball playing skill in what is technically known as headwork. In batting he had no superiors, if an equal, in really scientific play at bat. There was not a "trick of the trade" he was not familiar with. He invented the bunt, and some years later when trying to draw a bunt away from the third baseman, he discovered the fair-foul hit. He could place the ball in almost any part of the field he desired. In the Fall of 1865, a New York writer in speaking about Pearce, said:

"In his knowledge of the points of the game, in judgment and experience, he has no superiors. What he does not know of the points of the position is scarcely worth learning."

Cotemporaneous with Pearce on the Atlantics were several other great players, notably Ferguson, Smith and Start.

Charles J. Smith, the great third baseman of the old Atlantics, was a player of uncommon ability, active, graceful and he possessed all the qualities which go to make the rare class of players who have been so few that they stand out conspicuously in the pages of baseball history.

No one who ever saw him perform when in the full vigor of health and strength will ever forget him.

Smith joined the Atlantics on October 18, 1858, coming from the Enterprise Club, which was then one of the strongest junior nines in the vicinity of Brooklyn, and played third base for them almost continuously until the summer of 1867, when he replaced Crane at second base, the latter going to center field, and Ferguson to third base.

While playing third base Smith was conceded to be the model player in that position, with no other player in his class. In a Brooklyn afternoon paper dated August 14, 1868, will be found the following about Smith:

"Charley enjoys the reputation of being the best general player living, and the most reliable in his position, which is second base. He is captain of the nine and has an al-

THE NATIONAL GAME.

most magnetic influence over his comrades. He is a general favorite with every one with whom he is acquainted."

After Smith, Ferguson was considered the most useful player on the team.

WHEN THE ATLANTICS BEAT THE REDS.

Ferguson in that memorable game between the Atlantics of Brooklyn and the Red Stockings of Cincinnati which was played in Brooklyn on June 14, officiated as the captain of his team. He also caught the terrific pitching of Zettlein and this without the aid of glove, mask or chest protector. It was really Ferguson's fine playing and headwork that won this game for the Atlantics and broke the Reds' continuous record of victories.

The score was 7 to 5 in the Reds' favor when the Atlantics went to the bat in their last inning. Smith led off for the Atlantics with a sharp grounder past third base. Start hit to right field and when McVey tried to field the ball after it had hit the bank, one of the spectators jumped on his back and interfered with him so that Smith reached home and Start went all the way to third base. To get the ball away from George Wright, the Reds' short fielder, Ferguson, batted left-handed instead of right, and brought Start home with a scorching drive to right field. Start's run tied the score. Zettlein, the next man up, hit hard to Gould and the latter threw to second to head off Ferguson, but so badly that the ball got by Sweazy and went into the field, while Ferguson, by speedy running, managed to just get home with the winning run. Magnificent work like this made Ferguson's record as a player, a record maintained by him even after the famous Reds were disbanded and forgotten.

After quitting his position as catcher, Ferguson commenced playing at third for the Atlantics, and a Brooklyn paper in 1860 said of his work:

"For a number of years Charley Smith was considered the best third baseman in the country, but since he vacated that base it is claimed that Fergy is the best. In 1856 he joined the Atlantics and has been a member ever since. He is noted for his good humor as well as his great playing qualities."

After quitting as a professional player Ferguson commenced work as an umpire in the National League. In this latter position he was fearless, independent, impartial as well as capable and trustworthy. His fearlessness was shown on the field one day when surrounded by an angry mob who threatened to kill him, he seized a baseball bat and shouted:

"I'm only one man to your thousand, but if you don't think I can protect myself just pitch in and give it a trial."

FERGUSON AS AN UMPIRE.

"Fergy" was as kind and good natured as he was brave and honest. He belonged to the game during its time of trial and tribulation and when it was often at the mercy of the black leg and crook, but when he died, there was no one who could say aught against his good name and reputation.

George Zettlein, the pitcher of the Atlantics, was nearly a giant in build. While working at his trade as a barber he became interested in the amateur games played on the fields in and around Brooklyn and soon he became noted as a wonderful pitcher.

At that time the rules compelled the pitcher to pitch the ball and not throw it, and it required great strength to attain any amount of speed.

Zettlein had a great arm and pitched so well against the amateurs that in the sixties he was admitted to the Capitoline grounds where all the great players of Brooklyn were being developed.

Zettlein made such rapid headway that when the Atlantics got together in June, 1870, the strongest nine they could think of, Zettlein was selected as their pitcher and he had the distinction of helping administer to the Cincinnati Reds the first defeat they had ever met with during their wonderfully successful life.

That victory set the world talking about the Atlantics and when Chicago in 1870 set to work selecting her first Chicago White Stockings, Zettlein was secured with Ed Pinkham, another Brooklyn boy and great left-handed pitcher, to do the pitching for them. In the West Zettlein sustained the fine reputation he had made while with the Atlantics, pitching for the Chicagos when they defeated the Cincinnati Reds in that memorable series played at Dexter Park, Chicago, in September and October, 1870.

Lipman Pike, the second baseman of the Atlantic team was the son of a Brooklyn haberdasher.

Like John Burdock, Start and other great Brooklyn players, he learned to play on the lots in and around that city and as soon as he knew how to play the game well he moved into the Capitoline grounds and played with the best teams that held forth there.

In build Pike was a born athlete and beside being a fine fielder and base runner he was one of the hardest hitting left-handed batsman.

He played with the Atlantics at second base, but later developed into a great outfielder and it was to play in the outfield that he was signed by the manager of St. Louis' first professional team, the St. Louis Browns, who held forth in the National League in 1875, 1876 and 1877.

In 1875 Pike did wonderful work with the bat for St. Louis, leading his team in that direction with the fine average of 342.

Of McDonald and Chapman the other two fielders on the Atlantic team McDonald retired early, but Chapman continued in the game for years, first as a fielder and then as a manager of teams at Louisville, St. Louis and other places.

This covers all there was of the Atlantic team with the single exception of Joe Start, perhaps the most beloved of all the great players who in their day claimed Brooklyn as their first school ground.

The first series of games ever played for a World's Championship took place in New York City in October, 1884. The Providence Club, winners of the National League pennant,. and the Metropolitans of New York, champions of the American Association that year, were the competing teams. The result was as follows:

PROVIDENCE.	R.	H.	O.	A.	E.	METROPOLITAN.	R.	H.	O.	A.	E.
Hines, cf.	2	1	1	0	0	Nelson, ss.	0	0	2	2	0
Carroll, lf.	1	0	1	0	0	Brady, rf.	0	0	1	0	0
Radbourne, p.	0	0	0	1	0	Esterb'k, 3b.	0	0	1	3	0
Start, 1b.	0	0	13	0	0	Roseman, cf.	0	0	0	0	0
Farrell, 2b.	1	1	2	2	0	Orr, 1b.	0	0	13	0	0
Irwin, ss.	1	1	0	6	1	Troy, 2b.	0	1	0	5	0
Gilligan, c.	1	1	8	2	0	Reins'ger, c.	0	0	7	2	1
Denny, 3b.	0	1	0	2	1	Kennedy, lf.	0	0	0	0	0
Radford, rf.	0	0	2	0	1	Keefe, p.	0	1	0	1	0
Totals	6	4	27	13	3	Totals	0	2	14	13	1

```
Club.                1 2 3 4 5 6 7 8 9
Providence ...............2 0 1 0 0 0 3 0 x—6
Metropolitan ............0 0 0 0 0 0 0 0 0—0
```

Earned runs—Providence, 3. Bases on balls—Off Keefe, 2. Struck out—By Radbourne, 9; by Keefe, 8. Umpire—Mr. Kelly.

The following day Keefe repeated, as did Radbourne, but again Keefe was defeated, New York getting but three hits and Radbourne striking out six men. Radbourne, it will be noticed, was some pumpkins as a hitter, too, and batted third. The summaries of the scores in those days did not give as many details as they do to-day, hence it is hard to tell whether there were any long hits made. The score of the second game follows:

PROVIDENCE.	R.	H.	O.	A.	E.	METROPOLITAN.	R.	H.	O.	A.	E.
Hines, cf.	0	0	3	0	0	Nelson, ss.	0	1	1	2	0
Carroll, lf.	0	0	0	0	0	Brady, rf.	0	0	3	0	0
Radbourne, p.	0	0	0	0	0	Esterb'k, 3b.	0	1	1	1	0
Start, 1b.	0	1	7	0	0	Roseman, cf.	1	1	1	0	0
Farrell, 2b.	1	2	2	1	2	Orr, 1b.	0	0	7	0	0
Irwin, ss.	0	0	0	3	1	Troy, 2b.	0	0	1	3	0
Gilligan, c.	1	1	5	3	0	Hulbert, c.	0	0	5	1	0
Denny, 3b.	1	1	2	2	0	Kennedy, lf.	0	0	2	0	0
Radford, rf.	0	0	2	0	0	Keefe, p.	0	0	0	1	0
Totals	3	5	21	9	3	Totals	1	3	21	8	0

```
Club.             1 2 3 4 5 6 7
Providence ..................0 0 0 0 3 0 0—3
Metropolitan ...............0 0 0 0 1 0 0—1
```

Bases on balls—Off Keefe, 2. Struck out—By Radbourne, 6; by Keefe, 4. Umpire—Mr. Remsen.

There was no reason for Radbourne to exert himself in the final game. Keefe found the pace set by Radbourne too fast, and after pitching for two days in succession found that he could go no further. The result was that a youngster named Becannon was called upon to pitch and he was given a severe drubbing, so Radbourne had an easy game, which may explain why his opponents got five hits and two runs.

Paul Hines, who is now a government employe in Washington, was the center fielder of the Providence team, and he never tires telling of the wonderful pitching of Radbourne. The following is the score of the third and final game which was called after only six innings play:

PROVIDENCE.	R.	H.	O.	A.	E.	METROPOLITAN.	R.	H.	O.	A.	E.
Hines, cf.	3	2	1	0	0	Nelson, ss.	0	0	1	1	0
Carroll, lf.	1	1	0	0	0	Brady, rf.	1	0	2	0	0
Radbourne, p.	1	1	0	2	0	Esterb'k, 3b.	0	1	0	0	0
Start, 1b.	0	0	6	1	1	Roseman, c.	0	2	0	0	0
Farrell, 2b.	1	1	1	3	0	Orr, 1b.	0	1	12	0	0
Irwin, ss.	2	2	2	1	1	Foster, 2b.	0	0	1	4	1
Gilligan, c.	1	2	4	0	1	Reipsch'r, c.	1	0	1	2	0
Denny, 3b.	2	2	1	2	0	Kennedy, lf.	0	0	1	1	0
Radford, rf.	1	2	3	0	1	Becannon, p.	0	1	0	4	1
Totals	12	13	18	9	4	Totals	2	5	18	12	2

```
Club.             1 2 3 4 5 6
Providence ......................1 2 0 1 4 4—12
Metropolitan ....................0 0 0 0 1 1— 2
```

Bases on balls—Off Becannon, 2. Struck out—By Becannon, 1; by Radbourne, 1. Umpire—Mr. Keefe.

OLD RELIABLE JOE START.

Of old reliable, Joe Start, a newspaper man of the sixties had this to say: "Joseph Start, the first baseman of the Atlantics, is without doubt the best player

JOHN L. DENNIS.
The Speedy Pitcher of the Mutuals of Chicago Away Back in the Seventies.

in his position in the country. From his invariable good play he has been nicknamed 'Old Steady.'

"In 1862 he joined the Atlantics and has played with them ever since. It is claimed for him that he can catch any ball thrown to him, that is within his reach; also, that he can cover more ground than any player at first base.

"He is a very quiet player, hardly ever saying a word during the game."

Long after those lines were written, Start was playing baseball. He was covering first base in 1884 for the great Providence team, champions of the National League, who that year won the first World's Championship from the Metropolitans, the champions of the American Association.

These games in New York City in 1884 in which Start played and which were the first games ever played for a world's championship, form a memorable part of the history of the game in New York.

Twenty-five years ago the World's series did not amount to much. The crowds were small, and the players' share of the receipts was hardly more than the bat boy gets these days. But that fact did not effect the artistic part of the contests. They played earnestly in those days, though salaries were comparatively low. The only pitcher Providence had in shape to play in this series was Charles Radbourne, or "Old Hoss," as he was familiarly known. His team won the National League pennant in 1884, and a series of five games was arranged with the Metropolitans of New York, winners of the American Association flag.

It was to be the best three in five games, and Radbourne was selected to pitch the opener. He won his game, 6 to 0, and came right back the next day and won by a 3 to 1 score. The third day Radbourne also pitched, winning easily, 12 to 2.

So Radbourne pitched three consecutive days and won every one of his games. Perhaps the most remarkable feature of his pitching was the fact that he did not allow a base on balls in the entire three games.

It is questionable if there is a pitcher in the game to-day who could duplicate Radbourne's performance of twenty-five years ago in so important a series. Nowadays pitchers need at least two or three days' rest, and even then they show signs of the strain. But Radbourne was an artist, perhaps the greatest the game has ever developed, in that he never wasted a ball. Every time he pitched he had some purpose in view, and his control was his stronghold.

Walter Johnson of the Washington team established a record when he pitched three shut-out games against New York in a row. That record probably will stand in baseball as long as the game lives. But the series was not important, and the players were not under a strain, which, of course, makes a difference.

In this 1884 year the Metropolitans were the big six in that section, for the New York National League Club had not then fairly started.

But at this time the baseball fever had become epidemic in all parts of New York City and teams were springing up everywhere. On the far West side of the Metropolis at a point known then as "The Dump," many diamonds were laid out and from them came players who were afterwards famous the country over for their skill as fielders and batsmen.

A strange crowd of rough and ready fellows were these "Dump" players. They seemed to have a "patois" all their own and they were noted when off the field for their skill at handling "high balls" as well as the other.

Rooney Sweeny, Dasher Troy, Bug Shappert, Jack Warner and many other noted players were graduated from the "Dump."

Warner and Sweeny were great catchers of their time and it used to be said that either could sit in a rocking chair and catch the speediest pitching.

Sweeny caught for the Atlantic team of the eighties, the nine that Billie Barnie put in the field and Warner back-stopped for the New York Giants and the St. Louis Cardinals only a year or two ago.

I have not gone into detail in reciting the work each year of the leading teams of New York for there were times when the game was at a low ebb there and when but little could be said of it. The interest that has increased in baseball in New York City until now it is by long odds the best patronized sport there, had its real commencement in this 1884 season when the Providence and Metropolitan clubs played their series there for the World's Championship.

Those games showed what an open field there was in the metropolis and perhaps led to the organization of the great nine which in its day had no rival and which in all around strength and playing ability would perhaps hold its own against any other team that was ever put together.

I refer of course to the original New York Giants, the team that captured the National League pennant in 1888 and that subsequently defeated the St. Louis Browns, champions of the American Association in the race for world's honors.

The New York team that year included Buck Ewing, P. G. Murphy and William Brown, catchers; Tim Keefe, Mickey Welch and L. Titcomb, pitchers; Roger Connor, first base; D. Richardson, second base; A. W. Whitney and Buck Ewing, third base; John M. Ward, short stop; James O'Rourke, left field; M. J. Slattery, center field; Mike Tiernan, right field; George F. Gore and Elmer Foster, center field.

This team proved invincible in 1888 and 1889, winning the National League pennant those two years and capturing world's honors at the same time.

There were few changes from the 1888 to the 1889 team. All the 1888 players held over except Titcomb, Murphy, Slattery and Foster. Hank O'Day, at present National League umpire, took Titcomb's place on the pitching staff and Gil Hatfield was secured as general utility man. This 1889 team beat Brooklyn for world's honors as easily as it had beaten St. Louis the year before.

The original New York Giant team with the original Chicago White Stockings, captained by Anson, will always be remembered as the heroic legion of baseball. When

THE NATIONAL GAME.

they were in the field with all their great players in position they were head and shoulders over all other nines.

Never before or since have we had greater all around players than were Ewing, Keefe, Ward, Tiernan, Connor and other of the Giants, and never again will we see players who as fielders and batsmen could beat Anson, Kelly, Williamson, Flint, Pfeffer and others of the great Chicago team.

The Chicago nine went out just as the New York nine came in, and after their great 1889 season the great New York team, like the Chicago, began to disintegrate. And New York was not in the limelight of baseball again until 1904 when with John T. Brush as president and John J. McGraw as manager, the New York Giants came into life again, winning the National League flag that year as well as in 1905 and in the latter season beating the Athletics of Philadelphia in the series for the world's pennant.

In this 1904 team there was not a vestige of the great team of 1888. Ewing, Ward, Keefe and the renowned players of 1888 had made their exits and the team which Mc-Graw placed in the field was made up of J. J. Warner and J. Bowerman, catchers: J. McGinnity, George Wiltse, Christy Mathewson, Louis Taylor and Leon Ames, pitchers; Dan McGann, first base; W. O. Gilbert, second base; A. Devlin and John Dunn, third base; William Dahlen, shortstop; Sam Mertes, left; Roger Bresnahan, center, and George Browne, right field.

In 1905 Bresnahan went behind the bat for New York and Mike Donlin took a place in center, while Sam Strang took the place of John Dunn as utility man. This was New York's last season as a leader.

The New York League team was in exclusive possession of the field in New York until 1903, when the New York Highlanders, the American League club, entered the arena.

From 1903 to 1906 this New York American League team had for its president, Joseph W. Gordon, an office filled ever since by Frank J. Farrell.

This New York American League team was managed and put together by Clark Griffith, who remained with the team from 1900 to 1907 when he gave over the reins to George Stallings.

This team has not yet won a championship in its organization, but is always trying hard.

In the 1910 year the teams representing New York in the National and American League were made up as follows:

New York Giants, members of the National League: Pitchers—Mathewson, Raymond, Wiltse, Crandall, Ames, Marquard, Bell and Drucke. Catchers—Schlei, Meyers, Wilson and Snodgrass. Infielders—Merkle, Tenny, Bridwell, Doyle, Devlin, Fletcher and Shafer. Outfielders—Murray, Seymour, Devore and Becker.

New York Highlanders, members of the American League: Pitchers—Doyle, Carroll, Clunn, Fisher, Ford, Frill, Hughes, Manning, Quinn, Upham, Vaughan and Warhop. Catchers—Criger, Mitchell, Kleinow and Sweeny. Infielders—Chase, Gardner, Laporte, Knight, Foster, Roach, Austin and Johnson. Outfielders—Hemphill, Cree, Wolter, Engle, Daniels and Madden.

THE GAME IN CHICAGO.

THE EXCELSIORS AND THE ATLANTICS WERE THE TWO FIRST REAL BASE-BALL TEAMS CHICAGO COULD BOAST OF.

Next to New York, Chicago is the greatest baseball city in America.

She has two magnificent major league grounds, nearly a hundred semi-professional parks and enclosed fields and her roster includes many of the greatest baseball players in America.

There seems to be some doubt as to where the first baseball club was organized at Chicago, but it has been stated that a club called the Unions played town ball there in 1856. This may be possible as we have a record of town ball being played at Alton, Ill., on Saturday, June 19, 1858. The first item we can find that refers to baseball being played at Chicago is as follows, and it was taken from The Spirit of The Times, published in New York, May, 1859. The items reads:

"Chicago, Ill., May 1, 1859.

"Dear Spirit—The baseball clubs of this city are in active preparation for their season, which promises to be a lively one. There are three or four clubs here. The Excelsior is the most prominent one, and is one of the pioneer clubs, having been in existence for a year or more. It was the first club to adopt the new style game played under the rules and regulations of the National Association, known as the New York game. The Excelsiors make a nice appearance on the ball field in their new uniforms, which consist of long white pants and white shirts made of English flannel. Their practice days are Tuesday and Friday."   "CHICAGO."

It would appear from the above, therefore, that baseball was being played by several teams in the Garden City as early as 1859 or more than fifty years ago.

It was not, however, until 1865 or nearly five years after the Empire team had been organized in St. Louis that Chicago placed any real baseball teams in the arena.

The first teams of any consequence to be organized there were the Excelsiors and the Atlantics.

These teams were of such importance that in July, 1868, they were selected to meet the Cincinnati Red Stockings, the first real professional team who visited Chicago on June 21 and 22, 1868.

On June 21, the Cincinnatis defeated the Excelsiors by 43 to 22 and on June 22 the Cincinnatis got away with the Atlantics by 28 to 9.

These games were played on grounds located on the North Side of Chicago, the only enclosure, in fact, the Lake City could then boast of.

These games gave the Chicago people their first taste of real baseball and from this time forward the game commenced to increase its areas in the garden city.

In all corners of the town baseball teams sprang up like mushrooms, for while the city could boast of but one enclosure, there were diamonds built on the prairies which then surrounded Chicago on all sides.

Several later famous amateur and semi-professional teams played games out on these prairies. The diamonds on them at this time were so common and so many games were played that in later years players graduated from them and coming into prominence were called ex-prairie players.

At this time the Bull's Head Tavern at Ogden avenue and Madison street marked the Western city limits of Chicago.

South the town extended only to Twelfth street and the Northern city limits ended at Division street.

Playing on the prairies directly adjacent to these city limit lines were all the best players then located within the limits of the Lake City.

Playing on the Western prairies were the Actives, the Libertys, the Mutuals and the Neversweats.

The North Side was represented by the Atlantics, who afterwards became known as the Aetnas and still later as the Franklins.

On the South Side the Pastimes were cock of the baseball walk and in the center of the city the Excelsiors held forth.

A year or two after the visit of the Cincinnati Reds, 1868, to be exact, the Actives established for themselves a regular ground at Lake and Ada streets. It was not enclosed, however.

The Libertys at the same time were holding forth at Madison and Western avenue, the Mutuals at Leavitt and Van Buren streets, the Actives in the old Atlantic grounds on the North Side and the Pastimes on a ground of their own, in South Chicago.

At about this time, too, a wonderful non-professional team came into the Chicago field. It was called the Dreadnaughts and it became invincible when pitted against the other teams by reason of the fact that it had "Cherokee" Fisher, an already famous Eastern professional, pitching for it, and a wonderful first baseman, a Swede, called Ole Olsen.

From these non-professional teams in Chicago were graduated many players who soon after became famous in the professional field.

From the Aetnas came many great players, notably Jack Carbine, the famous first baseman of the Louisville National League team; Jimmy Hallinan, later the short fielder of the original Chicago White Stockings; Paddy Quinn, one of the first to catch up close to the bat without mask or gloves; Hughey Reid, one of the first and best of Chicago's great pitchers; Paddy Lynch, a fine first baseman; Graves, a great fielder, and others.

From the Actives were graduated the Foley brothers, Tom, John, Charles and William Foley, all great players of their day; Mike Brenock, W. B. Lapham, McClelland and others.

From the Pastimes came Em Gross, who later became famous as the catcher of the champion Providence team; Bill Phillips, afterwards the first baseman of Cleveland's great stonewall infield and others just as good as them.

From the Libertys came Ike Fleming, one of the great catchers of that day; Mike Hayes, a noted pitcher, and the O'Day brothers, Dan, James and Henry, the latter best known in later years as the pitcher of the New York Champion League team and now the dean of the National League's corps of umpires.

It was the games played on the prairie and single enclosure in and about Chicago and these early games between the Excelsiors and the Atlantics on the one side and the Cincinnati Reds on the other that led to the boom of the game in the Garden City, a boom that did not end until in 1869 when the first team ever known as the Chicago White Stockings was placed in the field with but one object in view and that to take the measure of the Cincinnati Red Stockings who were now going about the country beating the life out of every baseball team that dared to meet them.

The game in the Garden City at this time was so crude that the men who had gotten Chicago's first real professional team together had given no heed to the building up of a ground and when the team was gathered together in the Spring of 1870 it had to do its practicing out on the prairie. The playing ground even then had not been agreed on.

When at last the great games with the Cincinnati Reds were arranged for Dexter Park, the famous old race track then located near the Chicago Stock Yards was secured as the battle ground and the diamond was laid out in front of the race track grandstand.

No bleachers were erected and of the thousands who gathered to see the famous games between the first Chicago White Stockings and the Champion Cincinnati Reds, a few were given seats in the grandstand while the remaining thousands formed a ring around the players and were kept from interfering with them by ropes which were stretched all the way around the in and out fields.

The first of these great games between the Chicago White Stockings and the Cincinnati Reds took place at Dexter Park on September 7, 1870, and Chicago won by a score of 10 to 6.

On October 13, 1870, the second game between these two then great teams was played at Dexter Park and again Chicago won, this time by a score of 16 to 13.

I saw both of these games and shall never forget them. Chicago had scoured the country for players out of which to form a team that would take the measure of the crack Cincinnati Reds.

This team included William H. Craver, catcher; Levi Meyerle, Edward Pinkham and Tom Burns, pitchers; James McAtee, first base; Jimmy Wood, second base; Levi Meyerle, third base; Charley Hodes, shortstop; Edgar Cuthbert, left field; Fred Treacy, center, and Clipper Flynn, right.

The Reds on this day had Doug Allison, catcher; Asa Brainard, pitcher; Charles Gould, first base; Charles Sweazy, second base; Fred Waterman, third base; George Wright, short stop; Andy Leonard, left field; Harry Wright, center, and Cal McVey, right.

No finer looking teams have ever taken the field than were these two in these two great games.

Every player of each team was in perfect condition. Discipline and good order were in evidence, too, the men appearing in clean and showy uniforms.

The Chicagos wore white flannel caps, shirts and stockings and blue trousers, while the Cincinnati boys were dressed in white shirts and trousers with red caps and stockings.

Each and every player seemed to be in the very pink of condition and each of the two games were magnificently played and contested.

The skies were clear and lovely wather ruled at both of these games and crowds that taxed the capacity of the Dexter Park enclosure were in attendance. So great indeed was the attendance at the second game and so high was the enthusiasm that at its close the crowd pushed over the race track fences and walked over the fence boards as they pushed and jostled their way out of the grounds.

Before these games were played the Chicago White Stockings had played other games with other noted teams. One of these games was the first shut-out game ever played. This game took place in Dexter Park, Chicago, on July 23, 1870, the Chicago White Stockings then falling before the Mutuals of New York who defeated them by a score of 9 to 0. Just to show how the game was scored at this time and just how the Chicago nine was placed, I give the score of this game in full:

MUTUALS.	O.	R.	1B.	T.	CHICAGO.	O.	R.	1B.	T.
Hatfield, ss	4	1	1	1	McAtee, 1b.	4	0	0	0
Eggler, m.	3	3	1	1	Hodes, ss.	3	0	0	0
Patterson, lf.	4	1	1	1	Wood, 2b.	2	0	0	0
Nelson, 3b.	1	1	2	2	Cuthbert, lf.	3	0	1	1
E. Mills, 1b.	4	0	0	0	Flynn, rf.	2	0	1	1
Martin, rf.	3	0	0	0	Treacy, m.	4	0	0	0
C Mills, c.	4	0	0	0	Meyerle, 3b.	3	0	1	1
Wolters, p.	1	2	2	4	Craver, c.	3	0	0	0
Swandel, 2b.	3	1	1	1	Burns, p.	3	0	0	0
Totals	27	9	8	10	Totals	27	0	3	3

```
                Club.    1 2 3 4 5 6 7 8 9
Mutuals ................1 0 0 0 0 3 0 3 2— 9
Chicago ................0 0 0 0 0 0 0 0 0— 0
```

The following year, 1871, the Chicago White Stockings found a new and what they hoped would be a permanent home, these new grounds being located at what was then known as the Lake Front Grounds or what is now Lake street and Michigan avenue.

There was at this time no regularly organized baseball association and the White Stockings remained at home most of the time and met whatever teams could be induced to come into Chicago and cross bats with them; and so in this year (1871) these grounds were visited by the crack teams of the country, notably the Forest Citys of Rockford, which then had Anson, Hastings, Addy, Spalding and other famous players in its ranks: the Forest Citys of Cleveland, who brought to the Garden City later noted players like Jim White, Al Pratt and others; the Eckfords of Brooklyn, who came with Martin, their famous slow pitcher; Nat Hicks, their great catcher; Gedney, then one of the fastest outfielders, and a lot of other good men; the Stars of Brooklyn, who came with Candy Cummings, the first of the curve pitchers and other teams equally as well known as those named.

These games proved profitable and the Chicago team was going along beautifully until the great Chicago fire of October, 1871, came along and swept the ball park and all thoughts of baseball from that part of the earth—swept it so successfully that for a long while Chicago was without anything that looked like a professional baseball team.

It was not indeed until five years later, 1876, that Chicago again took a leading place in the affairs of the National Game.

During the early part of that year the picked players of the champion Boston team, the nine which had captured the league flag four years in succession, 1872 to 1875, both inclusive, were signed for Chicago, and in 1876 they landed the pennant for the Lake City. This Chicago team known then and later as the Chicago White Stockings had for its president, William A. Hulbert, while A. G. Spalding was its secretary, captain and manager, as well as its only pitcher. The record in 1876 of this team, which called itself National Champions of the United States, was as follows:

Games won, 52; lost, 14. Per cent, .788.

CHICAGO.	No. Games.	Pct. Won.	Field. Pct.	Bat. Pct	CHICAGO.	No. Games.	Pct. Won.	Field. Pct.	Bat. Pct.
A. G. Spalding, p.	60	.788	.850	.395	J. W. Glenn, lf.	56	....	.866	.291
A. G. Spalding, cf.	6	....	....	....	Paul A. Hines, cf.	64	....	.917	.330
Jas. White, c.	64	....	.701	.337	R. Addy, rf.	33	....	.800	.272
C. A. McVey, 1b.	55	....	.956	.345	O. Bielaski, rf	31	....	.702	.205
Ross Barnes, 2b.	66	....	.910	.403					
A. C. Anson, 3b.	66	....	.850	.342	Team Record	66	.788	.882	.323
J. P. Peters, ss.	66	....	.932	.348					

This team played its games on the grounds located west of State and south of Twenty-second street, a rough board enclosure with a grandstand not near as pretentious as those owned now by the poorest of the Chicago City League teams. It retained the pennant but a single season, its players scattering at the end, its great catcher and main stay, Jim White, going back to the Bostons the following year and taking the pennant back there with him.

It was not until 1880 that Chicago came into her own again. Hulbert was still the president of her club, Spalding was still the club's secretary, but A. C. Anson had taken up the reins of manager and captain. It was this year that the best known Chicago White Stocking team, the nine that was known ever afterwards as the historic legion of baseball came into being and remained at the head in the National League during 1880, 1881 and 1882.

The 1880 nine which gave Chicago her first real high place in the baseball world made this record in this particular year.

Games won, 67; lost, 17. Per cent, .798.

CHICAGO.	No. Games.	Pct. Won.	Field. Pct.	Bat. Pct.	CHICAGO.	No. Games.	Pct. Won.	Field. Pct.	Bat. Pct.
L. Corcoran, p............	56	.798	.939	.221	T. E. Burns, ss............	73	....	.863	.309
F. Goldsmith, p..........	24	.798	.931	.260	A. Dalrymple, lf..........	84	....	.857	.332
F. S. Flint, c...............	62	....	.829	.167	Geo. F. Gore, c.f.........	71	....	.871	.365
A. C. Anson, 1b...........	77	....	.977	.338	M. J. Kelly, r.f...........	62	....	.811	.292
Jos. Quest, 2b.............	78	....	.895	.245		—	—	—	—
E. Williamson, 3b........	61	....	.893	.255	Team record..............	84	.798	.891	.281

In 1881 this same team captured the flag again, the only addition to its roster being Hugh Nicol, their little right fielder. In 1882, Thomas E. Burns was the single addition to the old team which remained intact. In this year, however, A. G. Spalding became the president of the club, Mr. Hulbert, its original president and leader, having passed away.

In the National League from 1883 to 1884 Chicago was without a champion team.

It was in 1884 that Chicago put a team in the Union Association. This nine was organized and managed by Joe Ellick, then a well-known professional player, but now a prominent boniface of Kansas City.

This Union Association team was made up with players, most of whom had learned the game on the Chicago prairie grounds.

It was made up of Kreig, catcher; One Armed Hugh Daly, pitcher; Shoeneck, first base; Hengle, second base; W. Foley, third base; Matthias, shortstop; Householder, left field; Cady, center, and Ellick, right.

This team played its first game at St. Louis on April 20, 1884, and lost to the St. Louis Unions by a score of 7 to 2. It played one hundred and eight games, winning thirty-four of them and then in the very middle of the season disbanded, owing to lack of patronage.

In 1885 Chicago again secured a winner in the National League. Her team this season (1885) made this good record:

A. C. Anson, manager and captain. Games won, 87; lost, 25. Per cent, .700.

CHICAGO.	No. Games.	Pct. Won.	Field. Pct.	Bat. Pct.	CHICAGO.	No. Games.	Pct. Won.	Field. Pct.	Bat. Pct.
J. G. Clarkson, p..........	70	.790	.803	.215	E. Williamson, 3b........	111	....	.891	.238
J. McCormick, p..........	28	.740	.710	.218	T. E. Burns, ss............	111	....	.844	.271
F. S. Flint, c...............	67	....	.855	.208	A. Dalrymple, l.f........	113	....	.878	.274
M. J. Kelly, c.............	33	....	.760	.287	G. F. Gore, c.f...........	109	....	.884	.312
M. J. Kelly, r.f...........	67	....	.868	....	Wm. Sunday, r.f..........	42	....	.825	.255
A. C. Anson, 1b...........	112	....	.957	.310		—	—	—	—
Fred Pfeffer, 2b...........	109	....	.892	.270	Team record.............	113	.770	.859	.264

This team repeated in 1886 with the same nine that had captured leading honors in 1885, but with the addition of John Flynn as pitcher and James Ryan as right fielder. This year (1886) witnessed the commencement of the gradual decline and decay of the once famous Chicago Club and the team which had carried itself so proudly for many a day never won a flag after this year.

In the four years following the representative of the National League in Chicago did so poorly that in 1890 when the Garden City put a team in the newly organized Brotherhood or Players' League it was predicted by many that soon the old league would be lost altogether and forgotten.

In this Brotherhood year, 1890, the flower of the old Chicago National League Club was taken and placed in the Chicago Players' League or in other Brotherhood teams. The Chicago Brotherhood team started out with a team which included Boyle and Farrell, catchers; King and Baldwin, pitchers; Comiskey, first base; Pfeffer, second base; Latham, third base; Bastian, shortstop; O'Neil, left field; Duffy, center, and Farrell, right.

This great team lasted only through this 1890 season when it disbanded and many of the players returned to their old clubs.

From 1900 to 1905 Chicago continued without stellar honors, but in 1906 the Chicago Cubs, the present great representative of the Garden City in the National League under the leadership of President Charles W.Murphy and Manager Frank L. Chance, captured leading honors. The record of this 1906 team was as follows:

Games won, 116; lost, 36. Percentage, .765.

CHICAGO.	No. Games.	Pct. Won.	Field. Pct.	Bat. Pct.	CHICAGO.	No. Games.	Pct. Won.	Field. Pct.	Bat. Pct.
Edw. Reulbach, p.........	33	.826	.968	.157	Arthur Hoffman, r.f.......	21	....	.976	....
M. Brown, p..............	36	.813	.980	.204	John Evers, 2b............	152	....	.947	.255
Carl Lundgren, p..........	27	.739	.984	.174	Henry Steinfeld, 3b.......	150	....	.954	.327
Jack Pfeister, p...........	31	.724	.922	.048	J. Tinker, ss..............	147	....	.944	.233
Orval Overall, p..........	31	.667	.928	.179	Jas. Sheckard, l.f.........	149	....	.986	.262
John Kling, c.............	96	....	.982	.312	Frank Schulte, c.f......	146	....	.975	.281
P. Moran, c..............	61	....	.979	.252	Jas. Slagle, r.f............	127	....	.976	.239
Frank Chance, 1b.........	136	....	.989	.319		—	—	—	—
Arthur Hoffman, 1b.......	20	....	.990	.256	Team record	154	.765	.969	.262

MICHAEL J. KELLY.

Michael J. Kelly, better known to the baseball followers of the eighties as "King" Kelly, was in his day considered the greatest baseball genius in the history of the sport.

THE NATIONAL GAME.

It was in 1900 that the American League invaded Chicago and added new life and interest to the game in the Lake City by capturing the first pennant of the new organization.

This 1900 American League team had taken up the name of the old Chicago White Stockings and its record this season with Charles A. Comiskey holding the reins as president and Clark Griffith as manager, was as follows:
Games won, 82; lost, 53. Percentage, .607.

CHICAGO.	No. Games.	Pct. Won.	Field. Pct.	Bat. Pct.	CHICAGO.	No. Games.	Pct. Won.	Field. Pct.	Bat. Pct.
R. Denzer, p.	36	.724	.950	.212	Fred Hartman, 3b.	116	....	.876	.2i5
C. Fisher, p.	35	.581	.945	.225	Frank Isbell, 3b.	15	....	.815	....
John Katoll, p.	37	.500	.937	.155	Frank Shugart, ss.	98	....	.906	.283
Roy Patterson, p.	29	.739	.898	.191	Charles O'Leary, ss.	26	....	.876	.163
Joe Sudgen, c.	74	....	.974	.289	W. E. Hoy, c.f.	137	....	.976	.254
R. Buckley, c.	34	....	.968	.201	P. Dillard, l.f.	16	....	.976	.183
P. Wood, catcher.	28	....	.967	.307	Frank Isbell, l.f.	18	....	.967	....
Joe Sudgen, 1b.	43	....	.984	....	Herman McFarland, r.f	120	....	.946	.241
Frank Isbell, 1b.	54	....	.979	.248	E. Shearon, r.f.	114	....	.929	.277
R. Padden, 2b.	130	....	.952	.284	W. Brodie, l.f.	64	....	.919	262

In 1901 Comiskey's men captured the American League flag for a second time and by these figures:
Games won, 83; lost, 53. Percentage, .610.

CHICAGO.	No. Games.	Pct. Won.	Field. Pct.	Bat. Pct.	CHICAGO.	No. Games.	Pct. Won.	Field. Pct.	Bat. Pct.
Wiley Piatt, p.	24	.375	.952	.209	Fred Hartman, 3b.	120	....	.893	.315
Clark Griffith, p.	25	.774	.947	.300	Jim Burke, 3b.	74	....	.807	.223
Roy Patterson, p.	40	.571	.942	.288	Frank Shugart, ss.	107	....	.884	.251
J. Callahan, p.	27	.714	.938	.344	Jim Burke, ss.	31	....	.860	.223
John Katoll, p.	27	.521	.912	.125	W. E. Hoy, c.f.	131	....	.958	.293
Joe Sudgen, c.	43	....	.974	.283	Fielder Jones, r.f.	133	....	.933	.325
W. D. Sullivan, c.	98	....	.967	.245	Ed McFarland, l.f.	132	....	.953	.265
Frank Isbell, 1b.	137	....	.980	.261	Clarence Foster, utility	110	....	.934	.270
Sam Mertes, 2b.	132	....	.939	.280					

From 1901 when Comiskey's team captured the American League flag until 1906 when Comiskey's Chicago American League Club captured the American League pennant and the Chicago Cubs took leading honors in the National League, the Garden City was without a champion team. In 1906 when Chicago captured premier honors in both of the major leagues the baseball public went wild and record breaking crowds witnessed the tilts for the world's flag between those two teams. The play off resulted in a victory for the American League representatives (the White Sox) over their National League opponents (the Chicago Cubs). The teams were made up in this way:

Chicago Americans (White Sox)—Pitchers, White, Owen, Walsh, Altrock; catcher, Sullivan; basemen, Donahue, Isbell, Rohe; shortstops, Tannehill, Davis; fielders, Dougherty, Jones, Hahn.

Chicago Nationals (Cubs)—Pitchers, Brown, Reulbach, Pfiester, Overall; catcher, Kling; basemen, Chance, Evers, Steinfeldt; shortstop, Tinker; fielders, Sheckard, Hofman, Schulte.

In 1907 the Chicago Club of the National League again captured leading honors in that organization and subsequently defeated Detroit in the series for the World's Championship. This Chicago team considered by many the greatest team that ever took the field made this record in its 1907 season:
Games won, 107; lost, 45. Percentage, .704.

CHICAGO.	No. Games.	Pct. Won.	Field. Pct.	Bat. Pct.	CHICAGO.	No. Games.	Pct. Won.	Field. Pct.	Bat. Pct.
Edward Reulbach, p.	27	.816	.930	.175	Arthur Hoffman, ss.	42	....	.921	....
M. Brown, p.	34	.769	.990	.153	Arthur Hoffman, l.f.	23	....	.958	....
Orval Overall, p.	36	742	.968	.213	Arthur Hoffman, r.f.	35	....	.948	....
Carl Lundgren, p.	28	.720	.984	.106	John Evers, 2b.	151	....	.964	.250
Jack Pfeister, p.	30	.609	.881	.094	Henry Steinfeldt, 3b.	151	....	.967	.266
C. Fraser, p.	22	.615	.942	.067	J. Tinker, ss.	113	....	.939	.221
J. Taylor, p.	18	.583	1.000	.191	James Sheckard, l.f.	142	....	.975	.267
John Kling, c.	98	....	.987	.284	James Slagle, c.f.	132	....	.961	.258
P. Moran, c.	59	....	.973	.227	Frank Schulte, r.f.	91	. ..	.972	.287
Frank Chance, 1b.	109	....	.992	.293					
G. E. Howard, 1b.	33	....	.972	.253	Team record	155	.704	.967	.250
Arthur Hoffman, 1b.	18	....	.990	.263					

It was the above team that surprised the baseball world by beating Detroit in four games out of the five and tying the other after eleven innings of play. And this magnificent record was the finish of Chicago for the time being as a pennant winner.

Few other cities can boast of a better record in a pennant winning way than is shown by Chicago in the above figures. Since the real commencement of the real game the Lake City has always been a shining light and has had some club or another always knocking at the front door for leading honors.

The teams representing Chicago in the 1910 year in the two leading leagues were made up in this way:

Chicago Cubs, members of the National League: Pitchers—Brown, Overall, Reulbach, McIntyre, Pfeister, Kroh, Hagerman, Cole, Carson, Pfeiffer. Catchers—Archer,

Moran, Needham. Infielders—Chance, Evers, Tinker, Steinfeldt, Zimmerman. Outfielders —Sheckard, Schulte, Hofman, Beaumont and Miller.

Chicago White Sox, members of the American League: Pitchers—Walsh, White, Smith, Scott, Burns, Sutor, Olmstead, Lang and Young. Catchers—Sullivan, Payne, Block and Krueger. Infielders—Gandil, Muller, Zeider, Collins, Blackburne, Purtell and Tannehill. Outfielders—Dougherty, Parent, Hahn, Barrows, Cole and Messenger.

Friday, July 2, 1910, will ever be a red letter day in the history of baseball in Chicago. It marked the opening of the new American League baseball park in that city, an enclosure second to none in America and built under the guiding hand of Charles A. Comiskey, president of the Chicago White Sox, the American League's representative in Chicago.

The opening game in this new park was witnessed by over thirty thousand persons. The Chicago White Sox and the St. Louis Browns were the competing teams and the full score was as follows:

CHICAGO.	AB.	R.	H.	O.	A.	E.		ST. LOUIS.	AB.	R.	H.	O.	A.	E.
Zeider, 2b	1	0	0	0	1	0		Stone, l.f	4	1	3	0	0	0
French, 2b	3	0	0	1	0	0		Hartsell, 2b	2	0	0	2	3	0
Browne, c.f	4	0	1	3	0	0		Wallace, s.s	4	0	1	2	3	0
Collins, r.f	2	0	0	2	1	0		Newnam, 1b	3	0	1	11	0	1
Block, c	1	0	0	1	1	0		Schweitzer, c.f	3	0	1	0	0	0
Dougherty, l.f	4	0	1	1	0	0		Hoffman, r.f	3	0	0	1	0	0
Gandil, 1b	4	0	0	5	1	0		Truesdale, 2b	3	1	1	5	2	0
Purtell, 3b	4	0	0	2	1	0		Killifer, c	3	0	0	6	4	1
Blackburne, ss	3	0	2	2	2	0		Pelty, p	3	0	0	0	5	0
Sullivan, c	1	0	0	8	3	1			—	—	—	—	—	—
Payne, r.f	1	0	0	0	0	0		Totals	28	2	7	27	17	2
Walsh, p	3	0	1	2	4	0								
	—	—	—	—	—	—								
Totals	31	0	5	27	14	1								

Club.	1	2	3	4	5	6	7	8	9	
Chicago	0	0	0	0	0	0	0	0	0—	0
St. Louis	0	0	2	0	0	0	0	0	0—	2

Two-base hit—Stone. Three-base hits—Dougherty and Stone. Sacrifice hit—Hartsell. Stolen bases—Collins. Truesdale, Stone (2), Hartsell and French. Double plays—Zeider to Sullivan to Purtell to Blackburne. Left on bases—Chicago, 6; St. Louis, 1. First base on balls—Off Walsh, 1; off Pelty, 2. Struck out—By Walsh, 6; by Pelty, 4. Time of game —One hour and fifty-five minutes. Umpires—Connolly and Dineen.

There were many incidents in connection with this historic game that are worthy of a place in this book.

The first ball pitched by Walsh was a "ball." George Stone made the first safe hit in the new park and Hartzell the first sacrifice. Collins drew the first pass and stole the first base. Blackburne made the first Sox hit and also the second.

There were four bands of music at this game including the Seventh Regiment Band of Chicago.

Soon after the distinguished guests arrived a committee of local rooters subpoenaed President Comiskey to the home plate. On the journey he was supported by Chairman Herrmann of the national commission and president of the Cincinnati club, and Mayor Busse and other city officials. The regimental band stationed on the field played "Hail to the Chief," and at the plate the big chief was presented a tall banner of blue and white bearing the legend, enclosed in a large "C," "Chicago, Congratulations, Comiskey," and the date, July 1, 1910.

The cheers which had greeted the master of the Sox when he first appeared were renewed with tremendous energy as he bared his gray head and marched back to the stand beneath the graceful folds of the banner. There never was a prouder moment in the old Roman's life in all probability than this in which he was made to feel the sincerest and best wishes of so many thousands and their thanks for what he had done to insure their comfort now and as long as steel and concrete will hold together, which is a man's idea of eternity.

Just before the game started the most impressive feature of all occurred. The regimental band assigned to duty suddenly awoke from "parade rest" to "attention," and to the tune of a lively quick step marched out into the field. A half turn brought it face to face with the flagstaff in deep left and here the band halted.

Its leader picking a color squad from the bugle corps then grasped the fold of a beautiful new American flag. As they hoisted away at the ropes the band played "The Star Spangled Banner," and the great throng, rising to its feet, cheered the nation's colors frantically.

No more fitting bit of sentiment could have been devised than that which assigned those khaki clad representatives of Uncle Sam's regular army to the honor of raising for the first time at the new grounds the flag whose stars and stripes meant so much more to each of them than to any one else in the crowd under which each and every one of them may be destined to fight, and in defense of which they are pledged to give their own lives unquestioningly if necessary. With the flag belayed tightly to its mast, the soldier boys marched back again and disappeared modestly from view, giving the stage for the rest of the day to the athletes.

This game also marked the return of "Billy" Sullivan to the Chicago team. The great receiver of the White Sox was injured on the early spring training trip to California, running a nail in his foot and coming very near lock-jaw. He was laid up for months and was not able to appear until in this opening game in the new grounds. He was cheered as he took his place behind the bat.

THE NATIONAL GAME.

In this game, too, the Sox appeared in a new style of home uniform, all white, with blue trimmings.

THE GAME IN PHILADELPHIA.

THE ATHLETICS WERE THE FIRST GREAT PROFESSIONAL TEAM THE CITY OF BROTHERLY LOVE COULD BOAST OF.

Philadelphia, with Boston and New York, shares the honor of being the first city to harbor organized baseball teams.

Philadelphia has her own baseball writers, notably Francis C. Richter, the able editor of the Sporting Life, the great baseball paper; Frank Hough, the veteran baseball editor of the Philadelphia Inquirer; Horace Fogel, once known world wide as a baseball writer in Philadelphia, but now the president of the Philadelphia National League Club; Ray Ziegler, baseball editor of the Philadelphia Record, and George M. Graham, the baseball writer of the Philadelphia North American, all of them better able than I to write of the game's history in the City of Brotherly Love.

I will therefore, not dwell on the early history there, but simply commence with 1860 when the Athletic Club of Philadelphia was organized.

That will be fifty years ago this spring, which is going back far enough I think. For from this great team sprang those other baseball nines that in subsequent years made Philadelphia known, America over, and that won for her the highest honors within the gift of the National Game.

The Athletics and the Keystones of Philadelphia were the great teams in Philadelphia during the sixties.

In 1871, eleven years after the organization of the Athletics, that team entered the race for the National baseball championship, competing with all the great teams of the East and West and coming out victorious. This feat gives to Philadelphia the honor of having owned the first National Champion baseball team of the United States.

The Athletics of 1871, the champion team of America that year, won 22 games and lost 7, winning the flag by a percentage of .729. The full record of the team and the men composing it, was as follows:

ATHLETICS.	No. Games.	Pct. Won.	Field. Pct.	Bat. Pct.	ATHLETICS.	No. Games.	Pct. Won.	Field. Pct.	Bat. Pct.
Dick McBride, p.	25	.759	.792	.284	John Sensenderfer, c.f.	25	....	.905	.371
Fergy Malone, c.	27	....	.800	.365	Geo. Heubel, r.f.	17	....	.841	.290
West Fisler, 1b.	28	....	.961	.333	Geo. Bechtel, r.f.	19	....	.849	.350
A. J. Reach, 2b.	26	....	.905	.371	Tom Pratt, substitute	8	....	.909	.295
Levi Meyerle, 3b.	26	....	.881	.448		—	—	—	—
John Radcliffe, ss.	28	....	.934	.333	Team record	29	.759	.894	.342
Ed. Cuthbert, l.f.	28	....	.930	.278					

I call to mind this team as it appeared on the field this year (1871), and the one thing I remember best about it was the wonderful athletic looking appearance of the players.

Not one of them but that was the trained athlete and not one of them was much above the other in height and general build. Every man on the team was about the medium in height and weight. Cuthbert was the only short man of the lot, but what he lacked in height he made up in wonderful muscular strength and speed. He was at this time the fleetest base runner in America.

I recall too, that the Athletics of 1871 were a magnificently uniformed team, wearing the finest of white cricket flannel with blue stockings and caps. In fact in the forty years since then, Philadelphia has never sent a better dressed team to St. Louis than the Athletic nine of 1871.

Of this Athletic team Cuthbert was a butcher when not at play, and Malone a shoemaker. Reach, its second baseman, had early entered the sporting goods business and from the little acorn he planted then has come the A. J. Reach Company, the largest manufacturers of baseball and sporting goods in all the world.

Tom Pratt, its substitute, also prospered, and in 1884 he was the owner of the Keystones, the team that represented Philadelphia that year in the Union Association.

Cuthbert in the early seventies located in St. Louis and remained here the balance of his life playing with St. Louis' first National League team in 1875 and 1876 and then helping Von Der Ahe organize the first team to represent St. Louis in the American Association.

Of the other Athletic players of the first championship team Sensenderfer was known as "The Count," owing to his royal bearing, and Fisler, Meyerle, Radcliffe, Heubel and Bechtel also attained high rank as gentlemen sportsmen.

Meyerle was the only big fellow on the Athletic team. He remained in baseball for many years after most of the original Athletics had retired.

Hicks Hayhurst was the Athletics' manager in their 1871 season.

There were some funny games played by this Athletic Club in this 1871 year. The Athletics defeated the Haymakers of Troy, New York, by the awful score of 49 to 33.

The Eckfords of Brooklyn, the Bostons, the Haymakers, the Mutuals of New York, the Baltimores, the Forest Citys of Cleveland, the Kekiongas of Fort Wayne and the Chicago White Stockings were the Athletics' great rivals this year.

In 1872, 1873, 1874, 1875 and 1876 the Athletics remained in the National League, but won no pennants.

From 1877 to 1882 inclusive, Philadelphia was not represented in the National League. The Athletics played independently in 1878 and won forty-five games and lost sixteen, tying one.

In 1883, Philadelphia obtained membership in the National League and finished last. The new league addition opened its career by whitewashing the Ashlands of Philadelphia 11 to 0, and on April 7 defeated the Baltimores of the American Association at Baltimore 6 to 3.

THE NATIONAL GAME.

They repeated this performance on the 11th, winning again, 9 to 8.

The Philadelphia line-up of 1883 included Gross and Ringo, catchers; Hogan and Coleman, pitchers; Sid Farrar and Ferguson, first base; Charles Ferguson, second base; Purcell and Warner, third base; McClellan, shortstop; Manning, Harbridge and Purcell, fielders.

Farrar was none other than the father of the world-renowned prima donna, Geraldine Farrar. Ferguson was one of the finest players the game ever knew. He developed into a most effective pitcher, and his early death was a severe blow to the prospects of the Philadelphia Club.

It was in 1881 that the American Association was formed at Cincinnati, Ohio. The season of 1880 had been most disastrous to the Cincinnati Club and it went into bankruptcy. A team was organized, and played Sunday ball for the most part. An attempt was made to hold a meeting at Pittsburg, but it did not succeed. At Cincinnati, however, there were represented clubs from Cincinnati, Philadelphia, Louisville, Rochester, Toledo and Brooklyn and they were immediately admitted to membership.

The Brooklyns and Athletics disbanded in midseason, the latter team losing five stars by desertion. The Athletics made a good start, but dropped back in the middle of the season, owing to weakness in the box. They were in such straits in the middle of September that they were obliged to release their high-priced men and finish with a pick-up team that could scarcely win a game.

The second great era in baseball, however, really came in Philadelphia in 1883 when the Athletic Club won the championship of the American Association.

That team included Jack O'Brien and Ed Rowen, catchers; George Washington Bradley, Bobby Mathews and "Jumping" Jack Jones of Yale College, pitchers; Harry Stovey, first base; Cub Stricker, second base; Fred Corey, third base; Mike Monayhan, shortstop; Jud Birchall, left field; Bob Blackiston, center, and Lon Knight, right.

This team was put in the field and kept there by William Sharsig, Lew Simmons and Charley Mason, the Athletics' managers. These three started the Athletics of 1882 with a shoe string.

Sharsig's capital consisted of a stocking of gold, the life savings of his old mother, which he had borrowed, and the contributions of Simmons and Mason, his partners in ownership of the club.

Pretty much all this was eaten up in fitting up the grounds in the most simple manner possible—a small covered stand that would seat less than a thousand persons, a few bleachers and a skin diamond. The field was barely fit to play ball on when the season opened and was never, even in after years, anywhere near first class.

But Sharsig, Simmons and Mason had some very good ball players, even though barely enough to make up a team, and they won out in the first really close pennant race in the history of organized baseball.

Greatest and best of the Athletic players of this day was Harry Stovey who covered first or any other place on the team.

The Athletics won the championship of the American Association in 1883 with a record of sixty-six games won and thirty-eight lost.

St. Louis finished second with 65-37, and Cincinnati third with 62-36. The Metropolitan Club of New York; Eclipse of Louisville; Columbus, Allegheny of Pittsburg, and Baltimore were also in the circuit and finished in the order named.

A tenth-inning wild pitch by Guy Hecker of the Eclipse team, gave the Athletics a 7 to 6 victory in the game that decided the championship at Louisville on September 28, the last but one of the season. It allowed Stovey to score the winning run.

Old timers remember well how the Athletics won this game on this particular wild pitch. They remember it because it was the first and only time that a single run decided a championship. It was in the last game of the season. The Athletics needed one more victory to insure them the pennant. They had to wind up their season at Louisville with a series of four games.

The Louisville players, spurred on by offers of big money from Chris Von Der Ahe, whose St. Louis Browns had a chance to tie the Athletics, tried all they knew how to earn the cash promised them by Chris to take four straight games from the Philadelphians. The Athletics had played themselves out and were sadly crippled after the hard campaign they had gone through. Louisville had won the first three games and it looked bad for the Athletics. Then came the final game, and Guy Hecker, Louisville's great pitcher of those days, was sent in to administer another beating to Billy Sharsig's men. After a fierce struggle the score was a tie when the ninth inning opened.

Stovey, the Athletic's star hitter and greatest base runner in the country, made a hit in the ninth and worked his way around to third base by the time two of his teammates had been disposed of. Then, with two down, Hecker made a wild pitch and Harry raced home with the run that won the game and gave the Athletics the championship.

The Athletics, as already stated, had lost the other three games of this closing series while the St. Louis Browns had won three straight from Allegheny, but that margin of one game to the good was enough to land the pennant and a great reception and street parade were accorded the team when the players arrived in Philadelphia a few days later.

"Jumping Jack" Jones, the Yale pitcher, with his catcher, Hubbard, was paid $1,000 for one month's service (September), and Jones, by winning two successive games from St. Louis, 11-1 and 5-4 (September 6 and 7), broke the slump which the team was experiencing and started the boys winning again.

Bradley's fine playing won the third game from the Browns, giving the St. Louis men a terrible set-back just at a time when they looked like coming champions.

That was Comiskey's great St. Louis team, and one of the liveliest ever put on the diamond, which afterwards won enough American Association pennants to make the race look like a joke.

Jones followed his St. Louis victory by beating the Columbus team 5-2, but after that he was not much account until he pitched that deciding game at Louisville, which won the championship. He was bumped good and hard when put against the Browns

71

at St. Louis, and all told he pitched but seven games, of which he won but four. But those four games were well worth the salary paid the Yale battery—even though Hubbard was of no use whatever to the club, since he did not class with O'Brien as a catcher.

All but five of these old-time champion Athletics—Crowley, Birchall, Moynahan, Matthews and Rowen—are still living.

O'Brien (Bryan) is a teamster in Philadelphia; Bradley is a policeman in the Twenty-sixth Philadelphia district; Stovey is in the police department at New Bedford, Mass.; Stricker is keeping a cigar store near Twenty-third and Columbus avenue, in Philadelphia; Corey is a lather at Providence, R. I.; Blackiston is a sailmaker at the Mare Island Navy Yard, California, and Knight is in the highway department at the City Hall in Philadelphia. Of its three managers Sharsig is dead, but Simmons and Mason are still alive and well.

The success of the team in winning games was not due to discipline or adherence to the usual rules of training, for the players did pretty much as they liked both on and off the field.

. It was a happy-go-lucky crowd, both owners and players.

On the trips abroad the three owners took turns about accompanying the team, and Stovey, the field captain, was practically the manager, also.

In 1884 Tom Pratt put a team in the Union Association for Philadelphia and it lasted only through that year.

From this forward until 1890 the Athletics cut little figure in the American Association. In 1890 the Louisville's captured the association flag and the Athletics finished at the tail end of the procession.

In 1891 Boston landed the flag, and the Athletics finished in fourth position. This was the last year of the American Association for there followed the swallowing up of this organization by the National League, and, as a result, there was but one club in each of the cities of Boston, Philadelphia and St. Louis. This condition continued until Comiskey invaded Chicago in 1900, and in the following season the American League forced its way into Philadelphia, Boston and St. Louis, and in 1903 gained a foothold in New York.

With such an able leader as Harry Wright, it was to be expected that the Philadelphia Club of the National League would make a much better showing in its second than in its first year, and in 1884 the team finished in sixth place, landing ahead of the Cleveland and Detroit clubs. In this year Philadelphia had on third base Joe Mulvey, its standby for many seasons to come. George Ed Andrews was on second and "Jimmy" Fogarty was certainly a great find as an outfielder. The club was securing players of rank, and in the next season—that of 1885—the club climbed into third position. Charley Ganzell was a member of the team in the season of 1886 when the Phillies dropped to fourth place, being beaten by the New Yorks by only seven points. Chicago landed the pennant after a hot race with Detroit.

The Phillies had a strong team with Ferguson, Casey and Dailey as pitchers; Clements, Jim McGuire and Cusick, catchers; Farrar, Bastian and Mulvey on the bases; Arthur Irwin, shortstop, and Wood, Andrews and Fogarty in the outfield.

In the following season, the Phillies were but twenty-seven points behind the champion Detroits at the finish. Philadelphia had Charley Buffington, so long with the Boston Club, that year, and behind the bat had Tom Gunning, now a leading physician in Fall River. The Philadelphia team again made a brilliant showing in 1888, finishing in the third position, being excelled only by New York, the pennant winners, and by Chicago. It was during this year that the club lost its great player, Ferguson. This loss was, in part, remedied by the acquisition of that wonderful batsman, Delahanty.

It was not surprising that the Phillies dropped to fourth place in 1889, when New York again captured the pennant, followed by Boston and Chicago. Outfielder Sam Thompson, formerly of Detroit, was the only addition of note to the team.

The inroads of the Players' League or the Brotherhood, as it was also called, played sad havoc with the National League clubs in 1890. Still Philadelphia maintained a strong club and made a very good showing, finishing third. Brooklyn landed the pennant, and Chicago was second. Philadelphia had Clements and Schriver as catchers; Gleason, Smith and Vickery, pitchers; McCauley, Myers and Mayer, on the bases; Allen, shortstop; Thompson, Hamilton, Burke, in the outfield. In Hamilton was secured a player who made the greatest base-running record the world ever knew, while he was a member of this club. He came from the Kansas City Club and batted .324 in his first season—a very fine showing.

The baseball seasons of 1891 and 1892 were uneventful in Philadelphia. In these years the Phillies were a poor competitor, but two of her players did phenomenal work. In 1892, the first year of the big twelve club's league, Billy Hamilton of the Phillies again made a brilliant showing, hitting for .330, scoring 131 runs in 135 games, besides stealing 65 bases. Delehanty hit for .312 that season, and stole 35 bases.

In 1893, 1894, 1895 and 1896 season, the Phillies fared badly. In the 1897 race they landed in tenth place, and that with such players as Delehanty, Lajoie and Nash in the ranks. Delahanty again showed his hitting powers, batting for .377, and scored 110 runs in 129 games. Hamilton was traded to Boston for Nash—a fine move for Boston, as he batted for .344 and made 153 runs in 155 games, as well as stealing 70 bases.

The Phillies improved in 1898, and finished in the sixth position, Boston again taking first honors, with Baltimore second. Delahanty, Lajoie, Flick and Cooley of the Phillies all hit for more than .300, Del. leading the quartet with a percentage of .334. He scored 114 runs in 142 games. Lajoie hit for .378 and made 113 runs in 147 games.

In 1899, the Phillies landed in third position, but five points behind the Bostons, who were second to the Brooklyn Club, the latter being strengthened by a trade which sent some of the crack players of the Baltimore Club to that city. Delahanty, Flick, Thomas, Lajoie, McFarland and Childs all batted for over .300 in the campaign, and Delahanty again made a rare run-getting record by crossing the home plate 133 times in 145 games. Flick made 101 runs in 125 games; Thomas, 135 in 148 games, and Lajoie, 70 in 72 games,

CONNIE MACK.
The manager of the Athletics of Philadelphia, winners of the American League Championship in 1910.

Cornelius McGillicuddy, better known in the baseball world as Connie Mack, the manager and part owner of the great Philadelphia Athletics, winners of the championship in the American League, in the 1910 season, is one of the real big fellows in the baseball world. Mack is known among the ball players, close followers of the game and press as the "Wise Old Owl." He's the manager, who, since he has had charge of the Athletics, has been winning pennants with supposedly classless ball players.

That is to say, Connie seems to be able to pick up mere youngsters, inexperienced players, as it were, and without much to do, build them into steady, winning players. Being an old foxy catcher himself, he

has always been successful in picking unknown backstops and pitchers. He has a system of play—it is soft, slow and steady. He teaches his men much like the professors of old, in a systematic way. If the youth is capable of grasping just what Connie wants he becomes a successful ball tosser. In 1902, 1905 and again in 1910, he won the American League Championship with the Athletic team.

He has developed hundreds of good infielders and outfielders—for other clubs. The pitchers, however, he has held for himself. Eddie Plank and Bender were practically discovered by him. It will be this pair of veteran pitchers on whom will fall the brunt of work, when his nine ties up with the winners of the National League Championship in 1910.

The Phillies held their ground in the season of 1900, again finishing in third place, a good second to Pittsburg, the Brooklyn Club again assuming first honors. Flick led the Phillies in hitting with .378, and the great Lajoie was second with a percentage of .346, making 95 runs in 102 games. Thomas was third with .325, and Delahanty fourth with .319. Of the first thirty batsmen, eight belonged to the Philadelphia Club—a most remarkable showing.

The season of 1901 marked the entry of the American League into the East, and Philadelphia has had two clubs ever since. The Nationals finished second to the Pittsburgs that season. Delahanty was second in batting to Jesse Burkett, the latter batting for .382, and the former for .357. Flick ranked third in his team with .336.

Philadelphia was badly hit by losing some of its most valuable playing timber in the season of 1902, and finished in seventh place, New York bringing up the rear. Such a trio as Delahanty, Flick and Lajoie were much missed and it was not surprising that the club failed to make any improvement in the season of 1903, finishing again in seventh position. In 1904 the club finished in last position, just seventeen points behind Boston. The next season the Phillies made a good spurt and finished in the fourth position. In 1906 the club again was fourth, and in 1907 was third, twenty-five points behind the Pittsburgs, who were second to the Chicagos. In the 1908 season the Phillies landed fourth, Chicago again winning, with New York second and Pittsburg third.

While the Phillies were doing this sort of work in the National League the Athletics from 1902 to 1905 were cutting high capers in the American League. In 1902 the Athletics with a team which had Benjamin F. Shibe for its president and Connie Mack for its manager, won the championship of the American League and with the players named: Games won, 83; lost, 53. Percentage, .610.

ATHLETICS.	No. Games.	Pct. Won.	Field. Pct.	Bat. Pct.	ATHLETICS.	No. Games.	Pct. Won.	Field. Pct.	Bat. Pct.
Fred Mitchell, p.	19	.654	.945	.189	D. Fultz, 2b.	18	....	.939	....
Ed. S. Plank, p.	36	.571	.939	.296	Louis Castro, 2b.	33	....	.920	.248
Ed. Waddell, p.	33	.766	.927	.279	Lave Cross, 3b.	137	....	.947	.339
B. J. Hustings, p.	33	.714	.921	.169	Monte Cross, ss.	137	....	.926	.207
O. F. Schreckengost, c.	71	....	.957	.317	R. A. Seybold, r.f.	136	....	.963	.317
M. B Powers, c.	68	....	.947	.271	D. Fultz, c.f.	111	....	.960	.300
Harry Davis, f.b.	128	....	.983	.308	F. T. Hartzel, l.f.	137	...	.963	.286
D. F. Murphy, 2b.	76	....	.968	.313					

Three years later the Athletics again captured the championship of the American League with the same officers at the head and with these players and figures: Games won, 92; lost, 56. Percentage, .621.

ATHLETICS.	No. Games.	Pct. Won.	Field. Pct.	Bat. Pct.	ATHLETICS.	No. Games.	Pct. Won.	Field. Pct.	Bat. Pct.
Charles Bender, p.	35	.621	.968	.217	D. F. Murphy, 2b.	150	....	.956	.278
E. S. Plank, p.	41	.667	.946	.231	Lave Cross, 3b.	146	....	.928	.266
W. Henley, p.	25	.267	.935	.169	Monte Cross, ss.	76	....	.929	.270
A. J. Coakley, p.	34	.680	.907	.144	John Knight, ss.	81	...	.895	.234
Ed. Waddell, p.	46	.730	.872	.172	R. A. Seybold, r.f.	132	....	.983	.271
O. F. Schreckengost, c.	114	....	.284	.274	B. Lord, c.f.	60	....	.962	.239
M. B. Powers, c.	68	....	.947	.271	Dan Hoffman, c.f.	117	....	.942	.262
Harry Davis, 1b.	149	....	.986	.284	F. T. Hartzel, l.f.	148	...	.938	.276

It will be noticed by the above that while Philadelphia has generally been represented in all the leagues that were going she has since 1871 scarcely had her fair share of championships.

While the Phillies have had a long list of managers—Horace Phillips in 1883 and Harry Wright for the next ten seasons, then Arthur Irwin for two, Billy Nash for one, Shettsline for five and Zimmer for two, winding up with Billy Murray and Catcher Dooin the Athletics have had but one manager, Connie Mack, who came from Milwaukee, and has been successful from every standpoint. It took much hard work for Mr. Mack, and all his resourcefulness was brought into play, especially when he was prevented from playing Lajoie in Pennsylvania, and it became necessary to transfer that player to the Cleveland Club, in which he has been a power ever since he began to play there in 1902.

This brings us down to the present day, the two Philadelphia clubs commencing their 1910 season with these players:

The Philadelphias, members of the National League: Pitchers—Moore, McQuillen, Moren, Sparks, Ewing, Foxen, Humphries, Shettler, Maroney and Brennan. Catchers—Dooin, Jacklitsch and Cheek. Infielders—Bransfield, Ward, Doolan, Grant, Knabe and Walsh. Outfielders—Magee, Bates, Titus and Deininger.

The Athletics, members of the American League: Pitchers—Bender, Coombs, Morgan, Plank, Dugert, Krause, Atkins and Friere. Catchers—Livingstone, Thomas and Lapp. Infielders—Davis, Rath, Collins, Houser, Barry, McIvers and Baker. Outfielders—Hartsel, Oldring, Murphy, Strunk and Heitmuller.

THE GAME IN BOSTON.

THE CITY OF CULTURE WAS ONE OF THE FIRST TO CULTIVATE REALLY GREAT BASEBALL TEAMS.

Boston has always been a hotbed of baseball.

Many of the greatest players that ever lived were born there and learned to play the game on the Boston commons.

Two men who have done as much for the National Game as any two others living, have written baseball for the newspapers of Boston and boomed the game there for nearly half a century.

One of these veterans is Tim Murnane, who in the seventies and eighties played baseball and afterwards wrote about it, and the other, Jacob Morse, one of the best champions the game has ever had.

Mr. Murnane is the baseball editor and has been the baseball editor of the Boston Globe for so long we have forgotten just when he commenced there and he has also for years been the president of the New England League.

The other great Boston baseball writer is Jacob C. Morse, editor of the Baseball Magazine of Boston now, but for nearly a score of years baseball editor of the Boston Herald. Mr. Morse is also associated with Mr. Murnane in the New England League, being the secretary of that organization.

I have a soft spot in my heart for these two men for they were with me when I went to the Union Association and the Brotherhood in the long ago, and they were the only two Eastern baseball writers to give me the friendly hand when I set out to organize the American League in 1898.

Through the fine tact, judgment and advice given out by these two famous writers Boston owes much of the success her clubs have scored in the baseball world.

For Boston, be it remembered, has figured perhaps too often and has had far more than her share of the honors when it came to baseball championships.

It is true that in the past decade Boston has not done much in so far as winning National League championships is concerned, but from 1871 to 1898 her club was always near the top in the National League race, and always winning or finishing in the first division or just next to it.

Just to show the magnificent work done by Boston's representatives in her winning years from 1871 to 1898 inclusive, which includes the Boston team's five years' membership in the old Professional Association, from 1871 to 1875, inclusive; as also in the National League, with its eight-club circuit, from 1876 to 1891, inclusive, and in the major National League, with its twelve-club circuit, from 1892 to 1898, inclusive, I give these figures:

Year.	Name.	Vic- tories.	De- feats.	Pct. of Victories.	Posi- tion.
1871	Professional Assn	22	10	.688	Second
1872	Professional Assn	39	8	.830	First.
1873	Professional Assn	43	16	.729	First.
1874	Professional Assn	52	18	.743	First.
1875	Professional Assn	71	8	.899	First.
1876	National League	39	31	.557	Fourth
1877	National League	31	17	.648	First.
1878	National League	41	19	.707	First.
1879	National League	49	29	.628	Second.
1880	National League	40	44	.474	Sixth.
1881	National League	38	45	.458	Sixth.
1882	National League	45	39	.536	Fourth.
1883	National League	63	35	.643	First.
1884	National League	73	38	.658	Second.
1885	National League	46	66	.410	Fifth.
1886	National League	56	61	.478	Fifth.
1887	National League	61	60	.504	Fifth.
1888	National League	70	64	.522	Fourth.
1889	National League	83	45	.648	Second.
1890	National League	76	57	.571	Fifth.
1891	National League	87	51	.630	First.
1892	Twelve-Club	102	48	.680	First.
1893	Twelve-Club	86	44	.662	First.
1894	Twelve-Club	83	49	.629	Third.
1895	Twelve-Club	71	60	.542	Sixth.
1896	Twelve-Club	74	57	.565	Fourth.
1897	Twelve-Club	93	39	.705	First.
1898	Twelve-Club	102	47	.685	First.

The following were managers, respectively: 1871, Harry Wright; 1872, Harry Wright; 1873, Harry Wright; 1874, Harry Wright; 1875, Harry Wright; 1876, Harry Wright; 1877, Harry Wright; 1878, Harry Wright; 1879, Harry Wright; 1880, Harry Wright; 1881, Harry Wright; 1882, Morrill; 1883, Morrill; 1884, Morrill; 1885, Morrill; 1886, Morrill; 1887, Morrill; 1888, Morrill; 1889, Hart; 1890, Selee; 1891, Selee; 1892, Selee; 1893, Selee; 1894, Selee; 1895, Selee; 1896, Selee; 1897, Selee; 1898, Selee.

It will be seen clearly by the above record that in the year named the Boston Club stood credited with the highest percentage of victories known in the annals of the league, viz., that of 1875, when their percentage reached .899. Again, in no one single pennant race of the twenty-eight the club participated in in those years did the team fall lower down in any annual race than sixth place, and then only three times; while they occupied first place, twelve times; second position, four times; third place, once; fourth place, three times, and fifth position, four times.

The Boston Club of 1872, the National League champions of that year had for its president, Ira W. Adams and Harry Wright was its secretary, manager and center fielder. This team won thirty-nine and lost eight games in this season and won the flag with a percentage of .830. The playing team of this season (1872) and its record are given below:

BOSTONS.	No. Games.	Pct. Won.	Field. Pct.	Bat. Pct.	BOSTONS.	No. Games.	Pct. Won.	Field. Pct.	Bat. Pct.
A. G. Spalding, p	47	.830	.903	.338	Andy Leonard, l.f	45	....	.895	.341
C. A. McVey, c	45	....	.745	.306	Harry Wright, c.f	44	....	.878	.261
Chas. Gould, 1b	44	....	.970	.256	Fraley Rogers, r.f	44	....	.878	.294
Ross Barnes, 2b	44	....	.908	.404	Dave Birdsall, utility	16	....	.753	.179
Harry Schafer, 3b	47	....	.900	.262		—	—	—	—
Geo. Wright, ss	47	....	.948	.336	Team record	47	.830	.896	.324

This team with the addition of Jim White, a catcher, won the championship for Boston from 1872 to 1875 inclusive.

In 1876 Spalding, White, McVey and Barnes were away from Boston playing with Chicago and that year they won the flag for Chicago and Boston with Harry Wright still as manager finished fourth.

In 1877 Jim White returned to Boston and with Tommy Bond as their only pitcher, Lew Brown as their only catcher, White, Morrill, Sutton, Leonard and George Wright as an infield and John O'Rourke, Tim Murnane and Harry Schafer as outfielders, Boston again won the flag.

In 1878 with practically the same team with the exception of Jim White, who had gone elsewhere and the assistance of Charley Snyder, who caught Bond, instead of Lew Brown, Boston again came out victorious.

From 1878 until 1882 Boston was not so fortunate, but in 1883 her team again captured leading honors, the team that year having A. H. Soden for its president and John F. Morrill for its manager and captain. The playing team included:

BOSTONS.	No. Games.	Pct. Won.	Field. Pct.	Bat. Pct.	BOSTONS.	No. Games.	Pct. Won.	Field. Pct.	Bat. Pct.
Jas. E. Whitney, p	62	.643	.839	.282	Ezra B. Sutton, 3b	94	....	.872	.323
Jas. E. Whitney, c.f	32	....	.794	....	Samuel W. Wise, ss	95	....	.827	.270
Chas. G. Buffington, p	35	.643	.756	.237	Jos. Hornung, lf	98	....	.936	.278
Chas. G. Buffington, c.f.	49	....	.756	....	P. R. Radford, rf	71	....	.837	.205
M. M. Hackett, c	32	....	.760	.234	Chas. F. Smith, ss and rf	20	....	.904	.217
Michael Hines, c	56	....	.751	.228		—	—	—	—
Jno. F. Morrill; 1b	80	....	.974	.310	Boston team record	98	.643	.852	.276
Jno. J. Burdock, 2b	96	....	.923	.330					

From 1883 to 1889 Boston won no more championships with Morrill as her leader. In the latter year he turned over the reins of management to James A. Hart and the team ran a good second.

In the 1884 season Tim Murnane put a team in the Union Association for Boston and it lasted only through that one year.

After the one year in Boston, Hart retired as manager of the Boston League Club and Frank Selee took his place and put together the great Boston team which from 1890 to 1898, when it won its last championship was always in the hunt. This Boston team under the leadership of Selee won its first championship in 1891 with this team:

BOSTONS.	No. Games.	Pct. Won.	Field. Pct.	Pct.	BOSTONS.	No. Games.	Pct. Won.	Field. Pct.	Pct.
John G. Clarkson, p	25	.642	.840	.233	R. L. Lowe, lf	105	....	.929	.281
C. A. Nichols, p	47	.638	.870	.201	R. L. Lowe, 2b	17	....	.949	...
H. E. Staley, p	25	.638	.833	.184	W. S. Brodie, cf	134	....	.963	.266
C. W. Bennett, c	74	....	.942	.215	H. D. Stovey, rf	133	....	.903	.279
C. W. Ganzel, c	68	....	.927	.259	M. J. Kelly, rf	15	....	.815	.239
T. J. Tucker, 1b	140	....	.975	.272	Martin Sullivan, lf	16	....	.896	.224
Joseph Quinn, 2b	123	....	.906	.247		—	—	—	—
W. H. Nash, 3b	139	....	.904	.273	Boston team record	140	.650	.906	.257
H. C. Long, ss	139	....	.902	.287					

And this team remained a winner in 1892, 1893, 1897 and 1898. During the five years in which it was at the top, few changes were made in its personnel.

In 1903, however, the Boston American League team won the championship in that organization and followed it out in the Fall by defeating Pittsburg, the National League champions in the series for the championship of the world. The Boston American League team in this its most wonderfully successful season had for its president, H. W. Killelea, and for its manager, James Collins. The team's record is given below just to show who the men were that did such good work for Boston in this great year:

BOSTON AMERICANS.	No. Games.	Pct. Won.	Field. Pct.	Bat. Pct.	BOSTON AMERICANS.	No. Games.	Pct. Won.	Field. Pct.	Bat. Pct.
William Dineen, p	34	.656	.988	.160	George La Chance, 1b	141	....	.986	.258
Thomas Hughes, p	32	.730	.966	.283	Hobe Ferris, 2b	141	....	.944	.250
Denton Young, p	40	.757	.946	.330	James Collins, 3b	130	....	.943	.296
N. R. Gibson, p	25	.571	.944	.262	Fred Parent, sh	139	....	.934	.304
George Winters, p	23	.556	.942	.121	Charles Stahl, cf	74	....	.965	.279
Louis Criger, c	96	....	.978	.197	John O'Brien, cf	74	....	.959	.212
C. Stahl, c	26	....	.973	.239	P. A. Dougherty, df	139	....	.957	.302
Charles Farrell, c	17	....	.958	.404	J. Freeman, rf	141	....	.941	.285

In 1892 big Jack Stivetts came to assist Nichols and Staley in the pitching department. In 1893 Henry Gastright joined the team's pitching staff. In 1897 when the team won

THE NATIONAL GAME.

again Klobedanz had joined the pitching crew and Fred Tenney had taken Tucker's place at first base, but the team which Selee had put together years before outside of those two players remained almost intact. From 1898 on when Selee's nine won, Boston has won no National League pennant.

This 1910 year the National League and the American League team of Boston started out splendidly equipped with players and with every hope of giving a good account of themselves in their respective races. Their teams are made up as follows:

The Boston Club, members of the National League: Pitchers—White, Brown, Mattern, Curtis, Richie, Ferguson, Evans, Burke, Wolfgang and Tuckey. Catchers—Graham, Raridan and Smith. Infielders—Martel, Shean, Sweeny, Cooney, Siner, Getz and Herzog. Outfielders—Beck, Billy Collins, Leise and Moran.

The Boston Club, members of the American League: Pitchers—Arellanes, Barberich, Cicotte, Collins, Erman, Hall, Karger, Peroy, Pape, Smith, Steele, Thompson and Wood. Catchers—Bradley, Carrigan, Donahue and Madden. Infielders—Meyers, Stahl, McConnell, French, Wagner, Gardiner, Lord. Outfielders—Hooper, Lewis, Speaker and Niles.

THE GAME IN CINCINNATI.

HOW THE QUEEN CITY HAS GIVEN MANY GREAT BASEBALL PLAYERS AND BASEBALL WRITERS TO THE GAME.

Cincinnati may justly lay claim to being the birth place of organized and professional or salary-paying baseball.

And Cincinnati may also lay claim to having given to the professional world many of the greatest players known to the game.

Notable among the many famous players who were graduated from Cincinnati diamonds was Buck Ewing for years the catcher of the New York Giants and claimed by many to have been the greatest catcher and batsman the National Game has ever known.

Long John Reilly is another of the great players who claims Cincinnati as the place of his birth and early training ground.

During the past forty years Cincinnati, the real birth place of professional baseball has had two championship teams. ·The Reds of 1869 started the city off on the high tide of early baseball enthusiasm by their magnificent work, which was continued with a good measure of success throughout the season of 1870. In 1882 the Cincinnati team won the pennant in the old American Association.

That was the last baseball honor of importance to fall to the Queen City of the West.

For twenty-five years Cincinnati has been continuously represented on the baseball map, but without capturing any notable honors on the playing fields.

In the business end of the sport Cincinnati has kept to the front of late years by furnishing the chairman of the National Baseball Commission, the supreme court of baseball, in the person of Garry Herrmann, president of the Cincinnati Club, whose fame has spread to all corners of the baseball world. But on the field no Cincinnati team since 1882 has achieved a remarkable reputation.

Baseball began to be played in Cincinnati in 1860, being developed from the old game of town ball, and the first Cincinnati baseball club was organized in 1866. The club was composed of men prominent in the business and social life of the city.

The first officers were Alfred T. Goshorn, president; Aaron B. Champion, vice president; Henry Glassford, treasurer, and Edward E. Townley, secretary.

Among the active and enthusiastic players in the early matches were Bellamy Storer, J. William Johnson, John R. McLean, J. Wayne Neff, Samuel Kemper, John C. How, Charles E. Callahan, Holmes Hoge, O. H. Tudor, Drausin Wulsin, Nicholas Longworth, Stanley Mathews and Andrew Hickenlooper.

The new club played many match games in 1866 and in 1867 meeting the newly organized teams of Newport, Louisville, Indianapolis and other cities. Only one game was lost in 1867, the Nationals of Washington, D. C., then defeating Cincinnati by a score of 53 to 10. The largest score of the season was 109 to 15 in a game with the Holtz of Newport in which Cincinnati made 31 home runs.

In 1868 the Cincinnati team first adopted the uniform which is practically the same to-day that it was at that time. The marked feature was the red stockings, from which the club took its name and without which no Cincinnati team has taken the field in any championship games up to the present time.

Up to 1868 ball players had worn long trousers like cricket players, and the white flannel knickerbockers with long red stockings were an attractive novelty. This uniform was designed by George Ellard, who thus gave Cincinnati the Reds.

The team of 1868 was composed of Harry Wright, pitcher; Allison, catcher; Gould, first base; Brainard, second base; Waterman, third base; Howe, shortstop; Hatfield, left field; King, center field, and Johnson, right field. The club played forty-nine games that season, winning forty-two and losing seven, a record which stamped it as the leading baseball nine of the country.

Up to this time baseball had been an amateur sport the country over. There were four players in the Reds of 1868 who received some compensation for their services, but the balance of the team was composed of men who played just for the fun of playing. But the rapid and widespread growth of the game made it evident that a club to remain in the front rank, must be composed of players who were at liberty to devote their entire time and attention to baseball.

Therefore at the close of the season of 1868, a meeting of the Cincinnati Baseball Club, composed of the leading citizens of the town, was called and it was voted to eliminate the amateur element from the team and secure for the following year the services of the best players in the country regardless of expense.

The members of the club pledged themselves to meet the expense and George B. Ellard was appointed to select the players and negotiate with them. Mr. Ellard at once began correspondence with the crack players of various teams and in the end he secured the team which made Cincinnati famous as the home of the Reds of '69. This

77

was the first completely professional baseball team ever organized and Cincinnati has, therefore, been correctly termed the cradle of professional baseball.

Beside the great team which Cincinnati gave to the baseball world in 1869 that city also produced ten of America's best-known baseball writers, J. B. (Macon) McCormick, O. P. Caylor, Harry Weldon, Frank Wright, Ban Johnson, Ren Mulford, C. H. Zuber, Jack Ryder, F. W. Rostock and Charles W. Murphy, the latter now the president of the Chicago National League Club.

The first game of baseball played in Cincinnati took place on a field where the Cincinnati Hospital now stands.

The nines were drawn from the Excelsiors Town Ball Club, the first baseball nine ever organized in the Queen City.

From this town ball club to Cincinnati came the Buckeyes, a team organized on October 1, 1863.

This team secured grounds in the Mill Creek Bottom where a club house and open and covered stands were erected. The playing team of the Buckeye Baseball Club of Cincinnati in 1866 was made up in this way:

James E. Sherwood, catcher; George W. Smith, pitcher; Charles H. Gould, first base; George F. Sands, second base; B. O. M. DeBeck, third base; John B. Shiedemantle, shortstop; John L. Boake, left field; W. H. Boake, center field; G. P. Miller, right field.

During the season of 1866 baseball became popular in all ends of Cincinnati as well as over the river at Covington and Newport. As a result four very good nines were organized, all claiming local honors, and at this time the list of players on these four teams was:

LIVE OAKS.

Dr. John Draper, catcher and captain.
T. C. Frost, pitcher.
D. R. Powers, first base.
Si Hicks, second base.
Jas. Fogarty, third base.
R. B. Lee, right field.
J. Hicks, center field.
John R. Brockway, left field.
M. M. Tolston, shortstop.

COVINGTONS.

B. W. Foley, catcher and captain.
Matthews, pitcher.
Bertie, first base.
Moses Grant, second base.
W. L. Porter, third base.
Thos. Fallon, right field.
W. Grant, center field.
Parker, left field.
Ben Brookshaw, shortstop.

EAGLES.

Mahaffey, catcher and captain.
Pudder, pitcher.
Lyford, firse base.
Bricker, second base.
Southard, third base.
Kennedy, right field.
Lusk, center field.
Ford, left field.
Swift, shortstop.

BUCKEYES.

Skiff, catcher.
Smith, pitcher.
Shiedmantle, shortstop.
Gould, first base.
W. Wright, second base.
Fallow, third base.
Meagher, right field.
H. W. Boake, center field.
J. L. Boake, left field.

The first match game ever played in Cincinnati took place there on September 8, 1866, with the Eagles and the Live Oaks as the competing teams. The score was 52 to 12 in favor of the Live Oaks.

In 1867 the first baseball tournament in the history of the game was held at Cincinnati.

That year, too, the Cincinnati Red Stocking Baseball Club, the first to put an out and out professional team in the field, was organized.

The first promoters of this club were Aaron B. Champion, Alfred T. Goshorn, Henry Glassford, William Tilden, George B. Ellard, J. William Johnson, Holmes Hoge, Quinton Corwine and a few others.

They elected Alfred T. Goshorn president; Aaron B. Champion, vice president; Henry Glassford, secretary, and E. E. Townsley, treasurer. William Worthington was the club's first official scorer and George B. Ellard was its manager.

From the Cincinnati tournament and the interest which sprang from the playing of the clubs which developed right after, came the organization of the nine which later became famous as the Cincinnati Reds.

This regularly organized team was put together in the Fall of 1867 and the men who played on the nine that year were: Harry Wright, pitcher; Fred Waterman, third base; Douglas Allison, catcher; Charles H. Gould, first base; Asa Brainard, second base; J. William Johnson, right field; Rufus King, center field; J. V. B. Hatfield, left field; John C. How, shortstop; Moses Grant, substitute.

It was from this team that came the famous Cincinnati Red Stockings of 1869 referred to at length in the early pages of this book.

Cincinnati's next champion team came to her in 1882 when the American Association was formed.

The Cincinnati Club of 1882 was organized with Louis Kramer, as its president; Louis Herancourt, its treasurer, and O. P. Caylor, the famous baseball writer, as its secretary. Its chief backer was Aaron S. Stern.

The champion Cincinnati team, the first to win a championship in the American Association was made up with Charles Fulmer as its manager and Charles N. Snyder as its field captain.

The team included Dan Stearns, first base; John A. McPhee, second base; W. W. Carpenter (Old Hickory), third base; Charles Fulmer, shortstop; Joe Sommer, left field; Johnny Macullar, center field; Harry Wheeler, right field, and Harry Luff, who played twenty-seven games with the team at first base.

In winning this first championship of the American Association, the Cincinnati team sadly outclassed its opponents, winning fifty-four games during the season and losing only twenty-six.

O. P. CAYLOR.

O. P. Caylor was in his day perhaps the most famous baseball writer in America, doing duty on the Cincinnati Enquirer.

In 1884 Cincinnati had two clubs, one in the Union Association and the other still in the American.

The officers of the Union Association Club were, Justus Thorner, president; Frank B. Wright, secretary, and George Gherke, treasurer.

In 1893 and 1894 the National League and American Association battled for the possession of the baseball patronage in Cincinnati and at the end the older organization came into possession of the field and has clung to it ever since.

In the past ten years Cincinnati has had such famous leaders for her club as Buck Ewing, Charles Comiskey, Gus Schmelz, Joe Kelly and Clark Griffith, but she has never since the season of 1882 when she won the American Association flag, come near a championship.

Some of the greatest players of their day finished their professional work on the diamond at Cincinnati. Among those who rounded out their major league career in that city those most worthy of mention in this particular are Michael J. Kelly ("King Kell"), Charles Radbourne, Charles A. Comiskey, Louis Roger Browning, Bobby Caruthers, Curt Welch, Arlie Latham, Tip O'Neill, Joe Kelly, Bug Holliday, Kid Baldwin, Long John Reilly, Will White, Charley Snyder, Jimmy Clinton, Jim Keenan and many others.

Redand history would be incomplete without a reference to the good work of Buck Ewing, John G. Reilly, John Corkhill, Jim Keenan, Tony Mullane, Billy Rhines, Charles Jones, Gus Shallix, Tom Mansell, Ren Deagle, Jimmy Peoples, George Tebeau, "Germany" Smith, Jerry Harrington, Frank Dwyer, Phil Ehret, Elmer Smith, Kid Baldwin, Jim White, Lip Pike, Bug Holliday, Jake Beckley, Hugh Nicol, Lee Viau, Harry Vaughn, Frank Foreman, Frank Hahn and a host of others, some of whom have slid across the home plate of eternity, while the rest are still playing life's game. All of these great players in their day played in Cincinnati and either learned the game there or came to the Queen City to play with her professional teams.

In 1910 Cincinnati started with her one club in the National League, with Clark Griffith as her manager and these players under contract:

Pitchers—Fromme, Spade, Caspar, Beebe, Rowan, Castleton, Suggs, Coveleskie, Hosp and Anderson. Catchers—McLean, Clark and Roth. Infielders—McLean, Clark and Roth. Infielders—Hoblitzel, Egan, Downey, Lobert, Doyle and Charles. Outfielders—Mitchell, Bescher, Paskert, Miller and McCabe.

BASEBALL IN INDIANAPOLIS.

THE NINE WHICH WON THE CHAMPIONSHIP OF THE INTERNATIONAL ASSOCIATION AND OTHER TEAMS WHO PLAYED WELL THERE.

The City of Indianapolis has been prominent in professional baseball for many years.

In 1908 her team won the championship of the American Association.

In 1902 Indianapolis also carried off leading honors in the American Association with the fine average of .682.

In 1908, the Indianapolis team's average was .601, Louisville, with .575, pushing her very closely for the pennant.

But the team the Hoosiers were prouder of than any other that represented them on the diamond was the "Only" Indianapolis, the team that represented the Hoosier capital in 1877 and that won for her that season, the pennant in the International Association.

Three St. Louis boys were in that nine, Frank Flint, their catcher; "Trick" McSorley, their left fielder, and Charley Houtz, their first baseman.

Flint by his grand playing that year was known as the "Only" Flint, and Nolan for the same reason was called the "Only" Nolan.

Flint and Quest of this great team afterwards played for years on the Chicago White Stockings, Flint having no superior at that time as a receiver, and Quest being considered the prince of second basemen.

Flint, while on the Chicago team, was known as "Old Hoss," for he caught every day and handled the speedy pitching of men like Goldsmith, Clarkson and Corcoran with the greatest ease.

Flint was born in North St. Louis and learned to play on the open fields just north of what is now North Market street.

He died in the heydey of his career and his body lies in Bellefontaine Cemetery in this, his home city.

McSorley and Houtz, also of St. Louis, are now living in the Mound City, McSorley being on the St. Louis police force and Houtz being the manager of the Golden Lion of which establishment John W. Peckington, the old vice president of the St. Louis Browns, is the owner.

This great Indianapolis team really had its first start in St. Louis.

Early in 1875 Packie Dillon, Joe Blong and John "Trick" McSorley, went to Covington, Ky., to play with the Covington Stars. Their playing there was so good it caused a sensation and W. B. Petit who was looking about for players for a team at Indianapolis went to Covington and signed all of the St. Louis boys to play with the Hoosier team.

They made such a fine impression that when in 1876 Petit wanted more players for his Indianapolis team he came to St. Louis to find them.

Here he found Frank Flint, who was afterwards famous as the catcher of Anson's Chicago White Stockings, the heroic legion of baseball, and Charley Houtz, who had been playing a great game at first for the St. Louis Reds.

This 1876 Indianapolis team which later became known as one of the greatest winning nines in America, was made up of Frank ("the only") Flint, catcher; Edward ("the only") Nolan, pitcher; Charles Houtz, first base; Joe Quest, second base; John "Trick" McSorley, third base; Denny Mack, short stop; Edgar Cuthbert and Mike Golden, left field; Fred Warner, center, and Ad. Rocap, right.

In 1878, John Clapp came as catcher to help Flint; Arthur Croft, a St. Louis player, took the place of Houtz at first; Jack Nelson came from Brooklyn to cover short field and the great Ed Williamson was brought from the Alleghenys of Pittsburg.

One of the greatest and quickest thinkers on this Indianapolis team which was such a winner was John McSorley. He was so tricky that he soon became known the country over as "Trick" McSorley.

McSorley was born in St. Louis and did his first professional playing with the St. Louis Unions in 1872. He was the third baseman and change pitcher of that team and for that matter could play any place on the nine.

But the great success of the Indianapolis team was mainly due to the great work of their battery, Flint and Nolan.

Nolan pitched every game and every day in the week. He pitched 114 games during the season, every one in which the team took part and Flint caught in all of them.

Nolan went to Indianapolis from Patterson, New Jersey, and he is back there now as a policeman. He played with the Buckeyes of Columbus just before joining Indianapolis.

Joe Quest and Ed Williamson went to Indianapolis from the Alleghenys of Pittsburg. Denny Mack was a Philadelphian and so was Eddie Cuthbert. Golden was from Rockford, Ill., and William Riley from the Cincinnati and Westerns of Keokuk, Ia. Fred Warner and Ad. Rocap, like Mack and Cuthbert, hailed from Philadelphia. Jack Nelson was from Brooklyn, where he had played with the old Eckfords and Atlantics.

I am indebted to Houtz for the picture of the Indianapolis team of 1877 which appears in this history of the game.

The players composing that nine were Frank Flint, catcher; Edward Nolan, pitcher; Charles Houtz, first base; Joe Quest, second base; Fred Warner, third base; D. J. Mack, short stop; J. B. McSorley, left field; William Reilly, center, and Ad Rocap, right.

Indianapolis during her time has had professional teams in all the great baseball leagues.

Her first real venture in baseball or at least the first worth talking about, was when, in 1870, a team of local players was gotten together and called the Indianapolis. The mission of the nine was to put an end to the victorious career of the then already famous Cincinnati Reds.

The game which was to place Indianapolis on the baseball map and which was to send the Cincinnati Reds into oblivion, took place at Indianapolis on August 5, 1870.

It created great excitement and brought out the first great crowd that has ever seen a game in the Indiana capital. The score at the end was: Cincinnati Reds, 61; Indianapolis, 8.

Seven years later, or in 1877 to be exact, Indianapolis organized a first-class team of local and foreign professionals who with the aid of the "Only" Nolan made it very warm and interesting for every professional and non-professional team that cared to come to the capital city and cross bats with it.

That year it defeated all clubs in the International Association including the Canadian members of that organization and claimed for itself the championship of that body.

As a matter of fact in this 1877 year this really wild cat or non-league club was the best of its kind in the country.

It defeated every big league club that paid it a visit, except the Hartfords, and with the latter was never beaten worse than 2 to 0.

At the commencement of the 1878 year the directors of the Indianapolis non-league team, thinking they had a bononza in Nolan, christened him "The Only Nolan," joined the National League and set out to win the pennant of that organization.

The attempt, however, was a wonderful failure, the club not only failing to win the league flag, but to make good for its directors.

At a meeting of the club directors at the close of the 1878 season they found to their dismay that the playing year had closed with the club some $2,500 in debt and no money in the treasury to pay the salaries still due the players.

Just before this meeting was held a club for the following season, 1879, had been talked of, and Clapp, McCormick, Warner and McKelvey had signed to play in it, but the sorrowful discovery made knocked this programme into a "cocked hat," and the players who had signed were released. Clapp and McCormick went to Buffalo, Warner to Cleveland or Boston, and McKelvey and the other players elsewhere.

In this Fall of 1878 soon after the discovery of the shortage this special dispatch was sent out from Indianapolis:

"The Homeless Nine membership are still hanging about town awaiting payment by the stockholders in the busted baseball organization. The individual indebtedness to the players will average $250, on which $50 each has been paid. It is the understanding that will have to content, as they will get no more. The total indebtedness is said to exceed $5,000. Warner and Schaffer are threatening to place their claims in an attorney's hands, and the rest will probably join them. Petit, the president, is soundly cursed; still there is no apparent reason for the abuse beyond that he has not eminently distinguished himself as a financial manager. He has been absent from the city since the bust up, but he writes the consoling assurance to the stockholders, by mail, that he hopes they 'will make satisfactory settlement with the boys.' Not even a semiprofessional club will be maintained in this city next year, from the present outlook."

I give this special and tell the story just to show what a rough road these early professionals once had to hoe even in what is now one of the best baseball cities in America.

There were but six clubs in the National League in this 1878 year and they finished in this order: Boston, Cincinnati, Providence, Chicago, Indianapolis, Milwaukee.

The people of Indianapolis were so disappointed at the work of the team that had represented them so splendidly the year before that they repudiatd it and wearing uniforms like that previously worn by the members of the St. Louis League team the nine went barn storming through the country and wherever they went they were called the "Homeless Browns."

W. B. Petit, brought this team to St. Louis. I was writing baseball for the Missouri Republican at the time and to help Petit along I organized a picked team with Cuthbert, Pearce, Houtz, Croft and other left-over professionals, and arranged a series to take place at Grand Avenue Park, now Sportsman's Park.

St. Louis at this time was down and out in the baseball line and Petit and his men did not draw enough at the gate to pay carfare. It was the failure of these games to draw that led to the subsequent sudden disbanding of the team. The fate of this nine gave the game a black eye in Indianapolis and it was not until years later that she recovered from the blow, this from a baseball standpoint.

In fact it was not until 1887 that Indianapolis again took a place in the baseball world.

That year Mr. John T. Brush, now the president of the New York National League Club and an enthusiastic lover of the game, organized a team and secured for it a franchise in the National League.

This team held a membership in the National League throughout the season of 1887, 1888 and 1889. At the close of the latter season it resigned its membership.

In her three years in the National League, Indianapolis saw her team finish last in the eight-team league of 1887, and seventh in the eight-team league of 1888 and 1889.

In the early nineties, William H.Watkins went to Indianapolis and joined John T. Brush in the building up of the game in that city and he has been there ever since either as manager or president of the Indianapolis Club. At this time it was a member of the Western Association.

Mr. Watkins managed the great Detroit team of 1887, the team which won the National League pennant that year and which had in its ranks such famous players as Jim White, Brouthers, Richardson, Dunlap, Jack Rowe, Ned Hanlon and others. A better manager and organizer perhaps never lived and small wonder therefore, that he has been wonderfully successful in the managing and building up of the Indianapolis team.

In 1898 Indianapolis could finish no better than in the eight-team Western League of that year. In 1899 in the same league her team fought out the battle for the pennant to the very finish with Kansas City, the latter winning at the end, capturing eighty-eight games to Indianapolis' eighty-four and losing fifty-one games to Indianapolis' fifty.

In 1900 Mr. Watkins joined forces with his fellow members of the Western Association and Indianapolis became one of the charter members of the American League. Her team, however, remained in that organization but a single season.

In 1910 Mr. Watkins, with the others, helped put together the now powerful American Association, and Indianapolis has ever since held a prominent place in that organization.

At the beginning of this article I tell of the record of the Indianapolis Club in the American Association. It has won the championship in that organization twice.

The 1908 team which captured the American Association flag and which was owned by Mr. Watkins, was captained and managed by Charles Carr, its great first baseman and leading batsman, and a team coached by Perry Werden and made up of these players: Wakefield, Livingston, Lindsay, Davidson, Cook, Bush, Marquardt, Coulter, Siever, Slagle, Durham, Hayden, Howley, Williams, C. C. Carr, captain and manager; Druhot, Hopke.

In the winter of 1891 Indianapolis was the place at which the famous peace conference between clubs of the National League, and American Association was held. That meeting resulted in the National League buying out four of the American Association clubs and taking the other four into partnership, thus wiping out all opposition and combining all the major leagues of the country under the one banner.

In fact Indianapolis has always held a prominent place in the history of the National Game and has always been fortunate in having men like Brush and Watkins at the head of her baseball affairs.

CLEVELAND IN BASEBALL.

THE FOREST CITY, EVER SINCE THE DAYS OF HER GREAT NAMESAKE TEAM, HAS BEEN TO THE FORE IN THE AFFAIRS OF THE NATIONAL GAME.

In the affairs of the National Game the City of Cleveland has always taken a prominent part.

Her team, the famous Forest Citys of the sixties, was the first baseball team to represent Cleveland in the real field of professional baseball.

It was this great Forest City team that met the famous Cincinnati Reds at Cleveland, on May 12, 13 and 31, October 6, and November 5, 1870, and gave the Reds a good battle, although all the scores were against the Cleveland team, the figures being 12 to 2, 12 to 2, 27 to 13, 18 to 15 and 28 to 5.

In these days Jim White was catching for the Forest Citys and little Al Pratt was doing the pitching.

That they were a great team even at this early day was proven when in 1870 they defeated the crack Kekionga team of Fort Wayne, Ind., by the then unheard of score of 2 to 0.

In 1871, with a part of her great Forest City team reinforced by professional players captured in all parts of the country, Cleveland entered the only association then worth mentioning. This organization included in its ranks the Athletics of Philadelphia, the Boston Reds, the Chicago White Stockings, the Mutuals of New York, the Olympics of Washington, the Haymakers of Troy, the Forest Citys of Cleveland, the Kekiongas of Fort Wayne and the Forest Citys of Rockford, who in the race that year finished as I have named them.

The Forest Citys played but twenty-nine games that 1871 year and won but ten of them.

In 1872 Cleveland was in a league that consisted of eleven teams who that season finished in this order: Boston, Baltimore, Mutual, Athletic, Troy, Atlantic, Cleveland, Mansfield, Eckford, Olympics and Nationals of Washington.

Cleveland won but six games in this 1872 league and lost fifteen. So poorly indeed

THE NATIONAL GAME.

did her playing team do both from a playing and financial standpoint that from 1873 to 18.8 both inclusive, Cleveland was without the pale of organized baseball.

In 1878 Cleveland had but nine players under contract. The nine then was made up of Kennedy, catcher; Mitchell, pitcher; Phillips, 1b.; Streif, 2b.; Carey, ss.; Glasscock, 3b.; Eden, rf.; Warner, cf.; Riley, lf.

This nine had a hard road to hoe, so hard that the baseball writer of the Cleveland Leader at the end of the season said: "Many of the members of the Forest City nine will leave for home this week—that is providing they feel strong enough for the walk."

In 1879 a new company was organized at Cleveland with J. Ford Evans as its president and a team backed by this organization was admitted to membership in the National League. In 1882 Mr. Evans resigned the presidency of the club and C. H. Bulkely was elected in his place and remained president from 1882 to 1884. In the latter year the Union Association took from the Cleveland team many of its great players, notably Dunlap, Briody, Glasscock and McCormick and as a result Cleveland resigned her membership in the National League.

Five years later Frank De Haas Robison and Stanley Robison, his brother, who owned large street car interests in the Forest City, reorganized a team for Cleveland and were granted a franchise in the National League. This team with Mr. Frank Robison as its president, was made up of: Catchers—Zimmer, O'Connor and Criger. Pitchers—Cuppy, Young, Powell, Wilson and Frasier. First basemen—Tebeau and O'Connor. Second basemen—Childs and Tebeau. Third basemen—Wallace. Shortstop—McKean. Outfielders—Blake, Frank, Heidrick, Burkett and McAleer.

It was certainly a great baseball team to place in the field in a single and initial year and its caliber shows the kind of live men the Robison brothers were.

This 1889 team of Cleveland remained almost intact until 1899 when it was transferred almost entire to St. Louis, the Robisons coming to this city with their team.

This Cleveland team, great as it was, never did much in the way of winning championship flags.

In 1895 and 1896 at the close of its season, Cleveland contested with Baltimore for the Temple Cup.

In 1895 Cleveland beat Baltimore four out of the five games played. Cy Young won three of these games for Cleveland and Cuppy captured one for that team and lost one.

In 1896 Cleveland played Baltimore again for the Temple Cup, but this time lost all four games played.

Hoffer and Joe Corbett pitched the winning games for Baltimore and Young, Wallace and Cuppy pitched the losing games for Cleveland. Bobby Wallace was one of Clevelands regular pitchers that year.

It will be noticed by this recapitulation that Cleveland had a team in the National in 1879. It remained until 1884, when it returned its franchise to the league. In 1889 it re-entered the league and remained for ten years. It never had the honor of housing a flag winner. It did win first honors the last part of the double season of 1892, but Boston won the combined year, and so the Forest City had to be satisfied with second place. It also ran second in two other years and third twice. It ran last in 1899. fourth once, fifth and seventh four times and sixth twice.

Cleveland was admitted to the American League in 1900 with John F. Kilfoyle as the president of her club and James R. McAleer as manager. Mr. Kilfoyle acted as manager of the club from 1900 to 1907, both inclusive, but W. R. Armour took the place of McAleer as manager and held it from 1902 to 1904. In 1905 Napoleon Lajoie was made the manager of the club and he held that position until 1909, when he resigned to give way to the veteran catcher, James McGuire, who is now managing the team. Mr. Somers became president of the team in 1910.

In 1910 Cleveland had one team in the field and it a member of the American League. James McGuire was the manager of this nine and the players under contract were: Pitchers—Joss, Young, Berger, Falkenberg, Mitchell, Link, Kirsch, Koester, Doane, Griffiths, Harkins, Boise and Vance. Catchers—Clarke, Easterly, Bemis and Higgins. Infielders—Lajoie, Stovall, Turner, Ball, Nicholls, Cooney, Peck, Bradley, Perring and Cutting. Outfielders—Krueger, Birmingham, Lord, Flick, Graney and Gough.

PROVIDENCE IN THE BIG LEAGUE.

HER GREAT CHAMPION TEAM GAVE HER A PLACE IN THE MAJOR LEAGUE WORLD OF BASEBALL.

Providence deserves a prominent place in this history if only for the great team which she put in the field in the 1884 season.

That was really the first team to win a world's championship.

The Providence champion team of 1888 was made up of Gilligan and Nava, catchers; Radbourne and Sweeny, pitchers; Start, first base; Farrell, second base; Denny, third base; Irwin, shortstop; Carroll, left; Hines, center; Radford, right field.

Providence, during its eight years' career in the National, carried off two pennants. one in 1879 when George Wright was its manager and one in 1884 when Frank C. Bancroft was manager.

The Providence team first showed in the big league in 1878, and ran third with a record of 33 won and 27 lost. The next season it won a flag, then ran second three times in a row. During that time it won 434 games and lost 276—an average of .611.

THE HARTFORD CLUB.

Hartford, though it spent but two years in the National and is a small place compared with some of the other towns that have been in the league, has the second best combined record in the history of the old organization. It was in the league in 1876 and 1877 and ran third both seasons. Its average for the two years was .602, it having won 71 and lost 47.

The Hartford nine of 1876 and 1877 was run by a stock company whose capital stock

THE NATIONAL GAME.

was $5.000. This amount was gotten together in shares of $25 each by Lipman Pike; the famous old Atlantic outfielder who was the Hartford manager.

TROY LEAGUE RECORD.

THAT CITY WAS TWICE IN THE BIG LEAGUE, BUT NEVER RAN BETTER THAN FOURTH.

Troy was represented in the National League as far back as 1879. And Troy remained in the big league from 1879 to 1888.

Her first professional essay, however, was away back in 1871 when her famous Haymaker team of that year took the field with the Athletics of Philadelphia, the Boston. Chicago, Mutuals of New York, Olympics of Washington, Haymakers, Forest Citys of Cleveland, Kekiongas of Fort Wayne and Forest Citys of Rockford and those teams finished in the order named.

In the big league Troy won 134 and lost 191 games during four years for a percentage of .412. It ran fourth, fifth, seventh and eighth once each.

STARS OF SYRACUSE.

THEY ONCE REPRESENTED THAT CITY IN THE NATIONAL LEAGUE, BUT DID NOT FINISH WELL.

Syracuse was a member of the National League in 1879.

Hamilton S. White was the president of this club during its only year in the National League and in the race that year the team finished in sixth place.

The Star Club of 1879 included Kelly, c.; McCormick, p.; Carpenter, 1b.; Farrell, 2b.; Richmond, ss.; Allen, 3b.; Mansell, l.f.; Dorgan, c.f. and change catcher; Purcell, r.f. and change pitcher.

THE RECORD OF BALTIMORE.

IT WAS SURELY A GREAT ONE WHEN McGRAW, JENNINGS AND OTHER GREAT PLAYERS PLAYED THERE.

The game of baseball has been played in Baltimore since the early days of the sport and the monumental city has often held a high place in the struggle for leading honors.

In fact in the matter of winning pennants Baltimore, with the great work of Ed Hanlon and his famous Oriole bunch, stands third in combined records.

McGraw, Jennings, Kelly, Keeler and others sure did travel some for Baltimore in the early nineties.

Baltimore first entered the National league in 1892, the first year of the twelve-club circuit.

Its advent was not very impressive, as it ran absolutely last with the poor percentage of .313. The next season it was eighth with .462. Then for three seasons in a row the Orioles captured the flag. In 1897 and 1898 they were second, and the last season the city was in the National it finished fourth.

Baltimore's champion team in 1894 was made up in this way and made the record named:

THE BALTIMORE CLUB.

NATIONAL CHAMPIONS UNITED STATES.

Edward Hanlon, president and manager.
Games won, 89; lost, 39. Percentage, .695.

	No. Games.	Pct. Won.	Field Pct.	Bat. Pct.		No. Games.	Pct. Won.	Field Pct.	Bat. Pct.
J. McMahon, p	33	.758	.869	.286	F. Bonner, 2b	24	...	.909	.301
W. V. Hawke, p	25	.640	.887	.301	J. J McGraw, 3b	117	....	.895	.340
W. Gleason, p	21	.714	.841	.342	H. Jennings, ss	128	...	.928	.332
C. H. Esper, p	11	.818	.929	.239	J. Kelly, l.f.	129	....	.951	.391
W. Robinson, c	106	....	.914	.348	W. Brodie, cf	129	....	.944	.369
W. J. Clarke, c	22	....	.856	.270	W. Keeler, rf	127	...	.928	.367
D. Brouthers, 1b	123	....	.975	.344		—	—	—	—
H. Reitz, 2b	100	....	.966	.306	Baltimore team	128	.695	.914	.343

The above team really won championships for Baltimore in 1894, 1895 and 1896 and in 1896 and 1897 it captured the Temple Cup series from Cleveland and Boston respectively.

There were few changes in the Baltimore Club from 1894 to 1897.

In 1895 Arthur Clarkson, Hoffer and Hemming took the places on the pitching staff held the year before by Hawke and Gleason. The latter was placed at second base on this 1895 team, taking the place of Bonner and Reitz. Pond was added to the pitching staff in 1896 and Clarkson was dropped, but the rest of the team was preserved nearly intact.

This club represented Baltimore in the National League from 1892 to 1900. Its president in 1892 was H. R. Von der Horst, who had been at the head of the club representing Baltimore in the American Association for many years.

From 1893 to 1899 Edward Hanlon was the president of the Baltimore Club. In 1899 when the Baltimore Club resigned from the National League, Mr. Hanlon went to Brooklyn, took many of his great players there with him and that 1899 year won the flag for the city of churches.

The old Lord Baltimore team represented that city in the early days of the game

84

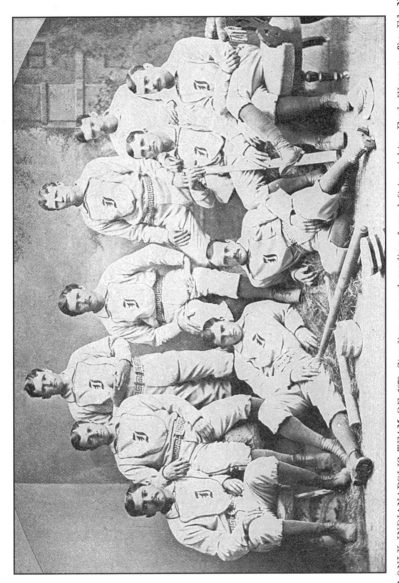

THE ONLY INDIANAPOLIS TEAM OF 1879—Standing up and reading from left to right: Fred Warner, 3b; Ed Nolan, p.; Denny Mack, s. s.; Frank Flint, c.; W. Reilly, rf. and substitute. Sitting down and reading from left to right: Charles Houtz, 1b; Trick McSorley, p. and f.; Adam Rocap, rf.; Mike Golden, lf. and change p.; Joe Quest, 2b. A story of them is given elsewhere in this book.

away back in the sixties, but the man who really placed baseball on a professional footing in the Oriole City was the late William Barnie of Brooklyn who managed and organized the club that represented Baltimore for years in the original American Association.

PITTSBURG IN BASEBALL.

THE ALLEGHENYS WERE THE FIRST CLUB TO BRING THE SMOKY CITY INTO PROMINENCE IN THE BASEBALL WORLD.

In recent years Pittsburg has held a high place when it came to the dealing out of baseball honors.

Fred Clarke, during his ten years as manager of Pittsburg, has given the Smoky City some of the finest baseball that has fallen to the lot of any city in the country. His record during that time has more than made up for the poor showing of the city in its earlier career.

So nice has Clarke moved during his career that he has never finished outside the first division once. The Smoky City during its twenty-five years has had four flags and five second-place teams. Third place has been its place once. The other thirteen years it ran between fourth and eighth place. It has won 1,769 games and lost 1,470. Its record is .546.

Denny McKnight and Horace Phillips were the first to give Pittsburg a real place on the professional baseball map.

Mr. McKnight was the first president of the American Asocciation and his famous old "Brewery" teams are still remembered by veteran followers of the game.

Fred Clarke has won four flags for Pittsburg, three of them being straight, in 1901, 1902 and 1903, and the other last season when his team, besides capturing the National League pennant, also won from Detroit in the play-off for the World's Championship.

The Pittsburg team in 1909 was made up in this way and made the record named:

THE PITTSBURG CLUB.

National Champions United States. Barney Dreyfuss, president; Frederick T. Clarke, manager. Games won, 110; lost, 42; percentage, .724.

	Na. Games.	Pct. Won.	Field. Pst.	Bat. Pct.		Na. Games.	Pct. Won.	Field. Pst.	Bat. Pct.
S. Leever, p	19	.889	1,000	.167	J. B. Miller, 2b	150	....	.953	.279
H. Camnitz, p	41	.806	.973	.138	R. Byrne, 3b	151	....	.929	.226
C. B. Adams, p	25	.800	.919	.651	E. J. Abbaticchio, ss	18	....	.965	.230
C. Phillipe, p	22	.727	1,000	.971	J. Wagner, ss	136	....	.940	.339
A. P. Leifield, p	32	.764	.952	.192	F. T. Clarke, cf	152	....	.987	.287
V. Willis, p	39	.667	.953	.136	T. W. Leach, cf	138	....	.969	.261
N. Maddox, p	31	.619	.968	.224	J. Wilson, rf	154	....	.957	.273
G. C. Gibson, c	150	....	.983	.265	H. J. Hyatt, f	40	....	....	.299
W. Abstein, 1b	135	....	.982	.250					

Pittsburg has always been one of the best ball cities in America and is now in possession of the finest and most commodious baseball enclosure ever built.

Pittsburg started the 1910 season with this team under the management of Fred Clarke: Pitchers—Howard Camnitz, Adams, Leifield, Maddox, Phillippe, Leever, Moore, Powell and Harry Camnitz. Catchers—Gibson, O'Connor, Bridges and Simon. Infielders—Flynn, Sharle, Miller, Wagner, Byrne, McKechnie and Abbatichio. Outfielders—Clarke, Leach, Wilson, Hyatt and Campbell.

THE BROOKLYN CLUB.

ALTHOUGH LOW NOW IT WAS ONCE AT THE TOP OF THE CHAMPIONSHIP LADDER.

There was a time when Brooklyn held a far higher place in the world of baseball than she does now.

That was in the days when she was well represented in the American Association, when Charley Byrne was the president of her club and when the old St. Louis champion players, Bushong, Caruthers, Foutz and others were playing under his management.

In 1899 and 1900 under the management of Edward Hanlon, Brooklyn won the National League flag. In 1900 her champion team was made up in this way:

THE BROOKLYN CLUB OF 1900.

National Champions United States. Chas. H. Ebbets, president; Edward Hanlon, manager. Games won, 82; lost, 54; percentage, .603.

	No. Games.	Pct. Won.	Field. Pct.	Bat. Pct.		No. Games.	Pct. Won.	Field. Pct.	Bat. Pct.
J. McGinnity, p	41	.769	.875	.185	Wm. Dahlen, ss	134	....	.942	.259
W. Kennedy, p	36	.600	.919	.301	Joseph Kelly, lf	78	....	.955	.318
Frank Kitson, p	30	.517	.848	.283	Joseph Kelly, 1b	28	....	.992	....
Chas. Farrell, c	73	....	.911	.277	J. Sheckard, lf	75	....	.934	.305
J. McGuire, c	68	....	.909	.280	W. Keeler, c.f	136	....	.947	.366
H. Jennings, 1b	110	....	.984	.270	F. A. Jones, rf	136	....	.959	.309
T. P. Daly, 2b	95	....	.926	.313	—				
E. DeMontreville, 2b	47	....	.956	.259	Brooklyn team	136	.603	.933	.287
L. Cross, 3b	133	....	.941	.293					

THE NATIONAL GAME.

The Trolley Dodger city has had a team in the National on twenty-one different occasions. Brooklyn first showed in 1876, when the Mutuals represented her. She ran sixth. The city then dropped out of the league until 1890, and has since continued in it.

During this time Brooklyn won three flags, ran second once and third twice. Though generally looked on as a cellar champion, the team has finished last only once—in 1905. During its twenty-one years it has won 1,392 and lost 1,481 games—percentage, .488.

Of the early days of the game in Brooklyn I have covered them thoroughly in another part of this work and have there made special reference to Brooklyn's first great baseball team—the Atlantics of the seventies.

I have also covered the story of the old Capitoline grounds, the first great baseball enclosure, which were opened to the public on May 5, 1864.

In 1910 Dahlen appeared as the manager of the Brooklyn National League team and these players under contract: Pitchers—Rucker, Bell, Scanlon, Wilhelm, Hunter, Schneiberg and Dessau. Catchers—Bergen, Erwin, Ulrich and Miller. Infielders—Jordan, Daubert, Hummel, Lennox, McMillan, McElveen and T. Smith. Outfielders—Wheat, Burch, Lumley, Davidson and Harry Smith.

DETROIT'S RECORD.

IT HAS ALWAYS BEEN A PROUD ONE AND THIS IN ALL SORTS OF ASSOCIATIONS.

The City of Detroit has always held a proud place in baseball history.

That city which is no longer represented in the National League, had a fair record during the eight years it was represented in that organization.

During that time it won a flag and finished second once. Fourth place was its lot on another occasion, and on the four other occasions it was lower than fourth.

It finished in the same position only twice. Running sixth in 1882 and 1885. Detroit won 426 and lost 437 games during the eight years in the National League with a percentage of .494.

William H. Watkins, now the owner of the Indianapolis Club gave Detroit her first great baseball team in 1887. It won the National League flag that year and its record was:

THE DETROIT CLUB.

National Champion United States. Fred K. Stearns, president; W. H. Watkins, manager. Games won, 79; lost, 45. Percentage, .637.

	No. Games.	Field Won.	Pct. Pct.	Bat. Pct.		No. Games.	Field Won.	Pct. Pct.	Bat. Pct.
Chas. Getzein, p.	43	.683	.906	.240	H. Richardson, lf.	58	....	.936	....
J. P. Conway, p.	17	.471	.876	.247	J. L. White, 3b.	106	....	.848	.341
C. B. Baldwin, p.	24	.565	.767	.347	Wm. Shindle, 2b.	19	.. .	.325	.340
C. W. Bennett, c.	50	....	.905	.363	J. C. Rowe, ss.	123	....	.906	.263
C. W. Ganzel, c.	50	....	.852	.285	L. Twitchell, c.	52	....	.867	.252
Chas. Briody, c.	32	....	.850	.277	E. Hanlon, cf.	118	....	.903	.316
D. Brouthers, 1b.	122	....	.869	.419	S. L. Thompson, rf.	127	....	.909	.406
Fred Dunlap. 2b.	64	....	.953	.326		—	—	—	—
H. Richardson, 2b.	62	....	.941	.363	Detroit team.	126	.637	.909	.347

Detroit remained in the National League from 1881 to 1888.

In 1900 with James D. Burns as its president and George F. Stallings as its manager, Detroit entered the American League race.

Frank Dwyer succeeded Stallings as manager in 1902 and Barrows, Lane and Armour followed him.

In 1907 Hugh Jennings took the management of the Detroit team and under his management they have won three pennants hand running and during the 1910 season made a grand bid for the flag, but failed. The record of Jennings' Champion team of 1909 is given below:

THE DETROIT CLUB.

American League Champions United States. Frank J. Navin, president; Hugh A. Jennings, manager. Games won, 98; lost, 54; percentage, .645.

	No. Games.	Pct. Won.	Field Pct.	Bat. Pce.		No. Games.	Pct. Won.	Field Pct.	Bat. Pce.
Wm. Donovan, p.	22	.533	.975	.200	Sam Crawford, 1b.	17	....	.971	....
E. Summers, p.	35	.679	.971	.106	Jas. Delehanty, 2b.	136	....	.951	.222
Ed. Killian, p.	25	.550	.984	.161	G. Moriarty, 3b.	133	....	.939	.273
E. Willett, p.	41	.710	.937	.202	Chas. O'Leary, 3b.	76	....	.922	.203
Works, p.	16	....	.900	.050	Owen Bush, ss.	157	....	.925	.273
Geo. Mullin, p.	52	.784	.973	.203	M. McIntyre, lf.	125	....	.975	.244
Chas. Schmidt, c.	84	....	.955	.209	D. Jones, lf.	69	....	.982	.279
Beckendorf, c.	15	....	.957	.250	Sam Crawford, cf.	139	....	.965	.314
Stanage, c.	77	.. .	.964	.263	Tyrus R. Cobb, rf.	156	....	.946	.377
T. Jones, 1b.	141	....	.988	.259					

Jennings' success with this team has given Detroit a fine reputation in the baseball world.

In fact the victories of Jennings' team and the great work done by the Detroit Big Four team in the olden time proves that the people of that city know a good ball player when they see him and that they are never content except when a winner is representing them.

THE NATIONAL GAME.

Detroit started the 1910 season with her old manager Hugh Jennings still at the helm and these players under contract:

Names.	Bats.	Throws.	Names.	Bats.	Throws.
Mullin, p.	R.	R.	Casey, c.	R.	R.
Donovan, p.	R.	R.	T. Jones, 1b.	R.	R.
Willett, p.	R.	R.	Delehanty, 2b.	R.	R.
Summers, p.	L.	R.	Bush, ss.	L.-R.	R.
Killian, p.	L.	L.	Lathers, s.. s.	L.	R.
Pernell, p.	L.	L.	O'Leary, ss.	R.	R.
Browning, p.	R.	R.	Moriarty, 3b.	R.	R.
Lelivelt, p.	R.	R.	Simmons, 3b.	R.	R.
Stroud, p.	R.	R.	McIntyre, l.f.	L.	L.
Works, p.	R.	R.	D. Jones, lf.	L.	R.
Stanage, c.	R.	R.	Crawford, cf.	L.	L.
Schmidt, c.	L.-R.	R.	Cobb, rf.	L.	R.
Beckendorf, c.	R.	R.			

It will be noticed that every one of Jennings' outfielders is a left-handed batsman.

THE GAME IN WASHINGTON.

THE CAPITAL CITY HAS NEVER HAD A GOOD CLUB IN THE MAJOR LEAGUE.

The capital city, truth to tell, has a poor baseball record. In the National League her showing of 573 won and 1,034 lost, is about the poorest in the league's history.

In the American League she has not done much better.

In the 1910 year with James R. McAleer as the new manager of the team in the American League, Washington started out with these players: Pitchers—Johnson, Gray, Groom, Walker, Witherup, Reisling, Foreman, Havelik, Ohl and Oberlin. Catchers—Street, Rapp, Hardy, Slattery and Killifer. Infielders—Unglaub, Schaefer, Elberfeld, McBride, Yohe, Kelley and Crooks. Outfielders—Gessler, Browne, Conroy, Milian, Lelivelt and Miller.

And out of this team, judging them by their early work in 1910, McAleer is going to build up a strong playing nine.

Of the early baseball days in Washington, the work of the old Olympics and of old Washington players like Hines and Start, I have referred to elsewhere in this work.

THE CITY OF BUFFALO.

AT ONE TIME SHE WAS FINELY REPRESENTED IN THE NATIONAL LEAGUE.

At one time Buffalo was well represented in the National League.

During her seven years in the big organization Buffalo won 312 and lost 333 games, for a percentage of .484. By so doing she has the honor of being given twelfth place in the National League records. The Bisons never won a flag or finished second. They did run third three times—in 1881, 1882 and 1884. Fourth and fifth place once each, and seventh twice is where the team finished the other years.

Worcester, Milwaukee and Kansas City were in the big league but a single year and ran unplaced.

HUGH JENNINGS.
Hughie Jennings is the dashing, prancing, popular and successful manager cf
the Detroit Tigers, one of the greatest of modern baseball nines.

THE NATIONAL GAME.

THE GREAT CATCHERS.

A LIST OF THOSE WHO LED IN THE RECEIVING DEPARTMENT IN THE OLD
PROFESSIONAL ASSOCIATION AND THE NATIONAL LEAGUE, AND A
STORY OF OTHERS WHO WERE JUST AS GREAT PLAYERS AS
THOSE WHO HAD THE TOP RECORD.

The following is the record of the catchers who led each year in the old Professional
Association and then in the National League in that department of the game, the list including the year 1871, when professional baseball first came into real notice, down to the
present day:

Year.	Catchers.	Club.	Fielding Games.	Pct.	Year.	Catchers.	Club.	Fielding Games.	Pct.
1871	Jas. L. White—Cleveland		47	.806	1891	R. D. Buckley—New York		66	.944
1872	F. G. Malone—Ath.-Phila.		27	.800	1892	M. Kittredge—Chicago		66	.921
1873	Nathan Hicks—Mut'ls, N. Y.		31	.818	1893	C. W. Bennett—Boston		58	.912
1874	Nathan Hicks—Philadelphia		58	.811	1894	C. L. Zimmer—Cleveland		88	.931
1875	Jas. L. White—Boston		79	.816	1895	W. Robinson—Baltimore		74	.952
1876	Jas. L. White—Chicago		64	.791	1895	J. Clements—Philadelphia		84	.952
1877	C. W. Snyder—Louisville		49	.913	1896	H. Vaughan—Cincinnati		57	.951
1878	C. W. Snyder—Boston		58	.841	1897	C. H. Peitz—Cincinnati		72	.956
1879	Frank Flint—Chicago		74	.839	1898	Jas. McGuire—Washington		92	.958
1880	Frank Flint—Chicago		62	.829	1899	C. H. Peitz—Cincinnati		91	.955
1881	C. W. Bennett—Detroit		67	.895	1900	M. Sullivan—Boston		64	.933
1882	C. W. Bennett—Detroit		53	.874	1901	C. L. Zimmer—Pittsburg		67	.969
1882	T. Deasley—Boston		62	.874	1902	M. Kittredge—Boston		72	.967
1883	C. W. Bennett—Detroit		65	.859	1903	J. J. Warner—New York		85	.979
1884	M. M. Hacket—Boston		67	.879	1904	J. J. Warner—New York		86	.973
1885	C. W. Bennett—Detroit		63	.885	1905	P. Moran—Boston		78	.986
1886	C. W. Bennett—Detroit		67	.912	1906	F. Bowerman—New York		67	.984
1887	C. W. Bennett—Detroit		50	.905	1907	F. Bowerman—New York		62	.990
1888	C. W. Bennett—Detroit		72	.911	1908	W. Bergen—Brooklyn		99	.989
1889	C. W. Bennett—Boston		80	.916	1909	C. Gibson—Pittsburg		150	.983
1890	C. W. Bennett—Boston		85	.914	1910	P. Moran—Philadelphia		56	.989

AMERICAN LEAGUE CATCHERS.

A LIST OF THOSE WHO HAVE LED IN THIS POSITION SINCE THE FORMATION
OF THIS BASEBALL BODY IN 1900.

The following is a list of the catchers who have led each year in the American League
since it was formed in 1900:

Year.	Catchers.	Club.	Fielding Games.	Pct.	Year.	Catchers.	Club.	Fielding Games.	Pct.
1900	Joe Sugden—Chicago		74	.971	1905	O. F. Schreckengost—Phila.		114	.934
1901	Louis Criger—Boston		69	.969	1906	J. O'Connor—St. Louis		54	.990
1902	J. Warner—Boston		63	.979	1907	O. F. Schreckengost—Phila.		99	.985
1903	J. O'Connor—New York		64	.988	1908	W. D. Sullivan—Chicago		137	.985
1904	Joe Sugden—St. Louis		79	.990	1909	L. Criger—St. Louis		73	.986
					1910	P. W. Donahue—Boston-Phil		18	1,000

Next to the great pitchers, the great catchers who have had so much to do with the
building up of the game are first worthy of mention.

Opinion is divided and history fails to prove just which of the veteran catchers was
the first to play up close to the bat with neither mask, chest protector or the commonest
kind of a glove to protect him.

The honor has been claimed in turn by the friends of Robert Ferguson of the Atlantics of Brooklyn, Fergy Malone of the Athletics of Philadelphia, W. H. Craver of
the original Chicago White Stockings, Douglas Allison of the Cincinnati Reds, Mart
King of the Haymakers and later of the Chicago White Stockings, Scott Hastings of
the Forest Citys of Rockford, Mike McGeary of the Haymakers of Troy, Jim White of
the Forest Citys of Cleveland, Charley Mills of the Mutuals of New York, Ad. Jouett of
the Eckfords of Brooklyn, and F. R. Boerum of the Atlantics of Brooklyn.

I saw all of these players in their work behind the bat in 1870 and not one of them
had mask, chest protector or glove to protect them from the swift pitching they then

faced. They were all fine, fearless players and took no heed of the injuries to face, head, body and fingers which came to them often.

There may, however, have been other catchers before those I have mentioned to play up close to the bat.

Thomas B. Flynn, in a recent article in the Boston Baseball Magazine devoted to "Old Time Catching," tells quite a story of the punishment the old catchers received when they were playing. He says:

"With their wire masks, pillow gloves and bed-mattress chest protectors, the present-day catchers, compared with the stalwart huskies who caught for the Athletic Baseball Club of Philadelphia, in the first decade of its existence, are as carpet knights to the weather-beaten veterans of an old-time army.

"In the good old days, when baseball was played more for glory and amusement than for business, such things as masks, big gloves and chest protectors would have been regarded with derision both by players and fans.

"This naturally recalls a story of Dockney, the old-time famous catcher of the Athletics, in the late sixties and early seventies. Dockney was one of the best catchers of his time, and perhaps the toughest of anyone who ever stood behind a bat. Robert Reach, a brother of Al Reach, at one time a great baseball player himself, vouches for the following story of Dockney's toughness

" 'It was somewhere around 1870, according to Mr. Reach, that the Athletic Baseball Club, accompanied by Dockney as catcher, paid a visit to St. Louis. On the night of the day prior to the game, Dockney went out with the boys to see the town and, getting into a bar-room brawl, was carried to a hospital, with his chest laid open from shoulder to shoulder by a razor or butcher knife, wielded by a St. Louis tough. He lay in the hospital all night in the care of the doctor, who stitched up his wounded chest and covered it with plasters. Notwithstanding his weakened condition from the loss of blood and the serious nature of the wound, he insisted on going into the game on the following day to catch for his club, nothing covering his wound except the plasters and a flannel shirt.

" 'He handled the swift delivery of the famous Dick McBride with all his old-time vigor. Every ball that missed his outstretched hands and struck him on the chest brought the blood in spurts from his wound, which was freshly laid open by the force of the ball; but, notwithstanding his condition, he resisted the advice of the physician who examined him, and finished the game. When he was finally carried from the field with his wound broken open and his shirt all clotted with blood, he was glad that he had caught the game. Imagine one of the modern catchers in scientific baseball catching a game like that.

" 'Perhaps the best catcher who ever stood behind the bat was Charlie Bennett, of the old Detroits. Lon Knight, the famous old Athletic player, tells how Bennett caught for his club, game after game, while suffering the most intense agony from a split thumb. Bennett never wore the catcher's mitt. The only glove he wore while catching was an ordinary kid glove with the fingers and thumb cut off. During one of the games his thumb was split open from the hand to the tip, clear to the bone. Instead of going to the hospital or taking a rest, he persisted in catching, day after day, with his thumb in this condition. Between each inning he would have to sponge the gash in his thumb with cotton soaked in antiseptic which he carried with him in his pocket, in order to remove the corruption which was continually flowing from the wound. This he did in spite of the fact that the doctor warned him that he must either stop playing ball until the thumb had entirely healed, or lose his thumb, or even his arm, as blood poison was liable to set in. He continued, however, to catch the game until it was impossible for him to do so any longer.

" 'And in the days of both Dockney and Bennett the pitching was swift and the ball was just as hard as it is to-day, the distance between the pitcher's box and the batsmen being even shorter than at the present time."

Now, right here, in connection with this very interesting article from the pen of Mr. Flynn, it might be well to refer to other great catchers beside Dockney and Bennett, who also played behind the bat in their day and faced the speediest of pitchers without the aid of mask or gloves.

When Frank Flint, for example, the great St. Louis catcher who played so long behind the bat for the Chicago White Stockings, quit playing professional baseball, he told his friends that every joint in every one of his fingers had been broken at least once and that his nose had been frequently put out of joint and his teeth smashed.

To protect the fingers was the first thing done when players commenced to wear ordinary buckskin gloves. Later a piece of rubber was used between the teeth to protect the molars and the mouth and then came the mask.

The story is that Thayer, captain of the Harvard baseball team wanted Tyng, one of his best players to catch close up under the bat. Tyng, a handsome fellow, having some respect for his frontispiece, demurred. Thayer one day in the college gymnasium saw a fencer wearing a mask and putting it on, caught a few balls as an experiment. He found that the wire covering the eyes interfered with his work, but he had a tin-smith remove that obstacle and then he offered the newly made affair to Tyng. It was the same mask really, in the rough, as is worn to-day. Tyng tried it on, liked it, found it practical and wore it in all the games he played afterwards. That was in 1877 and from then on the mask came into general use, being improved on each year by the sporting goods manufacturers until it became the perfect thing it is to-day.

After the mask came the chest protector, the shin guards and the catcher's big glove—things that made almost an entirely new business out of the art of catching.

THE NAMES IN THE RECORD.

Of the men whose names appear in the best catcher's record and who played behind the bat in the earlier days of the game before the mask, the catcher's glove and the chest protector had come into general use, Jim White, who tops the record, was one of the best.

Next to him came Fergy Malone and Nat Hicks.

Jim White is first remembered as the famous catcher of the Forest Citys of Cleveland in the early seventies. He caught the pitching of Pabor, Pratt and Matthews.

In 1873 Jim White was catching Spalding on the Boston team which won the National League Championship that year.

Now he was no longer the bare-handed catcher. He was fitted with gloves and mask and he handled the swift underhanded pitching of A. G. Spalding without any trouble whatever. White, beside being a great catcher, was one of the speediest throwers, as well as a great batsman.

That White was a really great player was proven, for many a day, even after he had graduated from the Forest City of Cleveland team of the early seventies, for after catching for the Boston champions in 1872, 1873, 1874 and 1875, he went to Chicago with Spalding in 1876 and helped him bring the flag to the Garden City.

In 1877 Jim White returned to Boston, this time to play at first base for that team and he took the championship back there with him.

Ten years later found Jim White still at work, this time covering third base for the Detroit Club who that year won the National League pennant and later took the world's flag from St. Louis.

So talking about the new and the old army, what man of the new can match Jim White when it comes to playing on championship teams.

Next to White on the record list is Fergy Malone who in 1872 was catching Dick McBride on the Athletics of Philadelphia.

Fergy Malone was the great catcher of the Athletics in the sixties. He and his pitcher Dick McBride were in their day the most famous battery in America.

They helped win the championship for the Athletics in 1871, the first year of real professional baseball.

Malone was one of the old army who caught up close to the bat without the aid of mask or gloves.

Next to Malone on the record list comes Nat Hicks of the Mutuals of New York.

Hicks, like Malone, was one of the old army who in their day caught up close to the bat without glove or mask to protect them. In that time Hicks caught the speedy pitching of Wolters and caught him well.

Next to Hicks comes Charles W. Snyder who in 1877 caught Devlin on the Louisville team and the next year faced the pitching of the speedy Bond in Boston. Snyder, like Malone, White and Hicks in the sixties and early seventies, had caught barehanded and without gloves, but when he worked with Louisville in 1877 and from then on he was as well armed as the rest. He was with White and Malone, one of the first of the really great baseball catchers.

He was indeed one of the greatest of the catchers who were playing their best in the seventies and he was also the receiver of the Cincinnati Club which captured the first American Association pennant in 1882.

Before joining Cincinnati Snyder was the catcher of the Louisville National League team.

In the late seventies while with that team he was one of the few able to handle the terrific pitching of Jim Devlin.

Cotemporaneous with Ewing, Flint, Bennett and other great catchers, were Tom Deasley and "Doc" Bushong, who caught for the St. Louis Browns when they were winning World's Championships for St. Louis; Charley Briody and Charles Ganzel, who caught for Detroit with Bennett in 1877; Mortie Hackett and Mike Hines, the receiver of the Boston World's Champions of 1883; Barney Gilligan and Vincent Nava, the receivers of the Champion Providence team of 1884; Pat Murphy and Billy Brown of the New York Giants; Tom Daly and Bob Clark of the Champion Brooklyns; Wilbert Robinson and W. J. Clarke of the Champion Brooklyns; Marty Bergen of the Champion Bostons of 1897; Charley Farrell of the Champion Brooklyns, Charles Zimmer and Jack O'Connor of the Champion Pittsburgs.

Like their rivals in the National League in their endeavor to develop classy backstops the American League managers have tried out almost 100 catchers in seven seasons. Of the receivers who were in the American League in 1902, which was the first season that the circuit assumed really big league proportions, there are only three left to-day, Bemis of the Naps, Sullivan of the White Sox and Criger of the New Yorks.

Others who were catching for the American League clubs seven years ago, were: McFarland for Chicago, Bobby Wood for Cleveland, Buelow for Detroit, Mike Kahoe, Joe Sudgen and "Jiggs" Donohue for St. Louis, Schreck for Philadelphia; Wagner for Boston, Bill Clarke and Lew Drill for Washington, and Robinson, Smith and Bresnahan for Baltimore.

Since then, Chicago has tried out Slattery, Roth, Hart, Armbruster (secured from Boston); Shaw (who came the same route); Weaver, Payne and Schreck.

Bobby Wood had as successors Fred Abbott, "Nig" Clarke, Buelow, Kittredge, Wakefield, Davidson and Land.

Davidson, however, caught so few innings that he can scarcely be counted.

Detroit started out with McGuire and Buelow in 1902 and has since used McAllister, Wood, Beville, Warner, Drill, Doran, Payne, Schmidt, Archer and Thomas. Beckendorf and Stanage are added to the list for 1909.

McAleer, while manager of St. Louis Browns, has used twelve catchers or so in his anxiety to get a winner.

Kahoe, Sugden and Donahue were his first backstops at St. Louis. They were succeeded by Spencer, Weaver, Roth, O'Connor, Rickey, Stephens, Blue, Smith and Criger.

Connie Mack of the Athletics of Philadelphia managed to get along with fewer receivers than any of his rivals. For years Schreck and Powers did all the catching, with occasional assistance from Noonan in 1904 and Smith, Blue, Lapp and Egan in 1908. Boston had a long string of catchers Warner and Criger were the backstops in 1902. Jack Stahl caught a few games the next year, while Duke Farrell helped out in 1903 and 1904. Then came a long list of youngsters—McGovern, Armbruster, Graham, Carrigan, Peterson and Donahue.

MICHAEL KAHOE.
One of the men to play behind the bat in the American League and now the official scout of the Washington American League Club.

THE NATIONAL GAME.

New York did not break into the league until 1903. O'Connor and Beville were slated to do the catching. Nineteen hundred and four, however, found McGuire and Kleinow on the job, Ira Thomas, Rickey, Blair and Sweeney being added later.

Washington had quite a bunch of catchers in seven years, Clark and Drill being followed by Kittredge, Heydon, Warner, Wakefield, Blankenship and Street.

The above list has included about all the catchers that caught games to get their names into the records. Of course, there were others who were tried out, but who failed to participate in many games. It shows that only five catchers have had seven years' experience in the American League, with Kleinow being a five-year man and Spencer and "Nig" Clarke four-year men. Schmidt, Thomas and Payne have been in the league three years, but most of the others have been in the circuit but one or two years, while several, touted as classy receivers, have yet to catch an American League game. Coming again to the catchers of the present period the man now considered the greatest catcher in his profession is John Kling, the one man who as much as any other helped the Chicago Cubs win National League and World's Championships.

But with Kling must be reckoned Jimmy Archer, who ranked right alongside the Cub's great catcher in doing really everything, who has no superior as a thrower to bases and who served the Cubs well while the great Kling in the 1909 year was sulking in his tent.

Talking of the great catchers recently, John Ward, the once famous player, had this to say about Ewing and other of the old-time catchers:

"Beginning with the catchers, 'Buck' Ewing was the best all-round man that ever put on a mask. He had a happy disposition that was seldom ruffled, knew every twist and angle of the game, could whip a ball like lightning to any base and got everything out of his pitchers there was in them. His signaling and throwing to bases kept the whole field wide awake and on tip-toe and he could "jolly" the spectators, cajole an umpire or good naturedly "kid" an opposing batsman with equal success. And as an "inside" man, as hitter, base runner and run getter, especially when it was most needed, there were few better men in the country.

"Kling is a splendid catcher, and Gibson did great work last season, but neither of them are in Ewing's class. But good as he was, there were others who, regarded solely as catchers, pressed Ewing hard. Robinson of the old Baltimore team was a grand catcher, as good as, or better than any man of to-day; and if you don't believe it, ask McGraw or Hughie Jennings or Ed Hanlon or Joe Kelly, teammates of his, who are still in close touch with the game.

"Then there was Charley Bennett, who caught day in and day out and was a veritable stone wall behind the bat, and could throw to second like a rifle shot. And what about old "Silver" Flint, who took his medicine every day, catching in turn at the 45-foot distance, such speed as was handed him by "The Only" Nolan, Teddy Larkin, Jim McCormick, Larry Corcoran and Fred Goldsmith? Why, even back of that set, Charley Snyder was turning tricks behind the bat that some of the present-day catchers have never yet learned."

M. Sullivan of Boston in 1900, C. L. Zimmer, then of Pittsburg, in 1901; M. Kittredge of Boston in 1902, and J. J. Warner of New York in 1903 and 1904 were the leading catchers in those years and they were all fine players.

Following them in 1905 came Pat Moran, then of Boston, but now one of the mainstays of the Philadelphia National League Club.

Now, cutting away from the record, I give a list arranged alphabetically of the catchers who have belonged to and who are now playing in the National League or American League and also of those who, in their day, at some time or other, played in one or the other of the old major leagues.

W. H. ALEXANDER—W. H. Alexander, known best to the baseball world in the eighties as "Nin" Alexander, was in his day one of the best professional catchers in America. Alexander caught in the days when it took pluck and bull dog courage to fill the catcher's place. He caught the speediest of pitching without the aid of mask or glove. Alexander was born at Pana, Ill., November 24, 1858. He commenced playing baseball on the lots of Pana in 1876. He caught for the then famous Meteors of Pana in 1883. In 1884 he was signed as catcher by the Kansas City Union Club management and he caught in the first professional game ever played in Kansas City. In 1885 he played with Jerry Whalen at St. Joe, Mo. In that year he helped Edward Murphy, John W. Brandon, Al Spink and others organize the old Western League, which took the field in the Fall of 1885 and lasted through 1886. In 1886 and 1887 Alexander managed the

St. Joe team and did most of its catching and that season brought out Silver King "Bug" Holiday, Pat Tebeau, Jack O'Connor, Sam Smith, "Jumbo" Harding, Bart Grether, Joe Herr and Arthur Sunday, all of whom made a record for themselves later in the major leagues. Alexander also gave St. Joe the best team she has ever had. Alexander was always an honor to the profession. He was ever and always steady, reliable and honest and he always worked to build up the game and to increase its areas. He is now a prosperous merchant at Pana, where he won his first honors as a ball player, and he comes down to St. Louis occasionally to see the game as it is played to-day.

FREDERICK ALLEN—Frederick Allen was one of the catchers of the St. Louis Browns in their 1910 season. He was released near the middle of the season to the Louisville Club of the American Association. He is considered a most promising player.

JAMES P. ARCHER—"Jimmy" Archer of Chicago, is the greatest throwing catcher in the world, according to Clarke Griffith of Cincinnati.

"Griff" has been "sweet" on the sturdy backstop for several years and declares that had he not been in Montana when Detroit asked waivers on Archer the catcher would never have been permitted to leave the American League.

Had he been taken to New York with the Highlanders he would have been widely known as one of the leading big-mitt artists of the profession.

"If I had that fellow I'd work him every day just to watch him peg," said "Griff," "and there is not another man in his class when it comes to shooting the ball. He is faster than chained lightning, and he never has to take a step to get the ball to any of the bases. Kling isn't in it when it comes to keeping the runners glued to the bags."

It is said that this "flat-footed" throwing of Jimmy's which is so much admired by many baseball men is what cost Archer his job with Detroit. Jennings, manager of the Tigers, is said to have undertaken to coach him to throw, and that because James showed preference for his natural style rather than that desired by the "hee-haw" boss, a release to Buffalo followed.

Archer caught the final game of the 1907 world's series, and attracted the attention of Chance at the time. His faultless, snappy throwing kept the Cubs from stealing, and had them diving to the bags each time they happened to stroll four feet from the cushion. Last season when the team was going East, on an off day, Chance stopped over at Buffalo to watch McConnell, a spitball slinger.

About the fourth inning a friend who was with Chance said:

"Well, what do you think of the pitcher?"

"Pitcher!" exclaimed Chance. "It's the catcher I've been watching."

The catcher was Archer, and negotiations were opened for his purchase immediately.

Several months later, when the peerless leader was in California, he learned that Archer had risen from a sickbed to catch McConnell on that day, as the other Buffalo backstops had positively refused to bang themselves up in stopping the spitters. This convinced Chance that James is just as full of grit as he is good at throwing.

Archer has had all the luck the able, conscientious ball player deserves—and then some. Away back some five or six years ago, Archer was an outfielder on the Atlanta team. He was all right in the field, but not a marvel at the bat—unless it was negatively. One day the manager ordered him to go behind the bat. "Never caught a game in my life," replied Archer. "Try it," returned the manager. He did—and made good.

He was tried by a big league club soon after, but turned back almost at once. Then Detroit looked him over, sized him up as a fair catcher, but a "flat-footed" thrower who could not be taught to take the usual step toward the base, and sent him to Buffalo. In the Fall of 1908 Chicago drafted him.

Chance let him throw naturally—often pegging them down in perfect form while squatting behind the plate—something impossible for other catchers to attempt—and Kling's disaffection gave him the chance he needed. It is said that the reason Archer can throw so speedily and accurately from a crouch, is that a sore on the arm from an old burn has affected the muscles in such a way that he gets power and control impossible for other catchers.

Archer is 27 years years of age, weighs 176 pounds and is five feet, ten inches tall. He was born in Dublin, Ireland, and his home is now in Toronto. Beginning to play professional ball at Fargo, in 1905, he was with Atlanta in 1905. Pittsburg drafted him, but shipped him off to a minor league club, from which Detroit took him for a mere look-over before sending him to Buffalo, from which club the Cubs secured him in 1908.

Archer, who jumped to the very front rank as a catcher in the National League in its 1910 season and who scored so well as the backstop for the Chicago Cubs last year, is a crack-a-jack against the big pins. Archer is considered one of the star bowlers of Northern New York. While he was a member of the Buffalo team of the Eastern League he conducted a bowling alley in the Bison City during the winter months.

Jimmy claims it has done him a world of good, and figures that it has given him the speed which he possessed in his mighty right, which, by the way, is feared by all base runners in the National League. Archer, while at Hot Springs last season, won a cup for the highest three strings made against Hammond candle pins, or "rubber necks," as they are known in the South. The Chicago backstop won this cup from a field of well-known diamond stars. Hal Danzig, who was then a member of the Red Sox training squad, was second, Archer winning out by three pins, connecting for 339 in his three strings.

GEORGE BAKER—One of the best and safest receivers in the olden time was George Baker, a St. Louis boy, who, in his day caught for Rochester and then for the St. Louis Browns and later for the St. Louis Unions.

He was the partner of Tom Dolan when those two, with Jack Brennan, another St. Louis boy, helped the St. Louis Unions win the championship of the Union Association in 1884.

Baker was one of the best and most effective catchers of his day, who in the early days of the Browns' success caught McGinnis and who in 1884 handled for the St. Louis Unions the speedy and erratic pitching of Boyle, Healy, Kirby and Hodnett.

ELMER BECKENDORF—Elmer Beckendorf, catcher of the Washington Nationals of the American League, is a New Yorker, 24 years old. Though used but little in 1909, while with Detroit, he has since shown himself of big league caliber. He is five feet nine inches tall and weighs 174 pounds. Before coming to Detroit he played with several Hudson River Valley clubs, and in 1907 with Toronto. In 1908 he helped win a New York State League pennant for Scranton.

Beckendorf is a native of New York City, and was born there June 15, 1884. He played with the Williams A. A., a strong semi-professional team, and also with Everett College. He was with the Kingston Club of the Hudson River League in 1904 and 1905, assisting to land the pennant in 1905. In 1906 he was with the Providence Club and in 1907 and 1908 with Scranton, Detroit purchasing him from that club and was later turned over to Washington.

HARRY P. BEMIS—Harry P. Bemis has been catching for the Cleveland American League team for several years and during that time he has held his end up splendidly.

CHARLES W. BENNETT—Next to Flint on the record list was Charles W. Bennett, who was the receiver of the Detroit Club which captured Worlds honors in the National League and he was one of the finest catchers that ever lived.

It was his magnificent work behind the bat that went far to win the National League Championship for Detroit in 1887.

He was not only a magnificent catcher and thrower to bases, but he was also a heavy batsman.

That he was a wonderful catcher was proven by the fact that he was at the top in the catcher's record in 1881, 1882, 1883, 1885, 1886, 1887, 1888, 1889, 1890 and 1893. No other catcher can begin to point to such a magnificent record as this.

The year Detroit won the League Championship and subsequently defeated St. Louis in the series for the World's Championship, Bennett had a batting percentage of .363 and his fine hitting did much to contribute to the success of his side.

Bennett's career was cut short by a railway accident in which he figured at Hutchison, Kansas. In it he lost both of his lower limbs. He is still alive and well, however, and in business at Detroit.

Bennett in his day was considered the king of all the catchers in the major league. He was on the crest of the highest wave of popularity when he met with the terrible accident that forced him to retire. In his time he handled such pitchers as Staley, Nichols, Stivetts, Clarkson, Shaw, Conway, Getzein and Baldwin, and in 1882, 1883, 1885, 1886, 1887, 1888, 1890 and 1893 he led the old league.

WILLIAM BERGEN—William Bergen, the leading catcher of the Brooklyn team is ranked with the best receivers in the business. He comes of a baseball playing family, his brother, Marty Bergen of the old Boston, being once considered the best catcher in the business. Bergen led the National League catchers in 1908, towering over Bresnahan, Kling, Phelps, Gibson and the best receivers in the business. Bergen is perhaps the best throwing catcher in the National League.

WILLIAM BLAIR—William Blair is the star catcher of the Rochester Club, Eastern League, and was formerly with the New York Americans. He caught in forty-two games for New York last year and made an excellent record that season.

JACK BLISS—Jack Bliss is the junior member of the St. Louis Cardinals strong catching staff, which is made up of Bresnahan, Phelps and Bliss, and other youngsters. Bliss was discovered by Stanley Robinson when the latter was visiting on the coast in 1907. He is a fine stalwart young player and is regarded as one of the brainiest and best receivers in the National League.

JACK BRENNAN—Jack Brennan played his best ball when catching for the St. Louis Unions in their 1884 season, and he wound up his professional career with the New Orleans Club of the Southern League. There were few brainier or more intelligent players than Brennan in his day. He learned all the fine points of the game from Captain Dunlap of the St. Louis Unions and understood inside baseball so well that he was generally selected as the captain or coach of the team he played with. Brennan was a fast, active receiver and a lightning thrower to bases. He was also a plucky and timely batsman. In his long professional career he won friends by the score, for in his playing he was always fair, open and conscientious.

ROGER BRESNAHAN—One of the great catchers of the present day is Roger Bresnahan, who did the bulk of the catching for the New York Giants when that team was winning the National League and World's Championships for the New York Giants.

In those years Bresnahan not only did royal work behind the bat, but he was one of the leading batsmen on the team, his average in 1904 being .284 and in 1905—with Mathewson, Donlin and McGraw, Bresnahan, while playing in the Metropolis, was one of the "Big Four."

It was in the Fall of 1908 that Bresnahan was signed to play with the St. Louis Cardinals in 1909.

President Stanley Robison of the St. Louis Club probably gave the fanciest price ever paid for a player, for Bresnahan, just to get a good catcher and some "brains" for his young ball club.

Whether he was successful still remains to be seen, but long ago Roger was recognized for his wisdom in running a ball club and recognized by that peerless manager, Johnny McGraw.

In 1908 Bresnahan caught in 139 games for Johnny McGraw. He practically led the National League receivers, as Jack Bliss and "Bill" Bergen, the only two catchers who outranked him, did not perform in anything like so many engagements. Bresnahan's notch was .985. Gibson of the Pirates got in 140 games. He alone was busier than Roger, and Roger beat him out 12 points in the averages. Furthermore, Bresnahan—and in one less game—worked in fifty more put-outs, four more assists and nine less errors than the clever Pittsburger.

In the same season Sullivan, who topped the American League catchers, ran up precisely the same percentage as Bresnahan. There was not a receiver in the Johnsonian organization who got in as many battles as Gibson and Bresnahan. As already said it was 140 matinees for Gibson and 139 for Bresnahan. Sulli, with 137, and Street, with 128, were the willing workers in the American League. Bresnahan also hit the sphere to the tune of .283 for New York. None but infielders and outfielders, and not many of them, excelled the Duke. To be exact, here's just who did outhit him: Wagner, Donlin, Doyle, Bransfield, Evers, Herzog, Lobert, Zimmerman, Titus, Bridwell, McCormick and Magee.

Appended you will get a record of Bresnahan's work each season from 1905, the year he was the king of the catchers, and the year when his team, the Giants, won the world's championship, to date:

	G.	AB.	R.	BH.	BA.	FA.
1905	95	331	58	100	.302	.970
1906	124	405	69	114	.281	.974
1907	104	328	57	83	.253	.986
1908	139	449	70	127	.283	.985
1909	69	234	27	57	.244	.960

In 1910 Bresnahan started his team with a rush and it played very fair ball in its early season games.

CHARLEY BRIODY — Charley Briody was the catcher for the Cleveland League team in 1883.

With Jim McCormick, the great pitcher of the Cleveland Club, Briody jumped to the Union Association in 1884.

He and McCormick were the battery this latter year for the Cincinnati Unions.

This was Briody's closing season in the major leagues of baseball, he taking on weight so fast that he was unable to get in condition for the following season.

LEW BROWN—Lew Brown was the catcher of the Boston Union team in its 1884 season. In his day he stood with the best receivers, handling the curves of Tom-

JACK BRENNAN.

The picture above is that of Jack Brennan, catcher of the St. Louis Unions
when they won the championship of the Union Assocation in 1884.

my Bond and other great speed merchants.

R. D. BUCKLEY—R. D. Buckley of the New York Giants was the leading catcher in 1891.

He was a fine, big fellow, and besides being a fine receiver and thrower, he was a good batsman.

After Buckley came Malachi Kittredge, who shone for two or three seasons with the Chicago Club.

Bennett bobbed up as the leading catcher again in 1893.

DICK BUCKLEY—Dick Buckley, a Philadelphia boy, stalwart and a corking good receiver, helped the St. Louis Browns when they won American Association pennants back in the eighties.

He was known in the nineties as the "man who made Rusie." He was a fine hustling player.

WILLIAM CARRIGAN — The Boston American League team was very fortunate when it succeeded in securing William Carrigan, the fine young catcher, who is one of the best batting catchers in the country.

He was born and brought up, and received his education in Lewiston, Me., and is 27 years of age. While at the Lewiston High School he captained the club. He then went to Holy Cross and his fine work there led to his engagement by the Boston American League Club. He was loaned to Toronto for the season of 1907 and did excellent work there.

It was not until 1909 that he was given an opportunity to show his talents to the best advantage, an opening being made for him by the release of Catcher Criger to the St. Louis Browns. He led the Boston Club at the bat a good part of the season and his backstopping and throwing have left little to be desired.

He did fine work behind the bat for the Boston American League team in their 1910 season. He is an experienced catcher and beside that is a good steady batsman.

J. F. CASEY—J. F. Casey is one of the junior catchers of Hughie Jennings' terrible Tigers. Casey was secured by the Tigers in the Spring of 1910, being purchased from the Little Rock Club, then a member of the Southern Association. Casey gives promise of becoming a first-class catcher with a little more experience.

JOHN CLAPP—John Clapp was one of the greatest catchers that ever lived. He was the leading catcher of St. Louis' first major league team away back in 1876. In 1878 he was the catcher of the famous Indianapolis team and later he played with the best nines in America. He was a wonderful receiver, handling the speediest pitching with the greatest of ease.

J. J. CLARKE—J. J. Clarke, known best as "Nig" Clarke, is the veteran catcher of the Cleveland Club of the American League. He was one of the greatest receivers of his day. He was a fine catcher and a magnificent thrower. He was also a hard hitting batsman.

THOMAS A. CLARKE—Thomas A. Clarke is the understudy of the famous "Larry" McLean the giant catcher of the Cincinnati Reds. Up to August in the 1910 season Clarke played in thirty games and his fielding and throwing were of a superior order.

W. H. COLGAN—One of the greatest of the early day catchers was W. H. Colgan, the receiver of the Nationals of East St.

Louis in the eighties. He and Florence Sullivan, also of the Nationals, became famous as a battery and wound up their professional careers with the Pittsburg Club of the American Association in the eighties. Colgan was a fine all-around player and batsman and one of the most popular players ever hailing from East St. Louis.

LOU CRIGER—Louis Criger, now a member of the Highlander catching staff, led the catchers in the American League in 1908 while with Boston.

He remained with the Boston American League team until 1908 when his release was sold to St. Louis. He played in St. Louis in 1909, but in speed and cleverness he was not up to his old standard and he was traded to the New York Americans.

In his day Criger was one of the cleverest of backstops and a fast and very effective thrower to bases.

He did his best work perhaps when he was the receiving end of the famous Young-Criger battery.

JOSEPH CRISP—Joseph Crisp is the name of the young catcher secured by the St. Louis Browns in August, 1910, from the Newark Club.

Crisp began his professional career back in 1906 with the Tulsa Club of the South Central League.

During that year he played wonderful baseball and was picked up by the Winnipeg Club of the Northern League the following Spring. He helped the Winnipegers win the pennant by catching every game his team played that year and was the sensation of the league both in sticking and fielding. The following year the Kansas City Club plucked Joe from the "bushes," and he made good from the start. He played in Kansas City, which is his home city part of the season of 1907 and in 1908. In 1908, however, like most players, he grew tired of playing in his home town and longed to play in the East, where the weather is generally cooler.

It was around this time that Manager McGinnity of the Tigers heard of Crisp and purchased him from the Kansas City Club. He played with Newark part of the 1909 season, but gave way to Blair toward the close. He started with a rush and was burning things up. Doubles, triples and homers were contributed by Joe this Spring in every game he played and he was the sensation of the league.

Big league offers came pouring in on McGinnity for Crisp's services from every side until May 15, when Newark and Buffalo jumped to that city for a game. With Starr at bat and a man on first the batter put up a high foul. Crisp went after it and made a sensational catch, but was unable to check his flight and fell into the depression at the visitors' bench. He injured his right knee, and it has never mended properly.

Crisp was born in Lone Jack, Mo., and spent much of his early life in the open air, so that he has acquired a rugged constitution. At an early age his family moved to Kansas City, and that town has since been his home. Before playing professional baseball he played with several amateur teams in and around the Missouri metropolis. Crisp has a big league career before him.

MICHAEL J. CULLINANE—Michael J. Cullinane, a St. Louis boy, was one of the greatest players in the Mound City in the eighties. He was at home behind the bat.

He was a tall, athletic built player who could hit the ball as well as field it. He did his first notable work behind the bat in 1882 for the St. Louis Amateurs, playing so well that he was called on frequently to catch the pitchers of the St. Louis Browns in their 1882 season. He might have played regular as a professional, but his business calling prevented that. He was, however, always a staunch and earnest friend of the game with a hand ever open to assist the deserving and needy player.

TOM DALY—Tom Daly was the crack catcher of the Brooklyn Club in the days of Byrne and Abell. He was a fine active receiver and held his own with the best for many a day.

TOM DEASLEY—In the race for catching honors in the National League in 1882 Tom Deasley, then catching for Boston, tied Bennett of Detroit.

A great catcher and thrower was Deasley, so great indeed that Ted Sullivan brought him to St. Louis and here he really wound up his career.

Deasley was a fine receiver and thrower, but too wild and jovial a fellow to last long in league company. His life on the center of the baseball stage was brief.

THOMAS J. DOLAN—Thomas J. Dolan, at one time one of the very best known catchers in the National League, now drives a fuel wagon for the St. Louis Fire Department.

Dolan learned to play ball with the old St. Louis "Reds" and he was graduated from there to the Buffalo National League team, where he handled the terrific delivery of Jimmy Galvin.

Ted Sullivan brought Dolan back to St. Louis in 1883 to play with the St. Louis Browns and he left the latter team in the middle of the playing season of 1884 to play with the St. Louis Unions.

On the Browns, Dolan caught the speedy pitching of George McGinnis, Silver King, Elton Chamberlain and Tony Mullane, and for the Unions he caught Boyle and Healy.

Before then Dolan faced the best League pitchers and had won a reputation of being one of the best and most reliable receivers in America.

P. W. DONAHUE—P. W. Donahue, the young receiver of the Boston American League Club was signed by that team in the Spring of 1909 on the recommendation of his brother, "Jiggs" Donahue, the once famous first baseman of the Chicago White Sox. Young Donahue made good with Boston from the jump.

CHARLES DOOIN—There are few players living to combine the qualities possessed by Charles Dooin, catcher, captain and manager of the Philadelphia Club of the National League in its 1910 year.

Frederick G. Lieb has written a fine sketch of this player. Of Dooin, Mr. Lieb wrote:

"Should the casual wanderer to Sleepytown happen to stray into the Phillies' rejuvenated baseball plant, and ask a friendly looking Quaker fan who, in his modest opinion exceeded all other catchers in regard to ability, knowledge of the game, etc., after the disturbance that would follow, a mutilated, hacked, unidentified body would find its way to the morgue, while the coroner's jury, composed of honest, honorable, law-abiding, peace-seeking Quakers, would find the verdict, 'Came to his death by a new and violent method of suicide.'

"In Philadelphians' hearts there is indeed but one catcher, and that is the beloved "Reddy" Dooin. Few ball players have won the popularity, good will, and almost adoration of the fans of their adopted ball towns as Charlie Dooin has with the army of Philadelphia baseball lovers. Undoubtedly, his is a case where earnestness, diligence and untiring, hard work against all odds has been fittingly rewarded.

"Charles S. Dooin was born in Cincinnati, Ohio, June 12, 1880. But to speak of Dooin as 'Charles,' does not sound exactly right. To refer to the auburn-haired little manager of Fogel's Phillies as anything else than 'Reddy' or 'Charlie' sounds harsh to the ear, and seems entirely out of place. It would sound as bad as a New Yorker speaking of 'Christy' Mathewson as Christopher, or to refer to our beloved ex-chief executive and foremost hunter as anything else than 'Teddy.' 'Reddy's' papa, James Dooin, was a cabinet maker, and one of those sturdy sons of Erin who have furnished Uncle Sam with a large majority of his stellar baseball talent. Charlie was educated in the public schools of Cincinnati, putting on the finishing touches at St. Xavier's school. He learned the trade of a cloth cutter, and but for his fondness for outdoor life and natural ability as a ball tosser, he might still be doing terrific execution with a pair of shears.

"Although frail of build, Dooin has worn well in his nine years of big league adventure. He is good for one hundred and forty games or more, and is almost immune from injury. The only injury of any account that kept 'Reddy' out of the game during the last half a dozen years, was received during an exhibition game between the Nationals and Quakers early this Spring. On that occasion, one of Walter Johnson's speed balls dented his left shoulder to such an extent that several ligaments were broken, and kept him out of the series with Connie Mack's White Elephants for the Quaker City Championship, and the first few games of the National League race.

"Another of 'Reddy's good qualities is his ability to block runners intent on scoring runs to the detriment of the Quaker cause. He can upset the heaviest player, and put the ball on him, yet with no apparent injury to himself. Quaker bugs, however, always dread lest one of these smashups between a ponderous two hundred pounder sailing into Dooin at the rate of a mile a minute, at some time may result in a big disaster to the little brick top. He is, however, absolutely fearless, and the chance of a serious injury to himself would not deter him in the least when, by blocking off a hefty runner, he can prevent a run being scored against Sleepytown.

"As a batsman Dooin does not rank high, but with men on bases he is one of the most dependable stickers on the team."

The present manager of the Phillies never forgets his first professional baseball engagement.

Born in Cincinnati, Dooin learned the game on the lots. Although small to the point of frailty, he made rapid strides, and while as young as 16 he was regarded as the best amateur catcher in Cincinnati. He kept on improving and shortly afterwards went to the St. Joseph (Mo.) team of the Western League.

"There is a wonderful catcher in Cincinnati by the name of Dooin. He is an amateur, and his release won't cost one penny. Give him a trial and you will never regret it."

That was the tip handed to the St. Joseph manager. The latter decided to give Dooin a trial, and he was ordered to report for duty when the season opened.

The next Spring Dooin boarded a train for St. Joseph. On arrival he sought the manager. There was certainly nothing impressive about his 130 pounds avoirdupois as he approached the manager and said, nervously: "I—I—I'm Dooin, your new player."

"Great Ceasar's ghost!" shouted the manager, sizing him up doubtfully. "I wanted a catcher, not a jockey. Why you havent strength enough to sweep out a parlor, let alone catch some of the six footers on my pitching staff. You've been misrepresented to me, and the best thing you can do is to take the next train home."

Dooin pleaded for just one trial and after some persuasion the manager consented. On the ball field Dooin showed what he could do. After the first day in practice the manager came up to him. Patting him on the back, he said:

"Laddie, you had better figure on staying here. I think I will need you.'"

Dooin soon became the best catcher in the Western League and the St. Joseph team received a handsome price when it sold his release to the Phillies.

THEODORE HENRY EASTERLY — Theodore Henry Easterly is one of the American League catchers who has advanced into the very front ranks of the sport. He was born in Lincoln, Neb., April 20, 1886. His folks went to San Diego, Cal., when he was but 7 years of age and he started playing independently in Pasadena and San Diego, Cal. He played with Los Angeles in 1908, in the Pacific Coast League, that club landing the pennant. He was recommended to the Cleveland Club, who secured him by draft. Owing to the disabilities of Clark and Bemis the new comer had an opportunity to show his mettle and sterling work for the Clevelands in 1909 and 1910. He stands five feet and weighs 165 pounds.

BUCK EWING—After the men who did yeoman work behind the bat in the early seventies and who worked without mask, gloves or chest protector, there came another army; an army that eclipsed the first, mainly because it was so splendidly equipped with the weapons of defense which were denied the first regiment.

And perhaps the greatest player behind the bat of this second army, if not the greatest catcher that ever lived, was Buck Ewing, a Cincinnati boy, who won his best spurs as captain and catcher of the New York Giants, positions he filled when that team was winning championships as early and often as it pleased.

Ewing was a giant in stature and an athlete in build. In the work of receiving the ball, in shooting it to any of the bases, in quick head work and all around fielding I have never seen his equal in the position he filled. But besides being a great catcher, no man that ever lived excelled him as a batsman, some of the great hits he made on the Polo grounds being record hits to this day.

DUKE FARRELL—For many a day Duke Farrell, a fine, stalwart fellow, was the leading receiver of the Chicago, Washington and Boston teams, and besides being a fine receiver, he was one of the hardest hitters in the business.

FRANK FLINT—The record says that Frank Flint, then playing with the Chicago White Stockings of the National League, was the greatest catcher in 1879 and 1880 and there the record certainly told the truth.

Up to those two years no catcher had ever ranked with Frank Flint, a St. Louis boy, known as "Silver" Flint, owing to his blonde hair, who was the famous catcher of the often champion Chicago White Stockings.

Flint, like Buck Ewing, who came after him, was a stalwart and it was his custom to catch nearly every game his team played during its whole season, handling each pitcher that faced him with equal ease and agility. As a fielder and thrower he ranked with Ewing, but the latter had away the edge on him when it came to hitting the ball, Flint being the weakest sort of a batsman.

When the Chicago team was winning world's championships Frank Flint caught nearly all their games for them.

In the thirteen years between 1877 and 1890 "Silver" Flint caught 935 out of 1,325 games played by his club, in most of which he never wore a mask or a protector.

In 1880 Flint caught sixty-two of the eighty-four games played by his team. In 1881 he caught in 77 of the 84 games played by his nine and he kept up this record until 1886 when the Chicagos again took the League pennant.

Flint was born in St. Louis and learned to play ball on the lots in North St. Louis. He caught for the St. Louis Artisans in the early seventies. His first important engagement away from home was with the "only" Indianapolis team, the nine that won the championship in the International Association in 1879.

On that team Flint faced the speedy pitching of Ed. Nolan and the two were always referred to as the "Only" Nolan and the "Only" Flint. That Indianapolis team included Flint, catcher; Nolan, pitcher; Charles Houtz, first base; Joe Quest, second base; Fred Weaver, third base; D. J. (Denny) Mack, shortstop; J. B. (Trick) McSorley, left field; Mike Golden, center field and change pitcher; Ad. Rocap, right field, and Billy Reilly, substitute.

Flint did such wonderful work with this team that he received a call from the Chicago Club with whom he remained through all the balance of his professional career. Beginning life here the great catcher when he died was brought home and now his body lies in Bellefontaine Cemetery.

GEORGE GIBSON—The World Championship games of 1909 in which Pittsburg defeated Detroit, brought to the front George Gibson, the wonderful young catcher of the Smoky City team.

Up to that series, Gibson was comparatively unknown outside the inner works of baseball. That series made him famous, for it proved him a catcher of the top flight.

Gibson is a Canadian, having been born in London, Ontario, July 22, 1880.

He is a fine stalwart young fellow, standing 5 feet, 11 1-2 inches and weighing 190 pounds.

He played with Buffalo of the Eastern League from September, 1903, to June, 1904. From June, 1904, to July, 1905, he was with

THOMAS J. DOLAN.

The above is a likeness of Thomas J. Dolan, who, in his day, was one of the best known professional catchers in America. Dolan caught Jimmy Galvin and all the pitchers of his day with the greatest of ease and was considered one of the best and most reliable of backstops.

THE NATIONAL GAME.

Pittsburg. While with the latter team Gibson has been called "The Iron Man" and has set new records in Marathon catching, having worked in 134 games in succession in the 1909 season.

Wagner, Clarke and Leach have been set above all others in alloting credit for Pittsburg's success, but there is a deep impression in many people's minds that "Gibby" was the one best bet.

Just figure where the Pirates would have been had George not been ready for duty when called upon in any of those 134 games. There is no doubt but that Gibson could have caught every game of the National League schedule had it been necessary for him to do so. However, the pennant was cinched many days before the wind-up and Clarke gave Gibson the rest he so richly deserved.

Gibson, in addition to throwing to the bases in wonderful manner, has coached the pitchers in masterful fashion and it is freely stated that it is due to his magnificent work in this regard that has made Adams so valuable.

Clarke has a long string of young pitchers and Gibson has starred in the role of developer. He is a likeable fellow, being popular with the players and is a man of sterling character in and out of baseball.

The Pittsburg team did not have a slump during 1909 and this fact is largely due to the way Gibson handled the team. Cub followers looked for a slump on the part of the Pirates. They said no team could go along without a fall down of some kind, and they were greatly surprised when Pittsburg upset all calculations in this respect.

Gibson was the team on the field. It can thus be seen what a potent factor the husky receiver really was in the machine representing Pittsburg. O'Connor and Simon, the other two catchers, are average youngsters. What a different front the Pirates would have presented with "Gib" out.

In addition to being a real field leader, Gibson is a topliner in both batting and fielding. He is always a timely hitter, batting equally well facing right-hand or left-hand boxmen, and as a batsman is considered as dangerous by the Pittsburg team's opponents as almost any man on the aggregation.

Gibson participated in 150 of the Pirates' 156 battles in 1909, and hit for an average of .267. "Gibby" was high for the National League backstops in batting, and, in addition, scored forty-two runs. Not only did Gibson have a good average, but many of his hits were good for more than a single base, twenty-three being doubles, nine triples and two home runs.

Gibson did not get off to a very good start in the hitting line, and made but three hits from April 14 to 25, for an average of .120. He picked up somewhat after this and from April 25 to May 1, he failed to hit safely in but one game, increasing his percentage to .231. He continued at this gait for the next month, and then gradually increased his mark to the .250 notch. From June 15 until July 9, he hit hard, making thirty safeties in seventy times at bat. At that time he had an average of .284, his high-water mark of the campaign.

BARNEY GILLIGAN—Barney Gilligan, the catcher of the Providence team in the eighties, was one of the best receivers of his day. He faced the hurricane pitching of Charles Radbourne and Charles Sweeny. Gilligan was a little fellow.

GEORGE F. GRAHAM—George F. Graham is one of the catching staff of the Boston Nationals, was born in Aldeo, Ia., March 23, 1880, and has been playing professionally for six years. He started with the Rock Island of the Three-I League in 1902 and played there also in 1903. In 1904 he was a member of the Colorado Springs Club of the Western League.

From there he went to the Minneapolis Club of the American Association in 1905, playing continuously with that team until the Fall of 1907, when he was purchased by the Boston National League Club for which he did splendid work in 1908, his first season as a major leaguer.

Besides being a fine backstop he is an excellent all-around player and has shown excellent capabilities in every position except that of pitcher. He stands five feet nine inches in height and weighs 175 pounds.

EM. GROSS—Em Gross in the seventies and eighties was one of the greatest receivers in the profession.

Gross was born in the south end of Chicago and learned to play ball on the prairies down there.

He was a fine big fellow and he perhaps did his best work while catching Sweeny and Radbourne for the Champion Providence team.

JOHN D. HARDY—John D. Hardy, who with Charley Street, holds down the receiving department for the Washington Americans, was born at Cleveland, Ohio, June 23, 1880. He is a big fellow, weighing 180 pounds.

Hardy played with Fort Wayne and Cleveland in 1904, and with Fort Wayne again in 1905, Nashville and the Cubs again in 1907, Nashville in 1908, Mobile in 1909 and Washington the end of that year.

A catcher on the Washington team has the supreme satisfaction of sitting on the bench, holding down the coacher's box, warming up pitchers, and watching Charlie Street work—which last must be admitted is a liberal education. However, Street, hard working as he is, has a rest coming to him some time, and gets hurt once in a while, when John D. gets his chance. It should not be omitted that John D. has a very big, deep voice and a world of enthusiasm, hence he is usually to be found on the lines during the game.

JOHN P. HENRY—John P. Henry, the Amherst College catcher, now with the Washington team of the American League, is an Amherst boy, the son of George L. Henry. He prepared for college in the Amherst high school, and during his preparatory course he made his mark as a catcher and all-round player and general athlete.

Making the varsity baseball team in his freshman year, Henry has always played a strong game, excelling in hitting as well as behind the bat. He weighs 180 pounds and is 21 years old. Last season he batted for .206 and fielded for .952. In 1910 he caught in every game. During the Southern trip he made an excellent record, scoring a home run at Annapolis and against the University of Virginia. He played a star game with Pennsylvania, permitting no stolen bases. In the ten games of the regular schedule he made but one error in the game with Princeton. In these games he made eleven hits in thirty-nine times at the bat.

RICHARD HIGHAM—Richard Higham was one of the greatest catchers of his day. He was with Providence in 1878 and later with other leading league teams.

BILLY HOLBERT—Billy Holbert in the early eighties was one of the best known men in baseball.

In 1883 he was the captain and leading catcher of the New York Metropolitans, the first and only team to represent Gotham in the American Association.

A handsome, jovial fellow was Holbert, and a good receiver too, for he handled speed merchants then like Tim Keefe, who was afterwards the firing end of the Giants' crack battery, composed of Buck Ewing and Tim Keefe.

FRANK JACKLITSCH—Frank Jacklitsch is one of the most active, able and aggressive receivers in the National League. He is a member of the Philadelphia Club. He is a fine batsman and occasionally fills utility roles.

JIM KEENAN—Jim Keenan was one of the great catchers of the early eighties.

He and Larry McKeon, his pitcher, were called the "Dago" battery, for they were dark-skinned, dark-eyed boys, but both great players.

At a benefit game in 1907 Keenan caught with all of his old-time cleverness.

MICHAEL J. KELLY—Next to Buck Ewing and Frank Flint as a handy man behind the bat, on the bases, in the field, or any old place, was Michael J. Kelly, Anson's right-hand man on the Chicago White Stockings.

Many of the players of the famous Chicago White stockings were prominent in the public eye by reason of their strong personality, their gift of making friends and their ready wit and repartee used on and off the field.

I have known all the great players since the game became a professional affair and I can recall no one of the lot who compared with Kelly when it came to a combination of those things in baseball which are known as quick wit and quick thinking, ability to see and to do the right thing at the right time and the strength, will and power to do it. Kelly combined all these essentials.

Thomas F. McCarthy, now a plain citizen of Boston, but at one time a crack outfielder of the St. Louis Browns, shares with me the belief that Michael J. Kelly was the greatest baseball player that ever lived. Talking about Kelly on one occasion, and I see no reason why the statement should not be made a part of this history, McCarthy said:

" 'Mike' Kelly or 'King Kel,' the name by which I knew him best, was the greatest player I ever knew.

"There were lots of crack players like 'Buck' Ewing and Bennett and Ganzel, but they all had to bow their heads before 'Kel' when it came to brains—baseball brains. Kelly was far and away the brainiest player I ever saw.

"Of course, there are plenty of folks who remember him when he played in Boston, and I suppose there are hundreds of anecdotes about him. He was a man about whom anecdotes could easily be written, for he was doing something all the time on and off the field. It would take a book just to tell of the doings of Kelly on the field in the heat of a hard-fought game.

"They don't play the kind of ball now that Kelly showed when at his best. The rules are against much of it. Not that his playing was dirty. It was nothing like that. He simply did lots of things for the first time, that's all, and rules were hastily made to provide against them in the future.

"For instance, on all hits to right field when Kelly was on first or second, he seldom touched third base. It used to make the bleacherites howl in glee when they saw him cut the base ten and fifteen feet and make home by a fancy slide.

"I remember when Boston got him for $10,000 from Chicago. He was a wonder then and in the first ten days he made more hits, stole more bases, and scored more runs than all the rest of the team. His work was truly phenomenal. The old records tell of his great playing better than I can in figures and all such-like, but the books do not tell how he did it.

"Kelly was a great base stealer for several reasons. In the first place, he always took plenty of room, more room than the average man of his time did. This counts a great deal in successful base-stealing. He wasn't particularly fast, not anywhere near as fast as Wagner or Ty Cobb, but he got there, and that's what counts.

"No man guarding a bag ever had more of Kelly to touch than his feet. He never came into a bag twice in the same way. He twisted and turned as he made his famous "Kelly slide," and seldom was he caught. He was a regular boxer with his feet when sliding into bases.

"Just to show what I mean by Kelly's brains, let me instance a play in the World's Series between Boston and Cleveland.

"Jesse Burkett was on third with two out. The batter hit to Herman Long at short and the Dutchman got the ball over to Tommy Tucker just a shade too late. The "Crab" started for home at the crack of the bat.

"The moment Kelly heard the umpire's "safe," he dropped his mitt as if the man had been called out. This slowed up Burkett. Then Kel turned like a flash, signaled for the ball and, catching it in his bare hand, stopped Burkett with his legs and got him just as easy as winking. Never was there any other player in the game who had the brain to think this play out in the heat of the game."

To distinguish him from the ordinary player he was often called "King Kell," and owing to his great all-around superiority he was worthy of that title.

Jim Hart, so long the president of the Chicago National League Club and at one time with Boston, tells this story about the "only" Kelly:

"Mike Kelly was a big-hearted, openhanded, kindly chap, the easiest man imaginable to manage as to the ordinary laws of baseball and the hardest to discipline that I ever had under my control, for a man who could hold any ill-feeling against Mike would have had ice water in his veins instead of blood. He was always ready to confess his lapses, his frankness and ever-prevailing good temper was too much for any manager to disregard. His earnings belonged to everybody but himself, the money he had just borrowed to take care of a pressing personal demand would be divided or given in whole to the first person who would ask for a piece of it or to any old friend who looked as if he needed a 'boost.'

"It was the practice of the treasurer of the Boston Club to advance money to the players between pay-days, taking their written receipts or acknowledgements

103

therefore. On pay-days he, armed with a little satchel containing the pay-day fuel, would hie himself to the park and take his station in the so-called directors' room, just next adjoining the players' dressing room under the grandstand at the old South End Park. He arrived usually just before the time for the home teams' practice and found the players in uniform. The routine consisted in him calling the name of a player who would respond by entering the presence of the treasurer, remaining a few moments and returning with his salary in his hands. For instance, the treasurer would call, 'Mr. Brouthers.' Big Dan would enter, remain but a moment and come back with his hands filled with cold cash. Later on 'Mr. Johnson' would be called, then 'Dicky' would make the trip, returning with cash in one hand and receipts for money advanced to him in the other. In due course 'Mr. Kelly' would be called; exit Mike into the presence of the cash bag, remaining some time, returning with both hands filled with cancelled receipts and no cash. I doubt if ever he had a real pay-day during his entire engagement with the Boston Club. Money was no object to him. The only use he had for it was to make somebody happier or more comfortable. He was dubbed 'King Kelly,' and if there was a king of good fellows it was 'His Royal Highness.' There will, in my opinion, never exist a player who will be so sincerely loved by the entire baseball public as was 'Dear Old King Kel,' who in life never had an enemy but himself.

"I honor, revere and respect his memory."

There was only one Mike Kelly. Certain men are born for things and Mike was one of those predestined for baseball. Mike was the inventor of the short route from second. He was the original. All others were imitators. He had a great weakness —that of getting under fly balls in front of him. To get one over his head for which he had to jump was soft for him. He was as full of expedients as an egg is full of meat, and there was no telling what he would do next. With all his trickery he was a very clean player and he would never stoop to do a mean thing to a fellow player.

M. KILLIFER—M. Killifer is the great little backstop of the St. Louis Browns. He has done some fine catching for them this year. Killifer did his first professional work with the Houston Texas Club. He is a brother of Wade Killifer of the Boston Club. He is only 21 and is a sure comer.

MALACHI KITTREDGE—Malachi Kittridge was for years with Anson as catcher of the Chicago White Stockings. Later he was with the Boston Nationals. Last year he distinguished himself by landing the pennant at Wilkesbarre, Pa., and is looking for pastures new in 1910. "Kitt" has shown himself to be a winner as in 1908 he landed a pennant at Scranton, Pa., in the same league.

The veteran catcher, now turned manager, is making an excellent showing with the Wilkesbarre, Pa., team of the New York State League.

JOHN KLEINOW—John Kleinow is the oldest member of the catching staff of the Boston Americans. Of late he has not been used much in regular games, his principal duty being the coaching of the young pitchers and acting as scout for the club.

JOHN G. KLING—The player, or rather the backstop to whom present day players hand the crown as being the leader in the profession is John Kling, the catcher of the Champion Chicago Cubs of 1906, 1907 and 1908.

In 1906 Kling caught ninety-six games for his team, in 1907 he caught ninety-eight, and in 1908, 117. In the winter of 1908-1909 Kling quarreled with the manager of the Chicago Club and retired to his home in Kansas City.

He did not play with the Chicago Cubs in 1909, neither did that three-time winner team capture the World's Championship that year.

Kling, besides being a great receiver, is great as a thrower and great as a batsman.

John G. Kling, now the great catcher of the Chicago "Cubs," is 33 years old, and has been in professional baseball fourteen years, having been secured by the Cubs from the St. Joseph, Mo., team, with which Kling began his professional career. Kling was looked on as the king of backstops for several seasons. His ease behind the bat is most marked. He throws and bats right-handed.

Although he remained out of baseball for a year and proved that champions can "come back," Kling now advises ball players to stick to the game until they are ready to step down and out for good. He claims—and his case is an example—that they can "come back," but says its a pretty hard job.

Because of some misunderstandings with the officials of the Chicago Club, Kling did not report to play with the Chicago team during the 1909 season. He played some in a semiprofessional league in which he was interested.

This year he decided to rejoin his club, and the question arose, "Can Kling regain his old form in batting, throwing and fielding?" He has done all of that, but not until after much hard work and under trying and discouraging conditions.

"Right now I am as good as ever, I believe," said Kling recently. "But after my own experience in getting back into condition I can readily understand why Jim Jeffries failed in his attempt to defeat Jack Johnson.

"I am not a drinking man. I don't even smoke. It was pretty tough for me to regain my old-time form, so I can see where these fellows who dissipate and carouse have their troubles after being out awhile and then try to be their old-time selves again."

MICHAEL KONNICK—Michael Konnick was one of the catching staff of the Cincinnati Reds at the opening of the 1910 season. He is a fine young player.

GROVER LAND—Grover Land, a catcher of the Toledo Club was transferred to the Cleveland American League team in August, 1910, and he is with that team now. Land is a wonderful player, a great fielder and thrower and a tremendous batsman. Two years ago he created a sensation with the Frankfort, Ky., team when they met the Cincinnati Reds by his wonderful work behind the bat. He was recommended to Cleveland by Pat Newman, a leading distiller of St. Louis, who saw Land play down in old Kentucky.

J. LAPP—J. Lapp is one of the promising young catchers of the great Philadelphia Athletics, leading member of the American League during the 1910 season. Lapp

CHARLES DOOIN.

Charles Dooin is one of the playing managers of the National League, being the main catcher as well as the "big noise" of the Philadelphia National League team.

has been working behind the bat for Connie Mack for the past two seasons and his work, taking it as a whole, has been high-class. He is a very fair fielding and throwing catcher.

PATRICK LIVINGSTON — Among the many young backstops who have broken into the major leagues in the last year or two and one who gives promise of developing into one of the stars of the American League circuit is Pat Livingston, whom the Philadelphia management obtained from the champion Indianapolis Club of the American Association last Fall. Manager Mack of the Athletics says that with a little more big league experience Livingston will make the crack backstops in Ban Johnson's league look to their laurels. Livingston is a heady catcher, an accurate thrower and good field general.

His good work behind the bat last season materially aided Indianapolis in capturing the flag. The Athletics have another promising backstop in young Lapp. Manager Mack thinks that with these two youngsters and Ira Thomas, the former Detroit catcher, to help out the Athletics will have as strong a backstopping department as several of the other clubs.

M. M. HACKETT—Mertie Hackett carried off record honors in the catching line in the 1884 season.

That year he was with the Boston Club and faced the speedy pitching of Whitney and Buffington.

THOMAS MADDEN—Thomas Madden in 1908 was one of the catchers of the Boston American League team.

Madden is a Boston boy and was born in the Roxbury district of that city in 1882. He played with local teams and afterwards with Ipswich and Beverly, Mass., before going to Lynn in 1907. He played with Lynn the following season. Daum was the regular catcher and when injured Madden relieved him and played in thirty-three consecutive games. Mr. Lake was scout for the Boston Americans and recommended him. He was secured by that club and in 1909 was traded to Portland, Ore., for Pat Donahue. He batted for .273 and fielded for .970 in 118 games. He weighs 183 pounds in playing condition.

JAMES T. McGUIRE—James T. McGuire, manager of the Cleveland Americans during the 1910 season, while catching for the Washington Club, had the best record in 1898.

To James T. McGuire, a National League catcher, too, belongs the record of being the oldest professional player in the business.

He was born November 18, 1863, at Youngstown, Ohio.

He has played professional baseball for twenty-five years.

He has never been fined, never put out of a game by an umpire. He has saved his money, and owns property at Albion, Mich.

He formerly enjoyed the nickname of "Pinch," because of his timely hitting. For ten years he has been "Deacon" to everybody.

He holds the world's record for continuous catching, officiating behind the bat in 142 straight games for Washington one season.

McGuire, who was with Cleveland in 1909, began his baseball career in 1883, twenty-five years ago.

He was then 21, and he was in every back lot game that offered opportunity to get into the spot light.

McGuire had a chance to shine in 1884, but baseball was fragile then, and Jim had small chance to show his worth. He was released and was signed by the Toledo Club of the American Association.

When the season of 1884 ended McGuire was transferred to the Detroit Club of the National League.

He was behind the bat in forty-eight championship games in 1885, and his work was so good that Philadelphia purchased him and he was with that team in 1886 and 1887.

McGuire went to Cleveland in 1888, playing with the American Association Club. The next year, 1889, found him with Toledo, then in the International League.

In 1890—when the National and Brotherhood were at war—McGuire was with Rochester.

The next year found him with Washington, where he participated in 106 games.

Jim stuck to Washington until 1899, when, in the middle of the season, he was released to Brooklyn, where he played for three years, going to Detroit in 1902 and playing with the Tigers until the close of the season of 1903.

When McGuire was signed by New York in 1904 it was given out that his salary was to be $6,000 a year. Whatever it was, McGuire earned it.

Then came the information, two years ago, that the Boston Americans had signed him as manager. McGuire "made good," and his release by President Taylor was regarded as an act of ingratitude and as a grave mistake.

McGuire was signed by Cleveland in 1908 when the chances for the pennant assumed formidable proportions. He became a favorite, almost rivaling in popularity Lajoie and Addie Joss.

Jim McGuire has no enemies among the players or umpires.

In 1909 McGuire succeeded Lajoie as manager of the Clevelanders.

Last season before he relinquished the management of the Boston team, a report came out of Washington that Jim had accused one of the arbitrators of unfairness.

Manager McGuire was shown the dispatch.

"All a dream," said Jim. "Even if the umpiring had been of the worst I wouldn't have said a word, but it wasn't; it was good."

That's Jim McGuire.

JOHN BANNERMAN McLEAN — John Bannerman McLean, the well-known backstop, is the tallest catcher in the National League.

He stands six feet five and one-quarter inches and weighs 228 pounds.

McLean was born in Cambridge, Mass., July 18, 1882, and was enabled to celebrate his twenty-seventh anniversary at his home, the Cincinnati Club playing in Boston at that time. He received his education in the Washington Grammar School and in the Cambridge Manual Training School in Cambridge. He first came to notice as a baseball light with the New-towns of Cambridge. He played with the St. John, N. B. Club in 1899 and 1900, and in 1901 went South with the Boston Americans, that being the first year of their existence.

McLean made a great showing while the club was in the south, but afterwards showed the need of further development. He played with and managed the Halifax, Nova Scotia, team in 1902, and the follow-

JAMES T. McGUIRE.
James T. McGuire. manager of the Cleveland Club of the American League
holds the record of being the oldest professional player in the business.

ing season was with the Nashua Club of the New England League, and made a splendid showing there that attracted a deal of attention, hitting hard and fielding splendidly.

Chicago, of the National League, and Cleveland of the American League, tried to secure him, and after being with the Cleveland Club for a week it developed that the Chicagos had the prior claim. He played three games with Chicago and was then traded with Pitcher Jack Taylor to the St. Louis Cardinals for Mordecai Brown and Jack O'Neil, the latter afterward being traded to Boston. He played with St. Louis in the season of 1904 and the following season was released to Portland, Oregon. Here he played until the middle of the season of 1906, when he was purchased by Cincinnati, and he has played with Cincinnati ever since.

The big Cincinnati backstop caught wonderful ball for the Reds during the season of 1910. Last season he fractured his knee and it was feared that he would be permanently disabled, but the injury has healed completely.

JOHN T. MEYERS—The only full blooded Indian playing baseball in the major leagues is John T. Meyers, the stalwart catcher of the New York National League team in 1910.

Meyers is a fine, stalwart fellow of swarthy complexion and dark eyes. He is a magnificent receiver, comparing indeed with the very best men in the big league. His home is at Riverside, California, and he was born out there July 29, 1882. In 1905 he was a student at Dartmouth College, but he was not eligible to play on the varsity nine. He played with Harrisburg in the Tri-State League in 1906 and the following season was with Butte in the Northwestern League. Butte sold him to St. Paul and that club sold him in 1908 to the New York Nationals for $6000. He played the season of 1908 with the St. Paul Club and started in with New York in 1909, proving a winner from the start. He stands five feet, eleven inches and weighs 194 pounds. He is a fine batsman as well as a first-class receiver and thrower.

John Meyers has been winning a lot of games for the McGrawites recently by his timely hitting and is one of the most popular players on the Lowland combination. The Chief has improved in his work behind the bat and has gained confidence in himself. Early in the campaign Meyers did some horrible pegging to the bases, but recently he has got the range of second and has been throwing most accurately.

GEORGE MILLER—George Miller, who caught Jimmy Galvin for Pittsburg nearly twenty years ago, was one of the great receivers of his day.

The old battery was known as "Pud" Galvin and "Doggie" Miller.

Galvin died a year or so ago, and Miller followed his old pitcher last April.

This is the second of the fine old batteries to be reunited in the Great Beyond within the past few years, for John Clarkson died the other day and went to seek 'Mike Kelly in the farther world.

Miller, a stocky little fellow, full of life and comedy, was a type of the old-time ball player—frolicsome, boisterous, playing the game for all there was in it every day and spending his money merrily at night.

He took no heed of the future, and when at last the arm was gone and the batting eye was dim, there was but little saved to help him in his later years.

Ever since 1891 until he died last April, Miller lived as best he could, quietly and inconspicuously, and the baseball world had completely lost sight of the little fellow who was one of its favorite stars. Miller was one of the liveliest, gamest catchers that ever donned the mask.

A contemporary of Mike Kelly, Silver Flint and Charlie Bennett, he was not the equal of those great men as a backstop, but was almost the rival of Kelly in jollying and gingering up a team, while the Pittsburg fans believed him to be a marvel in every way.

Jim Galvin, the burly old man of baseball, was paired with Doggie, and the two worked together like clockwork machinery for many seasons.

FRED MITCHELL—Fred Mitchell, one of the catchers of the New York American League team was born at Cambridge, Mass., June 5, 1879; receiving his education in the Allston district of Boston. When 16 years of age his parents moved to Concord, N. H., and remained there for two years. They then returned to Allston and Mitchell began his baseball career as a member of the St. John, N. B., club as a pitcher in 1900.

His excellent work there attracted considerable attention and Mike Moore, a brother-in-law of Hugh Duffy, secured Mitchell for the Boston Americans. He played with Collins' team in 1901 and a part of 1902, finishing the latter season with the Philadelphia Nationals in 1903 and 1904; with Brooklyn in 1905 and with Toronto 1906, 1907, 1908 and 1909, being secured by the New York Americans. Mitchell pitched up to the season of 1909, when he went behind the bat. He was behind the bat in ninety-two games last season and had a fielding percentage of .947. He batted for .285 in 109 games, standing fourth among the batsmen who played in 100 games or more. He stands five feet nine and one-half inches in height and weighs 189 pounds when in playing condition. His present home is in Hudson, Mass.

PATRICK MORAN—There are few greater catchers in the business than Patrick Moran in 1909, receiver of the Chicago National League Club, but now with the Philadelphia Nationals.

Moran was with Boston in 1905 and that year he topped the record for catching in the National League. He is one of the most intelligent players in the business and in the Baseball Magazine recently wrote a masterly article relative to the art of catching. He said in it:

"In almost every walk of life, it's the man behind who is the 'big man.'

"The man behind the gun is the man who kills the foe; the man behind the business concern is the man who makes it go; and the man behind the bat is the one who does most in making a baseball team a success or a failure.

"Ask any ball player what position he considers the hardest to play, ninety-nine times out of a hundred, he will declare that his own particular one is the most critical and important.

"Some will say that of course they have not as much to do as the players in some other places, but their work, when it does come, is difficult and can only be accomplished by a man who is especially adapted for it. Admitting this to be true, it is still my belief that the catcher is the most important man on a baseball team.

"On him falls the burden of the work. And this work is always important. He

JACK O'CONNOR.

In another part of this book appears a long story of the career of Jack O'Connor, once the manager of the St. Louis American League Club. In his day O'Connor was considered one of the best catchers in America. In his day he played behind the bat, catching speedy pitchers like Cy Young, Cuppy, Powell and men like them with the greatest of ease.

can never afford to take it easy or to be caught napping, for he is the pilot of the baseball craft. His are the eyes that must always look for the rocks, and see that his ship keeps to her course and avoids the reefs and shoals.

"At the present time the pitcher is the hero of the baseball lover. You hear the fans talking about the number of strike-outs this one had, and about the grand way that another kept his opponents from hitting the ball. Every day you hear some such remark as this:

"If they didn't have him pitching for them, they'd be nowhere in the race.'

"Now, I am not attempting to take away any of the pitcher's glory. The man in the box is deserving of great praise for the work that he does, but it is my claim that he should not get all the credit. The catcher should get some of it, for the good pitchers themselves, when questioned, will invariably admit that their catchers should be praised as much as they should, when credit is being given for victories on the diamond. Just stop and think for a moment. Where would a twirler, no matter what his ability, be, if he did not have someone catching him, who could help him in matching his brains against those of the batter, encourage him when things were breaking badly, and talk to him when perhaps a little hard luck had discouraged him and put him in the air? It is the catcher's brains oft-times that win the victories. The pitcher, of course, has the curves that will deceive the batsman, but the man on the receiving end tells him how to use his curves in such a way that the hitters may be fooled. The catcher, owing to the fact that he works in almost every game, knows the weaknesses of the various batters, and the pitchers set great store on this very thing, and are ever looking to the catcher to tell them what to do.

"On the playing field, the man behind the bat is, in reality, the manager of the team. He, before all others, can know when his pitcher is beginning to weaken, and he communicates his knowledge to the manager on the bench, who sees to it that another man is warmed up, so that, when the crash comes, the team will not be left in the lurch.

"The owners of teams are beginning to see that a man who makes a good catcher must have brains and an intimate knowledge of the game. Consequently, they are beginning to give their catchers the positions on the salary list which they have always filled on the playing field—the office of manager. Bresnahan is managing the St. Louis Nationals. Lake, an old-time catcher, heads the Boston team, while McGuire is now managing the Clevelands and Red Dooin leads the Philadelphia Nationals and catches nearly every game.

"To my mind the day is almost at hand when we will see every big league team with a catcher as manager."

Moran, while the Chicago Cubs' second catcher, did not get a chance in the World's Series of 1908, but he did some fine work for the champions during the season of 1908, when Kling was laid up with a broken thumb, and also did finely for Chicago in 1909. Moran is 31 years old, has been playing twelve years and broke into the business at Lyons, N. Y. He throws and bats right-handed.

Moran went to the Cubs from the Boston Nationals three years ago and remained with them until 1910 when he went to the

Philadelphia National League Club where he is playing now.

VINCENT NAVA—Vincent Nava, with Barney Gilligan, did the catching for the Providence team in the eighties handling the swift pitching of Sweeny and Radbourne. He was a little Cuban and his catching was the acme of grace and skill.

T. J. NEEDHAM—T. J. Needham is one of the catching staff of the Chicago Cubs. He was one of the regular catchers of the Boston National League team and in the east was considered a star.

JACK O'CONNOR—There are few professional players in the ranks to-day who have led as active a life and as long a one in the professional field as Jack O'Connor.

He is the man selected by President Robert Lee Hedges to manage the 1910 St. Louis Browns.

O'Connor is a St. Louis boy. He was born up on North Broadway forty-two years ago and learned to play ball on the prairies which were then numerous out there.

It was from these lots that graduated perhaps the greatest baseball catcher that ever lived, Frank Flint of the Chicago White Stockings, and next to Flint in the olden days there were few better receivers than this same O'Connor.

O'Connor first came into prominence as the catcher of the crack Shamrock team—a nine that hailed from North St. Louis and that could beat anything in that neck of the woods.

It included in its ranks such later famous players as Pat and George Tebeau, Sam Smith, Joe Herr, George Sharinghaus, Jack (Dutch) Reinagle and Ed Struve.

O'Connor's first professional engagement away from home was with the St. Joe Club of 1886. That team, managed by Nin Alexander, now of Pana, Ill., in the Western League, went through that entire season with ten men and came within one game of winning the pennant from Denver after they had spent thousands on their team to strengthen it.

The names of the old St. Joe's are familiar to almost every "fan" in the country even to-day, and are as follows: "Silver" King, pitcher; Bart Grether, pitcher; Jack O'Connor, catcher; "Jumbo" Harding, catcher; Sam Smith, first; Pat Tebeau, second and captain; Joe Herr, third; Will Fry, short; "Bug" Holliday, left; (one of the catchers played center, which would be a crime if done to-day); Art Sundy, better known as "Windy," played right, and Nin Alexander was the substitute catcher and manager.

O'Connor caught such grand ball for St. Joseph that he had no trouble in 1887 securing a position with Cincinnati. The following year he went to Columbus, and in 1890 he played American Association with Denver.

In 1891 he joined Cleveland, where he played until 1899, when with the rest of the Cleveland team, he was removed to St. Louis.

In 1900 he was sold to Pittsburg, where he played until 1902, when he jumped to the New York Americans. There he remained until 1906, when he joined the Browns. He remained in St. Louis until 1909, when he was signed by Little Rock. He played in that city for four months and did good work until he came to St. Louis in August, 1909. He acted as scout for the Browns during August, September and October, 1909.

As far as baseball knowledge goes, O'Connor bears the highest reputation among the best judges of play in the world. Baseball men say that he is without doubt one of the cleverest judges of play that has ever graced the game.

O'Connor has made a deep study of baseball, and few men in the game have a superior knowledge of the sport. He has a knack of doing the unexpected or outguessing his adversary. It was Jack, for instance, who, while catching the Browns, made big John Anderson, then with Washington, throw the ball against the pavilion. Jack pretended to be the Washington first baseman and "Big" John heaved the ball to him. Then Jack sidestepped and let the horsehide roll, while a pair of Brownies scored. This was only one of the tricks that earned for Jack the title of "Brains."

When playing ball in Columbus, Cincinnati, Cleveland, Denver, Pittsburg, New York and other big towns. O'Connor always spent his winters in North St. Louis. Jack is well fixed financially. He owns considerable real estate in the "Goose Hill" district, the scene of his early triumphs as a ball player.

Twenty years ago St. Louis became famous as the nursery of major league baseball players. Jack O'Connor, Pat Tebeau, Bill Joyce, "Bug" Holliday, Theodore Breitenstein, Heine Peitz, Sam Smith, "Kid" Baldwin, "Baldy" Silch and other National League and American Association stars of the two decades ago were developed here. Somebody started the story that they all came from "Kerry Patch," but as a matter of fact none of the great players that made St. Louis famous in the baseball world were from the "Kingdom of Kerry."

Pat Tebeau was the first St. Louis boy to be placed in command of a St. Louis major league team. He managed the Robison team of 1899 and part of 1900, when he was succeeded by Johnny McGraw.

O'Connor learned his baseball under Tebeau. The pair played together with the old Shamrocks, and were afterwards together with Cleveland and St. Louis. O'Connor, by the way, has played most of his major league baseball with the best clubs in the business. That's one of his strong points. He saw service under Tebeau at Cleveland when Oliver Patrick led the Temple Cup winners, the world's champions of 1895. O'Connor also was the premier catcher of the famous Pittsburg champions of 1901 and was the principal backstop of the New York Americans in 1903, the year Griffith's band ran Boston to a nose for the American League championship.

O'Connor's record justifies the confidence placed in him by President Hedges of the Browns. Mr. Hedges is a loyal employer. He stood by McAleer for eight years and never murmured when McAleer finished in the ruck year in and year out.

O'Connor is assured of a fair trial, and in order to make good as a manager he must, some day round up a first-division team.

To sum it all up Jack O'Connor is one of the best baseball men in the country, and there is every reason to expect that he will prove the success with the St. Louis Americans that President Hedges anticipates. No one knows the game any better and he has had the experience to build up a first-class team.

The St. Louis club of 1909 and 1910 was anything but a glittering success, and it can not very well make a more unsatisfactory showing during the seasons to come.

O'Connor, therefore, has nothing to lose and everything to gain. He has rare ability in that very important department—the coaching of pitchers—perhaps the most vital essential of the good manager. St. Louis has some very good material in all branches, and it's simply up to O'Connor. The new manager is very popular in St. Louis and will have the heartiest kind of support in his attempt to some day give St. Louis a champion team in the American League.

PATRICK F. O'CONNOR—Patrick F. O'Connor, one of the catchers of the World's Champion Pittsburg Club of 1909, was born August 4, 1882, in Windsor Locks, Conn. He stands five feet eight inches and weighs 168 pounds.

He played in 1902 and 1903 with Bristol, in the Connecticut State League; 1904 to 1907 with Springfield, in the Connecticut State League; 1908 and 1909 with Pittsburg. He is the junior member of the Pittsburg National League team's catching staff, being an understudy of the famous George Gibson.

WALTER OWEN—Walter Owen, one of the catchers of the Chicago White Sox has divided honors with the great Billy Sullivan in the receiving department of that team. Owen is a good steady backstop.

FRED PAYNE—Fred Payne is the utility catcher of the Chicago White Sox with whom he has been for several years. He is a fine reliable backstop and when Billy Sullivan was injured he caught all the speedy pitchers on the White Sox team and proved himself a receiver of the first class. He was the best fielding catcher according to the record in 1908 and 1909.

HENRY PEITZ—Henry Peitz, according to the record, was the greatest catcher in the 1897 and 1899 years.

Indeed in the nineties there were few better catchers in the major leagues than Heine Peitz, better known as "Heiny" a St. Louis boy, who was a fine receiver, a fine thrower, and a good batsman.

Peitz, in 1909, managed the Louisville Club of the American Association. He was born and brought up in St. Louis, where he got his first experience on the lots in North St. Louis.

His initial professional engagement was with an independent team at Hillsboro, Ill., in 1889. For the next two years he caught for a somewhat stronger independent team at Jacksonville, Ill. In 1892 he went to Montgomery, in the Southern League, which was his first job on a regular league circuit.

He did so well that before the year was out he had attracted the attention of major league managers, and he was sold to the Mound City team for the three following years, and went to Cincinnati in the Spring of 1896.

For nine successive years from that date he was the mainstay of the Cincinnati Reds behind the bat, and he established the reputation there of being one of the best and wisest catchers who ever wore a mitt. While a member of the Cincinnati Reds he handled some famous twirlers, including such famous stars as Amos Rusie, Frank Hahn, Billy Rhines, Theodore Breitenstein, Frank Foreman, Frank Dwyer and many others, and he was largely responsible for the success of these pitchers.

During the winter preceding the season of 1905 Peitz was traded to Pittsburg for Ed Phelps. He remained in Pittsburg two seasons, and was the most reliable of the Pirate catchers, but when George Gibson showed his ability to catch nearly every day, Heine was released to Louisville, where he did almost all the catching in 1907 and 1908. He was asked to assume the management of the Colonels two years ago, but preferred to serve in the ranks for the salary that was offered him at that time. In 1909 that club weighed in with a liberal offer and then Peitz accepted the management of the Louisvilles and piloted them through a most successful season in 1909.

EDDIE PHELPS—There are few better receivers in the major leagues to-day than Eddie Phelps, the stalwart catcher of the St. Louis Cardinals.

Phelps is not only a splendid receiver, but he is a fine and plucky batsman, being always a good man in the breach.

Eddie Phelps was purchased by the Pittsburg Club from Rochester in 1902, traded to Cincinnati in 1904 and returned to Pittsburg at the beginning of the 1907 season. He remained there during 1907 and 1908 and is now with the St. Louis Cardinals. Phelps is one of the heaviest-hitting catchers in the National League.

MICHAEL R. POWERS — Michael R. Powers, who did great work for the Athletics in 1908, was one of the best receivers in the business.

He was with the Athletics from the time they entered the American League in 1900 until last May when he died in Philadelphia.

Powers was not only a great player, but owing to his sterling character he was a universal favorite among the followers of the game in Philadelphia. On the field he was always manly, loyal, discreet, courteous and capable. He inspired confidence on the playing field, warm friendships among his associates and profound affection in his own cherished home circle.

In all his relations with the club's management and its players, Mr. Powers disclosed high qualities of sincerity, integrity and true comradeship. He was the soul of honor. To attain success by questionable means was beneath and apart from his nature.

The club management and his associates on the playing field trusted him implicitly; nor was their confidence in him ever misplaced or betrayed. Year in and year out he was the same earnest worker, faithfully devoted to duty. Enemies he had none, and wherever he went he grappled friends to him as with hooks of steel.

When Powers passed away someone in Philadelphia wrote these lines about him:

"RED CROSS MIKE."

You fans all knew of Red Cross Mike who played the game to win,
But always played it on the square and fought through thick and thin.
There never was a whiter man that caught behind the plate,
Who kindly cheered his comrades more and fixed an ailing mate.
When someone met a liner and was struggling hard for air,
Of all who helped the stricken man, "Doc" Powers first was there.

"Work hard, old man, work hard," said Mike, when things were going ill;

And by his true and steady work, he'd pull his team uphill—
To victory. But the fans cheered "Doc" with all their might,
He'd always give the credit to a teammate for the fight.
Calm in the midst of tumult, when the shouting split the air,
Doing his best in every play, "Doc" Powers still was there.

We'll have another catcher who will play in Powers' place;
We'll have another catcher who will fight to win the race,
But "Doc" has gone and passed beyond the umpire's strident call;
No more he'll rise to duty when we hear the words, "Play Ball!"
But though he's left a team to mourn and miss his kindly air,
Within the hearts of countless friends "Doc" Powers will be there.

So great and lasting was the love of the Philadelphia people for Powers that on Friday, June 30, 1910, no less than twelve thousand persons, one year after his death, attended the "Powers Day" celebration at Shibe Park, Philadelphia, where the memory of the dead player was commemorated by a benefit for his widow and children. Players from the Boston, New York, Washington and Philadelphia American league teams participated in the various events.

Lord of Boston beat a bunt to first in :03 1-5.

Donahue of Philadelphia won the prize for the most accurate throwing.

In the base circling contest Collins of Philadelphia equaled the world's record of :14 1-5; Austin of New York and Speaker of Boston tied for second at 14 3-5.

Hooper of Boston won the long distance throwing contest with a throw of 356 feet 4 inches. Speaker was second with 345 feet 7 1-2 inches.

Austin won the 100-yard dash for men weighing more than 200 pounds, with Vaughn of New York, second. The time was :10 2-5.

Dygert of Philadelphia won the fungo hitting contest.

Austin was the only contestant who succeeded in throwing the ball over second base from the catcher's position, beneath a bar six feet high at the pitcher's box.

In the relay race circling the bases, Boston and Philadelphia tied at 14 3-5. In the run off both teams again tied at 14 2-5. The local team won the toss.

Only six innings were played in the baseball game between the Philadelphia team and the team composed of players from the other clubs, the locals winning 5 to 3.

WILLIAM RARADEN—William Raraden is the young and promising catcher of the Boston National League team.

WILBERT ROBINSON—There were few better catchers in his day than Wilbert Robinson, the star receiver of the champion Baltimore team when McGraw, Kelly, Jennings, Brouthers and other great players were in its ranks.

A fine receiver was Robinson as well as a timely and plucky batsman.

Last Spring Robinson went to Marlin Springs, Texas, where the New York Giants were in training and there coached McGraw's green pitchers.

There is not to-day a man who can equal Robbie in this line of work, for he has not only the ability and experience,

NIN ALEXANDER.
One of the first of the old catchers to catch the ball up close to the bat and
alive and well at Pana, Ill.

THE NATIONAL GAME.

but as a salve artist he stands alone. Few men can detect and develop pitching ability as can this veteran. The history of Joe McGinnity in the big league is an illustration of this fact.

In 1899, when the Baltimore team was transferred to Brooklyn and Baltimore was represented by the cast-offs from the two clubs, Baltimore trained at Savannah and Brooklyn at Augusta. McGraw and Robbie had been left in Baltimore as the nucleus for the local club and they were to be given anything that did not look swell enough for Brooklyn.

Among the pitching candidates on the Brooklyn roster was Joe McGinnity, then unknown to the major circuit. It did not take long for Robbie to see that he was a real pitcher and when the time came to shuffle the discards he advised McGraw to take the Iron Man in preference to anything on the list. McGinnity's work for the Orioles was the sensation of the season and Brooklyn jumped at the opportunity to get him in 1900 and single-handed he pitched Ebbets' team into the championship that year, topping all other National pitchers.

Hughey Jennings declares that Wilbert Robinson was the best catcher that ever lived and the Tigers' leader is pretty good authority. "Robbie" of the Baltimore Orioles and John Clement of the old Phillies, afterwards with Cleveland and St. Louis, tied for top-notch honors in 1895, the former with seventy-five games and the latter with eighty-five.

FRANK ROTH—Frank Roth, one of the catchers on the staff of Clark Griffith, has shown to good advantage in the games he has played thus far with that team.

JACK RYAN—Jack Ryan was at one time the crack catcher of the St. Louis Cardinals. This veteran is now doing yeoman service as manager of Jersey City in the Eastern League, and asks no handicap for age, as he is doing about all that is expected of him.

GEORGE SCHLEI—George Schlei is the veteran catcher of the New York Giants who divides honors on McGraw's team with "Big Chief" Meyers. Schlei besides being a good receiver is an excellent batsman. He was with Cincinnati for several years before going to New York.

CHARLES SCHMIDT—Charles Schmidt, who caught in six out of the seven games for the Detroits when they played Pittsburg for the World's Championship in 1909, and again in 1910, when the Tigers and Pirates met, is a fine back-stop and a good batsman. If he has any weakness it is throwing to the bases.

Schmidt is a native of Coal Hill, Arkansas and is 30 years of age. His early baseball was played in Springfield, Mo., Little Rock and Minneapolis, Detroit purchasing him from the last mentioned club at the end of the season of 1905. Schmidt is five feet ten inches in height and weighs 184 pounds. He bats left-handed.

Schmidt is a marvel physically and a good receiver, thrower and batsman. He was drafted by St. Paul of the American Association in 1904 where one of Hughie Jennings' scouts discovered him. He has been with Detroit ever since.

O. F. SCHRECKENGOST — Osee F. Schreckengost is generally known throughout the baseball world as

"Schreck" and has had a long career on the diamond.

He was born in New Bethlehem in 1875, and played with the Williamsport, Pa., Club in 1895 when he was 20 years of age.

The next season he played with the Fall River, Mass., and Augusta, Me., clubs of the New England League, and in 1898 was with Cedar Rapids, Iowa Youngstown and Cleveland. In 1899 he played with St. Louis and Cleveland, and he played with Buffalo the following season.

In 1901 he was selected to play with the new American League Club of Boston under the management of "Jimmy" Collins, but he remained in Boston but one season, thence going to Cleveland. He joined the Athletics in 1902 and played in ninety games that season. He was later traded to the Chicago American League Club, which found itself crippled in the catching department. Schreck was retired to the minors in the Spring of 1910.

M. E. SIMON—M. E. Simon is the cub member of the Pittsburg Club's catching staff and is now in his first season in the big league. He is one of the coming great receivers. At least so says Fred Clarke.

HARRY SMITH—Harry Smith was the youngest manager in the major leagues in point of service, and a great catcher, being the manager of the Boston National League Club in 1909, when he succeeded Frank Bowerman.

In 1910 Smith was succeeded by Fred Lake.

Smith is a native of England and was born in Yorkshire, October 31, 1875.

When he was 7 years of age his people settled in this country, in Massillon, Ohio, which has always been their home.

Young Smith was a machinist by trade and during his spare time played baseball for which he had a great liking and he took to it so handily that he started a professional career at Canton, Ohio, in May, 1896. A month later he went to Warren, Pa. He did so well there that Buffalo gave him a trial in the latter part of 1896 and he remained with that club in 1897. The following year he was with Wilkesbarre and in 1899 he joined the Milwaukee team of the American Association, where he was also in 1900. He went with Connie Mack to Philadelphia with the launching of the American League there. Then he went to the National League and from 1902 to 1907 was with Pittsburg. In 1908 he was secured by the Boston Nationals with whom he did excellent work.

Harry Smith is the quietest and most peaceable of the numerous Smith family that has ever been in baseball. There was Broadway Aleck Smith, who was carried on the New York Giants' pay roll to put down bets for McGraw until he was ruled off the turf; there is Frank Smith, challenger of Jeffries and expert piano hustler, who is now the premier pitcher for the Red Sox, and a lot of other Smiths, but Harry Smith, in the past, had the big job of the baseball Smiths.

OSCAR STANAGE—Oscar Stanage, who caught one of the games for Detroit against Pittsburg in the memorable series of 1909, was born in San Diego, California, 23 years ago, and was graduated direct from the San Jose High School team to the St. Louis Cardinals in 1906. He was released to Cincinati and then went into the Eastern League. Detroit

114

THE NATIONAL GAME.

purchased him from Newark a year ago. He bats right-handed, is 5 ft. 9 1-2 inches tall, and weighs 185 pounds.

JAMES STEPHENS—There may be fancier, noisier and perhaps more accomplished catchers in the American League than little Stephens, but when it comes right down to clean, consistent, aggressive work, steadiness and ability the "Horseshoe Kid," as he has been dubbed, has few, very few, equals. The majority of so-called star boxmen, have usually been developed and seasoned while playing with first division clubs. Rarely, indeed, do we hear much praise sung about the deeds of the plugging catchers who are forced to work behind the weak-kneed twirlers of the tail end clubs. They are rarely exploited in the press outside of an occasional line when they happen to pull off a sensational play.

The St. Louis Browns were in a bad way indeed in 1907, when the scouts for McAleer, dug up in far Texas. one James Stephens, catcher of Waco, Texas. When he reported in St. Louis in the spring his appearance caused the wise ones to laugh outright. He was a mere strip of a boy and had not yet attained his majority. He weighed 125 pounds and was as shy and backward as a girl.

McAleer, however, had faith in the little lad's prowess and in the Spring games against the Cardinals he showed the Texas "child." It is needless to state how little Jimmy surprised the St. Louis fans. He caught the terrible shoots of the giant Powell and Glade with ease. His tossing to the bases was a revelation. Down in Texas, he had led the catchers with the stick and some of his long timely hits made in that first Spring show immediately won him a place in the hearts of the St. Louis fans.

In 1908, the Browns with a greatly improved team over the previous season, jumped out and fairly tin-canned in the van in the American League race. Little Stephens had developed into a steady, careful catcher and to him fell the brunt of the hard games. He participated in 50 games during the season and in the Fall when the Browns were fighting Detroit for the flag. Again in 1909 and 1910, Stephens continued to hold down the big job on the Browns catching staff. Manager O'Connor thinks the "kid" today is the premier big mitt artist of the American. Of late Stephens has developed into a sure batter and during the season of 1910 he hit in a dozen runs, which were the means of pulling his team out of the hole and to victory. Stephens is 23 years old, and is a native of Sharon, Pa. He is 5 ft. 2 inches tall and now weighs 165 pounds.

CHARLES S. STREET—The Washington Club made no mistake when it added to its ranks that excellent ball player, Charles S. Street, who was the principal backstop for the club in 1909.

Cincinnati had this player in 1904, having secured him by purchase from the Terre Haute, Ind., Club.

Cincinnati allowed him to go in 1906 and sold him to the San Francisco Club, but he joined the Williamsport, Tri-State Club, then not under the National agreement. When the Tri-State League joined organized ball, Street rejoined the San Francisco Club and did so well that he was secured by Washington. Street is a Southerner by birth, Huntsville, Ala., being his native place, and he was

28 years of age September 27. He played with Jackson, Tenn., in 1900 and after devoting two years to study played in the "Kitty" League in 1903, rapidly advancing thereafter to the highest company. He acquired national fame by his feat in catching a ball thrown from the top of the Washington Monument in Washington, D. C., August 21, 1908.

There are many, in fact, who consider Street the best of the present day corps of catchers.

But for George Gibson's immense season with the Pirates, also the Nationals' horrible showing in the American League race, Street would have attracted far more attention than he did.

Gibson worked in 150 of the Pirates' 154 games. Also in all seven World's Championship scraps with the Tigers. Street got in 137 of Washington's 156.

Gibson started his record-breaking career in 1909 when he put together his record of 140 successive performances.

Street, the busy Washingtonian, was the only American League receiver who took part in over 100 games in 1909. His total was 137, Sullivan, 97; Thomas, 84, and Schmidt, 81, were the other regular toilers.

Street would have raised his total but for quitting the Nationals; laying off, or becoming lost, or something or other, in midseason. He was gone a week or so. Otherwise he would have given Gibson a greater run—passed the 140 game notch anyhow.

JOE SUGDEN—Joe Sugden, once the catcher of the St. Louis American League team, was once a member of Anson's Chicago White Stockings and one of the best receivers known.

BILLY SULLIVAN—When Fielder Jones left the Chicago White Sox, Comiskey at the twelfth hour had to look about for another manager.

In the breach he selected his great catcher, Billy Sullivan, who managed the team all of last season.

Sullivan has been one of the leading catchers of the country for many seasons. He started his career with Dubuque and later signed with Columbus.

In 1899 he was sold to the Boston Nationals, and when the baseball war broke out in 1901 he joined the Chicago Americans.

Sullivan's first desire when he entered professional baseball was to shine as an infielder, and he played short until an accident left his team without a catcher. Without any previous experience he was put in to catch and found it was his natural position, and he remained in it with success ever since. Indeed, today there is no man playing behind the bat in either league that in all-round play has the edge on Sullivan.

On August 24, 1910, Catcher "Billy" Sullivan of the Chicago Americans repeated the feat of Catcher Charles Street of the Washington American League team last year, in catching a baseball thrown from a window at the top of the Washington monument, a drop of 542 feet.

The ball was tossed from the top of the monument by Pitcher Ed Walsh of the Chicago team. It was only after twenty-three attempts that Sullivan finally caught the ball, although he succeeded several times in so gauging the sphere as to get it in his mitt. The speed of the ball was so terrific, however, that he was unable to hold it. It is estimated that the ball was

115

traveling at the rate of 161 feet a second when caught.

Several members of the Chicago team, including Collins and "Doc" White. Trainer Quirk of the Washington team and a few government officials witnessed the feat.

While the feat has been attempted many times in past years, only Street heretofore was able to accomplish it. His feat was performed during the summer of 1908 on the thirteenth attempt.

Sullivan subsequently caught two more balls thrown from the monument window. After observing Sullivan's first attempts and ultimate success, "Doc" White suggested that the balls should be thrown farther afield. He ascended the monument and, standing well back within the window, hurled ball after ball as far out as he could. Sullivan caught the first one and to show that it was no accident he also caught the fifth. Of ten balls thrown by White the catcher could get under only one other and he was unable to hold that one.

TOM SULLIVAN—St. Louis catcher, who in his day was considered the best throwing receiver in the business.

St. Louis from the earliest days of baseball gave many great catchers to the major leagues.

Frank Flint, Tom Dolan, Tom Sullivan, George Baker, Frank Decker, Jack O'-Connor, Heine Peitz and Packie Dillon are only a few of them.

They were all of them great players and one of the very best of them was Tom Sullivan, who caught Jimmy Galvin's pitching when the latter pitched for the Reds on the old Compton Avenue grounds near the Missouri Pacific Railway tracks in St. Louis.

Sullivan caught Galvin's speediest delivery without the aid of gloves, mask or any of the present-day contrivances and caught them beautifully. He was a great thrower, too, this boy, and there were few stolen bases when he was doing the receiving.

Sullivan was a genial, kindly lad without an enemy in the world. After his day as a player he passed the time mostly with old friends in the "Patch." One night the boy started to walk from the "Patch' to the St. Louis Poor House. He had a friend out there employed in one of the city departments. It was a cold night and in the long walk over the hill Sullivan had his hands frozen and a few days later to save his life they were amputated. Thus the lad who was one of the first to catch the speediest delivery close to the bat and who was rated for his skill as a receiver, thrower and batsman was left a hopeless cripple and his scores of friends in the "Patch" always referred to him as "Poor Tom." When he died out there in the Fall of 1909 the Cullinane

brothers, William and Michael, who had been his life-long friends, saw that he was given christian burial.

EDWARD F. SWEENY—Edward F. Sweeny, is the fine young catcher of the New York Americans.

This promising young receiver was born in Chicago, July 19, 1888, and caught for St. Ignatius College in 1903. In 1904 and 1905 he played with Aurora, Ill., and in the following season was with Columbus, S. C., in the South Atlantic League, thence going to Atlanta, Ga., where his fine work attracted a deal of attention. This led to his purchase from the Atlantic Club by the New York Americans. He stands six feet, one inch in height and weighs 190 pounds.

IRA THOMAS—There are few better men behind the bat than Ira Thomas, the stalwart young catcher of the Philadelphia American League Club, who hails from Ballston Spa, N. Y., where he was born January 22, 1881.

In his boyhood Thomas' people removed to Collinsville, N. Y., and from there he went to Birmingham of the Southern League, where his work in 1905 caused him to be bought by the St. Louis Browns of the American League.

For the St. Louis team he played the outfield his first year and second base in 1907. By a trade he went to the New York Highlanders that Fall and after playing a few months with the Highlanders in 1908, figured in a deal whereby he became the property of the Boston Americans. In 1908 he was utility man, but in 1909 while starting out in the same capacity he played almost steadily either in the outfield or at second base. He has played better by far for Boston than he did for St. Louis or New York.

Thomas stands five feet, eight and one-half inches, and weighs one hundred and seventy-six pounds.

A. E. WILSON—A. E. Wilson is one of the junior members of the New York Giants' catching staff who finished his second season in the big league in the Fall of 1910. In 1909 season Wilson caught in seventeen games and out of sixty-eight chances he accepted sixty-seven perfectly. Of course, with Schlei and Meyers working regularly as the Giants' main catchers, Wilson was not given much chance to show his worth.

CHARLES L. ZIMMER—A great catcher and a stalwart fine fellow was Charles L. Zimmer, who led the catchers in the record of 1894.

Zimmer played with the Cleveland National League Club that season, handling the speedy pitching of Cy. Young.

He was one of the great Cleveland Club that had in its list such then great players as McAleer, McKeon, Burkett, Young, Childs and others.

JAMES P. ARCHER.
The Great Catcher of the Chicago National League Team.

THE NATIONAL GAME.

THE GREAT PITCHERS.

A LIST OF THE MEN WHO DID SPLENDID TWIRLING FOR THE CLUBS OF THE OLD PROFESSIONAL ASSOCIATION AND THE NATIONAL LEAGUE.

This is a list of the pitchers who did the best work in championship games in the old Professional Association and then in the National League from 1871 to 1909 inclusive. The list gives the complete record of pitchers who pitched in twenty-five games or over and who had the highest percentage of victories for each year in championship games from 1871 to 1909 inclusive:

Year.	Name. Club.	No. Games.	Pct. Won.	Year.	Name. Club.	No. Games.	Pct. Won.
1871	Dick McBride—Athletics, Phila..	25	.750	1891	William Hutchinson—Chicago....	63	.696
1872	A. G. Spalding—Boston............	47	.830	1892	John E. Stivetts—Boston.........	47	.702
1873	A. G. Spalding—Boston............	60	.729	1893	F. Killen—Pittsburg	44	.772
1874	A. G. Spalding—Boston............	60	.717	1894	J. Meekin—New York	47	.790
1875	A. G. Spalding—Boston............	63	.899	1895	W. Hoffer—Baltimore.............	35	.323
1876	A. G. Spalding—Chicago...........	60	.783	1896	W. Hoffer—Baltimore.............	35	.823
1877	Thomas Bond—Boston.............	49	.646	1897	Amos Rusie—New York..........	37	.784
1878	Thomas Bond—Boston.............	59	.683	1898	E. M. Lewis—Boston.............	34	.757
1879	John M. Ward—Providence.......	65	.702	1899	James Hughes—Brooklyn.......	34	.823
1880	L. Corcoran—Chicago.............	56	.798	1900	Joseph McGinnity—Brooklyn...	41	.769
1881	L. Corcoran—Chicago.............	45	.667	1901	Jack Chesbro—Pittsburg.........	30	.700
1882	F. E. Goldsmith—Chicago.........	43	.655	1902	Jack Chesbro—Pittsburg.........	33	.818
1883	Jas. E. Whitney—Boston..........	62	.643	1903	Sam Leever—Pittsburg...........	33	.800
1884	Chas. Radbourne—Providence....	72	.838	1904	Joseph McGinnity—New York ...	51	.814
1885	J. G. Clarkson—Chicago.......	70	.790	1905	Sam Leever—Pittsburg............	33	.800
1886	C. B. Baldwin—Detroit...........	56	.750	1906	Edward Reulbach—Chicago.......	33	.826
1887	C. J. Ferguson—Phila.............	35	.686	1907	Edward Reulbach—Chicago.......	27	.810
1888	Timothy J. Keefe—New York.....	47	.745	1908	Edward Reulbach—Chicago.......	31	.774
1889	John G. Clarkson—Boston........	72	.736	1909	C. Mathewson—New York	37	.806
1890	T. J. Lovett—Brooklyn............	42	.738	1909	H. Camnitz—Pittsburg	41	.806
				1910	Scanlon—Brooklyn	34	1.000

THE LEADING TWIRLERS.

A LIST OF THOSE WHO PITCHED BEST FOR THE CLUBS OF THE AMERICAN LEAGUE SINCE ITS INITIAL YEAR.

These are the men who led in the pitching record in the games played by the clubs of the American League since the initial season of that body:

Year.	Name. Club.	No. Games.	Pct. Won.	Year.	Name. Club.	No. Games.	Pct. Won.
1900	Miller—Detroit	26	.731	1905	Ed Waddell—Philadelphia.........	38	.730
1901	Clark Griffith—Chicago...........	31	.774	1906	Ed S. Plank—Philadelphia........	25	.760
1902	Ed Waddell, Philadelphia.........	30	.755	1907	W. Donovan—Detroit..............	29	.862
1903	Earl Moore—Cleveland.............	29	.759	1908	Ed Walsh—Chicago................	66	.727
1904	John Chesbro—New York.........	53	.774	1909	Geo. Mullin—Detroit.......:......	37	.781
				1910	Young—Chicago	27	1.000

At the top of the list of pitchers who have the best record for work done from 1871, when baseball first became prominent, to the 1909 season appears the name of Dick McBride, who in 1871 was the pitcher of the Athletic club of Philadelphia.

In 1872 A. G. Spalding held the proud place at the top of the pitchers' column, and that he was a remarkable player in his day is proved by the fact that he remained at the top for five consecutive years.

Both McBride and Spalding pitched underhand, delivering the ball from below the waist. They were both right-handed players.

Thomas Bond of the Bostons of 1877 and 1878 was the first of the great speed merchants and one of the first to throw the ball instead of to pitch it.

John M. Ward of the Providence team of 1879 was another of the speedy throwers.

Larry Corcoran of the Chicago White Stockings, who was the champion pitcher of 1880 and 1881, was a small man, but he had great speed and a great team behind him.

Fred Goldsmith, also of the Chicago White Stockings, who led in 1882, was a stalwart fellow, but much of his success might be attributed to the magnificent support received from the Chicago players that season.

THE NATIONAL GAME.

Jim Whitney of the Bostons, who led in 1883, and Chas. Radbourne of Providence, who was the leader in 1884, were both wonderful players and had terrific speed as well as perfect control.

John G. Clarkson of the Chicago White Stockings, who followed them, leading all in 1885, was a man of medium size, but with only moderate speed. His great success was due to his magnificent judgment, level head and wonderful control.

Charles Baldwin, leader in 1886, known by Detroit enthusiasts as "Lady" Baldwin, owing to his gentlemanly and kindly ways, was the first left-handed pitcher to reach the top, and he was the mainstay of the great Detroit team when they won the World's Championship in 1887.

Chas. J. Ferguson of the Philadelphias was the leader in 1887. He was at that time the pitcher and mainstay of Harry Wright's Philadelphia Athletics. Ferguson was perhaps the greatest pitcher that ever lived. He combined all the points to make him great. He had a magnificent arm, a clear eye, pluck and control. He could throw a ball with terrific speed, and he had absolute control of the sphere at all times. He was of great use to his team outside of his aid in the pitcher's points, for he was one of the best left-handed batsmen known to the game.

Tim Keefe of the New York Giants in 1888 succeeded Ferguson as premier pitcher of the National League. Keefe was a tall, powerful man, who had won fame as the pitcher of the Metropolitans of the American Association. He did wonderful work for the New York League team. Keefe's forte was speed and perfect control.

Clarkson, who had led all in 1885, came out as the leader again in 1889, this time being with the Boston Club and having even better speed and control than when he had first won the leading place.

Lovett of Brooklyn carried off the honors in 1891 and Jack Stivetts captured them while with Boston in 1892. They were morning glories, disappearing soon from the center of the baseball stage.

Killen of Pittsburg, the leader in 1893; Meekin, the prize pitcher of New York in 1894, and Hoffer, who carried off the prize in 1895 and 1896, while with Baltimore, were not remarkable as pitchers, their support having helped them greatly to their positions.

The year 1897, however, brought out a phenomenon in the person of Amos Rusie, a young Hoosier giant, who pitched remarkable ball that season for the New York Giants.

In 1898 E. M. Lewis of Boston, and in 1899 James Hughes of Brooklyn, took the leading place, but were not considered wonders.

Joe McGinnity of New York, who followed them, however, and who won leading honors in 1900, was a speed marvel and held his own so well that he was named "The Iron Man."

Jack Chesbro of Pittsburg was the champion pitcher in 1901 and 1902, and Sam Leever of the same club won the honor in 1903. The splendid work of these two was greatly aided by the magnificent support given them by the Pittsburg Club.

In 1904 "Iron Man" McGinnity came back into the limelight, pitching great ball for the New York Giants and helping them capture the League flag of that season, as well as leading honors for himself in the pitching line.

In 1905 Sam Leever carried off leading honors when it came to pitching in the National League. He was with Pittsburg.

Edward Reulbach, a St. Louis boy, playing with the Chicago National League team, followed Leever, leading the League pitchers in 1906, 1907 and 1908 and proving himself one of the best and speediest pitchers the baseball world has ever known.

Now, cutting away from record figures, I give a list, arranged alphabetically, of the pitchers who have belonged to and who are now playing in the National League, in the American League and who played in the old major league organizations. The list is as follows:

CHARLES B. ADAMS—Charles B. Adams, the young pitcher who officiated in the last and deciding game of the World's Series in 1909, between Pittsburg and Detroit, was never famous until then.

His success in that memorable game called attention to the fact that he had excelled all other pitchers in the great series, and that in coolness, fine, steady delivery, effectiveness and all that, he has never been excelled in a series of games where the real critical test had come as in this series of wonderful battles.

His great pitching, in fact, was the one thing that saved Pittsburg from losing the world's flag of 1909.

Compared to other great pitchers or the National League, Adams is only a spring chicken.

He commenced his professional career in 1905, playing with the Parsons, Kansas, team, which was then a member of the Missouri Valley League.

Adams was born in 1888 in Tipton, Indiana; he stands five feet eleven and one-half inches and weighs 180 pounds. He played in 1905 with Parsons, Kansas, in the Missouri Valley League; 1906 and 1907 with the St. Louis Nationals and with Denver, in the Western League; 1908 with Louisville, in the American Association, and in 1909 with Pittsburg.

Adams, a Mount Moriah, Missouri, boy, who probably made $6,000 by playing baseball last season and pitching for Pittsburg in three of the four games they won over Detroit in the world's championship games, thereby entering the class of the world's best pitchers, owes his success, in a measure, it is said, to a Princeton, Missouri, boy.

Walter Steckman, a member of the Princeton team about seven years ago, gave Adams his first instructions in pitching. While Steckman turned to the profession of making newspapers, Adams stuck to the curves and won fame. Pittsburg is now the champion ball club of the world, and Adams is its best pitcher. He has a fine record. Of twenty games he pitched last season, he won seventeen.

Charley Adams, or "Babe" Adams, as the ball players call him because of his youth, was reared on a farm near Mount Moriah, Missouri, a little inland town fifteen miles from Princeton. There he "skinned" mules and held the plow handles in the Summer time, and in the Winter attended school in the country districts. He grew to be a big, strapping fellow, and when Fred Coffman, the Mount Moriah barber, organized a base-

119

ball club among the boys in the neighborhood, Adams was put in as pitcher, because he had a good arm and power behind it.

Adams, then about eighteen years old, developed much speed and became known in the neighborhood as a good pitcher. The Mount Moriah Club won nearly all the games it played that season. Adams, however, was throwing only a straight ball.

The making of Adams came the next season, so the story goes. The Mount Moriah and Lamoni, Iowa, teams met at Blythedale to play a match game. Mount Moriah had quite a reputation, and Lamoni, in order to win, gathered a bunch of the best players in the country. With the Lamoni team were Walter Steckman and Joe Holmes. Steckman was shortstop and Holmes pitcher. The bunch landed on Adams hot and heavy and the Mount Moriah boys went down to defeat.

Adams felt badly over the defeat. After the game he and Steckman were talking it over, and Steckman tried to console him. While Steckman was not a pitcher, he was on to the curve, which then was rather new to the boys. He showed Adams how to grasp the ball for the different twists, and to let loose the whirlers which had so mystified the boys. Adams went home and got busy. In a short time he had mastered the curve and was the acknowledged champion of the neighborhood. His speed behind the twist did the business.

Adams' fame spread. When he was nineteen years old he signed with a salaried team playing at Parsons, Kansas. Next he went to the St. Louis Cardinals, then to Denver. The Denver team sold him to Pittsburg for $5,000. In 1908 Pittsburg "farmed" him out to Louisville. He made good there and in 1909 Pittsburg held him in its own club. That Adams has profited by the instructions given him by a Princeton boy is shown by his record last year.

Adams is now about twenty-six years old, and since quite young he has made his home with Lee Sarver, a farmer of Mount Moriah. Mr. Sarver recognized his ability as a pitcher and allowed him much time for practice. Now Mr. Sarver, it is said, is a typical baseball fan. At each game Adams pitched Sarver got the results by wire as soon as the game was over. Sarver's home in Mount Moriah in the last two weeks of the 1909 World's Championship campaign, was baseball headquarters for the entire neighborhood. Fans went there to get the results of the games and the wires from surrounding towns were kept hot asking for the news.

And Adams, although at the top, has not forgotten his benefactor. "Come out and see me. I'll pay all expenses and show you the best time of your life," is said to have been the message sent by Adams at Detroit to Sarver. Mr. Sarver was as much elated over the young man's success as Adams himself. And the whole town and the entire country about was just as proud of him. When Adams returned to Mount Moriah he was given a bigger reception than would be given President Taft should he light there.

In the spring of 1909 Adams was married to a boyhood schoolmate and sweetheart, a Miss Wright, at Mount Moriah.

Adams' great pitching ability was first recognized by John J. McCloskey, now manager of the Milwaukee Club, who has brought out many now famous players, among them both Adams and Captain Fred Clarke of the Champion Pittsburgs.

McCloskey brought Adams to St. Louis in 1906 to pitch for the Cardinals. He remained here in 1906 and 1907, but at the tail end of the latter season he was released to Denver. In 1908 he was transferred from Denver to the Louisville Club of the American Association, and he remained there until the commencement of the 1909 season, when he was drafted by Pittsburg.

NICHOLAS ALTROCK—Nicholas Altrock, a left-handed pitcher, now with Minneapolis and formerly with the Chicago White Sox, was born in Cincinnati, September 15, 1876. By trade he was a shoemaker, and while working at that also acquired distinction as a pitcher. He secured an engagement with Grand Rapids in 1898 and was purchased from that club by Louisville. He played with Oswego in 1900 and was traded by that club to Toronto. In 1901 he was with Los Angeles and in 1902 with Milwaukee. The Boston Americans had him in 1903, but didn't use him, as he was not in shape to work. He was with the Chicago White Sox when they were winning a World's Championship.

LEON AMES—Leon Ames is one of the right-hand speed merchants of the National League. He is a giant, with a world of speed. In the 1910 season, up to August, he pitched fifteen games for the New York National League team, winning eight of them. Ames is a veteran and he, with Mathewson, McGinnity, Wiltse and Dummy Taylor made up the pitching staff for the New York Giants in 1904 and 1905, when they were winning championships. In 1909, when New York ran Pittsburg a close race, Ames again showed his class, winning fifteen of the twenty-five games he pitched.

FRANK ARELLANES — Frank Arellanes of the Boston American League team of 1910 joined that team in their 1909 season. He was brought to Boston from the Pacific Coast League, being one of Fred Lake's discoveries. He pitched twenty-eight games for Boston in their 1909 season, winning sixteen of them. In 1910, up to August, he was not in the best form, pitching in twelve games and winning six of them.

FRANK ATKINS—Frank Atkins is one of the younger pitchers of Connie Mack's strong pitching staff and during the season of 1910 he pitched very fair ball. He was not a regular on the staff up to August, 1910, and had pitched in but three games. He won two and lost one. Atkins shows considerable promise and in the 1911 season should win a regular position on Mack's pitching staff.

LESTER BACHMAN—Lester Bachman joined the St. Louis Cardinal team in the Spring of 1909, he is a great big strapping fellow, possessed of a great deal of speed, but so far since showing in big league company, has shown a decided inclination to wildness. Bachman, so his manager thinks, should make good. Up to August, 1910, he took part in ten games, of which number he won three.

WILLIAM BAILEY—William Bailey is one of the pitchers of the staff of the St.

CHARLES B. ADAMS.

The above is a portrait of Charles B. Adams, the pitcher who did more than any other player with the Pittsburg team to win the World's Championship for that club in 1909.

Louis American League team. Bailey is a native of Fort Smith, Arkansas, where he was born April 12, 1889, so it will be seen that he has just attained his majority. He made Houston, Texas, his home when a boy, and still resides there. Bailey played with Austin, Texas, in 1906, and was with that club in August, 1907, when the St. Louis Americans secured his release. He joined the Browns in September of that year and has been with them ever since. Bailey made a very creditable record in 1909, landing eleven victories out of twenty-three games for the St. Louis Browns. Bailey, who is the youngest member of the Browns' team, has everything a pitcher should have but weight. The climate of his former home, Texas, is unsuited to the lad's constitution, and President Hedges brought Bailey to St. Louis to live.

JESSE BAKER—Jesse Baker is one of the pitching staff of the Chicago White Stockings. Comiskey purchased his release in August, 1910, from the Spokane Club of the Northwestern League, giving $6,000 and two other players in exchange for the release of Baker, who was said to be the most promising young pitcher in the Northwest in the 1910 season.

CYRUS BARGER—Cy Barger pitched good ball for the Brooklyn team in their 1909 season. Up to August, 1910, he had won ten out of seventeen games pitched for them, this being a fine record in view of the fact that Brooklyn this year was never a real contender for the pennant.

FRED L. BEEBE—Fred L. Beebe is one of the standbys of the pitching corps of the Cincinnati National League team. He is a native of Lincoln, Nebraska, and was born there December 31, 1880. He played with the University of Illinois at Champaign, Illinois, on George Huff's team, in 1901, and did fine work there that season and the two following—1902-1903. The next year he worked at his profession of electrical engineering, and played Saturdays and Sundays with semi-professional teams. In 1905 he played with Oshkosh in the Wisconsin State League, which finished second in the race. In the spring of 1906 he joined the Chicago Nationals, and in July was traded to St. Louis for Pitcher Jack Taylor. From St. Louis he went to Cincinnati, where he is now. He stands six feet and weighs 177 pounds when in condition.

GEORGE G. BELL—George G. Bell is one of the regular pitchers of the Brooklyn National League Club. He is a right-hander, and has been a consistent winner in the National League for years. He is another one of the so-called iron men of the profession. Each season he has taken part in as many as thirty or forty games. In 1909 he pitched in thirty-one games, and, with a weak team behind him, he won sixteen and lost fifteen. This year up to August he maintained his high standard, winning his share of the games.

CHARLES A. BENDER—Charles A. Bender is the Carlyle Indian University member who is now known as the crack right-handed pitcher of the Athletics of Philadelphia. He has for several years been one of the leading pitchers of the American League. He joined the Athletics in their 1903 season, and, with Waddell and Plank as his comrades in the

pitching department, helped the Athletics capture the 1905 pennant. He was the only one of the Athletics' pitching staff of that year to pitch a winning game against the New York Nationals in the world's pennant series, he winning his contest by 3 to 0. Bender is one of the biggest men in the business, standing six feet two inches and weighing two hundred pounds. In 1905 he pitched twenty-five full games, winning eighteen and losing seven. He promises to do even better in this 1910 year, proving that Indians are able to "come back" with a vengeance. Up to August in the 1910 season he had pitched twenty-nine games for the Athletics, of which he won seventeen.

REUBEN BENTON—Reuben Benton is the giant—six feet two inches tall—phenomenal pitcher whose release Clark Griffith of the Cincinnati Reds purchased from the Nashville Club of the Southern Association. Griffith paid $5,000 cash for this man, the highest price ever paid up to that time for an untried pitcher in the Southern Association.

CHARLES BERGER—Charles Berger is twenty-five years of age and was born at LaSalle, Indiana. He pitched for Muncie, Indiana, in the spring of 1903 and afterwards pitched for Piqua, Ohio. He did such good work in independent ball that he attracted the attention of the Columbus owners, and was secured in August of that season.

In his first season he landed six games out of nine; in 1905 he landed twenty-five and lost fourteen, Gus Dorner leading the league with twenty victories and eight defeats, Pat Flaherty being second with twenty-three victories and nine defeats.

JOE BLONG—Joe Blong, with George Washington Bradley, was the pitcher of the first St. Louis Browns, the team that represented St. Louis in the National League in 1875. A fine, speedy twirler was Joe and he held his own in the limelight of professional baseball for many a day. With his brother, Andy Blong, Joe was at one time a member of the St. Louis Reds. Both the Blongs are dead, but there are younger Blongs left who may some day be heard of in the professional baseball field.

THOMAS BOND—One of the fine pitchers of the olden days who had great speed and curves was Tommy Bond of the Boston Club.

He won his spurs with Boston's great League team and finished his career as the speedy pitcher of the Boston Unions, the team managed in 1884 by Tim Murnane, now one of the best-known baseball writers in America.

It was Bond who once and for all settled the question of curving the ball.

In 1878, when George Wright's Boston Reds, of which team Bond was a member, were playing in Cincinnati, two ten-foot fences were erected about twenty yards apart, with a post between them and all on a line.

Bond, a right-handed pitcher, stood at the left of one fence, and after two trials threw a ball which went to the right of the post, and then finished to the left of the second fence. He repeated the feat several times. Some of the doubters said the wind was responsible for the queer curve of the ball. To prove it was not, Wright stationed Mitchell, a left handed pitcher, to the right of the first fence.

JOHN M. WARD.

John M. Ward was the pitcher of the first and famous New York Giants and later their short-fielder and captain.

Mitchell threw a curve ball to the left of the post which finished to the right of the second fence. This settled it with all hands, and the news of the discovery of the curve ball was telegraphed to all parts of the country.

ASA BRAINARD—Asa Brainard, the premier pitcher of the Cincinnati Red Stockings of 1868 and 1869, was one of the first twirlers.

Brainard was quite English in appearance, being of rather delicate frame and appearing in the field wearing English mutton-chop whiskers.

He pitched an underhand ball, but with more speed than most pitchers of his time, and that helped make him effective.

With Harry Wright he did all the pitching for the Cincinnati Reds in the memorable tours they made in 1868 and 1869.

THEODORE BREITENSTEIN — Theodore Breitenstein was at one time the greatest left-handed pitcher in America.

That was in the middle 'nineties when he pitched for St. Louis.

And no left-handed pitcher has lasted longer in baseball than this St. Louis boy.

He did his first pitching in 1891 and is yet and in point of actual years service the only two pitchers that outrank him are Young of Cleveland and Bill Hart of Chattanooga.

Theo. Breitenstein saw the light of day for the first time on June 8, 1869, and St. Louis was the first place he ever played ball. When he was 22 years of age he joined the Grand Rapids team of the then newly-formed Northwestern league. This was his first attempt at professional ball, but he had already made a name for himself as an amateur pitcher on the lots of St. Louis.

He did not remain with Grand Rapids very long for Chris Von der Ahe, owner of the St. Louis Browns bought him from the Furniture City team, and August 3, 1891 he reported to St. Louis His debut in the big league was anything but a howling success as he lost both games he worked in.

In 1892 he was on the verge of being discharged time and time again, but Von der Ahe had faith in him and although he lost 20 games and won but five that season he was with St. Louis the following season. From this time on he developed into a wonder. The Cincinatti Club liked him so well that $7,500 was paid for his release. This was in 1897.

He remained with Cincinatti until 1901, when he once more returned to St. Louis It was while he was in Cincinnati that he pitched his first no-hit no-run game.

Ereitenstein's second advent as a St. Louis player was no more a success than his first, for he again lost the first two games he pitched. Then came the order for all major league clubs to cut down to 16 men and Theo. was let go to St. Paul.

He did not like the atmosphere of St. Paul any too well and he quit the team and returned to St. Louis to attend to his business interests. Charlie Frank, who was then manager of the Memphis club of the Southern league paid a short visit to St. Louis and when he returned to Memphis he had Theo's name to a contract.

The next season Frank left Memphis and took up the management of the New Orleans club of the same league and Breitenstein followed him there. This was back in 1903 and Theo is still there, pitching great ball for the Pelicans and it looks as though he would continue to pitch first-class ball for another season or two.

CHARLES E. BROWN—Charles E. Brown, known professionally as "Buster" Brown is the big right handed pitcher of the Boston Nationals. He played with the St. Louis Cardinals before going to the Hub previous to which he was the star boxman of O'Rourke's Omaha Western League champions.

MORDECAI BROWN—Mordecai Brown, the big-gun pitcher of the Chicago Cubs is one of the greatest men in his position that ever lived.

He has done as much as any other man to make the Chicago Cubs the invincible combination they are.

Brown was born in the coal mine regions near Brazil, Indiana. Talking about his wonderful career one day he said:

"I got my start as pitcher by accident in Brazil. I was playing with the Coxville team, which I do believe was the best amateur team ever got together. We were to play the Brazil salaried team. There was Schultz, a little pitcher from Chicago, who had the curves; Tub Noonan, Bob Berryhill and others who went to fast company afterwards. The boys at Coxville sent all the money they could raise to bet on us. Every player on our team was a coal miner. Just before time for calling the game our pitcher fell down. He was the only twirler we had. I was playing third, and had never pitched a game in my life.

"John Buckley, our manager, said to me: 'Brownie, we are up against it and you will have to pitch.' I told him I couldn't, but he said I had the best arm and would have to try it. Well, I went in and we beat Brazil 9 to 3. The game I pitched against the Giants in New York two years ago to decide the championship wasn't in it with this game in Brazil. I signed with Brazil and finished the season on salary which was a great treat to me. Good old days, those. All the fun is not to be had in the big leagues."

Although he has been pitching for a long while Brown did not come into his own until four years ago.

Although thirty-one years old and of eight year's experience in professional baseball, he did not loom up as the star that he is until the season of 1906, when his fine pitching was of chief aid in winning the cubs their first championship. Brown began playing professional ball at Terre Haute. He bats on either side of the plate, as every one knows, pitches with his right hand, which was maimed in his early youth by a piece of machinery. The fore-finger is off at the first joint.

He is the best fielding pitcher in the National League.

WILLIAM BURNS—William Burns is the big pitcher released by Washington to the Chicago White Sox in 1909, and with Cincinnati in 1910. He has surprised the best experts by his fine work in the box, for Cincinnati for it was the general impression when Comiskey released him that he was all out. Up to August 1910 he had pitched thirteen games for Cincinatti winning seven of them.

G. CALDWELL—G. Caldwell will be a member of the New York Highlanders' large pitching staff in 1911. Caldwell was purchased from the McKeesport (Pa.) Club where he had made a splendid record as a batsman. Caldwell made his first appearance in professional baseball in McKeesport in the Spring of 1910 and made good.

HOWARD CAMNITZ :— Before the World's Championship series of 1909 between Detroit and Pittsburg was commenced, the manager of the latter club depended largely on Howard Camnitz to help them land winner.

Camnitz had done great work for them in the regular league season. In that time indeed he had been their winning pitcher. But just before the commencement of the World Series of 1909, Camnitz was taken ill, and when he went in to face the Detroits in the second game of that memorable series he was in such a weak and deplorable condition that he was unable to do himself justice. In fact he proved a mark for the Detroit men.

In condition, however, there are few better pitchers in the business today than Camnitz. He is now in his twenty-eighth year, having been born Agust 22, 1881 in Covington, Ky. He stands five feet, eight inches and weighs 168 pounds. Camnitz played in 1902 with Greenville, Miss., in the Cotton States League; 1903, with Vicksburg, Miss.; 1904, with Pittsburg Nationals and Springfield, Ill., in the Three-I League; 1905 and 1906 with Toledo, in the America Association; 1907 to 1910 with Pittsburg.

Few pitchers have shown better work than was shown by Camnitz during the regular season of 1909 and but for the illness which befell him that fall he would undoubtedly have cut a prominent figure in the winning of that flag by Pittsburg.

HARRY CAMNITZ—The two Camnitz boys—Howard and Harry—have one thing in common. Each parts his name in the middle. The Pirate star's cognomen is S. Howard Camnitz, while the Pittsburg signs his name in this wise: R. Harry Camnitz, Jr. Heine Zimmerman of the Cubs, who often has batted against Howard, says that the elder Camnitz is one of those pitchers who puts something on every ball. "Cammy is always trying and never lets down when there is an alleged weak hitter up," declares the Cub player. "Howard is such a hard worker that I doubt if he will last as long as the man who occasionally eases up." Harry Camnitz was with the McKeesport last season and cost Dreyfuss $1,500. Barney says that Camnitz the younger will be just as good a pitcher as his brother in a couple of years. Harry won 27 out of 36 games in the O. and P. league last season.

CHESTER CARMICHAEL—Chester K. Carmichael, one of Billy Smith's pitchers of the Buffalo Eastern League earned a niche in the base ball hall of fame August 15, 1910, by not allowing a single player to reach first base in an Eastern League championship game. The feat was never before performed in the Powers' organization. Jersey City was the victim on its home grounds. Carmichael was farmed out to the Bisons this Spring by Cincinnati. He is due for another trial in the big league and will line up with the Cincinatti Reds in 1910.

ROBERT CARUTHERS—"Bobby" Caruthers who became famous as the pitcher for the St. Louis Browns in the eighties was a right handed pitcher and a very hard hitting left handed batsman.

Caruthers was a Chicago boy and it was his great pitching for the Champion St. Louis Browns in the World's Championship series of 1885 that resulted in the tie that took place in that year between St. Louis and Chicago. In 1886 when St. Louis defeated Chicago in the World's Championship series it was Caruther's grand pitching that had much to do with his side winning.

Caruthers had wonderful speed and perfect control and he was the first pitcher to take the real measure of the, up to that time, invincible Chicago White Stockings.

And besides being a speedy and effective pitcher Caruthers was one of the hardest pluckiest and most timely of left handed batsmen.

That he had a good head was proven later for after quitting the playing end he went to umpiring and for years was one of the best handlers of the indicator in the business.

CHARLES K. CHECH—Charles K. Chech, the well-known pitcher of the Boston American League Club is a native of Madison, Wis., and is 29 years of age. He first attracted attention by his work on the University of Wisconsin team, graduating from the school of pharmacy of that institution in 1901.

He played with St. Paul of the American Association in 1901, 1902, 1903 and 1904, the last two years as a member of a pennant winner.

In 1905 he made his first appearance in major league company with the Cincinnati Reds, pitching that season and a part of the next. He next pitched the latter part of 1906 and the next season, that of 1907 for Toledo. He did so well that Cleveland signed him. He is now playing in the American Association with St. Paul.

JACK CHESBRO—The "Iron Men" of the newer baseball era are no longer "iron men."

Jack Chesbro, leading pitcher of the American League in 1904, is farming today on a big homestead in New England.

Jack is done for, so far as the use of his big league arm is concered. He is not beset with any financial worries, because he saved a great deal of what he made in the days of success.

Jack Chesbro, the North Adams boy, broke into fast company with Pittsburg, reached the zenith of his fame in 1904, when he pitched the New York Americans to within one game of the pennant. He really pitched the pennant away, as well, because it was a wild pitch that gave Boston the deciding game. In that season, Jack, the mainstay of the club, pitched fifty-three games, and won forty-one of them the best major league record for nearly two decades.

That year Chesbro established the record of consecutive games won by pitchers in the American League, with a string of fourteen. Ed Reulbach just escaped passing it in the National League last season, the Giants clipping his wings after fourteen wins. Early in the season Ed worked like one of the backsliders.

Chesbro was born at North Adams, Mass., on June 5, 1877. He began with Springfield, Mass., in 1895; Roanoke, 1896; Richmond, 1897 and to the middle of 1898, when he was purchased by Pittsburg. He remained there until 1893, when he jumped to the New York Americans. He was sent to the Boston Americans last season, but has returned to the New York Americans.

EDWARD V. CICOTTE—Edward V. Cicotte is one of the cleverest pitchers of the American League and his work with the Boston American League Club has been decidedly sensational.

He was born in Detroit, June 19, 1884. He played his first base ball in that city and makes it his home.

He played with the Detroit Club in 1905 and then went to the Augusta Club of the South Atlantic League.

In 1906 he was with Indianapolis in the American Association and in 1907 with the Lincoln, Neb., team of the Western League, from which club he was purchased by the Boston Americans at the close of the season. He has proven one of the steadiest pitchers in the American League and his work has been instrumental in giving that club its high standing in the League race. Physically he is one of the strongest, if not the strongest member of the squad. He is a right-hander and is the originator of the "knuckle ball."

JOHN CLARKSON—Next to Michael J. Kelly and Adrian C. Anson, probably John Clarkson, who pitched for the famous Chicago White Stockings for several seasons, and who twice held leading honors as a twirler was perhaps the most remarkable figure in the history of the game in the Garden City.

Clarkson was a handsome fellow, of medium size, but he was possessed of great strength in his pitching arm and besides great speed he had as good command of the ball as any man that ever played in the position.

When Clarkson passed away in the winter of 1909 Captain Anson said:

"John Clarkson was one of the greatest pitchers that ever lived—many regard him as the greatest, but not many know what an amount of encouragement it took to keep him going.

"Scold him, find fault with him, and he would not pitch at all.

"Say to him after a game: 'Grand work, John, I will probably have to use you again to-morrow, for we've got to have that game,' and he would go out the next day and stand all the batters on their heads.

"In knowing exactly what kind of a ball the batters couldn't hit, and in his ability to serve up just that kind of a ball, John Clarkson probably never had an equal."

LEONARD L. COLE—Perhaps the most important find of the 1910 season is Leonard L. Cole, who last Spring made his debut with the Chicago National League team as a pitcher.

"King" Cole made good with the Cubs from the very beginning. Cole was born at Toledo, a little town of Tama County, Iowa. He is 24 years old and is six feet one and one-half inches tall and weighs in at 180 pounds. His right arm is the one that brings him good money and he is a right-handed batter—though he doesn't brag so much about that. For a youngster of such a short experience he is doing wonderful work, for he began to play professionally at Bay City in 1908. Bay City knew when it had a good thing and kept tight hold of him last year, until the Cubs picked him up at the end of the season. For Cole there was nothing in the farming line necessary. He made good from the start, and appears to have

before him a long and exceptionally brilliant career in the select circles.

ROY W. COLLINS—Roy W. Collins, one of the winning pitchers of the Boston American team in the 1910 season is a new comer to the major league ranks and has surprised all by his wonderful work in his initial season. It was mainly due to the fine work of Collins, Karger and Smith that the Bostons were for a long while during the 1910 season able to canter out in front in the American League race.

RAY COMSTOCK—Ray Comstock is the amateur pitcher of Toledo, Ohio, and was given a trial by the St. Louis Cardinals in the Fall of 1910. For an inexperienced youngster his work loomed up very fair. He will be given a thorough trial next Spring.

JACK COOMBS—Jack Coombs was perhaps the most reliable pitcher on the Athletic Club of Philadelphia during their 1910 season. On August 7, 1910, when the Athletics' crack right-hander defeated the St. Louis Browns at St. Louis, he marked down his twenty-eighth game of the season. He pitched more games than any other twirler in the American League up to that time in the 1910 season. Of the twenty-eight games he won eighteen and lost six, seven of his victories being of the shut-out variety.

Coombs is third in the list of American League twirlers. Ed Karger of the Boston Red Sox and Chief Bender of the Athletics being ahead of him up to August 1, 1910.

It will be seen that Coombs, really never considered a star before the 1910 season, is proving a sensation. He is not only pitching winning ball, but has gone to the mound oftener than any other pitcher in the league. It was Coombs who pitched almost every other day for two weeks at a time when Connie's twirling crew was a trifle to the bad during the latter part of the season.

Of Coombs, Malachai Kittredge, the once famous catcher says:

"Coombs has started to pitch great ball, because he has mastered the greatest of all pitching assets, the drop ball that does not break from the right-handed batters. I don't mean one of those outdrops, but a ball that comes up to the plate squarely in the center and falls from one to two feet without changing its lateral direction. Amos Rusie had that ball and he threw it with tremendous speed. Rusie pitched that drop thing and mixed it up with a fast one in close, and the batter who could meet it with any regularity never lived. They tell me that Ramsey and other old-timers depended on it extensively. Coombs certainly did give a fine exhibition of pitching on his recent appearance in Detroit. Batters like Sam Crawford, who usually hit the ball hard, swung and missed with great frequency. Time after time Crawford hit on top of the drop and nobody seemed able to do much with it."

FRANK J. CORRIDON—Frank J. Corridon is a product of the aristocratic summer resort, Newport, R. I., where he was born November 25, 1880. He pitched for the club of his native city and for Pawtucket in the New England League in 1898, and was with Providence the following season. Then he went to Chicago, playing there in 1903. In the Fall of 1904 he was sold to Philadelphia. In 1906 Corri-

HENRY BOYLE.
Henry Boyle, at one time the speedy pitcher of the St. Louis Unions, the St. Louis member in 1884 of the Union Association.

don, with Kruger and Abbott, were sold to St. Louis, but Corridon refused to come to St. Louis and went to Williamsport of the Tri-State League, but was back in Philadelphia again in 1907. He is six feet in height and weighs 168 pounds. He is now pitching for the St. Louis National League team. Baseball is considerable of a whirligig after all. Corridon was traded by the Philadelphia Nationals to the Cincinnati Club, and immediately afterward he learned that Cincinnati had turned him over to St. Louis. At this rate he was making the rounds with a vengeance.

HARRY COVALESKIE—Harry Covaleskie will line up as a member of the regular pitching staff of the Cincinnati Reds in the Spring of the 1911 season. Covaleskie was turned over to Cincinnati by the Phillies a year ago but he was a bit green and failed to make good. During the past season at Birmingham, Covaleskie recovered his form, and the chances are he will make good on the Reds' staff again.

OTIS CRANDALL—Otis Crandall is one of the star pitchers of the New York Giants Baseball Club who has been doing excellent work for this team for some few seasons. In 1909 Crandall pitched in ten games, winning six and losing four. In 1910 up to August he had taken part in ten contests of which number he won seven and lost three.

JIM CREIGHTON—John C. Chapman, who played in the outfield for the Atlantics of Brooklyn and who is still enjoying life in that city, thinks Tom Pratt, Dick McBride, Martin, Jim Creighton, Arthur Cummings, Bobby Mathews and Al. Spalding were the greatest of the pitchers of the long ago. And Creighton, he thinks, was as good as any of the others, if not speedier and better.

In a recent article in the Boston Magazine, writing about Creighton, Mr. Chapman said:

"I was present at the game between the Excelsiors and the Unions of Morrisiana at which Jim Creighton injured himself. He did it in hitting out a home run. When he had crossed the rubber he turned to George Flanley and said, 'I must have snapped my belt,' and George said, 'I guess not.' It turned out that he had suffered a fatal injury. Nothing could be done for him, and baseball met with a most severe loss. He had wonderful speed, and, with it, splendid command. He was fairly unhittable."

DODE CRISS—Dode Criss came to the St. Louis Browns as a pitcher, but soon was made their pinch hitter. When Abstein was released by the Browns early in the 1910 season Criss was tried at first base and did well there, but later he was retired in favor of Pat Newnam, who is now covering the initial bag for the St. Louis team. Criss is now the general utility player of the St. Louis American League team. He was born at Sherman, Miss., March 19, 1886. He played with the Cleburne, Tex., club in 1906, St. Paul, 1907, and was drafted from that club by St. Louis, where he has since played. He batted .341 in sixty-four games played in 1908, which was the top record of the season in the American League, he sharing honors with Honus Wagner of the National League. In forty-eight times at bat he hit .292 in 1909.

DOUGLAS CROTHERS—Douglas Crothers pitched for the St. Louis Browns in the American Association days of 1883. He also pitched for Cincinnati and other professional teams. Crothers was a fine player in his day and was born and died in St. Louis. At one time he was secretary to the postmaster at St. Louis and while filling that position he often pitched ball for St. Louis amateur teams.

ARTHUR CUMMINGS

The First Pitcher to Ever Curve a Baseball and the Man Who Is Credited With Being the Father of That Art.

ARTHUR CUMMINGS—When I visited the Capitoline grounds in Brooklyn in 1870 I saw Arthur Cummings, to whom old professionals give the credit of being the first pitcher to send in a curved ball.

Cummings was then the pitcher of the Stars of Brooklyn, who styled themselves the Champion Non-Professional Team of America.

When I saw Cummings at work he was facing the Fordham College nine, a team of no mean caliber, and capable of making the best nines of that day play ball.

The populace were amazed at the wonderful work of Cummings. He sent the ball in with such a curve that his opponents, not used to that sort of thing, often nearly broke their necks trying to reach after and hit the ball.

The story of his wonderful work spread so that when Cummings one day went to Boston with the Stars of Brooklyn to play the Harvards, he was called on after the game, which he had won easily, to explain the trick. He did so, claiming that the curve which made the ball shoot away from the batsman as it neared the plate, was acquired simply by the English put on the ball by a lot of deft fingers and aided by a powerful wrist. It was, however, simply the out curve ball which any old pitcher has to-day with other in and up and down shoots to match.

But Cummings got away with it so well that for years he held his own as the "King of the Curve Pitchers."

CLIFTON GARFIELD CURTIS—A fine pitcher is Clifton Garfield Curtis of the Boston Nationals.

Curtis did fine work for the Bostons in 1909 and 1910 and promises to be one of their star men in the future.

Curtis was born in Delaware, Ohio, July 3, 1882, and after gaining the rudiments of the game in that town, pitching for the High School team, he was secured for Fort Wayne in 1904. Cleveland drafted him and he went South with that club, but lacking proper seasoning, was turned over to Milwaukee and remained there until this year, when he was sold to Boston. His cleverest feat was his 1-0 defeat of the Pittsburg club in Boston after that club had won sixteen victories in succession from Boston. He stands six feet two inches and weighs 1.9 pounds.

WILLIAM DINEEN — When William Dineen, toward the close of the 1909 season, asked the management of the St. Louis Americans for his unconditional release, he exhibited an amount of foresight rarely shown by a baseball player. Few, if any, of the diamond stars ever realize the day of retirement is at hand, and generally have to be told by the manager.

"Bill" realized that his pitching arm was gone, and though he might come back for an occasional contest, he could never again pitch ball in his old-time form. He did the wise thing and quit.

It was Big "Bill's" pitching in 1904 for Boston that gave his team its second premiership in the American League race. In the closing days Dineen never faltered, and to his double defeat of Jack Chesbro, the pitching phenomenon of that year, on the last two days of the race, may be attributed Boston's second American League gonfalon.

Dineen, who at one time was a star pitcher for the Boston Club, more recently with St. Louis, and now one of Ban Johnson's umpires, is making good at the latter job. Dineen is right on top of all the plays, and there never will be any overruling of decisions while he is at work with Tom Connolly. They both work together very well. Dineen has been going along so well that the president of the American League, it is said, has boosted his salary. That's a very good sign that he is a good umpire.

FRANK DONAHUE—Frank Donahue, or "Red" Donahue, as he was always called, was at one time the leading pitcher of the Detroit American League Club.

Donahue retired in 1907 to go into the hotel business in Philadelphia.

He was known as the brainiest boxman in the history of latter-day baseball.

WILD BILL DONOVAN—"Wild" Bill Donovan, one of Detroit's great pitchers, is from Lawrence, Mass.

He was born there in 1877 and has played professionally with the clubs of Sunbury, Pawtucket and Waterbury, Mass.; Washington, D. C., Brooklyn and Detroit.

Like Mullin, Detroit's other great pitcher, Donovan is a giant and pitches, fields and hits equally well. He is right-handed in all things.

Donovan helped win the American League championship for Detroit in 1908.

He was Detroit's premier pitcher in 1908. Donovan, however, through the 1909 season with Detroit, could not get into his stride and he did nothing worth mentioning until he went in against Pittsburg in the second game of the 1909 world's series.

Donovan had been acquainted with major league baseball since 1898, when he made his big league debut as a member of the Washington National League Club. He played his first ball around Philadelphia and branched into the professional side of the game in 1895 with Sunbury, Pa., where he pitched for two years. He was with Pawtucket and Waterbury in 1897 and was purchased by Washington in 1898.

In 1899, when the Washington Club disbanded, Donovan went to the Brooklyn Club, with which he played four years. In 1902, just before the close of the war between the American and National leagues, Donovan signed a Detroit contract and has played there ever since. When in good shape Donovan has fine speed, a wonderful break on his fast ball and is one of the best fielding pitchers in the country. For the last two years Donovan has twirled great ball. In 1907 he won twenty-five out of twenty-nine games pitched, leading the league. In the 1908 season he won eighteen out of twenty-five.

JOE DOYLE—Joe Doyle was one of the pitchers of the New York American League team in its 1910 season. He pitched but two games for them in the first three months of the 1910 year. In 1909 he pitched fourteen games for the Highlanders, winning eight and losing six, a very good record with a losing team. In 1910 he started in with a lame arm and was unable to appear in his regular turn in the firing line. However on his 1909 form he showed class.

LOUIS DRUCKE—Louis Drucke, the youngest pitcher of the New York Giants, has come into the limelight of baseball like a meteor.

Drucke, known in Texas as "The Pride of the Brazos Valley," and in New York as the rising young athlete, was a college student one year ago. In three months he accomplished the step from college baseball to service in the major league, his minor league experience being brief, but long enough for Manager McGraw to recognize the lad's unusual ability.

Drucke graduated from Texas Christian University of Waco in June, 1909, and immediately joined the Dallas team of the Texas League. Drucke pitched twice a week and lost only two or three games. He was considered the best pitcher in the Texas League despite his lack of experience in professional baseball, and that was an honor, considering the fact that several twirlers from that league were corralled by major league scouts last Fall.

McGraw closed a deal for the purchase of Drucke in July, 1909, or, rather, he then exercised an option and bought the youngster's release for $2,000. But Drucke's experience with McGraw dates back to the Spring of 1908, when the giants made their first trip to Texas for training purposes.

The Giants that season won something like thirty-four exhibition games in the Lone Star State. They were beaten only once, and Drucke, then a green college pitcher, turned the trick.

Drucke is 21 years old and a strapping, long-armed fellow. He has been well advised by Matthewson, and to some extent has copied the delivery of the "Big Six." Like Matthewson, he indulges in no preliminary swing, but simply raises both hands above his head and lets go.

He has a very effective drop curve, something like Matty's "fadeaway."

J. DYGERT—J. Dygert is the toy pitcher of the Athletics of the American League. He only weighs 115 pounds, but this is made up mostly of nerve and muscle. Clubs who have opposed the Athletics say the little fellow has bluffed his way through the American League ever since Connie Mack discovered him at New Orleans in 1904 where he was the pride of the South.

CHICKERING F. EVANS—Chickering F. Evans of the Boston Nationals was born at Arlington, Vt., September 10, 1888. He first pitched for the Burnburton Seminary nine of Manchester, Vt., being the mainstay of his school nine in the box for three years.

Then he pitched semi-professional ball one season (1907) at Hoosick Falls. His work there attracted the attention of Tommy Dowd, the well-known coach of Williams College, who has managed successfully clubs in Holyoke, Hartford and New Bedford, and Dowd signed Evans for the Hartford Club of 1908.

Evans in 1909 pitched for the Hartford Club. Hartford gave Evans to Boston for Pitcher McCarthy and $1,500. On July 22, 1908, against Bridgeport, he allowed no hits, gave no base on balls, and did not hit a man with a pitched ball.

ROBERT EWING—Robert Ewing is the big right-hander, formerly of the Cincinnati Club, but now with the Philadelphia National League team, whom he joined this Spring. Ewing pitches with tremendous speed. He pitched twenty-three games for Cincinnati in 1909, winning eleven and losing twelve. With Philadelphia in the 1910 season up to August he had pitched fourteen games and won six of them.

FREDERICK P. FALKENBERG—Frederick P. Falkenberg of the Cleveland Club is perhaps the tallest man playing in the major baseball leagues.

He stands six feet four inches in height. Falkenberg was born in Chicago December 17, 1890. He pitched for the University of Illinois from 1899 to 1902, doing such good work as to attract general attention and cause a demand for his services from professional clubs.

He played with the Worcester (Mass.) Eastern League team in 1902, and in 1903 with the Pittsburg Club. The following season saw him with Toronto, and from 1905 to 1908 he was with Washington. Cleveland then purchased Falkenberg and Altizer for $5,000, and he is still with the Cleveland Club.

G. C. FERGUSON—G. C. Ferguson, one on the pitching staff of the Boston Nationals in their 1910 season, is one of the coming great pitchers of the major leagues. Ferguson made one of the most peculiar records yet chronicled in baseball in the game he pitched against the St. Louis Cardinals of the National League, on Tuesday, May 18, at Boston. He had the St. Louis team blanked up to the last inning when the visitors sailed in and made three runs, Ferguson passing the first four men at bat in that inning, after having struck out the three men who faced him in the eighth.

RAY FISHER—Ray Fisher was pitching fine ball for the New York Americans during their 1910 season. He was formerly the crack pitcher of the Dartmouth College team.

PATRICK FLAHERTY—In 1903 Patrick Flaherty was one of the crack pitchers of the Chicago American League team.

Flaherty is a native of Carnegie, Pa., which is also the home of Honus Wagner. He started with Jackson, Mich., in 1896, played with Patterson, N. J., in 1897 and 1898. His townsman, Honus, also graduated from that club. In 1899 he was in Richmond, Va., a club with which such brilliant lights as Jesse Tannehill and Jack Chesbro were once members. He pitched for Hartford, Conn., in 1900, was with Syracuse in 1901, Louisville in 1902 and Chicago Americans in 1903. Pittsburg secured him in 1904 and he stayed there the following season. He then went to Columbus and was back again in Pittsburg in 1907. Then he was turned over to the Boston Nationals together with Beaumont and Ritchey. He was in Japan with Mike Fisher's aggregation in the winter of 1908 and on his return was disposed of by Boston to Kansas City.

Flaherty, once a member of the pitching staff of the Chicago Americans, has proven a find for the Kansas City American Association team. In one of his best games he shut out Columbus and not a man on the opposing side saw third. Pat gave but one pass in the game and is credited with the only stolen base.

DAVID FOUTZ—On the St. Louis American Association team in 1883 to 1888 was Dave Foutz, who, with Bobby Caruthers, pitched for the St. Louis Browns in those years when they were winning American Association and then World's Championships.

Foutz was brought from the Bay City, Mich., Club to St. Louis and remained with the Browns while they were winning pennants.

In the Fall of 1888 Caruthers and Foutz, pitchers, and Bushong, pitcher, were sold to Brooklyn by President Von Der Ahe of the St. Louis Club. It was said he received enough for the releases of the trio to build a block of stone front houses on St. Louis avenue, just west of Grand.

When those three left St. Louis, however, the St. Louis Club's prestige went with them. With the aid of Foutz, Caruthers and Bushong, the Brooklyns won the American Association Championship in 1889 and 1890, but in the former year they lost in the fight for the World's flag with New York while in 1890 they tied with Louisville in the World's Championship series.

Foutz was perhaps the tallest and slimest pitcher in the history of the game. He was from all outward appearances a consumptive. But despite his appearance he was the possessor of considerable strength and while he was one of the speediest of pitchers he could also hit the ball an awful hard crack.

As a thoroughly gentlemanly player Foutz had few equals on the diamond. In his whole career no one ever saw him lose his temper or heard him speak a harsh word to his most formidable opponent.

When he left Brooklyn it was to go to Baltimore and he died in that city some years ago.

WILLIAM A. FOXEN—William A. Foxen, now one of the pitching staff of the Philadelphia National League Club, is a

HARRY SALLEE.
The Great Pitcher of the St. Louis Cardinals in 1911.

native of Tenafly, N. J., near Jersey City, and was born May 31, 1884.

Foxen played in semi-professional ball in his native town, and in 1903 played professionally with Jersey City and New Bedford. He was in Hartford in 1903 and 1904, and played in Jersey City in 1906 and 1907, thence going to Philadelphia. He is five feet eleven and three-quarter inches in height and weighs 178 pounds.

In July, 1910, Foxen was traded to the Chicago Cubs.

RUSSELL FORD—Russell Ford gained a reputation only in the last year. He is the leading right-handed pitcher of the New York American League Club. Ford hails from Jersey City, where, in 1909 he pitched thirty-two games, winning one-half of them, despite the fact that his team finished a bad last in the race for the Eastern League pennant. He is a well-built young fellow and there are many in New York who think him the peer of Matthewson. It was mainly due to his sensational pitching that the New York Highlanders were able to make a bold bid for the 1910 championship, they leading the American League a large part of the race. Ford in this time won thirteen straight victories. He lost his fourteenth game to Boston, the score being 1 to 0. Ford is considered the greatest find of the 1910 American League season. He is the possessor of great speed and is a thorough master of the spit ball and the originator of the knuckle ball, one of the hardest balls now to hit, in the game.

ARTHUR FROMME—Arthur Fromme, judging him by his work as pitcher of the Cincinnati National League team, is one of the coming great twirlers.

Fromme was born in Quincy, Ill., September 3, 1883, and began his baseball career playing with the team that represented that city in the Three-I League in 1905.

That year he won fame for Quincy by helping that team defeat the Chicago Nationals by 3 to 1.

He was with the St. Louis Cardinals in 1907, but poor health prevented him doing himself justice here and he was released to Cincinnati, for whom he has ever since pitched fair ball.

S. W. FROCK—S. W. Frock, one of the pitchers of the Boston National League team had taken part in fifteen games up the August in the 1910 season, winning five, and losing ten games, a pretty good record with a tail end team behind him. Frock was with Pittsburg in the 1909 season. This, therefore, is his first year with Boston.

HAROLD FRIENE—Harold Friene will be one of the aspiring pitching recruits on Connie Mack's pitching staff in 1911. Friene was signed up by the Athletics in the Spring of 1910, but was later farmed out for seasoning purposes. Friene is a remarkable young man and pitches ambidextrously, which means with either the right or left hand. He is said to be effective when working with either arm.

JAMES GALVIN—James Galvin, one of the great pitchers of the National League in the early eighties was a St. Louis boy. Galvin was one of the first great pitchers given to the baseball world by St. Louis. His first work was with the St. Louis Reds and his receiver was Tom Sullivan. On the Reds the two were known as

the Kerry Patch battery for they hailed from that portion of St. Louis.

From the Patch, too, came Tom Dolan, the great catcher, who was for years Galvin's side partner on the team that represented Buffalo in the National League. Nearly all the old players will easily call to mind the great work done by Galvin.

"Pud" Galvin was the name he was best known by and if you asked why he was called "Pud," they would tell you it was because that when he pitched, the opposition team was a pudding for his nine.

In other words, "Pud's" crowd generally ate the other fellows up.

There was not much curve to the ball that Jim Galvin pitched, but there was as much speed to it as though it had been hurled from a Gatling gun, and in true aim and accuracy he was simply perfection.

He did his best pitching perhaps in 1878 when he was with the Buffalo team, the nine that won the championship of the International Association.

That team was made up of Dolan, catcher; Galvin, pitcher; Libby, first base; Fulmer, second base; Allen, third base; Force, shortstop, and Crowley, Eggler and McGunnigle in the outfield.

Denny Mack and "Trick" McSorley were the substitutes on the Buffalo team that year. Trick, the St. Louis boy, could then play any old place, being a fine pitcher, an excellent baseman and in a pinch he could go behind the bat.

Mack, too, was an all-round man, but like McSorley, he was best as an infielder.

To-day, McSorley, looking as young and chipper as he did twenty-five years ago, is the night turnkey at the Dayton Street Police Station in St. Louis and there he often talks of the old days and such things.

George Miller and Jimmy Galvin were Pittsburg's great battery for years.

When the Brotherhood Rebellion came in 1890 the great battery split up—Galvin went with the Brotherhood and Miller stuck with the National League.

Miller passed from fast company in 1891, and Galvin, though he lasted a little longer, was never as successful as in the olden days when "Doggie" Miller was behind the bat.

Both Miller and Galvin died in Pittsburg, Miller passing away last April and Galvin a few years before that.

HARRY GASPAR—Harry Gaspar, one of the pitchers of the Cincinnati National League team is 26 years of age and was born at Kingsley, Ia., which is still his home. He played with Dubuque, Ia., four seasons ago and afterward with Wausau, Freeport and Waterloo, winning thirty-two out of thirty-six whole games in which he pitched. He gave only thirty-six bases on balls the entire season. Cincinnati drafted him and this is his third season with that club. This year in a game at Cincinnati he broke the chain of New York's nine consecutive victories.

CHARLES GETZEIN—He pitched for Detroit when they were winning a world's championship in 1887.

Charles Getzein was the leading pitcher of the Detroit Club when they won the championship of the world and the National League championship in 1887.

He and Ganzel, his catcher, were called the "Pretzel Battery."

The alliteration perhaps helped in keeping them before the public as a battery, but, of course, only slightly as compared to their usefulness.

The Detroits were the National League champions that year, and Getzein won more games for his team than any other pitcher—twenty-nine.

GEORGE GEYER—George Geyer, pitcher of the St. Louis National League Club, joined the Cardinals at the commencement of their 1910 season. He is a stout fellow and Bresnahan expects great things of him. Geyer comes from Columbus, Ohio, and his release cost Manager Bresnahan of the St. Louis Club, $6,000. In 1909 he was looked on as the best pitcher in the American Association. He pitches right hand. He possesses a peculiar drop ball and is a splendid fielding pitcher. In the Spring of 1910, while in training at Little Rock with the Cardinals, Geyer threw his shoulder out of joint. As a result he was unable to take his turn on the rubber during the season of 1910.

BARNEY GILLIGAN—Barney Gilligan will be a member of the St. Louis Browns' pitching staff in 1911. Gilligan came originally from Vancouver and was secured by the Browns from that place a year ago. He was farmed out in 1910 to the Toledo Club of the American Association. Gilligan showed considerable class while pitching in the minor organization and should win a regular position with the Browns the coming season.

WILLIAM DENTON GRAY — William Denton Gray, one of the pitchers of the Washington American League Club, was born in Houghton, Mich., December 4, 1878.

Gray is a six-footer and strips to 175 pounds. His professional career started with the Los Angeles, Cal., team in 1902, where he played for four years.

Then he had several shifts in one year, going in turn to the Johnstown, Pa., York, Pa., and the Cumberland, Md., teams in 1906, after which he returned to Los Angeles. Gray played with his first love during 1907 and 1908, after which Cantillon annexed him for the Nationals, with whom he played in 1909 and where he is still to be found.

Gray is a southpaw and when going right is a terror to the best stickman. Baseball wise ones will not soon forget the terrific eighteen-inning no-score tie played by Washington and Detroit in 1909, at Detroit, in which game Gray officiated for the whole route. To make the feat even more spectacular, what is not generally known should be taken into consideration—that Gray strained a ligament in his side in the ninth inning of that contest, but, perhaps not realizing the seriousness of the injury, pitched the game out and held Jennings' sluggers in the hollow of his hand the whole way.

Up to August, 1910, Gray had pitched in thirteen games for Washington, winning nine of them. Gray joined the Washingtons in the Spring of 1909 and pitched twenty-four games that season, winning five, not so bad a record when it is considered that Washington was the tailender that year.

ROBERT GROOM—Robert Groom, one of the crack pitchers of the Washington Club of the American League hails from Belleville, Ill.

He is a finely built young fellow, standing six feet two inches in height and weighing 170 pounds.

Groom played with the teams in and around St. Louis until 1904 when he went to Fort Scott, Kan. Leaving there he played in Springfield, Mo., in 1905 and 1906; Portland, Ore., in 1907 and 1908, and came to Washington in 1909.

Groom undoubtedly has a fine selection of curves and promises one day to be one of the greatest pitchers in the baseball world.

Groom's only trouble with Washington has been largely wildness and inability to find the corners at the right time. On the other hand, he has pitched some very fine games, not the least of which was the latter half of the eighteen-inning tie with Detroit in 1909, in which he relieved Gray in the tenth inning. Groom fields his position unusually well, and gets a fast and long start for first when he has to cover.

FRANKLIN HALL—Franklin Hall was one of the pitchers who fell into Manager O'Connor's big net, which was thrown out in a hurry during the closing days of the disastrous 1910 season for the St. Louis Browns. Hall had been pitching great ball for the Joplin Club of the Western Association all season. When the Browns made their final Eastern trip, Mr. Hall was taken along to be given a thorough tryout. On August 23, 1910, in Boston, Mass., the young Missourian was given his first baptism of fire. The big fellow opposed the Bostonians at a time when they were playing baseball and besides this it was his first attempt to do things in such big company and as a natural result the kid was nervous. He proved rather wild, passing eight and being hit safely eleven times. The final score was 5 to 2. Hunt is a great big, healthy youth, standing six feet two inches in his spikes, pitches with his awkward left hand and comes from Sacramento, Cal.

WILLIAM HART—William Hart, an old major league pitcher, was in his day one of the speediest pitchers in the business.

He began pitching twenty-five years ago and was at work this 1910 season in the Southern League.

In a recent interview Hart said: "People who think I can't pitch good ball because I have been pitching for twenty-five years are mistaken. I am just as strong as I ever was. The only trouble I have is getting in shape early; but after I am once in condition I think I can pitch as often and as long as any twirler in the business; I don't care if he has not pitched for more than a week. I want to show those folks in Chattanooga that I have not lost my cunning simply because I have seen twenty-five years flit past since I left there. Some of the fans who saw me work a quarter of a century ago may be under the impression that I am an old man, but I will fool them when I begin to burn them over."

EARL HAMILTON—Earl Hamilton is another aspiring young pitcher who was picked up by Scout Harry Howell of the St. Louis Browns last year. Hamilton was the crack pitcher of the Joplin minors, members of the Western Association.

JOSEPH HARRIS—The good pitching of Joseph Harris has led to his engagement by the Boston Americans. Joe was born at Melrose, Mass., February 1, 1884. He learned to play ball in the vacant lots of Melrose and his great speed attracted attention. He could not keep away from the game, and in 1902 received his first money from baseball playing on the semi-professional teams of Melrose, Malden and the Wellingtons of Dorchester. In 1903 he batted around the New England League, being twice released from Concord, by Jack Carney, then the manager of that club. After two trials at Concord, he went to Lawrence in the same league and finally finished out the season at Fall River. Manager McDermott was the only one who could get the right kind of work out of big Joe. He made the big fellow work hard and deliver the goods.

McDermott hung on to him for two more seasons, but in the Fall of 1905 he was sold to Boston. He pitched a few games for the club and was taken South the next Spring on the training trip. In 1906 he was with Boston all year, and, although he pitched some fine games, luck was against him, and he won very few of them. He started out with Boston in 1907, but in the middle of the season he was transferred to Providence and finished the Eastern League season with Duffy's aggregation.

Then he went back to Boston again for a few games. Southern training did not agree with him, in fact left him in a very bad shape, and he has been a long time recovering from the ravages done his system in that section.

ROBERT HARMON—Robert Harmon is the young giant right-handed pitcher of the St. Louis Cardinals in this 1910 season. Bresnahan considers him one of the best and speediest young pitchers in America. Harmon is a fine fielding pitcher, being intelligent and having all the earmarks of a comer. Harmon was born at Liberal, Mo., October 15, 1887. He played with Morenci, Arizona, 1907, joined the Portland, Ore., Pacific Coast League team next Spring, was released in May, and returned to the Morenci team March, 1909. He was with Shreveport, La., and did such nice work that he was purchased by St. Louis in June. He has done very fair work for his club this season and has a most promising future.

"PINK" HAWLEY—Pink Hawley was at one time a member of the St. Louis Browns. Last year Hawley was with La Crosse, Wis., in the Wisconsin-Illinois League, and he is handling the Oshkosh team this season. Oshkosh was once under the management of none other than the veteran Frank Selee. In his proclamation for the opening of the season in Oshkosh, Mayor Voss said: "A good baseball team is one of the best advertisements for a city, and I request every business man to observe the occasion as far as he can do so and to permit himself and his employes to have one-half day of genuine, wholesome excitement and recreation."

JOHN HEALY—John Healy was the pitcher of the Indianapolis Club of 1878. Six years later he was the pitcher of the St. Louis National League team, the nine that played in Union Park at Cass and Jefferson avenues and that was known as the St. Louis Unions. Healy's home was down in Cairo, Ill., and when he came to St. Louis he was nicknamed "The Egyptian." A tall, graceful player was Healy, popular with the public and his fellow players. There was another pitcher, John Healy, a St. Louis boy, who was at one time associated with Peoria and other minor league teams, but he was no relation to the tall and once famous "Egypt-

ian," who was a member of the St. Louis detective force when he died here a few years ago.

JOSEPH HORLICK—Joseph Horlick is the name of the big pitcher tried out by Washington in 1909 and returned to Peoria later. Horlick was born in Bohemia, August 16, 1884. He stands five feet ten inches and weighs 180 pounds.

THOMAS HUGHES—Thomas Hughes is one of the pitchers of the New York American League team. He is a right-hander. He had pitched nine games in the 1910 season for the Highlanders up to August and had won five of them, a very fair record for a newcomer who was not used in his regular turn.

THOMAS HUGHES — Thomas Hughes, the first, who up to the Spring of 1910 had been pitching in the big league for a dozen years with grand success, but who, owing to a lameness of the arm, was sent back to the minors, will again try to deliver in the American League. "Old Tom," as he is affectionately called by his comrades, experienced one of the best seasons of his career in 1910 while pitching for Joe Cantillons' Minneapolis champions of the American Association. Prize fighters might not be able to come back, but good, old, sturdy, big-hearted athletes like the grand old man, Hughes, can.

BENJAMIN HUNT—Benjamin Hunt is a member of the pitching staff of the Boston Red Sox of the American League and made his initial appearance in the big league in the Fall of 1910 when he defeated the St. Louis Browns handily, by a score of 5 to 2. Hunt stands six feet, two inches and is a well built chap, he is a native of California and pitched in the California State League before being picked up by the Boston Club.

WALTER JOHNSON—Walter Johnson of the Washington Club is considered to-day the greatest pitcher of all the present army of speed merchants.

Johnson was unearthed in the summer of 1907 by Joe Cantilion, then manager of the Senators. Since that time he has been creating a series of sensations by his clever work.

Johnson was born at Humboldt, Kan., on November 9, 1888. He did not play ball until going to California, at the age of 18, when he drifted into the amateur game. It was only necessary for him to show himself in two or three of these before he attracted the attention of Tacoma, of the Northwestern League, which signed him in a hurry. But, rather strange to recount, he got no chance to show his ability and went to Wesler, of the Idaho State.

He pitched ten games for that club, of which he won nine. Returning to California the following winter, he made an attempt to get on the Los Angeles Club, but no berth was open for him and that team did not recognize its opporunity.

He returned to Wesler the next year, winning thirteen of the fifteen games in which he appeared. He pitched eighty-five consecutive innings without allowing a run, averaging fourteen strike-outs in a contest. In his first twelve games he allowed a total of only twenty-five hits.

He was sold to Washington and to-day he is rated as one of the greatest young pitchers discovered by the majors in recent years.

ADAM JOSS—"Addie" Joss as he is best known gained the reputation of being the

CLARKE GRIFFITH.

As is well known, Mr. Griffith is the manager of the Cincinnati Red Stockings baseball nine. Foxy Griffith, as some unkind critics call him, is one of the live characters in the baseball history of America. The "Old Fox" was a pitcher in his day.

brainiest pitcher in the American League. He is a right-hander and one of the biggest men in the Cleveland American League team.

By the Cleveland people he is looked on as McGuire's right-hand bower. He is a fair batsman as well as one of the speediest and best pitchers in the business.

Joss is a native of Cleveland and has never pitched for any team outside of the one now representing that city in the American League. He has been with that team since its organization. He had a great record in 1908, pitching in thirty-five games and winning twenty-four of them. It was due to his consistent pitching in the latter part of the season of 1908 that his team was able to give the Tigers an awful run down the stretch for the pennant, the Clevelands losing out in the very last game by half a point.

Joss during the winter puts in his time as sporting editor of one of the Cleveland newspapers and his articles on inside play have a fine reputation.

EDWARD KARGER—Edward Karger, the left-handed pitcher of the Boston Americans, was born May 6, 1883, at Los Angeles, California. He played with Houston, Texas, in 1905 and was drafted by Pittsburg for 1906, which traded him to the St. Louis Nationals, where he did some very good work. St. Louis disposed of him to Cincinnati in 1909, but his work did not warrant his retention and he was sent to St. Paul. A deal was there made by which he was turned over to the Boston Americans.

Karger experienced a splendid season under Manager Donovan in 1910, proving one of the Red Sox's best winners and also one of the star Southpaws of the American League.

TIM KEEFE—Tim Keefe was one of the great pitchers of the New York Giants back in the eighties.

He now lives at Cambridge, Mass., where Tommy Tucker, one of the great first basemen of the olden days also makes his home.

MAT KILROY AND TOAD RAMSEY— At one time Toad Ramsey of Louisville and Matt Kilroy of Louisville were the leading left-handed pitchers respectively of the American Association and National League.

Elmer E. Bates, the famous baseball writer, now tells this story of these two:

The efforts of all club owners to sign a first-class southpaw pitcher these days recalls the time when left-handers occupied the center of the stage to the practical exclusion of the men who handed the ball up to the batters in the natural way.

"Toad" Ramsey, Louisville's famous left-hander, was one of the greatest of the great, but a more unassuming pitcher never lived. When with the Colonels, after pitching three shut-out games in a row, in which his smallest number of strike-outs for nine innings was ten, the team went to another city. As Ramsey asked for his key at the hotel—this was twenty-one years ago—a hanger-on said to the big twirler:

"Better get plenty of sleep, Toad. We'll take some of that conceit out of you to-morrow."

Ramsey dropped his key and grabbed the man.

"Take that back," he said; and he meant it. "Take that back, or I'll choke the life

out of you. If I thought there was one drop of conceit in me I'd cut off my left arm."

It was the next day that Ramsey made his record of nineteen strike-outs in a nine-inning game.

Mat Kilroy's fame as a southpaw was contemporaneous with Ramsey's. No other pitcher in all history held the base runners so closely to the bags as did Kilroy.

In one game when Kilroy was at his best the score was 1 to 1 in the ninth, when, by some chance, the home team got a man on first. Two men had already paid the penalty of venturing but a single step off the initial sack.

The captain dashed into the coacher's box. "Hey, fellers," he shouted, "we've got to have this game. I'll fine any man who gets ketched $50."

The base runner stood stock still on first. The next batter's hit to right field fence sent the runner to third. Kilroy made a throw or two to first, and then, wheeling, whipped the ball to third and caught the runner red-handed, a single step off the bag.

"Does that fine go, Cap?" asked one of the fans in the third-base bleacher seats.

"You bet it does," snapped the leader, and he meant it, too; but after a night's sleep decided to overlook the offense, for it was one of Kilroy's boasts that no base-runner dare take two steps off a bag when he was pitching.

HENRY KRAUSE—Although it was an undertaker who discovered Henry Krause, the boy hurlsmith of the Philadelphia Athletics, working in California jungles, and hustled him across the continent to Connie Mack, unbiased fans the country over unite in declaring the youthful left-wheeler is about the liveliest corpse a mechanic for the dead ever shipped over the Rocky Mountains.

But in all the work of the big league stars during the strenuous grind of 1909, nothing excited such wide comment as the phenomenal work of the 19-year-old lad, who received his early education on the San Francisco sand lots and was taken by Connie Mack direct from the St. Mary's College team on the recommendation of former Chief Deputy Coroner Peter McCormack of that city, an ardent fan, who knows a good ball player when he sees him, and who successfully steered Krause clear of the scouts of the minor leagues on the Pacific Coast and sent him direct to the big brush on the Atlantic seaboard.

It was at the beginning of the season of 1908 that Connie Mack was induced to come to the coast by McCormack and take a look at this "boy-wonder."

Krause was then hurling them over for St. Mary's College and was pitching his last game in an intercollegiate series that showed a string of twenty-six straight wins. The youngster did not know that the eyes of the big league magnate were upon him and he pitched the game of his life.

He was then in his 17th year, but Mack went wild over his work—slipping him a contract that was enough to make any youngster's heart stop beating, and went back East, happy when Krause had sufficiently recovered from the shock to affix his signature to a paper.

The youngster looked too much a child when he arrived at the stamping grounds of the Athletics and Mack decided to farm him out for a year to Harrisburg,

HARRY KRAUSE,
The Famous Left-Handed Pitcher of the Athletics of Philadelphia in 1911.

137.

in the Tri-State League. Krause set the Tri-State fans wild with his phenomenal work. His record was eighteen wins out of twenty-three games pitched, and the good work lost him to Harrisburg forever.

Mack gathered him into the fold and he led off with ten straight wins for the Athletics. Up to his eleventh game he had all the big league timber wielders eating out of his hand. From the record of his first lost game Krause kept on holding the opposing teams of the big league in hand up to the close of the season. He was easily the leading pitcher of his team.

Connie Mack declared him to be the greatest pitcher developed among the men who hurl from the starboard side since "Rube" Waddell broke into fast company, and fans all over the country have picked him for second place pitcher with the men who go to make up the All-American championship team for the season of 1910. Pretty fair for an undertaker's protege, eh?

FLOYD KROH—Floyd Kroh, who was one of the members of the regular pitching staff of the Chicago Cubs in the National League for two seasons past, but who, owing to having had a misunderstanding with the management in August, 1910, jumped the club and as a consequence was indefinitely suspended. Kroh experienced a splendid season of it in 1909, being rated one of the Cubs' winning pitchers. During the 1910 season, however, his form was not of the best and he did not take his regular turn on the slab.

JOE LAKE—Joe Lake was the leading pitcher of the St. Louis Browns in their 1910 season. A fine speedy right-hander is Lake with thorough command of the ball. He was by long odds the most effective and valuable of the St. Louis Browns' staff from the opening to the close of the 1910 season. Besides being a most valuable pitcher Lake won many a game for the Browns by hitting the ball safely at the right time. He is regarded as the best right-handed spit ball artist in the American League, barring Ed Walsh of the Chicago White Sox. Lake was secured by St. Louis from the New York Highlanders in the winter of 1909 in exchange for Catcher Criger. In 1909 though New York was not in the hunt, Lake held up his own beautifully, pitching twenty-five games of which number he won fourteen.

TED LARKIN—Ted Larkin was one of the pitchers of the Chicago Club back in the seventies. He was a New York boy who had played with teams in Brooklyn before coming West. He did about his last work with the Atlantics of Brooklyn, the team which Billy Barnie had in the field in the 1880 season. Larkin was one of the best pitchers of his day.

GROVER LAUDERMILK—Grover Laudermilk is the tall, wiry lad who pitched for the St. Louis Cardinals in 1909, who was turned over to the Springfield Club of the Three-I League in the Spring of 1910, and who was recalled by the Cardinals in the Fall, and who will start out on their regular pitching staff in 1911. Laudermilk is a fearfully speedy pitcher and his only weakness is lack of control. It was said by Owner Kinsella of the Springfield team that Laudermilk has finally secured control of the ball. If this is a fact he should prove a valuable member of the Cardinals' pitching staff in 1911.

SAMUEL LEEVER—Samuel Leever is still a member of the Pittsburg pitching corps. He was born December 23, 1872, in Goshen, Ohio; stands five feet eleven inches and weighs 175 pounds. He played in 1897 at Richmond, in the Atlantic League. He was with Richmond until the Fall of 1898, when he joined Pittsburg and has been continuously in the service of the Pirates ever since.

ALBERT P. LEIFIELD—Albert P. Leifield, one of the best pitchers on the Pittsburg team, was born September 5, 1883, in Trenton, Ill. He stands six feet one inch and weighs 178 pounds. He played in 1903 with Des Moines, Ia., in the Western League; September, 1905 to 1906, with Pittsburg. Albert (Lefty) Leifield is a son of Mrs. Margaret Leifield, who, until departing for the West recently, lived in St. Louis.

In the steady victorious progress of the Pittsburg team to the National League pennant, the work of Pitcher Arthur Leifield played no small part. Always cool, always in perfect condition, he has deservedly earned a reputation as one of the most dependable pitchers in the country.

LADDIE LINK—Laddie Link was pitching for the Cleveland American League team up to August, 1910, when waivers were asked on him by the Cleveland Club and he was bought in by the St. Louis Browns for the waiver price of $1,500. Up to the time of his leaving Cleveland in the 1910 season Link had pitched ten games for Cleveland, winning four and losing six.

WILLIAM LILIVELT—Another Detroit pitcher is William Lilivelt, whose release was purchased in the summer of 1908 by Detroit from the Mobile Club of the Southern League, Detroit giving Pitchers Sugg and Allen, the promise of a catcher and a check for a considerable sum for his release. Since joining the Tigers he has been troubled with a lame arm and has not made good his minor league promise. Prior to 1909 he played in the I. I. I. League. He is 22 years old and a younger brother, Jack, is now playing with Washington. Lilivelt lives in Chicago, which city is also his birthplace. He is five feet eleven inches tall and weighs 167 pounds.

Lilivelt is a big right-hander and admittedly the best pitcher developed in the Southern League in several seasons. He was loaned by Detroit to Minneapolis in 1910 and helped them win the 1910 pennant of the American Association.

JOHNNY LUSH—John Lush made his professional debut in 1903 with the Williamsport (Pa.) Club as a fielder. He attracted attention there and that Fall the Philadelphia Club signed him. He started in in 1904 as a southpaw pitcher, but in a short time was used in the outfield to get the benefit of his excellent batting. In midseason he was placed on first base, and in a short time he mastered the position so well that he finished the season at the bag. The following season, however, he was used as a pitcher, as Bransfield was secured as a first baseman from the Pittsburg Club. Lush remained with the Phillies until 1907, when he was traded to St. Louis for Pitcher "Buster" Brown. He has since been a useful member of the Cardinals' pitching staff. In 1906 Lush pitched a no-hit game against Brooklyn.

Lush was born in Williamsport, Pa., February 11, 1884. He played with Girard

College in Philadelphia in 1901, 1902 and 1903 and after graduating in the Spring of 1903, played with the Williamsport, Pa., Club. He attracted the attention of President Shettsline of the Philadelphia Club by his fine work with Williamsport, and was signed for the Phillies. In 1905 he jumped back to Williamsport, which was in the Tri-State League, which played independently, but came back to Philadelphia for the following year and played there in 1906 and until June, 1907, when he was traded to St. Louis, with which club he has been since. He stands five feet nine and one-half inches and weighs 165 pounds when in shape.

CARL LUNDREN—Carl Lundgren was one of the stars of the champion Cubs. He attracted attention by his pitching in 1904, and his work in 1906, when the Chicagos wrested the championship from New York was of the stellar order. In 1904 Lundgren won seventeen games and lost nine, and in 1906 he captured the same number and lost but six.

He had fallen behind the Cub speed in the Spring of 1909 and Frank Chance sent him to Toronto. He could not show there, and he dropped out. He is now pitching independent ball in and around Chicago.

Lundgren is 29 years old and graduated with the class of 1902 at the University of Illinois. He pitches and bats right-handed. He is due to again re-enter the big arena next season.

CHRIS MAHONEY—Chris Mahoney is the young pitcher secured in 1910 from Fordham College by the Boston Americans. He was with Fordham for four seasons and also pitched for the Milton High School team, the Dorchesters and Pittsfields. He is 23 years of age, stands five feet nine and one-half inches and weighs 165 pounds.

WALTER MANNING—Walter Manning is one of the pitchers of the New York American League team. He is a right-hander and has held his own so far.

NICHOLAS MADDOX—Nicholas Maddox, one of the pitching staff of the champion Pittsburg team of 1909 is but 23 years of age.

He made his first great hit when he disposed of Brooklyn without a run or hit in Pittsburg, September 20, 1907.

Maddox was born in Govans, Md., and after taking as naturally to baseball as a duck takes to water, he started in professionally for the Easton Club of the Eastern Shore League and also did crack work the next season with the George's Creek League.

In 1906 he did fine work for the Cumberland, Md. team of the Pennsylvania, Ohio, and Maryland League and then played with Wheeling, W. Va., where he was drafted by Pittsburg, but his work did not warrant his retention and he was returned to Wheeling for seasoning. He did so well this time that Pittsburg recalled him in the Fall, and in his first game in 1909 he blanked the St. Louis Club and allowed but five hits. Three days later he again won from St. Louis and afterward landed from Brooklyn and New York, and only lost to the Phillies 3 to 2, with Sparks pitted against him. He has done fine work in the box ever since.

Maddox is still one of the winning pitchers of the Pittsburg Club. In 1909 when the Pirates won the flag Maddox went to the firing line twenty-one times and won thirteen of his games. In the

world's championship series of 1909 Maddox won his game from Detroit 8 to 6.

REUBEN MARQUARD — Reuben Marquard is the big left-handed pitcher for whose release the New York Nationals paid Indianapolis $11,000, the largest price ever paid up to that time for a minor league player. In 1909 he pitched eighteen games, of which he won five. His poor record was due to lack of control although he possesses great speed and a wonderful array of benders. In 1910 up to August Marquard had only pitched four games for New York, winning two, his lack of control again proving his weak spot. Marquard is a perfectly built man, standing six feet three inches in height. He is said to possess as much speed as Rusie, considered at one time the speediest pitcher in the business. Marquard hails from Indianapolis and is only 22 years of age.

ALPHONSE MARTIN—Alphonse Martin, or "Phonnie" Martin, as he was called by the players of his time, was the first to pitch a slow curve ball that fooled the best batsmen of his day.

Martin first came into prominence in 1863 when he appeared in the points for the famous Eckford team of Brooklyn.

I saw Martin pitch for the Eckfords in Brooklyn in 1863 and eight years later I saw him again in the points, this time facing the original Chicago White Stockings on the old Lake Front grounds in Chicago.

Martin's fame had preceded him to the Garden City. Those who had seen him at the commencement of his career, and among this lot was Captain Jimmy Wood of the Chicago Club, who had played with Martin on the Eckfords, did not believe his slow delivery would last. But instead of wearing out it seemed to become the more effective the older it got and even as strong a batting organization as the Chicago team of 1871 could do little but drive Martin's curve high in the air.

His slow ball came to the plate at such a snail-like pace that it nearly drove the batsman crazy and when he got ready to hit it good and hard it seemed to carrom away from him.

Martin pitched the ball with a twist of the fingers and the wrist, manipulating the sphere about as you would a billiard ball when you wanted to put the English on it.

His delivery set the spectators as well as the opposing batsmen nearly wild. It was so long drawn out that it tired the spectators and so slow that it maddened the batsman so that he tried to kill it.

Instead of doing that he usually drove the ball high and generally to the left field where Al Gedney, the Eckfords' speediest and best outfielder, generally took good care of it.

The Martin ball was also a tantalizing affair to the catcher for it often curved away from him just before it crossed the plate, injuring his fielding and putting him in bad with the spectators who thought anyone should be able to catch that kind of a ball.

But Martin, through it all, prospered for many years as a famous pitcher, and now at 65 he is hale and hearty and an employe of the Madison Square Garden, New York.

Not long ago Arthur Cummings who is now a house painter in Hartford, Conn., was asked:

"Were you the first man to curve a ball when pitching it to the batsman?"

"No, I don't think I was the first man

to pitch a curved ball," was the reply. "I think that Martin of the old Eckfords had the curve—not mine, but a kind of curve; and I am sure that Zettlein, who was the great pitcher of the Atlantics when they were champions, pitched a curved ball, and that Pabor, who is now a policeman in New Haven, pitched a curve when he was playing with the old Unions of Morrisania, New York, with which George Wright once played.

"But none of these pitchers knew that he had a curve, and I suppose it is fair to say that I was the first to find out what a curve was and how it was done.

"Hicks was catcher and I was pitcher of the semi-professional Stars of Brooklyn. I noticed that very few batsmen could hit me, and finally I saw that when I pitched the ball it swerved outward before it reached the batsman. Then, when I had thought about this a little, I said to myself: 'That ball does not go in a straight line until it begins to fall; it curves outside of the horizontal line, and that is the reason why batsmen can not hit it.'

"Well, I studied and experimented until at last I found that if I held the ball between my fingers and thumb in a certain way, and gave it a certain twist of the wrist just as I delivered it, then the resultant motion that the ball took produced a curve. I wondered how that could be, and I made up my mind that the rotary motion of the ball created a vacuum on one side, the outside, and the pressure of the air on the other side caused it to swerve. I had found out the secret of the curved ball. I afterwards taught it to Tommy Bond, and he could make a ball curve either way."

In this modest way the discoverer of the curved ball, which has made modern baseball possible, narrated the story of his great find.

ROBERT MATTHEWS—Of the old-time pitchers who held their own in the limelight for many years was Robert Matthews.

"Bobby" Matthews was the name he was best known by.

In 1869 Matthews was pitching for the Marylands of Baltimore, a team almost unknown outside of that city.

But his fame spread when one day, while Matthews was pitching for them, the Marylands beat the Eckfords by 21 to 16, a great score, considering the fact that at this time the Eckfords were the champions.

It was Matthews' great pitching that did it all. He had the same curves that Martin and Cummings had introduced a year or two before and a little more. In fact Matthews had besides the curves of Martin and Cummings, a good deal of speed and this combination made him invincible. So much so that in a game in which he pitched for the Kekiongas of Fort Wayne in 1871 against the then famous Forest Citys of Cleveland, Matthews' side won by the unprecedented score of 2 to 0.

Some of the players of the present day claim that the ball which Matthews was pitching then was nothing more nor less than the "spit" ball used now by many of the best pitchers.

But this is hardly possible for the "spit" ball is fearfully wearing on the pitcher and soon retires him from service.

Matthews commenced pitching for the Marylands in 1869 and in 1883, fourteen years later, he was pitching his best ball, this time for the Athletic Club of Philadelphia, who captured the championship of the American Association that year. And that was not his last season in the business.

CHRISTY MATHEWSON—The pitcher of the New York Giants pronounced by present day pitcher that ever lived.

In speed, in perfect control, in curves and shoots, in headwork, the National League players who have faced him say that Mathewson is the hardest man to master in the business.

In build Mathewson is a fine big fellow and this grand physique helps him along wonderfully, but he adds to this natural strength a fine eye and an active brain, qualities which added to his native strength make him a master in his home position.

When Mathewson joined the Giants not quite ten years ago, he was a lad just from school, only 19 years old, and with practically no experience in professional baseball. But he had the gift of observation, and he put it to good use from the start of his career. He created no sensation the first year he was with the New York Club. He was just a recruit, who had the size and the make-up of a promising pitcher, and he was carried along with a view to the future.

The papers at that time seldom mentioned him, and he was an unknown quantity. But Matty put in that first year to the greatest possible advantage. He went around the circuit with his eyes wide open and his brain registering impressions which were to assist him in his work. He was a quiet athlete and said little, but he was always looking at things and coming to conclusions.

The next year he put his knowledge into practice and jumped at once into the front rank of the pitchers of the league and of the entire country. For nine years he has been the mainstay of the Giants in the box. Without him they would to-day be a second division team.

Matty, by the use of his calm, cool brain and his superb physique, holds them up in the race year after year. From present indications Matty is not much more than half through with his career as a successful pitcher in the major league. He knows how to work to the best advantage to himself. You never see him straining himself to the limit when nothing is to be gained by the exertion.

With no one on the bases, Matty looks like an easy pitcher to hit. He has it all figured out that the average batter has not one chance in three of hitting the ball to a safe spot, even if he is given a pretty good opportunity to do so. Therefore, Matty goes calmly about his business, relying on the eight men behind him. He puts the ball over and around the corners of the plate, using little exertion, and trusts to its not going safe. He saves himself for the time of need. If Matty pitches 125 balls in the course of a game —an extra large number for him, by the way—it is a safe bet that he does not use his full power on more than twenty of them, at the most. The rest are handed up easily and without undue strain or exertion. He never works hard until there are men on the bases, and then he can cut loose in the most terrific manner, for he has reserved his strength for just such an emergency. From his methods Matty

HARRY WHITE.
Veteran Pitcher of the Chicago White Sox in 1911.

141.

is not a no-hit pitcher, nor does he hold the strike-out record. He usually allows six or eight hits, and he seldom fans good batters, except when it is absolutely necessary to do so. But he almost invariably wins his game, and his opponents are lucky to get a run off his delivery.

That is because he is pitching to win, and to prevent the other side from scoring runs and not to establish a freak record.

It would be fun to see Matty go into a game some day with the deliberate intention of striking out as many men as possible. He would probably establish a record, but he will never try. His object is simply to win games for his side and he goes at the task in the easiest way, and the one which best preserves his strength for the next occasion. It is this constant care of his powers which makes it possible for him to pitch three games in five days in times of stress and hold the enemy to three runs in the three games. And he is always willing to go in out of his turn and deliver the goods. He is capable of doing so, because he never over-exerts or abuses himself, and he always has a little extra power to cut loose. He is the greatest example of intelligent force in the pitcher's box in the country to-day, and the chances are that he will remain at the pinnacle of fame for many years to come.

Mathewson was the pitching hero of the New York-Athletic series in 1905. Matty twirled the opening game for the Giants and blanked Connie Mack's men with Eddie Plank pitching against him, by a score of 3 to 0.

"Big Chief" Bender came right back and whitewashed New York with McGinnity pitching, 3 to 0. Mathewson twirled the third great game for the Giants and crushed Philadelphia by the one-sided score of 9 to 0. Mack's men made four hits off the peerless Christy. Plank defeated McGinnity 9 to 1 in the fourth game and Mathewson blanked Bender in the fifth, 2 to 0.

Christy Mathewson was born in Factoryville, Pa., August 12, 1880. The name of Mathewson is a prominent one in Factoryville; the family is the first in the town. It took Christy, however, to acquaint the world at large that the Mathewsons were really remarkable people. He was also instrumental in giving Factoryville a just and deserved rating on the Lehigh Valley Railroad folder, as duly behooves a town with a name of such imposing grandeur.

He first began to attract attention, though a youth of tender years, while performing on the slab for the Scranton Y. M. C. A. Later he entered Bucknell University, and in 1899 he pitched the Lewistown collegians to victory in every game he figured in on the mound. Christy had the highbrow college swatters of the big universities, as well as the backwoods performers, standing on their heads and swinging like gates. Even the hefty nines from the Universities of Princeton and Pennsylvania fell victims to his prowess; the famous "fadeaway" ball was in the first stage of its development, the college season over, "Matty" concluded it was about time to make a little spending money out of his twirling talents, so agreed to perform on the slab for the good country folk who inhabit Honesdale, Pa. "Mat-

ty" did not tarry long in Honesdale, however. The Taunton Club of the New England League offered better inducements, and he packed his grip and migrated.

He was pitching for Taunton when the eagle eye of Connie Mack, the Athletics' manager, fell across him. Connie had followed Mathewson's course from Bucknell University to Taunton and Norfolk. He made Christy an offer, which he accepted. Later, the New York Giants, after much persuasion, prevailed on him that he could win more glory in the big metropolis than in the smaller Sleepytown, so he signed another contract and remained loyal to Gotham reserve laws.

In the midst of the turmoil, warfare and strife, Captain Cunningham, who is alternately a baseball magnate and ship captain, then owner of the Norfolk Club, was having a lovely time trying to figure out to whom he had actually sold Mathewson. It was a query whether he should send his bill to Cincinnati, Philadelphia or New York. As neither of the three showed any symptoms of loosening up, he took his case to court and secured the purchase price from the Giants' coffers through a judicial ruling.

During the season of 1903, when the Giants leaped from last place to second, Christy cut his first niche in the hall of fame, and ranked with the leading twirlers in the league. In 1904 and 1905 he was one of the main factors in the Giants copping the National League pennants, and pitched himself into the glory of being admitted the premier twirler in the game.

His record in the world series of 1905, when he took Connie Mack's Athletics into camp three times in one week, on each occasion adding insult to injury by spreading it on with a whitewash brush, is a feat that will probably never be equalled. For twenty-seven innings not an Athletic warrior indented the plate with his spikes, and in the three games they made but fourteen hits, an average of 4 2-3 hits a game. In the three games he gave but one base on balls; his control may be said to have been nothing short of perfect. It is true Babe Adams equalled Matty's record for three straight victories when he blasted the hopes of Jennings' pets in the 1909 series, but Christy's kalsomine and control records stand forth as brilliant as ever.

Since then Matty continues each year to be the mainstay of the Gotham twirling corps; each season finds him at the top of the National League's pitchers, and generally about one-third of the Giant's victories have been wrested from the enemy through his untiring efforts. He has also been fitted by nature so that he can officiate in the box with much frequency. A day or two of rest after a hard conflict, and Matty is ready and eager to enter another fray.

Probably the game on which more depended than any other in which Matty has figured in his entire career, and the one which he tried hardest to win, resulted in a defeat. It was the fateful game at the close of the 1908 season, on which hung the National League championship, and which the Cubs succeeded in winning, 4 to 2, by bunching several hits and three runs off Matty's delivery in the second inning. Matty's brilliant pitching record is as follows.

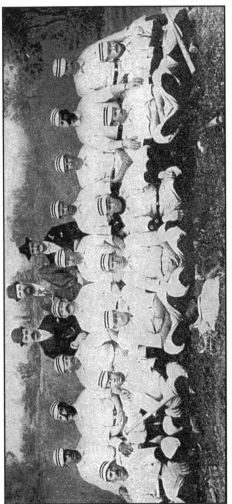

BALTIMORE'S FIRST PENNANT WINNING ORIOLES—THE TEAM OF 1894.

First row, standing, reading from left to right: Edward Hanlon, manager; H. R. Von der Horst, president; Herman H. Von der Horst, secretary.

Second row, reading from left to right: Walter Brodie, cf.; George Hemming, p.; Wilbert Robinson, c.; Dan Brouthers, 1b.; J. McMahon, p.; W. Clarke, c.; Charles Esper, p.; Joseph Kelly, lf.

Third row, reading from left to right: Henry Reitz, 2b.; W. "Kid" Gleason, p.; Frank Bonner, sub. 2b.; J. McGraw, 3b.; H. Jennings, ss.; W. Keeler, rf.; W. V. Hawke, p.

Grouped in the accompanying picture by close observation the reader can see the faces of a dozen or more lads who have played star roles in the baseball world. This is the old and genuinely original Baltimore Oriole Club. There is no question but that this was the greatest combination of talent and brains the baseball world ever saw. McGraw, Jennings, Keeler, Joe Kelly, and the greatest catcher of them all, Robinson, belonged to this wonderful team. Big Dan Brouthers on first, Henry Reitz on second, Jennings at short and one "Kid" McGraw at third made up an infield the like of which had never been seen up to 1894, nor has there ever been lined up since, for men who were so great in their respective positions.

Brouthers was a giant in size and was one of the most desperate batsmen of those days. In the line-up it was always big Dan "in the hole" to pull them out. Reitz was fast as lightning as a fielder and very tricky on the bases. He, with Jennings working to his right, made up a pair of extraordinary fielding talent. Both lads were there when it came to cleaning up the bases. Over at third stood a little quiet, graceful fellow, "Kid" McGraw. In those days the now famous leader of the New York Giants was not much bigger than a rabbit. He weighed about 110 pounds, and didn't appear strong enough to bat the ball out of the infield. But he fooled them all and has been fooling them all ever since. Then there was the greatest outfielder of them all covering left garden, Joseph Kelly. Kelly, with Walter Brodie, made up most of the famous outfields.

	Won.	Lost.
1900	0	4
1901	20	17
1902	13	18
1903	30	13
1904	33	12
1905	31	9
1906	22	12
1907	24	12
1908	37	11
1909	25	6
Totals	235	114

With the bludgeon Matty also fails to be the mark most pitchers are supposed to be. Instead of merely standing at the plate so that an out may be registered by the scorers, Matty can push out frequent bingles.

ALBERT ARTHUR MATTERN—One of the marked young figures in the National League in 1909 was Albert Arthur Mattern, the great young left-handed pitcher of the Bostons.

Mattern was born in West Rush, N. Y., ten miles from Rochester, June 16, 1882, and there he started in playing ball as a boy.

Mattern pitched such good ball in 1905 that he attracted the attention of Al Buckenberger, who was managing the Rochester Club at that time, and pitched eight games, winning seven, and was compelled to stop on account of a spiking in his pitching hand, received in a collision with his first baseman in trying to field a grounder. He was compelled to lay off the remainder of the season.

In 1906 he was secured by the Montreal Club and played under Manager Jimmy Bannon, winning nineteen out of twenty-seven. In 1907 he played with Holyoke under the management of Tom J. Dowd and was very successful.

Holyoke won the pennant that year and the brilliant work of Mattern was largely responsible therefor, his record being twenty-two out of twenty-seven games. The late president of the Boston Nationals, George B. Dovey, purchased the release of Mattern and in 1908 loaned him to Trenton, N. J., of the Tri-State League, of which Jack Carney was the manager. His record was twenty games won and twenty-one lost. His fielding average was .986. He stands five feet ten inches, and when in condition weighs 168 pounds. He returned to the Bostons in 1909 and did great work for them that season.

JOUETT MEEKIN—When the New York team won the Temple Cup in 1894, the pitching honors were shared between Amos Rusie and Jouett Meekin.

Meekin and Farrell were a great battery in their day. They were bought by the New York Club, then owned by E. N. Talcott, and went there from Washington as a battery.

Farrell was of the big, strapping type of catcher, a heady player and a fine handler of pitchers, and Meekin was a big, free-and-easy chap, who improved immensely under Farrell's tutelage.

Farrell will tell you now that Meekin had more speed than any pitcher he ever caught, and he caught the whirlwind Rusie.

JIM McCORMICK—Jim McCormick was one of the great pitchers of the eighties.

He pitched for Cleveland until 1884 when with his great catcher, Briody, he jumped to the Union Association.

He played with the Cincinnati Club of the Union Association in 1884 and pitched great ball for that organization.

McCormick was a heavyweight and when he and Briody were the leading battery for Cleveland, they were the heaviest pair in the business.

JOSEPH McGINNITY — Joseph McGinnity used to be the best "iron man" in the business. He could pitch a double engagement to-day, and go in and wheel again to-morrow.

And he used to win the majority of his games. That's why he was regarded as the best "iron man." Joe did his most superb work when McGraw was erecting pennant poles at the Polo grounds. This was more than five years ago. At present McGinnity is not twirling for the Giants.

Too many "iron man" entertainments made him lose his National League effectiveness. Now he is managing the Newark Club of the Eastern League, and pitching once or twice a week.

McGinnity was the leading pitcher of America in the 1900 season when he pitched for Brooklyn and he also led all in 1904 when he was with the New York Giants.

HENRY McINTIRE—Henry McIntire is one of the right-handed pitchers of the Chicago National League team. He joined them in the Spring of this year. Up to August of this year he had pitched in thirteen games, of which he won seven. McIntire is one of the veterans of the business. He was with the Brooklyn and Philadelphia National League teams for several years.

LARRY McKEON—Larry McKeon was the great pitcher of the "only" Indianapolis Club when that team won the championship of the National Association in 1869.

That year, with Frank Flint, a St. Louis boy, then the greatest catcher, Flint and McKeon were known as the "only" Flint and the "only" McKeon.

They were two great players. After leaving Indianapolis McKeon went to Cincinnati and he was for some time a pitcher on the team that represented that city in the American Association.

GEORGE McQUILLAN—George McQuillan has done some fine pitching for the Philadelphia National League team in this 1910 year.

He was born in Brooklyn, May 1, 1885, and moved with his parents to Paterson, N. J., while he was very young. He played with the Paterson High School team and was a member of the local team in 1904.

STONEY McGLYNN—Stoney McGlynn, another of the real iron men, released by the St. Louis Cardinals in 1908 because it was believed he was "all in," was the sensation of the American Association in the seasons of 1909 and 1910. He kept Milwaukee in the lead for weeks early in the season, and often appeared in three and four games a week.

H has worked as willingly in doubleheaders as in single contests and never complained when ordered forth to finish for his mates when they got into trouble. His willingness made him a great favorite with his fellows, with the manager, with the owner and with the fans and his greatest pitching, not only nearly landed Milwauee in the first place in the American Association race of 1909, but did land it a very close up second.

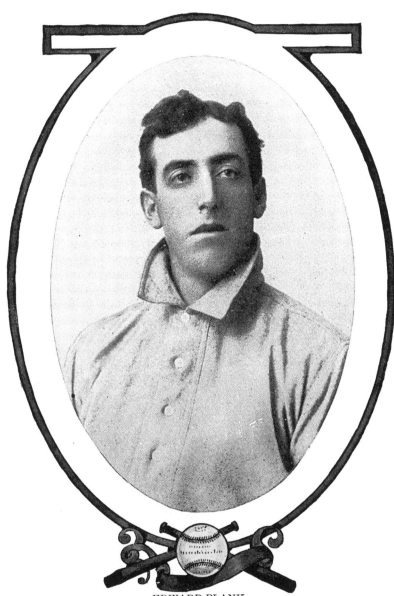

EDWARD PLANK.

Eddie Plank is unquestionably the most consistent winning left handed pitcher in the history of baseball of later days. Plank is a southpaw and it was due to his wonderful work in 1910 that good old Connie Mack won the 1910 championship.

145

WILLIAM MITCHELL—William Mitchell is one of the left-handed pitchers of the Cleveland Club of the American League. He is a youngster and so far has made a good record in the big league. In the season of 1910 up to August he won four games for Cleveland out of ten pitched.

LEWIS H. MOREN—Lewis H. Moren is the right-handed pitcher of the Philadelphia National League Club. He gets $100 from his father for every game he wins and on his team he is known as the "million dollar kid." He joined the Quakers in the Spring of 1909. He did his first pitching for the Fordham College team, Billy Murray, then the Phillies' manager, taking him right off the college campus. Moren was most successful in the 1909 season pitching thirty-one games of which he won sixteen. Up to August in the 1910 season he had pitched sixteen games, of which he won seven. Moren is only a college youth and will perhaps some day be one of the greatest pitchers in America.

EARL MOORE—This pitcher, once a great card of the Cleveland American League Club, proved of decided assistance to the Philadelphia National League Club in the 1909 season, figuring in eighteen victories and twelve defeats, while Frank Corridon, who made the best showing of the Philadelphia pitchers was just ahead of him in percentage with eleven victories and seven defeats. Moore was born near Columbus, Ohio, in 1889. He played with Cleveland from 1902 to 1905, but in 1906 was incapacitated by an injured foot. The Cleveland Club carried him until 1908 and then released him. Jersey City of the Eastern League then signed him. Here he won thirteen games and lost twelve. The Phillies gave him a trial in the Fall and had good reason to feel pleased with his work.

CYRUS MORGAN—Cy Morgan is doing the best work of his career for the Athletics of Philadelphia in this 1910 season. He is certainly pitching great ball and the team is playing brilliantly behind him. It takes that combination to produce a winner. Morgan hails from Martins Ferry, W. Va., the home of Dick Padden, former manager of the Chicago White Sox. Morgan, up to August, 1910, had pitcher twenty games for the Athletics, winning thirteen of them, tying another and losing six. he was in fact, one of the main standbys of the Athletics as they were leading in the American League in the 1910 season. In 1909 Morgan was secured by the Athletics from the Boston Americans and immediately developed into a winning pitcher. This was perhaps due to Connie Mack's careful coaching. In 1909 Morgan officiated in thirty-five full games besides which he helped out Plank, Bender and Dygert in a dozen more, winning the name of "Iron Man." Of the games he pitched in 1909 he won eighteen and lost seventeen. Morgan uses the spit-ball with tremendous speed. He is also a fine fielding pitcher. While with the Boston and St. Louis American League teams his lack of control only prevented him from being a winning pitcher. Connie Mack's coaching remedied his fault in that direction and he is now one of the steadiest as well as one of the speediest pitchers in the business.

Perhaps no player has had a more unique career than Morgan.

Until two years ago Morgan was the property of the St. Louis American League Club.

For three years previous Morgan's name always appeared on the roster of the Brown's team. Each Spring he would report and usually would start one or two games and then be shipped back to St. Paul in the American Association.

Manager McAleer, then in charge of the St. Louis Club, was certain that Morgan had the stuff to stick in fast company, but the fans refused to be convinced of the fact.

Just as soon as Morgan would step on the rubber the crowd would get after him, and it would not be very long until he was on the way to the clubhouse. It became evident to McAleer that Morgan would never do as a St. Louis player, and he was sold to the Boston Americans. Morgan then proceeded to make good. Perhaps no victory ever pleased him more than the one he scored against St. Louis on his first appearance in this city after drawing his release.

He shut the Browns out, 1 to 0, holding them down to something like two hits. For some reason or other Boston traded Morgan to Connie Mack last year, and it was a mighty good thing for the leader of the Athletics, as Morgan was a tower of strength in the gruelling battle for the pennant honors.

During the off season Morgan does a minstrel turn on the vaudeville stage.

GEORGE EMMETT MULLIN—Next to Adams, George Emmett Mullin of the Detroit team shone out as the pitcher par excellence of the great series played by Pittsburg and Detroit for the World's Championship in 1909.

Mullin is right-handed and a stalwart of stalwarts. He was considered the best hitting pitcher in the American League.

Mullin was born at Wabash, Indiana, in 1881 and has been playing professionally the past ten years.

The first two of these ten years he played with the Fort Wayne (Ind.) Club and the last eight years he has been with Detroit. No pitcher in the history of previous contests for the blue ribbon of baseball covered himself with more glory than did Mullin in this 1909 series.

Baseball experts agree that if Jennings had had another pitcher of Mullin's caliber Detroit would have won the world's championship in 1909 hands down. Even the Pittsburg fans admit that Mullin outpitched Adams in the inaugural game of that series and but for costly errors by Bush and Delehanty the Pirates would have lost.

Keen baseball men now rank Mullin with Mordecai Brown, Christy Mathewson and William Dinneen, three of the greatest pitchers that ever curved a ball over the plate. Mullin divided the pitching honors with "Wild Bill" Donovan in 1907, the first year Detroit won the American League championship. Mullin was the only Detroit pitcher to win a game from the Chicago Cubs in the world's championship battles of 1907-1908. Big Georgie beat Pfeister of the Cubs in the third game of the 1908 series, score 8-3, letting the hard-hitting "Teddy Bears" down with seven hits.

Mullin is also the boy that pitched Detroit to the front in the American League championship race the 1909 season. He won twenty-nine and lost nine games during the campaign and set a record for the league by winning eleven straight during the middle of the season. Mullin pitched the most brilliant ball of his career in 1909. His friends attribute his good work to the fact that he took off about forty pounds at the commencement of that season.

But best of all Mullin proved himself Detroit's greatest pitcher in the great series which that team played with Pittsburg for the World's Championship in 1909. But for the great work of Mullin, the Detroit team would have been disgracefully beaten in that series.

Mullin, who is the oldest member of the Detroit team in point of continuous service, and leading pitcher of the American League in 1909, was born in Toledo and is now in his 28th year. He went to Detroit after one year in professional baseball, spent in Fort Wayne. His 1909 season was his best, due largely to the fact that he consistently kept himself in good physical condition. Mullin is a fine figure of a man, just a half inch over six feet in height and kept his playing weight in the neighborhood of 180 pounds in 1909, in spite of the fact that in former years he carried about well over 200.

Mullin has been a member of the Detroit team for nine years. Prior to joining the Tigers he put in one campaign with a club in the Western Association. Detroit took him on trial in the Spring of 1902, after the Buffalo Eastern League Club had refused to carry out its contract with him.

Right from the start Mullin made good in the American League, and generally he has won more games than he has lost. Four years ago, however, Mullin was in disfavor with the Detroit management and public and came near being traded to another American League club. The Tigers held on to him—a move which never has been regretted.

Mullin, in 1908, did the best work of his career, topping off his splendid performance in the American League championship campaign by performing gallantly in the world's championship series with the Pirates. He won two games from the corsairs and came near figuring in another triumph.

Mullin is a great hitter, besides being a clever pitcher, and is a glutton for work. In the Spring of 1909 he won twelve games in a row for the Tigers, many of these being played in cold weather. He is one of the few veteran twirlers who is able to jump right in at the start of the season and do good work.

Mullin's 1909 record was twenty-nine victories and eight defeats. He seldom was batted out of the box and proved to be the steadiest and most reliable of all of Jennings' gunning corps. Without him the Tigers would have had a hard time winning the American League championship. Mullin weighs more than 200 pounds, and the only weakness he has, according to players, is that he isn't clever about making men who reach first hug that base.

Mullin, during his American League career, has twice batted for over .300. The first year Big George hit above the charmed mark was in 1902, when his stick credit was .328. Two seasons later Mullin walloped the sphere for .305. George got a big raise in salary from Frank Navin next season. The big fellow certainly deserves it.

MICHAEL MURPHY—Michael Murphy, better known as "Red" Murphy until August, 1910, was the star pitcher of the Ap-

pleton Club of the Wisconsin-Illinois League. He was then sold to the St. Louis American League Club for $1,500. Under the terms of the sale Murphy is to report to the St. Louis team at the close of the present season, or about September 15, and St. Louis will pay $1,000 more or return Murphy to the Appleton Club, May 15, next. Murphy is the first pitcher in the W.-I. League to be sold this year, and is the first in the history of the league to be sold to a major league club during his first year in the game. The Chicago Stock Yards Irishman is only 19 years old. He stands five feet ten inches in his stocking feet and weighs 175 pounds. He played semi-professional ball in Chicago last year, but this is his first season on a professional team. He has been the mainstay of the Appleton team, and it was more due to his pitching than to any other thing that Appleton led the league practically the entire season. Murphy took part in forty-six games in the 1910 season of the W.-I. League; thirty-three of them as pitcher and thirteen as outfielder. He batted .281 and fielded .945 in the forty-six games. He pitched and won twenty-four games, lost seven and took part in two other games which were won before he went in the box. In the thirty-three games Murphy allowed but 177 hits, seventy-three runs, fanned on an average of six men to the game and gave on an average less than three bases on balls to the game.

R. NELSON—"Red" Nelson, the Akron pitcher, bought by the St. Louis Americans, in August, 1910, was the leading twirler of the O. P. League during the season. He won seventeen games and lost only six. He was secured by Columbus in the middle of the season and bolstered up the Akron pitching staff and put a tail-end team in the fight for a pennant. As an "Iron Man" in the minors he was in a class by himself. He pitched and won both ends of three double-headers during the 1910 season, each time against the league leaders. Three years ago he was pitching for the Sands Diamonds, an amateur team of Cleveland. He was given a chance in the Three-I League and made such a good record he was picked up by St. Paul. In 1909 he went to Columbus in exchange for Infielder Zeke Wrigley. Later he was turned over to Lima, and finished the season at the top of the Ohio State League pitchers. Columbus turned him over to Akron, when the Senators persisted in going bad behind him. Manager Jack O'Connor and Scout Billy Doyle of the Browns watched him win several games and they decided to buy him.

JOHN NESS—John Ness, who was one of the stars of the Williamsport Club will line up as a member of the Detroit Tigers in the Spring of 1911. Ness has had a few years' experience in the minors and report has it that he is due to become a regular member of the Tigers' regular pitching staff next season.

EUSTACE J. NEWTON—Eustace J. Newton is one of the veterans of the staff of the New York American League Club's staff of pitchers and is in his thirty-second year.

Newton was born at Mt. Carmel, Ind., October 26, 1877, and acquired proficiency when a student at Morris Hale College. He played professionally with Norfolk, Va., in 1897 and 1898, and in 1899 was with Indianapolis and Cincinnati.

Newton signed with the New York American League Club before the Amer-

THE NATIONAL GAME.

ican and National League Club declared a truce with each other, but he was awarded to Brooklyn, and as he would not accept the offer of President Ebbetts of the Brooklyn Club, joined the Los Angeles Club, and remained there until 1905, when he was secured by the New York American League Club. In 1907 he played with the Montreal Club, and the following season came back to the New York Americans with whom he has played good ball ever since.

CHARLEY NICHOLS—Charles A. Nichols, who pitched for the Bostons when they won the National League pennant in 1891, 1892 and 1893 was one of the greatest pitchers of his day.

On the Boston Champions with him were the great Clarkson, Stivetts and Staley, but Nichols outclassed all of them.

He was the only one of that famous quartet remaining with Boston in 1898, the last pennant year of that organization.

Nichols was a fine, speedy pitcher and a great fielder in his position. He was for many a year considered the peer of any pitcher in the National League. Nichols was brought to Boston from the Omaha Club of the old Western League. Frank Selee was then the manager of the Omaha team, and when he went from there to Boston he took Nichols with him. "Nick" made a hit from the start and for many seasons figured heavily in the success of the Boston Club.

He managed the St. Louis Cardinals in 1904, and besides pitched high-class ball.

FRED OLMSTEAD—Fred Olmstead is one of the right-hand pitchers of the Chicago American League team in their 1910 season. Up to August in the 1910 year he had pitched ten games for Chicago winning four, a good average considering the losing streak which that team was then enjoying. This is Olmstead's second year with Chicago.

WILLIAM OTEY—William Otey is one of the enthusiastic young twirlers whom Manager McAleer of the Washington Nationals picked up last Fall. Otey was the star flinger on the Norfolk Club in the Virginia League during the early part of the 1910 season.

ORVAL OVERALL—Orval Overall, the big man from California, is one of the mainstays of the pitching department of the Chicago National League team, is only 29 years old and has played professional ball only five years, having been a member of the class of 1903 at the University of California. He broke into the game at Tacoma, joined the Reds in 1905 and was secured by Chicago the following season. He throws right-handed and bats from either side of the plate.

BARNEY PELTY—Barney Pelty, one of the clever right-handed pitchers of the St. Louis Browns, hails from Farmington, Mo., and is about 32 years of age. Pelty joined the Browns in 1903 and has always pitched good ball for them.

JOHN A. PFEISTER—In John A. Pfeister, the Chicago National League champions have one of the best left-handed pitchers in the country. He is a native of Cincinnati, Ohio, where he was born May 24, 1878. So he is 31 years of age. He played with Baltimore in the first year of the American League in that city in 1901, and in 1902 and 1903 was with Columbus, Spokane and San Francisco, and was signed in the Fall of 1903 by Pittsburg, but

in two months was released to Omaha, and it was from that club that he was secured by Chicago in 1906. He has played an important part in all of the Cubs' championships.

CHARLES PHILLIPPE—Charles Phillippe, also of the Pittsburg's pitching corps, was born May 23, 1872, in Rural Retreat, Va. He stands six feet and one-half inch and weighs 180 pounds. He played in 1896 with the Mankato (Minn.) Independents; 1897 and 1898 with Minneapolis, in the Western League; 1899 in the Louisville Nationals; 1900 to 1909, with Pittsburg Nationals.

Phillippe remained with the Pittsburg Club through their 1910 season and did so well that at the end of the playing season he stood third in the regular pitchers' record with a percentage of .875. Brennan, of Philadelphia, and Burke, of Boston, who played in only nineteen games respectively and who had an average of .1000 were the only two pitchers in the National League with a better record in the 1910 season than Phillippe. The big Virginian is a painstaking, earnest player whose services are invaluable to any team of which he is a member. He has been with Pittsburg so long that his friends in the Smoky City are legion.

JACK POWELL—Jack Powell is the big right-handed pitcher of the St. Louis Browns in this 1910 season. He is one of the old members of that team. He has been with them since the organization of the New Browns in 1902. Powell's great forte is pitching with fearful speed. He also has perfect control. He has been one of the standbys of the Browns and though the club for several season's past has rarely won half its games Powell has usually finished up each season with an average percentage of .500. In 1908 when the Browns made a determined effort to capture leading honors, Powell pitched phenomenal ball, winning a great majority of his games that season. During 1910, although pitching in his regular turn with a poor team behind him, the big boilermaker continued to pitch a steady, winning line of ball. Powell is one of the veterans of the game. He was born at Bloomington, Ill., where he was discovered by Patsy Tebeau in 1895. That year Tebeau signed Powell for the Cleveland Spiders. For years Powell, Cuppy and Young were the pitchers of that team and they were then the best trio in the business. Powell was one of the men brought by the Robinsons to St. Louis when they transferred their Cleveland National League team to this city. Jack is 36 years old.

WILLIAM B. POWELL—William B. Powell is one of the youngsters of the great Pirates' pitching staff and has been showing in fast company in the past two seasons. Powell took part in ten games during the 1910 season of which number he won four and lost six.

JOHN QUINN—John Quinn is one of the pitchers of the New York American League Club. He is a speedy right-hander. Quinn comes from one of the Eastern colleges and this is his second year with New York. He pitched fourteen games for New York in 1909, winning nine and losing five of them, a most creditable record considering the fact that the Highlanders were far down in the race that year. In 1910 he has held his own nicely, winning more than half of the games he pitched for the New York team.

148

BARNEY PELTY.
One of the best pitchers on the St. Louis American League team of 1910, is Barney Pelty, a sketch of whom appears elsewhere in this book.

CHARLES RADBOURNE—Charles Radbourne, who won the championship for Providence in 1884 and who led the National League that year as a pitcher, was born in Bloomington, Ill.

Clark Griffith, for many years leading pitcher of the Chicago National League team and who later played with Comiskey's Chicago White Stocking team, was a pupil of Radbourne.

Griffith himself admits that he never compared with Radbourne in speed and skill and the fact that Griffith was one of the best of the present day pitchers is itself proof that Radbourne would indeed easily rank with the very best pitchers of the present year.

I first saw Radbourne pitch in 1880 when he came to St. Louis with the Dubuque team of the Western League. We had gotten up a team of professionals to meet the Dubuque nine and expected to beat it, but thanks to Radbourne's great pitching, our team was beaten.

Then an obscure pitcher in a semi-professional nine, Radbourne, four years later was the leading pitcher of the peerless Providence team.

In action on the field Radbourne was magnificent. He was an athlete in figure as well as in action and beside being able to send the ball in with terrific speed, to curve it in any direction, he was always in complete control of his delivery and was seldom credited with a wild pitch.

And not only was Radbourne a great pitcher, but like nearly all of the great pitchers of his day he was a fine batsman. That he was a player of great nerve and skill, one who could hit the ball hard when a hit was needed, was proven on August 17, 1882, when the Providence and the Detroit National League teams met.

Eighteen innings had been played with Radbourne pitching for Providence and without either side having scored a run.

To bring matters to a finish Radbourne knocked the ball over the fence and his home run gave the great contest to Providence.

Jacob C. Morse of the Boston Baseball Magazine, says Radbourne was the greatest pitcher that ever lived.

In an article in the Baseball Magazine of January, 1909, Mr. Morse, in an article headed:

"The Greatest Pitcher That Ever Lived," has this to say about the Bloomington, Ill., boy, who for many a day was famous on the baseball field:

"Pitchers may come and pitchers may go, but the name of 'Old Hoss' Radbourne goes on forever. I have talked to many great ball players who have lamented to me the fact that baseball fame is so ephemeral, that it was not worth gaining; and, while no doubt this is in a great measure true, there is one pitcher who has left a name that promises to roll on for many, many years.

"Each year hundreds of pitchers claim attention from the world; and each year they are promptly forgotten. But Illinois has produced a man who, although eleven years deceased, has a brighter name than any of the great multitude.

"In the great campaign of 1884, when the Providence Club, then a member of the National League, was fighting a bitter game with Philadelphia, a catastrophe occurred that it was thought would disrupt its chances of winning the pennant.

"Charles Sweeny, who was pitching, was ordered to go into right field to change places with "Cyclone" Miller. At that time it was not permissible to take a pitcher out of the game. Whereupon, Sweeny promptly walked out of the game, leaving the team with only eight men and with one pitcher—Charles Radbourne.

"Two men tried to cover the field, with the result that Providence was completely snowed under. A meeting of the directors was held to decide whether or not the club should be disbanded. Certainly a professional team was never in a sorrier plight.

"Radbourne was approached, and the proposition put up to him.

"'I can win the flag, all right,' said he, quietly, and in a mater-of-fact tone.

"And then followed the most remarkable battle for a pennant that the world has ever seen.

"Radbourne then established a record that has never been equalled, one that will live when more expensive contests will have been blissfully forgotten. In twenty-seven consecutive games Radbourne won twenty-six of them. In four games with Boston he had three shut-outs; only one run was scored, and only seventeen hits were made. This defeat was suffered at the hands of Buffalo by a score of 2 to 0, and even then only five hits were made off him, showing that the defeat was not due to poor pitching. Needless to say, Providence won the pennant—or rather, Radbourne won the pennant.

"But the great player had to pay the price. No arm could stand that awful strain without great agony. Morning after morning when Radbourne arose he could not lift his arm as high as his waist. He had to brush his hair with his left hand. But he did not give up the game. He would slip out to the park about two hours before the rest of the team put in an appearance and would begin the excruciating process of limbering up. He could pitch the ball only a few feet when he would first go out; but he would keep on trying, time after time, rubbing his arm with his left hand. Sometimes his face would be drawn up into contortions, but never a word of complaint left his lips.

"Half an hour before the game was to begin, the players would slip out to see how 'Old Hoss' was getting along; they would sit patiently on the bench, waiting for his arm to get into condition. When he was able to throw from second to home base, a rousing cheer would go up, for they knew that meant the winning of the game for them.

"Radbourne claimed as his home, Bloomington, Ill. This city has other famous pitchers to its credit, namely, Jack Powell and Clarke Griffith."

Of Radbourne, Ted Sullivan, who perhaps knew him better than any other man, recently had this to say:

"Of the many funny incidents happening during my baseball career, none is funnier than 'the crooked baseball' story sprung at Prairie-Duchien, Wisconsin, in the early times of curved ball pitching in that section of America. When the reader understands that the scientific men of the country were at first skeptical of the possibility of imparting a curve to a pitched ball and boldly asserted that a ball could not change its course while in transit from the pitcher's hand to the catcher, you can imagine what a lot of villagers in a country town thought of it when they saw the great Radbourne bend the ball up and down, out and in.

EDWARD HANLON.
The former manager who played alongside Dunlap on the Champion Detroit team.

"It was the first professional club I ever handled and it was a team of stalwarts. It was composed of a lot of witty kindred spirits—Comiskey, Loftus and others, with the great Radbourne in his first year as a regular pitcher. He was then on the threshold of his greatness, with a constitution and physique that carried him through many a hard baseball campaign in later years in the National League. He was not only the greatest pitcher in any period of baseball history, but also a batter and general ball player. Before he made the unparalleled record of pitching feats in Providence in 1884, he alternated from right field to the pitcher's box with John M. Ward and also from shortstop to the pitcher's position when Ward essayed the infield position once in a while for the Providence team of 1882.

" 'Rad' was continually inventing some new delivery and trying to get control of it. He often said: 'Ted, any delivery without control, is no delivery at all.' He was in his element when pitching those country exhibition games, as we all considered them a little diversion from the serious work of the regularly scheduled championship games. Radbourne, as the posted followers of the game know, was the master of curves and deliveries.

"He had all of what they have to-day, and one or two that they have not. He had a jump to a high, fast ball, and an inshoot to a left-handed batter. He had a drop ball that he did not have to spit on, and called it a 'spit ball.' Added to that, he had a perplexing slow ball that was never duplicated on the ball field. The nearest approach to him in this delivery was by John Clarkson and Tim Keefe of Rad's time. To this slow ball he could give a lot of speed. It would come toward you and then change its route all of a sudden. It was the delivery they call to-day the 'fadeaway.'

"Of course, all those deliveries must have new names to-day or they would not be considered new. It's the same principle as at a French restaurant, where you get the same dish every day, but with a new name. According to a certain line of baseball logic, Smith is not 'Smith if he wears a different suit of clothes from that he had on when he was known as Smith. Vanity is a great thing in this world of baseball. One generation does not want you to tell it of the mighty deeds, or of the merits of that which preceeded. The present generation insists upon being regarded as the pioneer in the inventive or strategical features of the game. But Radbourne, as sure as you live, in his day had everything the very best pitchers of to-day could boast of."

After Radbourne's great season with Providence, managers all over the country were on his heels. Flattering offers poured in, and he was not under contract with Providence for the next season, either. When the contest was over the late Ned Allen, president of the team that season sent for Radbourne. He laid the release before him, and close beside it a blank contract. Radbourne looked at them both for several minutes, and then slowly took up a pen and filled the blank out for a sum only a little higher than he had been getting, and tore up the release. Allen almost fell on his neck and wept for joy.

Radbourne's last year in baseball was with Cincinnati in 1891, but it was a sad year. It seems a pity that the career of

so great a ball player should have ended so sadly. That year his work showed great deterioration, for the awful strain made in 1884 was beginning to tell on his arm. At the end of the season he was too proud to go into minor league baseball, and so entirely withdrew from the game. He returned to Bloomington, where he opened a billiard hall. He had little to say, and in unwinking silence would sit in a corner and watch the young men laugh as they played. He would talk about himself only when cornered, and then only a few short words. He had always been an ardent fisherman, hunter and sportsman, but he gave up the open life. Each year his taciturnity increased, until he became almost sullen.

After a time he gave up his billiard hall and retired into the obscurity of his home, seldom letting people see him. At last, in 1897, when he was 62 years old, he fell ill and soon passed away. Even when he was on his death bed, few of his friends knew that he was ill. The bitterness of senility had gripped him unrelentingly. And so lived and passed away the great Hercules of baseball.

WALTER RAY—Walter Ray, the right-handed pitcher, is perhaps the youngest player on the St. Louis Browns. He joined that team in the middle of the season of 1910, coming from Muscogee of the Western Association and made good from the start.

ARTHUR L. RAYMOND—Arthur L. Raymond, who was with the New Yorks until July, 1910, when he retired, is one of the greatest and speediest pitchers that ever lived. He is a man of wonderful physique and fearful strength. He has terrific speed and is really one of the fastest pitchers in America. He started out with Rockford, Ill., and Waterloo, Ia.

In Waterloo, Raymond won nine straight games, and attracted the attention of Ed Barrows, then the Detroit manager. Barrows thought better of his bargain after he had purchased Raymond and sold the eccentric pitcher to the Atlanta Southern League Club. The big chap was somewhat disgruntled at his failure to get at least a one-game tryout with Detroit, and he sulked in his new Southern surroundings. The manager of the team mistook sulkiness for inefficiency, and "Bugs" was let go to the Savannah team, another club of the same league.

At Savannah, Raymond made a wonderful record, pitching sixty-five games and losing but five of them. The money poured in on the happy pitcher, and it didn't take him long to learn the easy task of making money go as fast as it came. Therefore, the end of the season found him penniless, and he was glad to accept a position tending bar in Atlanta. In that city Raymond made many friends and met several baseball celebrities. While at his newly-found vocation of dispensing liquid refreshments he acquired a hankering to include the spitball in his pitching repertoire. Raymond read of the marvelous success Elmer Stricklett was having with it, and immediately determined to become famous as a spitball pitcher.

He started out in this line with the Jackson, Miss., team and from there he went to Charleston, N. C., where he was discovered by Manager McCloskey of the Cardinals.

Raymond stayed with the St. Louis Cardinals until 1908, when an enormous

EDWARD REULBACH.
Eddie Reulbach for several years led the pitchers of the National League, while a member of the great Chicago Champion Cubs. Reulbach belongs to old Missouri, having been born in the one big city of that State, St. Louis.

deal was pulled off by St. Louis. New York and Cincinnati, the Giants getting Raymond and Murray from St. Louis and Schlei from Cincinnati, St. Louis receiving Roger Bresnahan, the New York star catcher, for a manager, and giving Karger and Fromme, two pitchers, to Cincinnati, the Reds letting Schlei go to New York in part payment for Bresnahan.

On the baseball field Raymond is a strong drawing card. The big, red-faced fellow is always cutting loose with some queer antics, and when he makes a base-hit, which is rarely, he never fails to dance a weird dance, of his own invention, about the base, to which the hit has sent him.

On one occasion in Boston this year, Raymond drove a long foul over the left field fence. It was only a foul by a few inches and this nearness to a home run almost paralyzed the big chap with delight. "Whoopee!" he yelled, shaking his bat at his teammates, while the umpire called another strike on him. The next ball pitched was a strike also, and "Bugs" watched it as it went by, but he didn't care if he had struck out; he had nearly made a home run, and a real home run, all the way over the fence, too. All the way to the bench "Bugs" danced a brand new Raymond sidestep.

Raymond is a clever pitcher and he relies upon this cleverness to win games, as well as he does on his strength, speed and curves. Fully half the ball players in the National League to-day give Raymond no credit for possessing brains at all, and these same players are the easiest victims for the big fellow when they face him at the plate.

S. F. REISLING—S. F. Reisling is one of the most promising pitchers on the Washington American League team. He is a new comer to the major league ranks, hailing from California. He is a right-hander. In the 1910 season up to August he had pitched sixteen games for Washington, of which he had won eight, a pretty good record on a losing team. He is a medium sized man with plenty of strength and all the curves.

EDWARD REULBACH—Edward Reulbach was the leading pitcher of the National League for four years.

He joined the Chicago National League team in 1904 and in 1906, 1907 and 1908 he led the League in the pitcher's position.

He has the unique distinction of having in his first year pitched two record games, one of eighteen innings and one of twenty innings. Reulbach is six feet three inches in height and weighs 190 pounds.

In the World's Championship games of 1907 and 1908 it was his wonderful pitching as much as anything else that made the Chicago combination well-nigh invincible.

Reulbach is a native of Detroit, Mich., and was born there December 1, 1882. He budded into the game in the college world. He pitched for the Notre Dame, Ind., club in 1904, after having pitched for Sedalia, Mo., the previous year, and in the summer of 1904 was in the Vermont State League. Chicago secured him in 1905, so that this will be his fifth season with that club.

The best pitching percentage in the National League in the past twelve years is .826, made in 1906 by Reulbach. Hoffer, Hughes and Chesbro practically had the same percentages, but pitched only a dozen or more games, while Reulbach's average was for the whole season, he filling the pitcher's position in nearly fifty games each year.

DUTCH REVELLE—Dutch Revelle will line up as a member of the New York Highlanders' pitching corps in the Spring of 1911. According to E. P. Lyons, manager of the Colonial Theater, Richmond, Va., Revelle should prove a sensation in the big league. He is a port-sider and was drafted by the Highlanders in 1908-1909, but was only carried during the Spring trip. He is now seasoned and probably will make the team.

J. LEE RICHMOND—Not long ago Sam Crane, the veteran player who is now writing baseball for the New York Journal, New York City, had something to say about the once famous left-handed pitchers who gained renown at one time or another on the diamond. There were in all about thirty-three of them, but how Sam came to overlook Robert Mitchell of the Cincinnatis, of 1877; J. Lee Richmond of the Worcesters, of 1879-1880; Ed Morris of the old Pittsburgs; E. L. Cushman of the old Metropolitans of New York, and John F. Smith of Newark, Baltimore and other teams, can best be answered by himself.

They were in their day just as prominent in a baseball way as were any of those mentioned by Sam.

It was Mitchell and Tommy Bond who gave the curve ball pitching demonstration at Cincinnati in the Summer or Fall of 1877, before a bunch of professors—the college variety, not the barnyard species.

Richmond was the first pitcher to shut out a National League team without a run or a solitary safe hit. He did it twice —first in 1879, when Worcester was a member of the International Association, he shut out the Clevelands, and in 1880, after Worcester had been admitted to the National League, he turned the same trick on Chicago. Both were remarkable feats in those days against such heavy-hitting teams as Cleveland and Chicago.

J. Lee Richmond, who pitched a no-hit game thirty years ago—the first on record —lives in Toledo, Ohio, where he teaches in a high school. Elmer Bates, sporting editor of the Cleveland Press, visited him in his home and got the following interesting story of the ex-player and his achievement:

"Pitching a no-run, no-hit, no-man-reach-first game, thirty years ago, did not make the same sensation in the baseball world as such a feat does to-day.

"I do not recall that any particular fuss was made about it by any newspaper or any set of 'fans' when I was fortunate enough to set up this record in 1880."

Very modestly was this statement made by Prof. J. Lee Richmond, now one of the teachers in Toledo Central High School. Not only modestly, but somewhat reluctantly, did Prof. Richmond talk of that remarkable game of June 12, 1880, when pitching for the Worcester team, he did not allow a Cleveland player to reach first in a nine-inning game.

"I went from Geneva, Ohio, where I was born, to Oberlin, and then to Brown U.," said Prof. Richmond. I always loved baseball, and in the old days of underhand pitching acquired a degree of proficiency that enabled me to win some games at Brown somewhat handily.

"Now, this no-hit, no-run, no-man-reach-first game against Cleveland in 1880 was not exactly the first no-man-reach-first game I pitched. A year earlier, when Worcester was in the minor leagues, I had gone down there on request and pitched against Chicago in an exhibition game. Worcester won, 7 to 0. Later Anson's team came back for another game, and again I was appealed to. The invitation included my regular catcher, and the offer for our joint services was $20. We accepted. The game went only seven innings, as the Chicagos had to catch a train. Just twenty-one of the old White Stockings went to bat.

"We joined Worcester next season. My partner was a good catcher, but my favorite was Charley Bennett, the best backstop that ever lived in the world. He went after everything, he knew no fear, he kept his pitcher from going into the air. Later he went bad, but came back grandly and wound up his diamond career gloriously.

"Our captain was Lon Knight, a mighty fine fellow, who always kept us cheered up, always had a kind word for us."

"Arthur Irwin says that you were the best left-handed pitcher that ever lived," I remarked.

"Oh, I wouldn't lay claim to any such distinction," said Prof. Richmond, quickly. "I did have a fast jump ball that was hard to hit when it was working right, and it must have been working right on that hot afternoon of June 12, 1880, when not one of the Cleveland players reached first base.

"It is a singular thing that of that first no-man-reach-first-base game in 1880 I can remember almost nothing except that my jump ball and my half stride ball were working splendidly and that Bennett and the boys behind me gave me perfect support."

Here is the score of the great game in which Richmond set up the world's mark that all the pitchers in the country have been aiming at ever since:

WORCESTER.	AB.	R.	H.	O.	A.	E.
Wood, cf.	4	0	0	3	0	0
Richmond p.	3	0	1	1	6	0
Knight, rf.	3	0	0	3	1	0
Irwin ss.	3	1	2	2	3	0
Bennett, c.	2	0	0	0	2	0
Whitney, 3b.	3	0	0	0	2	0
Sullivan, 1b.	3	0	0	14	0	0
Corey, lf.	3	0	0	1	0	0
Creamer, 2b.	3	0	0	3	4	0
Totals	27	1	3	27	16	0

CLEVELAND.	AB.	R.	H.	O.	A.	E.
Dunlap 2b.	3	0	0	4	3	2
Hankinson, 3b.	3	0	0	0	0	0
Kennedy, c.	3	0	0	9	1	0
Phillips, 1b.	3	0	0	6	0	0
Schaefer, rf.	3	0	0	2	0	0
McCormick, p.	3	0	0	1	8	0
Gilligan, cf.	3	0	0	1	1	0
Glasscock, ss.	3	0	0	0	2	0
Hanlon, lf.	3	0	0	1	0	0
Totals	27	0	0	24	15	2

Innings—	1	2	3	4	5	6	7	8	9	
Worcester	0	0	0	0	1	0	0	0	*—	1
Cleveland	0	0	0	0	0	0	0	0	0—	0

Base on balls—By McCormick, 1. Struck out—By McCormick, 7; by Richmond, 5. Double play—Glasscock, Dunlap and Glasscock. Time—One hour and twenty-seven minutes. Umpire--Bradley.

LOUIS RICHIE—Louis Richie. one of the pitching staff of the Chicago Nationals was born in Amber, Pa., August 23, 1883, and got his schooling there.

He started playing in Wilmington, Dela.,

in 1903, having played independent ball previously. He was in Oxford, in County League, Pennsylvania, part of 1904, and finished at Williamsport and also played with that club in 1905. That club won the pennant. Philadelphia secured him in 1906 and he played with that club until the deal with Philadelphia, by which he was secured by Boston, July 15. He is five feet eleven and three-quarter inches in height and weighs 160 pounds.

JOHN A. ROWAN—John A. Rowan is a member of the pitching staff of the Cincinnati Club of the National League.

Rowan was born June 16, 1886, at New Castle, Pa., which is still his home. He began playing with Leavenworth in 1906, with Atlanta in 1907, to Dayton in 1908, and then to Cincinnati, where he has played ever since.

CLARENCE DICKSON RUSSELL — While "Clarence Dickson" may be little known, "Lefty" Russell's fame has been pretty well advertised by the announcement that Connie Mack paid $12,000 to the Baltimore Eastern League Club for his services. No check for that amount has ever been exhibited and the suspicion is strong that there was some cash and that the remainder has been or will be "taken out in trade."

"Lefty" is a pitcher, born in Baltimore on July 8, 1890. From the first he let it be known that he could throw out a bawl. In 1906 and 1907 Sunday School leagues flourished in Baltimore and "Lefty" became a Sunday School boy—a "bona-fide" attendant of the Twenty-fifth Street Sunday School, for which team he pitched. After the Sunday School business fell into decline, he donned a Hagerstown, Md., uniform. It was an independent team, but there were some hot old games up in the mountains of Western Maryland and Russell made such a showing that Manager Dunn of the Orioles corralled him for the Baltimore team in 1909.

The Orioles were long on pitchers of both ability and experience and as Russell needed steady work, he was farmed to Wilkesbarre. Breaking in badly there, he soured on the team and finally jumped back to that dear Hagerstown, where he was allowed to remain unmolested until near the close of the Eastern League season, when Manager Dunn could have used a pitcher of the caliber Russell had grown to be, very handily. Emissaries were trotted up to Hagerstown in a steady stream, but Russell would have none of their blandishments and remained until he took a notion to skip down to the Virginia League, where he pitched a game or two until "discovered" by Manager Dunn and his prompt rejection demanded.

Last winter, chiefly through the agency of Umpire McAtee, a close friend of Russell, the boy was made to see the harm he was doing himself by defying the laws of organized ball, and he signed his 1910 contract like a man. He has pitched some remarkably classy games this season and the fact that he has not shown much since his reported sale, does not worry—'twas ever thus.

Incidentally, Russell is a southpaw batter, as well as pitcher, and displaces sufficient atmosphere to accommodate five feet eleven and one-half inches and 165 pounds of vigorous personality.

An Eastern paper recently published an alleged interview with Russell. Here is the interview:

"I was a very sensitive youth," commenced the Priceless. "My parents felt sure that a great future was before me and I was not allowed to play with ordinary boys of my age. The lives of the great men of history constituted my daily diet in the world of literature. My boyish imagination was fired at turns by the genius of Shakespeare and of Keats, the valor of Alexander, Caesar and Napoleon, the sublimity of the work of Beethoven and Sousa and other masters in the domain of music. I felt that I possessed all the gifted qualifications essential to make me the poet warrior musician of the age. I was convinced that my destiny had been set in high places. Assiduously I applied to the work of development in the paths I had chosen in life, but I was mistaken. I was not to be a poet, a warrior, a musician. Carefully as I was guarded from all contact with the outside world, the day a copy of a daily newspaper fell into my hands, wherein I saw a picture of the great Tip O'Neill, who was then playing in the outfield for the St. Louis Browns and who was the idol of the baseball world, I decided that I, too, would rise to this eminence. I vowed to myself that I, too, would be a bright luminary in the baseball firmament. I told my parents of my full purpose, and after a vain endeavor to dissuade me from my mad career, they wished me Godspeed, and I went off to college to learn the art of the game. Through diligence and hard work I have succeeded as you know, and the end of my glory is not yet."

NAPOLEON RUCKER—Napoleon Rucker is one of the every day pitchers of the Brooklyn team and has been for several seasons past. Up to August in the 1910 season, he had pitched in twenty-two games and won eleven of them, a great record considering the fact that he was with a tail-end team. He is regarded as one of the classiest pitchers in the National League.

HARRY SALLEE—Harry Sallee is the star left-handed pitcher of the St. Louis National League team of 1910.

He helped the St. Louis team early in the season to win games from their most formidable opponents.

Sallee was born at Hagensport, Ohio, in 1885, and started his professional career for the Meridian (Miss.) Club of the Cotton States League in 1905.

The next season he pitched for the Birmingham (Ala.) Club, his brilliant work contributing much to help land the pennant for that club.

The New York American League Club drafted him, but turned him back again to Birmingham, and in the latter part of the season he was purchased by the St. Louis Nationals.

In 1908 he was farmed to the Williamsport Tri-State League Club, and again proved a winner among the minors. Since that season he has been on the roster of the St. Louis Club.

Sallee, when in condition, is regarded as one of the hardest pitchers in the business to beat. His poor record made during the latter half of the 1910 season, was due to lack of condition and illness.

W. D. SCANLON—W. D. Scanlon is one of the right-handed pitchers of the Brooklyn National League team. He has been with that team a long while and is one of their regulars. For several years he has pitched winning ball. In 1909 he was stricken down with a serious illness and was forced to retire for the season. Up to Au-

gust in the 1910 season he had pitched in seventeen games, winning four of them.

JAMES SCOTT—James Scott was one of Charles Comiskey's 1910 recruits. Up to August of the 1910 season he had taken part in sixteen games, winning four, losing eleven and tying one. Scott was worked mostly in the Spring before his teammates had hit their stride. According to Manager Duffy, the youngster has displayed considerable class and should be heard from next season.

CHARLES E. SMITH—Charles E. Smith is one of the veterans of the major league class.

Smith was born in Cleveland in 1880. He gained his first professional experience in 1902, Cleveland picking him up from the lots.

In his first game Smith twirled against the Athletics with the then great "Rube" Waddell pitching, and beat him. His next game was won from Baltimore, but going to Baltimore he was knocked out of the box and he weakened from that point, subsequently being released to New Orleans in 1903.

On account of illness he was also released from this club. The following season, when he was recovered, Smith pitched for Atlanta of the Southern League and led the pitchers of that organization. He twirled splendidly for Atlanta in 1904, and at the end of the season was drafted by Washington.

In 1906, 1907 and 1908, and up to the present he has pitched for Washington, and is the only player on the team who represented Washington before Joe Cantillon became manager. Smith is a right-hander and a cool proposition under fire. His work was for Washington, but should show better with the speedy Red Sox to support him.

FRANK SMITH—Frank Smith is the big right-handed pitcher of the Boston Red Sox. He is so big that the fans have dubbed him the "piano mover." He was traded in August, 1910, to the Boston American League by Comiskey, he and Purtell going to the Bostons in exchange for Harry Lord and McConnell. Smith and big Ed. Walsh were the pair who kept Comiskey's White Sox in the running for several years past. Smith was a member of Comiskey's pitching staff in 1906 when the club won the American League Championship and also defeated the Chicago Cubs for world honors. Since that time Smith has pitched winning ball each season and was only traded by Comiskey because the wonderful big fellow and Walsh could not agree. In 1910 up to August, Smith had won nine games for Chicago and lost four, a mighty good record considering his support. Like old Joe McGinnity, Smith is an iron man and could pitch every day in the week if necessary. In 1909 he pitched 44 games, winning 25, losing 17 and tying 2.

Smith was one of the oldest members of the White Sox team, having come to the South Side Club from Birmingham, Ala., where he was the star pitcher for several seasons before he was signed by Comiskey. He was a big help in winning the American League pennant in the memorable 1906 campaign. His great weakness is not being able to hold base runners on the sacks. Two such big pitchers as Walsh and Smith have no place on the same team, and it is a good

CHARLES SWEENY.

The partner of Charles Radbourne, the most famous pitcher of his day, was Charles Sweeny, considered the speediest pitcher in the eighties, and Sweeny was one of the players brought to Providence from California by Manager Harry Wright. He was a man of great strength and power, and one of the most skillful pitchers that ever lived. He left Providence in 1884 to join the S. Louis Unions.

thing for both of them to part. Smith never could win while Walsh was winning, and Walsh could not win while Smith was winning, for some unaccountable reason.

ROBERT SPADE—Robert Spade made the best record of any of the staff of pitchers of the Cincinnati Club in the season of 1909, landing seventeen games and losing twelve.

It was his fine showing with Atlanta in the Southern League the previous season that induced Cincinnati to secure him. While with Atlanta he figured in eighteen victories and twelve defeats, that club landing the Southern League pennant.

Spade was born in Akron, Ohio, January 4, 1879. His first work of note was with the Kent, O., independent team and this led to his engagement by the Youngstown, O., Club in 1898. He went back to independent ball until 1905, when he went to Jacksonville, Fla., in the South Atlantic League and was traded to Macon that season. The St. Louis Cardinals drafted him and let him go after a trial of two months, and he went back to Macon, winning sixteen, losing seven and tying one game; Macon finished third. Atlanta drafted him and then he went to Cincinnati.

Last Spring he was secured by the Browns from Cincinnati, but owing to ill-health and a strained shoulder was unable to do his best. Manager O'Connor turned him over to Newark of the Eastern League with "Rube" Waddell in exchange for Catcher Crisp.

FRANK SPARKS—Frank Sparks, for years one of the winning pitchers of the Philadelphia Nationals, is a right-hander. He is a small man. Up to August, 1910, however, he had pitched during the season only two games for his team and lost both of them which seemed to end his usefulness for he was not tried again. Sparks is well preserved for a veteran pitcher and will, no doubt, re-appear next season in shape to hold his own again.

GEORGE SPEER—George Speer, left-handed pitcher of the Detroit Tigers is a Missourian by birth, having first seen the light of day on a farm near Springfield. With the team of that town he was at one time a battery partner of Charley Schmidt, of the Detroits. Later he blossomed out as a star with Wichita in the Western Association. Speer is in his twenty-third year. He is five feet nine inches tall and weighs 152 pounds.

EDWARD STACK—Edward Stack is one of the pitchers of the Philadelphia National League team. He was born at Chicago twenty-two years ago. He played with the St. Viteurs College team at Kankakee, Ill., from 1904 to 1908. In 1909 he joined Callahan's Logan Square team from which he was secured by the Chicago Nationals. The latter team sold his release to Philadelphia.

WILLIAM STEELE—William Steele will line up as a member of the St. Louis Cardinals' pitching staff in the Spring of 1911. This, of course, will mark Mr. Steele's initial appearance in major league company. During the 1910 season he was regarded as one of the most efficient pitchers in the Tri-State League. He went to the hill twenty-eight times and managed to come home with the bacon

twenty-two times. Manager Bresnahan of the Cardinals expects to make Steele a regular member of his pitching staff.

JACK STIVETTS—Jack Stivetts, who pitched for the Boston National League Champions in 1892, 1893 and 1898, was a fine big fellow and much resembled the veteran Cy Young in build and delivery.

He was also a fine batsman and when not pitching for Boston he often played the field for that nine, his good batting in the pinch often proving useful.

He pitched his last big league game in St. Louis several seasons ago.

FLORENCE SULLIVAN—One of the best known major league pitchers in the eighties was Florence Sullivan, who first became famous as the pitcher of the East St. Louis Nationals. He pitched for many teams in the neighborhood of St. Louis until the early eighties when, with his great little receiver, "Billy" Colgan, he was signed to pitch for the Pittsburg Club of the American Association. Sullivan was a speedy pitcher and an excellent batsman and his friends in East St. Louis were legion.

EDGAR OREN SUMMERS — Following closely on the heels of Mullin and Donovan of the Detroit team which in 1909 ran Pittsburg such a game race for the World's Championship, is Edgar Oren Summers, a giant like Donovan and Mullin of the same team. He stands just one inch over six feet in height and scales in the neighborhood of 175 pounds.

He is a Hoosier, his birthplace and residence in the winter being the hamlet of Ladoga, Ind. Indianapolis tried him out in 1905, but farmed him to Grand Rapids, for which club he virtually won a pennant. He was back in Indianapolis in 1907 and was purchased by Detroit in the Fall. In his first season with Detroit, 1908, for a youngster, he made a splendid record in the box, winning twenty-four games and losing twelve. Summers has good control and a cool head, and manager Jennings says he is one of the best boxmen in the business.

THOMAS TUCKEY—Thomas Tuckey is one of the young and promising left-handed pitchers of the Boston National League team of 1910. His best feat this year was when on May 19, 1910, when in a pinch, he retired three of the St. Louis Cardinals in order on strikes. He is looked on as one of the coming pitchers of the big league.

JAMES J. VAUGHN—This strapping left-handed pitcher of the New York Americans, who stands six feet three inches and weighs 213 pounds, was born in Weatherford, Texas, April 9, 1888. While with the Fort Worth fire department in 1906 he was urged to go to Temple, Tex., and went thence to Corsicana, staying there until July 4, when the league broke up. He then went back to Fort Worth and resumed his connection with the fire department.

In the Spring of 1908 he went to the Hot Springs of the Arkansas League, and won 16 out of 17 games the first month of the season. This induced Clarke Griffith to secure him, and he joined the New York Highlanders in May 1908.

Vaughn has proven a valuable addition to the Highlanders pitching staff.

WILLIAM SUDHOFF.

William Sudhoff was one of the Browns' best pitchers several seasons ago. He is a native of St. Louis, where he is engaged in the clothing business.

GEORGE EDWARD WADDELL—One of the most eccentric and wonderful left-handed pitchers and greatest of drawing cards in the profession of baseball is George Edward Waddell, late of the St. Louis American League team, but who was traded to Newark, July, 1910. He was with the Athletics in 1902 and 1905, the years they won the American League Championship and with Plank he was considered the most effective pitcher in the American League ranks in those two years.

This wonderful left-handed pitcher, nicknamed "Rube," was born in Butler, Pa., October 13, 1876 and first played professionally in Oil City, Pa., twenty years afterward.

It was his verdant appearance that secured for him the sobriquet by which he is generally known. He pitched for Volant College in 1897 and the same year joined Louisville.

In 1898 he was with Detroit and Homestead, in 1899 with Columbus, 1900 with Pittsburg and Milwaukee, 1901 with Chicago of the National League, 1902 with Los Angeles and the Athletics of Philadelphia. He remained with the Athletics until 1908, when he was released to the St. Louis American League Club.

Despite his flighty conduct, he was a leading factor in helping the Athletic Club to land the two pennants that were secured by it, and he proved a decided accession to the St. Louis Club in its 1908 season.

These are facts about the most eccentric pitcher in the business.

Age—Just entering his thirty-fourth year.

Height—Six feet one and one-half inches.

Weight in condition—196 pounds.

Number of years in professional game—Fourteen.

First became prominent—1897, with Milwaukee Club.

Went to Louisville—Same year, 1897.

Dropped to Columbus—1898.

Went to Pittsburg—1900, when Louisville was consolidated.

With the Chicago Nationals in 1900, but was obstreperous and jumped to California.

With the Athletics—1902 to 1907, then came to St. Louis.

Largest salary he drew—$3000 per annum, with Connie Mack.

Salary in St. Louis—Dependent on performance. Contract called for $1200 with special increase for winning.

Waddell, who has been remarkable for his eccentric conduct as much as for his pitching prowess, was born in Butler, Pa., some thirty-six years ago. He came into prominence as a pitcher with the Western League team of Milwaukee, about 1897, and was purchased from that club by Louisville, then in the National League. In 1898 Waddell was sent back from Louisville to Columbus of the Western League for further fitting. In 1900 he came up to the Pittsburg Club, which took the players of the old Louisville Club on a consolidation deal. Waddell pitched wonderful ball in 1900. He was with the Chicago Nationals in 1901, but jumped to California, whence he was persuaded to return by Manager Mack of the Athletics who had the man in Milwaukee and who knew how to wheedle him.

For the following five years Waddell did wonderful things in a pitching way . Mack kept Waddell from 1902 to 1907, and then sold him to St. Louis for $5,000. He pitched fair ball for the Browns in 1908, but in the past two years had lost most of his famous speed and curve and has won few games.

In June, 1910, Waddell was turned over to Newark, New Jersey, of the Eastern League by the management of the Browns. At the time it was the understanding that Waddell had been relegated to the minors for all time, but such was not the case. In August the National Baseball Commission gave out Waddell's name as being one of the St. Louis Browns' reserves. The big eccentric southpaw will of course line up with the Browns in the Spring of 1911.

DIXIE WALKER—Dixie Walker is one of the young pitchers of the Washington team. In 1910, up to August he had pitched nine games for Washington of which he won three. This was his first season in the big league. Last year, 1909, Walker was the only man whose release was purchased from the minors. He is a most promising young player and with a year's seasoning is expected to hold his own with the best, for he is a big fellow and the possessor of great speed.

EDWARD A. WALSH—A player in every way worthy of special mention in this work is Edward A. Walsh, the giant pitcher of the Chicago White Stockings, whose wonderful pitching did as much to win a world's flag for his team as any other influence or force in that organization.

Standing six feet and over in his stockings and every ounce of the six feet whalebone and muscle, Walsh is a wonderful sort of a man. He was born in the rugged Pennsylvania mountains and grew tall and straight and vigorous as the pines of the hills where he rambled as a boy. He was 23 years of age five years ago when President Comiskey saw him playing with the Newark, New Jersey, team of the Eastern League.

Comiskey has no superior when it comes to judging a young player. He saw this great strapping boy, Walsh, playing with the Newarks. Walsh then had the rosy, healthy cheeks of a country boy, the clear eye of the mountaineer, and the loose, easy action of a man of wonderful power, and Comiskey saw in him the making of a great pitcher.

Almost at sight of Walsh, Comiskey put in a claim for his services. But the Chicago president had quite a battle trying to land Walsh in his camp, as Walter Burnham, manager of the Newark Club, claimed he was exempt from being drafted as the Newark Club had a prior contract with Walsh to play in Newark for 1904.

But the big player was finally awarded to Chicago and has done yeoman service for Comiskey the past seven years.

While with the Eastern League prior to his joining the Chicago White Stockings, Walsh was considered its speediest pitcher. He was not only a great twirler in his early days in the Eastern League, but a good all-round player, as he could play both in and out field positions; was a good, steady hitter and for a man of his size—he weighs 215 pounds—was fast on the bases.

He carried these good traits and even improved them after entering fast company and besides pitching wonderful ball for the Chicago White Stockings, his trusty bat has often pulled a game out of the fire for them.

Walsh started his career as a professional in 1902 with the Meriden (Conn.) team of

GEORGE EDWARD WADDELL.
The above is a portrait of George Edward Waddell, considered the best baseball card to-day in America. The "Rube" is a great pitcher, is now with the Newark Club of the Eastern League, but up to August this year he was the great left handed pitcher of the St. Louis American League team.

the New England League. He was reserved for the season of 1903 by that team. His phenomenal work attracted attention and after the Fourth of July he was sold to Newark, where he finished the season, winning over 70 per cent of his games.

Walsh was considered the "Iron Man McGinnity" of the Eastern League, as on four different occasions he won double headers on the same day for his club. And since joining the Chicagos he has kept up the record.

Walsh was born in Plains, Pa., May 22, 1882. He was a coal miner in his boyhood days and it was following that work that he first showed signs of excellence as a ball player, spending his leisure hours playing on the diamond and tossing the sphere. He made a hit almost immediately when he joined the Meriden Club of the Connecticut League as a pitcher. He was with Newark the following year and it was while pitching for that club that Comiskey saw and captured him.

Walsh's great effectiveness as a pitcher consists mainly of his ability to pitch what is called the spit ball.

He uses a trifle of slippery elm bark in his mouth and moistens a spot an inch square between the seams of the ball. His thumb he clinches tightly lengthwise on the opposite seam, and, swinging his arm straight overhead with terrific force, he drives the ball straight at the plate. At times it will dart two feet down or out, depending upon the way his arm is swung.

The American League, during the early days of the "spit ball," used it so much that Charlie Dryden, angler and scribe, remarked that: "The American League consists of Ban Johnson, the 'spit ball' and the Wabash Railroad."

Walsh is considered the "Charlie" Radbourne of the game to-day. Radbourne knew not the meaning of the word weary. Neither does Walsh. Other pitchers want to rest from four to five days between games. Walsh asks for no more than twenty-four hours rest between games.

The Chicago pitcher is one of the most perfectly formed athletes in the major leagues. Some say he is the Beau Brummel of balldom. Baseball players in general concede this honor to him. And Walsh is aware that he bears the distinction.

Whenever a discussion regarding the spitball comes up, rest assured that the name of Ed Walsh will be introduced, for he has used the salivated leather with more success than any other man in the business.

Sometimes Walsh is known as "the spitball trust." He uses the spitball more than any other man, and he is its best booster.

"If they would take away the spitball, would Walsh be the pitcher he is to-day?" asks a player.

The question will remain without an answer till the men who rule baseball pass some regulation which will bar the spitball in the future.

With the use of the spitball Walsh has wonderful control. The chief reason why so few twirlers use the spitball is because they can't control it. Walsh pitches few wild balls while using it.

Extra inning games never bother Walsh. Many claim he is the most powerful man playing in baseball to-day, and his record stands by the assertion, for Walsh has remarked repeatedly at the end of a

1 to 0 game that he felt no more fatigued than when he started the contest.

This brought him the title of "Iron Man." The White Sox played 154 games in 1908 and of these Walsh pitched fifty-five. He lost but fifteen out of that total of fifty-five.

It was not the pitching of fifty-five games that was so much of a feat, but the winning of forty of them that brought admiration and fame unto Walsh.

Defending the lightest hitting team in the American League, big Ed carried the White Sox through the year. He practically bore them on his shoulders, and when he set them down they were tied with the Tigers for the American League pennant. He had to win most of his games by holding his opponents down to one, two or no runs.

This is the seventh year that Walsh has been a member of a Comiskey organization. In the five years that are history he pitched 147 games for the Chicago Club, and of this number he won ninety-five.

Because of his wonderful work last year Comiskey gave Walsh a bonus, which brought his year's earnings up to something like $6,000.

There are thirteen in the Walsh family, and Ed, of White Sox fame, is the greatest of the thirteen.

This is some distinction, as every one of the thirteen has some recognized ability as an athlete.

JOHN WARHOP—John Warhop was one of the pitchers of the New York American League team during its 1910 season. He is the speedy right-handed pitcher of the Highlanders, joining them at the tail end of the 1908 campaign and holding his own in the big league ever since. A fine promising player is Warhop.

MICKEY WELCH—Mickey Welch, who, with Tim Keefe, shared the pitching honors with the New York Giants back in the eighties is now living at Holyoke, Mass., along with Tommy Tucker, at one time one of the crack first basemen of his day.

GEORGE WEIDMAN—George Weidman died on March 3, 1905, at the New York City Hospital after an operation for cancer of the throat.

In 1886 Weidman, with Getzein and Baldwin, was a member of the pitching staff of the great Detroit Club of that year.

He was a man of medium stature, but he had great speed and strength as a pitcher.

He had in fact all of the skill possessed by the cleverest pitcher of to-day and wonderful command of the ball.

GUY HARRIS WHITE—There are few greater pitchers in the business to-day than Guy Harris White, of the Chicago American League team.

White was born in Washington, D. C., April 9, 1879. He was educated at Georgetown University and pitched very effectively for the college team.

In 1900 he pitched for the Fleischman mountain team. He graduated in dentistry at Georgetown in 1902. He joined the Philadelphia National League Club in the Fall of 1901 and in 1902 joined the Chicago American League Club. White is associated with Charley Hickman in a sporting goods business in Washington, and off the field is an excellent dentist.

White is one of Comiskey's winning pitchers. White is a tall, sparely built man and is always in condition. It was

EDWARD A. WALSH.
Eddie Walsh is the great right-handed pitcher of Comiskey's White Sox team who came back again in 1910 and was a regular winner. Walsh is regarded in the American League as its best right-hander.

White's great work with the White Sox in their 1906 season that went far to win the world's championships for them from the Cubs.

During the 1910 season, despite the fact that the White Sox showed poor form, Dr. Harry kept up his good work, winning his share of games during the season.

IRVING K. WILHELM—Irving K. Wilhelm is one of the pitchers of the Brooklyn Club. This is his second season with that team. He took part in sixteen games in 1909, losing thirteen. Up to August in the 1910 season he had won three games out of nine pitched.

EDGAR ROBERT WILLETT—Last but not least of the Detroit pitchers, for he is a six-footer and weighs 185 pounds, is Edgar Robert Willett, a Kansan by residence, though born in Norfolk, Va., twenty-three years ago. He pitched a lot of winning games for the Wichita Club of the Western Association in 1906 and was purchased by Detroit. His record during the 1908 campaign was fifteen games won and nine lost, an average of .625. He was in eighth place in the list of pitchers in the American League race and but one Tiger was in front of him, this being Summers, who had an average of .667.

During the sessions of 1909 and 1910 Willett proved one of the steadiest and best boxmen on the Tiger staff.

JOE WILLIS—Joe Willis is the young pitcher whose release was bought by the St. Louis Browns in August, 1910, from the Springfield, Illinois team. Willis is a big left-hander who did some great pitching in the Three-Lamp League and the Browns expect great things of him. Willis is six feet tall, weighs 185 pounds and lets fly with the left. He has been with Springfield for two seasons and has made an enviable pitching record.

VICTOR C. WILLIS—Victor Willis, one of the Pittsburg pitchers, who took part in the World's Series of 1909, was born April 12, 1876, in Newark, Del. He weighs 185 pounds and stand six feet two inches. He played in 1894 with Wilmington; 1895 with Lynchburg, Va.; 1896 and 1897 with Syracuse, in the Eastern League; from 1898 to 1905, inclusive, with the Boston Nationals; from 1906 to 1909 with Pittsburg. At the close of the 1909 season he joined the St. Louis National League team for whom he is doing fine work now. Willis, for several years, was regarded as the Pirates' steadiest boxman. In 1909 he did much to help them capture the National League pennant, winning twenty-two games that year out of thirty-three played, an average of .667. In the 1910 season up to August he pitched thirteen games for St. Louis, winning seven of them.

GEORGE R. WILTSE—George R. Wiltse has been one of manager McGraw's most reliable twirlers for several seasons and his consistently good work on the slab has greatly helped to make the Giants pennant contenders during that time. Wiltse is a left-hander and played an important part in the World's Championship games of 1905 when he pitched winning ball for New York against the Athletics of Philadelphia.

PETER WILSON—Peter Wilson is one of the southpaw pitchers of the New York American League team. He is a most promising player.

JOSEPH WOOD—Joseph Wood, the fine young pitcher of the Boston Americans, was born in Kansas City, Mo., Oct. 25, 1889. He afterwards lived in Chicago and in Ouray, Colo.; afterwards returning to Kansas City to make his home in that city. He obtained his schooling at the Ouray High School and played the infield and outfield with the ball club of that institution.

When but 17 he played with the Hutchinson, Kas., team of the Western Association, which finished third in the race. He played with the Kansas City team in 1907 and 1908 and was purchased in July, 1908, by the Boston American League Club and from the first did very fine work showing remarkable speed and effectiveness. He stands five feet, eleven and a half inches.

Joe Wood is certainly a wonder. He is but a mere boy, yet his pitching will compare with that of any player in the country. He is but 19 years of age, but is no child in weight, turning the scales at 175 pounds. He may not be old but he is certainly "hefty."

RALPH WORKS—Ralph Works is one of the pitchers of Detroit's Champion American League team. He is a right-handed pitcher and batsman. Works is in his twenty-fifth year. He was with Medicine Hat and Syracuse before joining the Tigers in their 1908-1909 season. He is a most promising player and Jennings expects great things of him.

HARRY WRIGHT—It was in 1869, five years after Alphonse Martin had commenced pitching his slow curve ball, for the Eckfords of Brooklyn, that I saw Harry Wright try the same sort of a delivery against the Empires of St. Louis. It was so like the pitching of Martin that it might have been taken for that player's delivery by those best acquainted with it.

Wright was at this time the regular pitcher for the Cincinnati Reds, but his pitching must have lacked the effectiveness of that of Martin for the players soon commenced to hit it good and hard and Wright went to center field for his team while Asa Brainard, who had been playing out there was called in and made the regular pitcher of the team. In fact Martin was the only one of the famous slow pitchers who lasted over a night.

EARL YINGLING—Earl Yingling, one of the left-handed pitchers of the Toledo Club was transferred in August, 1910, to the Cleveland American League team, is with them now and promises to hold his own in the big league for an indefinite period.

DENTON T. YOUNG—If I were asked who was the greatest pitcher the game ever knew, I would say, Cy. Young, now the dean of the professional brigade of pitchers, a member of the Cleveland Club.

There have been other pitchers who have been more brilliant and successful than Young for a brief period, but none that have equalled him in long years of service and steady, faithful work,

Young has been pitching baseball in fast company since 1890. His first season out he won ten games and lost seven for the Cleveland team of that year.

Young is the author of three no-hit games, as follows: Cincinnati on Sept. 17th, 1897; Philadelphia, on May 5, 1904; and New York, on June 30th, 1908. Since 1890 when he joined the Cleveland Club, Young has won 478 of his 760 games. That's a

CYRUS YOUNG
Dean of Major League Pitchers and Considered by Many the Greatest Player in
His Position That Ever Lived.

percentage of victories of .620. His record in full is:

Year. Club.	Won.	Lost.
1890 Cleveland	10	7
1891 Cleveland	27	22
1892 Cleveland	36	10
1893 Cleveland	34	17
1894 Cleveland	25	22
1895 Cleveland	35	10
1896 Cleveland	29	16
1897 Cleveland	21	18
1898 Cleveland	24	14
1899 St. Louis	26	15
1900 St. Louis	20	18
1901 Boston	31	10
1902 Boston	32	12
1903 Boston	28	9
1904 Boston	26	16
1905 Boston	18	19
1906 Boston	13	21
1907 Boston	22	15
1908 Boston	21	11
1909 Cleveland	19	15
Totals	497	297

That he is a clever, hard working and conscientious player is proven by the fact that in all his long career he has played with but three clubs.

He was nine years with Cleveland and this will be the tenth year he has played in that city.

Then he was with St. Louis for two years, then for eight years with Boston, and the last two years with Cleveland.

Cy's real name is Denton T. Young, and when not outguessing the batter, he's trying to outguess the weather man down on his Ohio farm. For twenty years now, Cy has been leading this dual life.

His first big league engagement was Aug. 5, 1890, against Chicago, when he was given a workout with the Cleveland Club—the same with which he is now probably winding up the most unusual pitching career in the history of the game. In all the twenty years he has worked for big league clubs—once with the St. Louis team—Cy has never been a failure, but has been one of the reliables. It was at his own request that he was traded to the Boston Club. "The climate here did not suit him," Cy said. At that time Cy had seen long service, and the St. Louis Club did not think it would miss much anyway, when Cy went away.

But instead of growing old and stiff, Cy put on new youth at Boston and pitched championship baseball for that club. With Lou Criger, another St. Louis discard, he formed perhaps the most successful battery in the American League, in the 1908 year.

Then John I. Taylor took a chance at outguessing Cy. He figured it out, two years ago, that it was about the round in which Father Time was getting ready to administer the knockout to the Methuseleh of the baseball world. So he sold Criger to St. Louis and Young back to his old team, Cleveland, in exchange for Chech and Ryan and about all the loose coin the Forest City management could toss in.

But John I. was a bad guesser, Cy stalled off the Grim Reaper again and pitched great baseball for the Blues last year. This season he is still in fine form, according to McGuire, who relies on him to hold down the main post of all his slabmen.

And what is the secret of all this?

Old Cy has been asked this many times. But he takes it all soberly each time just as if it were a novelty, and says he doesn't know whether it's due to farming, wood chopping, chewing tobacco, or an occasional indulgence in the brew of the hops, all of which Cy is partial to.

"It isn't any secret," says Cy, "just outdoor life, moderation and a naturally good arm. I've slowed up some, of course, but it's in my legs, not in my throwing muscles. I don't know that I take any better care of myself than any other pitcher does, it just happens, this thing of my lasting. It isn't the result of any system."

Cy is now 44 years of age and pitching as good ball today as he did twenty years ago.

IRVING M. YOUNG—Irving M. Young is known as Cy Young the second. This left-handed pitcher was one of the phenomenons when he was with the Boston National League Club in 1905 and 1906. He was in 1909 a member of the Minneapolic Club of the American Association, and was drafted by the Chicago Americans as a result of his fine work.

Young was born at Columbia Falls, Washington County, Maine, July 21, 1877. He stands five feet nine inches in height and weighs 174 pounds when in condition. Young was recommended to the Boston National League Club and played in that city from 1905 to 1908 when he was traded to Pittsburg for McCarthy and Cy Young, 3rd. In 1909 he was released by Pittsburg to Minneapolis.

EDWARD ZMICH—Edward Zmich is the name of the young pitcher who joined the St. Louis National League team in June, 1910.

His release was purchased from the Marion Club of the Ohio State League for $1,500, the highest price ever paid for the release of a player in that organization.

Zmich is 24 years old, a man of excellent habits and one who is ambitious. He pitches a heady game, has an abundance of curves and speed at his command and is quick to analyse the weakness of a batter.

Zmich had a fine record in the Ohio State League up to the time he joined the St. Louis team in 1910.

Winning 15 out of 19 games was easy for him. In addition he did utility work in about twenty games. In the 39 games his batting average was .279, and more than one game was won by Marion through his great hitting when sent in as a pinch swatter in the ninth. Zmich is a willing worker in every sense of the term. No player will strive harder to win than he. An instance may be cited of his loyalty to his club. In several double-headers this year and last he worked the first game. Denied the privilege of working two in a day, he has forfeited his right to leave the grounds and change clothes, after pitching the first game, to wait around and bat for someone in the second, if he was needed.

EDWARD KONETCHY.

The above is a likeness of Edward Konetchy, the crack first baseman of the St. Louis National League Club. Elsewhere in this book appears a sketch of his career.

THE NATIONAL GAME.

THE GREAT FIRST BASEMEN.

A LIST OF THOSE WHO HAVE BEEN AT THE TOP WHEN IT CAME TO COVERING THE INITIAL BAG FOR THE BIG TEAMS OF THE OLD PROFESSIONAL ASSOCIATION AND THE NATIONAL LEAGUE.

These are the men who led in the fielding record at first base since the first years of the old Professional Association and the National League up to the present year:

Year. First Basemen. Club.	Fielding Games.	Pct.	Year. First Basemen. Club.	Fielding Games.	Pct.
1871 West Fisler—Ath., Phila	28	.961	1891 Tom Brown—Philadelphia	97	.986
1872 C H. Gould—Boston	44	.970	1892 Roger Connor—Philadelpnia	153	.985
1873 J. Mack—Philadelphia	45	.965	1893 W. Brown—Louisville	117	.987
1874 Jas. O'Rourke—Boston	70	.966	1894 A. C. Anson—Chicago	83	.988
1875 Ed. Mills—Hartford	64	.964	1895 O. Tebeau—Cleveland	52	.992
1876 Joe Start—New York	56	.963	1896 O. Tebeau—Cleveland	112	.987
1877 Joe Start—Hartford	50	.964	1897 O. Tebeau—Cleveland	91	.994
1878 J. F. Sullivan—Cincinnati	60	.974	1898 G. LaChance—Brooklyn	75	.989
1879 A. C. Anson—Chicago	49	.974	1899 W. Clarke—Pittsburg	79	.988
1880 A. C. Anson—Chicago	77	.977	1900 Dan McGann—St. Louis	124	.989
1881 A. C. Anson—Chicago	83	.975	1901 Dan McGann—St. Louis	113	.986
1882 D. Brouthers—Buffalo	84	.974	1902 W. E. Bransfield—Pittsburg	109	.988
1883 John Morrill—Boston	80	.974	1903 Dan McGann—New York	129	.988
1884 Joe Start—Providence	90	.974	1904 Dan McGann—New York	141	.990
1885 A. McKinnon—St. Louis	100	.978	1905 Dan McGann—New York	136	.991
1886 S D. Farrar—Philadelphia	118	.979	1906 Dan McGann—New York	133	.995
1887 John Morrill—Boston	124	.985	1907 Dan McGann—New York	81	.994
1888 A. C. Anson—Chicago	134	.985	1908 F. Tenney—New York	156	.990
1889 A. C. Anson—Chicago	134	.982	1909 F. L. Chance—Chicago	92	.994
1890 J. Virtue—Cleveland	62	.982	1910 Chance—Chicago	87	.996

THE AMERICAN LEAGUE.

LIST OF THE MEN WHO HAVE LED ALL AT FIRST BASE IN THIS ORGANIZATION FROM 1900 TO 1909.

Year. First Basemen. Club.	Fielding Games.	Pct.	Year. First Basemen. Club.	Fielding Games.	Pct.
1900 John Anderson—Milwaukee	90	.989	1905 Charles Carr—Cleveland	87	.991
1901 John Anderson—Milwaukee	125	.981	1906 J. Donohue—Chicago	154	.988
1902 George Carey—Washington	120	.991	1907 J. Donohue—Chicago	157	.994
1903 John Anderson—St. Louis	120	.987	1908 J. Donohue—Chicago	83	.994
1904 George LaChance—Boston	157	.991	1909 F. Isbell—Chicago	101	.994
			1910 Hauser—Philadelphia	**29**	**1.000**

Next to the batteries come the men who have played first base since the game became a real profession.

The first of the great first basemen were those who gained fame in 1871, the first year in which professional teams were at work in the leading cities of both East and West.

Of this lot West Fisler of the Athletics of Philadelphia was perhaps the most brilliant player in his position. He was noted for his clean and quick work and for his admirable coolness at all stages. Like all the players of the Athletic Club, Fisler was a man of medium stature. He led the country at first base in 1871. A year later the honor was taken from him by Charles H. Gould, the tall first baseman of the Boston Club of that year who had gone to Boston from the Cincinnati Reds with George Wright, another of the great players of that team.

Gould's idea of playing the base was standing very close to the bag, attending to the throws that came within reach, and allowing the second baseman to cover the territory lying between the first and second bag.

Gould won his first real spurs when he made the long tour with the Cincinnati Reds in 1870, and in 1872 he was playing the position for Boston.

McAtee, who at this time held down first base for the original Chicago White Stockings was not much of a fielder nor base runner, but he was good with the stick.

J. Mack of the Philadelphia Club was the champion first baseman of 1873. He was like Fisler, below the medium in height and general stature.

James O'Rourke of the Boston Club of 1874 was the leading first baseman of that year. O'Rourke was playing until last year and is best remembered by the old army, as the captain and manager of the Buffalo Club in the days when Jack Rowe, Dan Brouthers, Hardy Richardson and other great players were with it.

Mack, the champion first baseman of 1873 stood out in strange contrast to Edward Mills, the great first baseman of the Hartfords of 1875.

Mills was first known as the big first baseman of the Mutuals of New York who, in 1870 fought hard with the Athletics of Philadelphia for leading honors. Mills stood over six feet in height and swung a very heavy bat.

The leading first baseman of 1876 and 1877 was Joe Start of the New York and Hartford clubs. The baseball writers called Start the greatest first base player of his day, and he undoubtedly was. In fact proof of this was given, for years later Start was holding down the initial bag. To be exact, he was the first baseman of the Champion Providence team of 1884, the team that won the National League pennant of that year and then the World's Championship.

Honest Joe Start he was called, and beside being an honest and great first baseman he was a fine, hard-hitting left-handed batsman,

FRANK CHANCE.

Frank L. Chance, peerless leader of the Chicago Cubs, 1910, champions of the National League. Chance has the honor of having directed the Cubs through four pennant winning seasons.

Start came from the field at Brooklyn that gave Ferguson, Burdock, Pike, Mills, Pearce and other great players to the profession. He was playing great ball in the sixties, seventies and eighties. What player has ever beaten that?

J. F. Sullivan of Cincinnati led the first basemen of America in 1878. He was a fine heady player and an excellent batsman.

John Morrill of the Champion Bostons was the leading first baseman in 1883.

Tall, black haired and handsome was John Morrill, for years the captain and first baseman of the Champion Boston Club.

Morrill learned the rudiments of the game while playing with the Stars, an amateur team on the Boston common.

He afterward became a member of the Boston team and worked his way into a captaincy and managership. He was a great player in his day, great as a fielder and great as a batsman and a captain and manager of the first class.

Joe Start captured leading honors as a first baseman again in 1884, and a year later the honor fell to Alec McKinnon.

McKinnon, who played at first base for the first St. Louis National League team in the old Union Grounds at Jefferson and Cass avenues, was a fine fielder.

As a batsman, too, he had few superiors and he was an awfully good hitter in the pinch. When playing for St. Louis he was unusually thin and delicate looking, and he died soon after leaving here— but despite his apparently weak condition while in St. Louis, he could hit the ball an awful rap.

Jake Virtue of Cleveland was the leading first baseman in 1890 and in 1891 the honor went to Tom Brown of Philadelphia. They were two fine fielders and hard-hitting batsmen.

Roger Connor, a giant, much resembling Dan Brouthers, not only in size, but by reason of the fact that he was a hard-hitting left-handed batsman, was the leading first baseman in 1892. He is best remembered, however, as the first baseman of the New York World Champions when Ewing, Ward, Keefe and other great stars of the olden days were with that team.

Bill Brown of Louisville came after Connor—a stalwart, broad-shouldered fellow who could field finely and hit well.

Anson led the first basemen again in 1894 and then came Oliver Tebeau of Cleveland, who was the champion first baseman in 1895, 1896 and 1897.

Tebeau learned to play ball in North St. Louis.

There was a large family of Tebeau's and they all loved the game, loved it so well that two of the boys, Oliver and George became famous in its annals.

They learned to play on the prairie near the old Water Tower on Grand avenue.

"Pat" Tebeau, the name Oliver was best known by, and his brother George, were the star players of the Peach Pie team of North St. Louis and later they were the brightest on the Shamrock nine, which held forth in the same neighborhood.

Pat's first professional work was with the St. Joe team of the Western League in the early eighties and then he came into the limelight as the captain, manager and first baseman of the Cleveland League team.

It was Tom Loftus, then manager of the Clevelands, that saw in "Pat" Tebeau the sort of spirit needed to make a good commander, and when Loftus gave up the reins he put them in the hands of "Pat." That they were well handled goes without saying. Tebeau was not only a fine first baseman, but a hitter of the first flight.

George LaChance of Brooklyn was the leading first baseman of 1898 and W. Clark of Pittsburg carried off the honor in 1899.

Johnny Ward, one of the finest ball tossers in his day, a great pitcher and a wonderful infielder, now a prominent lawyer in New York City, after seeing Hal Chase of the New York team play, did not express the least hesitation in awarding to Chase the palm of all the players he had ever seen handle a ball, and Ward has seen them all, from times far back to the present day. Artists of the caliber of Chase are scarce indeed, and it means a deal to the New York Club to have him back in line once more.

Doyle of the Forest Citys of Rockford, Carleton of the Forest Citys of Cleveland, Fisler of the Haymakers of Troy, Allison of the Eckfords of Brooklyn, Dehlman and Croft of the St. Louis Browns of 1875 and 1876, Charles Houtz of the Indianapolis Club of 1879, and Carbine of the Louisvilles of the early eighties, were all great first base players in their day.

Referring to the great first basemen, the greatest the world has ever known, W. A. Phelon, baseball editor of the New York Telegraph in November, 1909, had this to say in the columns of that newspaper:

"Two of the classiest first basemen that ever played the game are, apparently, almost through, and when they leave the fast company it will take some great hustling to bring the standard of first base play up to the mark they set. Fred Tenney and Jiggs Donohue, a pair of players who never had a superior in the brilliant work of the position, have slowed up, started on the downhill trail, and seem to be almost done. It is, of course, possible for these two men—who are not old in years ——to come back and show former speed in another campaign, but the indications are all against it—the big league seems due to lose two of the most spectacular infielders that ever wore the big thick glove.

"The career of Tenney and Donohue was oddly similar. Each is left-handed, and each started in fast company as a catcher. Only one left-handed catcher—John Clements—was ever a star behind the bat. Fred and Jiggs, great backstops in their amateur days, found that they were frosts in the big league and both of them, with rare good sense, proceeded to try another job. Both became first basemen, both speedily grew into masters of the position, and now they are going out together.

"The wizardry which Tenney and Donohue worked in the art of first base play was something almost uncanny. Both of them could make dazzling pick-ups of wide-flung balls, hitting the ground in any old spot, they were enough to drive the fans hysterical. Both could leap high, reach up the gloved right hand and pull down frantic throws. Both were marvels at chasing foul flies, or snapping up grounder cutting across the line. Tenney was also the king of all first basemen when it came to mixing into plays around the bases. Old-time first-sackers contented themselves with working in a sort of sturdy, mechanical fashion, doing just what came straight into their hands to do, and never dreaming of interfering in the complicated plays that were coming off in other sections of the field. Tenney changed all that and forced himself

JOHN J. McCLOSKEY.

McCloskey, who has been directing the Brewers of Milwaukee for two seasons, is another one of the best bets when it comes to landing great lights from the baseball firmament. McCloskey has developed thousands of ball players and is even to-day recognized as one of the real judges of young ball players.

into every play that was happening around the circuit. He taught the other first baseman things they didn't imagine possible, and, even after they had learned his tricks, he still remained their king.

"Donohue was not as great in bringing off trick plays and mixing with the doings as was Tenney, but was the greater of the two when it came to impossible performances, stops and catches, that seemed beyond the power of any performer. Both were strong batsmen and valuable factors in all departments of the game, and, till they slowed up with the years, speedy base runners.

"The first base play of 1909, despite the slowing up of Donohue and Tenney, was of admirable quality, but does not promise any improvement for next season. Konetchy and Chase kept the standard up, but can hardly be any better next year, while the absence of Donohue and Tenney will make the general average of skill fall short to some degree.

"The Boston Nationals, with Beck, Stem and Autrey, fared but poorly on first during the recent campaign. Brooklyn had Jordan and Hummel, both good batsmen, and fairly strong infielders, though not of Chase-Tenney class.

"Frank Chance, with Del Howard as understudy, was again on deck for the Cubs. The Big Bear, who, like Donohue, and Tenney, was formerly a catcher, as a swell fielder, clumsy in style, but terribly effective, while his batting, base running and qualities of leadership make him a great figure among modern first basemen. Howard was not nearly as good as in the previous campaign, seeming to have an off year.

"The general class of the first basemen was largely saved from deterioration by Hoblitzell, the 20-year-old recruit of the Reds. This young fellow played fine field ball, though not of Tenney-Donohue class, and was the best batting first baseman in the country—a splendid slugger.

"Tenney, as has been said, is going back, and 1909 was too stiff in the legs to give McGraw his former service, either around the base or at the bat. His understudy, Merkle, did not do as well as in 1908, and does not appear to be a real big leaguer any more.

"Bransfield, of the Quakers, had a good year with the bat and fielded well, and seems to be something unusual—a player who was almost all in and then came back stronger than ever.

"Pittsburg worked a new man, Abstein, who hit strongly and fielded well, but got in bad at the finish by poor work in the world's championship. The unlucky Cardinals had one of the finest of them all. Konetchy the Greek, whose all-round play was magnificent. This man has developed slowly, and is now fully ripe—a strong and timely batsman and about as valuable as any first sacker in the land. McGraw wants him, but has a fine chance—nix—to land the boy.

"Harry Davis, the veteran first baseman of the Athletics, is not retrograding much, if any. He may be a little slower than four years ago, but can still hit and still plays a fancy game upon the bag.

"Jake Stahl, of the Boston Reds, in 1909, had the best year of his life. Free from managerial worries, he cut loose, and for the first time since he entered the big leagues, slammed the ball around as he has always been expected to.

"Comiskey, with Donohue slowing up,

has his troubles to fill the job. To the intense sorrow of the Old Roman, his other veteran, Isbell, likewise showed signs of retrogression, and the White Sox will have a new boy on the first base job for 1910.

"Stovall, the Cleveland first sacker, did not bat as high as usual, but played good, efficient ball, just the same.

"Claude Rossman, who had been gradually getting in Dutch at Detroit, was presented with the hook in midseason. Moriarity played some games on the bag, doing well, and Tom Jones was obtained from St. Louis for the latter part of the season. Jones is a good batter, but a mechanical player, without much snap and brilliancy.

"Hal Chase, the Highlanders' wonderful first baseman, is now the premier without dispute, since the backing up of Tenney and Donahue. He always had swarms of advocates who claimed that he had Fred and Jiggs beaten as it was, but now that they are passing out he reigns supreme. Chase has Donohue's skill on fielding difficult chances and mixes into the play as Tenney was wont to do—a combination that ought to make a first baseman incomparable, especially when, as is the case with Hal, it is coupled with strong batting and good base-running.

"Jones did most of the work for McAleer till he was traded to Detroit. Griggs was on the job afterward and, though at a new position, fielded fairly and batted well.

"Donohue and Unglaub, with a few volunteers, took most of the work for Washington. As has been said, Jiggs is passing out, while Unglaub is a good performer any place you put him."

Now, breaking away from the record list, I give a list arranged alphabetically of the players who have and who are now playing in the National League, American League and who played in the old major league organizations. That list is as follows:

WILLIAM ABSTEIN—William Abstein, first baseman of the champion Pittsburg Club of 1909, was born February 2, 1885, in St. Louis, Mo. He stands six feet and weighs 185 pounds. He played in 1903 with Belleville, Ill., in the Missouri-Illinois League; 1904 with Houston, in the Texas League; 1905 and 1906 with Shreveport, in the Southern League; 1907 and 1908 with Providence, in the Eastern League; 1909 with Pittsburg, in the National League; 1910 with St. Louis, in the American League, until June 1, when he was given his release.

Abstein was turned over to the Jersey City team of the Eastern League by the Browns. He played nice ball on first for the Easterners. He recovered his old form in the Eastern League, and enjoyed a prosperous season, both in fielding and at the bat.

CAPTAIN ADRIAN C. ANSON—A. C. Anson was the leading first baseman according to the figures in 1879, 1880 and 1881, and as if that were not honor enough he captured the lead again ten years later, or to be exact, in 1888 and 1889, and then again in 1894, five years later. In brief, even as a fielder, Anson was at the top of his profession for full fifteen years. For twenty years he was at the top as a batsman.

For years, in fact, the best known figure in the baseball world of Chicago was

Adrian C. Anson, the old Roman of the baseball field.

I first saw Anson playing on the old Lake Front grounds at Chicago in 1870 or nearly forty years ago.

He was then covering third base for the Forest Citys of Rockford, Ill., a team that had come to town to play a series with the Chicago White Stockings of that year.

I shall never forget the wonderful work he did then. He stood over six feet in height, was straight and slender as an arrow, could run with the fleetness of a deer and could hit the ball harder than any man I had ever seen.

I was told then that this great young player had been imported from Marshalltown, Iowa, where he was known as the "Marshalltown Infant," and where he and his father and brothers had the distinction of all playing on the one nine.

Anson's days with the Forest Citys were few. He left that organization to go to the Athletics of Philadelphia, but after a season there he returned to the Garden City and for more than twenty years after he was the most picturesque and most familiar figure on the Chicago League team.

It was Anson who put together the famous Chicago White Stockings which in its palmiest days had such great and famous players as Flint and Kelly, catchers; Goldsmith, Corcoran, McCormick and Clarkson, pitchers; Anson, first base; Quest and Pfeffer, second base; Burns, third base; Williamson, short field, and Kelly, Dalrymple, Gore, Sunday and Nicol in the outer works.

Writing of Anson, Tim Murnane, the veteran sporting writer of the Boston Globe, the other day said:

"Anson looked his best in '74 when he went to England with the American ball players.

"Six feet in his stockings and weighing 190 pounds, while as straight as an arrow, it was no wonder that John Bull saw in the young American a boy who might do some clean fighting as a soldier in the ranks.

"I was strolling with Anson in Hyde Park, London, in the summer of '74 when we were stopped by a man who smilingly asked if we would like to become members of the British Army. We listened to the proposition and then informed the English officer that we were Americans, when a very clever apology followed."

Of Anson, in a recent letter the veteran Ted Sullivan had this to say:

"A. C. Anson, the gallant old commander of the Chicago White Stockings, was the most aggressive batter that ever faced a pitcher. He was not only aggressive, but the greatest batsman in the entire history of baseball. He showed his sterling character in the thickest of that greatest baseball storm of 1890—known as the Brotherhood War—when the National League ship was shaken from stem to stern by the assaults of the Brotherhood ship. The players of the National League ship were deserting it in this terrible storm by getting on board the Brotherhood craft, but the form of big Anson was still seen on the National League ship ——refusing to leave her, but ready to sink with her if she went down. This is the end of my tribute to his integrity and steadfastness to the old National League ship."

JAKE BECKLEY—Jake Beckley, who played with Pittsburg, St. Louis and other major league teams, was one of the hardest hitting first basemen in America.

For twenty-three years his name was a by-word to the fans of the big league circuit. For twenty years he was a familiar figure in the National League. Years ago he was the idol of the Pittsburg fans. That was before the days of Honus Wagner, Fred Clark and even Barney Dreyfuss. In those days Barney Dreyfuss was head of the Louisville team and Wagner, Clark and a few other stars of the Smoky City had not been thought of.

To-day Beckley's name is but a memory in the Smoky City and none but the oldest fans remember his playing. Beckley joined the Pittsburg team June 22, 1888, and remained there until 1896, when he was sold to the New York Giants.

Pittsburg was not Jake's first professional job, as he broke into the game as a pro two years before that as a member of the Leavenworth (Kan.) Club. The following Spring he was sold to the Lincoln, Neb., team. After finishing the season with this club he beat it to the coast and played all that winter with a team at Stockton, Cal., where he made a great record for himself. The next Spring he was secured by the St. Louis Whites and the St. Louis team in turn sold him to Pittsburg in June of the same year.

Beckley was born in Hannibal, Mo., August 4, 1867, is now in his forty-third year and twenty-four of these years were spent in playing professional ball, a record any man may well be proud of. Of these twenty-four years spent in professional ball, Jake has put nineteen of them in the big leagues.

His first big league game was with St. Louis in 1888 and his last big league game was with the St. Louis Cardinals in 1907. Now let us go back to Pittsburg, that is where we left Jake as a big league player. He remained with Pittsburg until 1896, when he was secured by the New York Giants.

The Giants did not hold on to Jake long, for the next year, 1897, he was found putting up his same old game as a member of the Cincinnati Reds.

A Red he remained until 1903, when we once more find him back in St. Louis, this time a member of the Cardinals. Jake held down his job in St. Louis until 1907 and that is going some.

In 1907 George Tebeau, owner of the Kansas City team of the American Association, bought his release from St. Louis and placed him at the head of his club. He succeeded Monte Cross as manager of Kansas City. Jake, however, was not a howling success as a manager and he was relieved of the job by Danny Shay and it was he who gave Jake his unconditional release on April 23, 1910.

Jake will play with Topeka in 1911.

HUGH BRADLEY—Hugh Bradley, who is playing a grand game at first for the Washington Americans, was last year the first baseman of the Worcester Club. He is a nephew of Michael H. Bradley of Lawrence, also a former New England Leaguer. Several clubs were after Bradley. He has been with Jess Burkett of the Worcester Club the past three years and under the fine guiding hand of Jesse has developed into a first-class first baseman.

WILLIAM E. BRANSFIELD—William E. ("Kitty") Bransfield, first baseman of the Philadelphia Club, was born at Worcester, Mass., on January 7, 1875. Began at Grafton, Mass., in 1897, going to Boston in 1898, though he did not play enough games to get recorded. He caught for Worcester in 1899 and in 1900 was played at first base. Pittsburg got him in 1901 and he remained there until 1905, when he was released to Philadelphia.

He is probably the most popular ball player in the National League. The pitchers, though, never did like to see "Kit" step up to the plate, as he is one of the most dangerous sluggers, in a pinch, in the game to-day.

DAN BROUTHERS—Dan Brouthers led all the first basemen in 1882. He was a member of the Buffalo team of that year. Brouthers was a great, tall, magnificently built man and one of the hardest hitting left-handed batsmen that ever lived.

Brouthers went with Jack Rowe and Hardy Richardson to Detroit, and they were members of the World's Champion Detroit team in 1887.

FRANK L. CHANCE—Perhaps the most valuable man to any major league team in America is Frank Chance, the manager, captain and first baseman of the Chicago National League Club.

At home he is well called "The Peerless Leader."

The "Peerless Leader" of the Chicago National League Club has been described and interviewed in newspapers and magazines until it would seem that his very trait and peculiarity ought to be familiar to the public. And yet one of his most marked characteristics has been strangely overlooked. It is the strong contrast between his demeanor in private life and his behavior as soon as he gets into his baseball uniform.

Such a contrast is not unusual. The most domineering business man often turns into the meekest of lambs when he gets home to his wife; the most learned doctor will sometimes be made a fool of on the witness stand by a quick-witted, clever lawyer; that lawyer himself might very well be a stammering craven in a big Stock Exchange deal.

With Chance it is a case of a rather quiet—perhaps even diffident—man, being transformed, as soon as he gets out on the ball grounds, into a determined, able, and magnetic leader of men. He becomes a fighter, to put it briefly.

His fighting spirit inspires his men with extraordinary enthusiasm and at the same time his honor system with them (there is no supervision of the men after hours on the Chicago team) gained their friendship. Combined with these, his cleverness in meeting an unexpected situation and general effectiveness have helped give him his great success.

The great manager and first baseman of the Chicago Cubs was born thirty-one years ago in California, Fresno being the exact spot of his nativity. Chance, or "Husk," as he is popularly known to the fans, was in the class of 1894 at the University of Washington, Irvington, Cal., but left college to join the Chicago National League team eleven years ago. Chance has never played with any other professional club. He was used as a catcher when he first joined Chicago, but Manager Selee made a first baseman of him. Chance succeeded Selee as manager of the Cubs during the season of 1905, and since then has piloted his team to three National League pennants and two World's Championships. He throws and bats right-handed.

Frank Chance is a "Native Son," having first seen daylight in Fresno, Cal., on September 9, 1877. He comes of Scotch and English extraction. He is the son of William Harvey Chance, who stars as vice president for the First National Bank of Fresno, and even though he hadn't happened to be the "Pop" of the famous Peerless Leader, his name would have gone down in history as one of Fresno's premier citizens.

HAL CHASE—There are many who claim that Hal Chase of the New York Americans is the best first baseman in America. By others he is considered the best that ever played the bag.

It is true that his ability as a base runner, as an inside player, his speed and quick grasp of points add to his reputation; but as a first baseman pure and simple he also excels.

He doesn't make any less errors than his contemporaries—he may make more—but a majority of these are due to his superior ability in getting to a ball and planning and making the play before his companions are ready for it. His style, too, adds to his reputation. He has magnetism on the field.

Perhaps were he a bit more of a plodder, had a bit more stability, so to speak, he might be still better.

Style and rapidity of action aside, Chase has solid ability as a first sack guardian, and we come back to the main point, which is that in spite of the long list of first basemen there have been few of the Chase class.

Chase, who is a left-hander, thinks that players using that hand are better fitted to cover the initial bag than any other.

He might have cited Joe Start, Fred Tenney and other left-handed players who covered the bag so well in their day.

In a recent article on this very subject Chase had this to say:

"I believe a left-handed first baseman is better fitted for the position than a right-hander. He uses the left hand for throwing. This makes a snap throw to second or third much easier. He naturally faces these bags. The right-hander has to turn around, losing valuable time. As to throwing to the plate, there is no advantage at either style. I believe the time will come when a right-handed first baseman will be almost as rare as a left-handed third baseman now is. Fred Tenney was the pioneer southpaw first sacker. He originated the sacrifice killing play. That is, on a bunt to him, he tried for the man that was to be advanced. I did the same thing before I heard of Tenney. It was as natural for me to do it as to play for the plate with bases full and none out. For a right-hander, the play is more difficult. He loses too much time in turning after getting the ball."

JOHN F. COLLINS—John F. Collins started out in the 1910 season as the left fielder of the Chicago American League team, but later was made the regular first baseman of the club.

Collins commenced playing baseball in Newton, Mass., at the age of 16, and for a number of years pitched for the strongest semi-professional teams in Massachusetts. He later played with the Marlboro team, and then went to Haverhill of the New England League. Collins played shortstop for Haverhill during the season of 1907, and in 1908 signed to play first base, but on account of injuries was kept out of the game almost the entire season.

JOE QUINN.
As he looked when he first played first ba se for the St. Louis Union team of 1884.

In 1909 he played second second base for Springfield, Mass., of the Connecticut League. He had a fielding percentage of .906 and a batting average in eighty-eight games of .322. He scored sixty-four runs, stole twenty-four bases, and made twenty-one doubles, twelve triples and eight home runs

DICK COOLEY—Dick Cooley, once famous as a first baseman in the major leagues, is now managing the Topeka Club of the Western League.

A fine first baseman and a heavy hitting left-handed batsman was Cooley in his day.

He is one of the players who made a batting record of .300 or better for four years from 1896 to 1908, inclusive, in all major leagues.

In 1895, 1896, 1897 and 1898 Cooley batted .340, .300, .327 and .317.

CHARLES A. COMISKEY—First and foremost of the greatest first basemen the game has ever known, comes Charles A. Comiskey, now the president and owner of the Chicago White Sox of the 1909 American League.

As a fielder and all-round guardian of the initial bag, I do not believe there ever lived a player who could compare with Comiskey when he played at first, managed and captained the for a long while, invincible St. Louis Browns.

My first impressions of Comiskey were gleaned in the early seventies when I saw him pitch for the prairie teams who played their games on the west side of Chicago.

There were two ball grounds on the West side in Chicago then frequented by the amateur players at almost all hours of the day. One of these was located at Harrison and Ada streets and the other at Madison street and Western avenue.

In the early and late seventies the Libertys, the Dreadnaughts, the Actives, the Mutuals and the Neversweat baseball teams played games on these grounds.

On the Libertys were the O'Day brothers, Henry and Jim, the former now a National League umpire; Hayes, lke Fleming and other players then famous in Chicago's amateur baseball world.

One day among these players appeared Charles A. Comiskey, tall, lean and awkward. He came when a pitcher was needed and filled the bill so well that his fame spread.

T. P. Sullivan, famous afterward and now in baseball, at this time was living in Dubuque, and wishing to get together a team of semi-professional players for that city, he came to Chicago. What Sullivan wanted was train boys who would act as train butchers, sell newspapers and peanuts on the trains and when not engaged in that occupation, who would go out and play baseball.

The year before Sullivan had had a real professional team in Dubuque, but it had proven a costly experiment. Now, he wanted to try the semi-professional game. The 1879 team which Sullivan had placed in the field had in its ranks several players who later became famous.

This team included Thomas J. Sullivan, catcher, a St. Louis boy who had made good as a receiver with the Worcesters of 1878; L. P. Reis, pitcher of the Chicagos of 1878; W. B. Lapham, first baseman of the Worcesters of 1878; Thomas J. Loftus, second base; Jack Gleason, third base; W. Gleason, shortstop; Charles Radbourne, fielder and change pitcher; T. P. Sullivan,

fielder and pitcher, and J. Ross, right field.

Now, this team, having been a failure financially, Sullivan set out to organize one of players who would follow business pursuits when not actively engaged in the playing of the game, and it was players of this sort that he looked for on the Chicago prairies.

Comiskey, who Sullivan had known at college, measured right up to the latter's standard and he was taken to Dubuque and set to work there for the Western News Company. When not thus employed in 1880 he could be found on the field playing with Ted Sullivan's Dubuque "Rabbits," which included in its ranks Jack Ross, catcher; Ted Sullivan, pitcher; Comiskey, first baseman and change pitcher; Tom Loftus, second baseman, and any other players, amateur or professional that happened along. It was this semi-professional nine which Ted Sullivan, at my solicitation brought to St. Louis in the Summer of 1881 and it was then and there that we selected Charles A. Comiskey the first baseman of these same Dubuque "Rabbits" to cover first base for our St. Louis Browns of the American Association during their initial season, 1882.

To climb from the humble position of train butcher to the head of a baseball club representing the greatest city of the West.

To hew the way from comparative poverty to a place high up in the financial world these days is an undertaking that requires pluck, push, brains and enterprise and Comiskey possesses all of these traits.

His life reads like a romance and it might be summed up in this way:

1880—Newsboy and member of the Dubuque semi-professional baseball team.

1881—Newsboy and first baseman of the Dubuque semi-professional team.

1882—First baseman of the St. Louis Browns, St. Louis' representative in the American Association, which had just been organized.

1883—Captain and first baseman of the St. Louis Browns.

1884—Captain, manager and first baseman of the St. Louis Browns.

1885-1886—Captain and manager of the St. Louis Browns, who these two years captured the championship of the American Association and subsequently defeated the Chicago Club of the National League in the games each Fall for the World's Championship.

1887-1888—Captain and manager of the St. Louis Browns who again captured the American Association flag, but who these years failed to win the World's Championship.

1889—Captain, manager and first baseman of the St. Louis Browns.

1890—Captain, manager and first baseman of the Chicago Brotherhood Club.

1891—Captain, manager and first baseman of the St. Louis Browns.

1892-1893-1894—Captain, manager and first baseman of the Cincinnati Reds.

1895-1896-1897—Captain, manager and first baseman of the St. Paul Club of the Western Association.

1898-1899—Captain, manager and first baseman of the Chicago Western Association Club.

1900 to 1908, inclusive—Owner and president of the Chicago American League Club.

In brief, Comiskey has been actively connected with the game from 1878 to 1909, a period of thirty-one years, in which time he has never been idle for a moment, but

THE NATIONAL GAME.

ever and always actively engaged in building up his team and enlarging its activity.

Four times in the American Association Comiskey headed the St. Louis Browns, the team which won the championship.

Twice while commanding the St. Louis Browns his team carried off World's Championship honors.

Three times his Chicago White Stockings have captured the American League pennant and three times under his guiding hand they have captured the championship of the world.

Three times in his thirty years' career has Comiskey seen his nine land at the very top when it came to a division of leading baseball honors. What other professional player can point to a record equal to this?

Perhaps no baseball writer of the present day has enjoyed a closer acquaintance with Comiskey than I have. We have been close and dear friends from the day Ted Sullivan smuggled his Dubuque "Rabbits" to town. That was nearly thirty years ago and ball players by the caravan have come and gone since then, but Comiskey seems to go on forever.

In all the years I have known Comiskey I have always found him the pink of kindness with always a respect and consideration for the rights and feelings of others.

Often asked as to why he had been more successful than other baseball managers I always attributed his success to his gameness more than to any other one thing.

When commanding a nine Comiskey never knew what it was to be beaten. Often and often, as the saying is, by his quick wit and gameness he snatched a victory out of the very jaws of defeat. He was never known to weaken and he never could hit the ball so well as when in the breach and when a hit was needed the most.

He had no use for the grandstand player who could hit the ball over the fence when the bases were clear and his side a mile ahead, but he loved the man who could hit the ball right on the nose when a run was needed and a good clout meant the game.

Comiskey instilled this idea into the hearts of his players and Curt Welch, Billy Gleason, Tip O'Neill, were three of the boys after his own heart and were sure to join him in doing the right thing at the right time and place.

It was this quality of gameness that won championships for St. Louis long ago and it is this quality that he has instilled into his Chicago team and that has made them always awfully troublesome even to their most formidable opponents.

And this quality of gameness in Comiskey was never better exemplified than just before the second games for the World's Championship between the St. Louis and Chicago teams were played in 1886.

A. G. Spalding, then at the head of the Chicago Club, champions of the National League, acted as though he did not care to put his team against the St. Louis Browns, winners of the American Association pennant of that year.

When pressed to play he said he would only allow the Chicago Club to play the St. Louis Club on condition that the winning team take all of the gate receipts.

Some of the St. Louis players demurred to this proposition, but Comiskey, backed by Von Der Ahe, promptly accepted Spalding's terms and the series was played with the understanding and the contracts drawn that the winning players should take every penny of the gate receipts.

How the games were played and how Comiskey and his men won the majority of them and with the games a great bag of gold is now a matter of history.

It was in the Fall of 1889 that Comiskey was asked to join the Brotherhood of Baseball Players, to leave St. Louis and to head the organization that was to represent the Brotherhood in Chicago.

Comiskey had all to lose and nothing to gain in leaving the St. Louis Club, but he felt it his duty to stand loyal to the players and so he left here and joined the Chicago Brotherhood team.

This one act will show that Comiskey was full of real sentiment, and this is the quality that has made him the idol of the baseball world and helped to fill his treasure box with real gold.

After all these years Comiskey has purchased the very ground in Chicago where the Brotherhood played its home games, and has erected a monument in the way of a baseball plant.

From a poor lad to the possessor of $500,000 in less than twenty years, is the record of Comiskey, who broke into the game eight years after Anson, and for a number of years fought the National League for all in sight. Comiskey was never with the National League at heart, while Anson was always a staunch supporter of the old organization.

Ted Sullivan, who put Comiskey in the business, has this to say of the great Chicago leader:

"As a captain, Comiskey outclassed any man who ever gave orders to ball players. Four times in succession he won the American Association pennant. After Von Der Ahe had disposed of all his star players in the winter of 1888—Gleason, Curt Welch, Bushong, Foutz and Caruthers—the last two named the crack pitchers of the Browns—Comiskey took the remnants of that classy team and filled it with others who came within a small margin in 1889 of winning the pennant for the fifth successive time.

"He was great as a captain and he is still greater as a president and club owner. As his baseball position advanced, his personality developed and became greater—meeting all demands of the occasion as he went on. He is as plain and as democratic in his manner and ways as he was in his humble boyhood days with me over in Iowa. His manner and dealing with the Chicago public, the city of his nativity, has given him such a hold upon the public that it would overlook things with him as a tail-ender that it would not from another man at the head of a winner.

"He is the only player in the entire history of baseball who attained the heights of success by legitimate ball playing and the strength and magnetism of his personality. A. G. Spalding and Al Reach were ball players, but they made their fortunes by the manufacture of the implements and necessities of the game, not by any means on their personality. Comiskey came to work for me in a mercantile way as chum and college friend. He began his minor league playing at $60 per month and his major league playing at $75 per month when he joined the St. Louis Browns, and when he left that team he was getting $6,500 per year. He then became a club-owner in the Western League.

"When conditions arose in the baseball

world that made plenty of room for another major league, he was the first to perceive it. The rules then existing, formulated by the National League, the then dominant power in baseball, asserted that no minor league could expand or leave the territory it occupied except by permission of the National League—just as if it had got a patent from the United States Government or a Divine order that no one should trespass on the sacred territory of the self-appointed barons of the game.

"While the Western League was in its timid state about exposing or invading the sacred territory of the senior league, then did a lion appear—Charles Comiskey. He said, come what may, rules or no rules, I will put a team in Chicago, my native city and I am not going to ask "by your leave," either. Then the lambs became lions. The invasion and expansion took place. The Western League became the American League, founded on the aggressiveness and fearlessness of the old Roman, Chas. A. Comiskey, who, in my humble opinion is the greatest baseball man that ever figured in the national sport of America.

"His baseball career began at $50 per in the city of Milwaukee, to which city I smuggled him—to my home town Milwaukee, to which I came back from St. Mary's College, Kansas, where I met "Commy." He was with me there two weeks before I went into business at Dubuque, Ia., and Charley was the only professional on the Milwaukee amateur team.

"He received the $50 in an odd way and indirectly from the hands of a man who is now not only one of the railway kings of the world, but the conceded statesman of Canada—Sir Thomas Shaughnessy of the Canadian Pacific Railway. In my academic days in Milwaukee, Sir Thomas was my desk mate at school, prior to my knowing Comiskey. When Charley was seen playing on the amateur team in Milwaukee, Mr. Shaughnessy said to me: 'Ted, where did you get the lone professional from?' I said, 'Tom, he is from Chicago, and the $50 you gave me to have a carpenter fix the back fence, I gave to that young willowy fellow on third.' Shaughnessy smiled and that was the beginning of Comiskey as a real live professional. To-day Charles Comiskey is a millionaire, when you take into consideration his half million plant at his new ball park and the franchise in the American League, which is worth to-day, $500,-000. No one is more elated to see him worth that much than his first tutor and adviser."

This summer George McGinnis, the veteran pitcher, paid royal tribute to the skill of Comiskey as a player and manager. McGinnis was the star twirler of the St. Louis Browns in 1885, the year Comiskey won his first pennant. McGinnis was also with the Browns in 1886. He finished his professional career with Baltimore in 1887. George is now employed at the City Hall in St. Louis.

"Comiskey's success as a player, manager and club owner," said the veteran pitcher, "is a tribute to his ability. 'Commy' was always a hard worker. The men he worked for and the men who played ball for Comiskey will tell you that he is the finest character in baseball. No man has done more to boost baseball and make it the great national game than Charlie Comiskey. I remember his first game in St. Louis, away back in 1881. Al Spink

signed him for the Browns of that year. He came here to play the outfield. The first day he started to play center field he found himself unable to judge a fly ball and asked to be shifted to first base. I told Oscar Walker, our first baseman, to switch with 'Commy.' That switch cost Walker his job, for 'Commy' played first base thereafter for the Browns until he signed with the Chicago Brotherhood team of 1890. C. Comiskey was the 'Hal Chase' of his day.

"He played a deep first base and was the first man to field the position as it should be covered. When 'Commy' started to play first base all the first basemen were big men of the Pop Anson, Dan Brouthers, Dave Orr, Roger Connor order. Dave Orr weighed 250 pounds. He was a left-handed hitter and could kill a fast ball, but he couldn't run a lick and never covered an inch of ground around first base. Dan Brouthers was another giant. Like Orr, he could fairly murder the pigskin, but he held his job on his hitting, not for any ability he ever displayed as a fielder around the initial sack. Connor handled the sack more acceptably than Brouthers or Orr, but he was never in the hunt with Comiskey as a fielding first baseman. About the only man of that period that classed with Comiskey as a fielder was Long John Reilly of the old Cincinnati Reds.

"I was with Comiskey the year the Browns beat Anson's Chicago White Stockings for the World's Championship in 1885. The teams played seven games. St. Louis won three, Chicago won three and one game was tied. Comiskey had a shade on Anson that year because one of the Chicago victories was obtained by a forfeit. The next year Comiskey's Browns beat the White Stockings decisively for the world's championship. That makes two world's championships to Comiskey's credit for he also won the blue ribbon of baseball in 1906, when the Chicago White Sox beat the Cubs. The Detroit sluggers beat Comiskey's Browns in 1887, and the New York Giants beat Comiskey's Browns in 1888. Comiskey came to St. Louis to work for $75 per month. He left here at the end of 1891, getting $6,000 per annum. The 'Old Roman' is now rated a millionaire."

ARTHUR CROFT—Arthur Croft, a St. Louis boy, was holding down first base for the Indianapolis team of the National League in 1878. Later Croft returned to St. Louis and in the early eighties he covered first base for the St. Louis Browns. Croft was really a graduate of the St. Louis Reds, being a co-laborer in that club of Tom Loftus, Jim Galvin, the Gleasons, Jack and Billy, and other players, who later became famous.

HAROLD DANZIG—Harold Danzig, the first baseman, who was under the control of the Boston Americans last season and played most of the season in Lowell, Mass., has been turned over to the Sacramento Club of the Pacific Coast League.

H. DAVIS—Harry Davis, who is the captain and first baseman of the Philadelphia Athletics, is the only surviving American League championship infielder—that is, the only survivor of the championship clubs prior to 1909—who is still playing his regular position in the infield of the team with which he played when the pennant was won.

Naturally, all of the Chicago champions

HARRY DAVIS.
The Brilliant Player and Captain of the World's Champion Athletics of Philadelphia in Their 1910-1911 Seasons.

of the first two years of the American League have passed out of sight. The Athletics won in 1902 with an infield composed of Davis, Murphy, Monte Cross and Lave Cross.

Davis is the only one left on the infield, as Murphy is playing in the outfield. Boston won the next two years with LaChance, Ferris, Parent and Collins in the infield. La Chance is but a memory, while Parent is with Chicago and Ferris and Collins are minor leaguers. In 1905 the Athletics won again with the same infield as in 1902. Then came the Chicago White Sox, with an infield composed of Donohue, Isbell, Davis, Tannehill and Rohe. Tannehill is still with the club, but is only a substitute. Taking the place of the famous heroes of 1906 we find Gandil, Zeider, Blackburne and Purtell, not one of whom was a professional player four years ago.

Davis is considered the best home run hitter of the American League and he is chief aid to Connie Mack, the wise one. Davis is the axis on which the Athletics revolve. On the field he is supreme. Every Spring the report is shipped North that Davis is "all in," but when the season opens Davis is always found guarding the first sack, and guarding it well. But playing first base is only a habit with Harry. It is in pelting the ball that he has always delivered the merchandise.

Of course Davis is not banging the ball to all corners of the parks as he did some time back, his eye is not as clear as it once was, but at the same time he places the willow against the leather in a very healthy manner every now and then, and often he breaks up the game. Davis did not head the list of home-run hitters last year nor the year before, but in nine years he has made a total of sixty-seven home run drives, which is somewhat more than any other player in the league can show in the 1909 records. In addition to the home-run hits, Davis is credited with ninety-two two-base hits and seventy-six triples.

Davis topped the record for home run hits in the American League for four consecutive years. He made ten homers in 1904, eight in 1905, twelve in 1906 and eight in 1905, twelve in 1906 and eight in 1907. "Wahoo Sam" Crawford made his bow about this time in the ranks of the home run clubbers, replacing Davis as the leader in 1908 with seven four-base smashers. Davis had five. In 1909 Cobb led the league with nine, Davis having four. But the record made by Davis in his nine years of play in the American League will stand a lot of hammering before being replaced.

One by one the old stars of the American League are giving way to the rising generation, and Davis himself is grooming a very clever young man for his place. Ben Houser is the name of the young man. With Davis it is the team first, player afterwards.

When he is ready to quit he wants to have Houser ready to take his place, and not until Davis gives the word will Mack take him off the bag.

JACK DAUBERT—Jacob Daubert, the crack first baseman of the Brooklyn Club was in 1909 the first baseman of the Southern Association Club at Memphis. He was regarded as the best first baseman the South has ever seen and was the champion of that league in the season 1909 as well as being the best fielding first base-

man in that league. Daubert was born in Memphis and is about 24 years of age. He succeeded Tim Jordan, the slugging first baseman of the Brooklyns of 1909, which proves him to be a first-class player in every respect.

JIGGS DONOHUE—At one time this great first baseman had no superiors in his home position.

When the Chicago White Sox defeated the Chicago Cubs in the World's Championship series of 1906, no player on either team did better work than Jiggs Donohue, the first baseman of the Sox.

Donohue remained with that team until 1908 when he was transferred to the Washington Club.

Donohue was one of the chief individual factors in the capturing of the world's championship for the Chicago White Sox in the Fall of 1908, his fielding being phenomenal and game saving and his batting most timely. Donohue was born in Springfield, Ohio. He played his first professional game in Marietta, Ohio, in 1896, starting as a catcher. In 1900 he joined the Pittsburg Nationals. He finished the season with Minneapolis, then went to Milwaukee in 1901. At the close of 1903 he was purchased by the White Sox management and joined them in 1904. He throws and bats left-handed. Donohue led the first sackers in the American League in fielding for the three years.

JACK FLYNN—Jack Flynn, the recruit from the St. Paul American Association Club, for whom Pittsburg paid $4,000 last Winter, is holding down first base for the Pittsburg team in fine shape in the this 1910 year. "Bud" Sharpe, the Eastern League graduate, who cost the club little more than one-third of the sum invested in Flynn, will cover the initial cushion for the Boston Doves.

With Sharpe, Pitcher Sam Frock, who was with the Pirates all last season but worked in only one or two games, goes to Boston, while Pitcher Kirb "Red" White is transferred to Pittsburg by Manager Lake.

On the day that the deal was announced as having been consummated, Flynn won a game, from Cincinnati for the Pirates by clouting the horsehide over the left field wall at Forbes Field with two runners on bases. The score was a 2-to-2 tie at the time, two were out and Miller had been passed intentionally by Pitcher Beebe to bring up Flynn, who had fanned on his previous turn at bat. He had two strikes and two balls when he hammered out the wallop that won the game.

J. GAINOR—J. Gainor is another youngster who will wear a Detroit uniform in the spring of 1911. Gainor was the regular first baseman on the Fort Wayne, Ind. club in the 1910 season and his record was a very meritorious one.

J. GANDIL—J. Gandil is one of the first basemen of the Chicago White Sox. He was the man brought from the Pacific coast by Ted Sullivan to take the place at first base on the Chicago Club filled so long and well by "Jiggs" Donahue. He made good from the start, proving himself a player of the very highest flight. Gandil is a native of Sacramento, Cal., where he did his first professional playing three years ago. He developed fast and in the season of 1909 was regarded as the best fielding and hitting first baseman on the coast. Gandil joined the White Sox in the spring of 1910 and made good from the jump. In 1909 with the

Sacramento Club, Gandil participated in 200 games, scored ninety-five runs, 214 hits, stole twenty-seven bases and had a batting average of .282. He ranked sixth as a batsman in the Pacific Coast league.

GUS GETZ—Gus Getz is the first baseman of the Boston National League team in their 1910 season. He is a new comer, an excellent fielder and a promising young player.

RICHARD HOBLITZEL—Richard Hoblitzel is now playing a great game at first for the Cincinnati National League team.

Hoblitzel made good for Cincinnati during the 1909 season, playing first in 142 games with a fielding percentage of .982, Konetchy of the St. Louis team being the only player to take part in more games.

Konetchy and Bransfield were the only players on first base who had more assists. He showed up very strong in the batting department, his average being .308, and he ranked third among the players who competed in 100 games, Mitchell, his team-mate, hitting for .310 and Wagner .339.

This was a remarkable showing for a lad of nineteen, for he was born in Parkersburg, W. Va., Oct. 26, 1889. He played with Clarksburg, W. Va., in 1907.

In 1908 he was for six weeks with the Reading, Pa., club and then went to Newark, N. J., where he played three weeks and then went to the Wheeling, W. (Va.) Club and after being there two months was bought by Cincinnati. The investment in this player proved very satisfactory, for he proved to be a genuine find and without doubt has a splendid future before him.

Richard Hoblitzel made good for Cincinnati during the 1909 season, playing first in 142 games with a fielding percentage of .982, Konetchy of the St. Louis team being the only player to take part in more games. Konetchy and Bransfield were the only players on first base who had more assists. He showed up very strong in the batting department, his average being .308, and he ranked third among the players who competed in 100 games, Mitchel, his teammate, hitting for .310 and Wagner .339. This was a remarkable showing for a lad of 19, for he was born in Parkersburg, W. Va., Oct. 26, 1889. He played with Clarksburg, W. Va., in 1907. In 1908 he was for six weeks with the Reading (Pa.) Club and then went to Newark, N. J., where he played three weeks and then went to the Wheeling (W. Va.) Club, and after being there two months, was bought by Cincinnati. The investment in this player proved very satisfactory, for he proved to be a genuine find and without doubt has a splendid future before him.

J. HUNTER—J. Hunter is booked to hold down the first base position on the Pittsburg Pirates Club during the 1911 campaign. The management of the Pittsburg Club have experienced considerable difficulty in endeavoring to secure a capable man to hold down first base. During the season of 1909 and 1910 Manager Clark tried out no less than half a dozen players inside and outside of Flynn, who was tacked on the base when the 1910 season was concluded, none of the hopefuls showed sufficient class to warrant their retention. In securing Mr. Hunter, President Dreyfus made an excellent move. Every club in both the American and National Leagues made offers to Manager Shay of the Kansas City Club for the services of Hunter. At one time during the season, it is said, Dreyfus offered six players for Hunter, three of them of long experience in the National League. It is known that President George Tebeau, owner of the Kansas City Club, refused a cash offer of $7,500 for Hunter. While it is not known precisely what President Dreyfus paid the management of Kansas City for Hunter's release, those who know declare that the big fellow cost the Pirates a small fortune. Hunter played the entire season with the Kansas City Club and was considered the brightest star in the American Association. He is an excellent batsman, clever, fast fielder and should make good with the Pirates.

FRANK ISBELL—Isbell played with the Chicago White Sox at first base from 1900 until the 1909 season.

In the latter year he was granted an unconditional release by President Charles A. Comiskey, all the major leagues having granted waivers.

Isbell is a part owner of the Wichita Western League Club and is now acting as the playing manager of that team.

Comiskey was willing to release Isbell two years before, but some of the other major league clubs would not waive on him. Isbell was the only member left of the original team that Comiskey brought from St. Paul when the American League was organized in 1900.

First Baseman Gandil, last season with the Sacramento (California State League) team, took Isbell's place at first base on the Chicago White Sox and promises to be a fixture there.

THOMAS JONES—Thomas Jones, the first baseman of the champion Detroits of 1909 and 1910, is a veteran, having played since 1903 at that position for the St. Louis Browns, prior to which time he was with Baltimore. He is a native of Locustdale, Pa., and played his first ball on the semi-professional diamonds of his native state.

Jones is five feet ten inches in height; bats and throws right-handed. His weight is about 170 pounds. He is one of the best fielding first basemen in the American League.

TIMOTHY JORDAN—Tim Jordan covered first base for the Brooklyn National League team for several seasons.

In 1907 Jordan was one of the best hitters in the older organizatin and a fair fielder. Jordan made his professional debut with the Senecas of New York in 1899. In 1901 he was a substitute on the Washington Americans. During the season of 1902 he played with the Newark team of the Eastern League and in 1903 with the Nashua Club of the New England circuit. In 1904 he became a member of the Baltimore team. He did fine work that year and in 1905 attracted the attention of the Brooklyn Club. In 1906 he made twelve home runs, leading the league.

EDWARD KONETCHY — Edward Konetchy, the first baseman of the St. Louis Cardinals, is perhaps the best player in that position now in the game.

He is also the leading batsman of his team.

Konetchy is a youngster and is coming so fast that he promises to surprise the natives before another season rolls around.

Only six years ago Konetchy was a candymaker in La Crosse, Wis. Eddie earned $50 per month making chocolates, and thought he was doing well. He played baseball for fun and soon became recognized as a star among the amateurs of La Crosse. In the spring of 1905, when Konetchy was 19 years of age "Pink" Hawley acquired control of the La Crosse ball team.

Konetchy applied for a position with the club. Hawley told him to bring his uniform to the park and practice with the squad.

"I dallied around nine days before Hawley took any notice of me," said Konetchy. "Then he tried me in the outfield. My good right arm impressed him favorably and he signed me for the La Crosse Club.

"Hawley inquired what salary I was making in the candy shop, and when I told him $50 per month, he said: 'We'll give you the same pay.' I was slated to play the outfield for La Crosse, but the day before the season opened our first baseman failed to materialize and Hawley sent me to the initial bag. I played my first game on first base for La Crosse in an exhibition contest with the Galesburg (Ill.) team. Playing the bag was easy. I hit .222 that year. In 1906 I hit .277 and in 1907 I stung the horsehide to the tune of .405.

"My hitting that season attracted the attention of John J. McCloskey, manager of the Cardinals and he purchased my release. I've heard various stories about the deal. Some people said McCloskey paid $500 for my release; others had it that La Crosse got $1,000 for me. But I was glad to get here, and never bothered much about the deal. I like St. Louis and have been treated handsomely by Mr. Robison. He's a good man to work for and nothing would suit me better than to play for him as long as he remains in baseball."

Konetchy's improvement in batting was the feature of his work with the Cardinals last season. When asked how he fattened his batting average, the big first baseman said:

"Hard work. I made it my business to study closely the pitchers who bothered me most in 1906. Rucker, of Brooklyn, had a high, fast ball that he curled around my neck. It gave me a lot of trouble in 1908. Last Spring at Little Rock I got Harry Sallee and Johnny Lush to use it while I was taking batting lessons against them. After three weeks of constant practice I got 'next' to the ball and could whale the stuffing out of it. The first time I faced Rucker in 1909 I clouted his fast, high curve all over the lot. After the game Rucker came over to our bench, called me aside and said he wanted some information.

" 'You couldn't hit that ball with a plank in 1908,' said 'Nap,' 'but it doesn't fool you this year, does it?' How did you succeed in mastering it?'

"I then told him about practising with Lush and Sallee in the Spring, and Rucker had to smile. I had another weakness in 1908 that Roger Bresnahan corrected. He watched me work at Little Rock and said I was hitting the ball to left field too often.

"They are all onto your little game, said Roger, 'The fielders guess you right too often. You must learn to pull the ball to right field.'

"It took a lot of hard work, but I finally succeeded in becoming fairly proficient. I could see myself placing the ball and worked all the harder. As the season progressed I kept getting better and about 49 per cent of my safe drives during the season were hit to right center. The outfielders never knew where to play for Eddie. When they looked for me to hit to left field I would whip the ball to right, and when they got set for a drive to right center, I'd pull the pill to left. It was fine and dandy and boosted my batting average forty points. Any young ball player can do the same. But it takes a lot of hard practice and a man must have patience.

"I made some fearful long wallops in 1909," continued Koney. "One of the longest drives of the season at League Park was a home run punch I manufactured during a series with Cincinnati. The ball went over the shortstop's head on a line and never quit rolling until it disappeared under the bulletin board. Another long drive of mine hit the left field bleacher at League Park, on the first bounce— and say, it takes some poke to send the leather that distance. If you don't think so, go out and try it yourself.

"Wheat, of Brooklyn, robbed me of a home run during the last series in St. Louis with the Superbas. I drove one over his head, but he turned and traveled with the ball, getting it with one hand just before it hit the ground. It was the greatest catch I ever saw on a ball field. Another long drive of mine was a home run smash at Cincinnati. The ball hit the left field wall at Redville on the fly. Jack Ryder, sporting editor of the Cincinnati Enquirer, said it was the longest drive of many years in the Cincinnati ball yard."

Konetchy is the biggest kind of a favorite with St. Louis fans. They worship the gigantic first sacker and are unwilling to admit that any other man playing ball has anything on him. One thing about Konetchy that endears him to the rooters is his ability to work. The big boy is always on the job, trying every way he knows how to bring victory to the Cardinals. His big stick has broken up more games for St. Louis than the bats of any other two men on the team. His speed and cleverness on the base lines is another brilliant feature of his work. No first baseman in the game can dig them out of the dirt or reach higher for wild throws than Koney. Eddie will have a great infield to work with the coming season, and will doubtless shine more brilliantly than ever. President Robison has been offered as high as $20,000 for the big fellow.

PETER LESTER—Peter Lester is the young first baseman drafted by Detroit from Williamsport, Pa., for the season of 1910. He was born at Savannah, Ill., July 29, 1882, and lives in Rock Island, Ill. His professional baseball career began with Lemars, Ia., in the Iowa and South Dakota League in 1902, and for the next two years he was with Rock Island of the Three-I-League. In 1906 he played with Portland, Ore.; in 1907, Birmingham, Ala.; and Nashville, Tenn., in the Southern League, finishing the season with the Cleveland American League Club. In 1908 he went to Toledo, and in 1909 he was with Williamsport, Pa., in the Tri-State League, leading the league in batting with .350 and fielding for .982.

FRANK LUDERUS—Frank Luderus was the understudy of the peerless Frank Chance, the regular first baseman and manager of the Chicago Cubs in their 1919 season. Luderus played several good games, but as there was little chance of

FRED MERKLE.
Fred Merkle is the crack first baseman of the New York Giants in their 1910 season

THE NATIONAL GAME.

using him regularly he was transferred in August, 1910, in a trade to Philadelphia for Pitcher Foxen. Luderus is a fine first baseman and showed ability with the stick. He will probably be the Quakers' regular first baseman in their 1911 season. Luderus has already made himself solid with the Philadelphia fans. He looks even better than Bransfield and it is likely that he will soon supplant the veteran for keeps.

LEE MAGEE—Lee Magee is the finely built athletic-looking youth who was picked up by the Cardinals in the winter of 1909-1910. He was played at first base on the Cardinals' second nine in the early spring games, and but for the magnificent playing of Konetchy at the initial bag, would have easily made the team. He was farmed out to the Louisville American Association where he played all the season of 1910. He was recalled by the Cardinals in the fall of 1910 and will start out with them next spring as utility infielder. There are many who say Magee resembles the famous Ty Cobb, both in build and action and he certainly looks like a comer.

DAN McGANN—Dan McGann, of St. Louis and New York, was the leading first baseman according to the record in 1900, 1901, 1903, 1904, 1905, 1906 and 1907. The first two of these years McGann was with the St. Louis National League team and the last five with the New York Giants. He has been the Brewers' regular first baseman for three years.

The record proves that McGann in his day was certainly a great first baseman. He became a star under the tutelage of Ned Hanlon in the days when the Baltimore Orioles were annexing championships, and then under the leadership of his old team-mate, John McGraw, continued to be regarded by many as the premier first baseman of the National League when he helped New York win that pennant in 1904 and 1905 and aided in the Giants winning the title of World's Champions in the latter year.

McGann began to show signs of going back during the season of 1907, and McGraw, ever on the alert to better his team, allowed Dan to go that winter, Boston taking him in one of the historic trades of the game, and he finished his Major League career with that team.

Dan played Major League baseball the greater part of two decades and is perhaps the best known of the men who have sought a refuge in the minor leagues after a thrilling career on the diamonds of the big circuits.

WILLIAM E. BRANSFIELD—In 1902, Bransfield, of Pittsburg, was the leading first baseman according to the National League records.

Wm. E. Bransfield, "Kitty," as he is called, was born in Worcester, Mass., some 34 years ago and during the off season he always lived there. He started to play ball as an outfielder with shop teams in his home city. In 1894 he went behind the bat and the following year was tried out as a backstop by John Smith, of Pawtucket, but did not make good. In 1896 he played on the Westboro and Grafton teams, leading the latter in batting. This drew the attention of Selee, Connie Mack and Tom Burns to him, and Selee managed to land him for Boston. He caught but five games for Boston and in 1899 was released to the Worcester team. Playing first base he made a name for himself,

and in 1900 Fred Clarke secured him for the Pirates. With this team he remained until 1904 when he was signed up for the Philadelphia Nationals.

AL M'KINNON—Al McKinnon was the first baseman of the St. Louis National League team in 1885. He came to St. Louis from the New York League team. He was a fine fielder and a corking good batsman.

FRED MERKLE—Fred Merkle is the regular first baseman of the New York Giants. He succeeded the great Tenney on that team, who had in his time stepped into the shoes of Dan McGann, the best fielding first baseman in the National League for many years. Merkle has been with the Giants for three years playing general utility roles and always making good both as a fielder and batsman.

PAT NEWNAM—Pat Newnam is the big Texan now covering first base for the St. Louis Browns. He was discovered by Jack O'Connor while playing with the Houston team of the Texas League. Pat was for several years the star batsman, fielder and base runner of the Texas League. He made good with the Browns from the jump. He more than filled the place of Tom Jones, who had been the first baseman of the Browns for six years.

LONG JOHN REILLY—Long John Reilly, who covered first base for the Cincinnati American Association team in the early seventies, was a magnificent first baseman.

He was a tall, slender lad with great length of limb, and no first baseman could beat him in reaching far out for badly thrown balls and fielding them in.

As a batsman, too, Reilly was grand, being always a good man in the breach. As a base runner, too, he was valuable to his team.

In temperament Reilly also excelled, having an excellent disposition and a temper that made him always a prime favorite with his fellow players.

CLAUDE ROSSMAN—There were few finer looking and more promising first basemen than Claude Rossman who held down the initial bag for the Detroit Champion team during its great years of success.

In 1909 in the midst of the playing season Rossman and Manager Jennings of the Detroits fell out and the big first baseman was released to the St. Louis Browns.

He was unwilling to come to St. Louis, and after a couple of games which he played with the Browns, he left them and refused to re-join them during the balance of the playing season of 1909.

Rossman, when in form, played a great game at first for the Detroits and he was one of the safest, best and most reliable batsmen.

Claude Rossman, discarded by Columbus and apparently bound for the bushes so far as baseball is concerned, took on a new lease of life when Manager Joe Cantillon got him from Columbus in June, 1910, and his newly acquired batting eye has been considerable of a factor in the Millers' recent victories. To the surprise of his team-mates the former Nap actually got to throwing runners out at the plate on balls hit into his territory.

Rossman will probably be returned to the St. Louis Browns in 1911.

ED SHARPE—Ed Sharpe is one of the aspiring youngsters who broke into the

184

R. P. KENNEDY.
The tall first baseman of the Uniontown, Pa., Club in its early days and now the best known National League rooter in America.

THE NATIONAL GAME.

big league a year ago. Sharpe was used in utility roles on the Boston National League Club during the season of 1910. He is a promising baseball player and should win a steady berth on his club next season. In August, 1910, he had played in eighty-five contests and had stacked up a batting record of .267.

J. SOMERLOT—J. Somerlot is a first baseman whom the Washington Nationals purchased from the Terre Haute Club of the Central League. In sixty-one games he showed a batting average of .310 and a fielding average of .992. He had also stolen eighteen bases.

GARLAND J. STAHL—Garland J. Stahl was born in Elkhart, Ill., April 3, 1881, and shone in baseball and football with the University of Illinois, with whom he played in 1900 and 1903. He attracted much attention in baseball and that caused him to be widely sought by professional clubs. Among those who made overtures to him was the late Frank Selee, the manager of the Chicago Nationals.

The Boston Americans secured him, however, and he played behind the bat for them in 1903. Washington then took him and he remained with that club from 1904 to 1906, being manager the last two seasons. Washington sold him to the Chicago Americans in 1907, but he refused to go there and coached the Indiana University Club and played with the Logan Squares, an independent club of Chicago. Chicago traded him to the New York Americans and he played with them until July, 1908, when Boston secured him and he has played with that club ever since, in a very satisfactory manner. He batted for .294 last season and fielded .984. In 1901 he made an exceptionally fine showing.

Stahl, now the first baseman of the Boston American League team, is a grand player in his position and a wonderful batsman.

In fact, if Stahl could get a case of swelled head and begin to think he is really as good as he is, he would be the greatest of them all.

Modesty has held him back and I have feared he would finish his career without finding out how good he is.

GEORGE STOVALL—George Stovall, of the Cleveland Club, is a fine, active first baseman. He had more assists than any American League first baseman last season; Tom Jones, of the St. Louis and Detroits, being second, both with over .100.

George Stovall, the regular first baseman of the Cleveland American League team, is next to Hal Chase, the real goods in the American League when it comes to first basemen. He is a fine, big fellow and beside being a great fielder, is a corking good batsman. He is a native of Texas and has been with the Clevelands for several seasons. He is one of the great players Ted Sullivan picked up in the Texas League. Beside being a fine all-around player, Stovall is one of the most popular men in the American League. He comes from a family of baseball players, four of his brothers being professional players.

HARRY STOVEY—Harry Stovey, whose right name was Stovie, was the captain as well as the first baseman of the Athletics of Philadelphia, who captured the American Association pennant in 1883.

Although an outfielder, Stovey played the initial bag for the Athletics that year

and so well that at the close he had the best average of any first baseman in that body.

Stovey was a most remarkable ball player—a good batsman—except against such left-handed pitchers as Matt Kilroy, a fast fielder and a phenomenal base runner. Standing upward of six feet in his stockings, he would slide to a base, feet first, and regain a standing position with less effort and greater speed than any other man who has ever played baseball.

He always slid feet first, but was not "nasty" with his feet in the way of trying to hurt the baseman, as some of his imitators were.

Stovey always wore a pad on the left hip to protect the bones, and when some twenty feet from a base he would make a great forward feet-first plunge, plowing along on the side of his feet with his face turned toward the man making the throw intending to catch him. His hip would strike the ground about the time his feet reached the base bag, and, rebounding, he would come to a standing position fully prepared to continue his chase around the bases in case the throw was not right on the mark. His speed and daring drew many wild throws, and it was not at all infrequent to see Stovey, after making a base hit, complete the circuit of the bases on steals or wild throws before the succeeding batsman had been retired. In one season Stovey stole 156 bases, which is a greater number of steals than were ever recorded by any other player up to the present time.

HARRY SWACINA—Harry Swacina, the St. Louis boy, once the Pittsburg regular first baseman, but now with Mobile, Ala., in the Southern Association, was in 1910 one of the leading sluggers of the Association. In the late fall Swacina was batting at a .310 clip, was fielding like a whirlwind and all in all was rated as one of the best players in that fast organization.

FRED TENNEY—The National Game has had few greater first basemen than Fred Tenney, for years the first baseman of the Boston National League team and for the past two years with New York. He led the National League in his position in 1908.

Tenney is a college graduate. He was the first baseman of the Brown University team until he joined the professional ranks. And as a player and gentleman, he has always been an honor to the profession.

In fielding at first base Tenney had a method strictly his own and that it was effective was proven by his great number of grand plays and his wonderful quick handling of low and badly thrown balls.

The story of Fred Tenney is a remarkable proof of the fact that many able players make serious mistakes in the selection of their playing positions.

Sometimes the player gets wise to himself and voluntarily makes a shift; sometimes a manager, more sensible than the player, forces him to take a new position, but in most cases the man who thinks he can play a certain place and is a frost, has not sense enough to change, or else is released before the chance comes to show his worth in some spot where he really belongs. Many a youth of great natural ability has passed out of the fast company just because he was wrongly placed, and never made a fielding change.

Fred Tenney, at college, was a catcher. He is left-handed and left-handed catchers

186

have not been successful as a rule, John Clements being the only great left-hander who worked behind the bat. Nevertheless, Tenney could catch well enough for a college team, and his batting was a daily feature. When Boston engaged him he proved to be a serious frost as a backstop. He was erratic in his throws, and his all around mask work was anything but what a big league man should show. But he could bat, and on batting only he held his job. They tried him in the outfield, but he was nothing much as a gardener, and it looked to be a case of back to private life for Fred.

Tom Tucker had grown old, and there was need of a first baseman on the Boston team. Frank Selee, watching his left-handed failure doing the best he could, decided that Tenney was meant by nature to be a first baseman, and ordered him to take up the job.

Tenney did so, and within a few weeks had become one of the finest first sackers that the game has ever seen. It was plain at the start that Tenney belonged right there on first, and should have always played the bag.

The mere mechanical work of the job—taking the throws, scooping the low shots, etc.—seemed wholly natural to him from the jump, but it was only a few days before Fred began to develop the possibilities of the position as if he had been schooled thereto for years. Tenney played first base like a moveable cog of the infield machine, not like a stationary hub. He got into the play with intelligence and foresight, and no man, to this day, has anything on him when it comes to quick thinking and quick action. In two weeks it was evident that a great first baseman had arrived, and one who should have been there years before.

Tenney's batting did not suffer through the change in fielding jobs. On the contrary it was rather improved, and the collegian, a failure at the start, settled down to spend years and years as a star amid the fastest company. The story of Tenney therefore is one for the younger players to figure on and make extremely useful. Tenney tells this story of his breaking into baseball:

"During my baseball career I have been asked many times what induced me to take up baseball as a means of livelihood. My answer to that question always has been that I was delighted at the idea of someone being willing to pay me for doing what I loved. While I was at college I became quite proficient as a player, and naturally wondered if I really could play well enough to hold a job on a major league team.

"In June, 1894, during the week of commencement exercises at Brown's University, I received a telephone message from Manager Selee of the Boston Club, saying that all his catchers were disabled and asking me to come up the next day and help them out. I had known them all for several years and was only too glad to play with them, as it would give me the long-sought-for opportunity of finding out just how fast baseball was played in the league and whether I could hold up my end of it or not.

"I went up to Boston the next day, and caught five innings of the game, and was getting along nicely when I was unfortunate enough to get a foul tip on the forefinger of my throwing hand, breaking it at the second joint. That accident forced me out of the game and I knew that I would not be able to play again for a month.

"This was quite serious for me, as I figured on making enough money in the summer vacation through ball playing to pay my expenses all the rest of the season.

"I was feeling pretty blue over the outlook for an enforced month's idleness, but after I got my finger dressed, Manager Selee told me that Mr. Billings, one of the owners of the club, wanted to see me at his office. When I got there he told me that he had been watching my work for some time past, and from the showing in the game I had caught for them he had been empowered to offer me a contract calling for $300 a month, dating from that day.

"I did not then know how they did business in the big leagues, and $300 looked like a young fortune to me, but I could not understand why they should be willing to give me all that money when I had just broken my finger and would not be able to play for a month. Naturally I thought they were trying to have a little joke with me, and I concluded that I could do a little kicking myself.

"I thought I would call their bluff by asking for some advance money. I screwed up my courage and asked Mr. Billings whether, if I signed the contract at once, I could get some advance money. He asked me how much I wanted and I thought I would mention a big sum in order to call their bluff good and strong. I asked for $150. He consulted with Mr. Conant, another director, and said I could have the money.

"He immediately wrote out a check for $75, counted out $75 in cash, shoved the contract over to me to sign, laying the cash and the check beside it. I signed the contract and put the money and the check in the most accessible inside pocket I could find. I had never seen as much money at once in my life before, and was so scared that I would lose it that I was feeling for that roll every ten steps on my way down the street.

"That is how I broke into the league, and in the years that have followed, I have never regretted signing that first contract."

TOM TUCKER—Tom Tucker of the Baltimore team was one of the finest fielders of the first basemen who flourished in the early nineties.

Tom was also an excellent batsman and base runner.

He was a left-handed hitter and often came to the rescue of his side with a good stroke.

Tucker is now living in retirement at Holyoke, Mass., where also are "Smiling" Mickey Welch of the old New York champions, "Jack" Doyle and Jack Hanifin of the Boston Nationals.

ROBERT UNGLAUB—Robert Unglaub, a small, wiry fellow, fast, aggressive and a good hitter, as well as a good fielder, is the regular first baseman of the Washington American League Club. Unglaub has been playing in the big league a long while, most of which time was spent with the Boston Americans. He was at one time their first baseman and manager.

PERRY WERDEN—A fine, stalwart player was Perry Werden, at one time one of the best known of major league players. Werden's home position was at first base, although he set out as a pitcher. Werden won his first honors in the baseball line while pitching for the Peach Pies of St. Louis. His first professional engagement came to him in 1882 when he joined the Lincoln (Neb.) team. He was with other teams in the Western League until 1884 when he was signed to pitch for the St. Louis Unions with Jack Brennan as his receiver. After the Union smash-up Werden set out as a first baseman and he held down the initial bag for several major league clubs, notably St. Louis. Three years ago Werden went to Indianapolis and was the coach and trainer of the American Association Championship team of Indianapolis. Werden is a giant and while he has been playing ball for nearly thirty years, he is still active and can get around as well as the liveliest youngster. In his day he was a fine first baseman as well as one of the hardest hitters in the business.

JOHN EVERS.
Here is the great and brainy second baseman of the Chicago Cubs.

THE SECOND BASEMEN.

THESE ARE THE MEN WHO SHONE IN THIS POSITION IN THE OLD PROFESSIONAL ASSOCIATION AND THEN IN THE NATIONAL LEAGUE.

Of the great players who covered second base in the days of the old Professional Association and then in the National League, Fred Dunlap was perhaps the greatest player that ever covered this particular position. But this is the record of the men who took part in the games of the two associations named:

Year.	Second Basemen. Club.	Games.	Fielding Pct.	Year.	Second Basemen. Club.	Games.	Fielding Pct.
1871	Ross Barnes—Boston	43	.950	1891	J. A. McPhee—Cincinnati	138	.960
1872	Ross Barnes—Boston	44	.908	1892	L. Bierbauer—Pittsburg	153	.956
1873	West Fisler—Ath., Phila	43	.911	1893	L. Bierbauer—Pittsburg	128	.959
1874	West Fisler—Ath., Phila	37	.953	1894	H. Reitz—Baltimore	100	.966
1875	Ross Barnes—Boston	78	.915	1895	R. L. Lowe—Boston	90	.957
1876	Ross Barnes—Chicago	66	.916	1896	J. A. McPhee—Cincinnati	116	.982
1877	John Burdock—Hartford	49	.905	1897	J. A. McPhee—Cincinnati	80	.965
1878	John Burdock—Boston	60	.917	1898	C. J. Crooks—St. Louis	65	.962
1879	Joe Quest—Chicago	79	.926	1899	E. DeMontreville—Chi'go, Balt...	61	.966
1880	Dave Force—Buffalo	49	.926	1900	R. J. Lowe—Boston	127	.960
1881	Dave Force—Buffalo	53	.936	1901	William Hallman—Philadelphia..	89	.977
1882	John Burdock—Boston	82	.929	1902	C. C. Ritchey—Pittsburg	114	.965
1883	John Farrell—Providence	93	.925	1903	C. C. Ritchey—Pittsburg	137	.961
1884	John Burdock—Boston	84	.927	1904	C. C. Ritchey—Pittsburg	156	.958
1885	Fred Dunlap—St. Louis	106	.933	1905	C. C. Ritchey—Pittsburg	153	.961
1886	C. J. Bastian—Philadelphia	86	.944	1906	C. C. Ritchey—Pittsburg	151	.966
1887	Fred Dunlap—Detroit	64	.953	1907	C. C. Ritchey—Boston	144	.971
1888	C. J. Bastian—Philadelphia	65	.946	1908	W. Knabe—Philadelphia	151	.969
1889	Fred Dunlap—Pittsburg	121	.949	1909	D. Shean—Boston	86	.960
1890	Chas. E. Bassett—New York	100	.951	1910	McKechnie—Pittsburg	36	.971

AMERICAN LEAGUE.

THESE ARE THE MEN WHO HAVE LED AT SECOND BASE IN THE AMERICAN LEAGUE FROM 1900 ON.

In the American League since the 1901 season Napoleon Lajoie of the Clevelands has always been at, or near the top in the position. The record follows:

Year.	Second Basemen. Club.	Games.	Fielding Pct.	Year.	Second Basemen. Club.	Games.	Fielding Pct.
1900	L. Bierbauer—Buffalo	110	.954	1905	N. Lajoie—Cleveland	59	.931
1901	N. Lajoie—Philadelphia....—	130	.963	1906	N. Lajoie—Cleveland	130	.973
1902	N. Najoie—Cleveland	87	.974	1907	N. Lajoie—Cleveland	128	.969
1903	B. McCormick—Washington	83	.964	1908	Murphy—Philadelphia	56	.965
1904	Hobe Ferris—Boston	156	.964	1909	E. Colins—Philadelphia	152	.967
				1910	Collins—Philadelphia	153	.970

The story of the second basemen will perhaps be found as interesting as any written in this book of baseball for the great players of their day who filled that position were all famous and held high rank in the professional baseball world.

The record starts off with Ross Barnes, who in 1871 and 1872 covered the second bag for Boston.

In those two years many other great second basemen were at work, but Barnes was really the star of the army.

He was a magnificent fielder and thrower and a royal batsman and base runner.

It was Barnes who was the first to master the fair foul hit and he mastered it so well that in 1872 and 1873 he led the Boston Club in batting; in 1872 with the high average of .404 and in 1873 with the wonderful average of .453. This splendid record was mainly due to Barnes' ability to hit the ball so that it would land fair and then swing in foul, just out of the reach of the third baseman. Barnes' ability to make these fair foul hits, and his speed in beating the ball to first base, made him a terror to the opposing pitchers.

Cotemporaneous with Barnes in the 1871 and 1872 years were many other great second basemen, among them A. J. Reach, Al Reach, as he was then called, and now the richest and most influential man connected with the game.

Reach in 1871 was the second baseman of the Athletics of Philadelphia and he was one of the greatest players on that team. He was a left-handed batsman, one of the truest and most timely of hitters, and a fielder of the first class.

It is claimed by many that Reach was really the first professional baseball player, that is to say, the first baseball player who ever received a regular salary.

Reach had been playing with the Eckfords of Brooklyn, when Philadelphia enthusiasts, who wanted to get a great team together for the Athletics of that city, offered him a salary which he accepted and it was the first ever paid a professional player. Subsequently Dockney and Fike of the Atlantics of Brooklyn were also offered salaries to join the same team.

Reach started out under salary for the Athletics in 1864 and Dockney and Pike followed him to Philadelphia as paid players in 1866. So Reach was really the first salaried player.

In this 1871 year, too, Jimmy Wood of the earlier Eckfords of Brooklyn team was playing a great game at second for the original Chicago White Stockings.

A fine fielder was Wood, a splendid captain and trainer, and a fine, hard-hitting, reliable batsman.

And while Wood was playing at second for Chicago, another great Brooklyn player was at work for the Atlantics of Brooklyn, John Burdock, or "Burdy," as he was called.

I first saw Burdock playing on the Capitoline Grounds at Brooklyn in the late sixties. He was a finely built lad, black-eyed, of dark complexion and an athlete all over. In the early games on these grounds he was often pointed out when a boy as a promising player and he had no trouble whatever when the professional era arrived, in finding a prominent place with the best teams.

Ross Barnes and Wes Fisler of the Athletics of Philadelphia, were the leading second basemen of their day according to the old record from 1871 to 1872, inclusive.

Barnes led in 1871 and 1872 and in 1875 and 1876 and Fisler was the leader in 1873 and 1874. Fisler in these two years had taken the place on the Athletic team of Philadelphia which Al Reach had filled so well.

When Reach quit the game in 1871 to look after his then fast-growing sporting goods business, Fisler who had been playing at first for the Athletics, was moved up to second and he finished his career on the diamond playing that position. In our list of first basemen we have already passed on Fisler's ability as a great infielder.

John Burdock led the second basemen of the country in 1877 and 1878. He was with the Hartfords in 1877 and with Boston in 1878. He remained with Boston a long while and he led the league second basemen while with that club in 1878, 1882 and 1884.

In 1879 a new name appeared at the head of the National League's second basemen. It was that of Joe Quest, who had made a name for himself while covering that point for the only Indianapolis team who in 1878 captured the pennant of the International Association.

Quest was a brilliant second baseman, a fine fielder and an excellent batsman.

After Quest as a leader of the army of second basemen came Davy Force, who was top man in 1880 and 1881.

Force was a dwarf, standing about five feet in height; but he was a wonderful fielder and a very fair batsman. He was with Buffalo in the two years mentioned.

After Burdock had captured the leading honor again in 1882 it was taken by Jack Farrell of the Champion Providence team. Farrell was a fine, big fellow, an excellent fielder and batsman.

Fred Dunlap led the National League second basemen in 1885 and again in 1887.

He was one of the cleverest, wide-awake professionals that ever took the field and besides being a clever fielder and base runner, he was a fine heady batsman.

There are perhaps other great second basemen, or there were perhaps other great second basemen not mentioned in the above list, among them Hughey McDonald, who played on the co-operative St. Louis Browns of 1880; Smiley of the Athletics of Philadelphia in their off 1880 year; Cub Stricker, who covered the bag for the Athletics, the first American Association Champions from 1883 forward; Cupid Childs, who played the bag for the Cleveland and St. Louis National League teams in the nineties; Dundon, who took turns with Isbell and Rohe in covering the bag for the Chicago White Sox in 1906; Murphy of the Athletics of 1906; Dick Pad-

den, who played the bag for the St. Louis Browns until 1906, and Moran, who shared that honor with him; Kahl and Stovall of Cleveland; Nill and Hickman of Washington, and many others of whom we will make more extended mention in the next issue of this book.

After Bierbauer, Reitz of the Champion Baltimore, was the leading second baseman. Reitz carried off that honor in 1894 and Lowe of Boston took it away in 1895.

In 1896 and 1897 McPhee, who up to that time had been playing professionally for fifteen consecutive years, again captured the honor, demonstrating the fact that he was still one of the most skillful although one of the veterans of the profession.

After McPhee came Jack Crooks, the second baseman of the St. Louis Cardinals. Jack topped the record in 1898 and played fine ball that year. He was a fine, heady player, could cover a great deal of ground, and was one of the best of pinch hitters.

Eugene DeMontreville, of Chicago and Baltimore, held the record in 1899. He was a fine, active young second baseman and created something of a sensation during his brief stay with the big league.

And now breaking away from the record list we give the names in alphabetical order of the players who have taken part in games played in the old Professional Association, the National League, the American League and all other major leagues from 1871 on:

EDWARD J. ABBATICHIO—Edward J. Abbatichio, in 1906 the clever second baseman of the Pittsburgs, is of Italian parentage and was born in Latrobe, Pa. He first came into prominence as a football player. Then he did so well as second baseman of the Greenburg, Pa., Club that he was recommended to Al. Reach of the Phillies in 1897 and was given a trial but met with an injury and was unable to complete the season. He played with Milwaukee in 1900, in Nashville, in 1901 and 1902, and was then secured by Boston. He quit baseball in 1906 to give entire attention to his hotel in Latrobe but figured in a deal the winter of 1906 by which he was traded to Pittsburg.

He then turned over to the Boston Nationals with which club he has been playing ever since. Abbatichio is one of the veterans of the National League and is considered a very fair man. Since joining Boston he has been one of its most consistent players. During the season of 1910 his duties consisted mostly of playing at second and short.

CHARLES ASCHENBACH—Charles Aschenbach was the regular second baseman of the Milwaukee Club of the American Association during the season of 1910. Aschenbach was born at Phillipsburg, N. J., in 1883. He played with Atlantic City in 1903, Brandywines of Chester in 1904. Williamsport, Pa., claimed him in 1905-6-7, and in the fall of 1907 he was drafted by the St. Louis Cardinals. In the fall of 1909 he was turned over to the Cincinnati Club by the Cardinals who in turn transferred him to Milwaukee. Charles is an excellent fielding second baseman, he is fast on the bases and a fair hitter. He is known in baseball circles as the "millionaire kid."

LOUIS BIERBAUER—Louis Bierbauer, who led the second basemen of the National League in 1892 and 1893, was with the Pittsburgs those two years.

Bierbauer won his first laurels while covering second for the Athletics of Philadelphia.

At the time he was considered the greatest second baseman in the American Association.

And he was a magnificent fielder and a fine batsman.

Bierbauer, one-time king of second basemen and all around player, first blossomed into promise as a ball player with the old Erie Penn. Malleables, twenty-five years ago. His first engagement away from home was with the Warren, Pa., team, then in a bitter baseball struggle carried on in the oil regions. Shortly after this he jumped over to Hamilton, Ontario, in the Primrose League, where Joe Quest, the famous second baseman of the late twenties found him and induced Bierbauer to go to Philadelphia and play with the Athletics.

Bierbauer's position was behind the bat, but Quest gave him a trial at second, and so brilliant did he play that position that shortly afterwards he supplanted Quest and became the leading favorite with the fans of the Quaker City. He remained with the Athletics for six years and when the celebrated war inaugurated by Johnny Ward and others against the contract system was waged Bierbauer joined the Brotherhood and was assigned to Brooklyn, where he played one year, until the Brotherhood disrupted, leaving him free to sign elsewhere. Managers at once got busy for his services.

Ned Hanlon, then managing Pittsburg, went to Erie in the depth of the Winter to secure a contract from Bierbauer. He found him on Presque Isle Peninsula, his favorite "hang-out." Hanlon had to cross the ice on the harbor in a bitter storm, but he finally reached Bierbauer's shack and before leaving had secured his signature to a contract to play with Pittsburg.

The announcement made by Hanlon upon his return to Pittsburg created a ferment in baseball circles. Philadelphia advanced prior claims, contending that he had been under contract to them when he jumped to the Brotherhood. The matter was fought out in court and the decision was in favor of Pittsburg and with the Pirates, Louis continued for six seasons.

He was a great favorite there up to the time he came to St. Louis, where he remained two years—his last in the National League, then he played a year with Columbus, and two with Buffalo in the Eastern League. His last appearance as a professional was with Hartford.

To-day he works daily as a molder in the Jarecki shops at Erie, Pa. He is the same old Bierbauer, enthused with the great American game, and his son, Louis, Jr., is the pride of his heart. Father and son are much alike in demeanor and in stature. The young man played last season in the Erie City League, where he was the star. He is a left-hander and a whirl-wind. Manager Broderick of the Sailors watched him work and last Winter quietly took him in tow and trained him for the opening of this season. Despite the fact that he is but 24 years of age and new to professional baseball he has proved himself a real find, and Erie fans will be greatly disappointed if he does not follow the footsteps of his father and make good in "higher company."

The Bierbauer family is a family of ball players. Young Roy J. Bierbauer, 15, brother of Louis, Jr., promises to be a good one. His father says he will be the best of them all. Young Roy is manager of an Erie amateur team and is a wonder for a boy of his years.

PETE BROWNING—A great player in the eighties was Peter Browning of the Louisville Club known then as the Gladiator.

He was the leading batsman of the American Association in its 1885 season.

Pete could play any place, either in the in or outfields. He was most at home, however, in the outfield, but he often covered second and short for the teams. He played with Louisville.

EDWARD COLLINS—Standing only second to Ty Cobb in the American League in both batting and base running is Edward Collins, the brilliant young second baseman of the Philadelphia Athletics. Through the entire season of 1909 his splendid playing kept his team in the pennant fight. No youngster ever made a greater impress on on the baseball public than Collins.

Collins was born in Millerton, Dutchess County, N. Y., on May 2, 1887. His father John R. Collins, is quite a famous citizen of the community for twenty-five years, holding down the office of General Freight Agent of the New York Central Railroad, and at present doing deserving service to the town of Tarrytown, N. Y., as chief of its Water Department. Eddie was educated in the Irving School, Tarrytown, and entered Columbia University in 1903. Eddie took up the regular college course, and graduated among the leaders of his class in 1907, receiving the degree of Bachelor of Arts as a fitting reward for four years of diligent highbrow researches. He was a member of the Columbia baseball nines of '04, '05, and '06, and did excellent work in the shortstop department. He was also a member of the football team in 1905, the last year the gridiron game was permitted at the Gotham institution. After the season of 1906 he was elected captain of the 1907 baseball team, but was barred from playing because of having played summer baseball during the season of 1906. During this summer he had quite a varied experience while performing with Plattsburg, N. Y., Rutland, Va., the Northern Outlaw League and Rockville, Conn. During the early part of 1907 he acted as head coach of the Columbia baseball squad.

He did not do much on the 1907 Athletic team, and did not even creep into Ban Johnson's official averages at the close of the season. In the great seventeen-inning tie game between Detroit and the Athletics for the title in 1907 Eddie was sent in to do the sticking for Rube Oldring in the seventeenth inning, under the most trying conditions, not only for a juvenile, but for a seasoned vet as well, and made good with a beautiful bunt which yielded him the occupancy of the initial sack, but his brother, Mackmen, failed to bring him around. During this season Mack concluded that Eddie needed a little minor league education and shipped him to the Newark, (N. J.) Eastern League team. After a brief season there he was called back to the Athletics.

Early in 1908 Eddie was down with typhoid fever and did not report until the season was under way. From the very first he was used almost daily by Mack as an emergency clubber and invariably made good. It made no difference how he got to first, whether by a hit, base on balls

EDWARD COLLINS.
The great second baseman of the Athletics of Philadelphia in their wonderfully successful 1910 season.

or an error by the enemy, Eddie would always manage to get there. He soon earned the sobriquet through Quaker fandom of "Lucky Eddie." Horace Fogel, the president of the Phillies, and then a leading Quaker City baseball scribe, would daily come forth with the announcement that there was no luck to Eddie's success, and declared he was the nerviest kid who ever broke into baseball, and that not many seasons would pass by before he would be one of the game's leading stars. Horace seemed to have the right dope, for there surely are mighty few Eddie Collins.

Connie soon came to the conclusion that Eddie was too valuable a man to decorate the bench, awaiting a twirler to blow up that he might represent him at bat while other regular Athletics were hitting in the .200 class. "Socks" Seybold, the ponderous White Elephant outer gardner of a few years ago, and a Mackman famous for ability to wield the bludgeon, was out of the game with a broken leg, and Eddie was tried out in the right garden. He didn't seem to look like an outfielder, so Mack switched him to short, his original job. He was a fine fielder at times, but rather erratic, and showed an inclination for heaving the sphere into the right-field bleachers in hurried attempts to peg speedy runners on their way to first, which wild flips often were very disastrous to the Mack cause. "Topsy" Hartsel's job in left field being temporarily open, Eddie was given another chance to prove his worth as an outfielder, and again did Connie decide he would not do. During all these shifts "Lucky Eddie" was mauling the pill with much frequency, and at such opportune moments when hits featured most in Athletic runs. Connie decided it was absolutely necessary to find the juvenile slugger a steady job. As Eddie didn't fill the bill in the outfield, Mr. McGillicuddy came to the conclusion that an infield position must be vacated to give Eddie an opportunity for showing his prowess with the willow. He accordingly switched Danny Murphy, the regular Athletic second sacker, to right field, and entrusted the care of the middle cushion to the Columbia kid.

The season of 1909 began the real career of Eddie Collins. On the Spring-training trip he performed at second base and captained the Athletics Yanigans. As soon as the regular season commenced, however, he was switched back to the regular team, and from the first day he has done valiant service, both with the stick and in the field. In one season he has jumped from being an erratic youngster, reputed as having lots of nerve, to the second most brilliant star in Ban Johnson's select organization. With his speedy base-running, sharp fielding and heavy clouting, up-to-date baseball, he is regarded as the premier second baseman in the game to-day, even eclipsing the wonderful Larry.

For three-quarters of the stretch for first hitting honors Eddie ran well ahead of Tyrus Cobb, of Royston, Ga., and finished a close second with the worthy average of .346. In base running he also followed right at the famous Detroiter's heels, pilfering sixty-seven sacks to Ty's seventy-six. In fielding he ranked first among American League second basemen, with an average of .967, as against Shean's (Boston) average of .960, who topped National League second sackers. To make these fielding figures more noteworthy,

and to prove **conclusively** that Eddie is not a player who plays for averages, it may be remarked that Eddie last season handled more chances than any other second baseman in either branch of the fast set, and made but twenty-seven misses in his 806 chances.

He is the real "live wire" of the Athletic team, and was one of the main reasons for the brilliant success achieved by Mack's team last year, composed as it was of a bunch of old vets, reputed to have grown stale from years of service, and an assortment of untried youngsters.

JAMES DELEHANTY—James Delahanty is the regular second baseman of the Detroit team and was one of that nine who deported himself more than well in Detroit's memorable series with Pittsburg for the World's Championship in 1909.

Delehanty joined the Detroit team in August, 1909, as the result of a trade whereby Detroit gave Washington, Schaefer and Killifer. He is the third brother of the famous Cleveland baseball family, and is probably the nearest to his late brother Ed. in batting ability. Prior to his work in Washington he played at Cincinnati, St. Louis and Boston. He admits to twenty-nine years of age, is five feet ten inches tall and bats right-handed.

Delehanty was one of the batting heroes of the Detroit-Pittsburg series of 1909. In fact his aggressive playing, desperate base running and timely bingling was probably one of the real features of this series. Delehanty took the place of the famous Dutch Schaefer on the Tiger team and though he had won the mitt of one of the popular players of the American League, the little brother of big Ed, retained his popularity. Delehanty is looked upon as one of the "classy" boys of the American League. He is a most graceful fielder and a congenial sort of a fellow both on and off the field.

THOMAS J. DOWD—Thomas J. Dowd is well and favorably remembered as a major league player.

Dowd played at second and other positions when with the St. Louis National League team.

Dowd was born at Holyoke, Mass., April 20, 1875.

In 1891 he made his debut with the American Association Club of Boston. He played in St. Louis from 1893 to 1898 acting as captain and manager of the St. Louis League team.

He went from here to the Philadelphia Nationals to Cleveland in 1899 and to the Chicago Americans in 1900 with whom he finished his major league career.

Since retiring from big league company, Dowd has been doing big things in the minor leagues.

LAWRENCE DOYLE—Lawrence Doyle, the brilliant young second baseman and captain of the New York National League Club, is regarded as one of the finds of baseball.

He was born at Caseyville, Ill., and will be only 26 years of age next July 19.

By trade he is a coal miner. He embarked in a baseball career with the Mattoon Club of the K. I. T. League in 1905 and was with Springfield, Ill, in the Three-I League in 1906.

In 1907 the youngster created a sensation by his fast work and many clubs endeavored to secure him, but it was not until New York offered $4,500 for the player that

MILLER HUGGINS.

Miller Huggins is an old-timer in the National League and requires but little boosting. He experienced one of the greatest years during his long career in baseball in 1910 as star second baseman and captain of the St. Louis Cardinals. He batted well, fielded splendidly and was one of the main stand-bys of Roger Bresnahan.

the Springfield club consented to part with him.

Doyle did not particularly distinguish himself in his first season with New York and many thought that he would not do, but he did great work in 1908, batting in sensational style, got .308 for the season and ranking third in the League in fielding. In 1909 he eclipsed the fine work he had done for the Giants the year previous and proved himself a royal player of the very first flight.

In 1910 he played grand ball and was one of the leading batters in the National League.

FRED DUNLAP—I have seen all the great second basemen from the time Al. Reach covered second for the Athletics of Philadelphia in the early sixties down to Nap. Lajoie, of the Clevelands and Johnny Evers of the Chicago Cubs who are considered the greatest men in the position in this 1909 season.

And I would easily pronounce Dunlap the greatest player that ever filled the position.

Dunlap was born in Philadelphia and learned to play ball there at about the time that Al. Reach, Jimmy Wood, and the old army of second basemen were beginning to retire.

Cotemporaneous with Dunlap were such great second basemen as Bid McPhee of Cincinnati, Fred Pfeffer and Joe Quest of Chicago, Joe Gerhardt of Louisville, Danny Richardson of New York, Nap. Lajoie of Philadelphia, Cupid Childs of Cleveland, Sam Wise of Boston, Reitz of Baltimore, Ritchey of Pittsburg, Joe Quinn of St. Louis and Boston, and others.

But none of these players could begin to compare with Dunlap in all around work or in covering the bag.

I say this because I had excellent opportunity to judge of the work of nearly all of these players. I saw them play with their respective teams in the major league and on other occasions when they occupied places in what might be termed wild-cat organizations where there was no discipline and where each and every player did about as he pleased.

And after viewing the men under these conditions I am free to say that Dunlap was far and away the greatest second baseman that ever lived.

The baseball world will perhaps never again see his equal; and I say this for several reasons. First of all, Dunlap was the right size for a second baseman, being just a little above the medium height, and he was built so close to the ground that it was an easy task for him to get down quick and handle the meanest hit grounder or the poorest throw.

He never wore a glove and his hands were as small as a woman's, but he could handle any sort of a throw or hit, running at the ball from either right or left and never halting at bad throw, or difficult ground hit.

Dunlap was ambidextrous. In covering second he would run and catch a badly thrown ball as well with his left as with his right hand and in rapid work, and in putting the ball swiftly on the runner with either hand he has never had an equal.

Dunlap used to say: "Ball players are made, not born." And he was certainly one of this kind.

When Dunlap was a lad of ten the baseball craze had begun to spread its wings.

On the outskirts of Philadelphia the prairies were dotted morning, noon and night with street gamin who played hookey from school and who put in their mornings and afternoons playing baseball. Dunlap had neither father nor mother in that early time and the people he lived with cared little where he went. So when he was not "at home" eating his meals he was out on the prairie hitting fungoes, catching the ball, throwing it or something else. The lad learned nothing but ball-playing. It was his only source of delight. He learned every trick and turn of the game. He had such a good eye that he could follow the hardest hit easily from the crack of the bat until the sphere landed in his hands. If a ball was thrown low he could tell where the rebound was to come. Thus he handled throws and hits that many of the second basemen of the present day would not try for.

Great as a fielder, he was even greater as a thrower. His aim was as accurate as the best rifle shot. He seldom, if ever, missed the mark. And as he was accurate, so was he speedy as lightning. His double plays were made with a single swing and he shot the ball so low that it seemed to tip the top of the short grass.

Mike Kelly, himself an erratic thrower, called Dunlap "Sure Shot Fred." Dunlap swung the ball, rather than threw it. This single motion gave him a marked advantage over other throwers. And there was no limit to the length of his low throw. He would run far out on the field after a fly ball and after capturing it he would shoot it home to head off the runner for the plate and with such fearful speed and accuracy that the ball seemed to sing as it flew.

And great as Dunlap was as a fielder and thrower he was also wonderful as a base runner. He ran low to the ground and with fearful speed and in making long dives for the bag or home base no one could beat him.

In the seventies managers of the baseball teams who were trying to get along in the professional arena often went to the Philadelphia prairies to hunt for material. From the lots there hundreds of great players were graduated. One day one of these experts espied Dunlap. A year or two later, in 1881, to be exact, he was playing at second base for the Cleveland National League team. And soon the news of his wonderful work spread. He was with Cleveland when that team had perhaps the greatest infield ever known. It included Big Bill Phillips, first base; Dunlap, second base; Jerry Denny, third base; Jack Glasscock, short field.

It was while Dunlap was playing with Cleveland that Henry Lucas of St. Louis, got him to sign with his St. Louis Union team. Strange to relate, Dunlap although the greatest player, knew absolutely nothing but baseball. He had grown up in the game and learned nothing else. While his little comrades were going to school Dunlap was learning the alphabet of baseball. His knowledge of the game was acute. He knew every letter of it. He could turn the neatest trick in a jiffy and he always sent the ball in the proper direction.

Playing ball, too, made him an athlete. He was as supple and free with his limbs as though made of rubber. Continual play from his youth not only made

RICHARD PADDEN.

"Brains" Padden, as he is best known to players and baseball enthusiasts who have viewed his work on the diamond for years, is to-day looked on as one of the most successful baseball scouts in America. Padden has been beating the bush leagues for talent for the Washington Nationals. Padden in his time was a great second baseman.

THE NATIONAL GAME.

him active and athletic, but gave him wonderful strength.

Once one of his players in the St. Louis Union Clubhouse rebelled, abused his captain and threatened to beat him to death. Dunlap explained that it would not be right for them to disfigure each other. Such disfigurement would result in their being unable to appear in the next day's game and render service to their club.

Dunlap suggested that they repair to a room accompanied by a friend each, that they strip to the waist and fight it out, but with the understanding that neither should hit the other a blow in the face.

Dunlap's opponent being a giant compared to his captain, eagerly accepted the proposition made him. The two with a friend each stripped to the waist and went at it with their bare fists.

The fight was a terrific one, but ended in a few minutes, Dunlap giving his opponent the worst beating a man ever received.

At another time Curt Welch, then the center fielder and the toughest man on the St. Louis Browns, came in from Sportsman's Park to the Union Grounds to take the measure of Captain Dunlap. He was sent back in a jiffy crushed and badly beaten. Dunlap had given him an exhibition of his fearful strength.

This great strength, too, made Dunlap a great batsman. He was one of the old men in the National League who made a record of .300 or better for four years. In 1881 Dunlap had a batting average of .420. Three years later when with the Detroit team who won the National League Championship and the World's flag in 1887, Dunlap's average was .326. He was not only a hard hitter, but a plucky and timely one, and he never fielded or batted better than when put to the supreme test in some all-important game.

When Dunlap quit Detroit to go to Pittsburg it was on his own terms. And when he left the Pittsburg Club in the early nineties, it was to return to Philadelphia with a small fortune.

Strange as it may seem, however, Dunlap although the quickest baseball mind ever known, was dull in other directions. He could neither read nor write. This ignorance, however, did not handicap him as much as one might suppose. This was due to the magnificent appearance of the man on and off the field. He had the finest features, the nose of an Indian chief and the brown eyes of a beautiful woman. From long service under the sun he had grown almost almond-skinned, but this color, added to the brown eyes, only made his face look the more noble and handsome. Off the field he always dressed elegantly and in raiment, looks and conduct he was ever and always the perfect gentleman.

As Mike Kelly praised Dunlap's throwing he also praised his raiment and referred to that player often as: "The best dresser in the business."

Although the greatest of second basemen, it was only in 1885 and 1887 that Dunlap led the National League in the position.

This was perhaps due to the fact that he was anything but a record breaker. He was never known to shirk a hard hit or to try and save himself an error. He loved the game so well that once in a contest all but the one thought of winning for his side vanished from his mind. When Dunlap quit the game his real life went out. He was never the same man afterwards. The great fortune he had earned during his long and brilliant career was dissipated in no time and long before old age had claimed him he passed away. His funeral, which took place in Philadelphia, was ignored by the professional players of the Quaker City with whom he was never a favorite. One who was in attendance at the obsequies said to me afterwards:

"There were not enough friends of Dunlap at his funeral to bury him and we had to call on the hack drivers to make up the list of active pall-bearers.

"When Dunlap came back to Philadelphia he brought nearly $100,000 with him. He died a pauper and what he did with the money he brought with him no one appears to know."

"Who do you put down as the greatest second baseman the game has ever known?" said Mr. Stanley Robison to me one day this summer.

"Fred Dunlap," said I without hesitation.

"There, at least," said Mr. Robison, your history is certainly correct. I speak from experience, for I was a citizen of Cleveland when Dunlap was playing at second for the club there. He was not only the greatest second baseman, but take him in all the departments of the game, he was perhaps the greatest player that ever lived."

As Mr. Robison spoke we ran into Judge James J. Spaulding, once the captain of the famous Empire Club of St. Louis, and John D. Sullivan, the veteran Postoffice Inspector at St. Louis.

"Who was the greatest second baseman that ever lived?" I asked Judge Spaulding.

"Fred Dunlap," he replied promptly.

"I never saw Dunlap's equal in the position," added Mr. Sullivan.

ROBERT J. EGAN—Robert J. Egan is the second baseman of the Cincinnati National League Club. He joined that organization in 1909 and succeeded Miller Huggins at the middle bag, a position which the latter had held down in Cincinnati for nine years. Egan is a little fellow like Huggins. He hails from the far West. He is a fast, fiery player, a good thrower and base runner and an excellent batsman. Egan is a new comer. He has done wonderfully well in the big league.

JOHNNY EVERS—By almost common consent the army of baseball fans of the 1909 season are a unit in declaring Johnny Evers of the Chicago National League team the greatest second baseman in the present organization.

Evers is not only a great fielder and base runner but he is a resourceful, all-around man and one of the best batsmen in America when it comes to the pinch.

And while Evers is today one of the greatest second basemen, he is also one of the youngest players in the big league. He is in his twenty-seventh year.

He joined the Chicago Cubs in 1903 being practically given to that team in a trade which it made with the Troy, New York team. Evers was the "boot" in the deal.

He is a right-handed thrower, but bats left-handed.

In build he is of medium height and

198

weight and just the shape to make a grand athlete and player.

When it comes to discussing the leaders of second base position of our great National Game, Mr. Ever's name should be mentioned first. Johnny, according to the wise ones, is regarded as the smart fellow of baseball. For seven years Evers has been the keystone of the Cubs' great baseball aggregation. He was not very well known until the season of 1903 when Chicago secured him on a trade from the Troy team. In those days the now famous Cubs were an unknown quantity. So was Johnny. He first became prominent in the season of 1905 when his wonderful fielding, timely batting and great inside play brought him into notice. Again in 1906 when his club won the championship of the National League, and then tied up with Comiskey's White Sox for the world's greatest title, Evers exhibited a brand of baseball which the fans had not seen since the days of Dunlap, Robinson and other second sackers of days agone. In 1908 when the Cubs and New York Giants were fighting down to the very last game of the season for the championship, Evers was credited with outgeneraling the enemy and winning for his club a championship. It was due to Johnny's quick wit in a pinch that Merkle was declared out. Thus started the famous saying, "touch-second." In 1910 Evers played his usual great game, batting and fielding like the champion he is. He will as usual be one of the real high lights in the World's Champion series of 1910.

PADDY EVERS—Paddy Evers, a younger brother of the king of all second basemen in the United States, or in any other old state, made his initial appearance in the professional baseball field in Chicago on Sunday, August 28, 1910 as a member of the West Ends of the City League in Chicago. Evers was recommended to the manager of the West End team by his big brother, Johnny, who stated when the "Kid" was delivered in Chicago that he would easily make the team. Evers success during the Fall of 1910 as a member of the West End is well known. Like his brother he is fast on his feet, graceful and he proved himself an excellent pinch hitter. The chances are Young Evers will be a member of the Chicago Cubs before the 1911 season is very old. Many say he is even a better fielding second baseman than his big brother.

CHARLEY FRENCH—Charley French is one of the infielders of the Chicago White Sox nine of the American League. Up to the time when McConnell was secured from the Boston Club, French was playing regularly on the Sox infield. French is a very fast, aggressive ball player and there is little question but that he will win a regular position with the White Sox in 1911.

EARL GARDNER—Earl Gardner is one of the second basemen of the New York American League Team. He is 25 years of age and comes from Sparta, Illinois. He went from there to the Houston Club of the Texas League. He was purchased by the Browns in the Spring of 1908. Later he was sold to the Hartford Club of the Eastern League and was recommended to the New York Highlanders by Bob Connery. Gardner has within the past year developed into a very high class infielder as well as winning the

reputation of being one of the hardest hitting infielders in the American League. On August 14, 1910, Gardner was batting close to .300 and fielding grandly.

JOE GERHARDT—Joe Gerhardt, in his day, was famous as a second baseman. He was with Cincinnati in 1878 and later with Louisville. He was the manager, Captain and second baseman of the Louisville American Association Team which played great baseball in the eighties. He was one of the best natured and popular of professionals and when he quit the game to open a buffet in New York he met with great success.

WILLIAM GILBERT—William Gilbert was one of the live fielders and folks will have to go a long way to find any better second base work than the people of New York saw in 1903, 1904 and 1905, when Gilbert was at his best.

Part of the time he covered as much or more ground than any infielder who has lived in years, and when the old fellows get around and swap yarns about the territory which was covered by Fred Pfeffer, Dunlap and some of those other old chaps who had quite a reputation in their day, be it known that for real ability to be everywhere between first base and second, behind the pitcher and over in the third base orchard picking up apples which had dropped to the ground, this nimble young Gilbert had about as much temperament as any of them.

He concluded his great career as a second baseman in 1909 while with the St. Louis Cardinals.

WILLIAM GLEASON—One of the oldest second basemen in the National League in 1908, was William Gleason of the Philadelphia Club.

"Kid" Gleason, for that is the name he has been known by in the base ball field for nearly a score of years, and even now in his veteran days, started off as a pitcher.

He was a fine speedy twirler at that but when his arm gave out he was easily able to obtain a position as an infielder for besides being a ball player of all-round capacity, he was a batsman of the first flight.

He covered second base for the New York Team for several seasons and then went to Philadelphia. He was not related in any way to William Gleason, the great short fielder of the St. Louis Browns.

JOHN E. HUMMEL—John E. Hummel has been the main stay at second base for the Brooklyn National League team for several seasons. He is one of the heaviest hitters in the business. He is a tall well built fellow and as a fielder covers a great lot of ground. Up to August 1910 he had retained his high record of the past and was batting close to .300.

MILLER HUGGINS—Miller Huggins, the clever second baseman of the St. Louis National League Club came to that organization from the Cincinnati National League team. Huggins' debut with St. Louis was made in the Spring of 1910, and he not only made a good record from the start but he was pronounced by experts the best second baseman that had played in a St. Louis professional team since the days of Dunlap. Huggins covers much ground and runs the bases so well that he became known to St. Louis followers of the game as "The Rabbit." Huggins has been playing ball a long while and his work in the 1910 season was a revelation to the St. Louis

followers of the game, who up to the time
of his debut here had never recognized
the true worth of the little fellow. He
made a world of friends here by his play
at second base and by his work as Captain
of the Cardinals. He is a native of Cincinnati and has only played there and in St.
Louis.

W. L. KILLIFER—W. L. Killifer is the
regular second sacker of the Washington
Club of the American League. Killifer
has been drawing a good salary in big
League circles for several years past. He
is considered a good batsman, a fair fielder
and should hold his own next season.

OTTO KNABE—One of the greatest second base players in the National League
today is Otto Knabe who has been filling
that position for the Philadelphia Club
since 1907.

Knabe is a native of Carrick, Pa., and
was born June 12, 1884. He gained valuable
experience in Clubs in the vicinity of
Pittsburg, Pa., and in 1905 tried his hand
with the Colorado Springs, Colo., Club and
went to Pueblo, Colo., when his team was
transferred there.

His work attracted considerable attention and among those who watched the
youngster was Barney Dreyfus, who secured him. He played several games with
Pittsburg in the fall of 1905, and showed
well for the future. Pittsburg had no opening for the youngster and sold him to
Toledo. Knabe made a fine record with
the Toledo Club and was recalled by
Pittsburg. Afterward Pittsburg decided to
take Pitcher Camnitz of Toledo, so Knabe
again became the property of the Toledo
Club, and he was drafted by Philadelphia.
He started the season of 1907 as a spare
man, but an accident to the veteran
"Kid" Gleason enabled him to get into the
game, and he has held the base ever
since.

Knabe proved a veritable find for the
Phillies, and has much endeared himself
to the lovers of the game in the Quaker
City. Last season he had more put-outs
and more assists and consequently more
chances than any National League second
baseman, his fielding percentage being .969.

NAP. LAJOIE—Almost any one asked to
name the best second baseman in the field
today would point to Evers of Chicago,
Doyle of New York, or Lajoie of Cleveland.
They would at the same time, perhaps,
prefer the latter, owing to his great ability
as a batsman.

Lajoie led the American League as a
batsman from 1901 to 1905. His record
those four years was: .422, .355, .381, .329.

He was with the Philadelphia Club from
1896 to 1900 and from 1901 to 1910 with
Cleveland and in all these years he has
been close to the top as a batsman.

Should there ever come a time when
the official baseball records contain not
only averages year by year, but grand
averages, the name of Lajoie, the best
batter of modern times, will be found
at the top. Close to him will be found
the names of Edward Delehanty, now
dead and Willie Keeler. Imagine what
sustained batting ability it requires to
have a grand average covering a period
of ten years of .370. That is Lajoie's
record for the last ten years and in that
time his lowest average was .328. Once he
went as high as .422. The grand batting
average of Delehanty for the period of
1898 to 1903, inclusive, was .363, while
Keeler's grand average for ten years is

.361. In 1897 Keeler's average was .432,
which is the best made by any batsman
in either big league in the last ten years.

The respective leaders in batting in the
American and National Leagues in 1905,
were Lajoie of the American League, and
Seymour, of the National League. It was
no spasmodic outbreak of hard hitting that
landed these two men at the top. By right
of sustained ability covering a stretch of
years in professional baseball, they are
entitled to rank at the top. They are two
of a small group of batsmen who year after year have hit the ball at a .300 clip,
that group including, in addition to the
two men named, Keeler, Fred. Clarke,
Wagner, Beaumont, Elmer Flick, Joe. Kelley, Mike Donlin, Jessie Burkett and Jake
Beckley. Of this list Clarke, Burkett,
Beckley and Kelley failed to reach the
.300 mark in 1906, but previous long records
of hard and consistent hitting entitled them
to a place among the small band of excep-
tional hitters named.

Of players now in the game Clarke, Lajoie, Keeler, Beckley, Kelley and Burkett
have grand averages of over .300 per cent.
for the last ten years.

Those who in the last ten years never
have hit below .300 are Lajoie and Keeler.

In the last nine years in the National
League John Wagner has not hit below
.300. The lowest he ever went was .305
in 1898 and the highest .363 in 1905. His
grand average is .347. John McGraw in
the last seven years that he played did
not bat below .300 and has the fine grand
average for that period of .343.

Batters who in the last ten years have
hit better than .400 are: Clarke, Lajoie,
Keeler, Delehanty, and Burkett. Burkett
is the only one who twice has gone over
.400, in 1896, and in 1899.

Following is a list of two batsmen and
their records, who for the last ten years,
or part of that time, have wonderful continuous records with the stick, whose
luster as clouters extraordinary the best
pitching skill in the baseball arena has
not been able to dim:

Lajoie—1896, .328; 1897, .363; 1898, .328; 1899,
.379; 1900, .316; 1901, .422; 1902, .369; 1903, .355;
1904, .381; 1905, .329. Grand average, .370.

Seymour—1898, .273; 1899, .337; 1901, .302;
1902, .349; 1903, .342; 1904, .312; 1905, .377.
Grand average, .326.

Perhaps no better compliment was ever
paid a player than that paid Lajoie by
Hugh Duffy, now the manager of the
Chicago White Sox. Of Lajoie he said:

"There is one fellow playing baseball to-
day who could play for me if he had only
one arm. I would make room for him
despite the fact he has reached the veteran age in baseball, for I believe he has
six or seven banner years before him. I
refer to Larry Lajoie, the grand fielder
and great slugger of the Cleveland Naps.
I have seen stars come and go, but I
don't believe that any one has ever had
anything on the Frenchman. Good Old
Ed Delehanty could clout the horsehide
some, but Larry seemed to be just as
powerful, if not a little more so.

'Well do I recall the day we thought
we had discovered Lajoie's weakness at
bat. With Klobedanz pitching for Boston
we beat the Phillies, and Larry struck
out twice. He didn't get anything that
looked like a hit. Klobey fed them in
close to Larry's neck. We were a jubilant
crowd in the club house after the game, for
we thought Larry would be a dead duck

NAPOLEON LAJOIE.

LARRY LAJOIE, ONE OF THE VETERAN SECOND BASEMEN OF THE
AMERICAN LEAGUE, AS WELL AS ONE OF THE GREATEST
BATSMEN IN THE WORLD.

Big Larry, who, during the season of 1909, was the leading batsman of the
American League and for the best part of the 1910 season requires but little introduction. Lajoie, since being relieved of the managerial reins has recovered his old-
time form. About a year ago, while the wonderful French athlete was managing
the Cleveland Club, it was said that the duties of trying to manage a baseball
nine and play besides was having the effect of weakening the big fellows' ability
as a fielder and a slugging batsman. Big Larry was of this opinion himself and
asked that he be relieved of the job of manager. In the 1910 season the big fellow danced onto the field around second base and began exhibiting flashes of his
old-time form. He began early to hammer out the slants of the pitchers and it
was not long when the name of the old champion slugger was being heralded
throughout the baseball world. Cobb, Crawford and big Larry took turns in leading the league with the big stick.. Up to September 1, Lajoie was on top, though
Cobb was giving him a close, hard fight.

in the future. The next day Ted Lewis was on the rubber for us and he was instructed to dish them up to Larry neck high and close in. He did. The first time up Lajoie slammed the ball over the left field fence. The second time he bounced the sphere against the brick wall in center field with such force that by the time I reached the spot where I figured the ball would land on the carom return, it had traveled back toward the infield about as fast as it had come out and was ten feet away from the third base, toward home plate. All Larry got on the drive was a double. Later he cracked out two singles and a triple. Lewis didn't have to tell us that he followed instructions to the letter the first three times, for every Boston players' eyes were focused on the big Frenchman. The fourth and fifth times Lewis fed him something else, but it was the same story.

"That afternoon in the club house we agreed that Klobey had caught Larry on one of his few off-days and that weakness hunch was all a hallucination. The greatest feat I ever saw Lajoie perform as a batsman was at Milwaukee, and it is because that feat is still fresh in memory that I say he could play with me if he had only one arm. With two men on base the pitcher tried to walk Larry. He pitched the ball three feet outside the plate. Larry let the first two pass without offering. On the third ball he took a mighty swing with the bat held in his right hand and met it fair and square, sending it on a line over the center field fence."

Napoleon (Larry) Lajoie, Ex-Manager of the Cleveland Americans, and a second sacker and swatter of much prominence and fame was born at Woonsocket, R. I., September 5, 1875, of French parentage, and, next to Senator Aldrich, he is the most important personage in American history born in Rhode Island since the Revolution. When the elder Monsieur Lajoie attached the name of the famous French Emperor to his young hopeful, it is doubtful if he ever thought that the baby Nap would be known from the Atlantic to the Pacific as "King" Napoleon. Even the Little Corporal might receive a rude shock himself were he to know that the Cleveland Americans were to go down to posterity as the "Naps" entitled such, not because of Nap, the Emperor, but because of Nap, King of Ball Tossers. He was educated in the public schools of his native town, and being compelled at an early age to eke a livelihood out of the cruel, world, found the cabby profession, clerking in a dry goods store or similar genteel occupations.

The New England League teams were wont to occasionally drop into Woonsocket, and play exhibition games with the aggregation of local talent, and the young slugger who caught for the Rhode Islanders began to acquire quite a reputation. In the Spring of 1896 the dreams of future fame began to materialize, for Nap was signed by the Fall River Club of the New England League as a catcher, and the Cabby business was shelved for keeps. In a few weeks he was the rage of the circuit, and had the decendants of Cotton Mather, Roger Williams, Miles Standish, and kindred folks, doing handsprings and turning cartwheels from sheer delight in the bleachers of Fall River and other towns in the league. For surely never before

had such doings with the bludgeon been enacted on Pilgrim soil.

Larry was not destined to entertain in their midst for any length of time.

On August 12, 1896, he made his debut as a major league player. His first appearance was at first base but he was soon moved along to second. And he has been there ever since. And a fine fielding second baseman is Lajoie. But his best forte is hitting the ball. As a batsman in fact there is probably no player today who can tell where he will hit the ball as well as Larry. He hits them to left, right or center with equal ease. No fielder can play for him, as one field is as easy as another. Another feature of his remarkable batting is the apparent ease with which he makes his longest hits. The writer remembers an instance when Larry met one of Rube Waddell's fast ones with no more swing than is applied to an everyday sacrifice bunt, yet the ball almost cleared the left field fence, and netted him a long two bagger.

FRANK LAPORTE—Frank Laporte played second base during the entire season of 1910 for the New York Highlanders in the American League and up to late Fall his work was nothing short of sensational. Laporte though a young man can be classed as a veteran in the American League at this date. Up to August 15, 1910, he had taken part in ninety-five games, lined out one hundred base hits and showed an average of .300. He was rated one of the real slugging infielders in the American League during the season. Laporte of course, will be the Highlanders' regular second sacker in 1911.

R. J. LOWE—R. J. Lowe was the leading second baseman of the National League in the 1900 season.

A fine, active fielder and base runner was Lowe and he was also something as a batsman.

In 1896, on Decoration Day, while playing at second for Boston against Cincinnati, Chamberlain pitching for the latter team, Lowe made a batting record of seventeen bases, four home runs and a single. Two of his home runs were made in a single game. Of late years Lowe has been doing scout duty for the Detroit Club. He has turned up some of the best youngsters shown in the American League.

AMBROSE M'CONNELL—There are few better all around players than Ambrose McConnell the little second baseman of the Chicago Americans. A star at the bat in the field and at running the bases he seems destined for a wonderful career. He was formerly with the Boston Americans being traded with Harry Lord to Chicago in exchange for Frank Smith and William Purtell.

MIKE McGEARY — Mike McGeary, a Philadelphia boy, was the captain and second basemen of St. Louis' first team in the National League.

This was away back in 1876 and in 1879 McGeary was playing this same position for the Providence Club, that year the Champions.

On this Providence team with McGeary were such great players as John Ward, Robert Matthews, Em. Gross, George Wright, Tom York, Paul Hines and Jim O' Rourke. And among these great players McGeary held his own.

JAMES A. McPHEE—James A. McPhee, or "Bid" McPhee, as he was always called, was the leading second baseman in the National League averages in 1891. He was with Cincinnati that year.

McPhee's real career on the diamond commenced in 1882 when he helped win the first American Association pennant. He was with Cincinnati that year and he was also with that club for over ten years afterwards.

McPhee was a magnificent fielder and thrower and a very timely batsman. He stood so well with the people of Cincinnati that for years they refused to part with him and a Cincinnati team seemed never complete without the old reliable McPhee guarding the second bag.

JOHN B. MILLER—John B. Miller surprised his most ardent admirers in the magnificent game he put up at second base for the Pittsburg Club in their great series with Detroit in 1909.

Miller is one of the youngest players in the National League. He was born Sept. 9, 1886, at New York City. He stands six feet and weighs 160 pounds. He played May to July, 1908, with Easton in the Atlantic League; July to September, 1908, with McKeesport in the O. & P. League, and in 1909 with Pittsburg.

Miller's parents moved to Kearney, L. I., eight miles from New York, between Newark and New York, when Miller was an infant, and there he gained his knowledge of the game, showing such aptitude that he gained a place on the Parkways of Kearney, where he played short.

In the 1908 season Sutton secured him for the Easton (Pa.) Club of the Atlantic League, and he played third base until July, showing up well. Pittsburg then secured him and turned him over to McKeesport in the Ohio and Pennsylvania League, playing short-stop. In 1909 the Youngster started with Pittsburg and gained a place as a regular and has done splendid work, both at the bat—ranking with the best—and in the field.

Miller was the find of the Pittsburg team in the 1909 season. He was then a power with the stick, hitting for .262, and his strong work kept Abbatichio, the Pirate veteran, out of the game.

SIMEON A. MURCH—Simeon A. Murch was born in Castine, Mo., November 21, 1880. When a youngster he came to the Jamaica Plain district of Boston and lived there until his marriage six years ago, when he moved to Brookline, Mass., and a year and a half afterwards moved to Roxbury. He played ball with the Lynn, Leominster, Dorchester, Hyde Park, West Roxbury, Sharon, Brookline, and Jamaica Plain Clubs before embarking with Billy Hamilton in Haverhill in 1902. He had always played second base before embarking in minor league ball, but Hamilton placed him on third. The next season Hamilton traded him and Bernard to Lawrence for Mike Murphy and Leon Demontreville. In 1904 he hit for .285 with Lawrence. The St. Louis Nationals secured him in 1905. He went to the minors the next two years, but in 1908 returned to Brooklyn. Later he was secured by the Indianapolis Club of the American Association, and during the 1910 season played grand ball at third base.

FRED PFEFFER—Fred Pfeffer was the second baseman of the historic Chicago White Stockings from 1884 until that great team was dissolved.

He was the field partner of such great players and infielders as Anson, Ed. Wil-

liamson, Tom Burns and Mike Kelly. He took Quest's place on the team.

Pfeffer was the tall, slender athlete of this bunch, but what a grand fielder and thrower he was and how beautifully he could hit the ball when a good, hard clip was needed.

Pfeffer shone as a star with the famous Chicago White Stockings for many years.

Always a gentleman both on and off the field he had made friends the country over and nowhere was he thought more of than in Chicago, for whose club he labored long and faithfully.

He was playing his very best in 1886, the last year the great Chicago aggregation won the National League Championship.

JOE QUINN—Joe Quinn, the second baseman of the Boston Club when they won the National League pennant in 1891 and 1892, is now a resident of St. Louis.

He played his first professional ball in 1884 with the St. Louis Unions, having been brought from Dubuque, Ia., by Ted Sullivan to play at first base for that team.

Dunlap was the captain and second baseman of the Unions that year. Quinn followed closely in Dunlap's footsteps, copied his every move, and so well that he was able for years afterwards to hold his own as a second baseman with the best clubs in the major league.

Quinn was a very lively sort of a lad at second, fielding finely and being a good hitter when a hit was badly needed.

He is now engaged in the livery business in St. Louis, and is rated one of the Mound City's most prominent and popular citizens.

DAN RICHARDSON—Danny Richardson, who covered second base for the New York Giants when they were winning National League and World's Championships in 1888 and 1889, much resembled Robinson of the St. Louis Browns in his style of play.

He was a very rapid fielder, a splendid thrower and base runner and in his last years with New York a hard hitting batsman.

For years he, Roger Connor, Arthur Whitney and John Ward formed New York's peerless infield.

WILLIAM ROBINSON—William Robinson, the second baseman of the four-time winner St. Louis Browns, was one of the most brilliant second base players of his day.

Robinson was one of the old "Stonewall Infield," the infield that included Comiskey at first, Robinson at second, Latham at third and W. Gleason at short field.

Robinson covered a fine lot of ground. He was especially good at backing up quickly and grabbing the short flies that were hit just over second base. He was a fine fielder and thrower and a fine emergency batsman.

HERMAN SCHAEFER—Herman Schaefer, best known as "Germany" Schaefer, was the second baseman of the Washington American League team in the early part of the season of 1910. Prior to joining Washington he was the captain of Hughey Jennings' Champion Detroit team in the season of 1907 and 1908. He is now the official scout of the Washington Club. In his day Schaefer was one of the best fielders and batsmen in the business.

DAVID W. SHEAN—David W. Shean is the second baseman of Fred Lakes' Boston National League team. He is a tall, rangy fielder, covers a lot of ground and is a fair batsman.

Owner Harris of the Bostonians considers Shean the peer of any second baseman in the National League.

GEORGE SMITH—George Smith several years ago was the second baseman as well as the captain of the New York Giants.

That was just before John McGraw took hold of that organization.

Smith fielded his position finely, but he was not heavy enough a batsman to hold his own in the big league.

Smith went to New York from the Rochesters of the Eastern League.

After quitting New York he managed and captained and played at second for the Buffalo team. He is now just a player on that team.

A fine character is this George Smith. Always reliable and trustworthy and one of the most valuable fielders in the business, there will always be a demand for his services just outside the big leagues.

Were he as good a hitter as he is a fielder, he would never want for a position in the major leagues.

FRANK TRUESDALE—Frank Truesdale, a great little player hailing from Kirkwood, Mo., and who was graduated from the Dallas Club of the Texas League is holding down second base for the St. Louis Browns. Though not a star, one man on the Brown team is entitled to much credit. That is this Truesdale. From the start of the training trip in Texas up to the time he began to show good form in June, 1910, it was "thumbs down" all along the line on Truesdale. From Texas went up frantic, fanatic wails for Olson, to come to the rescue and play second base, though Olson's ability was unknown to everyone. Truesdale just kept on biding his time and finally landed the position. Truesdale is the ideal second baseman in build. He is only twenty-one years of age and has a bright future before him.

JAMES T. WILLIAMS—James T. Williams played great ball for the St. Louis Americans in 1908, thereby contributing not a little to the standing of that club in the American League race that year. He is a native of St. Louis and was born here December 20, 1876. He first played with the Pueblo (Colo.) Club in 1895 and was with the Leadville and Albuqerque Clubs the following season.

In 1897 he played with the St. Joseph (Mo.) Club and then for two seasons made good with Kansas City. Pittsburg secured his services in 1900, and the next year he was with McGraw in Baltimore with the expanded American League. He stuck to Baltimore when McGraw went to New York, and in 1903 started in with the American League Club in New York. He remained with the Yankees until the season of 1908, coming to St. Louis in the trade which landed Ferris and Hoffman in St. Louis and Glade, Niles and Hemphill in New York. In the winter of 1909, Williams was sold, with Hobe Ferris to the Minneapolis Club of the American Association.

HENRY ZIMMERMAN—H. Zimmerman is the general man of all work on the Chicago Cubs of the National League. Zimmerman is without a peer in the role he occupies as the man who is supposed to do the impossible whenever he is called upon. He plays first, second, short, third and the outfield positions, and in a pinch, they say he could go on to the hill and pitch even with the best of them. In the several World's Championships in which the Cubs have taken part, Zimmerman's work has been one of the sensational features. He is a natural batsman and most of his drives go to the fence. He is also very fast on the bases and plays the game for all it is worth. A year ago President Murphy of the Cubs was offered fifteen thousand dollars cash by three owners of National League Clubs for the services of the great and only "Heine." In fact President Murphy told President Ebbetts of the Brooklyn Club that he would not trade the great Zimmermann for Mr. Ebbett's entire basball aggregation.

JOE QUINN.

At one time Joe Quinn, now a St. Louis business man, was one of the best known second basemen in America. He commenced playing in 1884 with the St. Louis Unions.

THE NATIONAL GAME.

THE THIRD BASEMEN.

BY COMMON CONSENT ED. WILLIAMSON OF THE CHICAGO WHITE STOCK-
INGS OF THE EIGHTIES AND JIM COLLINS OF THE BOSTON AM-
ERICANS WERE THE GREATEST PLAYERS IN THIS
POSITION IN EITHER THE OLD PROFES-
SIONAL ASSOCIATION OR THE
NATIONAL LEAGUE.

This is the record of the players who excelled at second base in the old Professional Association and then in the National League.

Year.	Third Basemen. Club.	Games.	Fielding Pct.	Year.	Third Basemen. Club.	Games.	Fielding Pct.
1871	A. C. Anson—Rockford	25	.886	1890	Jas. McGarr—Boston	115	.933
1872	Harry Shaffer—Boston	47	.896	1891	C. E. Bassett—New York	122	.910
1873	R. Ferguson—Atlantics, Brooklyn	57	.927	1892	Wm. Dahlen—Chicago	68	.943
1874	W. White—Baltimore	15	.925	1893	Jas. McGarr—Cleveland	63	.941
1875	E. B. Sutton—Ath., Phila	60	.930	1894	W. M. Nash—Boston	132	.932
1876	Joe Battin—St. Louis	63	.867	1895	Lave Cross—Philadelphia	124	.930
1877	A. C. Anson—Chicago	47	.872	1896	Lave Cross—Philadelphia	63	.945
1878	W. L. Hague—Providence	60	.918	1897	W. Clingman—Louisville	115	.949
1879	John Morrill—Boston	51	.878	1898	J. Wagner—Louisville	62	.945
1880	E. Williamson—Chicago	61	.893	1899	Lave Cross—St. Louis, Cleveland.	141	.950
1881	E. Williamson—Chicago	74	.909	1900	Lave Cross—St. Louis, Brooklyn	133	.941
1882	E. Williamson—Chicago	82	.880	1901	H. Wolverton—Philadelphia	92	.920
1883	Jerry Denny—Providence	93	.875	1902	E. Greminger—Boston	140	.954
1884	E. B. Sutton—Boston	106	.906	1903	H. Wolverton—Philadelphia	123	.941
1885	E. Williamson—Chicago	111	.891	1904	S. Woodruff—Cincinnati	61	.932
1886	J. Denny—St. Louis	117	.895	1905	J. Casey—Chicago	142	.949
	T. Esterbrook—New York	123	.895	1906	Harry Arndt—St. Louis	75	.965
1887	A. Whitney—Pittsburg	119	.924	1907	H. Steinfeldt—Chicago	151	.967
1888	W. M. Nash—Boston	104	.913	1908	A. Devlin—New York	157	.947
1889	Jerry Denny—Indianapolis	133	.913	1909	E. Lennox—Brooklyn	121	.959
				1910	Zimmerman—Chicago	23	.987

IN THE AMERICAN LEAGUE.

THESE ARE THE MEN WHO LED AT THIRD BASE IN THE AMERICAN
LEAGUE SINCE THE FIRST YEAR OF THAT ORGANIZATION.

In the American League, Bradley, formerly of Cleveland, is the only player at
third base who has led in that position in more than one year since the American
League came into the field. The American League record shows these men at
the top during the years named:

Year.	Third Basemen. Club.	Games.	Fielding Pct.	Year.	Third Basemen. Club.	Games.	Fielding Pct.
1900	W. Coughlin—Kansas City	130	.920	1905	W. Bradley—Cleveland	145	.944
1901	W. Bradley—Cleveland	133	.936	1906	W. Bradley—Cleveland	82	.966
1902	J. Collins—Boston	105	.951	1907	Wm. Shipke—Washington	63	.949
1903	Lave Cross—Philadelphia	136	.954	1908	Hobe Ferris—St. Louis	148	.952
1904	Lee Tannehill—Chicago	153	.948	1909	W. Bradley—Cleveland	87	.957
				1910	Conroy—Washington	48	.961

Third base has always been considered
one of the most difficult positions to play
on the ball field.

The man covering that bag has always
had to face the hardest hit balls and no
man not a fast and capable thrower has
been able to make good at this corner.

Third base was an especially difficult
place to fill in the early days of the professional game before fielding gloves were
known and when the third baseman had
to handle the hardest hit ground balls
with his bare hands.

In 1871 Adrian C. Anson, afterwards the
peerless leader of the historic Chicago
White Stockings was playing at third
base for Rockford, Ill. He led the National League in that position that year
and captured the honor again in 1877 when
he played the bag for Chicago.

Harry Shaffer of the Boston Reds had
the best record of any third baseman in
1872. He was a fine active player.

Captain Robert Ferguson, "Old Fergy,"
as he was afterwards called, had the best
record of the third basemen in the big
league in 1873. He was playing the position that year for the Atlantics of Brooklyn.

Ferguson was one of the first of the
original band of professionals who played
their first ball on the field near Brooklyn
and then took up their place in the Capitoline Grounds, the first real enclosure.

In our resume of the great catchers we
referred to Ferguson as one of the best
back-stops of his day and one of the first
of the great receivers to work close to
the bat without the aid of a mask, gloves
or chest protector. When not catching he
generally covered third for his nine.

As he was great as a catcher, so was
Bob Ferguson great as a third baseman.
He was a man about the medium height
and of wiry and muscular build. He was
a fine batsman as well as a great fielder
and base runner.

After a long career as a player he won
fame as an umpire and he filled that position in the major organizations almost
to the time of his death.

White wore spectacles and players who
saw him playing at third often wondered
how he ever escaped with his life. He
was a brother of Jim White, the famous
catcher.

Sutton was a great third baseman, great
as a fielder, thrower and batsman.

JACK GLEASON.
The famous third baseman of the old St. Louis Browns in the uniform he wore when with that team.

Battin, who, like White and Sutton, was of medium size, played a pretty game at third and was a fine reliable fielder and thrower.

Denny led the National League as a third baseman in 1883 and in 1886 he tied Tommy Esterbrook for the place.

Esterbrook was the third baseman that year of the original New York Giants. His partners in the infield were Connor, Richardson and Ward.

An eccentric fellow was Esterbrook. All New York called him "The Dude."

But outside of his eccentricity he was a fine player, covering third base finely and being a heavy and timely batsman.

Esterbrook went to the Giants from the Metropolitans when they were champions of the American Association, he going to the older club with Holbert, Keefe and others.

Arthur Whitney, then with Pittsburg, led the league third basemen in 1887. He was a fine fielder and thrower and so was Billy Nash, who led all in 1888 while with Boston.

Denny led again in 1899 and then Jim McGarr, Bassett and Dahlen followed in the order named. They were three great players, Dahlen, one of the best of the lot, is still playing and has been at it now for nearly twenty years.

McGarr repeated in 1893 and Nash came again in 1894.

Other third basemen who have been prominent in the National and American League games since 1900 are Sheehan of Pittsburg, Mowrey of St. Louis, Beam of Boston, Courtney of Philadelphia, Kane of Cincinnati, Sweeny of Boston, Shipke of Washington, Bradley of Cleveland, Yeager and Hartzell of the St. Louis Browns, Knight of Boston, O'Brien of Washington, LaPorte of the New York Americans, Delahanty of Washington and Quillin of the Chicago White Sox.

This brings us up to the players whose names do not appear in the top record, but who in their day were brilliant third basemen. Below in alphabetical order is given a list of players who in their day played at third base for the clubs of the old Professional Association, the National League, the American League and all other major league organizations since 1871:

JAMES PHILIP AUSTIN—James Philip Austin is the captain and third baseman of the New York American League team. For a youngster, he having entered the American League in the Spring of 1909, Austin is simply a wonder. He is a Cleveland boy and was born December 8, 1880. Playing in the lots around that city he attracted attention by his fine work for the Franklin A. C. He played with Dayton, O., in 1904-5-6, and with Omaha, Neb., in 1907-8, being drafted from that club by the New York Americans. He stands five feet seven inches and weighs 154 pounds. Austin is a timely hitter and a cracker jack third baseman. He is also one of the fastest baserunners in the American League. In his work as captain he is bold, fearless and quick as lightning.

F. BAKER—F. Baker is the third baseman of the Athletics in this their 1910 season. He is a speedy young player, a fine fielder and a cracker jack batsman. He is in fact one of the hardest hitters in the American League and has been a good batsman ever since he made his debut in fast company.

WILLIAM JOSEPH BARBEAU—William Joseph Barbeau, third baseman of the Kansas City American Association team, 1910, was born in New York City, June 10, 1884, and made that city his home until he was 18 years of age.

He is a printer by occupation and confined his early ball playing, like many youngsters, to Sundays.

While visiting relatives at Marquette, Mich., he went with the Baraga, Mich., club in the copper country to play at Soo, Mich., and played three games there and then went back to Marquette. That was in 1903. He also played in Soo the following season and in 1905 was with Columbus and was purchased by Cleveland in 1906.

In 1907 he was in Toledo and played short-stop that season and in 1908 Philadelphia drafted him for 1909 and turned him over to Pittsburg. On August 29 he was traded with Alan Storke for Byrne of the St. Louis Nationals, and in June, 1910, was turned over to Kansas City by the Cardinal management. He is five feet four and one-half inches in height and weighs 150 pounds. Barbeau is known as "Jap" owing to his swarthy appearance and he got his nickname from the pen of a Columbus newspaper man.

HENRY BATCH—Henry Batch, a native of Brooklyn, and born there 31 years ago, started out with Waterbury, Conn., in 1899 and went to Holyoke in 1903. There he won a name by his hard hitting and attracted a deal of attention.

Brooklyn tried him in 1904 but returned him to Holyoke after a short trial, but he gave such a good account of himself upon his return to the Holyoke club that he was again taken to Brooklyn.

In 1895 he played 145 games at third for Brooklyn and batted that season for .252. The following season he was worked in but fifty-two games, fifty of them in the outfield and he hit for .250. In 1906 he played in 106 games, 101 of these being in the outfield and he batted for .347. Last season he played with the Rochester club of the Eastern League and batted for .260 in 134 games, playing second, third, short, left and right with that club. He is again on the Rochester roster this season.

ROY BETCHER—Roy Betcher, utility infielder of the St. Louis Cardinals during the season of 1910, gives promise of making a name for himself in 1911. Betcher is a tall fellow, fast as lightning on the bases and fields beautifully. In the Spring of 1909 he was farmed out, but was later recalled and played many good games for the Cardinals during the late Fall.

WILLIAM BRADLEY—Another great strategist who looks after the third corner is William Bradley, who up to July, 1910, had been the Cleveland's best third baseman for years.

Like Lord, of Chicago, he is very heady and outwits his opponents more often by head work than by the mechanical perfection of his playing. "Dutch" Schaefer of Washington fell, one day, a victim to his wiles. "Dutch" was on third, taking a long lead. Harry Bemis, who was catching, threw to Bradley to try and get "Germany" napping.

The throw was a trifle high and the third baseman made no atempt to spear it. The base runner started back to third, saw the throw go high and put for the

THOMAS LEACH.
He played at third and in the outfield for the Champion Pittsburgs.

plate. He had failed, though to notice Turner, the short-stop. Terry was about ten yards back of third and Bemis' heave went directly into his hands. He shot the ball home and the chagrined Schaefer found it waiting for him when he arrived at the plate. Asked who had devised the play, Turner said:

"Bill Bradley doped it out one day and told me to watch for the sign and we would try it. We could have used it earlier, but we wanted to get one of the fast base runners on it."

JAMES BURKE—James Burke, manager and third baseman of the Fort Wayne club, began at Peoria in 1896, remaining there in 1897. Peoria, Minneapolis and Milwaukee, 1898; Rochester, 1899; Milwaukee, 1900; Milwaukee and Chicago Americans, 1901; Pittsburg, 1902; Pittsburg and St. Louis Nationals, 1903; St. Louis Nationals, 1904, and manager in 1905; Kansas City, manager, 1906 and 1907; Louisville, manager, 1908; Indianapolis, 1909, and Fort Wayne, manager, the past season.

ROBERT M. BYRNE—Robert M. Byrne, or "Bobby" Byrne, as he is always called, is the third baseman of the Pittsburg club of 1909, champions of the National League that year and champions of the world.

He was the third baseman of the St. Louis Cardinals in August, 1909, when the critical eye of Manager Clarke of Pittsburg fell on him.

Clarke offered Storke and Barbeau, two of his playes, for Byrne, and the offer was accepted.

Since August ,1909, when he joined Pittsburg, Byrne has been honored with the place at the top of the batting list for that club and he has played a magnificent game at third base.

Byrne was born December 31, 1885, in St. Louis, Mo. He stands five feet eight inches and weighs 150 pounds. He played in 1905 with Springfield, Mo., in the Western Association; 1906 with Shreveport, in the Southern League; 1907 to August, 1909, with St. Louis Nationals; joined Pittsburg Nationals August 19, 1909, and is with them now.

Byrne is always a dangerous man for the reason that at all times he is cool, nervy and smart. In his 1910 season Byrne commenced hitting like a fiend and in August of this year he had a batting record of .336 and was practically leading the sluggers of the National League, beside being the leading run getter of that organization, he having up to August 10, 1910, sixty-nine runs to his credit.

JAMES CASEY—James Casey was the third baseman of the Brooklyn club when it won the World's Championship in 1899.

That was the year that the old Baltimore quartet, composed of Kelly, Jennings, Keeler and McGann, joined the Brooklyn team and helped it win a world's flag.

Casey was a very small man and while he was a fine fielder he was weak as a batsman, a failing that got him out of the major league before his time.

JIMMY COLLINS—Jimmy Collins when with the Boston National League Champions of 1898 was considered the best third baseman then in the business.

With that great team Collins led in the number of games played, he taking part in 149 and in batting Billy Hamilton was the only man of the team to outhit him.

Collins also played a wonderful game on third, not only in fielding, but in throwing. In fact, he was perhaps the best thrower from third to first the game has ever known.

Collins, while in the National League, was a veritable marvel, and when the war between the American and National Leagues was inaugurated in 1899 he was selected to play at third base and captain and manage the Boston American League team. He was the third baseman of the Bostons when they won the American League pennants in 1903 and 1904, and when they captured the World's Championship in the series with Pittsburg in 1903.

As a member of the Puritans during their victories in the new circuit Collins starred and was a corner stone of the Boston defense. His fielding and batting were features of the series in which the Boston team defeated Pittsburg for the World's Championship.

Collins was traded to the Philadelphia club in 1908 and played with the Athletics the greater part of that season, but it was evident that he was "through" and his sale to the Minneapolis club by Connie Mack, which took place in the summer of 1908 was not unexpected.

W. COUGHLIN—W. Coughlin covered third base for Detroit in 1907 and 1908 and in both years he helped that team win the American League pennant. In his best year Coughlin was a fine all around player.

LAVE CROSS — Lave Cross, was one of the greatest third basemen from 1885 to 1907, twelve years in all.

He was with Philadelphia when he led all rivals in 1895 and 1896, with St. Louis and Cleveland when he led in 1899 and with St. Louis and Brooklyn when he led in 1900.

Cross, who was a man of athletic build, less than medium in height, was a great all around player. He has perhaps never been beaten in covering his position and then, too, he could throw beautifully, while as a batsman he ranked with the best.

That he was a fine heady player was proven when in 1906 he captained the Athletics of Philadelphia, who, that year, captured the American League pennant.

JAMES DAVIS—James Davis is another one of the great aggregation of Mound City boys who won his spurs in the major league twenty years ago. Jim learned to play the National Game on the lots in Kerry Patch, the neighborhood which turned out hundreds of many famous big league ball players. He donned his first professional uniform as a member of the old St. Louis Browns and lined up at third base. He was a winner from the outset and developed into a cracking, fast, hard hitting third baseman. After playing with the Browns a few seasons he was transferred to Kansas City and finally wound up a most successful career with the old Baltimore Orioles.

JERRY DENNY—One of the greatest of the greatest third basemen of his day was Jerry Denny, who covered that bag for the Providence Champions and then for the Cleveland, St. Louis and other teams.

In the early eighties Denny was often referred to as the king of the third base players of his day.

He was a member of the famous Cleveland infield in the early eighties when it had Phillips at first, Dunlap at second, Denny at third and Glasscock at short

LAVE CROSS.
The captain and third baseman of the Athletics of Philadelphia when they won the American League flag.

field and Denny was as speedy as any of these players.

He was a lightning fielder and thrower and a batsman of the first class.

ARTHUR DEVLIN—Arthur Devlin of the New York Giants, who led the National League at third base in 1908, also played a great game for that team in the 1909 and 1910 seasons.

Devlin is a first-class all around third baseman and an excellent batsman .

"Greatest of third basemen" is the title which this star of the New York Nationals has earned by his grand playing during the past five years. Always striving to win, never giving up in the face of defeat, ever a clean player, he is a credit to our National sport.

JIM DONNELLY—Jim Donnelly was the third baseman of the champion Baltimore team in 1896.

He took McGraw's place on that combination, the latter having retired as the result of a serious injury.

Donnelly made good in this champion team, fielding his position finely and batting nearly as well as any other man on the team.

NORMAN ELBERFELD—Norman Elberfeld, third baseman of the Washington club of the American League, is called "The Tobasco Kid."

This is due to the life and ginger he puts into the game, he being an unusually wide-awake and active player.

Elberfeld was born at Mason City, W. Va., April 13, 1876. He shone as a catcher and short-stop when quite young, and broke into professional baseball with Detroit of the Western League in 1897 and continued with that team the next season and in 1899 with Cincinnati.

From that club Elberfeld went to Washington, where he is playing now.

The name of Elberfeld—the Tobasco Kid—has been a household word for aye these many years, that is, in every home where baseball has been discussed. One would think the kid was 40 years old.

He was playing with Lajoie at Philadelphia before the year 1900 rolled around. He was with Detroit, New York and is now with Washington. The latter may be his last stand, but the Kid expects to play baseball for seven or eight years to come, for he is only 33 years old and is as lively as a cricket and as energetic on the ball field as at any time in his career.

It is sixteen years since Elberfeld broke into the game as a professional. He went from his home to Clarksville, Ky., and, according to his own story, he was a sorry looking spectacle when he reported to the manager. There had been a wreck the night before and instead of making the trip in a few hours the Kid was on the road all night. He was sleepy, dirty and hungry, as a youth of 17 can become overnight. He wore knee trousers and the manager looked at him askance when he walked up and said:

"Are you the manager? Well, I'm Norman Elberfeld, your new player."

A few minutes later the Kid heard the manager confide to one of the old players that "that half pint of cider will never do." However, he gave the Kid a chance that very day and he won the game for Clarksville. The same evening as they were walking along the main street, the manager turned to the Kid and after looking him over from head to foot, said: "I guess you are a ball player all right,

Kid, but if you stay with this team you will have to wear long trousers."

"I'm willing, boss," replied Elberfeld. "You buy them for me. You see, I'm dead broke and couldn't buy a shoe lace."

Elberfeld is a little bigger to-day than when he started on his long career sixteen years ago. His earthly belongings, however, amount to considerable more than in 1894. When the Kid reported at Clarksville he was the proud owner of a baseball cap and a pair of shoes. To-day he is well off in this world's goods.

You would be surprised to see the Kid in action. He is a different ball player than when he helped shoulder the burden with Clark Griffith at New York and later carried it all himself. He is the equal of any third sacker in the major leagues and he has instilled fight and ginger in the Washington club that is really good to behold. Nobody knows any more baseball than Elberfeld and the younger members of the team are only too happy to receive the many valuable tips from the Kid.

CLYDE ENGEL—Clyde Engel has been prancing around third base for the Boston Americans in very nifty fashion during the season of 1910. Previous to joining the speed boys in the Spring he was a member of the New York Highlanders for two seasons. Engel has proven himself a valuable player, his batting, fielding and speed on the bases earning him much favorable boosting during the past season. Clyde looms up as the main candidate for the second base position of the Red Sox for the season of 1911. He was born in Dayton, Ohio, on March 10, 1884, and started in professionally in Nashville, Tenn., as a pitcher.

He was with Augusta, Ga., in 1904, playing second base, and the following season was transferred to the outfield.

In 1907 and 1908 he played with Newark, N. J., playing in the outfield the first two seasons, but going to third base in 1908, as the club was in want of a third baseman and Engle volunteered to fill the gap and did so most satisfactorily.

New York purchased him and he has done excellent work in the big league ever since, one of his feats being five hits five times at bat in Boston, Labor Day, 1909. He stands five feet seven and one-half inches and weighs 190 pounds.

ALBERT FERRIS—Albert Ferris, better known in the big league as "Hobe" Ferris, was in his day one of the topnotch third basemen. When Hobe was with the Boston club he was paired with Parent, the short-stop, and both young men, starting in as major league players, created a great sensation. The veteran Comiskey said he never saw anything better than the playing of Ferris in his early years. It is his weakness with the bat that has caused his undoing. From .270 in 1908 he fell to .250 in 1909 and this led to his retirement from the big league ranks. He is now playing great ball for Minneapolis, the 1910 Champions.

E. L. GRANT—E. L. Grant is the third baseman of the Philadelphia National League Club. He is a grand player and perhaps the best hitting third baseman in the National League, barring Bobby Byrne of the Pittsburgs. On August 14, 1910, Grant had taken part in ninety-three games, scored forty runs, a hundred hits and stolen twenty bases, and making a batting record of .280.

W. E. KELSOE.

One of the St. Louis veteran baseball writers and still one of the best known journalists.

W. L. HAGUE—W. L. Hague was the third baseman of the St. Louis Browns of 1876.

This was the first team St. Louis had in the National League.

"Bill" Hague was a fine fielding third baseman and a very fair batsman.

FRED HARTMAN—Fred Hartman, who played at third base for the Chicago White Sox in 1900 and 1901 was a fine fielder and a good slugging batsman.

CHARLES LINCOLN HERZOG—Charles Lincoln Herzog is the sensational young third baseman of the Boston Nationals, who has made a decided hit by his superb work at third base for that club, a position which he is now assuming for the first time. He is a native of Baltimore, Md., where he was born July 9. 1885. He played short-stop for the University of Maryland for two seasons and later played independently. His first full-fledged professional engagement was with the York, Pa., club of the Tri-State League, and he acquitted himself so well that he was purchased by the New York National League, where he served with distinction as utility player and soon showed himself to be one of the best available men in the country. It was his success in filling the shoes of Larry Doyle at second when that player was injured in the season of 1908 that helped very largely to keep New York in the race for the pennant. In fifty-nine games he batted for .300. He played in forty-two games in 1909. Last April he was traded to Boston in return for Outfielder Beals Becker.

SCOTTY INGERTON—Scotty Ingerton, who was the best fielding as well as one of the slugging third basemen of the Tri-State League during the 1910 season, was purchased by the Chicago Cubs of the National League in the Fall of 1910. It is said President Murphy paid $1,500 for the youngster. Ingerton should make a decided hit in the National League the coming season, that is, judging from the reports of his work exhibited while a member of the Altoona Club.

WILLIAM JOYCE — William Joyce, "Scrappy Bill," a born and bred in St. Louis player, finished his professional career as the third baseman, captain and manager of the New York Giants. Joyce in his day was one of the greatest of third basemen, and he was a great left-handed batsman. He commenced playing in the eighties with local teams of St. Louis and started from here on a professional career that ended at the very top of the ladder. He was known around the baseball circuit as "Home-Run Bill." He was one of the grandest ball players ever sent into the big leagues by St. Louis.

WALTER A. LATHAM—Walter A. Latham now chief coach of the New York Giants, was the third baseman of the four-time winner St. Louis Browns, the team that captured the American Association and then World's Championships.

In his day he was the only rival of the famous Ned Williamson.

And, next to Comiskey, Latham contributed perhaps more than any other man to the success which attended the St. Louis Browns during their long championship career.

Latham played his first baseball in the early eighties with the semi-professional teams that were then numerous in Philadelphia.

It was while playing there that Ted Sullivan, then out looking for players for the St. Louis Browns, set eyes on him. He saw in Latham, then but a lad in his teens, the making of a great player. Sullivan, at sight, signed Latham for St. Louis, brought him into this city, planted him on third base and he stayed in that position through all the successful times of the St. Louis club. He was with them when they won the American Association Championship four years in succession and he was with the Browns when they battled for the World's Championship with Chicago, Detroit and New York.

A wonderful fielder and thrower was Latham, one of the speediest and brainiest base runners of his day and a bright, intelligent and effective batsman. 'But Latham's most valuable asset outside of his natural gift as a ball player was his ability as a coach.

At the game of standing on the base line and advising the batsmen and base runners Latham has never had a superior. As a witty and jovial master of the coaching lines he was admirable. His wit and joviality served two purposes. It brightened and put ginger into his fellow players. In all the baseball world in the eighties there were two bright particular stars on the coaching line. One was Latham of the St. Louis Browns, often called "The Clown," and the other, "King" Kelly, the highest star of the old Chicago White Stockings.

"Kel" would invent plays on the spur of the moment that it would take most men a season to work out. He was quick as a flash, a wonder for a man so large. As a baseball genius, he fairly towered over other chaps and the diamond lost a king when his powers failed him. He was as a new dollar on and off the field, a rare entertainer. In fact it was often said that if "Kel" had the powers of enlivening an audience on the stage that he had of enlivening a crowd at a baseball game that he would be the same attraction in vaudeville that he was on the diamond.

Latham, like Kelly, was full to the brim of fun and native wit and nearly as quick a thinker as Kelly.

As coachers, in fact, the two were brainy, intelligent and resourceful and with it all they knew every curve of the game.

In turning a quick trick Kelly was the king of perfection and he held Latham some there, but in quick wit and repartee "The Clown" had the King beaten. At that game indeed Latham was superb.

It was Latham's quick wit and resourcefulness that won an important World's Championship game for St. Louis one day from Chicago.

With Welch on third and Gleason on second Latham came to the bat. A hit meant the game for St. Louis and Latham knew it.

"Play a little farther out Mr. Dalrymple," said Latham to the Chicago's left fielder. "I am going to make a long hit to left and if you don't play a little farther out it will get away from you and go sailing over your head."

Quite naturally following the old rule, Dalrymple believing that Latham was going to do the very opposite of what he boasted he would do came in from the field, stationed himself right back of the Chicago short fielder and then shouted to Latham that he knew his game.

JIMMY BURKE.
Manager of the Indianapolis Club of the American Association in Their 1911
Season.

Latham hit the next ball with all his might and it sailed to left field. Dalrymple would have captured the ball had he been playing deep as Latham had advised him to do. But instead it sailed over Dal's head and the game was won for St. Louis.

But this lucky play and fine work of Latham on this particular occasion was only one of hundreds of great turns that he made while a member of the invincible Browns.

Latham's wit on the base lines, his cheery "Come now, everybody pull together and stop this nonsense," and his ever willing and ready spirit did much to make the Browns the fighting, invincible team they were.

On and off the field Latham was a kindly, genial spirit and a fine mate to that other prince of good fellows and king of third basemen, Ed Williamson of the Chicagos.

After quitting the playing end of the game Latham set out as an umpire, but in the 1909 season he was the coach of the New York Giants, a place given him by his old friend, John J. McGraw, and which he filled with all his old time spirit and energy.

EDWARD LENNOX—Edward Lennox is the regular third baseman of the Brooklyn team. He has held down this position for them for several seasons. He is a fast fielder and base runner and an excellent batsman.

HARRY D. LORD—Harry D. Lord, the crack third baseman of the Chicago American League team, is a Portland, Me., boy and is 26 years of age. He made a hit with the Bridgeton, Me., Academy. He afterwards played with Bates College. In 1904 he joined the Portland club and his fast work in all departments that season and the next attracted outside attention and he was secured by Jess Burkett for Worcester and his fine playing went far to help land the pennant for that club in 1906. His progress was so rapid that Providence secured him for the following season and in 1908 he became a member of the Boston Americans—no slight undertaking for one new to major league company, but he proved to have the pluck, the nerve, the speed and the ability and it was on that account he was picked out as the premier American League third baseman. He lives near Boston.

Lord was the captain and third baseman of the Boston Red Stockings up to August of the 1910 season, when he was replaced by Engle and his services placed on the market.

On August 10, 1910, Lord was transferred with Ambrose McConnell of the Boston American League team to the Chicago American League Club. They went to Chicago in exchange for Pitcher Frank Smith and Third Baseman William Purtell of the White Sox. Lord had played at third for Boston and McConnell at second and they went to play those positions on the White Sox.

LEVI MEYERLE—A big, stout fellow was Levi Meyerle, the third baseman of the Athletics of Philadelphia in 1871, when they were the Champions.

Meyerle in 1872 went to the original Chicago White Stockings and he was one of that famous infield which included McAtee, first base; Wood, second; Meyerle, third, and Hodes short field.

Meyerle was a very fair fielder, but his best asset was his ability to hit the ball hard.

He was at the top as a batsman in the champion Athletic team, with an average of .448.

GEORGE J. MORIARITY—George J. Moriarity, third baseman of the champion Detroits of 1909, is a Chicagoan, and had his first league try-out with the Cubs in 1904. He was released to Toledo, where he stole fifty-one bases in 1905, and was sold to Detroit in the winter of 1908-9. He has won particular renown by his success in stealing home in important games. Moriarity is six feet tall and weighs 169 pounds. He is a right-handed batter.

Moriarity of Detroit will have one record this season. He has tried five steals of home and has been successful four times. That is going some. Moriarity has played brilliant ball this year and has proven a very valuable man for Jennings' team.

H. H. MOWREY—Harry H. Mowrey is the third baseman of the St. Louis National League Club in its 1910 season, a position which he has been holding down splendidly. He is a fine fielder, a daring base runner and was one of the pluckiest and most timely of batsmen. Mowrey hails from the Far East, is a graduate of the Eastern League and was discovered by Billy Murray when the latter was manager of the Philadelphia Club in 1908. In the Fall of that season Mowrey was transferred to Cincinnati. He played there through 1909 and then came to St. Louis, where he made good from the start. He is regarded as the best fielder of bunts in either league.

GEORGE B. PINKNEY — George B. Pinkney was for a long while one of the best thought of third basemen in America.

He was the third baseman of the Brooklyn Club when they were World's Champions in 1890.

Pinkney was of medium stature and besides being a good fielder he was one of the best batsmen on the champion Brooklyns.

WILLIAM P. PURTELL—William P. Purtell is one of the great players of the Chicago White Sox.

Purtell was born in Columbus, O., January 6, 1887. He played with an independent team in Newark, O., in 1903, and played with Columbus a part of 1901, being but 17 years of age and needing ripening. This he secured with the Decatur, Ill., club of the Three-I League, where he remained until the Sox bought him.

Chicago secured him in August, 1907, but he played that season out with the Decatur Club. He batted for but .130 in twenty-six games last season, but fielded for second and did splendid work in both positions and promises to be a fixture on the team in 1910. He stands five feet eight inches and weighs 158 pounds.

WILLIAM SHINDLE—William Shindle was one of the great third basemen in the late eighties.

He played at third for the World's Champion Detroit team of 1887, covering that bag when Jim White, the regular third baseman, was resting or playing in some other position. A fine, active all-around player was Shindle.

HARRY STEINFELDT—Harry Steinfeldt, the Cubs' third baseman, whose glorious fielding kept the dashing Ty Cobb off the base paths in a couple of world's

JACK GLEASON.
As he looked when playing at third for the St. Louis Unions in 1884.

THE NATIONAL GAME.

series, and whose lusty wallops sent many a fellow-Cub scampering across home plate in the last few years, is another who was dubbed unfit by an erring leader in ill-fated Cincinnati. Harry left the haunts of the Reds, jumped in and completed Frank Chance's sterling infield, and still holds his court there, a veritable terror to seekers of base hits and stolen cushions.

EZRA SUTTON—Ezra Sutton was for many a day considered the greatest third baseman living. He was playing with Boston in the seventies. He succeeded Harry Schaefer as third baseman of the Boston Club of the National League and was with that team when it won pennants in 1877, 1878 and 1883. He was not only a great fielder, but he was one of the best batsmen of his day.

LEE TANNEHILL—Lee Tannehill was the one third baseman of the Chicago White Sox when they not only won the championship of the American League but also beat out the Chicago National League team in the race for world's honors.

Tannehill for years has been regarded as one of the finest fielding infielders in the American League. He played good ball in 1910.

ARTHUR WHITNEY—Arthur Whitney was the third baseman of the old Boston National League team of a decade ago, when they were winning championships.

ED WILLIAMSON—In 1880, 1881, 1882 and 1883 Ed Williamson, then with the famous Chicago White Stockings, was considered the greatest third base player that ever lived.

On that team at this time was the famous infield which included Anson at first base, Pfeffer at second, Williamson at third and Burns at short field.

Williamson, although a big man, nearly six feet in height, of deep chest and well rounded limb, was quick as lightning on his feet, and although a heavy man, he covered a great deal of ground and was one of the speediest of runners.

But Williamson's strongest forte lay in his ability to throw the ball. He sent it from third to first like a shot and at a lower range than is used by any of the

players of the present day. He was in his day the longest thrower in America.

Williamson was also a magnificent base runner and batsman. He was a hard, heavy hitter to left field, being fond of driving the ball along the left foul line.

In September and October, 1888, there was a contest given in Cincinnati under the auspices of the Cincinnati Enquirer.

In it Williamson threw a ball 133 yards and 11 inches.

Williamson at this time was throwing against the record of John Hatfield when on the Union Grounds at Brooklyn in October, 1872, Hatfield threw a ball 133 yards, one foot, seven and one-half inches. So it will be seen Williamson came within eight inches of beating Hatfield's throw, something no player living has been able to do.

But besides being a great player, Williamson was one of the finest fellows that ever lived.

No one of his comrades ever saw him lose his temper. At all stages he was the pink of coolness and no matter how strenuous the battle he was always a gentleman.

When he retired from the game it was to become a boniface at Chicago, a position that paid him well, but that owing to his kindly, easy, congenial spirit led to his early death. When he passed away all Chicago mourned him as the most favorite of her baseball sons, the kindliest and most indulgent spirit ever connected with the game in the Garden City.

WILLIAM C. YOHE—William C. Yohe, now in the Texas League, made a fine record in the 1910 season.

Yohe is a native of Mattoon, Ill., and was born September 2, 1879, stands five feet eight inches and weighs 180 pounds. He played independent ball all over Illinois before he played third base for the Jonesboro, Ark., club of the Arkansas State League in 1902. In 1903 he was with Poplar Bluff, Mo., in the Missouri Valley League, and in 1904-1905 played with Pittsburg, Kas. He was with Temple, Tex., in the Texas League in 1906 and managed the Greenville, North Texas League, in 1907. In 1908 he managed the Waco, Tex., club.

WILLIAM ROBINSON.
He was the second baseman of the St. Louis Browns in the eighties when they
were winning American Association and World's Championships.

THE NATIONAL GAME.

THE SHORT STOPS.

GEORGE WRIGHT WAS CONSIDERED THE LEADER OF THE FIRST BRIGADE, BUT HANS WAGNER EASILY LEADS ALL IN THE RECORD OF THE OLD PROFESSIONAL ASSOCIATION AND THEN OF THE NATIONAL LEAGUE.

These were the players who led in the old Professional Association and the National League from 1871 up to the present day:

Year.	Short-Stops. Club.	Fielding Games.	Pct.	Year.	Short-Stops. Club.	Fielding Games.	Pct.
1871	Geo. Wright—Boston	27	.937	1891	J. J. Cooney—Chicago	118	.924
1872	Geo. Wright—Boston	47	.948	1892	D. Richardson—Washington	91	.944
1873	Geo. Wright—Boston	59	.940	1893	Geo. J. Smith—Cincinnati	130	.935
1874	Geo. Wright—Boston	60	.929	1894	J. Glasscock—Pittsburg	86	.934
1875	Geo. Wright—Boston	79	.936	1895	H. Jennings—Baltimore	131	.943
1876	John Peters—Chicago	66	.932	1896	F. Connaughton—New York	53	.920
1877	Dave Force—St. Louis	42	.903	1897	H. Jennings—Baltimore	115	.923
1878	Geo. Wright—Boston	59	.947	1898	H. Jennings—Baltimore	114	.944
1879	Geo. Wright—Boston	84	.926	1899	Geo. S. Davis—New York	111	.944
1879	Dave Force—Buffalo	77	.926	1900	Geo. S. Davis—New York	113	.942
1880	John Peters—Providence	83	.898	1900	W. Dahlen—Brooklyn	134	.942
1881	J. Glasscock—Cleveland	79	.911	1901	Geo. S. Davis—New York	113	.943
1882	Dave Force—Buffalo	61	.907	1902	H. C. Long—Boston	108	.947
1883	J. Glasscock—Cleveland	90	.918	1903	Wm. Dahlen—Brooklyn	138	.946
1884	Dave Force—Buffalo	90	.901	1904	T. Corcoran—Cincinnati	152	.936
1885	J. Glasscock—St. Louis	109	.917	1905	T. Corcoran—Cincinnati	151	.952
1886	Dave Force—Washington	56	.908	1906	J. Tinker—Chicago	147	.944
1887	J. M. Ward—New York	129	.919	1907	A. Bridwell—Boston	140	.942
1888	W. J. Kuehne—Pittsburg	83	.915	1908	J. Tinker—Chicago	157	.958
1889	J. Glasscock—Indianapolis	131	.915	1909	A. Bridwell—New York	145	.942
1890	J. J. Cooney—Chicago	135	.936	1910	Doolan—Philadelphia	148	.948

AMERICAN LEAGUE RECORD.

BELOW IS A RECORD OF THOSE WHO HAVE EXCELLED AT SHORT FIELD IN THE RECORD OF THE AMERICAN LEAGUE SINCE ITS FIRST YEAR.

Year.	Short-Stops. Club.	Fielding Games.	Pct.	Year.	Short-Stops. Club.	Fielding Games.	Pct.
1900	L. Smith—Minneapolis	129	.918	1905	George Davis—Chicago	151	.948
1901	W. Clingman—Washington	137	.938	1906	T. Turner—Cleveland	147	.960
1902	R. Wallace—St. Louis	33	.951	1907	M. Cross—Philadelphia	74	.954
1903	J. Moran—Washington	96	.946	1908	R. Wallace—St. Louis	137	.951
1904	R. Wallace—St. Louis	139	.955	1909	G. McBride—Washington	15	.947
				1910	Turner—Cleveland	94	**.973**

The position of short field was not considered important by the early professional teams, until Dickey Pearce of the Atlantics commenced playing that position in the sixties.

Then it was that the beauties of that portion of the field were brought into the limelight for the first time.

Pearce was the first to study the opposing batsmen, fielding very close in for the weak hitters and backing deep when the hard hitters came up.

It was Pearce who turned the first double play by dropping a fly ball and then forcing the runner out, an act performed in the famous game in which the Atlantics of Brooklyn, administered to the champion Cincinnati Red Stockings of 1869, their very first defeat.

Since Pearce's time there have been many famous short-stops, Jack Glasscock of the Cleveland Club, of the eighties being considered the King in his day and he was acknowledged by all his fellow players to be the greatest in his position and, in his time undoubtedly was.

The king of short-stops to-day, however, without question is John P. (Hans) Wagner of the Pittsburg team the 1909 National League Champions and champions of the world.

Since baseball became a real profession there have been many great short fielders, notably George Wright of the Cincinnati Reds, who was easily the king in 1869

and following closely in his footsteps, Johnny Ward of the New York Giants, Arthur Irwin of Providence, Herman Long of Boston, Shorty Fuller of Washington, Bob Allen of Boston, George Davis of Philadelphia, Hugh Jennings of Baltimore, George Smith of Brooklyn, Ed McKeon of Cleveland, William Gleason of St. Louis, William Dahlen of Brooklyn, Joe Tinker of Chicago, T. Corcoran of Cincinnati, Charley Fulmer of the Philadelphia Athletics, Monte Cross of Philadelphia, Robert Wallace of the St. Louis Browns, George McBride of the Senators and Herman Long of the Bostons.

Undoubtedly, the two greatest short fielders of their day were George Wright, who was the king in the seventies and eighties and Hans Wagner, who has had few rivals in the position in the ten years between 1900 and 1909.

Wagner's name does not appear at the top in the fielding record. This is perhaps due to the fearful and wonderful chances he always takes and to the fact that he is always playing for his side regardless of his individual record.

But as a batsman in the National League Wagner's name always appears at the top or close to it. So take him all around he is the most useful short-stop in the business.

In the record the name of George Wright appears for seven years at the top as a short fielder. Five years in succession he

220

HANS WAGNER AND TYRUS COBB.
The king short-stop of the National League and the leading fielder of the American League as they appeared on the field shaking hands just before the first World's Championship game.

THE NATIONAL GAME.

led the major league short fielders. That was from 1871 to 1875 both inclusive. In 1878 he captured the honor again and in 1879 he tied with Davy Force for the honor.

When it comes to playing short-stop there have been so many high class performers that the really good players far outnumber those who are not quite first class. They are numerous from the time of George Wright down. The illustrious Wagner is among the lot, and the roster contains such names as Williamson, Glasscock, Fuller, Fred Ely, Irwin, Herman Long, Bob Allen, Geo. Davis, Hugh Jennings, George Smith and Ed McKeon. Still on deck are Bill Dahlen, Freddie Parent, Bobby Wallace, Terry Turner, Kid Elberfield, Wagner, Bridwell, Tinker, Doolan and McBride, not to mention Bush of Detroit. There is not a short-stop in the lot who was not or is not high class in his position.

Often the question of which is the hardest position on a ball field arises. It is discussed frequently by fans and players.

Owing to the sharpness of many of the hits to third base, that place is generally conceded to be the most difficult on the diamond. However, the figures disprove this assertion. Short-stop is the real hard job.

At least a short-stop makes more errors than anybody else, though in proportion to the chances offered the third baseman falls down just about as often.

The trouble with short-stopping seems to be the great amount of work coming that way.

In thirty leagues only one third baseman and one second baseman made the most errors.

In all the remainder, the short-stop got away with the most slip ups. This proves that short field is the real key to the infield and the place where the demands on the player are greater than in any other position.

In 1890 and 1891 J. J. Cooney played at short-stop for the Chicago Club and he led the National League those two years in the position. He was a fine fielder.

We have referred in our resume of second basemen to Danny Richardson, who in 1892, while with the Washington, had the top record among the short-stops.

After Richardson, George J. Smith was top man among the League short-stops. He was a fine fielder and thrower.

Then came F. Connaughton, who played at short field for New York in 53 games of their 1896 season.

After Connaughton in the 1896 season came Hugh Jennings, who for many a year was the King pin short-stop of America.

Now breaking away from the record, I give an alphabetical list of the players who in their day since 1871 have played at short field for the clubs of the old Professional Association, the National League, the American League and all other major organizations:

NEAL BALL—Neal Ball, one of the utility infielders of the Cleveland Club of the American League, during the season of 1910, might now be called a veteran, as he has been playing with Cleveland for several seasons. On July 19, 1909, Ball was the star actor in an unassisted triple play. Here's how it happened: Wagner of Boston was on second base and Stahl of Boston was on first base. Both men started with a rush, in a hit-and-run play, when McConnell drove a line drive straight into Ball's hand. Ball ran over to second base and touched it before Wagner could get back, and then ran towards Stahl and touched him out before he could return to first base, thereby making the triple play complete. He made the play in the second inning and in the same inning, when at bat, he hit out a home run. Subsequently he made a two-base hit in the game.

Ball played excellent ball during the 1910 season.

J. BARRY—J. Barry, shortfielder of the Athletics is one of the most promising players in the business.

In "Connie" Mack's opinion Barry is the most reliable of them all in the American League. "Barry is of the type of player who always does his best work at the right time," observed the lanky Cornelius. "I don't believe there is an infielder in the game who can handle a ground ball like he can. He seldom allows one to get through him, no matter how mean a bound it may make. It was Barry's injury, when he was spiked by 'Ty' Cobb that knocked us out of the flag in 1909.

"We were fairly thundering down the stretch. Detroit came along and we beat them the series. I was confident of winning the championship. I didn't see how we were going to lose any more games. The only question was, would the Tigers drop enough to allow us to land on top. Well, Cobb got Barry and that finished my band.

"Collins was never the same thereafter. Ed was thinking of Barry all the time and his all-round work was away below his usual clip. The Browns followed the Tigers into Philadelphia and we didn't see how they had a chance to take a single game. Bailey pitched in the first one. He had as much as any southpaw I ever saw and gave us a sound beating."

RUSSELL A. BLACKBURNE—Russell A. Blackburne, the brilliant young short-stop of the Chicago American League Club, is a native of Palmyra, N. J., where he was born 22 years ago. From boyhood up he was an expert at football, baseball and basket ball, and he is almost as expert a pitcher as he is an infielder. He began playing ball four years ago with the Frankford Club of Philadelphia. The following season he played with North Philadelphia, where his work attracted the attention of Manager Mack of the Athletics, who secured him for the Worcester Club of the New England League for the 1908 season. He performed so well for that club that the Providence Club of the Eastern League purchased him. His playing with Providence in 1909 attracted national attention, notwithstanding the fact that during the season he broke his leg and the Providence Club was deluged with major league offers for Blackburne. The Chicago American League Club finally secured him for 1910 for $8,500 in cash and the choice of two Chicago players, making Blackburne cost the Chicago Club about $11,000—the highest sum ever paid for a minor league player up to that time with the exception of Marquard. He is a youth of pleasant disposition, good habits and plays the game for love, as he is quite wealthy in his own right through inheritance and his parents are also well-to-do.

He displayed very fair ability during the 1910 season.

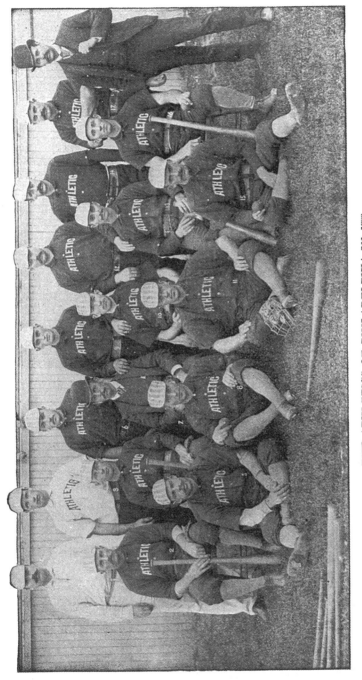

THE ATHLETICS OF PHILADELPHIA IN 1888.

First row, reading from left to right and standing up: Farmer, c.; Lyons, 3b.; Mattimore, p.; Larkin, 1b. and captain; Stovey, lf.; Curt Welch, cf.

Second row, seated, and reading from left to right: William Gleason, ss.; Bierbauer, 2b.; W. Sharsig, manager; Gunning, c.; Poorman, rf.; Blair, p.; Kame, secretary.

Last row, seated on field, reading from left to right: Townsend, c.; Seward, p.; Robinson, c.; Weyhing, p.

THE NATIONAL GAME.

ALBERT BRIDWELL—Albert Bridwell, the regular short-stop of the New York Giants, outside of being regarded as one of the prettiest fielders in the business, is also a splendid batsman. Bridwell has been covering short for McGraw's team for several years, previous to which he was the star infielder of the Bostons.

OWEN BUSH—Owen Bush, the midget short-stop of the champion Detroit team of 1909, is one of the best players that ever filled that position.

Bush weighs 155 pounds, though but five feet four inches tall. He was born in Indianapolis and played his first league ball with the Saginaw Club of the Interstate League in 1906. Indianapolis got a string on him that fall and used him as a main factor in its pennant winning campaign of 1908. He throws right handed, but bats from either side of the plate, depending in the style of pitching which he faces. He is 22 years old.

There are few short-fielders in the game to-day who excel Owen Bush, the great little player of the Detroit American League team.

Bush, although a major league youngster in 1909 stood second in the American League in runs scored, third in stolen bases and well up in the hitting list. Bush, the grand little Detroit short-stop, has in a single year won a reputation that others stars well may envy. No member of the Tiger nine is more respected by opposing teams.

TOM CAREY—Tom Carey is the best remembered of the famous short-fielders of the famous Hartford and Providence Clubs. Carey was with Providence in 1878, playing alongside the great Joe Start and Bill Hague, George Wright succeeded Carey on the Providence team in 1879 and they won the League pennant that year.

H. CORRIDON—H. Corridon, who originally hailed from Keokuk, Ia., of the Central Association, will line up as a member of the St. Louis Browns team of 1911. Corridon is a short-stop and was secured by the Browns in the Spring of 1910, but was farmed out to Omaha of the Western League, where he played splendid ball all season. His recall means that he will most likely be given a steady position on the Browns' infield.

MONTE CROSS—When Monte Cross, the veteran short-stop of the Phillies went to manage the Scranton, Pa., Club a few years ago the well wishes of all Philadelphia went with him. Cross had been for years the short-fielder of the Phillies and was one of the most popular players of the Quakers.

He was a first-class short-fielder in his day, as well as a fair batsman and base runner.

GEORGE DAVIS—George Davis, once the short-fielder of the Chicago American League Club was considered one of the greatest and brainiest players of the present day.

Davis was born at Cohoes, N. Y., August 23, 1870. He played with Albany in 1889, and the next season saw him in Cleveland.

He remained with that club the two seasons following and in 1893 became a member of the New York National League team and remained there until 1902, when the American League Club of Chicago succeeded in inducing him to join the ranks of that club. He was with the Chicago White Stockings in their ever-varying fortunes until 1909. The New York National League signed him to a two-year contract in 1903, but Comiskey fought this stoutly and won, and Davis was forced to remain with the Chicago Club.

In 1899 while a member of the New York National League Club Davis led all the other short-stops in the fielding line. In 1900 he tied William Dahlen for leading honors in the same position and in 1901 he again captured the leading honors.

So for three years he was the leading short-fielder of the major organization. And in the American League he has also done magnificent work, leading the short-stops of that organization in the 1905 season, when he played in more games than had ever been played in one year by any short-stop in the American League up to that time and with a better record than had ever been made before by any short-stop in this organization.

After a long and honorable career with the Chicago White Sox, Davis terminated his connection with that team at the close of its 1909 season.

He had been with Comiskey's team since 1902, and up to the 1909 season always put up a splendid game. He was at all times a clean player and his departure from the big league circles will be regretted. He should be a decided success as the handler of some minor league club.

MICHAEL J. DOOLAN—Michael J. Doolan, the clever captain and short-stop of the Phillies, is one of the best ever. He was born in Ashland, Pa., 29 years ago, and played with the Villanova College team in 1900 and 1901, thence going to Jersey City under Manager Billy Murray.

In 1903 he was drafted by Brooklyn, but that club lost him, erroneously drafting Catcher Dillon instead. Philadelphia then made a trade for him, surrendering Keister and $2,500 to make the deal. Doolan has played with the club ever since 1905, and is one of its strongest and best assets.

ARTHUR FLETCHER—Arthur Fletcher is the young and promising utility infielder of the New York Giants of the National League. Fletcher is a native of Edwardsville, Ill., and learned the game while playing about the lots of that town. In 1907 he was discovered by Joseph Gardner, president of the Dallas Club of the Texas League. He proved a winner in this league and during the season of 1908 was sold to the New York Giants, with which club he has been associated ever since. Fletcher is a tall, rangy fellow, fast on his feet and is one of the surest infielders in the National League. He gives promise of winning a regular position on the Giants' team in 1911. He stands five feet ten inches, is a right-hander and is 22 years old.

DAVY FORCE—Dave Force led the National League short-fielders in 1877, 1879, 1882, 1884 and 1886.

For ten years Davy Force was considered one of the best short-stops in America.

For nearly ten years he led the National League in that position.

Force was perhaps the right size for a short-stop. He was a dwarf and built so close to the ground that he could easily get to the hardest hit daisy cutters.

He did his first great work in 1877 when he came to St. Louis and joined the National League team which the Mound City had put in the field the previous year.

HERMAN BADER.
Herman Bader was at one time the fleetest base runner in America and one of the greatest outfielders.

While with the St. Louis Club this season Force excelled all other short-fielders.

From St. Louis he went to Buffalo and remained with the club that represented that city in the National League until 1886, when he went to Washington.

Force, in his day, besides being a fine fielder despite his dwarfish stature, was one of the hardest hitters and most effective batsman.

E. C. FOSTER—E. C. Foster has been the mainstay of the New York Highlanders' short-field during the season of 1910, which was his first experience in the big league. Foster comes from Jersey City, and made quite a creditable record there during the season of 1909, despite the fact that his nine finished a bad last in the pennant race in that organization. He played in 148 games, crossed the rubber fifty times, clouted out 130 hits, pilfered thirty-seven bases and was handed a batting record of .242. This was all very fair for an infielder. In a fielding way he accepted a great number of chances successfully. Since joining the Highlanders Foster has continued to play winning ball.

ROBERT GILKS—One of the best of the old short-fielders was Robert Gilks, or "Bobby" Gilks as he was called by his fellow players.

Gilks, who is now doing scout duty for the Naps, joined the old Cleveland (American Association) Club in 1887—twenty-two years ago. He was a versatile player, going into the box in the first game of a series, dropping down to third the next day and playing in center or left field, perhaps, in the third game.

With Gilks on the 1887 Cleveland team were Hotaling, McKeon, Allen, Sweeny, McGlone, Stricker, Mann, Reccius, Snyder, Carroll, Reipschlager, Morrison, Troy, Crowell, Daily and others.

In 1881 Gilks played eighty-four games at third, fifty-eight games in left and twenty-six games in center, besides making an occasional appearance in the box. Cleveland went back into the National League in 1889 and Gilks led the outfielders of that organization with an average of 1000 in twenty-nine games. He played in fifty-two games, in all, getting a batting average of .238. Gilks drifted out of the majors in 1890, but has been prominent in minor league baseball ever since.

JACK GLASSCOCK—In the 1883 season by common consent Jack Glasscock, then a member of the Cleveland Club of the National League, was considered the greatest short-fielder.

Glasscock was a member of Cleveland's famous stone wall infield, which included Bill Phillips at first base, Fred Dunlap at second, Jerry Denny at third and Glasscock at short-field.

These four were all great players, but in fielding none of them had the edge on Glasscock. He was such a great player that when the Union Association was organized in 1884 and its manager went hunting for phenomenal players, men who would draw the crowds, Glasscock was among the many selected.

He was one of the trio of Cleveland players, Briody and McCormick, being the others who left the Cleveland team in the midst of the 1884 season to join forces with the Cincinnati Club of the Union Association. At this time Glasscock's playing was simply wonderful and his accession by the managers of the Union Association gave that organization a mighty boost.

When the Union Association was disbanded in 1884 Glasscock joined his old partners, Dunlap and Denny, on the St. Louis National League Club, which held forth at the old Union Grounds at Jefferson and Cass avenues for a single season. The St. Louis infield that year included Alex McKinnon, first base; Fred Dunlap, second base; Jerry Denny, third base, and Jack Glasscock, short-field.

St. Louisans were very proud of this organization and expected great things of it. But the team was not successful, either from a playing or financial standpoint and before the season was half over its owners were plunged into bankruptcy. But Glasscock's great playing was often talked of afterwards.

After leaving St. Louis, Glasscock went to Indianapolis, where he led the league short-stops in 1889 and then went to Pittsburg, where, in 1894, he again bobbed up as the leading man in his position.

Glasscock is now a carpenter working at his trade in Wheeling, W. Va. He was one of the greatest players from a fielding standpoint the game has ever known.

While Glasscock was playing a great game at short field for Cleveland and St. Louis another player fairly shared honors with him. That was Arthur Irwin, the famous captain and short-fielder of the champion Providence Club of 1884.

HARRY GLEASON—Harry Gleason, the youngest brother of the famous "Kid" Gleason, since retiring from big league company has been playing in the minor leagues. During the past season Gleason held down short-field for the Harrisburg Club of the Tri-State League and his batting was one of the sensations of the league. Gleason stands five feet three inches, weighs 145 pounds and is 28 years old. He was born in Philadelphia.

JACK GLEASON — Jack Gleason and William Gleason, brothers, started out playing ball with the Stocks team of St. Louis in the seventies. Later they joined the St. Louis Reds. They also played with the St. Louis Browns, the co-operative team of 1881. In the following year both Jack and Billy joined the St. Louis Browns, the first member from this city to join the American Association, the baseball organization that took the field in that 1882 season. Later Jack Gleason went to Louisville, while his brother remained here with the four-time winners, St. Louis Browns. Jack Gleason was the hardest hitter St. Louis ever gave to the professional field. He was one of the few men able to drive the ball over the left field fence in old Sportsman's Park, a feat he accomplished early and often. He was also one of the best of third basemen.

JAMES HALLINAN—James Hallinan was one of the greatest short-stops of his day. He commenced playing professionally with the Aetnas of Chicago in the sixties. In 1873 he was the short-fielder of the Chicago White Stockings, which were then just coming to the front as a great team. Hallinan was a wonderfully speedy short-fielder, covering a great lot of ground and being able to send the ball with lightning speed to first. He was also a fine left-handed batsman.

ARNOLD J. HOUSER—Arnold J. Houser, the brilliant young short-stop of the St. Louis Cardinals of the National

WILLIAM GLEASON.

This is a photograph of "Old Brother Bill Gleason," now a captain of the St. Louis Fire Department. It is hardly necessary to say that Brother Bill was the great short-stop on the "Four-Time Winner" St. Louis Browns.

League in the 1910 season, is one of the cleverest and fastest short fielders shown in big league circles in years, and this notwithstanding the fact that it is his first year in fashionable company. In fact, many knowing ones consider the little fellow the best fielding short-stop in the business. He is especially good at pulling off lightning double plays, putting the ball on the runner and breaking up, hit and run plays, attempted by the opposition. Houser is a Chicago lad having been born in that city on September 25, 1888, and is therefore just 22 years of age. He played independent ball before joining Dubuque, Ia., last season and was drafted by the St. Louis Cardinals last fall. He stands five feet, five inches and weighs 145 pounds. Besides being a good short-stop he is a timely and intelligent batsman. At Dubuque in 1909 he led his team at bat with the fine average of .279, and he was also one of the leading base stealers of the Three-I League during the season.

Houser with Miller Huggins, who covered second for the Cardinals in 1910, made up a pair of little fellows hard to beat. The "Kids" held up Bresnahan's infield beautifully during the first half of the season when the team was playing very nice ball. Houser bids fair to rank with Tinker, Bridwell and even Honus Wagner in 1911.

ARTHUR IRWIN—Of the players who flourished in the eighties there was no speedier or brainier fielder and batsman than Arthur Irwin, now the New York Highlander's best scout.

He was the captain and short fielder of the World's Champion Providence team of 1884 and a better coach and more reliable batsman perhaps never lived. He was a member, too, of the famous Providence infield which in 1884 included Joe Start at first base; Jack Farrell at second; Jerry Denny at third and Irwin at short field.

Irwin is in the game to-day active and wide awake as ever, although many a good story is told of the great work he did on the baseball field full thirty years ago.

In the early eighties the Boston Club and the Providence Grays, then members of the National League, one day battled for sixteen innings on the South End grounds in Boston. Arthur Irwin, then a South Boston boy, playing short-stop for Providence and at the present time doing scout duty for Stallings of the New York Americans, made what old-timers who were fortunate enough to witness the contest, claim was the most remarkable or lucky hit ever made in baseball.

For fifteen innings both teams struggled to a 0 to 0 score.

High above the fence on the South End grounds, was erected a high wall of lattice work to prevent people on the adjoining house tops from witnessing the games.

In a section of this lattice work, was a small hole about fifteen to twenty inches square. No one knows just why it was there, or for what purpose it was intended.

In the sixteenth inning with two men down, and the excitement intense, Irwin started for the plate with bat in hand, and hit the ball high in the air towards the right field slats.

To the spectator it looked as if the ball would hit the wall, bound back, and entitle the runner to about two bases providing he could make two.

But not so. The ball sped right on its course, and to the surprise of all in attendance, went right through the opening as if it had been made for this occasion.

Then what a scene followed. Such a bedlam. Cheer after cheer rent the air.

Irwin was the hero. He was fairly lionized by his many Boston friends, and no doubt, if his eyes should happen to see this story, he will recall with joy, as he looks back to the days of Charley Radbourne, Charley Sweeney, Barney Gilligan, Joe Start, Jerry Denny, Cliff Carroll, Farrell and Paul Hines, all of whom were members of the famous Providence team, when "Old Hoss" Radbourne was the peer of any pitcher in the land, and poor John Clarkson, (now dead) had not yet reached fame as a professional baseball pitcher.

To Arthur Irwin, too, the famous short-stop and captain of the famous Providence team of 1884, belongs the distinction of being the first to introduce the fielder's glove. It was in that year that Irwin one day broke the third and fourth fingers of his left hand. In those days the best team only carried ten or twelve men. There was no one to take Irwin's place and so he consulted a glover, bought a buckskin glove many sizes too large for his injured hand, padded it, and sewed the injured fingers together to make way for the bandages. Irwin knew the spectators who knew of his injury would forgive him for appearing on the field with one hand looking much like a boxing glove. He discovered quickly that with the glove even in his injured condition he could meet the ball solidly, and so even after his broken fingers mended, he continued the use of the glove.

John Ward, the short-stop of the New York Giants, followed the lead of Irwin and soon infielder's gloves came into general use among the professional players.

It might have been because he wore these infielder gloves that Irwin was so effective as a short infielder, but one thing is certain, no player of his day excelled him in his position when it came to raking up difficult and hot grounders and getting them over to first base. Irwin was also a fine hard hitting left handed batsman.

HUGH AMBROSE JENNINGS—Hugh Ambrose Jennings was the leading short-stop of the National League in its 1895, 1897 and 1898 seasons.

Those were the days when Jennings played at short field and captained the Baltimore team which in 1894, 1895 and 1896 captured the National League Championship.

Jennings was in those three years one of the main stays of the club. His companions on the Baltimore infield in those days were Dan Brouthers, G. Carey and Jack Doyle at first; H. Reitz at second and John J. McGraw at third base.

It was a snappy, fighting organization and there was no livelier, wide-a-wake and aggressive player on the team than Jennings. He was a magnificent fielder, thrower and batsman and one of the most intelligent players in the business.

In fact during his major league career

DAVE ROWE.
Dave Rowe, who played with the St. Louis Unions in 1884, was one of the fastest center fielders and best hitters in America.

Jennings was not only one of the most brilliant of short-stops but he was one of the National League's most effective batsmen.

Jennings was born in Moolic, Pa., April 2, 1871, and got his start in baseball with the Leighton (Pa.) semi-professionals in 1890.

He played with Louisville in the National League the following year, being traded to Baltimore in 1893. Here he played for five years, being a most important cog in Ned Hanlon's World's Champion team.

Later he played in Brooklyn and Philadelphia, being finally sent back to Baltimore, then in the Eastern League, where he acted as manager.

His Winters he spent at Cornell and finally took a collegiate degree. Detroit tried to purchase his release in 1906, but Baltimore refused to sell. The Tiger management then drafted him, and since with that team he has been winning championships right along for Detroit in the American League.

Jennings, although a wide-awake and aggressive manager, is one of the most honorable and popular managers in the business.

He has always been bold and aggressive on the field but off it he is one of the most pleasant and good natured and mild mannered of gentlemen. When he quits the game which may not be for years, he will follow the practice of law, a profession he has mastered and in which he can shine whenever the time and place pleases him.

After Jennings as the greatest short infielder of his time came John P. Wagner, known in the baseball world as Hans Wagner.

Talking about his professional career the other day Jennings said:

"Jack Chapman, who was managing Louisville back in the early 'nineties, gave me my first professional engagement. I was catching for an independent team back in Pennsylvania when Jack wired me for my terms. 'Two hundred and fifty dollars a month and $100 advance,' was my reply. Jack wired back that I was asking too much. 'How much will you give?' I queried. Jack said $200 per month and $50 advance. I took a train for Louisville that night and soon after made my debut as a catcher.

"After a couple of seasons with the Louisville team, Harry Taylor and myself were traded to Baltimore for 'Voiceless Tim' O'Rourke. Billie Barnie made the deal. I played in Baltimore off and on until 1907, when Detroit drafted me. I was glad to get away from the Maryland burg. It's about the worst baseball town on the map. Ed. Hanlon won his first pennant in 1904, and the club made $50,000. The next year we repeated and the team made $25,000. The third year we won the flag the club was lucky to break even. That's what cost Baltimore her major league franchise. I took $3,600 worth of stock in the Baltimore Eastern Club League and never drew a dividend in three years. I was tickled to death to get my original investment back when I shook the town in 1906."

TEX JONES—Tex Jones, who was the star short-stop of the Enid Club of the Western Association in 1909, will line up as a member of Comiskey's White Sox next Spring. Jones experienced one of the best seasons of his career in Enid and the wise ones say he will make good in the big league. He is an excellent fielder and batsman.

W. J. KUEHNE—W. J. Kuehne, a St. Louis boy, led the National League shortstops in 1888. He was with Pittsburg that year. He had previously played with the Louisville and Columbus clubs. Kuehne is now employed in a wholesale dry goods house in St. Louis.

PHILLIP LEWIS—Phillip Lewis, the fine short-stop, who went to Baltimore this year, after going from there to Brooklyn in the Fall of 1904, is a native of Pittsburg and in his 25th year. It was by fine work at Cornell that he attracted attention and this led to his engagement by the Baltimore Eastern League Club in 1905. He batted for 294 and fielded for 301 for Baltimore in the season of 1904. His fine showing was sufficient to make him a much sought after player and he filled the bill for Brooklyn for the next four seasons.

HANS LOBERT—Hans Lobert played a great game for Cincinnati at short field in their 1908 and 1909 seasons.

He was third in the National League list of short fielders in 1907. The next season, however, he was switched to third base and he is now a permanent fixture in that position. He is a fine fielder and a useful man to any club.

HERMAN LONG—In his day Herman Long was considered the fastest and best playing short-stop in the National League.

He led all in that organization when he was famous as the short-stop of the Boston National champion team of 1891, 1892, 1893, 1897 and 1898.

Long was without a superior in his day and was the sensation of the baseball world. He covered a vast amount of territory and his ability to send the ball to the bag after a remarkable stop, without pausing to recover, was phenomenal.

Long was without a peer in his skill in handling thrown balls, and all in all was one of the most remarkable figures ever connected with baseball. He was of German extraction, which won for him his nickname of "Dutch" Long. Boston originally obtained him from Kansas City, and it required $6,500 to secure his release from the latter team.

Long died of consumption at Denver, Colo., on Sept. 16, 1909. He died penniless and friendless and his condition caused so much comment that soon after when Long died in poverty the late Harry Pulliam, then the president of the National League, talked about getting up a home for old professional players, who after quitting the game in old age or illness, found themselves poor and friendless. But Pulliam's death which came a little later, ended the proposition of establishing such a home for indigent players.

After Long and Dahlen came Thomas Corcoran of the Cincinnati Club, who led the short fielders of the National League in the 1904 and 1905 season. A fine fielder was Corcoran.

DENNY MACK—Denny Mack was at one time the crack short fielder of the old Louisville and Pittsburg team. He captained and managed the old Eclipse Club of Louisville and was a fine player and batsman in his day.

THE NATIONAL GAME.

GEORGE McBRIDE—George McBride, the first short fielder of the Washington Nationals, of the American League, has been dancing in the big arena for several years past. McBride is conceded to be the cleverest fielding short-stop in the country. For three years he has led such infielders as Wallace, Turner and Wagner, in chances accepted. McBride played his first big league baseball in St. Louis in 1905, when he was discovered by John McCloskey, who then managed the Cardinals. Owing to inability to bat and lack of experience, McBride was returned to the minors. The following year, however, he was purchased by Washington, and ever since has played grand baseball.

He topped the short-stops of the American League in 1909. McBride has also developed into a hard, timely batter.

THOMAS McMILLAN—Thomas McMillan, the midget short fielder of the Cincinnati Reds, won a permanent home for himself in the major leagues by his great work for his team in the 1910 season.

The midget, under the wise tutelage of Manager Griffith, has developed into a wonder in his position and he's there with the club at stated intervals.

He was particularly nifty in the games with the Brooklyns, thereby causing many pangs to chase themselves in various directions over the anatomies of President Ebbets and Manager Dahlen, who had let him go to the Reds. McMillan will stay with the Reds of Cincinnati and he's glad of it, for which simple reason that they didn't discover just where his little weakness lay.

JACK NELSON—Jack Nelson was one of the greatest short fielders of his day. Jack was playing at short field for the Indianapolis Club in 1878 and he was also the short fielder for the Metropolitans of New York when they won the championship of the American Association.

CHARLES O'LEARY—Charles O'Leary, infielder of the Detroits, who was used as a utility man, owing to the sensational work of "Donnie" Bush, was, for five years, the team's regular short-stop. He is a Chicagoan and was born in the stock yards district, 28 years ago. After a brilliant showing in semi-professional ball he was tried out in 1901 by the White Sox but drifted to Des Moines, where he was purchased by the Detroit management in the fall of 1903. He is 5 feet, 8 inches tall and weighs 158 pounds.

In 1910 O'Leary enjoyed a splendid season, both in fielding and batting.

JAMES PEEPLES—James Peeples was one of the most noted short-stops playing the game in the early eighties. He was a lightning fast fielder, wonderful thrower and besides was a corking good man with the bat, particularly when a hit was needed.

JOHN PETERS—John Peters led the National League at short field in 1876 and 1880.

He was the short fielder in 1876 of the Chicago White Stocking and on the infield that year were Cal McVey at first base, Ross Barnes at second and A. C. Anson at third.

Spalding was really the only pitcher of this organization, McVey assisting him occasionally but with all its lack of pitching material it captured the flag in 1876. Its outfield this latter year included John

Glenn, Paul Hines, Robert Addy and Oscar Bielaski.

Peters held his own with this great team. He was a short, stocky built man, a splendid fielder and accurate thrower.

Peters after quitting Chicago went to the Providence team and in 1880 while a member of that organization he again led the National League at short field.

Peters was born in St. Louis and now holds a position in one of the St. Louis city departments. He was a member of the St. Louis Reds in the sixties and was one of the many of the great players given to the professional field by that once famous organization.

ARTHUR REDMOND—Arthur Redmond who was playing at short field with Milwaukee in the National League in 1878, was a St. Louis boy. At one time he was a member of the St. Louis Reds. He was a fine fielder and hard hitting left hand batsman.

T. SMITH—T. Smith is one of the utility infielders of the Brooklyn Club in the National League. Smith is playing his second full season in fast company and so far appears to have held his own. He is an excellent fielder, very fair batsman and a good run getter.

W. J. SWEENEY—W. J. Sweeney is now holding down short field for Fred Lake's Boston team. In the early part of the season he was tried out at third, first and short and finally landed at the latter base where Beck and Martel had played before him. Sweeney is experiencing his first real season in fast company and seems to have certainly delivered the goods. He had played ninety-nine games with Boston up to August of the 1910 season. His batting average at that time was .261, showing that he was one of the real comers.

JOSEPH B. TINKER—Joseph B. Tinker, the crack short-stop of the Chicago National League Club, is 29 years of age and a native of Muskoda, Kas., where he was born July 27, 1880. He played with the Coffeyville, Kas., club in 1899, and was with Denver the following season. He played in Great Falls and Helena, Mont., the same season. In 1901 he was with the Championship Portland, (Ore.) Club and thence went to Chicago. He stands 5 ft. 8 1-2 inches and weighs 170 pounds.

He contributed greatly to the great victories which the Chicago Cubs scored when they won the National League and World's Championship in 1906 and 1907. He is a fine fielder and base runner and one of the most effective and timely batsmen. Tinker led the National League short fielders in 1906 and 1908. In 1907 Arthur Bridwell of the Bostons was the leading shortstop in the National League. Bridwell is a fine heady player in the position.

T. L. TURNER—T. L. Turner is the veteran short fielder of the Cleveland Club of the American League. Turner has been one of the leading fielders, base runners and batsmen of the American League for several years. Up to the coming into the league of George McBride, Turner was considered in the same class with the great Bobby Wallace of the Browns, when it came to perfect fielding and general all around play.

CHARLES WAGNER—Charles Wagner, short-stop of the Boston American League team, though not given as much publicity as his more famous namesake, Honus

231

Wagner, nevertheless is considered every bit as clever a fielder as the big Pirate infielder, though of course he is not as strong with the stick. Wagner has been playing with the Bostons for several years. He is 26 years old, five feet, eight inches in height, and weighs 175 pounds. When Harry Lord, who was captain of the Taylor aggregation, was transferred to Chicago, in August, 1910, Owner Taylor appointed Wagner captain of the team. He is an aggressive, intelligent player and very popular with the fans.

JOHN P. (HANS) WAGNER—Undoubtedly, and with little fear of contradiction, John P, (Hans) Wagner of the Pittsburg Club is the greatest baseball player living.

That he is the greatest batsman has been proven by the fact that he again leads the National League in hitting, it being his seventh season as the league's leading batsman.

That he is also a wonderful fielder was proven in the Pittsburg-Detroit World's Championship series of 1909 when he led all sides in fielding and base running.

The complete record of Wagner since he joined the Louisville's in 1900 up to the 1909 season is given in full below and at a glance it proves the wonderful player he is:

	Position.	Average.
1900—Wagner	1	.380
1903—Wagner	1	.355
1904—Wagner	1	.349
1906—Wagner	1	.339
1907—Wagner	1	.350
1908—Wagner	1	.354
1909—Wagner	1	.341

RECORD WITH LOUISVILLE.

	G.	AB.	R.	G.	SB.	Ave.
1897	61	241	38	83	27	.344
1898	148	591	80	189	25	.305
1899	144	549	102	197	56	.358

RECORD WITH PITTSBURG.

	G.	AB.	R.	G.	SB.	Ave.
1900	134	528	107	201	36	.380
1901	141	556	100	196	48	.352
1902	137	538	105	117	43	.329
1903	129	512	17	182	46	.355
1904	132	490	97	171	56	.319
1905	147	548	114	199	57	.363
1906	140	516	103	175	52	.339
1907	142	545	98	180	61	.350
1908	151	568	100	201	53	.354
1909	137	392	92	165	35	.341
Average for 13 years						.348

Wagner started getting noisy as a batsman in 1900, though at that, right from the start of his career in the parent body, in 1897, he always stood well to the fore in the hitting list. However, in 1900, he topped all. He hit .380 to Elmer Flick's .378 and Willie Keeler's .366. In 1901 Jessie Burkett, the late Ed Delahanty and Keeler were termed the "Big Three," in 1902 Clarence Beaumont, "Cy" Seymour and Keeler were the three monarchs.

Starting with 1903 Wagner has been particularly abusive to the pitchers. He led the artillery that year. Mike Donlin and Fred Clarke were the youths who trailed him. In 1904 Hans was supreme again. Donlin and Beckley pressed him the closest. In 1905 Seymour landed on top. "Cy" batted .377 to Wagner's .363. Donlin was No. 3.

Four years running now, making six out of the last seven, the awkwardly constructed German has landed first among the base-hit manufacturers. He did .339

in 1906, .350 in 1907, .354 in 1908 and .539 in 1909.

As all "fans" know, it isn't only as a batsman that Wagner is loved by Pittsburg and despised but revered by the other cities in the National League circuits. He's also the greatest base stealer and run-getter the game has ever known. Also its premier short-fielder. He's the player without a weakness and the artist extraordinary and the good fellow well met always.

Wagner is less symmetrial than massive. When it comes to throwing, the Dutchman can vary his style, just as he can for batting. Sometimes when the time is short his arm describes a swinging, swishing arc and then he cuts loose with great force.

I might try and describe the greatness of Wagner as a player, but a far better description of his ability in that direction than I could possibly write comes from the pen of Tip Wright, the keen and able baseball man of the Omaha Daily News. Of Wagner Mr. Wright wrote as follows.

"I've just seen the world's greatest ball player—this goes as it lays—Hans Wagner, in action, and I want to tell about him.

Imagine a Dreadnaught, powerful, majestic, all-compelling—a leviathan of the sea, with the latent power of unaccounted volcanoes behind her steel sides—frisking at thirty knots, starting, stopping, turning, darting, dodging like a destroyer, and you have an idea of the "Flying Dutchman" in action.

I saw Wagner at his best, playing at his best, playing against Chicago. To win meant to clinch first place for the Pirates. Brown, Tinker and Evers were in the game. It was the Cubs' best line-up.

Wagner lost no time. In the first, with one Cub out and men on first and second Hoffman hit the ball a mile-a-minute over second, seemingly for a hit. But Wagner interfered with the plan.

With a ten-foot leap, crouching close to the ground, he tore across the diamond and fairly hurled himself on the ball as it was passing. With one movement, seemingly, he tossed the ball to second, where Miller received and whipped it to first, turning back Hoffman and completing as dazzling a double play as I ever saw.

I have often wondered how Wagner accomplished his startling feats in the field, but the explanation is simple. He has the largest hands in baseball, and once he grasps a ball it is lost in his palm. He is a marvel of muscular strength and activity. About five feet, ten inches tall, he carries his 200 odd pounds as lightly as a featherweight. His bow legs give him an awkward appearance, yet, he turns the most startling plays with astonishing ease.

When fielding or running the bases he runs close to the earth and he runs as fast in this position as a sprinter. I saw him go to first on an infield hit in 3 2-5 seconds, which is tall traveling.

Quiet, unassuming, obliging, the big fellow is not given to talking of his performances. Playing each batter with a sixth sense, he is always on top of a ball hit in his direction, fairly smothering it. Because he plays so close to the ground it makes no difference to him how suddenly or poorly the ball hops; he grabs it, and, with his wonderful arm, fairly shoots it across the diamond.

I saw Wagner make a play that I never

WILILIAM GLEASON.
As he appeared at short field in the uniform of the four-time winner St. Louis Browns away back in the eighties.

would have believed possible. Steinfeldt hit the ball along the third base line past Barbeau, so fast that that player didn't get a look at it. But Wagner made a couple of jack rabbit jumps, speared the ball with his right hand way back of third, and, without straightening up, whizzed it to first, turning back the runner by a step. It was simply marvelous.

And he made it look easy. That's what makes him such a wonder. Built like a scow, for slow and easy motion, he moves like a flash and thinks faster than a lightning calculator.

And at bat. Ah, there's where Honus really shines. They all fear him. Even the great Mordecai Brown. In the first inning, with two down and Clarke on first the hit and run was signaled for, and Wagner came through. He smashed a fast breaking hook against the center field fence with such ease that it looked easy.

In the seventh, with the bases full and a run needed to tie the score, Wagner drove the ball to Steinfeldt so hard that the great third baseman could not handle it, and Barbeau crossed the plate. Thus, in two emergencies, he delivered the goods called for.

Wagner stands in the far corner of the box when batting. He swings his bat in a small circle until the pitcher starts his delivery, then, if he likes the ball he steps forward, swinging his bat at the same time, and when he hits it square that ball has an engagement somewhere else.

I was impressed chiefly with Wagner's earnestness. He played ball every minute, seeming to think that winning the game depended upon his every movement. Yet he played not for himself, but for the team. He is a great inside ball player.

Compared to other stars, Wagner is the baseball marvel of the day, and the Lajoies, Tinkers, Bresnahans, Hoffmans, and all the others may as well take their caps off to him. He has something on every one of them.

Barney Dreyfuss knows a good thing and John Peter Wagner, at $10,000 a season, is far cheaper than a lot of other high-class players would be at a $1,500.

And what Mr. Wright said about Wagner is not the whole story. Han's playing at short is really without an equal. He is as fast as lightning and gets almost as many plays at second and third as he does at his regular position. Age does not seem to wither the wonderful ability of the mighty German. In the last three years he has led the league in batting each season. He had a higher average last year than in either of the two preceding years. In the past twelve years Wagner's lowest average was .305 and his highest .380. He is the only man that has ever led a league in batting for seven different seasons. Wagner's base stealing ability has almost kept stride with his wonderful work with the bat, as he has stolen 533 bases in twelve years. His best year came in 1907, when he pilfered sixty-one sacks. In the last five years he has stolen more than fifty bases each season.

That Wagner besides being a great fielder and batsman is also a great thrower has already been proven.

At a benefit game given the Louisville Club on October 16, 1898, Hans Wagner, then the Colonel's big first baseman, and all-around player, made a new record for a long distance throw, although the performance will not be recognized because of the unofficial nature of the judging. Wagner threw the ball 134 yards, 1 foot and 8 inches. Exactly twenty-six years before to the day Hatfield, then with the Mutuals, made the world's record of 133 feet one foot seven and one-half inches at the Union Grounds, Brooklyn.

RODERICK J. WALLACE—Roderick J. Wallace, the clever short-stop of the St. Louis Americans, is one of the veterans in professional baseball. He was born in Pittsburg, Pa., November 4, 1874. He made his professional debut in Clarion, Pa., as a pitcher.

Cleveland purchased his release the latter part of the year. He was tried at third base in 1897 and made good. Ever since that time he has been played at third base and short-stop. When the American League started in St. Louis he was secured at a high salary and is one of the best paid players in the country.

He has been with the St. Louis Browns ever since they commenced playing in the American League in 1900 and in 1904 he was the leading short-stop of the organization. He was in poor health in the 1909 season and so did not play up to his usual standard that year. He has always been considered the leading short-fielder of the American League.

JOHN WARD—John Ward was at one time considered the most brilliant short-stop in the business.

He started out as a pitcher, but when his arm failed him he went to short-field and for years he was one of the kings in that position.

He was the leading short-stop of the National League in 1887 and he was playing just as great ball in 1895, nearly ten years later when he quit the game of his own accord.

Ward, for many years the captain and short-fielder of the New York Giants, was one of the greatest players the game has ever known.

And Ward, besides being a great player, was a gentleman and a man of brains and he gave the fine points of the game great thought and study.

Ward has written many sterling articles on baseball, that show the fine education of the man and the keen relish and interest he took in the pastime out of which at one time he made a living.

The New York captain, in fact, was one of the first to contribute a book to the National game.

To newspapers, magazines and in other directions Ward has contributed articles on baseball which have done much to increase its areas and to educate the masses up to the inner beauties of the great sport.

It was Ward who had the brains to see the injustice being done the players when the salary limit was being held at a low figure and it was his brain that set the machinery in motion which led to the organization of the Brotherhood, or Players' League, and to the reforms brought about by that league taking the field.

Besides being one of the brainiest and most intelligent men ever connected with the game, Ward was a magnificent all-around player. He was royal as a captain, superb as a fielder and thrower, great as a batsman and at the very top as a base runner.

He did wonderful work at short-field for the New York Giants when they won the National League and then the World's

ROBERT WALLACE.

Sir Robert Wallace is probably the king of short-stops in a fielding way. Little Bobby is a veteran ball player and previous to joining the St. Louis Browns ten years ago he was a member of the great Cleveland Spiders. Wallace is rated as being one of the wealthiest of ball players.

Championship in 1888 and 1889. He retired to the practice of law at a time when he was still one of the greatest players in the profession and in New York City he has been as successful in the game of law as he was in that other game at which he played so long and well and so profitably for his manager, for his fellow players and for the game's patrons at large.

Ward was one of the few who gave up baseball when he was on the top wave. He was manager and captain of the New Yorks when they won the Temple Cup in 1895 and could have served several years more of usefulness both as manager and player.

He was playing well at second base when he retired and was as skillful as ever with the bat, but he had made up his mind that it was time to get to his law practice, and nothing could induce him to stay in the game.

He is now a most successful lawyer in New York.

GEORGE WRIGHT—Coming down to the record of the short-fielders it will be seen by the figures that George Wright was the very best of the great players in that position.

In fact, George Wright in the sixties and even in the seventies was considered the greatest short-fielder of his day.

I first laid eyes on him when he came to St. Louis in 1869 with the Cincinnati Red Stockings.

I also saw him a year later when he with the Cincinnati Reds faced the Chicago White Stockings in that great game at Dexter Park, in which the Whites came out victorious.

A marked figure was George Wright at this time. He was a man just a trifle above medium height and with the build of an athlete. He had bushy, curly hair and fine teeth which he was always showing.

For a long, long while he was the king short-fielder. As Hans Wagner excels all others in that position in 1908 so did George Wright excel all the great short-fielders of the sixties and seventies.

He was a magnificent fielder and as fine a thrower as ever lived. He was also a magnificent batsman.

And besides being a fine fielder, thrower and batsman he was a speedy runner and quick thinker. And besides possessing all the fine points of a great player George Wright on the field was exceedingly graceful.

It was the custom of George Wright, Fred Sweasy, Andy Leonard and Fred Waterman of the Cincinnati Reds before each game to give an exhibition in juggling the ball at short-field, and the clever work never failed to gain for the great quartet a hearty round of applause.

George Wright was for many a day considered the model baseball player. He had no weak point. He could play any position on the team. He called short-field his home position, but when called on he was equally at home on any of the bases. He could catch as well as the best catchers of his day and was a fine, emergency pitcher. But he shone best of all at short-field and in that position he was superb.

He was able to play deeper than any man that ever filled the position and he was able to do this owing to his fearful speed and strength as a thrower. He was great at picking up ground balls and equally expert when it came to running out and

pulling down high short or deep flies. He backed up the pitcher and third and shared with his second baseman the honor of covering second when a base runner was on his way there. Take him all in all he was the model short-stop.

As a batsman, too, Wright shone with the top-notchers, not only of his own day, but of those who came later. As a base-runner no one of the Reds could beat him.

A. G. Spalding, writing not long ago about the players of the Cincinnati Red Stockings of 1869, said:

"The two Wright brothers, Harry and George, left their impress on the game; the former for his high principles and managerial ability, as well as being a skillful player; and George on account of his wonderful skill as a short-stop. His skill as a batsman, base runner and his attractive figure on the field, have never been excelled. I had a good opportunity to judge of George Wright's skill as a player. I pitched against him several times while he was a member of the Cincinnati team and I was the pitcher for the Rockford Club. I also played along with him in the Boston Club from 1871 to 1875, inclusive. Wright's then sunny disposition, athletic figure, curly hair and pearly white teeth, with a good-natured smile always playing around them, no matter how exciting the game was, together with his extraordinary skill in all departments of the game, made him in my opinion one of the most attractive and picturesque figures in baseball. I consider him one of the best all-around players the game ever produced."

George Wright played his first professional baseball with the Nationals of Washington in 1867. He had played with the Gotham team of New York before joining the Nationals. The Gothams were a team organized in March, 1852, so that George Wright was one of the earliest players. After the Nationals he joined the Unions of Morrisania, New York, and in 1868, while playing with that team he was signed to cover the short-field position for the Cincinnati Reds in their 1869 season.

When Wright stepped on the field with that team in 1869 they were the first full professional and all-salaried team got together in this country. What the Reds did that year with George Wright as their captain and short-fielder we have told elsewhere in this book. More of George Wright's record, too, is given in another part of this work, especially in that part where the games of the Cincinnati Reds of 1869 are referred to.

J. ZEIDER—J. Zeider was one of the regular short-fielders of the Chicago White Sox during the season of 1910. Zeider was one of the high-priced infielders which President Comiskey secured from the San Francisco Club of the Pacific Coast League during the Fall of 1909. Zeider covered third base for Frisco in the season of 1909 and was looked upon as one of the best infielders developed on the coast in years. During this season he played in 189 games, counted 141 runs, made 204 base hits, stole 93 bases and had a grand batting average of .289. Zeider player ninety-two games with the White Sox during the 1910 season and in a fielding way he lived up to his great coast reputation. On the bases he showed up a fast man, and also scored a goodly number of runs. He did not, however, find the pitchers of the American League such easy marks as were those on the Coast the year previous.

THE NATIONAL GAME.

THE LEFT FIELDERS.

CUTHBERT, YORK, GEDNEY, LEONARD, JONES AND HORNUNG WERE ALL LEADERS IN THIS POSITION IN THEIR DAY IN THE OLD PRO-FESSIONAL AND THE NATIONAL LEAGUE.

Year.	Left Fielders. Club.	Fielding Games.	Pct.
1871	Ed. Cuthbert—Philadelphia	44	.935
1872	Thos. York—Baltimore	24	.930
1873	Al. Gedney—Mutuals, N. Y.	61	.942
1874	Al. Gedney—Athletics, Phila	39	.943
1875	A. Leonard—Boston	77	.940
1876	Thos. York—Hartford	67	.899
1877	John Glenn—Chicago	31	.941
1878	C. W. Jones—Cincinnati	49	.893
1879	C. W. Jones—Boston	83	.933
1880	Thos. York—Providence	50	.932
1881	Joe Hornung—Boston	83	.947
1882	Joe Hornung—Boston	83	.930
1883	Joe Hornung—Boston	98	.936
1884	Jas. Fogarty—Philadelphia	75	.915
1885	P. Gillespie—New York	102	.941
1886	Jas. Fogarty—Philadelphia	56	.953
1887	Joe Hornung—Boston	97	.934
1888	Jas. O'Rourke—New York	87	.959
1889	W. Wilmot—Washington	107	.919
1890	M. Sullivan—Boston	121	.951

Year.	Left Fielders. Club.	Fielding Games.	Pct.
1891	W. O'Brien—Brooklyn	102	.958
1892	W. O'Brien—Brooklyn	121	.959
1893	Joseph Kelley—Baltimore	124	.952
1894	W. R. Hamilton—Philadelphia	131	.961
1895	E. J. Delehanty—Philadelphia	100	.945
1896	Joseph Kelley—Baltimore	130	.955
1897	E. J. Delehanty—Philadelphia	127	.970
1898	Joseph Kelley—Baltimore	123	.973
1899	Joseph Kelley—Baltimore	144	.976
1900	A. Selbach—New York	141	.957
1901	Fred Clarke—Pittsburg	127	.967
1902	Jas. Sheckard—Brooklyn	122	.964
1903	Sam Mertes—New York	137	.973
1904	Fred Clarke—Pittsburg	70	.976
1905	W. P. Shannon—St. Louis	140	.983
1906	Jas. Sheckard—Chicago	149	.986
1907	Fred Clarke—Pittsburg	144	.987
1908	J. Delehanty—St. Louis	138	.977
1909	Fred Clarke—Pittsburg	152	.987
1910	J. Collins—Boston	151	.977

AMERICAN LEAGUE LEADERS.

SINCE 1900, THE OPENING SEASON OF THIS ORGANIZATION, McINTYRE HAS TWICE LED THE MEN IN THIS POSITION AS A FIELDER.

Year.	Left Fielders. Club.	Fielding Games.	Pct.
1900	Ketchum—Milwaukee	73	.958
1901	Hugh Duffy—Milwaukee	78	.973
1902	Delehanty—Washington	110	.967
1903	F. T. Hartsel—Philadelphia	97	.968
1904	Jas. Barrett—Detroit	162	.979

Year.	Left Fielders. Club.	Fielding Games.	Pct.
1905	M. McIntyre—Detroit	131	.968
1906	P. Dougherty—Chicago	86	.978
1907	D. Jones—Detroit	125	.971
1908	M. McIntyre—Detroit	151	.977
1909	B. Lord—Cleveland	67	.992
1910	George Stone—St. Louis	145	.972

Left field has always been considered the hardest place to fill in the outer works.

It was especially hard in the early days of the professional game, when the pitching was slower than it is now, when the ball contained more rubber than the ball used at the present time and when hits to the left field, long rangy hits, were the order of the day in nearly each and every game.

So it happened that in the earliest days of the professional game the fleetest men on each team were assigned to positions at left field.

The first five leaders at left field in the National League, from 1871 to 1876 inclusive, Gedney having led for two years, were all wonderful runners.

Cuthbert's record for running bases stood for years and he was equally fleet in covering ground in the outfield.

York was much like Cuthbert and Gedney was perhaps the superior of both in covering great stretches of ground. I saw Gedney playing with the Eckfords of Brooklyn against the Chicago White Stockings on the old Lake Front Grounds at Chicago. That was in the early seventies.

Martin, the slow pitcher of the Eckfords, was doing the twirling and the Chicago boys were hitting the sphere high to the far outfield.

Gedney went out like a sprinter after many of these high flies and nearly always landed the ball. Eight or ten put outs in the game were frequent occurrences with him.

Cuthbert set out as a fielder with the Keystones of Philadelphia and in the early seventies he was secured by the Athletics of Philadelphia.

He was with the Philadelphias when he led the National League as a left fielder in 1871.

Edgar Cuthbert, one of the great left fielders of the seventies and early eighties was a Phila boy.

He learned to play ball professionally with the Keystones of Philadelphia, and from them was graduated to the Athletics of the same city. Later he joined the Philadelphias.

Cuthbert was a wonderful fielder, thrower, base runner and batsman.

When Jimmy Wood set out to select a professional baseball team for Chicago in 1870, a team that would annihilate the Champion Red Stockings of Cincinnati, he selected Cuthbert as his center fielder and it was the latter's magnificent batting and fielding that went far to win the two great games at Dexter Park, Chicago, September 7, and October 13, 1870, which Chicago captured from the Cincinnati Reds by ten to six and sixteen to thirteen. Cuthbert also belonged to the famous Athletic team of Philadelphia which in 1871 won the National Baseball Championship and his work that year stamped him as the most valuable all around man playing in the outfield. He was then at the very top as a fielder, batsman and base runner. He played great ball, too, later when he was with the Chicago White Stockings and the St. Louis Browns of 1876.

Cuthbert was a short, stout built man, a modern athlete in muscle and strength. He was great all around as a player being able to hit the ball hard as well as to field and throw it. Cuthbert is one of the silent army.

Tom York, like Cuthbert, was a fine fielder and a heavy hitting left handed batsman. He led in 1872 and Gedney was top man in 1873 and 1874.

After Gedney came Andy Leonard, who had won fame and reputation with the Cincinnati Red Stockings but who in this 1875 year was with Boston.

Leonard made the easiest work of the most difficult fly balls, and was a strong and accurate thrower.

John Glenn, a fine fielder and batsman, came after Leonard and then for two years, 1878 and 1879 Charles W. Jones of Cincinnati and Boston captured leading place.

Glenn and Leonard were medium sized men, fine athletes and fielders, but Jones was a great big husky fellow, who, besides being a fine fielder could hit the ball an awful clip.

After Jones came Joe Hornung the leading left fielder of the National League in 1881, 1882, 1883 and 1887. Hornung was a man of medium size, of rather light build, but he was a fine batsman and he not only covered a great stretch of ground in the field but he was a fine base runner and a sure catch.

After Hornung came Jimmy Fogarty, who led the National League left fielders in 1884 and 1886. He was then a member of Harry Wright's Philadelphia team. The people of the Quaker City who knew Fogarty best insist to this day that he was the greatest outfielder that ever lived.

And they nearly speak by the card for Fogarty was speedy as lightning, could cover ground like a deer and could throw the ball as well as field it. He was also great as a base runner and batsman. He died long before his time.

P. Gillespie who followed Fogarty as the leader at left field was of greyhound build, a fine fielder and runner and excellent batsman.

There are many other great left fielders whose names will be mentioned in another edition of this work; among them Dave Eggler of the original Eckfords of Brooklyn, John V. B. Hatfield of the Atlantics of Brooklyn, Jack Remsen and Tom York, Brooklyn players, and many others like them.

And now leaving the old record I give an alphabetical list of the men who have played at left field in the old Professional Association, the National League, the American League and all others major leagues since 1871:

HERMAN BADER—Herman Bader, now a prominent business man and politician, is another St. Louis professional who made his mark in the olden days. St. Louis has given many great players to the profession, catchers like Flint, Peitz, Dolan, Brennan and Sullivan; pitchers like Breitenstein, Galvin and Blong and great in and out fielders. To the profession, too, she gave Herman Bader, at one time the fastest base runner in America. This record he made while with the Dallas Club, in the Texas League, in 1888. While with that team in that season he stole eleven bases in one game and he had a record of stealing 156 bases during the season, a record that has never since been equalled or beaten. Bader was born in North St Louis and played his first games with the Enterprise team of North St. Louis. In 1884

Ted Sullivan, then managing the St. Louis Unions, saw Bader at work and liked him so well that he got him to play in the outfield for the St. Louis Unions at times when the regular outfielders of that team were out of commission. Bader's first real professional engagement was in 1884 when he played with the Lincoln team of the Western League. Later he was with the Omaha Western League team the Dallas, Tex., and the Albany, N. Y., team. When Washington joined the National League in the early nineties Bader went to that team and played a great game for it in the field. He was one of the speediest left fielders ever in the big league, a king base runner and a fine, timely, heavy hitting batsman. Bader having quit the game, is in business in St. Louis and is a thriving and popular citizen of the Mound City. His son, Arthur, the crack fielder of the Western League has taken his place in the profession. Like his father, he is a cracking hard hitter, fine fielder and good on the bases.

ROBERT BESCHER—There are few better players in the business to-day than Robert Bescher, the left fielder of the Cincinnati Club.

And besides being a great fielder Bescher is great in other directions, being the champion base runner of the country.

Although performing in but 117 games in the 1909 season, Bescher easily topped the sack pilferers. He stole fifty-four pillows. This is almost at Ty Cobb's rate.

Much has been said about the relative merits as base runners of Bescher, the National League star, and Tyrus Cobb, the best man on the paths in the American League. According to Griffith, Bescher is the Tiger's superior.

And Bescher's record bears Griffith out. Bescher made 107 hits in the 1909 season and stole fifty-four bases. Cobb rapped out 216 hits, more than twice as many as the Red and stole seventy-six bases. That gives Bescher the better of the work by a big percentage. For if Bescher got or first as often as Cobb there's no tellin; what he might do.

He accomplishes all his work in his start. He's off faster than any other player in the business. Then after he gets going he has as much speed as the next fellow.

Bescher joined the Cincinnati Club in the Fall of the 1908 season. He was obtained from the Dayton Club. He played in a majority of the games last season for the Reds in left field. The remarkable part of his work is the fact that he's such a big fellow to possess such remarkable speed. A little football playing in his early career is the only experience he has had in sprinting or running. According to Griffith he's just a natural born runner.

JOSEPH BIRMINGHAM — Joseph Birmingham, the clever left fielder of the Cleveland Club, is one of the best in the business. He is a native of Elmyra, N. Y., and is in his twenty-sixth year.

He played on local nines in 1901 and with Mercersburg, Pa., Preparatory School in 1902 and 1903. He played football at Cornell in 1903 and 1904.

In 1906 he played baseball professionally with the A. J. G. Club of the New York State League and was secured by Cleveland in August of that year. He is one of the most graceful fielders, a wonderful thrower, and his fine work the past season contributed materially to the good showing made by his club.

JESSE BURKETT.

Jesse Burkett, who for many years pranced about left field in the big league and who is now manager of the Worcesteer Club of the Massachusetts State League. He was one of the greatest batsmen of modern days. There is some talk of his being asked to manage a big league club in 1911.

JESSE C. BURKETT—When Jesse C. Burkett played baseball for Cleveland in the National League he was the hardest hitting outfielder in the business.

He also did fine work for the St. Louis Browns in left field until five years ago, when he quit the big league to go into business for himself.

In his late years in St. Louis he was called "The Crab" owing to the lively way he got back at his critics in the left field bleachers.

Since Burkett quit the major league he has shone brilliantly as a minor league manager.

Four times in succession he has piloted the Worcester, Mass., team to the championship in the New England League. This equals the league record. Fall River having four successive wins back in the '90s. Burkett, however, has the greater glory, for his team was a member of the league only those four years in which it won the championship; it was never anything but first.

It is no wonder that Worcester baseball fans think very highly of Burkett, and believe he would make a good major league manager, for he has won their admiration against heavy odds.

There was no enthusiasm when Burkett started on his managerial career in Worcester. There was condemnation on the other hand. Baseball fans did not know Burkett. Although he had made his home in Worcester since his early days of professional baseball few had even a bowing acquaintance with him. There was lacking that personal interest in him which many another man who has worn a Worcester uniform would have aroused.

From the first Burkett showed ability that even those who knew him did not suspect he possessed. Largely through his work a plot of ground was secured which insured the financial success of baseball in Worcester. For several years teams of three different leagues had vainly tried to make baseball a success, using Worcester Oval for their grounds. The grounds are handsome, but are a long distance from the center of the city.

Burkett and his associates secured a plot of land less than a mile from the center of the city, which had been a public dump for years. This was in mid-winter. Nobody believed it could be made into a baseball field in time to open in the Spring. But in doing so Burkett showed the trait that has won him his four successive championships.

St. Louisans will never forget Burkett, who played left field for the Browns in the first days of that team in the American League. He was one of the grandest batsmen and bunters the big leagues ever owned.

In those days Burkett was a royal fielder, base runner and batsman, but he was so fast to first that after a year or two of play, when he commenced to slow up, the exacting "fans" got after him.

Burkett retaliated and so forcibly that in his last year in St. Louis he was nicknamed "The Crab."

Burkett was born in Wheeling, W. Va., the home of Jack Glasscock, another great ball player, December 4, 1870.

His first professional engagement was when as a boy of 16 he played with the Scranton, Pa., team. That was in 1886.

In 1888 he went to Worcester and he was afterwards traded to New York.

At this time Burkett was a pitcher, but he was so wild that New York farmed him out to Lincoln, Neb., for a couple of seasons.

In 1891 New York sold his release to the National League team of Cleveland and there he developed into one of the hardest hitting outfielders the game has ever seen.

When the St. Louis Americans took the field Burkett joined them and remained with them until 1905, when he was traded to the Boston Americans for George Stone and $2,500 in cash.

He remained in that club but one season and then went to his old love, Worcester, where he is now the owner of one of the finest baseball grounds in Massachusetts.

JOHN C. CHAPMAN—One of the famous fielders of the seventies was John C. Chapman, who, in 1870, was the left fielder of the Atlantics of Brooklyn.

Jack was one of the first of the little army of professionals who set out in 1870 and swept all before them.

Cotemperaneous with Jack on the Atlantics were such later famous players as Charles Mills, George Zettlein, Joseph Start, Robert Ferguson, Charles J. Smith, Dickey Pearce, Lipman Pike, George Hall and Daniel McDonald. Leaving the Atlantics, Chapman played with many great teams, notably St. Louis and Louisville.

Pike, Hall and McDonald played the outfield with Chapman, but none of them could beat Jack at all around play.

In a Brooklyn newspaper published on August 14, 1868, the writer said:

"John C. Chapman is considered the best left fielder in the country. In 1862 he joined the Athletics and played with them continuously until 1867, when he joined the Quaker City, which was being organized by Tommy Pratt. This year he returned to the club and took his accustomed position at left. Among other qualities he has besides being a long thrower and a sure catcher, is that of being a swift thrower. Socially he is a genial fellow that everybody likes."

After it had been announced that Chapman had gone to Philadelphia, the following item appeared in The Clipper:

"Chapman will electrify the natives of the Quaker City with his phenomenal one-handed catches. We have seen him run at full speed, either toward the diamond or into deep left field and make the most surprising one-handed catches as we have seen no other fielder do."

Mr. Chapman is doubtless the veteran Elk of the country among baseball men, as he is No. 22 of the Brooklyn Lodge, which is oddly enough No. 22. Mr. Chapman joined the lodge in the year 1883 when it was instituted and has ever since taken the warmest interest in all matters relating to the order.

FRED C. CLARKE—Fred C. Clarke is to-day the foremost figure in the baseball world.

He holds that position by virtue of the fact that the Pitsburg team, of which he is the left fielder and manager, won the World's Championship of 1909.

In 1901 Fred Clarke was the leader among the left fielders of the National League. He has been very close to the top. in that position ever since leading the league in that position in 1901, 1904 and 1907 and 1909.

In the last ten years he has proven himself one of the greatest all-around baseball players that ever lived.

Fred Clarke was born at Des Moines,

OLD SPORTSMANS PARK FIELD AT ST. LOUIS.
On these grounds Comiskey, leading the St. Louis Browns, won four American Association and two World's Championships.

Ia., October 3, 1872, and is therefore in his 38th year.

He commenced his professional career in 1892, when he joined the Hastings, Neb., Club, and the following year he went to the St. Joe Club of the Western Association. In June of 1893 the St. Joe Club disbanded and Clarke went to Montgomery, Ala., where he played out the season.

In 1894 he started in with Savannah and it was at the commencement of that season that John J. McCloskey, then managing the Louisville Club, set eyes on him.

McCloskey, even then a great judge of players, saw in Clarke the making of a wonderful fielder and batsman and when the Savannah team disbanded McCloskey signed Clarke to play in the field for Louisville. Clarke created something of a sensation in Louisville his very first season by participating in seventy-six games, in which he batted at a .275 clip, and in that period stole twenty-four bases. He was one of the great run-getters of that period and scored fifty-five runs in seventy-six battles.

The year following he hit .354, scored ninety-four runs and stole thirty-six bases.

He continued with Louisville until 1899. He had a grand year his farewell season in the Kentucky metropolis. In 147 games he batted .348 and scored 124 runs, an average of .84 per game.

The great run-getters of to-day are Leach and Cobb in the National and American Leagues respectively. When it is taken into consideration that Cobb, a base runner and run-getter par excellence, scored 116 runs in 156 games, the real brilliancy of Clarke's performance can be seen.

In those days it must be remembered Louisville was hardly ever in the race for the flag, and though Louisville had a fair hitting team it was never a great machine.

Wagner and Leach were associated with Clarke at Louisville. Honus played right field, while Leach was in the infield.

Clarke went to Pittsburg in 1900, but slumped somewhat and hit but .281. He still retained his run-scoring proclivities, however, and tallied eighty-five times in 103 games. He continued with Pittsburg, where he has been ever since, and was a .300 hitter to the last three years.

He went to his lowest notch in 1908, when he hit .265. He came back brilliantly in the 1909 campaign, and had one of the banner years of his career. He was well over the .300 mark for 75 per cent of the season, but finished with an average of .299. He scored ninety-two runs and stole twenty-four bases.

Clarke has always been noted for his fielding and made but six errors during the past season, handling 374 chances. This netted him a fielding mark of .984. Clarke has always had an accurate throwing wing.

Taking the sixteen years into consideration, Clarke played in 1,968 games. In that period he has been to the bat 7,731 times and made 2,449 hits. He has scored 1,475 runs, stolen 450 bases and sacrificed 190 times. For the sixteen years Clarke has a grand average of .317.

The fielding figures of the Pirate leader are every bit as creditable as his batting record.

During his big league career he had 4,274 put-outs to his credit. He had 257 assists from the field, and in 1,968 games turned but 224 errors. His combined number of

chances totaled 4,755, and this would give him a gross fielding average of .953.

Clarke's record is meritorious when it is remembered that he is 38 years old. He hails from Kansas and has been in the game since he was a child. John McCloskey, last year's manager of the Milwaukee American Association team, and just prior to that leader of the St. Louis Cardinals, discovered Clarke. He was manager of the Louisville team in those days.

It was a twelve-club organization. McCloskey found Clarke in the South and brought him to Louisville. Two years later Clarke went to Pittsburg, when the Smoky City outfit and the Colonels were consolidated.

Since that time Clarke's team has never finished outside the first division.

Clarke is one of the best judges of young ball players in the country, and his success the past season is due to this fact. Miller and Adams are two of Clarke's 1909 "finds."

Clarke is one of the wealthiest players in the game, owning two ranches near Winfield, Kas. His averages for sixteen years follow:

CLARKE'S BATTING AVERAGES.

Year.	G.	A.B.	R.	H.	AV.	SB.	SH.
1894	76	316	55	87	.275	24	1
1895	132	556	94	197	.354	86	3
1896	131	317	93	169	.327	31	4
1897	129	525	122	213	.406	60	3
1898	147	598	115	190	.318	14	16
1899	147	601	124	209	.348	47	19
1900	103	398	85	112	.281	18	9
1901	128	525	118	166	.316	22	13
1902	114	461	104	148	.321	34	6
1903	102	427	88	150	.351	21	13
1904	70	278	51	85	.306	11	8
1905	137	525	95	157	.299	24	22
1906	110	417	69	129	.309	18	20
1907	144	501	97	145	.289	37	16
1908	151	551	83	146	.265	24	22
1909	147	535	92	156	.290	24	22
Totals	1968	7731	1475	2449	.317	450	190

Year.	PO.	A.	E.	TC.	Ave.
1894	166	14	29	202	.856
1895	338	25	41	404	.899
1896	276	17	31	324	.904
1897	283	23	24	330	.927
1898	346	22	14	322	.963
1899	324	21	13	358	.963
1900	263	9	16	288	.944
1901	283	14	10	307$	.967
1902	217	12	9	238	.962
1903	168	19	7	185	.962
1904	135	4	3	142	.979
1905	270	16	7	293	.976
1906	209	15	6	230	.974
1907	298	15	4	317	.987
1908	346	15	10	371	.973
1909	352	16	6	374	.984
Totals	4274	257	224	4755	.953

The manager of the four-time pennant winners is justly popular owing to the successful manner in which he has handled his men. The Kansan gets there because he is on the level with his players. Clarke is a grand ball player himself and a man of sterling qualities, but perhaps the most important of all is his absolute fairness to every man under him.

Clarke does little jollying. He seldom praises his men and never pounds them too hard. The last thing in the world he would think of doing would be to tell

Johnny Miller or Bobby Byrne, or, for that matter, any youngster on his team that he was the best young player in the game. Therefore he keeps out of a lot of holes. He never has anything to take back.

If one of his players gets a call for a stupid play that player cannot come back at the Pirate Chieftain with the remark:

"Why, I guess I know what I am doing. Last week you said I knew all about playing this position. Guess I haven't changed so very much since."

If Clarke calls a man that player knows that there is some good reason for it. Fred is a friendly fellow in a way, but he is no flatterer, neither is he a booster. When he called Abstein in the world's series Bill knew it was coming and took his medicine like a man and went in the final game and lived down many of his shortcomings of prior battles.

Clarke is serious about his work, both on and off the field, and he very rarely overlooks a point. He knows baseball about as well as any of them. He is one of the few managers that work from the outfield, and, like Fielder Jones, is one of the few managers that use judgment in changing pitchers.

Clarke has the character and determination to enforce his knowledge to the best advantage. He gets the best possible work out of his players day in and day out.

WILLIAM SHIRLEY COLLINS — William Shirley Collins, is the left fielder of the Boston National League Club of 1910. He was born in Chesterton, Ind., near Chicago, March 17, 1884. He played with Muskogee in 1905, Sharon, Pa., in 1906 and 1907, Cedar Rapids in 1908 and 1909. The New York Nationals drafted him for 1910 and gave Herzog with him for Becker. He stands five feet ten and one-half inches and weighs 165 pounds. His home is in Frankfort, Ind. During the 1910 season Collins showed improvement and is fast becoming one of the steadiest outfielders in the National League.

FRANK CREE—Frank Cree, the great young left fielder and batsman of the New York Highlanders, was born at Pittsburg, October 23, 1882. He played with the Pennsylvania State Normal School from 1901 to 1904 at third base and short-stop. Cree began to play professional ball during the summer of 1904 with the Washington team of the Pennsylvania State League. From 1905 till 1908 he was with the Pennsylvania State College nine. During the summer of 1906 he played at Burlington, Vt., and was with the Williamsport Tri-State team in 1907 and 1908. Connie Mack signed him for the Athletics of 1909 and later released him to New York.

ABNER DALRYMPLE—Abner Dalrymple, the left fielder of Anson's Chicago White Stockings, was one of the greatest players in the eighties. He belonged to that invincible combination which Anson held together for Chicago for so many years. Dalrymple was great as a fielder, strong as a batsman and speedy as a base runner.

He was with Chicago in 1878 and remained with Anson's historic legion for several years.

JOHN DALTON—John Dalton is a member of the Brooklyn Club of the National League and is experiencing his first season in stylish company. Dalton comes from the Far West and up to Fall had played very creditable baseball in the out-

field. He is a little fellow, fast on his feet and an excellent run-getter. He should win a regular berth in the line-up of the Brooklyn Club next season.

E J. DELEHANTY—Edward. J. Delehanty, the stalwart left fielder of the Philadelphia Club, carried off leading honors in the National League in 1895 and 1897.

Delehanty was a royal fielder, but his best forte was his ability to clout the ball hard, to send it in all directions and with such speed that his low hits often got by the best infielders.

Although he led the league left fielders in fielding but a single year he was for twelve years either at the top or very near the top as a batsman.

During the season of 1896 while with the Philadelphia team Delehanty made four home runs and a single off Terry, then pitching for Brooklyn, or a total of seventeen bases out of five times at bat.

Delehanty came from the famous Delehanty family of Cleveland, Ohio, that has given so many great players to the major leagues.

Edward Delehanty's first playing was done with the Wheeling, W. Va., team. His good batting on that nine attracted world-wide attention and the Philadelphia Club in the Fall of 1891 paid the Wheeling management $1,900 for Delehanty's release. It was claimed that this was the largest amount up to this time ever paid for the release of a minor league player.

Delehanty remained with the Philadelphia Club until he joined the Washingtons of the American League.

Delehanty's batting record for the twelve years he played in the big leagues was as follows and has perhaps never been beaten:

Years.	G.	A.B.	H.	Ave.
1892	120	470	247	.312
1893	132	588	218	.370
1894	114	498	199	.400
1895	116	481	192	.399
1896	122	505	199	.394
1897	129	530	200	,377
1898	142	545	183	.334
1899	145	573	234	.408
1900	130	542	173	.319
1901	138	538	192	.357
1902	123	474	178	.376
1903	43	154	52	.338
—	—	—	—	—
12	1454	5900	2167	.367

Delehanty might have continued his splendid baseball career for years, but in 1903 while riding on a train across the bridge at Niagara Falls, he accidentally fell off and was killed.

Like Wagner, Dunlap, Wright and other great players, Delehanty in his day was a marked figure in the baseball world and head and shoulders as a batsman over nearly all the players who were with him and beside him during the decade in which he ruled a king.

JOSH DEVORE—Josh Devore, a youngster, is one of the regular left fielders of John McGraw's New York Giants Club in the National League. Devore has been drawing pay on the Giants team these two years past. He is one of the smallest outfielders in the National and one of the speediest as well. He developed into one of the hardest hitters of the younger crop the past season. Up to August, 1910, he was batting .280, had scored sixty runs and stolen nineteen bases. Devore looms up as one of the real stars of the past season and is looked upon as the regular left fielder of the Giants.

MIKE DONLIN—Mike Donlin, who, with McGraw, Mathewson and Bresnahan, three years ago formed the backbone of the New York Giants, has probably quit the game for good.

He and his wife, Mabel Hite, are now in vaudeville and Mike may never again return to the ball field. But Mike will always be remembered as one of the greatest hitters and throwers in the business.

Donlin came to St. Louis ten years ago in the days when Lou Criger and Schreckengost, both of whom are practically out of it, were kid catchers and Cy Young and Jack Powell were the mainstays in the box.

It was the old Cleveland team that had been moved to St. Louis and it was on the verge of breaking up. Patsy Tebeau, the manager; Cupid Childs and Ed McKeon, three members of the great infield, passed out that year. Donlin came as a pitcher, but McKeon was all to the bad and Mike was put in to play short-stop that Sunday. Say! But he was a wonder! The whole town was talking about the sensational work of the southpaw short-stop.

But the next day and the next—a difference. Mike bruised the fences with balls he kicked out of the diamond. Then he was tried at first base. Not much better there, though the way he could slam the horsehide had the fans daffy with delight.

Mike won further fame by giving Schreckenghost a fine licking one evening while the team was about to start on a trip. Schreck said Mike had a million dollar arm and a ten-cent head. No good Irishman could stand that from a Dutchman, so the fight went on. There was no one but Mike around when it was over.

Mike passed out of the big show shortly after that and drifted to Baltimore. He was always a good ball player—one of the winning kind—but he did not find the right place until after he left St. Louis. McGraw put him in the outfield and when McGraw went to New York he took Mike with him.

Mike came from Pennsylvania originally, but as he played ball in California before coming to the National League he is now claimed as a native son of that State. They do that with all the boys who tarry a few minutes in California anad then become proficient in any line of sport out there.

PATRICK H. DOUGHERTY—Patrick H. Dougherty, the left fielder of the Chicago Americans, was born in Andover, N. Y., October 27, 1876. He played ball in his early days in Bristol, Conn. In 1898 he was with Dayton, Ohio, and in Canandaigua, N. Y. In 1899 he pitched for Bridgeport, Conn. The Boston Americans secured him in 1902 and he remained with that club until the middle of the season of 1904, when he went to New York. He left New York to join the Outlaws on the Coast, and returned to organized baseball to join Comiskey's team in July, 1906.

Dougherty is six feet in height and of stout and muscular build. He is an excellent fielder and batsman. In fact, there are few outfielders in the American League to-day who have anything on Dougherty. He's a beautiful fielder and a cracking thrower, a perfect bunter, and is especially good at the bat in a pinch. He was one of the live White Sox in 1906

when Comiskey, and his wonderful band, won the world's greatest prize in baseball, the World's Championship.

HUGH DUFFY—Hugh Duffy, selected by Charles A. Comiskey to manage the Chicago White Stockings of 1910, was one of the greatest left fielders of his day.

Duffy played with the Boston Champions when they won the flag in 1892 and 1893. He was their center fielder those two years. When they won the flag again in 1897 and 1898 he was switched to left field and he remained in that position during the balance of his career.

When he quit the National League it was to go to the Milwaukee Club of the American League.

Up to the closing days of his career as a player Duffy was a magnificent fielder and batsman.

Although below the medium in height he was a strong, husky figure on the field and he was one of the best men in an emergency the game has ever known.

GEORGE W. ELLIS—George W. Ellis, "Rube," the regular left fielder of the St. Louis Cardinals of the National League, made his debut in fast company with Cincinnati in the Spring of 1909. Ellis previously had played in California and had won the reputation of being a terrific slugger. The change of climate, however, affected his health his first season out and as a result he did not play up to expectations in Cincinnati. Last winter he was exchanged to St. Louis and ever since has shown considerable class. He is a left-handed batsman and throws with his left hand. Up to August, 1910, the Rube was batting at a .251 clip and fielding finely. He is five feet nine inches, weighs 165 pounds and is 23 years old.

ELMER FLICK—After being a star outfielder and batter for eleven years Flick, one of the most famous players the game has ever known, was in June, 1910, given a ticket for the minor leagues. The Cleveland Club disposed of him then to Kansas City. Elmer was a top-notcher from 1897 until the spring of 1908. Then his stomach went back on him and he played but little, either that year or the succeeding season.

In the Spring of 1908 he seemed to be in his old-time form until the water at New Orleans got the better of him. He finally recovered but his former speed seemed to be missing and McGuire benched him in favor of the youngsters. Then he was sold to George Tebeau.

Flick commenced his major league career in Philadelphia.

CURRY FOLEY—Curry Foley was one of the greatest left fielders of his day. He was famous in the late seventies and early eighties as the crack fielder and base runner of the Milwaukee, Buffalo and other teams. He came from the famous Lowell team of 1877, which that year had Sam Crane and other later noted players in its ranks. Foley was one of the star players of the seventies and eighties.

ALFRED W. GEDNEY—Alfred W. Gedney was the left fielder of the Athletics of Philadelphia when they, with the Boston Club made the famous baseball invasion of England in 1874. He now lives in Hackensack, N. J., and often runs over to New York and Boston to see the baseball games played in those cities.

Gedney was the left fielder of the great Eckford team of the seventies when

HUGH DUFFY.
Once one of the greatest outfielders and now the manager of the Chicago White Sox.

"Slow Ball" Martin depended on his fielders to help him out of the tightest situations.

Gedney in those days was wonderfully fleet of foot and covered as much ground as the fleetest outfielders of the present day.

BILLY HAMILTON—W. R. Hamilton, better known as Billy Hamilton, in his day was one of the greatest fielders and hardest hitters in the business.

He was a left-handed batsman and was very fast in getting to first base.

He was the champion left fielder in the National League in 1894.

But Hamilton's best card was his base running. For four years he stole more bases than any other player in the National League.

He was the leading base runner in that organization in 1890, 1891, 1894 and 1895.

In 1891 he stole 150 bases—a record never beaten in the major organization since and twice as many bases as were stolen by Wagner, the leading base runner of the National League in 1908.

JACK HATFIELD—John V. B. Hatfield, or plain "Jack" Hatfield, as he was best known in professional baseball circles, was at one time one of the best known professional players.

By general consent he was the champion of all the long distance throwers. He made his throwing record at Brooklyn, October 15, 1872. He threw the ball 400 feet seven and one-half inches. Many have been the attempts since that time to excel this record, but that of Mr. Hatfield is the only one that stands on the books to-day. Doubtless the best man in long throwing in the days of Hatfield was Edward Crane of Boston. Crane undoubtedly made more long throws than any man who ever attempted long-distance throwing, but his throws were never authenticated. Hatfield's were.

Jack Hatfield was playing at left field in the sixties for the Eckford and Mutual Clubs of Brooklyn, N. Y. In 1879 he came West and was with the Cincinnati Reds of that year.

When "Jack" quit the game he came to St. Louis and became associated as pool seller with Richard Roche, who then conducted a big turf exhange here. Later Hatfield returned to Brooklyn and he died there February 20, 1909, of heart disease. He was 62 years of age at the time of his death.

WILLIAM HOLMES—William Holmes, or "Ducky" Holmes, as he was called in the big league, was at one time one of the best known left fielders in the major league line. He is now the manager of the Sioux City team of the Western League.

He began playing professional ball in 1892, playing with the Beatrice team, in the Nebraska State League. From that time to this he was with the following teams: 1893, St. Joe, Mo., Western League; 1894, Des Moines, Ia., Western Association; 1895, Louisville, Ky., National League; 1896, New York, National League; 1897-8-9, Baltimore, Md., National League; 1900-1-2, captain of Detroit, Mich., American League; 1903-4-5, Chicago White Sox. After playing with the White Sox for three years Manager Holmes purchased his release and bought the St. Joe, Mo., franchise, Western League, and transferred it to Lincoln, Neb. After giving that city a very successful ball team for two seasons, 1906-1907, he disposed of his club to Guy Green and

purchased the controlling interest in the Sioux City Club, giving that city a pennant winner the first season of his management. In 1900 he lost out to Des Moines by the narrow margin of two points.

HAMILTON HYATT—Hamilton Hyatt played a good game in the field for Pittsburg whenever called on in their successful 1909 season.

He was their utility man and pinch hitter.

Hyatt when sent up as a pinch hitter—that most trying job—hit .310 for Pittsburg in the 1909 season. The pitchers all looked alike to him, right or left handers, no difference—he soaked them as they came.

When he got in for a few games as an active fielder he kept right on hitting incidentally he showed that he is no big dub after the flies no unwieldly cow, depending only on his batting for a job. He moved up and down the field with the agility of a cat, although he is a giant in size, he caught the long ones with beautiful judgment and he thew with accuracy and tremendous power.

In other words, young Mr. Hyatt showed that he is a classy ball player.

CHARLES JONES—Charles Jones, the first, who was at his best in 1878 when he played at left field for the Cincinnati League team and who later covered that position for Cincinnati's Champion American Association team was in his day one of the hardest hitters in America. Jones was a fine stalwart player and knew all the points of the game. He could field and throw finely and he was the home run hitter of the team. He is now living in New York.

DAVID JONES—David Jones, one of the left fielders of the Champion Detroits of 1909, was secured by that team in 1905 in the same deal with Schmidt, both having played with the Minneapolis Club, in the American Association.

It was not Jones' first essay in fast company, he having been in 1902 with the St. Louis Browns and the Chicago Cubs, jumping the latter team for the former. Jones started the season of 1901 with Dixon College and was successively employed that season by Rockford, Milwaukee and St. Louis.

Cambria, Wis., was Jones' birthplace and he admits to 29 years. He is five feet eight inches in height and weighs 161 pounds. He throws right-handed, but bats from the left side of the plate.

He is one of the speediest base runners in the American League.

JOSEPH KELLEY—Perhaps the greatest left fielder the game has ever known, is Joseph J. Kelley, who led the National League in that position in 1893, 1896, 1898 and 1899.

Kelley was with Baltimore those years the famous team that had such stars as Brouthers, Keeler, Jennings, McGraw, Doyle and Brodie. He was perhaps the king pin of this great lot of players, able to do all things well, being magnificent as a fielder and thrower and superb as a batsman and base runner.

Kelley is of heroic build and figure and a man of great nerve and strength. He held his own at the top of the National League for many years.

He was with the famous Baltimores through all their successful years.

SHERWOOD N. MAGEE.

Sherwood Magee is one of the veteran players of the National League and has been for years noted as a real slugging batsman. He plays left field for the Philadelphia Nationals. In 1910, up to September 5, Magee was right close to the top as a batsman.

Kelley commenced his baseball career as a pitcher for the Lowell, Mass., Club and did so well for that team that in 1891 he was given a trial by the Boston National League team.

Lacking steadiness he was released and he went to Omaha, where he gained such an excellent reputation that in 1892 he was signed by Pittsburg. The same year he was transferred to Baltimore, where he immediately rounded into championship form, and he remained with the Baltimore team until 1901 when he joined Brooklyn. In 1902 he returned to Baltimore, but in 1903, 1904 and 1905 he went to Cincinnati, where during those three seasons he managed the Cincinnati National League Club. In 1906 Ned Hanlon took Kelley's place as manager of the Cincinnati team, but Kelley remained with it that season as a player. In 1907 he managed the Toronto, Canada, Club and the next season Kelley returned to his first love, Boston.

WILLIAM LANG—Bill Lang, when he was with the Chicago Nationals a few seasons ago, was a fine batter, a fine fielder and a fine base runner.

Lang was head and shoulders above the general run of ball players.

He was so good a player that it was a pity that professional baseball had to lose him. He married a California girl, went into business out there, and has not played ball since. He, too, was in his prime as a player when he stepped down and out.

Lang was of gigantic size—one of the tallest and biggest men that ever wore a uniform. And he was as fast as a feather weight and led the old National League in stealing bases for at least two seasons. What other man of such tremendous bulk ever ran bases like a whirlwind?

Lang was a splendid batsman, a free, natural hitter, able to place the drives and to take extra bases on them, as Ty Cobb does now. He was a great thrower, true and accurate, and a superb outfielder, as Cobb is to-day. The best description of Lang would probably be this: Ty Cobb enlarged fully as great in speed, batting skill and base running and a much heavier man.

Besides all these things, Lang could pitch, catch, play any position of the infield and do all those things well, while Cobb can't? Why, then, was Lang not a better player than Cobb? Those who remember him best are of that opinion anyway.

Lang was one of the last individual idols—the players who had an immense personal following, a throng of admirers who went to the game to see Bill Lang, not to see his team. Now-a-days most of the baseball fans go to see the great work of some baseball machine—then they went to look at Rusie pitch or Ewing catch, or Lang run bases.

Lang had an ever-present and contagious smile and was an incessant practical joker—one of the little squad who made Anson's life a burden during his final baseball years.

He was a humorist and a josher, and also the greatest masher that ever trod State street or Broadway. Whenever Lang arrived in any city on the circuit a pile of tinted notes, sweet scented, were waiting on the desk at the hotel—and Bill never slighted one of them.

As is often the case with big fellows who are comedians and apparently care for nothing but foolishness, Bill Lange had the best and kindest heart any one could desire. A little sample is recalled as follows: Long after Lang left the diamond, the father of a Chicago friend died in San Francisco. Lang figured that the Chicagoan could not get in San Francisco in time for the funeral. He went out, bought a superb floral offering, attached his friends card to the flowers and sent them to the obsequies, taking no credit to himself, but giving the impression that the offering had in very truth been made by the son 2,000 miles away.

Bill Lang had many great afternoons when he roused the fans to frantic uproar. Perhaps the most thrilling of them all was one day when the Boston and Chicago teams went into extra innings. In the thirteenth Boston crowded the bases. Two were out, the sacks were filled. The next batter smashed the ball with tremendous power, and it went blazing, bent for the outer wall. Lang tore after it and charged down the full length of the field. He neared the fence. He crashed into it, but the ball was in his hands, not two inches before he reached the barrier.

With the score tied, Lang came up. Two out, none on. One gigantic biff and the ball went down through center while Lang, running like a maddened wolf, cleared the bases and slid home, just as the catcher reached up for the relay throw. There have been many individual feats in baseball, but such a combination of deeds in one inning has been but seldom known.

Lang turned squarely about when at the zenith of his career, he married a little California girl, who objected to his playing ball, quit the game, became a wealthy real estate dealer, and is now a big man in San Francisco. He ought to be for there are few like him, and his equal, all in all, may never wear the big league uniform again.

L. LELIVELT—L. Lelivelt is the left fielder of the Washington Club in the American League. He has been playing big league baseball for three years and is gradually developing into a most valuable man to the Washington outfit. He is a steady, hard hitting batsman, and an accurate thrower. In August, 1910, Mr. Lelivelt was clouting the leather to the tune of .263.

ANDY LEONARD—Andy Leonard, who was the left fielder of the famous Cincinnati Red Stockings, was playing the position years afterwards with the best teams in the National League. He was a member of the Boston Champion League team in six of its victorious campaigns, playing at left field and occasionally at short. He was a remarkably speedy player and one of the heavest batsmen of his time.

DUFFY LEWIS—Duffy Lewis, the left fielder of the Boston American League team, performed well during 1910, his initial season in the big league. Lewis came from Cincinnati to the Boston team last Spring and has made good with that team not only as a fielder but as a batsman.

The Boston Americans promise to show in Duffy Lewis, their California outfielder, a worthy companion to Tris Speaker, Lewis has done some wonderful stunts in the fielding line since he joined the club.

248

B. LORD—B. Lord is one of the mainstays of Connie Mack's great hard-hitting outfield. Briscoe with Rube Oldring and Murphy have been batting in a great majority of the Athletics' runs of the 1910 season. Lord is a big fellow, fast as lightning on the bases and a very fair rungetter. In August, 1910, he had scored forty-nine runs and was batting .253.

Before joining the Athletics he played with Cleveland.

SHERWOOD A. MAGEE—Sherwood A. Magee, the left fielder of the Philadelphia Club of the National League, is to-day considered one of the best outfielders and batters in the business.

He is a fine, all-around player, for besides being a fine fielder, he is one of the best batsmen in the business.

Magee was born at Clarendon, Pa., August 6, 1884. He played in Allentown in 1903, finishing the season with Mt. Carmel. In 1904 he played with the Lindnor Club of Carlisle, Pa., and was then secured for the Philadelphia Club. He has proved a success from the start and has been a member of the Philadelphias since.

MATTHEW M. McINTYRE—Matthew M. McIntyre, left fielder of the Detroits of 1909, is 29, and was born in Stonington, Conn., though he learned his baseball in Staten Island, N. Y. He played with Augusta, Me., in 1901, and was drafted by the Philadelphia Athletics, who released him to Newark. Later he was traded to Buffalo. Detroit bought him in the Fall of 1904. Matty is five feet ten and one-half inches tall and tips the scale around 170 pounds. He throws and bats left-handed and is one of the best fielders, throwers and batsmen in the business.

McIntyre is a neat and artistic hitter, not landing as frequently as Cobb, but having much of the same versatility in the alternation of long drives and short singles. He is a good base runner. But his legs are none too strong, and he does not show the lightning nerve and daring slides of Cobb.

RUSS McKELVEY—Russ McKelvey was the left fielder of the Indianapolis team in 1878. A fine fielder and batsman was McKelvey.

JOSEPH MOWREY—Joseph Mowrey will line up as one of the young men who will endeavor to win a steady position in the New York Highlanders' outfield in the Spring of 1911. Mowrey is a native of St. Louis and has been playing baseball in the Texas League for four seasons past, the majority of the time with the Houston Champions of that league. During the season of 1909-1910 Mowrey easily won the reputation as being the most capable outfielder in the Lone Star State. He is small of build, is fast on his feet and was the leading batsman of the league up to the late Fall of 1910.

TIM MURNANE—Tim Murnane, now one of the best known baseball writers in America, was one of the great fielders in the late seventies.

In 1871 he played on the Champion Boston Club twenty-one games at center and sixteen at left field. He was a fine fielder and a heavy hitting left-handed batsman.

In the early eighties Murnane was a very lively man on the bases and it was worth while to go to the games to see him get around.

Murnane, always the player's friend and always one of the best of good fellows, helped form the Union Association in 1884 and the Brotherhood of Baseball Players which followed a few years later.

He was the manager of the Boston Unions in 1884 and when they came here that year with Bond and Brown as their battery Murnane played an excellent game at first for them.

That was about the close of his career as a player, he devoting his time afterwards to the writing up of the game.

In the 1884 season Murnane showed the ability that was in him, as well as his loyalty to the professional players by organizing the team that represented Boston in the Union Association that year and preserving it intact through the full playing season.

It was a team picked up mostly on the commons near Boston and as near as I can remember the Boston Union team which Murnane brought into the old Union Grounds at Jefferson and Cass avenues in St. Louis in the Fall of 1884 included Tommy Bond and Ed Crane, pitchers; Lou Brown and Walter Hackett, catchers; Murnane, first base and captain and manager; J. O'Brien, second base; W. Riley, third base; W. Hackett, short-stop when he was not catching; Crane, left field when not pitching; Mike Slattery, center field; right field, C. Daniels.

Like Murnane, this 1884 year was nearly the last in the big league of Bond, who had been one of the great pitchers and of Brown, who had been in his day one of the famous receivers.

But the same year marked the coming out of Crane and Hackett, who subsequently ranked high in the National League ranks.

Murnane not only captained and managed and played at first base for the Boston Unions, but he led off in the batting list and the way he clouted the ball to right field was a caution.

He was a left-handed batsman of the best sort and in his day could send the ball as high and far to right field as the next.

But Murnane, besides being a great player and organizer in his day, has been one of the game's greatest and best friends, his entertaining baseball articles in the Boston Globe and his letters to the various sporting papers for which he corresponded winning many converts to the game and helping widen its areas in every direction. He also gave many of the famous players their first real start and among his best discoveries were such later great players as Hugh Duffy, Ned Crane, Charley Buffinton, Martin Sullivan, Tom McCarthy, Charley Farrell, Mike Slattery, Walter Hackett, John Irwin and many others.

For many years Mr. Murnane has been the president of the New England League, and he has done more to build up baseball in that section than any other man.

DAN O'LEARY—Dan O'Leary in the late seventies and through the eighties was one of the great players and characters then connected with the National game. Next to Mike Kelly in those days O'Leary was most in the limelight. He was one of the great players who had the courage to join in the Union Association movement of 1884, and he was the manager, captain and left fielder of the Cincinnati member of that organization. Sam

249

Crane, now one of the best known baseball writers in New York, played at second base on Cincinnati Unions with O'Leary and he tells this good story on Dan:

'Dan O'Leary was one of the many unique characters that figured in baseball some twenty-five years ago. He was a player and also a manager, but his managerial efforts were mostly confined to independent clubs, where he had the opportunity to perform many freak acts, that would have hardly passed in organized baseball, but which were to his natural bent.

"In 1886, O'Leary had taken up baseball in Scranton, Pa., as a venture, and, as usual, Dan had entered into the speculation on a shoestring. In those days Daniel was not blessed with any surplus coin, as he has been lately.

"O'Leary, several years previous to his Scranton venture, had undertaken the precarious job of handling a team made up of players, who afterwards starred with the Old Mets of New York. "Dump lots," most of them, but all could play ball like chained lightning. Dan still had a liking for his "grass-eaters" and the latter dearly loved their old manager, for O'Leary was never guilty of making any rules of conduct or habits. They, therefore, gladly flocked to the O'Leary standard when the Scranton proposition was unfolded to them.

"There may not be much money in it," said Dan to "Dasher" Troy, "Paddy" Callahan, "Billy" Taylor and others of his henchmen, "and again there might. If we make any coin you will get three squares a day and scuttles of suds, enough every night to float a ship, besides your salaries. No mon—no eats; no mon—no beer. But I think we can cop."

"So Dan started at Scranton, and completed arrangements sent for his players and started proceedings. Scranton was in those days perfectly satisfied with any old ball team, if it could could only beat Wilkesbarre, and as Dan and his crew were lucky enough to do that right off the reel, and three straight, they became popular favorites in the jump.

"The club made money and rolled in wealth, and luxury, or what they considered those necessary ingredients to happiness three squares and plenty of 'high ones.'

"There was a team playing in Williamsport at that time that had beaten every club they had met that season, and were anxious to meet the Scrantons, also an undefeated team. The game was arranged to be played in Scranton and many Williamsport sports acompanied their teams. The Williamsport boys had a day or two previously beaten the Athletics of Philadelphia, and their backers were feeling very cocky in consequence and imagined their team invincible.

"They came to Scranton with big wads of money and as a feeler offered to bet at odds of 100 to 80 on their pets. Not much Scranton money materializing at these figures, the odds gradually increased to 100 to 70. O'Leary laid low, it was pay day for his players and he had $3,700 tucked away in a saloon safe with which to pay his men their monthly stipends. But Dan didn't hesitate a minute when those odds were named—the whole amount went down on his team. Not satisfied with getting that amount down, for he never was a piker, Dan went to the saloon proprietor,

who owned the place where his players hung out, and mortgaged his share of the afternoon's gate receipts for $800, which he also bet on his team.

"The night before the game, Dan had, by offering to buy everything the saloon proprietor had in his place the next night, induced him to close his place and a meeting of the players was called by O'Leary. The manager had prepared himself by having a full stock of drinkables in his own room, and he kept his players under his own eye, until every saloon in town was locked up for the night.

"Next day the players heard about the heavy betting their manager had done and were suspicious that it was the pay money. "'Isn't this pay day?' they asked Dan.

"'Maybe,' Dan replied, and then he told them how he had placed the money.

"Well, talk about ball playing, why, those 'dump rats' went at the Williamsport fellows like playing fiends and made nine runs the first inning. The full score was something like twenty to six.

"Did the 'Dan O'Leary's' get the eats and drinks that night? Did they not? The manager set up the wine by the case; champagne, too."

Dan O'Leary is now living in Chicago and is known best there now in theatrical circles as the leading "first nighter."

He is one of the most enthusiastic baseball fans in Chicago, and rarely misses a game.

Not since 1879—and that's a long time ago—has a ball player repeated the great trick made by Dan O'Leary, now a popular clubman in Chicago, and in those days a player of considerable skill. Dan was with the old Indianapolis team, and was having an awful batting slump. In some twenty games poor Dan landed nothing that resembled a base hit, and he was fairly furious at his own ill luck and the joshings of his friends. Finally, at a critical moment of a desperate game, Dan leaned upon a fast ball and whooped for joy as the ball went shrieking down the field. Round the bases loped the delighted slugger, while the fielders madly pursued the leather. On and on he went, and at last, in one great slide and a storm of dust, Dan burst across the plate—only to be informed that he was out. He had run the wrong way, going to third instead of first and circling the bases in reverse order. Dan was so badly broken up over the affair that he gave up the game.

TIP O'NEILL—When the St. Louis Browns were winning American Association and World's pennants, there was one man on the team who was always doing more than his share of the hitting.

That man was J. E. O'Neill, or Tip O'Neill, as he was then called.

He was the fine, stalwart fellow who covered left field for the Browns in the halcyon days of that St. Louis team.

In 1887 O'Neill had a batting average of .492, a record that has never been excelled before or since. This proves the kind of a batsman he was.

All pitchers looked alike to him and when he faced the speedy pitchers of the National League in the World's Series he hit them as hard as he had hit the pitchers of the American Association.

O'Neill, besides being a star batsman, was an excellent fielder.

He was engaged originally for the Browns as a pitcher, but when his arm gave out Comiskey, wanting to retain his

CURTIS WELCH.
The once famous and world-beater ce nterfielder of the four-time winner St.
Louis Browns.

batting strength, sent him to the field and kept him there.

O'Neill was the leading batsman of the American Association in 1887 and in 1888, and was fourth in 1889 with .337, Tom Tucker of the Baltimore Club ranking first that season, with Milligan of the Athletics second with .370 and Stovey fourth with .330.

O'Neill is a Canadian and after retiring from the game went into the saloon business at Montreal, where he lives at the present writing.

While a member of the St. Louis Club, O'Neill was most popular and by his gentlemanly and pleasant demeanor won a host of friends and he was perhaps the most popular player with the local public ever known.

JAMES O'ROURKE — James H. O'Rourke, known in those days as "Jim" O'Rourke and "The Orator," was the leading left fielder of the National League in its 1888 season.

O'Rourke was playing ball in the 1909 year. He first played with the Unions of Bridgeport, Conn., in 1867. So for forty-two years he has been on the diamond.

O'Rourke was born in Bridgeport, August 4, 1854. So he was playing ball professionally in his fifty-fifth year.

In his life on the diamond O'Rourke won the respect of not only his fellow players but of baseball patrons the country over for besides being a player of the first class he was always a thorough gentleman.

When not engaged during the playing season O'Rourke put in his time studying law and in the teams he played he was generally the big brother and adviser of his fellow players.

To them he was always a kindly, gentle spirit in whom they placed all confidence His word was his bond and he never descended to a mean or contemptible action either on the field or off it.

O'Rourke started off as a catcher, pitcher and all-around man with the Unions of Bridgeport in 1867. He played so well with them that four years later he won a place with the Orioles of Hartford, Conn. In 1872 he quit the Hartfords to join the famous Mansfields of Middleton, Conn., a team which then had in its ranks John Clapp and Tim Murnane, two players of later world wide reputation.

From the Mansfields' O'Rourke went to the great Boston Redstocking team and he remained with them from 1875 to 1878. In their 1874 season O'Rourke made the memorable trip to Europe with the Bostons.

In 1879 O'Rourke went to Providence with George Wright and helped to land the pennant. The next season saw him back in Boston again. In 1881 and 1884 he captained and played with Buffalo and from 1885 to 1889 he was with the New Yorks, who won the pennant in 1888 and 1889. He was identified with the Players' League team of New York, in 1890, but was back again with the New York Giants in 1891 and 1892, and in 1893 he ended his career with the major league team in Washington. He tried his hand at umpiring in 1894, but did not find that occupation congenial and he finished the season with the St. Josephs at Bridgeport. In 1895 he managed the Victors of Bridgeport, and in 1896 organized the Naugatuck Valley League, and was manager and captain of the Bridgeport Club.

In 1897 he assisted to organize the Connecticut League and was its first president, secretary and treasurer. He has been secretary of the league ever since its organization.

In 1903 his only son, James H. O'Rourke, Jr., played on his father's team and continued there until the Fall of 1908, when he played with the New York Americans and is now with the Columbus American Association Club. In nine seasons the elder O'Rourke missed very few games in which the Bridgeport club took part. It is estimated that he has played in 1950 National and Players' League games, and in over 900 Connecticut League contests.

O'Rourke is not only a baseball magnate and manager, but a member of the National Board of Arbitration. He is also a practising attorney. The esteem in which he is held in Bridgeport is shown by the fact that he has served on the Board of Public Works and on the Board of Fire Commissioners. He is a prominent member of the Elks, the Royal Arcanum and the Knights of Columbus.

In his day Jim O'Rourke was one of the grandest batsmen and fielders in the major organization. He could fill almost any position on the team and fill it well. He was often known to pitch, to catch and to play on the bases or in the field, all in the same day. But while he was great all around his pet position was that in the field where, in the year named, he excelled all others.

ROY RALSTON—Doctor Roy Ralston, outfielder from Akron, Ohio, in the O. & P. League, was purchased by James J. McAlester, manager of the Washington Club in the Fall of 1910 for the reported price of $3,500. Ralston is rated as a wonder in all departments, and was earnestly sought by several other major league clubs. Detroit, for one, was after him in a hurry and Bill Donovan looked him over. Donovan recommended him highly but while Jennings was hesitating McAleer's offer was accepted and as a result he owns the promising youngster.

JAMES SHECKARD—James Sheckard, the greatest of latter day fielders, is the veteran left fielder of the world's renowned Chicago Cubs of the National League, the team which has been leading the other clubs in the league a merry chase during the entire season of 1910. Sheckard up to August 15, 1910, had performed in over 100 games and as usual, he ranked high with the stick and his fielding was brilliant in the extreme. Sheckard has been drawing big pay in the National League for a dozen years. He first came into notice while a member of the Baltimore and later the Brooklyn Club. Several years ago when Charles Murphy assumed command of the Chicago Cubs, Sheckard was secured from Brooklyn in exchange for four players. At the time Brooklyn was not playing good ball and many said the playing days of Sir Jimmy were over. He came back grandly during his first year with the Cubs, and in the World's Championships of 1906, 1907 and 1908, his playing was one of the distinct features of the shows.

GEORGE STONE—George Stone, the modest and unassuming left fielder of the St. Louis Browns, is one of the greatest batsmen in the business.

George's failure to reach the .300 mark last season can be assigned to his sickness, which no doubt prevented him from going at his true gait.

GEORGE STONE.

Mr. George Stone has been one of the steady outfielders of the St. Louis Browns. Stone is always high up in the averages with the stick, is a good base runner and is popular with the fans all over the cir cuit.

THE NATIONAL GAME.

Nevertheless, in all fairness to the great player, it must be said that few, if any satellite in the American League has anything on "Silent George" when it comes to bringing in the results.

He is ever willing to do his share of the work, be it ever so hard. He is known never to complain, and for that reason it has made him one of the most popular players that ever wore a St. Louis baseball uniform.

Should Stone regain his 1907 batting eye he will certainly be seen flirting with the leaders throughout the season.

GEORGE TEBEAU—George Tebeau, who played in the field for the old Cleveland, Cincinnati and other major league clubs, is today one of the wealthiest and most influential men connected with the National game.

At one time Mr. Tebeau was charged with running syndicate baseball, it being alleged that he owned the Denver, Kansas City and Louisville Clubs.

Today, however, it is generally admitted that Mr. Tebeau controls only one club in the American Association—the Kansas City.

George Tebeau is sure enough a self-made man.

He began his baseball career on the lots in North St. Louis where the Water Tower stands now.

He first gained prominence locally when he played with the Shamrocks of North St. Louis in 1885. While with them he proved himself a great all around player, filling all the positions on the team, pitching when a pitcher was needed and catching when the regular receiver was down and out, but his home position was left field. He was so alert and plucky in his work that in 1886 he received a call from Denver and he did so well out West that Denver clung to him for seven years.

In 1903 his fame as a player spread and he came into major league company playing in turn with the Cincinnati, Columbus, Grand Rapids and Cleveland Clubs.

In the three last named organizations he was associated with Loftus and from the latter Tebeau perhaps learned those rudiments of the game that in later years made him the most successful and wealthy of minor league managers.

Tebeau, although a most aggressive and pushing player and manager, had many fine traits, his reputation for honesty and square dealing being always above par.

Tebeau comes of a family of ball players in St. Louis, his brother, Oliver (Pat) Tebeau, being famous as the third baseman of the great Cleveland Club.

Tebeau, who played right field under his brother Pat at Cleveland some fifteen years ago and who was much pleased with his $1,200 salary, is rated a millionaire.

Tebeau earned a little money out of the old Western League and is getting good money, out of the American Association. Two years ago he ran three clubs. First of all he sold Denver. Last August he disposed of Louisville for $100,000. He can get $175,000 for his Kansas City Club, it is said. Incidentally he will probably make $60,000 out of the latter club this year, as he evidently has an improved team, and Kansas City, just like every other town in the land, is baseball enthusiastic, and anything like a winning article will get the fans out in force.

Some seven or eight years ago Tebeau leased a hole in the ground, a poor bit

of real estate, for an annual rental of $900. He likewise got an option to purchase it for $65,000 at any time during a period of ten years. Now Kansas City is going to have its new railroad station. Tebeau's ball park is so located that it must be grabbed up. The railway people have kept on increasing their bid until now there is a chance of Tebeau getting a million or so out of the ground and he deserves every penny he can get.

GEORGE E. VAN HALTREN—One of the greatest batsmen and left fielders that ever lived who has just rounded out his baseball career as an umpire out in California, is George Van Haltren. He started the career, which was crowned with glory, with the old Greenhood and Morans, a kind of semi-professional (if the term may be used) team, which played a couple of games a week. He was a pitcher and as good left-handed twirlers were scarce in those days, he soon attracted attention of the Eastern magnates, and in 1884 he signed a contract with the famous old Chicago White Stockings, then under the leadership of the peerless "Captain" Anson.

His control was lacking, however, and he was forced to give up pitching. He was given a trial in the outfield and "made good" from the jump; and old-time fans in cities where big leaguers were wont to romp, will recall the brilliant work of the famous Giant.

Van Haltren played with Brooklyn and with Pittsburg, with Baltimore and with New York. It was with the latter club that he achieved what is probably his best record. Gotham devotees of the sport will remember distinctly the old war horse, for he played for ten consecutive seasons in the Eastern metropolis, starting in 1894, and leaving in 1904.

It was in 1903, while sliding to second I believe, that Van Haltren sustained a broken ankle which eventually caused his retirement from the ranks of the "big ones." He could probably have stayed another year or two with the majors, but he thought best to accept the flattering offer to captain the Seattle team, then in the Pacific Coast League but now in the Territory of the Northwestern.

Van Haltren batted over .300 for over twelve years, all told, and one year—the fourth—spoiled the continuity by a drop of four points below the standard. Mr. Van Haltren's major league service extended over some seventeen years. He began with Pittsburg and Chicago in 1887, starting out at a .278 clip in 1887 and reaching .283 the next season. In 1889 he batted .322, .346 in 1890, .336 in 1891, .296 in 1892, .350 in 1893, .333 in 1894, .338 in 1895, .353 in 1896, .332 in 1897, .315 in 1898, .301 in 1901. The next year he dropped to .250, which he raised to .257 in 1903, when an injury to his leg terminated his big league career.

ZACH DAVID WHEAT—There are two real Indians playing in the National League. One of them is Chief Meyers, the stalwart catcher of the New York Giants and the other Zack David Wheat, the fine left fielder of the Brooklyn Club in this 1910 year.

Wheat, who was born at Hamilton, Mo., had a full blooded member of the Cherokee Indian tribe for a mother. Mrs. Wheat is an enthusiastic reader of baseball and takes a great interest in her son's career. During the winter Zack lives on a farm near Kansas City.

254

GEORGE SHAFFER.

George Shaffer, when he played with the St. Louis Unions, was considered the fastest right fielder in America.

Wheat is making a great hit with the Brooklyn fans this season. Zack broke into professional baseball with the Shreveport Club, then a member of the Texas League. He was less than 20 years old. After leaving the Kansas City high school, Wheat began playing independent ball with the Enterprise team. He was recommended to Shreveport and says at that time he was about the worst fielder that ever played the game.

He was playing first base with the Enterprise team, but was like a wooden man on a ground ball, and his efforts to catch a fly ball were awful and frequently resulted in failure. About all he could do was to catch a thrown ball, but even then it was not always a sure thing that he would hold it. However, there was one department in the game in which he did excel and that was hitting.

He played a few games at first base, but his manager took him quietly to one side one day and told him that he never would make a first baseman if he lived a century. During the summer of 1908 Wheat had his left arm broken by a pitched ball and was out of the game for a month, the greater part of which time he passed on the bench watching the game. He had been playing right field. Along about August, 1908, Shreveport had need of a twirler and put through a deal with the Mobile Club whereby it secured a cash consideration and a pitcher for Wheat and he finished the season of 1908 with the Southern team.

Wheat played strong baseball for Mobile in 1909 and his work attracted the attention of the Brooklyn Club scouts. He was secured and reported to Brooklyn in the Fall of 1909 and he started out and held his own with them during the 1910 season. He at once showed in the limelight by his splendid work with the stick.

HARRY WHEELER—Harry Wheeler, who played professional baseball for Providence in 1878, was with the Cincinnati Champion Association team in 1882 and later he played at left for the St. Louis Browns in the American Association.

WALTER WILMOT — Walter Wilmot was at one time one of the greatest left fielders in the National League.

Ted Sullivan, then managing the Washington Club, introduced Wilmot to major league company.

That was in 1888. Wilmot was the equal of the best of outfielders for many years in the league, batting and base running being his strong points. In fact, those two men, Hoy in center and Wilmot in left, set the pace for the rest in 1888. Wilmot was sold years after by Washington to Chicago, and he played with Anson's team for several years. Sullivan took Wilmot from the St. Paul team of the old Western League.

THOMAS YORK—Thomas York was the left fielder of the Champion Providence Club of 1879, the Providence outfield of that year including York at left, Paul Hines at center and Jim O'Rourke, perhaps the greatest fielding and hitting combination ever together in one outfield. York besides being a fine fielder was a hard hitting left-handed batsman.

THE NATIONAL GAME.

THE CENTER FIELDERS.

IN THE OLD PROFESSIONAL ASSOCIATION AND THE NATIONAL LEAGUE
PAUL HINES PERHAPS EXCELLED ALL OTHER PLAYERS IN
THIS POSITION.

This is a record of those who led in the position of center field in the old Professional Association and then the National League:

Year. Center Fielders. Club.	Fielding Games.	Pct.	Year. Center Fielders. Club.	Fielding Games.	Pct.
1871 Mart King—Chicago	18	.911	1891 W. S. Brodie—Boston	134	.963
1872 David Eggler—Mutuals, N. Y.	29	.943	1892 M. Griffin—Brooklyn	121	.969
1873 A. J. Reach, Athletics, Phila.	13	.943	1893 M. Griffin—Brooklyn	93	.960
1874 Paul Hines—Chicago	59	.935	1894 M. Griffin—Brooklyn	106	.963
1875 Jas. O'Rourke—Boston	69	.933	1895 M. Griffin—Brooklyn	131	.972
1876 Paul Hines—Chicago	64	.917	1896 W. S. Brodie—Baltimore	132	.971
1877 John Remsen—St. Louis	29	.902	1897 W. S. Brodie—Pittsburg	100	.983
1878 John Remsen—Chicago	55	.934	1898 M. Griffin—Brooklyn	134	.979
1879 David Eggler—Buffalo	77	.918	1899 W. S. Brodie—Baltimore	138	.982
1880 Paul Hines—Providence	73	.925	1900 Roy Thomas—Philadelphia	139	.966
1881 P. Gillespie—Troy	83	.932	1901 Roy Thomas—Philadelphia	128	.973
1882 Geo. A. Wood—Detroit	81	.891	1902 C. Beaumont—Pittsburg	131	.972
1883 Paul Hines—Providence	98	.913	1903 John Dobbs—Chic. & Bkln	126	.970
1884 Paul Hines—Providence	107	.895	1904 Roy Thomas—Philadelphia	139	.974
1885 Jas. O'Rourke—New York	112	.939	1905 Roy Thomas—Philadelphia	147	.983
1886 D. Richardson—New York	58	.951	1906 Roy Thomas—Philadelphia	142	.986
1887 P. Gillespie—New York	74	.946	1907 Roy Thomas—Philadelphia	121	.980
1888 Wm. Sunday—Pittsburg	119	.938	1908 J. F. Slagle—Chicago	75	.981
1889 Jas. Fogarty—Philadelphia	128	.960	1909 E. T. Oakes—Cincinnati	112	.979
1890 J. W. Holliday—Cincinnati	131	.948	1910 Artie Hofman—Chicago	110	.975

AMERICAN LEAGUE RECORD.

THIS IS A LIST OF THE CHAMPION CENTER FIELDERS OF THE AMERICAN LEAGUE SINCE THE FIRST SEASON OF THAT ORGANIZATION.

Sullivan of the Bostons was the only man to lead at center field for more than one season in the American League. The leading center fielders in that baseball body since 1900 were:

Year. Center Fielders. Club.	Fielding Games.	Pct.	Year. Center Fielders. Club.	Games.	Pct. Fielding
1900 W. E. Hoy—Chicago	137	.976	1905 Charles Stahl—Boston	134	.977
1901 J. Jackson—Baltimore	97	.967	1906 Fielder Jones—Chicago	144	.988
1902 Fielder Jones—Chicago	135	.980	1907 D. Sullivan—Boston	143	.975
1903 Fielder Jones—Chicago	137	.988	1908 D. Sullivan—Boston, Cleveland	99	.982
1904 H. Bay—Cleveland	132	.990	1909 Tris Speaker—Boston	142	.973
			1910 Oldring—Philadelphia	134	.978

In 1871, the first year of the National League, Martin King of the original Chi-White Stockings, led the country as a center fielder.

In those days the lively ball, the slow underhand pitching and the heavy hitting which followed, made things very lively and unpleasant for the outfielders.

So a man to hold his own out there had to be a speedy runner and a sure catcher.

Mart King and Eddie Cuthbert alternated at center field for the first Chicago team.

They were both great players, but Cuthber was the fastest of the two.

King was a giant in build, with massive shoulders and gnarled fingers. When not playing in the outfield he would go behind the bat and he handled the speediest pitching with the greatest of ease and without the aid of mask, gloves or chest protector.

King came from the famous Haymaker team of Troy, N. Y., the nine from which graduated McAtee, Steve King and Clipper Flynn.

This Haymaker team played its first game with each and every player on the team appearing in bare head and bare feet.

When Jimmy Wood of the Eckfords of Brooklyn set out to pick a team for Chicago that would surely defeat the invincible Red Stockings, he went to Troy and there picked up Mart King to play behind

the bat and in the field, McAtee as his first baseman and Clipper Flynn as his right fielder.

That Wood made no mistake was proven later when the Chicago White Stockings beat the hitherto invincible Cincinnati Reds twice hand running.

King was a giant in these games. His fielding and hitting were a feature of them.

David Eggler followed King as the champion center fielder of his day. He was with the Mutuals of New York when he captured the leading honor. A man below the medium height was Eggler, with a slender frame and a Punch and Judy face. He was a fine fielder.

After Eggler at the top came A. J. Reach, who, in 1873, played at center in only thirteen games for the Athletics of Philadelphia, his regular position being at second base.

After Reach at the top of the list came Paul Hines, who, in this 1874 year, was playing at second for the Chicagos.

Hines was at the top of the ladder off and on for many years.

In 1877 and 1878 John Remsen of St. Louis and New York were the leaders. When Remsen first appeared in the field it was with long beard and these whiskers attracted considerable attention in later years when professionals made it a practice to appear on the field with clean shaven faces. But Remsen, besides the whiskers, was a player of the first class.

P. Gillespie, then of Troy, was the leader in 1881. We have referred to him in sizing up the left fielders, where he played in later years. He led at center in 1881 and in 1887.

George A. Wood, while with the Detroit Champions, was the leader in the 1882 year. But the greatest center fielder of them all the five years following was Curt Welch of St. Louis.

William Sunday led the center fielders in 1888. I shall place him with the right fielders for that was where he shone the brightest in the heydey of his power.

James Fogarty was the leader in 1898. I have referred to him in my recapitulation of the left fielders.

In 1890 J. W. Holliday of the Cincinnati Club, was the leader. "Bug" Holliday, the name by which he was best known, was a St. Louis boy. He played on St. Louis and Western League teams before joining Cincinnati. He was a fine, rapid fielder, a splendid base runner and a useful batsman.

After Holliday came Brodie of Brooklyn, a fine fielder and base runner. He was at the top in 1890, 1896, 1897 and 1899.

Cotemporaneous with Brodie was George Gore, who played a great game at center for the Chicago and New York Champion teams. Gore was a fine fielder and base runner and a heavy hitting left-handed batsman.

With Dalrymple and Mike Kelly, he once formed the famous Chicago out-field and later he was part of the great New York field, which was made up of three of the greatest batsmen in the business, Jim O'Rourke, Mike Tiernan and George Gore.

Edward Hanlon, the center fielder of the Champion Detroit team in 1887, was one of the famous center fielders of his day. Besides being a great fielder, Hanlon was a hard hitting, left-handed batsman. I have more to say of h.m in my recapitulation of the managers.

John S. Corkhill of the Cincinnati and Brooklyn teams, was one of the best center fielders of the late eighties and the early nineties. He played fine ball in the field for both these teams and was an effective batsman.

"Ginger" Clarence H. Beaumont, center fielder of the Boston National League team, until he joined the Cubs, in 1910, had played the game for several years. It was only advancing age which showed him up a bit, but since being a member of the great Chicago Cubs, who copped the big prize in the National League in the season of 1910, the old boy has again exhibited signs of coming back. He was at his best while playing center field for the Pittsburg champion team of 1902. He for years was regarded as one of the heaviest hitting outfielders in the business.

W. E. Hoy was the leader at center field in the American League in 1900 the first year of that organization.

Hoy had previously played great ball in the field for the Cincinnati and other National League teams.

"Dummy" Hoy, he was called for the reason that he is a deaf mute.

A fine left-handed batsman, fielder and base-runner is Hoy.

J. Jackson of Baltimore and H. Bay of Cleveland, led the American League, respectively, in 1901 and 1904.

Bay was a clever player in his day. He is now a member of the Nashville, Tenn. Club of the Southern League. He was born at Pontiac, Ill., Jan. 17, 1878, and learned to play ball on the lots of Peoria and the next year was with Lincoln, Ill. In 1899 he was with the Rock Island, Ill. Club, and finished with Troy, N. Y. In 1900 he played with the Detroit, Elmira and Youngstown, O. Clubs. In 1891 he played such good ball with Indianapolis that he was transferred to Cincinnati. He did not bat well enough to hold on to his place in Cincinnati, and so went back to Indianapolis. He received another trial from Cincinnati in 1903, and was then released, unconditionally. He then went to Cleveland and remained there until the season of 1908. He was unable to play much in the season of 1907 with Cleveland, owing to a lame knee. He batted for .296 with Nashville last season and fielded for .956, having fifteen assists.

This brings me up to the center fielders of the past decade. Below, in alphabetical order, is given a list of the players, who in their day played center field for the clubs of the old Professional Association, the American League and all other Major League organizations, since 1871:

ROLAND BARROWS—Roland Barrows, the new center fielder of the Chicago Americans, was born in Raymond, Me., October 2, 1886, and started in playing baseball with the Gray High School team, Gray, Me., from 1903 to 1905. In 1905 he finished the season with the Pine Trees of Portland, under "Pop" Williams, Harry Lord of the Boston Americans being third baseman, and in 1906 played left field and pitcher for the Biddeford, (Me.) Independent Club. In 1907 he was centerfielder for the Portland Club of the Maine State League, and was then secured by Jimmy Canavan for the New Bedford Club, where he also played in 1909, whence he was bought by the Chicago Club. He stands five feet, eight and a half inches and weighs 155 pounds.

JOHN BATES—Johnny Bates is the fast hard hitting and great throwing centerfielder of the Philadelphia National League Club. Bates has been playing in the big league for three seasons. He began with Boston in the Spring of 1908 and made good from the outset. He maintained his excellent reputation as a slugger during the past season and was batting at a .277 rate in the Fall of 1910.

CLARENCE BEAUMONT — Clarence Beaumont is one of the old timers in the National League who seems to be able to hold his own regardless of the fact that there are coming into the league each season hundreds of enthusiastic youngsters who are anxious to take the places of the veterans. Beaumont for many years was one of the star members of the Pittsburg Club. He was always regarded as one of the leading sluggers in the league, and even to this day while acting as the general utility and pinch hitter of the great Chicago Cubs he continues to uphold his great reputation as a terrific batsman. Beaumont up to August, 1910, participated in forty-two games mostly of course as a pinch hitter. During this period he batted in dozens of runs and his record with the stick was .271.

ARTHUR H. BADER—Arthur H. Bader is one of the most promising juveniles playing ball in the Western League to-

ARTHUR HOFMAN.
Arthur, known wherever baseball is played as "Circus Solly," is the center fielder of the Chicago Cubs, Champions of 1910.

day. Bader is a native of St. Louis and a son of Herman Bader, a prominent business man and politician here. Bader, Sr., in his day, was regarded as a grand ball player. He too, like his son, made his initial appearance in the old Western League years ago. Bader, Jr., has been playing professional ball for four years. He was first heard of playing in the Trolley leagues around St. Louis. In 1905 the young man was signed as a second baseman by the Denver Club. He played there during that season and ranked high as a fielder and batsman. In the Spring of 1908 he was sold to Des Moines, (Iowa) team and has been with that club ever since. In 1910 he fielded at a .937 clip and batted .320, practically leading the league with the stick. In 1909 he made up his mind to play in the outfield. The move was a good one and during the 1910 season the St. Louis boy was rated as the leading outfielder, and one of the heaviest batsmen in the league. Bader is 23 years old and is an attorney at law, having been graduated in that profession last Winter. It is almost a certainty that the lad will line up in the American League as a member of Comiskey's White Sox team.

FRED BECK—Fred Beck, the clever young center fielder of the Boston National League, was born at Havana, Ill., in 1888. He started his diamond career with semi-professional teams in his native city.

So classy was his playing that after one year with the independents he was signed by the Bloomington Three-I League late in 1906. In 1907 Bloomington tried to use him as a pitcher, but he had no control, and after a month he was put in the outfield and was a hit from the start, both in fielding and batting.

San Francisco drafted him in 1908, and he made good as an outfielder and first baseman. At the close of the year he was signed by Boston, and 1909 won a regular place as first baseman. He is in the outfield in 1910, and promises to win laurels for himself by his clever fielding and stick work. He still makes his home at Havana, Ill. Up to August, 1910, the big fellow was getting his share of base-hits, his batting average being .288. Beck stands six feet one inch, weighs 180 pounds and is 24 years old.

VINCENT CAMPBELL—One of the young players who have broken into the National League with every promise of staying there, is Vincent Campbell, who is now playing at center field for the Pittsburg club.

His wonderful work in this, his first season in major league company, has surprised the patrons of the game in the Smoky City.

Campbell, whom Fred Clarke of the champion Pittsburg team, bought from Aberdeen of the Northwestern League in 1909, is perhaps the most promising of the whole St. Louis bunch of aspirants. Clarke is reported to have paid $4,000 for Campbell's release. Originally a catcher, Campbell was switched to the outfield in Aberdeen.

Campbell has been up with the big leaguers before. Frank Chance, of the Chicago Cubs, signed Campbell when he finished his schooling at Smith Academy, where he first gained attention as a ball player.

Campbell was taken South with the Cubs in 1908, but with Johnny Kling and Pat Moran as the Cub's catchers, Campbell had little chance of a regular berth. He was transferred to Decatur, of the Three-I League, and later drifted to Aberdeen.

At one time the Cardinals could have gotten Campbell. Manager McCloskey did not want him then. Afterwards, when McCloskey did want him, he couldn't get him. So that's how near Campbell came to being a Cardinal.

Campbell was born in St. Louis in 1888. He is a finely built young fellow, standing six feet, one and one half inches and weighing 180 pounds.

Campbell got his higher education at Vanderbilt University and began playing professional ball at Bartlesville, then in the Oklahoma-Arizona-Kansas League, in 1907. He played with Decatur in 1907, finishing the season with Aberdeen of the Northwestern League. He remained with Aberdeen in 1909 and was secured by Pittsburg at the beginning of the present season.

Campbell has been known to catch a few games, particularly in the early part of his career, though of late years he has been regarded as an outfielder.

Pittsburg has been using him to fill in whenever needed and he has generally distinguished himself by his steady batting and clever fast fielding wherever stationed.

SAMUEL CRAWFORD—Fielder Jones' only real rival in the American League from 1900 forward was Sam Crawford, the big left-handed batsman and center fielder of the Detroit Club.

Crawford, a grim veteran of the game, is much on the old-fashioned style when it comes to batting. He is a long, clean-up hitter of the kind our daddies loved—the Brouthers-Anson pattern—and how that old boy can line them through.

Sam Crawford is about the hardest hitter in the American League. Maybe "Wahoo Sam's" averages have not been as high as a good many sphere maulers after a season's play, but "Wahoo Sam" drives the ball harder than any of them.

His own weakness rests in the fact that he does not run out the little ones the way he might.

Samuel is so used to knocking the cover off the ball that the scratch kind does not appeal to him. This, coupled with the fact that he is the original hard luck batter, keeps him from hitting around the 400 mark.

In a recent game in Detroit Crawford put the ball over center field for a home run. It was the longest hit ever made in Bennett Park.

Crawford was born in Wahoo, Neb., and is in his 29th year. His advent in Tigertown dates back to 1903, and was the result of a baseball war, the player being wooed away from Cincinnati by the offer of a big salary. Prior to this Sam had played with Grand Rapids and Columbus, and in the Canadian League. Sam is 6 feet and 190 pounds heavy. He is the Tigers' leading clean-up hitter, and is regularly among the league leaders in extra-base hits. He hits and throws left-handed.

Crawford can only be regarded as a jumper in its generally accepted baseball sense. He was playing under the usual reserve clause contract with the Cincinnati Club in 1902, when, on the second trip East he yielded to the better salary inducements offered by Detroit and signed with that club for 1903 and 1904. At that time John T. Brush owned the Reds. In a few weeks, however, the club passed into the hands of August Herrmann, who

CHARLES HEMPHILL.
Charles Hemphill is one of the veteran outfielders of the American League.

heard the rumors of Crawford having signed with Detroit—rumors that Crawford denied. Crawford also voluntarily signed a Cincinnati contract for 1903 and even after it was learned definitely that Crawford had signed the Detroit document, he insisted that he intended playing in Cincinnati When the peace agreement was signed, Detroit claimed Crawford on the strength of holding the first signed contract and as Crawford himself elected to play in Detroit, Cincinnati made no effort to hold him. Crawford's work during 1902 was careless, which accounts at least partially for the Reds' lack of interest in his loss.

BERT DANIELS—Bert Daniels who has been holding down center garden for the **New York Highlanders** with such great success is said to be one of the real finds of the season. Daniels was recruited from the ranks of the Eastern League in the Spring of 1910. He is fast on his feet, a beautiful fielder and his throwing was probably the best in the American League. He gives promise of becoming one of the real outfielders in the American League.

L. PHILLIP GEIER—The baseball history of L. Phillip Geier, now manager of the Burlington Club is as follows: Born, November 5, 1865, at Washington, D. C. Began with Norfolk, Va., 1895, with Fall River in 1896, finishing season with Philadelphia; Montreal, 1897; St. Paul, 1898 and 1899; Cincinnati, 1900, and turned over to Indianapolis for the greater part of that season: Philadelphia Americans, 1901; St. Paul, 1902 and 1903; Boston Nationals, 1904; St. Paul, 1905 and 1906 and part of 1907, finishing the 1907 season with Milwaukee; St. Paul, 1908; Topeka, 1909, and now manager of Burlington.

MIKE GRIFFIN—For four years straight Mike Griffin, then of the Brooklyn team, led the center fielders of the National League.

He was at the top in 1892, 1893, 1894 and 1895, and he was at that time given credit for being the greatest and best player in the position in America. He also led all in 1898.

Outside of the record he was conceded by all to be a really great player.

Griffin was a great player for many years and he was as good as ever when he terminated his connection with professional baseball. The Brooklyns sold his release to the St. Louis Club without his consent. He said he would quit rather than come to St. Louis under the conditions, and he kept his word.

EMMETT HEIDRICK—Emmett Heidrick was one of the greatest center-fielders of his day. He was with Cleveland when McAleer, Tebeau and other famous players were on the team and he was also a member of St. Louis' first American League team. Heidrick was a fine fielder and one of the heaviest left handed batsmen of his time. He tried to come back playing with the Browns in the last part of their 1908 season but failed.

PAUL HINES—To Paul Hines of Washington belongs the palm of longest service in Major League baseball.

He was in the leading leagues from 1870 until 1891, twenty-one years in all and always near the top as a batsman.

In 1879 he led the National League with a percentage of .387 and took the McKay medal which that year was given to the leading batsman in the leading baseball organization.

Paul Hines' career on the diamond ranks in the same category as that of Joe Start, Charley Radbourne, James O'Rourke and Adrian C. Anson, with the most credit to Hines in point of service.

Hines started out to play ball in Washington in 1870, his first club being the crack junior organization known as the Rosedales, then champions of the "Island," as South Washington was then called.

His work there was so good that he next joined the Junior Nationals, but your Uncle Nick Young's attention was called to his playing and he was soon playing on the Olympics of Washington.

In 1872 and 1873 he was a member of the Nationals of Washington and played on the Washingtons a part of 1874, finishing that season with the White Stockings of Chicago.

He remained in Chicago during 1875, 1876 and 1877, during which time he was twice a world's champion.

From Chicago Hines went to Providence, R. I., where he made the record of his life and became unquestionably the leading player of America.

He led the country in 1879 as a batter and fielder, and, in fact, during his professional career from 1875 down to 1892, he was always among the first ten players of America in batting.

It was in Providence in 1879 that Hines made the famous triple play, unassisted, that stood unparalleled in baseball history for years.

Hines was center fielder and this play was made on a short fly caught just behind second base, that every one thought impossible to catch.

Second and third base were occupied by base runners, who, believing the catch out of all reason, had started for home as fast as they could sprint.

Hines caught the ball on a hard run and, being quick witted, saw his opportunity, and keeping up his stride, ran over and touched second base, and going to third base, did likewise, completing a most remarkable play.

He played on the champion Providence team from 1878 to 1885, then going back to Washington, where he played until 1887.

In 1888 and 1889 he was a member of the league team of Indianapolis, playing the latter part through of 1889 in Pittsburg, then going to Boston, where he played until the close of the season of 1891.

Then in 1892 he was back again in Washington, but left in the middle of the year to become manager of the Burlington, Iowa, team, also playing first base, remaining there for one year and a half, thence going south to Mobile, Ala., where he acted as playing manager of that team until 1896, when he retired from active service.

He was actually in the game for a little more than twenty-five years.

Hines was a great player in every respect. He had splendid eyes and was a magnificent judge of light and difficult flies to the outfield. He was also a magnificent batsman and base runner.

Hines was the leading center fielder of the National League in 1874, 1876, 1880, 1883 and 1884.

ARTHUR HOFMAN—Arthur Hofman, the great young center fielder of the Chicago Cubs, is a St. Louis boy.

EMMETT C. HEIDRICK.

Several years ago the young man who-e photo appears above, was a player on the St. Louis Browns. He did not quit the game because of any disability, but entered the contracting business. Heidrick was a leading batsman in the American League, a desperate base runner and one of the most lovable characters baseball has ever known.

The fans in Chicago call him "Circus Solly," on account of the vast number of sensational plays he has made during his career with the Cubs as utility player. It was only last season that he was placed permanently in center field. Hofman is only twenty-four years old and began playing at Des Moines six years ago. He bats and throws right-handed

DAN HOFFMAN—Danny Hoffman, the center fielder of the St. Louis Browns, is one of the speediest outfielders in the business. He is a fine heady batsman.

Besides being a fine fielder, Hoffman is a base runner of first flight.

That Hoffman is qualified to speak, one need only to glance over the records made by this speed marvel in the past. In 1902, with Springfield (Connecticut League) he stole forty-one bases in 105 games. The following year he came in fast company and pilfered eight bases in seventy-three battles, the next season he annexed seven bases in fifty-three contests. In 1905, his last year with the Athletics, he gathered in forty-six sacks in 119 games. Under Clarke Griffith, in 1906, in 107 battles he stole thirty-three bases. In 1907 he pilfered thirty in 136 games. In 1908, under a manager who held his men in leash, Hoffman could steal but seventeen sacks, and last year but twenty-four with a batting average of .269. Hoffman has stolen 2_6 bases in eight years.

According to Hoffman, this is one of the most important accomplishents in baseball. Base running means the work of encircling the bases in the most effective way. It means, in short, to improve every opportunity on the way; absolute to take the least risk of being put out.

Hoffman's career as a professional commenced in 1902 when he played with the Springfield, Conn. Club.

He was with the Athletics of Philadelphia in 1903, 1904 and 1905, with the New York Americans in 1906 and 1907 and since the latter year he has been a member of the St. Louis Browns.

TOOTS HOFMAN—Toots Hofman, a brother of the famous Artie Hofman, the renowned center fielder of the champion Chicago Cubs and who was given a trial by President Murphy of the Cubs a year ago was one of the star members of Jimmy Ryan's Rogers Park Semi-Professional Team, Chicago, during the 1910 season. Hofman is a younger brother of the more famous Arthur and the chances are he will line up as a member of the Cubs in the Spring of 1911. Toots is an outfielder and is said to be even faster than the ten-thousand dollar beauty Sir Arthur. Toots is a native of St. Louis and learned the game while playing in the Trolley League.

W. E. HOY—William E. Hoy, a deaf mute, was at one time one of the greatest outfielders in the National League.

Ted Sullivan found Hoy in 1888 playing at Finlay, Ohio, and signed him for the Washington League Club.

He made good there as he did later at Cincinnati and other places, made a good salary, took care of it and with his deaf and dumb wife is now living on Easy Street in Cincinnati.

In 1900 Hoy was the leading center fielder of the American League. In the National League as a center fielder he always ranked near the top.

FIELDER ALLISON JONES—Fielder Allison Jones, outfielder, captain and manager of the Chicago White Sox from 1900 to 1908 was undoubtedly one of the greatest players in the business.

He was the leader of the White Sox when they captured the World's Championship from the Chicago Cubs and it was his fine work as a leader and player that did as much to win that series as anything else.

As a centerfielder Jones led the American League in 1902, 1903 and 1906.

Jones is a native of Shinglehouse, Pa., where he was born August 13, 1871. He started his baseball career in 1903 with the Oregon State League as catcher and fielder.

The following season he was in Corning, N. Y., and in Springfield, Mass.

His work was of a caliber that attracted the attention of the major leaguers, and in the next five seasons he played in Brooklyn, casting his fortune with the Chicago Americans, when the American League invaded the Eastern country.

When Jimmy Callahan left Comiskey, owner of the Chicago White Sox, to seek his fortune as manager of an independent team, Jones was chosen his successor, and from June 8, 1904, until the close of the season of 1908 he was in charge of the fortunes of the club. At the close of the 1908 season he retired from the game to go into the lumber business at Seattle. Jones was a rare outfielder, being possessed of remarkable judgment in caring for the most difficult of drives, and he handled his club with rare ability. Three times his club finished third, once second and once first under his stewardship.

The lure of the diamond is so strong that few, very few, professional baseball players have retired from the game as Fielder Jones did, in the heyday of his career. Jones, who was the captain and manager of the Chicago Americans and once led them to victory in a world's series after winning the pennant in his own league made a complete renunciation of the game.

With Jones it was purely a matter of business. He had interests in Oregon which demanded his personal attention. Much as he loved the National game and strong as was its hold on him, he was firm in his intention to say good-bye to the diamond.

Just before Jones quit the Chicago Club to retire to business life, he was considered the quickest thinker and one of the most valuable managers and players in the game, and the baseball world looked on the retirement of Jones as the passing of the greatest exponent of "inside" baseball that ever played.

His wonderful brain work earned for the White Sox the title of "hitless wonders."

Under his regime the team won games without hits—won them merely on superior head work. In St. Louis on one occasion Fielder Jones gained grand evidence of his ability as a manager when, after three men were on the bags, he warmed up all his pitchers and put in a new twirler for each batter that McAleer sent forth, retiring the side without a run.

It was a play without precedent in the American League, and only emphasized the fact that Jones was the game's brainiest member.

When he left the Chicago Club, Comiskey visited him in Portland, Oregon, and did his best to get him to return to the White

Sox but Jones was determined to quit and when considered at his best as a player he did the remarkable thing of then retiring from the game for good.

THOMAS W. LEACH—No fielder on either side did more effective work in the World's Championship Series between Pittsburg and Detroit in 1909 than Thomas W. Leach, the center fielder of the former team.

Leach's hitting was timely, his fielding wonderful and his base running superb.

Leach was born November 7, 1877, at French Creek, New York.

He stands five feet, six inches, and weighs 150 pounds. He played in 1896 with Hanover, Pa., in the Cumberland Valley League; 1897 with Geneva (O.) Independents; 1898 Auburn (N. Y.) State League; 1899 Louisville National League; 1900 to 1909 with Pittsburg in the National League. He played third base until the 1909 season.

This sterling ball tosser equally at home in the out or in fields, hails from Cleveland, Ohio, and started out as a professional in the New York State League in 1888. Louisville then secured him and since that time he has played under President Dreyfuss in that city and in Pittsburg, going to the latter city in the consolidation of the two teams in the season of 1900.

HARRY McCAFFERY — Harry McfERY, a St. Louis boy, did some great baseball playing in the seventies and eighties. He played first professionally with the Davenport, Ia., team of the Western League and when St. Louis entered the American Association in 1882 McCaffery became a member of that organization. McCaffery was a fine all around player. He filled every position on the team and filled it well. He could catch or pitch in a pinch and he was at home anywhere in the infield. He played at center for the St. Louis Browns and on account of his great strength as a batsman he held his own in the ranks for a long while. Always a gentleman on and off the field and one of the most popular and intelligent members of the profession, McCaffery naturally had a large following and there were many regrets when he quit professional baseball for the postal service where he is now employed.

OWEN MILAN—Owen Milan has been a member of the Washington Club of the American League for several seasons past. He is a fast, steady player, an excellent thrower and is considered one of the sluggers of his league.

WARREN MILLER—Warren Miller will line up with the Washington Nationals in the Spring of 1911 as their regular center fielder.

W. NORTHEN—W. Northen will be one of the aspirants for outfield honors for St. Louis Browns' new 1911 Club. Northern was recruited from the Houston Club of the Texas League in the fall of 1910. Judging from his record made at Houston the youngster should win a new Brown uniform in the Spring. He is a good hitter, knows how to field and is very fast on the bases.

E. T. OAKES—E. T. Oakes, best known as "Rebel" Oakes, is the regular center fielder of the St. Louis Cardinals, which position he held down for the first time in the Spring of 1910. During the season of 1909 Oakes played the out field for Griffith's Cincinnati Reds in the National League. He was turned over to the Cardinals in trade in the winter of 1909-1910.

Oakes is a native of San Francisco and began his professional career out there three years ago. He is regarded as one of the smartest hitters in the National League and besides which he possesses a great throwing arm. He is five feet, eight inches in height, weighs 170 pounds and is 24 years old.

R. OLDRING—R. Oldring is the regular center fielder of the Philadelphia Athletics of the American League. Oldring has been cavorting in the Athletics outfield for several seasons and is regarded as one of the real stars of the league in every department. He is very fast on the bases, an excellent run getter and in August 1910 he ranked third in the American League batting with an average of .314.

FRED PARENT—Fred Parent has made good with the Chicago Americans in this 1910 season. His work at center field has been first class and has proven himself one of the best of emergency hitters.

He also worked at short and third during the 1910 season.

He is a valuable utility fielder.

GEORGE PASKERT—George Paskert, now the regular man at centerfield for the Cincinnati National League team, was born Aug. 28, 1886, at Cleveland, Ohio. He played in Dayton, O., in 1904, and after playing three seasons in that city, was drafted by Atlanta of the Southern League. There his showing was of such a high degree of excellence that Cincinnati secured him. He batted for .243 in 1908, his first seson with Cincinnati, and in 1909 hit for .251 in 88 games and fielded for .968. In 1910 he is up near the .300 mark as a batsman.

ALBERT SELBACH—Al Selbach, formerly centerfielder for the Boston Americans, will again direct the fortunes of the Harrisburg (Penn.) Club of the Tri-State League, Selbach in his day was one of the crack outfielders of the major leagues.

CYRUS BENTLEY SEYMOUR—Cyrus Bentley Seymour, the New York outfielder, was transferred to the Baltimore Eastern League team on August 22, 1910. For years Seymour was one of the great hitters of the National League. He led the team in batting one season. Seymour inaugurated his major league baseball career as a pitcher with the Giants when Bill Joyce was managing the team. Seymour was a left-hander with a wonderful assortment of curves, but he never could control his curve ball and finally became an outfielder on account of his great hitting. He developed into a star outfielder while with Cincinnati and then went back to New York. He covered center field for the champion New York team of 1905. Ames, Devlin and Mathewson are the only men of the 1905 team still with McGraw. McGann, Gilbert and Dahlen were the infielders of that team, while Mertes, Devlin and Seymour covered the outfield. Bresnahan and Bowerman, catchers, and Mathewson, McGinnity, Ames and Taylor were the pitchers.

JAMES SLAGLE—James Slagle, who is now one of the stars of the Baltimore Club in the Eastern League, playing center field, was up to 1909 one of the most valuable outfielders owned by the Chicago Cubs. Slagle had held down the middle garden for Chances team in perfect fashion for several years, and was sold to Baltimore, not because he had gone back in a fielding way, but because he had experienced a slump in his batting. Since joining Baltimore the "rabbit" has regained his old-time form and the past season records show him to be one of the best in the fast league.

He was with Boston in 1897, Pittsburg 1898 and 1899, finishing that season with Washington, Philadelphia and Boston Nationals in 1900, remaining at Boston until 1902, when he was secured by the Chicago Nationals.

HOMER SMOOT—Homer Smoot, formerly a member of the St. Louis National League team, now is a member of the Kansas City club of the American Association team playing center field. Smoot is a great big strong fellow and during the past season played no unimportant part in the success attained by Shay's Kansas City Blues. He stands five feet ten inches, weighs 180 pounds and is 28 years old. He is, and always has been, noted for his great ability with the bat. He still is pounds better than many outfielders in the major leagues.

FRED C. SNODGRASS—Fred C. Snodgrass was the meteor of the 1910 season. He has been playing in center field for the New York Giants and as late as August of this year he was the leading batsman of the National League, holding the phenomenal average of .377. He then led such great sluggers as Campbell, the wonderful young Pittsburger, Magee of Philadelphia, for years the recognized slugger of the National, and "Honus" Wagner, the king for many seasons. Snodgrass is a right-handed batsman and besides possessing great ability as a hitter, is a beautiful fielder and thrower.

He came to the Giants from the Pacific Coast League in the spring of 1908, sat on the bench for the Giants and caught an occasional game. McGraw saw the good that was in him, set out to play him regularly in the outfield and helped develop him into one of the best batsmen in America. He is also very speedy on the bases and a good run getter for his club. He hails from Ventura, Cal., where he was born on October 19, 1887. He stands five feet, eleven inches and weighs 170 pounds. He was catching for the St. Vincent team in Los Angeles, during the season of 1907-1908, when McGraw set eyes on him and signed him for the New York Giants, but it was not until the fall of 1909 that he was played regularly in the outfield.

TRIS SPEAKER—There are many experts who consider Tris Speaker, center fielder of the Boston American League club, the fastest man now playing that position.

In fact Speaker is considered by many the greatest of the present day center fielders, and though past baseball age, there never has been but one man who was his superior. Lange, the famous outfielder of Anson's White Stockings, was a greater player, but no one before or since has equaled Speaker.

Lange excelled him in height and reach; equaled him in speed; hit harder and was infinitely a better man on the bases. This is no criticism of Speaker, as Lange was with the possible exception of Hamilton, the greatest base runner the game has ever known.

Speaker's tremendous speed and his beautiful judgment on fly balls, his perfect sense of direction and his ability to throw make him the best fielding center fielder in the game. He can hit, bunt, push and poke. His one failure to score perfect is his work on the bases and that is improving.

President John I. Taylor of the Boston American League club believes he has in Speaker, the wonderful outfielder from Hubbard City, Texas, the finest player that has seen service for several years. Speaker is a wonderful ball-tosser. He is great as a batsman, as a base-runner and as a fielder. As a batsman he has a wonderful eye for the ball, and is very quick and graceful in his actions. He is a natural hitter and is bound to finish with the best in the country. As a fielder he has remarkable judgment and is an adept in handling balls that are batted either in front, behind or on one side of him. He is very fast on the bases and runs them with splendid judgment.

Speaker is 28 years old, weighs 180 pounds and stands five feet eleven high. He has the rough complexion of one who has spent most of his life in the open air. He has heavy, buddy, bloodshot eyes, not the kind one would imagine could pick out a good ball and paste it to the far corner of the field, or could start after the ball at the crack and judge to an inch where that ball is going to land.

He has a voice like rumbling thunder, and his softest words sound like the growl of a mastiff. He has large powerful hands, freckled.

Speaker lives in winter in Hubbard City, Tex., which is not a city at all, but a small post-village near Dallas, having a population of 894 in summer and 895 when Speaker is there.

He goes back home at the close of the baseball season and spends the first few weeks hunting, and then turns his hand to the cattle industry. He is a regular Texas cowboy in the saddle, and can do as much with a horse as he can with a baseball bat.

Speaker is only a boy in actions. Trifling things amuse him. He cares nothing for books, and as for newspapers he simply glances at the Red Sox score to see if the reporters have given credit to all the base hits he made. He wants to be out of doors all the time. Most of the Boston players live together in an apartment house on Huntington avenue. Many of them like to loll around their rooms when they are not playing ball. Not so with Speaker. He gets out and roams around if he has nothing else to do.

Recently he bought an automobile and next winter it will be the only car in Hubbard City, Tex. He has learned the mechanism of the machine and now spends his mornings speeding on the suburban roads. And doubtless this same automobile has affected his batting eye. No one can guide an automobile for twenty miles without returning with a kind of squint in the eyes. So it is with Speaker. It is a good bet that he will bat better on the Western trip than he has on the home grounds recently.

Hans Wagner of the Pittsburg club, who owns and operates an automobile, had to stop riding it because his batting fell off to nothing. Since then he has picked up wonderfully. Speaker could easily bat for .400 if he would leave the automobile alone.

ROY THOMAS—Roy Thomas is one of the utility fielders of the Philadelphia club who was the leader in his position in the National League for six years.

TRIS SPEAKER.
Tris Speaker is the wonderful young center fielder of the Boston Americans, who is considered one of the fastest men in the game to-day.

He was at the top in 1900 and 1901 and again in 1904, 1905, 1906 and 1907.

His record speaks for itself and proves him one of the greatest players that ever filled the position.

CURT WELCH—Curt Welch, the center fielder of the St. Louis Browns, when they were winning American Association and World's Championships in the eighties, was by long odds the greatest fielder of his day.

Welch was a rough diamond, uncouth, uneducated but a born athlete and player.

He did more than his share in the winning of championships for the St. Louis Browns during their wonderful success in the eighties.

Welch at this time was one of the most enthusiastic and aggressive players in the business. In fierce and offensive play he had no superiors. He would take any chance when running the bases and would buck a stone wall if that sort of thing was necessary.

He was a fine, plucky player, being always a good man in the breach and it was his ability to hit the ball when a hit was needed, or to steal a base when the steal meant a victory, that won many a game for his side.

But it was at fielding the ball that Welch excelled all other fielders of his day.

It was claimed that his skill in fielding the ball was due to his keen sense of hearing. It was said that he could tell by the sound of the crack of the bat just how far the ball was going to go. One thing is certain, no man that has ever played at center has excelled Welch when it came to rapid work in the field. In judging all kinds of high hits Welch was superb. He covered a great stretch of ground and seldom went after the ball without landing it.

In base running, too, he had no equal when it came to terrific head slides.

Curt Welch, Tip O'Neill, Walter Latham, William Gleason and Charley Comiskey were the five great and aggressive St. Louis Browns when they were at the top of the list for many seasons.

EDWARD ZWILLING—Edward Zwilling played in quite a number of games in centerfield for the Chicago White Sox in the fall of 1910. Zwilling is a native of St. Louis and played his first professional ball in the trolley leagues around St. Louis. Eddie Herr, now manager of the Flint (Mich.) team, discovered Zwilling and took him to the Bay City team. The youngster failed to play well with Bay City and he was traded to Battle Creek, where he proved a sensation, because of his hitting and fielding. When he was discovered by President Comiskey he was batting at a .329 clip. After joining the White Sox the young man continued his good work.

THOMAS LEACH.
This is Thomas Leach as he appeared when at bat for the Pittsburg Champions in 1910. This year he played in the field.

THE NATIONAL GAME

THE RIGHT FIELDERS.

LIPMAN PIKE, JOHN MANNING, MIKE TIERNAN, GEORGE SHAFFER, JAKE EVANS, HUGH NICOL, TOM McCARTHY, SAM THOMPSON, WILLIAM KEELER, J. B. SEYMOUR AND SAM CRAWFORD WERE AMONG THE GREAT PLAYERS IN THIS POSITION IN THE OLD PROFESSIONAL AND THEN IN THE NATIONAL LEAGUE.

This is a record of the players who excelled at right field for the clubs of the old Professional Association and then of the National League.

Year. Right Fielders. 'Club.	Fielding Games.	Pct.	Year. Right Fielders. 'Club.	Fielding Games.	Pct.
1871 Lipman Pike—Troy	28	.919	1891 Sam Thompson—Philadelphia	133	.946
1872 Levi Meyerle—Athletics, Phila	15	.862	1892 Sam Thompson—Philadelphia	151	.945
1873 Wes. Fisler—Athletics, Phila	51	.908	1893 Hugh Duffy—Boston	131	.958
1874 John Radcliff—Philadelphia	23	.926	1894 S. Thompson—Philadelphia	102	.961
1875 John Manning—Boston	64	.904	1895 S. Thompson—Philadelphia	119	.961
1876 W. Holdsworth—New York	49	.901	1896 Wm. Keeler—Baltimore	127	.973
1877 Geo. Shaffer—Louisville	47	.815	1897 Wm. Keeler—Baltimore	128	.970
1878 Geo. Shaffer—Indianapolis...—..	60	.844	1898 M. Tiernan—New York	103	.986
1879 Geo. A. Strief—Cleveland	56	.903	1899 Henry Blake—St. Louis	86	
1880 Jacob Evans—Troy	46	.906	1900 J. Wagner—Pittsburg	117	.969
1881 Jacob Evans—Troy	81	.933	1901 Wm. Keeler—Brooklyn	125	.985
1882 Jacob Evans—Worcester	67	.915	1902 Wm. Keeler—Brooklyn	132	.928
1883 Jacob Evans—Cleveland	85	.902	1903 P. J. Carney—Boston	92	.953
1884 Jacob Evans—Cleveland	85	.902	1904 W. P. Shannon—St. Louis	133	.978
1885 Geo. Shaffer—St. Louis	69	.917	1905 Otis Clymer—Pittsburg	89	.986
1886 S. Thompson——Detroit	122	.945	1906 Frank Schulte—Chicago	146	.975
1887 H. Richardson—Detroit	58	.936	1907 Joseph Bates—Boston	118	.979
1888 M. Tiernan—New York	113	.959	1908 F. Schulte—Chicago	89	.992
1889 A. J. Maul—Pittsburg	61	.946	1909 J. Titus—Philadelphia	149	.971
1890 W. S. Brodie—Boston	132	.953	1910 J. Titus—Philadelphia	142	.976

AMERICAN'S BEST MEN. .. ....

THESE WERE THE LEADERS AT RIGHT FIELD IN THE AMERICAN LEAGUE SINCE THE INITIAL YEAR OF THAT ORGANIZATION.

This is a list of the men who have excelled at right field for the clubs of the American Association since the initial year of that organization:

Year. Right Fielders. Club.	Fielding Games.	Pct.	Year. Right Fielders. Club.	Fielding Games.	Pct.
1900 T. Dowd—Milwaukee	68	.965	1905 Sam Crawford—Detroit	103	.988
1901 R. A. Seybold—Philadelphia	99	.965	1906 W. Keeler—New York	152	.987
1902 J. B. Seymour—Baltimore	72	.975	1907 E. Hahn—Chicago	156	.990
1903 Sam Crawford—Detroit	137	.964	1908 E. Hahn—Chicago	119	.965
1904 R. A. Seybold—Philadelphia	129	.985	1909 D. Murphy—Philadelphia	149	.976
			1910 Murphy—Philadelphia	151	.974

The early managers of the professional teams paid far more attention to right field than do the managers of the present day.

In the seventies and eightiest the fleetest fielders were placed at right field and they were asked to pick up right field hits rapidly and try and throw out the batsman before he reached first base.

This play is seldom scored by the right fielders of the present day, but in the earlier days of the professional game it was pulled off three or four times in each and every contest.

William Sunday of the Chicagos, Tommy McCarthy of the Champion Bostons and little Hugh Nicol of the Champion St. Louis Browns, all speedy right fielders, often threw batsmen out at first base.

Jake Evans and George Shaffer were two other veteran players who often turned the trick.

The first of the great right fielders, the man who led all in that position in the National League in 1871, its first season, was Lipman Pike, who, that year, was playing with Troy.

Pike came from the Atlantics of Brooklyn, and was one of the great players who mastered the game on the famous Capitoline Grounds.

When Pike came to St. Louis in 1876 to play with the St. Louis Browns, the first team entered by this city in the National League, he was a handsome-black-eyed, curly-haired boy and a fielder and left-handed batsman of the first flight. He remained at the top in his profession for a long while.

Levi Meyerle was the next leader at right, but third base was his home position.

Wes Fisler of the Athletics and Johnny Radcliffe followed Fisler as leader, but they were really playing out of their position as was Fisler before them.

After Fisler came, John Manning, one of the first of the right fielders to see the inner beauties of the position and to attempt to throw out batsmen at first base.

John Manning was the right fielder of the champion Boston team when they won the League Campionship in 1875 and 1878.

Manning played his first ball with the Tremonts on the Boston Common. He is still alive and at work in the Palace Theater in Boston. He was a fine fielder, thrower and batsman.

W. Holdsworth of New York led the right fielders in 1876 and after him came the first of the really great players in the position, George Shaffer.

They called Shaffer "the Orator" for the reason that he was a great stickler for his rights and talked to himself when not talking to the Umpire.

But Shaffer was a good player. He led the National League as a right fielder and great player for ten years.

He was with the St. Louis Unions in their 1884 season and in the Old Union Grounds at Jefferson and Cass avenue he won many friends for his fearless, aggressive and always earnest and effective work.

He was a baseball player, every inch of him, and was equally at home at the bat, in the field or on the bases.

George A. Strief of Cleveland led in 1879. He played at second later for the St. Louis Browns.

After Strief came another worthy rival of Shaffer, Jacob Evans, who led the National League as a right fielder for five consecutive years.

Many of the old players claim that Evans was the king pin in the position, being like Shaffer, a fine thrower and capable of often throwing the batsmen out at first.

This is quite a compliment, for while Evans was playing great ball, William Sunday and Hugh Nicol, two of the fleetest players that ever lived, were covering right for the Chicago and St. Louis teams.

This brings me up to the right fielders of the past decade. Below, in alphabetical order, is given a list of the players who in their day played right field for the clubs of the old Professional Association, the American League and all other major league organizations since 1871:

JAMES H. BANNON—James H. Bannon was at one time one of the best known professionals. He was born in Amesbury, Mass., almost 37 years ago. He played independent ball with Amesbury, South Groveland and other teams.

His first professional engagement was with the St. Louis Nationals in 1895. He played right field for the Boston Nationals in 1894-5-6. In 1897 he was with Kansas City. The next year saw him in Springfield, which team was then in the Eastern League. He was tied with Walter Woods for second place in the batting. He started the season of 1890 with Springfield, but finished with the Montreal club. In 1900-1-2-3, he played with Toronto in the Eastern League. In 1902 Toronto won the championship.

During his four years with Toronto he never batted less than .300. In 1894 he captained Columbus (O.) team and finished as manager. He managed Montreal in 1905 and 1906. In 1907 he was with with Rochester in the same league. In 1908 he was with Binghamton, in the New York State, being a part owner. He sold out his interests in early Spring of 1909. He bought the Hotel Rochester in Rochester, N. Y., in 1909, and still runs it. He played a part of the season of 1909 with the Syracuse team. He has a brother, Bill Bannon, who is an umpire in the National League. Bill played polo in Lawrence and baseball in Nashua. Jimmy has brothers playing in New York State, Connecticut and New England leagues.

TOM BROWN—Tom Brown, who played with Providence, Louisville and Boston, was at one time considered one of the best right fielders in America. Tom was also at one time one of the best base runners in the country and a member of Mike Kelly's Bostons in the days of the Play-

ers' League and the Association. He turned umpire after his playing days came to a close and had a National League try. He is now working for the Tri-Staters.

ALBERT BURCH—Albert Burch, one of the outfielders of the Brooklyn Club of the National League, was born at Albany, N. Y., 27 years ago. His home is now in Brooklyn, and he has lived in that city a dozen years. He made a hit in that city with such prominent teams as the Marquettes and the Ridgewoods.

Burch then branched out with the Poughkeepsie Club of the Hudson River League, and for three seasons was with Altoona Tri-State League team. He ranked high in hitting, both in Poughkeepsie and in Altoona. McCloskey secured him for the St. Louis Nationals in 1906 and the following season saw him in Brooklyn, where he has since played.

TYRUS COBB—Tyrus Cobb, the right fielder of the champion Detroit Club, is conceded by all to be the greatest player in this 1909 year in the American League.

Tyrus Raymond Cobb, right fielder and the American League's star batsman and base runner, has just turned up, but has been with the team since the Fall of 1905, coming from the Augusta Club of the South Atlantic League as the result of a deal in the Spring of that year, by which, in exchange for Richard Cicotte, Detroit received first choice of the Augusta players.

Cobb was the one selected, after a long hesitation as to whether the club should take him, Cicotte or Engle, all of whom are now in the American League. Cobb is a half inch less than six feet in height and weighs, stripped, 174 pounds. He throws right-handed, but bats left-handed.

Cobb's complete record since he began playing ball professionally is as follows:

LED AMERICAN LEAGUE.

Years	Position	Average.
1907—Cobb	1	.3:0
1909—Cobb	1	.377

RECORD WITH DETROIT.

	G.	AB.	R.	B.	SB.	AVE.
1906	97	310	44	112	23	.3.0
1907	150	685	97	212	40	.350
1908	150	581	88	188	39	.324
1909	156	575	118	217	91	.377

Average for four years 313

In the fall of 1908, at Augusta, Cobb was only a substitute, but he looked good to Bill Armour of the Tigers. So good, in fact, that Armour paid part of the purchase price himself.

When Cobb appeared in a Detroit uniform in the fall of 1906 he received no more than passing attention. Inside of a week he had them all sitting up and taking notice.

Inside of two weeks he was being heralded near and wide as the find of the year. There is no more shining light in baseball to-day than Cobb, yet as a minor leaguer he was regarded as only ordinary.

Since Cobb made his mark at least a dozen outfielders have drifted into the majors with the reputation of having Tyrus backed off the board, but most of them are again doing duty in the minors. Ty's crown remains undimmed. Many are bought as the real things, but players like Cobb, Wagner, Lajoie, Mathewson, Kling and a host of other big league stars are the exception to the rule. If such was not the case the major league club owners wouldn't spend money so lavishly each year in an effort to dig up high-class material

As fine a judge of playing as President Comiskey has pronounced Cobb the peer of diamond heroes.

In an article which Mr. Comiskey wrote for the Chicago Tribune and which appeared in that newspaper on April 17, 1910, the writer, among other things, had this to say about Cobb:

"The greatest ball player of all times.

"That question would have been a problem three years ago, and may appear so to a great many people now, for there probably are more differences of opinion about the relative merits of exponents of the greatest game in the world than about any thing else one can think of.

"But in my opinion no fair minded follower of baseball who has seen the great players in action and who has studied their strong and weak points, can come to any conclusion other than the one I have arrived at—that Ty Cobb, out fielder of the Detroit American League Club, is the real answer to the above query.

"I take it that the answer should mean the greatest all-around player, the one with the greatest all-around ability, the one most valuable to his team and not the one most proficient in any single position. There might be grounds for an argument if I were to say select Cobb because he was better as a right fielder than Wagner as a short stop, or Lajoie or Evers as a second baseman.

"I pick the Detroit man because he is, in my judgment, the most expert man of his profession and is able to respond better than any other player to any demand on him. I pick him because he plays ball with his whole anatomy—his head, his arms, his hands, his legs, his feet—and because he plays ball all the time for all that is in him.

"Why is Cobb a great ball player? The first and most important reason is that he loves the game. I never have seen a man who had his heart more centered in a sport than Cobb has when he is playing. There never was a really good ball player who didn't think more of the game than he did of his salary or the applause of the fans. Cobb, being a bright young man, naturally wants to be paid and is paid what he is worth in his profession. Furthermore, he probably has no objection to commendation from the people watching him; many ball players deny they care anything for the cheers of the crowd, and few take any stock in these denials. But I believe Cobb would continue to play ball if he were charged something for the privilege and if the only spectator were the ground keeper.

"In considering Cobb's ball excellence it is only natural to think first of his batting, for batting is the part of the sport that appeals to the big majority. After his record of last season I believe that the statement that he is the best hitter of to-day is indisputable. Averages tell a great deal about a man's ability to hit and the mark of .377, hung up by the Detroit man in 1909, cannot be overlooked. It would be folly for me to discuss the relative pitching strength of the National and American Leagues, for I have not seen any National League pitching aside from that of our world's series. But I will say that any man that can hit at that figure against present day pitching in either big league is nothing short of a marvel.

"When Cobb first joined the Detroit club word went around that he ,like most of the rest of the craft, has his weakness at bat. It was noised about that a left-hander could 'make him look foolish.' And it was true that Cobb was not as strong at first against the southpaws as he was against the right handers. But ask the left-handers about it now. They will tell you that he is any thing but a boy in their hands at present. The fact of the matter is that Cobb has overcome his dislike for that style of pitching and is as effective against it now as against the other kind.

"Cobb is not an in and outer, although he, like all of us, has his slumps. With him they never last long, and are so infrequent that none of his opponents ever are counting on one of them. Cobb is dangerous at all times, and a pitcher working against him knows he must pitch the hardest and never let up until the Georgian either has been retired or has added another hit to his long list.

"Cobb hits when hits are needed, and when they are not needed. He is as strong in a pinch as any one, besides being able to hit the ball farther away than the majority of 'clean up' hitters. However, he hits in all directions, some of his extra base drives going down the left foul line, some of them down the right, some of them to right center, some of them to center, some of them to left center and, in fact, in all directions.

"In addition to his ability to tire out the fielders with his long smashes, Cobb is one of the most expert bunters, and, of course, his speed makes him doubly effective in this particular accomplishment. With a runner or two on bases and Ty at bat, he has the entire opposing infield at sea. No faint hearted third baseman could live through a series against the Detroit club. Cobb may look the 'bunter' all over when a bunt is expected to advance a base runner, and may draw the third baseman in, confident that the ball will be laid down and then make him call on all his dodging ability to get out of the way of a terrific smash right at him, I don't blame infielders for being 'crossed' by Cobb. He has the head to fool them and the ability to carry out his schemes.

Although the left handers have been convinced that they were no more effective against him than their right-handed brothers, the latter still have some ideas about his 'weak spot' and those ideas are almost as many as are the pitchers. But every little while a pitcher will serve up one of the things a Cobb 'can't hit,' only to see it soaring over the fence or toward it.

"Another common fallacy, when Cobb first served in the American League, is that he was a 'fool' on the bases; that he 'ran wild.' There has been a reversal of the verdict, too. Undoubtedly, Cobb has pulled off some base running 'crimes,' but he loved to run and just couldn't hold himself in. If any one had kept track of Cobb's successes, and failures in his 'crazy' base running stunts it is sure that he would have found that the former far outnumbered the latter. And I am also sure that this 'crazy' running has won a lot of ball games for Detroit.

"There may be ball players that can run a hundred yards as fast as the Georgian, but there are none who can go from the plate to first base as fast and none who

ARTHUR BADER.
Arthur Bader will probably play in the outfield for the Chicago White Sox next year. He is now the fleetest outfielder and heaviest hitter with the Western League.

can equal his speed between any two bases or around the whole circuit.

"As for Cobb's fielding prowess, no manager could ask for a better man to play in right field, although doubtless there have been men who played the batsman better and men who throw more accurately.

"As one will question the assertion that Cobb covers as much ground as any player ever did, and as he catches almost everything he reaches, and reaches lots of balls that other fielders could not reach. I don't see what more any one could ask of him. He has a good throwing arm, and, what is better, he is not afraid to use it."

P. DAVIDSON—P. Davidson is a recruit of the Brooklyn Club playing his first season in fast company. So far the young man has exhibited some ability as a fielder, batsman and base runner.

R. DEMMITT—R. Demmitt was secured by the St. Louis Browns from the New York Highlanders at the close of the season of 1909 but he was released early in the season of 1910.

Few outfielders have the throwing ability of Demmitt. It is exrtemely dangerous to take any chances with this speedy youngster. But he was not a good enough batsmman to hold a place on the St. Louis Browns.

A. L. EVANS—A. L. Evans, Jake Evans as he is best known to the fans, is the right fielder of the St. Louis Cardinals.

Evans has more than made good with the Cardinals, not only as a good fielder but as a timely, hard hitting batsman. Evans was born in Cleveland, O., Feb. 17, 1885, and still makes that city his home in the Winter.

HARRY H. GESSLER—Harry H. Gessles, the hustling right fielder of the Washington American League Club, is one of the hardest hitting outfielders in the country and since his first appearance in professional baseball, he has been noted for his work with the stick.

Gessler was born at Indiana, Pa., December 23, 1880. He started out as a ball player with Greensburg, Pa., High School, and then went to Mercersburg Academy, where he played third base and pitched.

He then entered Washington, Jefferson College, and later went to Ohio University, playing on the Varsity nines of both institutions. Completing his medical course at Johns Hopkins, Gessler played independent ball with Puxsutawney, going from there to Jersey City.

Brooklyn drafted him and subsequently sold him to the Chicago Cubs, who sent him to Columbus, of the American Association. From this team the Boston Americans purchased him, and in the season of 1908 led the team in batting with a mark of .308. Later in the season he was traded by Boston to the Washington team, and strengthened that aggregation considerably.

BERT GRAHAM—Bert Graham, the hard-hitting outfieilder who played with Muskogee in 1909 and was a member of the Jackson team in the Cotton States League in 1910, was sold to the St. Louis Browns in the late fall. Graham seems to be the goods both at the bat and in the field.

ARTHUR GRIGGS—Arthur Griggs was one of the right fielders and general utility men of the St. Louis Browns during the American League season of 1910. Griggs is a youngster in the big league and has just finished his second season with

the Browns. He is a native of the Lone Star State and began playing professional ball at Shreveport, La., four years ago. In 1908 he lined up with the San Antonio club of the Texas League and during the season played behind the bat at first, second, short and in the outfield. He finished high up with the stick and his fielding was good. He was picked up by one of the Browns' scouts and ever since has been playing very satisfactory ball for Manager O'Connor. Griggs stands five feet ten inches, weighs 175 pounds and is 26 years old. He is a comer.

EDWARD HANKINSON—Edward Hankinson was the right fielder of the Chicago Club in the late seventies. He was also a good fielder. He played with teams in Brooklyn and New York before coming west.

CHARLES HEMPHILL—Charles Hemphill, the right fielder of the New York Highlanders of the American League has been playing big league ball for ten years. Hemphill is a native of Youngstown, Ohio, and before joining the professional ranks he played with amateur teams near his home town. In 1898, he played in the Ohio State League and later went to Kansas City. He was discovered by Pat Tebeau in 1899, when Sir Patrick was manager of the famous Cleveland Spiders. Hemphill made good while with Cleveland and when that club was transferred to St. Louis was installed as a regular on the old Cardinals. Hemphill was released to St. Paul, by the St. Louis team several seasons ago but he did not remain there very long being returned to the St. Louis Browns the following season. He has been playing in the outer garden for New York three years. He is considered one of the best run getters in the American League, is a cracking good batsman and when right is a hard man to beat. During the 1910 season Hemphill was looked upon as the star of the Yankee's outfield.

HARRY HOOPER—Harry Hooper is the regular right fielder of the Boston American Club. Hooper has been dancing in the big league for just two seasons and judging him on his 1910 career can be classed as one of the stars in the outer garden. Hooper's work during the season of 1909 was very good. He played in eighty-one games and finished up with a batting average of .282. Up to August, 1910, Hooper had played in 109 games, scored fifty-six runs, cracked out 104 base hits, pilfered twenty-seven bases and was batting .246.

WILLIAM A. KEELER—William A. Keeler, the right fielder of the New York American, was in his day one of the best of fielders and the greatest of batsmen.

He was with the Baltimore team when they won the National League pennant and he has been with other champion organizations.

He is a left-handed batsman and is considered the most skilled hitter in the business.

Keeler was born March 3, 1872, at Brooklyn, and has therefore completed his thirty-eighth millstone. He played with the Flushing, Arlington, Acme, N. Y., and Plainfield, N. J., teams before starting in with Binghamton, N. Y., in 1892. He led the Eastern League in batting, and was signed for the New York Club, but was injured and unable to play, and so his release was secured by Brooklyn for $700. At the close of the season, Ed. Hanlon of Baltimore gave Shindle and Treadway

J. R. McALEER.
In his day the fastest outfielder in America and now the manager of the Washington American League Club.

for Keeler and Dan Brouthers. Keeler played with Baltimore until 1898, figuring in three championships, and then went to Brooklyn, where he was again a member of two more pennant winners. Since 1903 he has been a member of the New York Americans.

JOHN T. MAGNER—John T. Magner, a St. Louis boy, was one of the greatest fielders and batsmen this city has ever given to the professional field. Magner was member of the St. Louis Reds in the seventies. He went from them to the Tecumsehs of the International Association and he soon became known as the heaviest batsman and the speediest base runner in the organization. He was also a magnificent fielder and thrower. Magner, in 1881, played with the St. Louis Browns, the team that that year played on the co-operative plan at Sportsman's Park. Later he played with the Standards and other local teams. Magner in the seventies and eighties was one of the best beloved players in the business, being of a genial, sunny disposition, with a hand ever open to help a fellow player. Magner is now living in St. Louis and is employed in the mailing department of one of the St. Louis newspapers.

THOMAS McCARTHY—Thomas McCarthy is now the regular scout for the Cincinnati Club and when not at work for that organization spends his time in Boston.

McCarthy in the days of the old and decidedly famous St. Louis Browns, was one of the star outfielders of that organization. "Little Mack" was the "Kid" who took the place in the Browns outfield of dear old Hughie Nichol. McCarthy was as fast as lightning in the outfield, a pretty man standing up at the plate and taking him all in all he might be termed one of the wonderful outfielders of the early eighties.

CALVIN A. McVEY—Calvin Alexander McVey, who played his first great baseball as right fielder for the Cincinnati Reds in 1896, was playing years later with the Cincinnati National League, Boston and other teams. McVey is now living in San Francisco. He was born at Montrose, Lee County, Iowa. When 10 years old he moved with his parents to Indianapolis and he was only 16 when he joined the University team there. Later he played with the Westerns and Actives of Indianapolis. He was with the latter when Harry Wright picked him up for the Cincinnati team. McVey played at right for the Cincinnati team but he was also a speedy pitcher, went behind the bat and caught with the best of them and stood ready at all stages to play any position on the team. As a batsman George Wright was the only man of the Cincinnati Reds who excelled him.

Long after the disbandment of the Cincinnati Reds, McVey held his own with the strongest and best players in the major leagues.

R. MELOAN—R. Meloan, up to August of the 1910 season proved to be the biggest find in the way of a recruit of the entire season. Meloan was purhased by Owner Charles Comiskey of the White Sox, from the Springfield Club of the Three I League, on July 15. The youngster was immediately put to work in right field and he made a decided hit from the jump. For several weeks, day in and day out the wonderful youth pounded out hit after hit and his fielding caused the critics of Chicago to go into raptures. In one game he lined out five safe hits in as many times at bat. George Rice, the veteran baseball authority of the Chicago News, a man who has seen the coming and going of thousands of ball players declared that Meloan was the grandest kid outfielder he had ever seen. Rice even went so far as to state that had Comiskey been able to show Meloan in the outfield in June, the White Sox would have won dozens and dozens of games more. Meloan is a well put up fellow, is fast on his feet and covers a world of ground. He is a native of East St. Louis, Ill., and previous to being discovered by Kinsella of the Springfield Club, played semi-professional ball. He is 22 years old, stands five feet, eight inches and weighs 170 pounds.

MICHAEL MITCHELL—Michael Mitchell is the big strapping right fielder of Clarke Griffith's Cincinnati Reds, the club which showed such vast improvement during this 1910 season in the National League race. Mitchell is probably the heaviest hitter in the National, a name which he had won because of his liking for nailing out three baggers and home runs just when a hit is needed. He joined the Reds three years ago, being recruited from the Portland Club of the Pacific Coast League. He made a decided hit from the outset and has hit close to .300 ever since. He is a splendid fielder, fast as lightning on the bases, and can throw with the best of them.

DANIEL F. MURPHY—Daniel F. Murphy, formerly the crack second baseman but now the regular right fielder of the Athletics of Philadelphia in 1909, was born in Philadelphia 32 years ago.

In his initial essay in professional life he received a try-out by Worcester, but did not pan out well, and he then went to North Attleboro, Mass., the same club with which "Hobe" Ferris of the St. Louis Browns shone.

In 1900 he went to Norwich, Connecticut, and did splendid work there.

The New York National League Club was attracted by his splendid playing and purchased his release. He played the latter part of the season and the first part of 1901 with New York and then went back to Norwich. The following year he was purchased by he Athletics to take the place of Lajoie who had been enjoined from playing with the Athletics by the courts, and he has played great ball with that club ever since.

Murphy is now the regular right fielder of the Philadelphia American League team and during the past season he, as usual, was regarded as one of the big fellows in the American League.

Murphy is one of Connie Mack's old guard and with Plank and Davis, is all that is left of Mack's old champions. For several years little Danny looked after second base and there were but few better infielders than he. It was his desire to move to the outfield and last spring Mack place him in right field. Murphy is an aggressive, steady fellow, is a splendid fielder and still a greater hitter and run getter.

JOHN MURRAY—John Murray is the regular right fielder of New York Giants of the National League season of 1910. Murray has been playing splendid ball in the National League for several seasons past. He was secured from the St. Louis Cardinals three years ago, where he had been playing steadily for three seasons. Under McGraw's careful handling Murray developed into a heavy hitter, a fast base runner and a rather fair sort of a fielder. In the season of 1909 he stood at the top as one of the best run getters in the National League, as well as one of the longest hitters. Murray played his usual good game the past season.

HARRY NILES—Harry Niles was born at Buchanan, Mich., September 10, 1881. His professional start was with the Binghamton Club of the New York State League for whom he played second base in 1903 and 1904.

He played at second for McAleer's Browns until 1907, when he was released to the New York Americans.

Niles was covering the right garden and short field for the Cleveland Club during the latter part of the 1910 season. Niles broke into the big league as a member of the St. Louis Browns four seasons ago. He was played at second and third bases while a member of the Browns team but when traded to New York two seasons ago he was moved to the outfield where his work showed much improvement. Niles is a very fast, aggressive ball player, and he has always been regarded as a good man with the willow. He has had a very fair season and seems to be marked for a good year in 1911.

FRANK SCHULTE—Frank Schulte is the regular right fielder of the Chicago Cubs of the National League. Schulte is one of the original Cubs, the team put together by Frank Selee, several years ago. He developed into a wonderful fielder and a slugger under the watchful eye of Frank Chance, and has played wonderful ball each year. Schulte stands five feet, ten inches, weighs 170 pounds, and is a perfect specimen of an athlete. Up to August 15, 1910, the speed merchant was clouting the ball to the tune of .280, had scored his share of runs and all in all had experienced another grand season.

WALTER SHALLER—Walter Shaller is a youngster who will attempt to win a steady position as a member of Hugh Jennings' Tigers outfield staff during the 1911 season. Shaller is a graduate of Pop Anson's Colts in Chicago. He is said to be a very fast fellow and many compare him with the youngster Meloan, who was captured by Comiskey last Fall.

W. L. SCHWEITZER—W. L. Schweitzer is a member of the St. Louis Browns Club of the American League, and during the past season he was used in the outer works, being played in right, left and center at times. Schweitzer is a native of Cincinnati, Ohio, and he began his big league baseball career as a member of the St. Louis Browns in the Spring of 1908, previous to which time he had played in the O. & P. League. Schweitzer is regarded as a promising young ball player, he is a good batsman and is fast on his feet and is a good thrower.

JOHN TITUS—John Titus has been looking after the right field garden of the Philadelphia Quakers of the National League for a dozen years. He is one of the old boys who has been able to appear each season in condition to play fast ball and compete with the hundreds of aspiring youngsters who are trying to win steady berths in the big arena. Titus is still considered one of the stars of the National League. He is a smashing batter, a beautiful thrower and a fast and dangerous man on the bases.

During the 1910 season he played his usual fine game, held up his end with the stick and scored his share of runs.

He is five feet, nine inches, weighs 166 pounds, and is 29 years old.

J. O. WILSON—J. O. Wilson, the regular right fielder of the Pittsburg Pirates, is one of the steadiest and most popular players in the big leagues. Wilson has been holding down the outerworks for the Pirates for four years and each season he has covered himself with glory. He is a splendid batsman, a true fielder and an excellent thrower. Before joining the Pirates he played three years with the Fort Worth Club of the Texas League. He was mainly responsible for that club winning the flag in the Texas League several years ago, his timely hitting doing the work.

H. W. WOLTER—H. W. Wolter was one of the fast hard hitting right fielders of the New York Americans during the season of 1910. Wolters was secured from Boston by the Highlanders and the change of club seems to have benefitted him much-ly. Wolters is considered one of the fast men on the bases in the American League and up to August of the 1910 season he had appeared in ninety-nine games, scored sixty-five runs, cracked out eighty-one bingles and had stolen twenty-three bases. His batting average was .244.

THE NATIONAL GAME.

THE BASEBALL MANAGERS.

AFTER THE PLAYERS COME THE MEN WHO PICKED THE PLAYING TEAMS IN THE OLD PROFESSIONAL ASSOCIATION AND THEN IN THE NATIONAL LEAGUE.

Year. Winner. Manager.	No. of Clubs.	Year. Winner. Manager.	No. of Clubs.
1871 Philadelphia—Hicks Hayhurst	6	1891 Boston—Selee	8
1872 Boston—Harry Wright	6	1892 Boston—Selee	12
1873 Boston—Harry Wright	6	1893 Boston—Selee	12
1874 Boston—Harry Wright	6	1894 Baltimore—Hanlon	12
1875 Boston—Harry Wright	6	1895 Baltimore—Hanlon	12
1876 Chicago—Spalding	8	1896 Baltimore—Hanlon	12
1877 Boston—H. Wright	6	1897 Boston—Selee	12
1878 Boston—H. Wright	6	1898 Boston—Selee	12
1879 Providence—G. Wright	8	1899 Brooklyn—Hanlon	12
1880 Chicago—Anson	8	1900 Brooklyn—Hanlon	8
1881 Chicago—Anson	8	1901 Pittsburg—Clarke	8
1882 Chicago—Anson	8	1902 Pittsburg—Clarke	8
1883 Boston—Morrill	8	1903 Pittsburg—Clarke	8
1884 Providence—Bancroft	8	1904 New York—McGraw	8
1885 Chicago—Anson	8	1905 New York—McGraw	8
1886 Chicago—Anson	8	1906 Chicago—Chance	8
1887 Detroit—Watkins	8	1907 Chicago—Chance	8
1888 New York—Mutrie	8	1908 Chicago—Chance	8
1889 New York—Mutrie	8	1909 Pittsburg—Clarke	8
1890 Brooklyn—McGunnigle	8	1910 Chicago—Chance	8

AMERICAN LEAGUE CHAMPION MANAGERS.

JENNINGS, THE MOST SUCCESSFUL OF THE MANAGERS IN THIS BASE-BALL ORGANIZATION SINCE ITS BEGINNING.

No manager in the American League, or any other league, has been so successfull since its beginning as Hugh Jennings of the Detroit Champion team. The list of winning managers in the American League since its initial year is as follows:

Year. Winner. Manager.	No. of Clubs.	Year. Winner. Manager.	No. of Clubs.
1900 Chicago—Comiskey	8	1906 Chicago—Jones	8
1901 Chicago—Griffith	8	1907 Detroit—Jennings	8
1902 Philadelphia—Mack	8	1908 Detroit—Jennings	8
1903 Boston—Collins	8	1909 Detroit—Jennings	8
1904 Boston—Collins	8	1910 Philadelphia—Mack	8
1905 Philadelphia—Mack	8		

After the players in the two leading baseball leagues of America come those who manage the teams, select the players and show the way.

By common consent the men considered the best managers are those who have been the most successful in winning championship pennants.

According to this theory, Hicks Hayhurst was the first of the great managers. It was he that placed the famous Athletics of Philadelpia in the field and who was their manager in the 1871 season, the first year, in fact, in which the professional game commenced to flourish and to widen its areas.

After Hayhurst came Harry Wright, perhaps the first real manager of the first real professional team, for he held that position with the Cincinnati Red Stockings of 1869. He was with them when they made their memorable tour that year.

In the sixties there was a team playing at Morrisania, then a village in Westchester County, New York, called the Unions.

Morrisania was at this time a sort of suburb of New York. It laid ten miles from the New York City Hall on the New York, New Haven and Hartford Railroad. It was annexed to New York as far back as 1873. In the sixties it was a place of few residences and broad fields. Here the youth of New York went when they sought fresh air, a ramble in the wild wood or a jaunt through country lanes.

Upon the broad fields of Morrisania the fine youth of New York, with athletic or baseball blood in his veins helped organize a baseball team in the sixties that later became famous the baseball world over as the Unions of Morrisania.

Upon this great team in the sixties were playing such noted players as the Wright brothers, George and Harry, first famous at cricket and then at baseball, and on the Union team were such later great players as Charley Pabor, at the top in his day as a pitcher; Dave Birdsall, in after years one of the first flight of catchers and players like them.

The Cincinnati people in 1868 were wild for a winning baseball team, and they appointed George B. Ellard and Alfred T. Goshorn to get a great team together.

These gentlemen scoured the country for material. On the field at Morrisania they found the Wright brothers and signed them, Harry to captain and manage their team and George to cover their short field. George and Harry Wright, beside playing with the Unions, had been with the Knickerbocker and Gotham clubs, semi-professional teams of New York City.

From that day in 1868, when he signed with the Cincinnatis until the close of his career many years later, Harry Wright was one of the best and most formidable builders up of the National game.

He was above all things a gentleman and an honest and ever earnest sportsman. That he knew all the curves and tangents of the great game is proven by his magnificent record.

He was for six years the manager of the champion Boston Club and he also did yeoman service as the manager of the Philadelphia Club of the National League.

Of all the men who helped the game when it was but an infant in arms, I know of no one who did better or grander work than Harry Wright.

He witn his brothers, George and Sam, were of English parentage. They had learned to play cricket before they took up baseball. They played cricket at Morrisania before they played anything else.

Next to Harry Wright as a champion manager, came A. G. Spalding, the manager of the champion Chicago White Stockings in their 1876 year.

I first saw Spalding at play with the Forest Citys of Rockford in the sixties. He was then a tall, slender youth. His home position was in the pitcher's box.

He was the only real pitcher the Bostons could boast of when they won the National League flag in 1872, 1873, 1874 and 1875, and he was the only real pitcher the Chicago White Stockings had when they won the flag in 1876.

Think of that, you one-day-a-week pitchers. Here was a man who went into the box every day for his side, pitched a- games without a rest and helped win five championships in succession.

Before his retirement, Spalding had grown to be a man of fine physique and great strength. He pitched underhand, the rules then forbidding the overhand throw.

Perhaps the two men in the baseball world, the men who have done more to widen the game's areas than any other two in the business are A. G. Spalding and A. J. Reach.

It was Mr. Spalding who planned the "All Around the World" tour of the players, the tour that went so far to introduce the game into England, Ireland, Scotland and other countries.

And to Mr. Spalding must also be given the credit of having helped as much as any other man in placing the game in this country on the solid foundation on which it rests today.

In the Spalding Guide of 1905 Mr. Spalding, talking of his first association with the National game, said:

"I am indebted for my first acquaintance with baseball to a disabled Illinois soldier returning from the war in 1863, when as a lad of 13, I listened to his account of baseball as played in the camp and under this old soldier's coaching, I became a member of the boys' club in Rockford, Illinois, which I believe was one of the first baseball clubs organized in the West.

"From 1865 to 1870 baseball clubs sprang up everywhere and the rivalry between cities became intense. The National Club of Washington was the first Eastern club to make an extended trip through the West in 1867 and met with only one defeat, and that at the hands of the Rockford Club, at which I had the honor to be the pitcher.

The result of this game was the indirect cause of my afterward becoming a professional player.

"Every effort was made at this period to keep the game on an amateur basis, but the rivalries between cities became so intense and the demand of the high-class public so urgent, that it was utterly impossible to keep the game on a strictly amateur plane. Veiled professionalism became the order of the day, and while the amateur status was insisted upon in the rules, young men possessed of skill as ball players, were offered lucrative positions in commercial houses with the understanding that they could play baseball all they wanted to, yet a large part of their salaries were provided by the local club or by some of its enthusiastic members.

"I recall my own experience when in the fall of 1867, I was surprised with an offer of a salary of $40 a week as a bill clerk in a wholesale grocery house in Chicago, which I accepted with the innocent satisfaction that my business abilities were so highly appreciated. I learned afterwards that the business concern appraised my service at $10 per week and that the Baseball Club made up the balance. This so-called amateurism or veiled professionalism, was in general vogue throughout the country during the latter part of the decade of the sixties and became so intolerable to players and club officials that it finally resulted in the organization of the National Association of Professional Baseball Players in 1876. From this date baseball playing has been recognized as a regular profession, and the game has since been under the management and control of regularly organized professional clubs, banded together in associations and leagues."

George Wright was the Champion Manager of the 1879 Providence Club and Anson and Morrill followed him. I have referred to these three great players elsewhere in this book.

Bancroft, then with Providence, was the champion manager of the 1884 season.

A man known the world over in baseball circles, and universally beloved is Frank C. Bancroft, now business manager of the Cincinnati Club.

"Banny," the name he is best known by in the baseball world, has been connected with the National game ever since it was worth talking about.

He has been in Cincinnati since 1890, nearly twenty years in all, but long before then he was connected with the game in some active way.

Mr. Bancroft, one of the deans of the profession, was born at Lancaster, Mass., May 9, 1906, and he was the proprietor of Bancroft's Hotel there until 1877 when he commenced taking an active part in the management of baseball teams.

In 1877 he organized the New Bedford team and so well that it won the state championship the following year. Elated at that success he organized the later famous Hop Bitters team and in the winter of 1879 he took that team to New Orleans and thence to Cuba where it helped wonderfully in the way of introducing the game into those parts.

In 1880 Bancroft went to Worcester, taking with him Arthur Irwin, who later became famous as the champion short fielder and captain of the Providence team, and J. Lee Richmond, a famous left handed pitcher of Brown University who later became one of the greatest pitchers of his day.

In 1881 and 1882 Mr. Bancroft was manager of the Detroit National League team and in 1883 he managed the Clevelands.

It was in 1884 that he managed the famous Providence team, the nine that with the aid of Irwin, Start, Farrell, Radbourne and other great players captured the first World's Championship from the Metropolitans then the leaders in the old American Association. He remained with Providence in 1885 and then went to Rochester for the 1886 season. In 1887 he was the business manager of the Athletics of Philadelphia and then after a season's absence in the theatrical world he returned to baseball, taking hold of the Indianapolis Club.

In 1889 was with Cincinnati and Milwaukee. In 1890 he found himself back with his Cincinnati friends and he has never since left the Queen City.

In 1877 when Mr. Bancroft was managing the New Bedford Club he had with him Jim Mutrie, afterwards manager of the New York Giants. On the New Bedfords Mutrie officiated as short-stop and captain and was paid $60 per month for his services. For the same New Bedford team Mr. Bancroft engaged Harry Stovey, afterwards a great star, as change pitcher at fifty dollars per month. George Washington Bradley, the pitcher, was paid the enormous salary of ninety dollars, and his catcher, Charley Reilly, got fifty dollars, Geo. Gore, Jesse Evans and Roger Connor, corresponding salaries. In a benefit in 1878 George Wright gave an exhibition on a rowing machine; his brother Sam swung Indian clubs; Harry Stovey gave a negro impersonation; Charley Foley (Curry) the pitcher, sang Irish songs; Jim Mutrie and George Gore engaged in a ten-mile walk, and Bancroft managed all these things.

Bancroft, although one of the veterans of the game, is still one of the livest and up-to-date men when it comes to the business management of a professionaal team.

W. H. Watkins was the manager of the champion Detroits in their successful 1887 year.

That was the year when Detroit had such great players as Brouthers, Dunlap, Rowe, Hanlon, Richardson, Bennett, White and Ganzel, and Watkins had much to do with getting this great team together.

He was always successful as a manager leading the St. Louis Club and then going to Indianapolis, where he now owns the club that represents that city in the American Association and where he has made a fortune out of baseball.

After Watkins at the top of the National League managers came big hearted, genial and loving James Mutrie, in 1888 and 1889 the manager of the Champion New York team.

When Jim Mutrie managed the Metropolitans and afterwards the New York Giants, he had a night key to all the newspaper offices in New York.

The newspaper boys of his time all swore by him and small wonder for he was a royal good fellow.

A good judge of players, too, was Jim, for it was he that got together the great New York team of which Buck Ewing, Tim Keefe, Johnny Ward, Mike Tiernan, Smiling Mickey Welch, Roger Connor, Danny Richardson and other great players were members. Mutrie used to be a shortstop, and came from the New England country from Chelsea, Mass., hard by Boston.

McGunnigle was the manager of the champion Brooklyns in their 1890 year. He was at one time a fine fielder and batsman.

After McGunnigle came one of the grandest characters connected with baseball and who honestly deserves a place in this book.

This was Frank G. Selee, who managed the Boston Club of the National League for nine years and who captured five championships with that team.

Few men in baseball were ever more popular than Mr. Selee. He had a host of friends. He was a gentleman by birth and breeding. His methods were of the quiet kind. He ruled his players gently, yet firmly. He believed the best results could be secured by bestowing confidence in his men and it was very rare indeed that his confidence was misplaced.

Mr. Selee was generous to a degree and extremely charitable. He was always ready, by word or deed, to promote a good cause. There will be recalled the splendid benefit that was arrangel for the crippled catcher, Charley Bennett, and was made a brilliant success largely through the efforts of Frank Selee. He has gone but will long be held in pleasant memory by all who ever had the good fortune to know him.

In 1896 Charley Mason, Billy Sharsig and Lew Simmons were the managers and the owners of the Philadelphia Athletics when they won the championship of the American Association in 1883.

The Athletics were a great money maker at home and abroad and their three managers kept no books but divided the receipts after each game, each taking his share home in a bag at the close of each day's business.

They were three good fellows all right. Simmons was a minstrel in his early days. He was the senior partner in the Philadelphia Minstrel Company known as Simmons, Slocum & Dixey.

The only baseball he ever played was on the stage.

Sharsig, his partner in the baseball business, was a thrifty Dutchman who died too early and Mason, his other partner, knew more about high balls than about that other ball on the diamond.

Still they were three good fellows and their Athletic team, thanks to the fine work of their captain, Harry Stovey, won championships and coined more money for the good-natured triumvirate.

Callahan of late years has been conducting one of the fastest semi-professional teams in Chicago, the Logan Squares.

Edward Hanlon, one of the greatest managers of his day, was at the top for five years. He first made winners of the great Baltimore team and then won two championships for Brooklyn. Hanlon is one of the brainiest men ever connected with the national game and besides being a great manager was one of the greatest players of his day.

Clarke was the leading manager in 1901, 1902, 1903 and 1909 and I have referred to him at length as a fielder.

Following Clarke in the 1904 and 1905 year, John J. McGraw, then leading New York, was the champion manager.

And of the present day lot of managers I think John J. McGraw of the New York Giants deserves a place at the very top.

The nine he manages always wins the flag or is so near the goal that it is always a drawing card.

The New York Giants under McGraw's management have always been a success from a box office standpoint and they have always played up-to-date and interesting baseball.

McGraw has often been accused of rough work and rowdyism. This is due to his always hustling and aggressive work on the field, which is not always understood by those who write for the press.

Those who know McGraw best know him to be a thorough little gentleman, generous and kind to a fault and a prince of good fellows.

His players speak well of him and that is the best test of his work as a manager.

Christy Mathewson, the great pitcher of the New York Giants, the other day told in this way the secret of McGraw's success as the leader of that team.

"I have often been asked to what I would atribute John McGraw's success as a baseball manager. In the first place, his method of handling his players conduces to getting the best possible results out of them. All players cannot be treated in the same manner. One man has to be patted upon the back, while another needs a sharp reprimand to make him put forth his best efforts to remedy his faults.

"McGraw has the supreme tact to employ these opposite methods in the way that causes no friction with the team, with the result that all of the men pull together for the success of the club. Every one knows that harmony is essential to a winning baseball team. Many teams on paper appear strong enough to win the championship, but because of some internal friction they fall short of their possibilities. On the other hand McGraw landed the pennant for New York with a team that was not seriously rated as a contender for first place. The good fellowship and pull together spirit that animated that team could not be excelled and John McGraw's lubricating tact kept the internal machinery working smoothly from first to last.

"A second great factor in McGraw's success is his knowledge of inside baseball. He is constantly planning to pull off the unexpected and in the execution of his plans he always takes into consideration the abilities of the players called on to carry out his scheme of play. The squeeze play, so popular with some managers, does not appeal to McGraw, but every other trick or device by which a run can be put across the plate has been sucessfully used in his campaigns on the diamond. He objects to the squeeze play because he believes that a brainy pitcher ought to break up the play and prevent its success by pitching the ball so wide that the batsman is not able to bunt it.

"The delayed steal, or the clean steal of third are all plays that can be worked with a first degree of success by certain men against particular teams. These and many other plays that contribute to team work or inside baseball are constantly practiced by McGraw's team, ready to be sprung whenever the watchful eye of the alert manager sees an opening.

"Of course, the plays are not always successful, for quick thinking opponents may anticipate them and break them up, but if a play fails because of some act of omission or commission on the part of the players, McGraw is quick to detect the fault and devise a remedy. Some managers have considered baseball and lacrosse as suitable for Spring practice for baseball players, but the Giants are drilled and drilled in baseball, not only physically, but mentally. Tactics play a large part in McGraw's method, and a player who cannot learn the fine points of the game under him will never excel in our national pastime.

"In the selection and retention of players McGraw's judgment is rarely at fault. When he became manager of the Giants one of his first acts was to release ten or twelve players. People who thought they knew declared he was letting some good material slip through his fingers, but only one man in the lot has retained a major league berth.

"The trade by which New York acquired Tenney and Bridwell was much criticised, but the result has justified McGraw's judgment. McGraw has the nerve to stand by his own judgment, and this was never better exemplified than when Larry Doyle made good at second base last year. McGraw had faith in Doyle from the beginning of Spring practice, and was deaf to the general criticism that he was making a mistake.

"I have been asked if I shall not miss Bresnahan. Indeed, I shall miss him, but as a catcher and a companion; but I believe that the deal by which we lost Bresnahan will strengthen the team in two departments of the game where we were weak. When the season of 1909 and 1910 is finished it is my belief we shall again applaud McGraw's wisdom in engineering an advantageous deal."

The manager of the New York Nationals was born in Truxton, N. Y., April 7, 1873, and is therefore 37 years of age. He played with Olean, N. Y., of the New York and Pennsylvania League in 1890 and in 1891 was the short-stop of the Cedar Rapids Club of the Illinois and Iowa League. Baltimore secured him that year and his career on the famous Baltimore champion team and since then with the New York Giants is known to every lover of the game.

Ask any of the players of the present day who is the best baseball manager in America and they will name John J. McGraw, Fred Clarke or Frank Chance.

Chance was the champion manager in 1906, 1907 and 1908, when he showed the Chicago Cubs the way. He is their manager, captain and first baseman yet and he is superb in all his positions.

In the American League Comiskey was top man in 1900, when he won the first pennant in that organization. We have referred to him in our sizing up of the first basemen.

Clark Griffith followed Comiskey as the leader of the Chicago White Sox in 1901. There was a time when Clark Griffith was only known as a great pitcher. That was when he pitched ball for the Chicago rival league teams.

Griffith hails from Bloomington, the town that gave Charley Radbourne, once the great pitcher, to the baseball world.

From Radbourne Griffith learned many of the great points of play that later made him famous as a pitcher.

From Chicago Griffith went to New York to manage the Yankees, but he was not at home there and when he quit them and signed up with the Cincinnati Club, to command the destinies of the Reds, many people said that one of the "brainiest" little managers in the American League was making his exit. Griffith was the first manager to make a success of changing pitchers.

He yanked out the tiring twirlers so fast it made their heads swim, and put his club up in the race long before any of the other managers took up the practice. He went in himself in pinches and was reputed to have nothing but his "head"—no speed or no curves—but still he was fairly successful on the slab. Fans are awaiting with a certain degree of expectancy, however, Griffith's showing in Redland. Success in his new berth means that he will continue to wear the title "Brains." So far he has more than made good over there.

After Griffith, as leading manager in the American League, came Cornelius McGillicuddy, better known as Connie Mack, in 1905, the manager of the Athletics of Philadelphia, champions of the American League that year.

Collins succeeded Mack as the leading manager in the American League in 1903 and 1904. We have referred to him in sizing up the third basemen. After Collins came Fielder Jones and Jennings, of whom we have also written extensively in another portion of this work. All of these we have mentioned were champion managers in their day. But there have been other managers not champions, it is true, but all worthy of mention in this work.

Stallings, the energetic and aggressive manager of the New York Americans, won the "first" pennant in the Southern League in 1893—there being two.

In 1893, there were twelve clubs in the Southern League circuit, and Augusta, under the management of Stallings, and the captaincy of the veteran third baseman, Jerry Denny, won the flag after the most strenuous baseball campaign ever waged in the land of Dixie.

Stallings has been doing great work ever since and is one of the best hustling managers in the business.

James J. Callahan, who managed the Chicago White Sox in 1901, was in his day a manager of the first class.

Callahan is now the clever manager of the Logan Square Independent Club of Chicago. He is a native of Fitchburg, Mass., and will reach his 36th year March 14, next. By trade Callahan was a plumber and he devoted as much time to baseball as he could.

Pitching was his great forte and he made such progress that he became noted there for his proficiency in that line. In 1891, when he was but 17 years of age, he won twenty-eight games, lost one and tied two as a member of the Pepperell, Mass., Club, and had a record of twenty-two strike-outs in one game. He played in Northampton, Mass., in 1892, with New Bedford in 1893, with Philadelphia in 1894, beginning that season with the Phillies in the National League and finishing with the State League team. In 1905 Callahan played with the Springfield, Mass., Club and made a fine showing there.

And, now breaking away from these managers, written about at random, I give an alphabetical list of the men who, since 1871 have held down that sort of a position with the clubs of the Professional Association, the National League, the American League and others of the major league organizatains that have flourished since that time.

JOSEPH CANTILLON—There are few more popular members of the profession to-day than Joe Cantillon, who managed the Washington Club of the American League and who is now at the head of the Minneapolis Club of the American Association.

Joe was the first heard of as a ball player 'way back in the eighties as a member of the Terre Haute (Ind.) team. He had played a lot of prairie ball before that around his old home in Janesville, Wis.

There were seven boys in the Cantillon family and every one of them played ball. With the help of two other boys they made a team that could beat anything in their part of the country. Strange as it may seem, Joe was the only one of the seven that has followed baseball through all the stages of the game. Mike is now a magnate, being a joint owner with Joe in the Minneapolis Club of the American Association, but he did not stick to the game through all the years that Joe did, but went into the railroad business with the other brothers, and worked himself well up before quitting and going back to his first love. All of his brothers have made good, and those that are in the railroad business to-day are among the highest officials of their roads.

Joe railroaded a good deal, but ball playing was more to his liking. In 1890, when Colonel Robinson wanted a few players to fill out his team in Oakland, Cal., Joe was recommended to him, along with Danny Sweeny and Sam Shaw. "Robby" signed the three easterners.

The boys were young and small, and when they landed in Oakland they were met by their new owner, who would not believe that they were his men, and imagined he was the victim of a joke.

Morris O'Neill, now president of the Western League, was there, however, and he convinced the club owner that there was no joke to it, and Robinson soon learned to his satisfaction that they were ball players. Joe remained in California three years and then came East and was manager of several minor league teams.

He was at Rock Island in the Three-I League, and then went to Dubuque, where he discovered Billy Sullivan, the present manager of the White Sox, in 1897. After that he umpired in the Western League, later in the American and still later in the National. He went to Milwaukee as manager in 1904, and for three years was at the head of the team there; then took charge of the Washington team in 1907 and remained there three seasons. He built the foundation of a very strong team in the Capital City. He went in with his brother, M. E., and bought out the Des Moines team in the Western League several years ago, and later sold it and bought the Minneapolis Club in the American Association. When the Washington people failed to renew his contract in 1909, he made arrangements to handle his own team in Minneapolis.

Cantillon was born at Janesville, Wis., Aug. 19, 1866. He was second baseman at Green Bay, Wis., in 1884; in 1885 with Tom Loftus in Dubuque, Ia., managing that club in '86; in '87 with Rockford, Ill. In 1888 he was in the Eau Claire, Wis., while Ted Sullian managed in Milwaukee. He was in Terre Haute in 1890; in that year he went to the Pacific slope and was with Oakland, Cal., until the close of 1893.

He was manager in Rock Island in 1894, and in Dubuque in 1895. In 1896 he managed in Columbus.

From 1897 to 1901, inclusive, he was in the Western Association and in the National League in 1900 and 1902. In 1903 he managed in Milwaukee and was there four seasons with the club, playing at second and from Milwaukee he went to Washington. Among the great players developed by Cincinnati during his managerial career were George Stone, "Jiggs" Donahue, Billy Sullivan, Howard Wakefield, "Lefty" Leifeld and Bob Ganley.

CHARLES C. CARR—Charles Carr, a fine stalwart fellow is the present manager of the Indianapolis club of the American Association who have won a pennant and stood high in that organization.

Mr. Carr is one of the strongest and best hustling first baseman in the game today. Mr. Carr was born in Coatesville, Pa., December 27, 1876. He played with the Atlantic City team in 1898, finishing with Toronto; 1902 managed in Jersey City.

In 1903 he went to Detroit and finished the season and part of the following one when he was sent to Cleveland. He remained with the Naps for a second season and in 1908 went to Indianapolis of the American Association as manager. He captured the pennant in that organization in 1908 and was in the fight to the finish in 1909. In the season of 1910, he made a grand fight for the pennant. While Carr was in the big leagues he was one of the most popular of players and besides he could bat some, and field some. He stands six feet, two inches and in playing condition weighs 195 pounds.

WILLIAM DAHLEN—William Dahlen, manager of the Brooklyn Club, was the leading short-stop of the National League in 1900. He was with Brooklyn that year and helped them materially in winning the championship that season.

Dahlen also played with Brooklyn when they won the championship. Dahlen was also the short-stop of the New York Giants when they won the championship in 1904 and 1905. He is still a fine heady player and was always a clever fielder, thrower and batsman.

PATRICK DONOVAN—Patrick Donovan was born March 16, 1865, in Lawrence, Mass., and his professional career began in 1886, when he played for the Lawrence Club, in the New England League. He continued with this team in 1887, the year it disbanded. He finished the season with the Salem Club, of the same league.

In his first two years in professional ball he did excellent work at the bat, ranking twelfth in the official averages of the league in 1886 and eleventh in 1887. In 1888 and 1889 he played center field for the London, Ontario, club and distinguished himself by his hard hitting and fine fielding, leading the International Association in 1888.

At the opening of the season of 1890 he was engaged by the Boston National League team, with which club he remained a few weeks, when he was signed by the Brooklyn Club, to replace Corkhill, who had fallen off in his playing. He proved a valuable addition to the Brooklyn Club hitting excellently, being a fine base runner and superb outfielder.

In 1893 he joined the Pittsburg Club and then went to the Louisville and the Wash-

ington teams. In 1898 he returned to Pittsburg and remained with the Pirates until they were consolidated with the Louisville team in 1900. He then became manager of the St. Louis National League team and remained in that position for four years.

He was next taken by Washington, in the American League. In 1895 he remained idle, owing to poor health. In the Fall of that year he was signed by the Brooklyn Club as manager and captain, where he remained until the Fall of 1908.

HUGH DUFFY—Hugh Duffy, who is now managing the Chicago White Stockings, is no novice in the handling of a major league team. Way back in 1890 he played with Comiskey's Players' League team, so that the "Old Roman" is no stranger to the abilities of his new manager. It will not be Duffy's first season in the American League either, as he managed in the season of 1901 when the Milwaukee team was in the organization. Duffy will have a great advantage in his new essay into major leaguedom of being identified with such an able connoiseur of baseball as is Comiskey. He will have full swing and at the same time will have the full sympathy and assistance of a man who knows the game from A to Z. It means a lot to a manager to have such a man associated with him. It is not often that suffiient financial inducements are made to prevail upon a man to relinquish such a position as Hugh Duffy had in the Providence Club, of which he was a part owner and manager, but Comiskey is willing to spend any sum within reason to further his end. Duffy certainly has some great talent with which to build a winning combination.

JACK DUNN—The man who was spoken of to manage the Boston Americans in 1910 is Jack Dunn, last year manager of Baltimore Eastern League Champions. Dunn was born in Meadeville, Pa., in 1874, and first attracted attention by his work with the New Jersey Athletic Club at Bayonne, N. J. Then he secured a professional opening with the Binghamton Club, champions of the New York State League, showing his versatility by pitching and playing the in and out fields. In 1896 he pitched for the Toronto Club of the Eastern League. He was purchased by the Brooklyns and remained with that club until the close of the season of 1900. The next season saw him with McGraw in Baltimore as a third baseman and the next three seasons he was a mamber of the New York Nationals. From New York he went to Providence to manage the Eastern League Club there for Pat Powers, and he landed the pennant there. In 1907 when the Providence Club changed hands he was signed by Ned Hanlon to handle the Baltimore Club, and acquitted himself so successfully that he landed the pennant after a terriñc struggle in which the Providence Club proved to be his closest rival.

EDWARD HANLON—Edward Hanlon has done much for the national game.

In his day he organized and managed many professional teams and in his earlier days he was a great fielder, batsman and base runner.

Hanlon will be remembered best by the old guard as the field captain and center fielder of the Detroit National League Champions of 1887. This team defeated Charlie Comiskey's St. Louis Browns for the championship of the world. Hanlon was a brilliant outfielder. He was the Fielder Jones of his time, playing the entire outfield for Detroit. Sam Thompson and Hardie Richardson, two tremendous sluggers, played the outfield with Hanlon in Detroit. They were carried for their hitting.

Hanlon was the whole show in the Detroit outfield, just like Fielder Jones was the whole works for the Champion Chicago White Sox. Hanlon saved his money while playing ball and when his playing days were over he was well fixed financially. Then he got a chance to show what he could do as a manager with the Baltimore National League team, and developed a great winner for the Maryland metropolis. When the Baltimore champions were transferred to Brooklyn, Hanlon bought stock in the club. He made a lot of money in Baltimore and Brooklyn. But he fell down as a manager after losing Johnny McGraw and Hughey Jennings.

Hanlon finished up his managerial career with the Cincinnati National League team. His record at Cincinnati was disappointing and there was no bidding for his services when his contract with the Reds expired. Ned then returned to Baltimore and was elected president of the Baltimore Eastern League Club in which he held the controlling interest. He sold out his holdings in the Baltimore Club recently to Jack Dunn and is now a free lance. Hanlon owns valuable real estate in Pittsburg, Baltimore and Brooklyn and is said to be worth $500,000. He is probably the wealthiest retired ball player in the history of the game.

FRED LAKE—Decidedly sensational was the engagement of Fred Lake, manager of the Boston Americans of 1909, by the Boston National League Club.

When Lake was given charge of the Boston Americans in the latter part of the season of 1909, he was the scout of the club. Such was his work that he was retained the season of 1909 and it became necessary to look about for a scout to succeed him.

P. J. Donovan, manager of the Brooklyn Club for the season of 1909, had been succeeded by H. C. Lumley, and was therefore at liberty. He was secured by President John I. Taylor of the Boston Americans.

It was the ambition of Lake to land his club in the first division of 1909, and he succeeded in so doing. It was not until late in the season that there was any suspicion that Lake would not succeed himself. Having received a bonus for landing his club as high as he did, Lake thought he was entitled to a substantial raise if he signed for the season of 1910, but President Taylor was unwilling to accede to Lake's demands and proceeded to do business with his scout, P. J. Donovan, who had ample experience in the management of major league teams and who made the last trip with the Boston Americans in the season of 1909.

No sooner had President Taylor signed Donovan than Lake signed to manage the Boston National League team of 1910.

Lake is now the fifth manager the Boston Nationals have had in five seasons. Tenney was the first one to take the reins under the Dovey regime, and he was followed by Joe Kelley in 1908. Frank Bowerman tried his hand in 1909, and after his resignation, Harry Smith took up

the running, and conducted the club to the end of the season.

Considering conditions and other things Lake's administration during the 1910 season might be called successful. He has rounded up what looks like a fair team for 1911, and should be heard from.

HARRY C. LUMLEY—Harry C. Lumley, who is one of the youngest of the major league managers in point of service in 1909, was born in Forest City, Pa., in 1880. He played with Rome, N. Y., in 1891, and was drafted by the St. Paul Club. He was with St. Paul in 1902 and with Colorado Springs the following season, finishing the season with Seattle. Then Brooklyn drafted Lumley, and he has been with that club ever since, at once making good with that team by virtue of his fine work at right field and his hard hitting, ranking as one of the hardest hitters in the country. The determination of President Ebbetts to secure a playing manager for the club for 1909 and the inability to effect a trade by which William F. Dahlen, of the Boston Nationals would have the position of manager paved the way for Lumley to secure the position and he has acquitted himself most creditably in his new place.

CONNIE MACK—If I were asked to name the four cleverest generals in the baseball business today I would unhesitatingly name Chance, Clarke, McGraw and Bresnahan in the National League and Connie Mack, Hughie Jennings, Hughie Duffy and Jack O'Connor in the American League.

And at the very top of even that list I believe I would place Connie Mack.

In clever generalship, in being able to always control his temper even under the most trying circumstances, in handling all sorts of ball players, and in handling them gently but firmly I know of no one to compare with the Athletics' manager.

In developing new material without running his club in debt for the purchase money, Mack also excels all others.

Connie Mack, the popular founder, manager and part owner of the Athletic Club of Philadelphia of the American League, was born at Brookfield, Mass., near Worcester, in 1862, and has had a long career in baseball. He played behind the bat with Meriden, Conn., in 1884, and with Hartford in 1885 and 1886. The latter part of 1886 he was with Washington, and he continued in that city in 1887, 1888 and 1889. Buffalo claimed him in 1890.

The next six seasons he was with Pittsburg as catcher and managed the club of that city from August, 1894, until August, 1896. In 1897 he managed the Milwaukee club of the Western League and in 1901 transferred his franchise to Philadelphia, thrice landing an American League pennant while in control of the Athletic Club. Mack's right name is McGillicuddy, but he is universally known as "Mack."

The game has no finer character than this leader of the Athletic Club. He is bold, fearless and aggressive as a manager, but on and off the field is always the real thoroughbred and gentleman.

Jake Morse, in a recent issue of his baseball magazine, had this tribute to pay to Connie Mack and a more deserved one was perhaps never written:

"Connie Mack, the astute gentleman who sits on the bench for the Philadelphia Athletics and pilots his 'White Elephants' to victory, is one of the marvels of baseball. He always manages to finish away up in the race, no matter how poor his chances may look at the opening of the season. His Athletics landed second in the American League in 1909, and gave the Tigers a desperate battle for the honors, the fight ending only two days before the season closed. And yet in the Spring the team was looked on as sort of a joke by the fans, players and scribes of the circuit. His pitching staff was its only bright feature.

"For catchers he had only material that other managers had turned down. Death robbed him of his star backstop, 'Doc' Powers, at the opening of the struggle. He had to depend on Ira Thomas, whom Hugh Jennings had dropped the previous season from his Detroit squad. His infield boasted one veteran, Harry Davis at first, Baker at third, Nichols at short, and Collins at second; all practically novices to the big league. In the outfield he two veterans, Hartsel and Murphy, were reputed to be 'going back.' The team went along smoothly for the first month. " 'Baseball luck,' declared the wise ones; 'wait until the others hit their gait, then watch the Athletics drop.'

"But somehow or other they didn't. Nichols, the short-stop, was about the only player who seemed slow. When the college season, closed, Barry, a youngster from Holy Cross, was brought into the ranks, put in at short, and at once began to show the fans along the line just how the game should be played. Baker, the tyro at third, was breaking up games every way with his trusty bat, and fielding in wonderful fashion. Collins, the guardian of second, was winning the unwilling admiration of his opponents, by his brilliant work in every department. He was even threatening to wrest the batting honors from the mighty Cobb.

"'Mack has a classy bunch, no doubt of it,' the critics began to admit along toward August; 'but they'll blow up soon. The youngsters are all right when things go smoothly. but they'll never be able to stand the strain. Detroit will walk away from them in the last month. Wait and see.' But as we have already stated the team from slowtown was in the fight up to the last ditch.

" 'How did they do it?'

" 'What kept them together.'

"There is but one answer—the baseball brains of Connie Mack. The shrewd leader knew the game from every angle. He knew how to get the most out of his players. He, better, perhaps, than any other, knew how to manage the erratic youngsters. He it was who handed out that panacea of all baseball ills—confidence—to his nervous proteges. And, above everything else, he instilled the spirit of team play. He kept after his men morning and night 'Play together' was his slogan from the opening day of the battle until the fatal afternoon last Fall, when an unexpected defeat by the White Sox called down the curtain on the Athletics' chances. The nine men were the units in a smooth working machine. Each one knew his part, and knew what to expect from his fellows. And so they were successful."

JAMES H. MANNING—James H. Manning was for many years one of the best known and most successful managers of baseball teams in the West.

As late as 1898 Mr. Manning was the president and manager of the champion Kansas City team of the Western League. He was engaged in professional baseball for sixteen years.

He started out with the Springfield (Ill.) Club in 1883. In 1884 and 1885, he played with the Boston team and 1886 found him in Detroit.

The following season he went to Kansas City, playing there in 1887, 1888, 1889, 1890, 1891, and a part of 1892. He finished the season of 1892 with the Birmingham (Ala.) Club. In 1893 he first became a magnate, being the owner and manager of the Savanah team of the Southern League.

The season of 1894 found him again in Kansas City, as the owner of the club, and he has remained there since, and has met with great success. In 1897 he entrusted the management of his team to another, and it fared so poorly he resolved to again assume actual control of the men, and during 1898 when his club won the pennant, he was on the bench in every game save one.

In 1900 Manning put his team in the American League and it remained there untill the reorganization which came a year later. Manning was not only a capable manager but an excellent player in his day,

JOHN J. McCLOSKEY — There are those who call John J. McCloskey, now the manager of the Milwaukee Club of the American Association "Columbus."

That is because he has discovered more great players than any other man.

He gave Fred Clarke to Pittsburg, Bugs Raymond to New York and Ed. Konetchy to St. Louis and these are only a few of his gifts.

And then, too, there are few better baseball generals than McCloskey.

As many of his campaigns are poorly executed he has often failed, but if he ever gets a team together that will carry out his orders, that team never will lose a game.

One of McCloskey's most brilliant plans was conceived when he was managing the Cardinals. He had an idea his team could beat Reulbach of the Chicago Club by bunting, and he sent the first seventeen men to bat with orders to bunt or to push the ball down the infield, no batter being allowed to hit the ball hard until after two strikes had been called.

The first six innings passed without a run being scored by St. Louis and then two bunts went safe in succession, another advanced the runners and the next man pushed the ball toward first base. It was thrown to the plate, two runs scored and St. Louis kept bunting until the game was won. All during the early stages of the game the players were frantic, begging to be permitted to hit hard, but McCloskey stuck to his plan of campaign and won.

McCloskey, who was with the St. Louis National League Club in 1907 and 1908 is one of the best known managers in the business.

McCloskey has been in baseball for over twenty years, and has doubtless handled more ball clubs than any man in the country. In 1887 he started with the St. Joseph, Mo. Club. From Missouri he went to Texas and handled the Austin and Houston teams.

He was on the Pacific slope in 1891, caring for the Sacramento teams' interests, and then hied back to Texas, casting his fortune again with Houston.

Since then he has been the leader of teams in Montgomery, Ala.; Savannah, Ga.; Louisville, Dallas, Grant Falls, Mont.; Tacoma, Wash.; Butte, Mont.; San Francisco, Cal.; Boise City, Idaho; Vancouver, B. C.; Wichita, Kan.; St. Louis, and Milwakee. He was in the latter city in 1909 when his Milwaukee team came within a game or two of winning the championship of the American Association. Again in the 1910 season McCloskey's team played very fair ball.

JOHN F. MORRILL—John F. Morrill, now the manager of the firm of Wright & Ditson, of Boston, formerly manager and captain of the Boston Club, and one of the best all round players of all time, has well maintained his interest in the game, and despite his great love for golf, manages often to attend ball games. Mr. Morrill also distinguished himself in the past by his articles on baseball in the Boston Journal. Lately he figured in a new role, being drawn on the jury and there he served with distinction as foreman.

RICHARD PADDEN—Richard Padden was the manager of the Chicago White Sox in their 1900 season. He was also their captain and second baseman. He was one of the foxiest and best second basemen in America. In 1902 he joined the St. Louis Browns and played at second for them. He was also their captain. That year the team made a great showing in the fight for the championship. The Browns went out in front early in June, and up to the final weeks of the season led the race. It was only because the Brown's pitchers went bad that Captain Padden's nine did not win out. It certainly was not his fault as "Brains" held the balance of the team together and fought beautifully against Mack's great Athletics. Before becoming a member of the White Sox and St. Louis Browns in the American League, Sir Richard had played with the old Pittsburg Pirates.

Padden was one of the real foxy fellows of the baseball world. He could field beautifully and was never better than when being hard driven. On the bases he was a very, very hard man to catch. It was not because he was unusually fast on his feet, but because he usually outgeneralled the battery. He was never more at home than when called to the plate in a pinch. He was not a slugger, but a cool, determined, careful, timely batsman. Padden is a native of Martin's Ferry, W. Va., the home of Cyrus Morgan, one of the Athletic's best pitchers. It was no one else but old "Brains' Padden that discovered Mr. Morgan and signed him for the St. Louis Browns. When James McAleer was made manager of the Washington Club a year ago, he signed the great Padden to act as chief scout for the Washington team. Padden is doing great work as a scout.

HARRY SMITH—Harry Smith deserves a word of credit for his work as manager of the Boston Club of the National League in 1909, and President John Dovey had the most implicit confidence in him. After Frank Bowerman resigned the position of manager, he was asked to designate his successor, and without the least hesitance named Harry Smith. Smith had no easy position to fill. He had to take a team that was a rank tail ender and going worse all the time. The club showed manifest improvement when the close of the season was reached. Under Smith's management, New York was twice blanked 3 to 0 and the team displayed an ability better than at any other time during the season.

In the Spring of 1910, Smith was succeeded by Fred Lake, who had managed the Boston American team the year previous.

T. P. SULLIVAN—"T. P. Sullivan, Writer and Dramatist. "That is what he calls himself; to others he is known as the "Scout" of the Chicago White Sox, the man to whom Comiskey goes for advice in so far as the worth of this, that or the other professional player is concerned. To me he is today and always has been plain Ted Sullivan, the best judge of a ball player in America, the man of widest vision in the baseball world, who predicted much for the National game years ago, and whose predictions have all come true.

You will find in nearly every college in America, stout, short, stocky lads, who seem to have the love of sport born in them.

It seems to be in their blood to excel at baseball, at football, at boxing, at rowing or at anything else in the way of outdoor sport.

And added to this love of manly games they have the keen sense of good judgment and in picking men to assist them and in bringing about an esprit-de-corps, proper team work and showing the way to successful play in all lines they excel.

John Ward, who captained the first New York Giants, was one of the sort. John J. McGraw, who now manages the New York Giants, and Hugh Jennings, the Detroit leader, are two others. I might mention others who ranked with these men when they were at their best as players, organizers and that sort, but none that would excel Ted Sullivan when it came to the picking of a team, placing it and getting all to take hold of one end of the rope and pull together.

Sullivan early proved the worth that was in him and proved it at a time when real players were scarce, when club discipline was a thing unknown and when the conduct of the so-called professionals often tried the soul of the best and most patient of managers.

Built on the lines of McGraw and Ward, with a face and eyes that beam intelligence, and a head which reflects nothing so much as the wide awake, go-ahead and aggressive spirit of the owner, Sullivan is a marked figure in any gathering. His long experience in the baseball world, his travel and brisk acquaintance have added to his natural fund of Irish wit and make him delightful as a raconteur. No man in the baseball world, indeed, can compare with Sullivan as a story teller.

He will tell you the story of the young player who has come in the spring determined to conquer all and show you the same young man meandering homeward before the real fight has begun, and do it by word gesture and grimace till you lose yourself and forget it is only Ted after all telling a story. He can and has mimicked a German Jew so well that men of that race have been deceived. He can talk the Irish brogue from the Limerick and Dublin twang to the bloody far down and no man on earth can better mimic the Texas farmer or the Southern gentleman. As has been said, often, Ted can "Scout" in all languages and in all garbs.

CHAS. DOOIN

The Crack Catcher and Manager of the Philadelphia National League Club in 1911

Ted Sullivan and Charles Comiskey grew up together. In their boyhood days they went to school together at St. Mary's, Kansas College and, Sullivan being the elder, a born wit and a leader in sport, even then Comiskey received his first real lessons from him. That was in the early seventies.

When they left school Sullivan and Comiskey went to Dubuque, Iowa, Sullivan to accept the news agency of all the roads running out of Dubuque to Chicago, and Comiskey to act as his assistant in that line. Later, Sioux City, Iowa and La-Crosse, Wis., were added to Sullivan's territory.

But while acting in this capacity Ted's mind still ran often to baseball, and almost alone and unaided, he organized the first minor baseball league ever known, its roster including the cities of Dubuque and Davenport, Iowa, Rockford, Ill. and Omaha, Neb.

It was in this league that Sullivan first showed his skill in picking players for in its playing teams were men like Charles Radbourne, Charles Comiskey "Bid" McPhee, Jim Whitney, Jack and Dave Rowe, Tom Loftus, the Gleason brothers, Jack and Billy; and many others, who subsequently shone as stars in the major leagues and nearly all of whom owed their real start to Sullivan.

It was in 1881 that I first met Ted Sullivan. I was then managing the co-operative St. Louis Browns, and was looking about the country for teams to play them. I had heard of Sullivan and I wrote to him at Dubuque and asked him to bring a team to St. Louis to play three or four games. In another part of this work I refer to the team he brought here then. It included, among others, Comiskey and Loftus, and it was this visit that led to Comiskey's coming to St. Louis a year afterwards to manage the St. Louis Browns. It was from this team, strengthened a year or two later, that came the four-time winner, St. Louis Browns, the team that won successive pennants in the American Association, and then captured world's honors. During the time one of the building up of this team, Sullivan was the leader. Comiskey, true enough, was even then the team's first baseman, but he had not yet mastered the inner points, nor did he possess the spirit, nor the aggressiveness needed then by the real commander.

It was not indeed until Sullivan had put the St. Louis team into real shape that Comiskey took hold of it as its captain and manager. That was in 1885. Prior to that, the work of building up had been done by Sullivan for the strong and aggressive personality of Comiskey did not really mature until later. The great players who went to make up the wonderful winning combination for St. Louis were gathered together from all parts of the country by Sullivan.

One of his first strokes was to bring little Hugh Nicol here to play right field.

He took him from the champion White Stockings. Then he went East and picked up Tom Deasley, the Boston catcher, and Arlie Latham, the crack third baseman of the Athletics of Philadelphia. He got other players from other directions, put together a stone wall infield and an outer works to match and then turned the guns over to Comiskey.

In 1884 Sullivan's active mind and aggressiveness led to his joining forces with Henry V. Lucas of St. Louis and that combination resulted in the organization of the Union Association of baseball players, the most powerful and widespread movement of independent players that up to this time had ever been taken in opposition to the owners of the clubs of the National League and American Association.

When this organization disbanded in 1885, Sullivan set out as an organizer of minor baseball leagues and that year he organized the Western League, with clubs in Kansas City, Omaha, Milwaukee, Toledo, Indianapolis and Cleveland.

In 1888 Sullivan appeared as the manager of the Washington Club of the National League.

In 1900 he established the Atlantic League and in 1902 and for a couple of years later he organized the Texas League and put the game on a proper footing in the Lone Star State. In 1904 he put the strong Virginia League in motion.

In recent years he has devoted nearly all his time to the selecting of players for the major league teams.

In the early days he introduced Charles Comiskey and Charles Radbourne, peerless players, to the game. More recently he has brought out such wonders as John Kling and Overall of the Chicago Cubs and Purtell, the great young player of the Chicago White Sox.

I might go on forever telling of what Sullivan has done for the game, for his labors have been increasing and have been continued from the earliest days of the real professional sport up to the present time, and so I will conclude this sketch of him with a few words spoken on the same subject by Charles Comiskey, Sullivan's life-long friend:

"Ted Sullivan's standing in the profession of baseball," said Comiskey, "cannot be measured by modern standards. He is in a class all by himself. He is ever and always ahead of his time, with a knowledge of the game and a versatility that no other baseball man of my acquaintance has ever possessed.'

Of what Sullivan did to bring about the organization of the American League, I have told elsewhere in this work.

JAMES A. WILLIAMS—James A. Williams was the manager of the St. Louis Browns in 1884.

Mr. Williams had been the secretary of the American Association and knew more about clerical work than the managing of a baseball team. So that part of the work was left to the team captain, Charles A. Comiskey, who the following year took Mr. William's place as manager.

THE NATIONAL GAME.

THE BASEBALL PRESIDENTS.

A LIST OF THOSE AT THE HEAD OF THE CLUBS OF THE OLD PROFESSIONAL ASSOCIATION AND THE NATIONAL LEAGUE.

These were the men who filled the high office of president for the club members, first of the old Professional Association and then of the National League:

Year.	Club.	Presidents.
1876-1881	Chicago	William A. Hulbert.
1882-1891	Chicago	A. G. Spalding.
1892-1905	Chicago	James A. Hart.
1906-1910	Chicago	Charles W. Murphy.
1876	—Boston	N. T. Appolinio.
1877-1906	—Boston	A. H. Soden.
1907-1909	—Boston	George B. Dovey.
1909-1910	—Boston	John S. C. Dovey.
1876	—Mutuals	W. H. Cammeyer.
1876	—Athletics	Thomas J. Smith.
1876-1877	—Hartford	Hon. Morgan G. Bulkeley.
1876	—St. Louis	J. B. C. Lucas.
1885	—St. Louis	Henry V. Lucas.
1892-1897	—St. Louis	Chris Von der Ahe.
1898	—St. Louis	B. S. Muckenfuss.
1899-1906	—St. Louis	F. DeHass Robison.
1906-1910	—St. Louis	Stanley Robison.
1876-1877	—Cincinnati	J. L Keck.
1878-1879	—Cincinnati	J. M. W. Neff.
1880	—Cincinnati	Justus Thorner.
1890	—Cincinnati	A. S. Stern.
1891-1902	—Cincinnati	John. T. Brush.
1903-1910	—Cincinnati	August Herrmann.
1878	—Indianapolis	W. B. Pettit.
1889	—Indianapolis	John T. Brush.
1878	—Milwaukee	J.R. Kaine.
1878	—Providence	John D. Thurston.
1879-0-1-4-5	—Providence.	Henry T. Root.
1882-1883	—Providence.	Henry B. Winship.
1879	—Buffalo	E. B. Smith.
1880	—Buffalo	John B. Sage.
1881-1885	—Buffalo	Josiah Jewett.
1879-1881	—Cleveland	J. Ford Evans.
1882-1884	—Cleveland	C. H. Bulkeley.
1889-1898	—Cleveland	F. DeHaas Robison.
1899-1900	—Cleveland	Stanley Robison.
1890-1897	—Brooklyn	Charles H. Byrne.

Year.	Club.	Presidents.
1898-1909	—Brooklyn	Chas. H. Ebbets.
1892	—Baltimore	H. R. Von der Horst.
1893-1900	—Baltimore	Edward Hanlon.
1876-1877	—Louisville	W. N. Haldeman.
1892	—Louisville	T. Hunt Stuckey.
1893-1896	—Louisville	Fred Dresler.
1897-1898	—Louisville	Harry C. Pulliam.
1899	—Louisville	Barney Dreyfuss.
1900	—Louisville	Harry C. Pulliam.
1879	—Syracuse	Hamilton S. White.
1879-1880	—Troy	Gardner Earl.
1881	—Troy	A. L. Hotchkiss.
1882	—Troy	Francis N. Mann.
1880-1882	—Worcester	Hon. C. B. Piatt.
1881-1884	—Detroit	Hon. W. G. Thompson.
1885-1886	—Detroit	Joseph A. Marsh.
1887	—Detroit	Fred K.Stearns.
1888	—Detroit	Chas. W. Smith.
1883-1892	—New York	John B. Day.
1893-1894	—New York	C. C. Van Cott.
1895-1902	—New York	Andrew Freedman.
1903-1910	—New York	John T. Brush.
1883-1902	—Philadelphia	A. J. Reach.
1903-1904	—Philadelphia	James Potter.
1905-1908	—Philadelphia	W. J. Shettsline.
1909	—Philadelphia	Israel W. Durham.
1909-1910	—Philadelphia	Horace S. Fogel.
1886	—Kansas City	Joseph J. Heim.
1887-1890	—Pittsburg	W. A. Nimick.
1891	—Pittsburg	J. Palmer O'Neill.
1892	—Pittsburg	A. C. Buckenberger.
1894-5-6-7-9	—Pittsburg	W. W. Kerr.
1898	—Pittsburg	W. H. Watkins.
1900-1910	—Pittsburg	Barney Dreyfuss.
1886-1888	—Washington	Robert C. Hewett.
1889	—Washington	Walter T. Hewitt.
1892-1900	—Washington	George W. Wagner.

AMERICAN LEAGUE PRESIDENTS.

A LIST OF THE PRESIDENTS OF THE CLUBS OF THIS ORGANIZATION SINCE IT WAS FORMED IN 1900 TO THE PRESENT TIME.

This is a list of the men who have held the office of president for the clubs of the American League since the first year of that body.

Year.	Club.	President.
1900-1910	Chicago	C. A. Comiskey.
1900	—Indianapolis	W. H. Watkins.
1900	—Kansas City	James H. Manning.
1900	—Buffalo	James Franklin.
1900	—Minneapolis	Clarence Salspaugh.
1900-1901	—Milwaukee	Matt Killelea.
1900-1910	—Cleveland	John. F. Kilfoyl.
1900-1901	—Detroit	James D. Burns.
1902-1903	—Detroit	Samuel F. Angus.
1904-1907	—Detroit.	W. H. Yawkey.
1908-09-10	—Detroit	F. J. Navin.
1901-1903	—Washington	Fred Postal.

Year.	Club.	President.
1904	—Washington	Thomas J. Loftus.
1905-1910	—Washington	Thomas C. Noyes.
1901-1902	—Boston	Charles W. Somers.
1903	—Boston	Henry J. Killilea.
1904-1910	—Boston	John I. Taylor.
1901	—Baltimore	Sidney W. Frank.
1902	—Baltimore	John J. Mahon.
1901-1910	—Philadelphia	Ben. F. Shibe.
1902	—St. Louis	Ralph Orthwein.
1903-1910	—St. Louis	Robert L. Hedges.
1903-1906	—New York	Joseph W. Gorden.
1903-1910	—New York	Frank J. Farrell.

After the managers comes a story of those who were the presidents of the great baseball teams since the game first really began.

And I suppose it is only right that I should place at the head of this list, Alfred J. Reach, who for twenty years held the office of President of the Philadelphia Club of the National League.

No other League president in years of service can approach Mr. Reach and best

of all when he retired as the head of the Philadelphia Club in 1902, after having served in that capacity for a round score of years, he was still in the heydey of his skill and strength as a baseball president and business man.

But beside being the dean of the baseball presidents, Mr. Reach is at the head of the baseball profession in so far as goes wealth and business standing. Mr. Reach is today by long odds the wealthiest man connected with the game.

And besides possessing great wealth, Mr. Reach is perhaps the best posted baseball man in America, having won his early education in that line on the famous old Capitoline Ball Ground in Brooklyn, from which in the early seventies were graduated the maiden crop of great professional players.

Mr. Reach is, perhaps, one of the only baseball presidents living who can remember the work of the earliest great players, the pitchers like Pabor, Martin, Pinkham, Zettlein and McBride, the catchers like Allison, Hicks and Mills; the first basemen like Start, Fisler and McAtee; the second base players like himself, Jimmy Wood, Sweasy and Smith; the third base players like Meyerle, Ferguson and Waterman; the short-stops like George Wright, Pearce and Radcliffe, and the great fielders like Gedney, Chapman, Pike, Cuthbert, Remsen and Sensenderfer.

Mr. Reach was associated with those players in the early days of the professional game. Later with the aid of the veteran Harry Wright, Mr. Reach gave to Philadelphia many of her greatest baseball players.

It was Mr. Reach who found for Harry Wright, the first great manager of professional teams, a place that he filled until the last days of his honorable career, and it was while associated with Mr. Wright that Mr. Reach became familiar with all the inside of baseball as it is played by the best experts of to-day. And so to-day Mr. Reach is wise in old and new baseball knowledge and all around in that line is excelled by no other person.

Mr. Reach, although a veteran of veterans, is to-day the picture of health and strength. He walks with steady stride and moves with all the life and activity of a man of thirty.

Looking at him one can scarcely believe that he was the great second baseman of the Athletics of Philadelphia in 1871, the team that won the championship of the Professional Association for Philadelphia that year. That was nearly forty years ago.

Two or three baseball generations have come up since then and the old players with whom Mr. Reach was associated on the old Athletic team have nearly all of them struck out.

But Mr. Reach in spirit, action and all is as young and brisk today as he was forty years ago, and he never is so happy as when talking of the games of the early seventies in which he took so active a part.

Mr. Reach was a member of the famous old Eckford team of Brooklyn in the late sixties, but in 1871 he went to Philadelphia to join the team which won the championsip for the Quaker City that year. He has made that city his home ever since.

It was while a member of the Athletic team that Mr. Reach started the A. J. Reach Company, the great sporting goods house of Philadelphia, which still bears his name, and which is the largest manufacturer of base balls and baseball goods in the world.

Mr. Reach started out a poor boy and out of his indomitable energy and business enterprise, he has placed himself at the very top of the great baseball world.

A man of medium size is Mr. Reach, of bright eye and intelligent and good natured face. As a player he was noted for his sterling integrity and steady conduct on and off the field, and these traits he brought into his business life and they helped him score the great success he has attained there.

After Mr. Reach perhaps should come the presidents of the three leading clubs of the National League, the Pittsburg, Chicago and New York clubs.

JOHN T. BRUSH—John T. Brush, president of the New York Club of the National League is the most aggressive and resourceful of all the great baseball presidents. Mr. Brush has always been a leader.

He was the brains of the American Association and when that organization was wiped off the face of the baseball map Mr. Brush, who was really its chief executive, went to the National League and ever since then he has been the most rapid thinker in that body.

He has in his day been at the head of the Indianapolis, Cincinnati and New York Clubs. He has been interested in professional baseball off and on for twenty years. He was identified with a clothing store in Indianapolis when he became president of the club of that city and sold his players to John B. Day of the New York Club in 1880 for $80,000.

By a strange combination of circumstances Mr. Brush got the Cincinnati Club in 1881 for absolutely nothing and he held on to it for nearly ten years, when he sold out to Garry Herrmann for almost $100,000. Mr. Brush then purchased a controlling interest in the New York Club from Andrew Freedman, and with McGraw at the head of the team he proceeded to score a series of phenomenal successes.

In 1908 the Giants, who lost the pennant by a single game, made $320,000 for Mr. Brush and his partners, while last season, it is said, nearly $200,000 was cleaned up at the Polo Grounds and on the road.

In all the great baseball movements Mr. Brush has been a leader. He was with the National League in their great fight with the Brotherhood and the Union Association and in those fights he saw that his side came out victorious at the end.

As an organizer and most resourceful leader there is no one in the National League to compare with Mr. Brush. Although a man of frail physique and for a long while in poor health he has controlled the National League meetings and it was he that placed Thomas J. Lynch at the head of that body.

From the time that John T. Brush got into baseball he was madly infatuated with the idea of winning the championship. When he was the owner of the Indianapolis Club his one idea was to put together an organization which would be strong enough to bring terror to the hearts of the New York, Chicago and Boston teams, which carried off the lions' share of baseball honors.

He bent all his energy to get together a team which would make a fine showing in the National League. "The only trouble that we had at that time," said he one day, when he was discussing baseball with his usual dry humor, "was that those of us who were 'small fry' had to dig down in our jeans and pay for the fun that we had in traveling around to New York and Boston, while the New York and Boston people had money thrown at them and traveled in superior

W. H. WATKINS.
Snapshot of the Veteran President of the Indianapolis Club, As He Sat in the Bleachers in the Spring of 1911 Watching His Boys Training.

style out to our cities and lorded it over us."

After he acquired the franchise of the Cincinnati Club he was still bent on winning a championship. One day while in the East, attendant upon a league meeting, he was joking with Frank DeHass Robison, his warmest personal friend in baseball. The Cleveland owner, as usual, was laughing at Mr. Brush because he never had won a pennant, and referred to the fact that Cleveland had at least finished second, which was more than could be said for Cincinnati.

"Never mind," replied Mr. Brush, "I'm not through yet. I'll bet you that I win a championship in the National League before you do."

They made a wager of a dinner and Mr. Brush won, although at that time neither of the men had the faintest idea that the championship would be captured by Mr. Brush as the owner of the Giants, one of the most famous clubs in all baseball history.

The present New York owner spent money right and left when he was with Cincinnati. He purchased release after release, that seemed as if it would do the Cincinnati Club good, but the usual run of misfortune which had followed Cincinnati for years, it seemed out of the question to get championship work from the players.

One day there came an opening to buy the New York Club. But one or two men in the United States knew that it could be purchased. John T. Brush was one of them. He lost no time in acquiring the necessary amount of stock which would put him in control of one of the oldest baseball organizations in the United States. There was no publicity in regard to the deal, until after it was completed, although there were a very few who knew that it would possibly be made.

With the New York Club he secured the services of John J. McGraw as manager, turned the playing end of the organization over to him, and, after waiting a year, finally had the hope of a lifetime realized when the Giants won the championship and he was the president and owner of the organization.

For years suffering from an illness that has at times almost been unbearable—rheumatism of the most painful description—it is rarely that this baseball pioneer has been heard to utter a word of complaint. Now and then the malady has been so violent that involuntary groans of agony have escaped the invalid, but so far as personal courage is concerned, John T. Brush bears his illness with the fortitude that he bears adverse legislation and the criticism of others.

In the last two years, especially, the Giants and the Polo Grounds have been his hobby. Started on the way to improve the field in New York, on which the games are played for the championship of the National League, he has determined that it shall be the handsomest baseball ground in the United States. He is wrapped up in the idea of giving New York baseball patrons a finer home for professional baseball than can be found in other cities.

Perhaps the rebuilt stand on the Polo Grounds may lack the stability of those magnificent new structures which are to be erected in other cities, but it is unquestionably true that the New York

owner has so improved the buildings in his home city that he has one of the most artistic parks in the United States and when all the details are completed it will most certainly be a feast of beauty.

Divided with the attention which he puts on the fitting for the game, is that which he puts on the players for his team. "I am going to win that National League championship once more," said he to the writer. "I had it won in 1908, but they euchred me out of it. I'll have it won in the year to come, or in some other year to come, merely to show that I am still in baseball. The law, they said, took the championship away from us in 1908. It wasn't a case of law, but justice. Poetic justice will give it again to the Giants where it belongs."

THOMAS M. CHIVINGTON—Thomas M. Chivington, the new president of the American Association, has had but three years actual experience in baseball, but he has been a student and critic of the national sport for a great many years as a semi-professional player, newspaper writer and scorer. He has written ball for newspapers of Chicago, Milwaukee and Louisville and has been identified with sports for nearly a score of years. Early in the year of 1907 the Louisville Baseball Club was turned over to him and for three years he was in entire charge of both the playing and business departments. He considers himself fortunate in having kept his team in the race each of these three years, finishing second in 1908 and winning the pennant in 1909.

GEORGE DOVEY—Baseball lost a staunch friend when on July 19, 1909, George Dovey, president of the Boston National League team passed away.

Mr. Dovey was a native of Philadelphia. Early in life he was interested in coal mining in Central City, Ky., and was compelled to abandon this enterprise owing to the inundation of the mines.

Thereupon he went into the traction business and was for many years identified with the Johnsons, and was with the Brooklyn road under Al Johnson for eleven years. It is worthy of remark that Mr. Johnson died very suddenly, in the prime of his life, much the same as did Mr. Dovey.

After leaving Brooklyn, Mr. Dovey was identified with St. Louis railway interests, being connected with the St. Louis Transit and the St. Louis Car Companies, always considered a valuable and trusted employe.

Baseball was no new thing to him when he determined to purchase the franchise of the Boston National League Club from Messrs. Soden and Conant, the sole owners. He was a close friend of Barney Dreyfuss early in life; in fact, played on Barney's team in Paducah, Ky., for it was in that city that Mr. Dreyfuss received the education in baseball which afterwards resulted in his devoting himself to it for life. Mr. Dovey and Mr. Dreyfuss were warm and fast friends and the former, always a great lover of the game, made the acquaintance of all the owners of the big clubs before he had any other than a sentimental interest in it.

In the season of 1906 a change in the Boston Club being thought desirable, the suggested itself that Mr. Dovey was the one man who could take hold of the club and make it a winner. The matter was brought to his attention, and after due consideration the deal was put through. Mr. Dovey was called upon to put up a deposit of $5,000 and to follow this up with a further payment of $70,000 in cold cash, for which the franchise, players, grounds and appurtenances were turned over to him, the owners of the real estate taking a back mortgage of $200,000 at three and a half per cent. The club that was handed over to him was a tail-ender, but he went to work on it with a will and commenced the building up of a first-class baseball team when death put an end to his endeavors.

Mr. Dovey was one of the most considerate of employers and held the respect of his players. He always had a kind word for every one with whom he came in contact. His warmth was infectious, and where George Dovey was there was good fellowship.

BARNEY DREYFUSS—There are all kinds of men at the head of the major league clubs of the country.

Undoubtedly the cleverest, and not far from the wealthiest, the owner of unquestionably the grandest baseball plant in the universe, as well as the World's Championship team, is Herr "Barney" Dreyfuss, the Pittsburg magnate.

Fred Clarke, Tommy Leach, "Hans" Wagner, "Deacon" Philippe and Sam Leever have never had any other boss than the little gentleman, who got his start on prosperity boulevard by dealing in whiskies and wines, first of all in that dear Paducah and then in Louisville.

The late Harry Pulliam, they say, taught Dreyfuss how to speak and write English. Anyhow, poor Harry did teach "Herr Barney the baseball business. As a reward he became secretary of the Louisville Club, then president, next secretary of the Pittsburg Club and for a grand wind-up, president of the National League.

According to most well posted souls in balldom, Clarke gets $12,500 per. Philippe and Leever, although little else but pensioners, are receiving their old pay. They were Dreyfuss' first two winning pitchers and there's work for them on the Pittsburg team as long as they wish to play ball. They've been told that. Neither will draw the pink envelope. When they discontinue their stay with the Pirates it will be when they have handed in their resignations.

So much for Dreyfuss' liberality and loyalty. Now for his sound sense. The 1909 season came by his team winning the National League Championship, and then the World's Series. Originally, the Pirates were going barn-storming.

Dreyfuss, also the fair city of Pittsburg, arranged so many festivities in honor of Fred Clarke and his players, that they called off the money-grabbing trip. Promoters wanted the Pirates to go to California. They left that to the Athletics.

Other promoters besought them to go to Cuba. They left that to the Tigers. A week later when the second outfit of filibusters set out for Havana it was thought that Messrs. Adams, Camnitz, Miller and Hyatt of the World's Champions would be in the party. As soon as Dreyfuss got wind of the scheme he wrote his men and showed them the foolishness of the winter trip. One by one they whisked along their regrets. Later they won a World's

Championship for Dreyfuss and incidentally paid tribute to his good sense and wise management.

ISRAEL W. DURHAM—Israel W. Durham, who was the president and a large owner in the Philadelphia National League Club, died in June, 1909, after a long illness. He was one of the staunchest and best friends the game had in the Quaker City.

Senator Durham was a leader in Philadelphia politics for years and was recognized as a man of great executive ability.

Some time before his death he found it necessary to lessen the burden of his political cares and so he turned it over to his partner, Senator James P. McNichol.

Previous to their acquisition of the Philadelphia Club from a syndicate, Senators Durham, McNichol and Clarence Wolf were always loyal followers of both the American and National League Clubs and always attended the games in Philadelphia when it was possible for them to do so.

Although this trio were very fond of the game, much surprise was expressed when they secured the club. In assuming the presidency, Senator Durham said:

"We are going to give Philadelphia a pennant winner if possible. No price will be too high to pay for a player if we want him for the money."

Following the acquisition of the club, extensive improvements were made on the plant, already one of the finest in the country, so that now it is a model establishment in every respect.

CHARLES EBBETS—Charles H. Ebbets, the president of the Brooklyn Club, of the National League, has worked his way from the ranks.

He has gone from the humble place of ticket seller to the position of president and he is now the virtual owner of the club and its property.

Mr. Ebbets has been identified with the game in Brooklyn for the past eighteen years.

He was engaged as a ticket seller by the originators of the club, Byrne, Doyle and Abell, when the Brooklyns began playing at old Washington Park.

Later he was appointed secretary of the club and remained on the job for a number of years. When the club was consolidated with Baltimore nearly ten years ago Mr. Ebbets owned ten per cent of the stock. In the course of time he secured sufficient backing to purchase more than 40 per cent of the stock from the late Harry Von der Horst of Baltimore, thereby putting Edward Hanlon and Abell in the minority. Mr. Ebbets elected himself president in 1898, but the club was quickly involved in litigation. He then dug up another bank roll and bought out Abell and Hanlon and to-day he is the leader in baseball in Brooklyn. Mr. Ebbets has no occupation other than baseball at present, but he has been a member of the Assembly and the Board of Aldermen of Brooklyn.

FRANK FARRELL—The New York American League Club, known as the Highlanders, have Frank Farrell as their president.

Before entering baseball Mr. Farrell was a turfman of note for many years. At one time he was a partner of Julius Fleischmann, former mayor of Cincinnati, and together they campaigned a powerful string of horses, including the famous Blues. When Fleischmann retired from racing Farrell went ahead on his own hook, buying many thoroughbreds with a lavish hand and always betting extensively.

At the tracks he met John McGraw, who was anxious to transfer his Baltimore American League Club to New York, and after some persuasion Farrell agreed to put up the money for the venture. But McGraw suddenly signed with the Giants and Farrell then determined to get into baseball at any cost.

When the American League, having lost Baltimore, decided to invade New York City, Farrell got the franchise and spent $110,000 in building the present park on the hilltop before he opened the gates.

Mr. Farrell has had a rough time in baseball, his team failing to come up to expectations, but this 1910 season his nine is doing well and promises to be a real winning attraction for its owner.

HORACE FOGEL—Horace Fogel, the new president and controller of the Philadelphia Club, has been in the game for nearly thirty years.

He was manager of the Indianapolis team in 1889 and later handled the Giants for a short time in 1896. At other times he was a newspaper writer in Philadelphia and was busy scribbling when a short time ago the chance was offered to get hold of the Quakers.

Fogel got somebody to put up $350,000 for the ball park.

It was said at the time that the money was supplied by Charles P. Taft of Cincinnati, but Fogel has denied this emphatically and has named several wealthy Philadelphians as his backers.

It is believed that E. F. Albee and Percy G. Williams, well known theatrical managers have a piece of the club, as the secretary and treasurer of the concern is Morris Scheck, who is identified with them in the show business.

Fogel is one of the livest and up-to-date baseball men in the business.

JAMES A. HART—James A. Hart was the president of the Chicago Club of the National League from 1892 to 1905 inclusive, fourteen years in all.

It was during his incumbency that Anson managed and captained that team and made it known as the heroic legion of baseball.

Mr. Hart went to Chicago from Boston in the Fall of 1889 and was clever enough to see an opening for a clever business man. He fully enjoyed Anson's love for the game and played cards that finally landed him at the head of the Chicago Club. Finally both men lost out and Charles Murphy holds forth where once Anson was king.

Hart did many things while at the head of the Chicago Club that left their impress.

It was he in conjunction with George Munson of St. Louis that arranged the big tour to California taken by the Chicago White Stockings and St. Louis Brown Stocking teams.

GARRY HERRMANN—One of the foremost figures in the baseball world today is Mr. Garry Herrmann, president of the Cincinnati Exhibition Company operating the Cincinnati Baseball Club, and chairman of the National Baseball Commission.

A leader in the sport world, successful in business and politics and a leader among men, Mr. Herrmann is a national figure.

Besides his keen interest in baseball "Garry," as Mr. Herrmann is called by his friends is an enthusiastic devotee of bowling and is president of the American Bowling Congress, under whose direction all the national bowling matches are held and at the present time is chairman of the executive committee that is to make arrangements for the thirteenth annual festival of the North American Gymnastic Union, to be held in the Queen City in June.

Besides his activity in the sport world, Mr. Herrmann is a highly successful business man and politician. He is president of the Board of Trustees of Cincinnati, Commissioner of Water Works, a new system that is to give the Queen City one of the finest water works in the country and has been active in all work for the betterment of his home city.

In the business world he is known as one of Cincinnati's most successful men. He is a director in many big firms, banks and trust and insurance companies and identified with a great number of private enterprises.

While Mr. Herrmann is one of the most active men in baseball, he first became interested in the national game out of civic pride when the Cincinnati Reds were owned by a non-resident of the Queen City and when the clash was on between the National and American Leagues, Mr. Herrmann purchased a controlling interest in the club and it was through his efforts that peace was brought about between the warring organizations.

He was interrupted in organizing the National Commission and several times his diplomacy has prevented strife between the two organizations.

He is one of the men who are responsible for the healthy condition of the game to-day.

Mr. Herrmann has been the president of the Cincinnati Club from 1903 up to the present time and he is also the chairman of the National Baseball Commission, the supreme court of the major leagues.

THOMAS J. LOFTUS—Thomas J. Loftus was the president of the Washington Club of the National League in its 1904 season.

He was also the manager of the Washington Club from 1902 to 1904 and during his sojourn in Washington made many friends.

He did much to bring the game into its proper sphere in the nation's capital and to win lasting and influential friends for it. In fact one of the great builders up of the national game, a player, captain, manager and magnate in his day was Thomas J. Loftus, who died at his home in Dubuque, Iowa, on April 16, 1910.

In his day Tom Loftus, as he was called in the professional world of baseball, was known and beloved by all, being one of the kindliest, jovial and best natured spirits ever connected with the National Game.

Mr. Loftus was born in St. Louis, November 15, 1856, his father being John Loftus, a life-long resident of this city. Tom attended Christian Brothers' School here and in his early youth developed remarkable ability as a ball player. At the

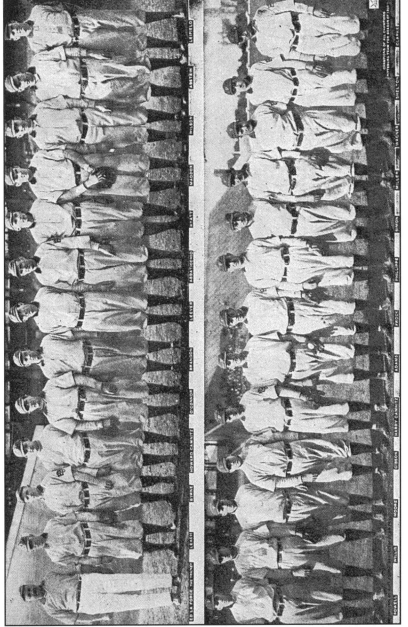

THE PITTSBURG CLUB, NATIONAL LEAGUE CHAMPIONS IN 1909.

age of 20 he was a member of the St. Louis Red Stockings, then the crack ball team of the city and he was regarded as the best player on the team.

In 1877 he signed with the then crack Memphis nine and was instrumental in winning the championship for that team. The next year he went to Peoria and was captain and manager of that club.

Ted Sullivan had gone to Dubuque from Milwaukee in 1874, having secured the contract for the news privilege on the Illinois Central. He was a baseball enthusiast, and he was organizing a team. He made such a showing with the team he had in 1878 that the merchants of Dubuque raised a purse to encourage him to get together a winning nine and the team he had that year was the sensation of the country. He secured Loftus from Peoria to captain and manage the team. Sullivan had had Alveretta the year before. With Loftus he obtained from Peoria the two Gleasons and Billy Taylor. He picked up Radbourne at Bloomington, Ill., and the other members of the team were Chas. Comiskey, William Lapham and Larry Reis of Chicago and Tom Sullivan of St. Louis.

The Dubuques of 1879 was one of the greatest teams ever gotten together and it gave Ted Sullivan and the players national reputations. Radbourne, who was afterwards known as "Old Hoss," was the first pitcher in the West to throw a curve. The team won the championship of the Northwest League, of which Rockford, Davenport, St. Paul and several other cities were members. Radbourne was only a youth, but news of his curve and his great pitching went all over the country, with the result that Capt. Anson brought his crack Chicago team to Dubuque, and Radbourne beat them, holding their heavy hitters powerless. Loftus played second base and his hitting and the inside baseball which he instilled into the team were the contributing factors in its remarkable record.

The success which Sullivan had in Dubuque prompted the business men who were backing the St. Louis club to engage him as manager and he came here in 1882, bringing Loftus to captain the team and Comiskey and several of the other Dubuque players. Loftus was taken sick and returned home, being succeeded by Comiskey, who had been a pitcher, went on to first base and this was the beginning of his great baseball career.

In 1884 Loftus, having recovered his health, signed to manage the Milwaukee team. He played with that team part of the season, but finally retired from active playing and devoted his time to the management of the nine. In 1885 he came to St. Louis to take charge of the St. Louis White Stockings and in 1887 he went to Cleveland where he developed a great team. He remained there until 1890, when he accepted the management of the Cincinnati team, remaining there two seasons. In 1894 he assisted in the organization of the Western League, which afterwards became the American League, and he took charge of Columbus, holding that team until 1899, when he disposed of his interests to accept the management of the Chicago National team.

He was in Chicago two years, 1899 and 1900, and resigned there to take the Washington franchise in the American League and remained there two years. He then disposed of his interests in Washington and retired from the game, returning to Dubuque to devote his attention to his business. He was given several good opportunities to return to the game and also to engage in business in Chicago and elsewhere, but he preferred to live in Dubuque and to keep out of the game. While he, therefore, was not active in the game from 1902, he was one of the counsellors of both big leagues and was regarded as one of the substantial men in baseball. His advice was sought and heeded and he was largely instrumental in shaping the game and making it the great American pastime.

Ted Sullivan who attended the funeral of Loftus at Dubuque, paid the latter a glowing compliment. He said that Lofus was twenty years ahead of the game when he was playing thirty years ago, and that he had always kept that far ahead, looking into the future and forseeing exigencies that were to arise and planning to meet them. In all his writings Ted Sullivan has accorded Loftus the place of highest honor among ball players and baseball men and Henry Chadwick, the "Father of Baseball," and who devoted his efforts exclusively to writing about the game and the men in it, gave Loftus the same prestige and place of honor.

C. W. MURPHY—Charles W. Murphy, president of the Chicago Cubs, the Garden City's representative in the National League, is one of the livest and energetic men connected with professional baseball.

Mr. Murphy's career in the baseball world has been meteoric. He became president of the Chicago Club in 1906 and in 1906, 1907 and 1908, with Mr. Murphy at its head, that team won the championship.

And perhaps it was a lucky thing for Mr. Murphy that the team did win these successive pennants for he had bought the nine on speculation and counted on paying for it out of its profits.

It happened in this way: In 1903, when John T. Brush was president of the Cincinnati Club, Murphy was writing baseball for the Cincinnati Enquirer and the two became fast friends. So when in 1903 Mr. Brush became the president of the New York Club he took Mr. Murphy to the metropolis and made him the press agent of the Giants.

It was while acting in this capacity that Mr. Murphy received a tip one day that John R. Walsh, the owner of the Chicago National League Club, had failed and that the baseball property was on the market.

Hurrying to Cincinnati Mr. Murphy hunted up Charles Taft and told him that he wanted to buy the Chicago Club and needed $125,000 to swing the deal. He got the money, bought the Cubs and they proceeded to win the world's championship the following season. The Chicago Club cleaned up $165,000 in profits on that campaign and Murphy promptly returned the money he had borrowed from Mr. Taft. Since then Mr. Murphy has had all kinds of luck. He has $400,000 all his own and is planning to build a great plant in the Garden City.

Writing of Mr. Murphy and his wonderful career, Ted Sullivan the other day had this to say:

"The president of the Chicago National League Club, Charles Murphy, came to Chicago as a stranger and bought one of the richest baseball plants in the United

States. It is a plant that has been in existence since the birth of the National League in 1876. He did not burglarize nor steal a franchise to get into baseball, but he bought the franchise with solid cash under the eyes of the most watchful and alert people in the business world—the Chicago public. The cash to buy the club was furnished him by the brother of the President of the United States—Charles P. Taft. There must be some class to the president of the Cubs if a man like Mr. Taft allows him to invest his money in a business about which Mr. Taft knew nothing.

"Mr. Murphy has given the city of Chicago a clean-cut team and a champion one at that. Coming to a large city like Chicago, where things are done on a large scale and where not only the politics of baseball were new to him but very often shown in a false light the least that Mr. Murphy has said has been exaggerated and what he did not say has often been manufactured by people who had no other motive than malice. There is not a profession in the world that will misrepresent a man like baseball. He may have the most honest motives for doing a thing, yet the wrong construction some time will be placed upon it.

"I have dealt, during my baseball career, with nearly all men of note in the game, either at one time or another. I can only speak of people as I find them, and when I hear a gentleman I know misrepresented, I like to tell my friends that it is false. I have had business dealings with Charles Murphy, president of the Cubs, and I have found him as liberal in his dealings as the most of them. Now, if in some person's mind it is a baseball crime to have culture and education, then Mr. Murphy is guilty. If it is also a crime in the same person's mind to be affable and courteous to those you meet, then Mr. Murphy is guilty of that crime also. If it is an insult to the National game to have the president of the United States become his guest and lend his presence to the nation's pastime, then Mr. Murphy disgraced the game by asking President Taft to attend.

"To close the chapter on the president of the Chicago Club—which is written at no solicitation from him, but of my own volition—let me say this to my friends who read my articles—it matters not to a broad-minded man of the world, and especially to a true American, of what extraction or from what lineage a man may come. In the assimilation of races, in our country, the personality of a man should rank higher with us than his nationality. During my travels throughout the country I hear of many races to which Mr. Murphy is said to belong. For the information and edification of curiosity seekers throughout the country, I will assert that Charles Murphy is not masquerading under a false label. He is what his name implies—an Irish-American, born in Ohio, of Irish parents who came from Ireland."

FRANK J. NAVIN—Frank J. Navin, president of the Detroit Club, is one of the big, broad, liberal-minded men who are to-day associated in the carrying on of major league baseball.

The champion Detroit Club is owned by Mr. Navin, who is the president, and a rich lumber merchant named Thomas Yawkey.

President Navin is strictly a baseball fan. He has large business interests in the West which occupy his time during the winter months, but the summer he devotes entirely to baseball.

Mr. Yawkey does not take an active interest in the affairs of the Detroit Club, but he follows the doings of Jennings' champions closely.

Mr. Navin was so enthusiastic when the Tigers won the pennant in 1908 that he gave the players $15,000 bonus in addition to their share of the world's series receipts ,and last Fall, when they captured the pennant again he raised salaries with extreme liberality.

THOMAS C. NOYES—Thomas C. Noyes in 1905 succeeded Tomas J. Loftus as the president of the Washington Club of the American League.

The Washington club has had many owners since the American League took that city into the circuit, but the most progressive and enthusiastic is Mr. Noyes, owner of a newspaper in the Nation's capital. Mr. Noyes has set out to get a winning team, and last Fall he secured James McAleer as manager at $10,000 a year.

The latter has put together a fine team and in this 1910 season Washington's baseball prospects seem better than they have seemed for many a year.

HARRY CLAY PULLIAM—One of the many who did much to build up the National game, not only in the Kentucky blue grass but in all corners of the earth, was Harry Clay Pulliam, who although but a boy in years from 1903 up to the time of his death on July 29, 1909 held the high office of president of the National League.

Mr. Pulliam, the fifth president of the National League of Baseball Clubs, was elected to the office during the December meeting of that organization in New York City in 1903. He was born in Paducah, Ky., on February 8, 1869. He served continuously in office as League President from the date of his election until his death in 1909, and was a little more than forty years old when life terminated.

A graduate of the High School of Louisville, Ky., he entered the Law School of the University of Virginia later, and subsequently chose to embark in daily newspaper work. His greatest success as a newspaper writer was in Louisville, and while a city editor of one of the newspapers of that place, he formed the acquaintance of Barney Dreyfuss, at the time President of the Louisville Baseball Club, which was then a member of the National League.

It was due to his friendship for Mr. Dreyfuss that he was induced to quit the newspaper profession and accept the position of secretary of the Louisville Baseball Club. From that time until the end of his days he was identified with the national sport.

When it became necessary for the National League of Baseball clubs to curtail its roster of members owing to the unwieldiness of a twelve-club circuit, Barney Dreyfuss acquired an interest in the Pittsburg Baseball Club. He moved to that city, and with him went the young secretary to act in a like capacity at Pittsburg.

He served with the Pittsburg club until

he was elected president of the National League. Mr. Pulliam was one of the real builders of the game. He won his spurs honestly and cleverly and was of no mushroom growth.

From the baseball reporter's place he was graduated into the manager's chair and from it to the highest place in the baseball world.

Poor, without influential friends and backing, Pulliam went to the front only through his own hard work, honest and conscientious efforts.

Others having the same experience and success might have become proud, arrogant and swollen in the region of the cranium.

But in the higher place Pulliam was always the same kindly, good-natured, considerate gentleman that marked him once as the best baseball writer in Kentucky and the best friend the game had in the blue grass.

There have been other league presidents, but none so democratic, so true to all and so able and active as Pulliam.

When through illness he was compelled to seek rest a few weeks before he died, the prayers of all who love the game and who knew Pulliam best went with him.

CHRIS VON DER AHE—No history of baseball would be complete without reference to Chris Von der Ahe, from 1881 to 1897 President of the St. Louis Browns.

Mr. Von der Ahe in his time was a remarkable figure in the baseball world. He was the main promoter of the American Association which came into the field in 1882.

In 1881, when the game was in a bad way in St. Louis, Mr. Von der Ahe was one of the first to come to the front and offer to subscribe liberally to the placing of a professional team in St. Louis and to the organizing of a new baseball association.

In 1882, when the American Association came out for its first season, Mr. Von der Ahe saw to it that none of its clubs fell by the wayside and it was mainly through his efforts that the organization finished its first season with a full roster.

Mr. Von der Ahe at this time was a modest grocery man of small means who had kept a little grocery store at Sullivan and Spring avenues, in the west end of St. Louis and who had branched out from there to a more commodious establishment at St. Louis and Grand avenues.

In baseball, from the commencement Mr. Von der Ahe proved wonderfully lucky, cleaning up hundreds of thousands of dollars in a few seasons and at one time he was rated as a millionaire.

His first set back came during the Brotherhood year of 1890 when he lost a small fortune, and these losses were followed by others which came through his connection with racing.

He was so hard pressed for funds that the National League leaders, who never had much use for him, owing to his too independent and combative spirit, succeeded in 1898 in depriving him of his National League franchise and forcing him out of the field of organized baseball.

In the American Association, Mr. Von der Ahe had been the ruling spirit, but when in 1892 he left that body to join forces with the National League his influence waned and he was not only treated badly but when the first opportunity presented itself he was deprived of what had

once been to him a wonderful money-making business.

His eight years in the National League proved disastrous and when he retired from that body in 1890 his great fortune had been dissipated and he was a comparatively poor man.

I was associated with Mr. Von der Ahe very closely in the baseball line not only during his most successful days, but during the closing period of his public life, when things were not so prosperous and roseate.

In wealth and in the subsequent disastrous time which overtook him, I found him always the same kindly, generous spirit.

I shall never forget his speech to me at the closing of the first game in Sportsman's Park. The team which Caylor had brought here to play and which he called the Cincinnati Reds, had been been beaten by our co-operative St. Louis Browns and all hands were jubilant at the victory and at the fine attendance. Mr. Von der Ahe, happier, apparently, than any of the rest, grasped me by the hand at the finish and said:

"What a fine big crowd! But the game, Al, the game. How was it? Was it a pretty good game? You know I know nothing about it."

From this co-operative team of St. Louis Browns, Mr. Von der Ahe, aided by Cuthbert, Ted Sullivan, Loftus, Comiskey, Munson and others, built up a team of world beaters.

Four times Vondy's Browns won the championship of the American Association and twice they captured the world's championship.

In the season of 1888 the St. Louis Browns, winners of the American Association championship, played the New Yorks for the world's championship, and I will here relate a brief story in connection with that series to prove the liberal and good fellow Mr. Vonder Ahe was in his palmy and most prosperous days. He was in Cincinnati with his team at the close of their season there and he wrote me this letter from the Queen City:

"Cincinnati, Sept. 30, 1888.

"A. H. Spink,

"Sporting Editor Globe-Democrat,

"St. Louis, Mo.

"Dear Al:—We will close our season here and three days before the closing George Munson will go on to New York direct from here to arrange for the world's series with the New York Giants. I wish you would arrange for a special train to take our party to New York and back to the other cities in which we will play.

"I wish you would have this special train decorated on the sides with banners and that you would go around to all our friends in St. Louis and ask them to accompany us on the trip, insuring them carte blanche in so far as their railway, sleeping car, buffet and hotel service is concerned. Tell Wetherell to fix up the train in fine style and to see that there is plenty to eat and drink on board.

"Also invite a representative from each of the St. Louis newspapers to make the trip at my expense. You take care of every one from St. Louis to New York and Munson will arrange with the Grand Central Hotel people in New York to take care of all the people you bring along.

"You must leave with your crowd Sun-

BENJAMIN SHIBE.
The veteran president of the Athletics of Philadelphia in their 1910 year.

day morning, arriving at Columbus with the special tra.n Sunday night. We will leave here after the game Sunday on the regular train and you will hold the special at Columbus until we join you there. Then from Columbus we will travel together to New York.

"Now please attend to all these details carefully and some day I'll do as much for you.

"Respectfully,
"CHRIS VON DER AHE."

On receipt of this letter I called on W. D. Wetherell, then local agent of the Vandalia, and told him of the special train Mr. Von der Ahe wanted over the Vandalia and Pennsylvania lines to New York and return. Wetherell, after we had talked the matter over, said:

"Why, Al, its nonsense talking about a special train. One like Chris wants wi'\ cost nearly $20,000 for the round trip. You write and tell him he'd better travel on the regular trains."

I wrote Mr. Von der Ahe immediately and the next day I received a telegra.1 from Cincinnati in which he said:

"Tell Wetherell to mind his own business and fix up that special as I want it."

The special train was arranged for and it cost Mr. Von der Ahe nearly $20,000.

I recall the merry party that went on that train. I recall, too, that just before our departure Gus Thomas, now the famous playwright, came to me and said:

"I understand you have charge of the baseball party that is going to New York. I understand you are going to take a representative from each of the St. Louis newspapers and that you have a man from all of them with the exception of the Missouri Republican. Take me along as the representative of the Republican. I want to get to New York."

"I will," I said, "but I am afraid Chris will jump me if I do. He knows every ball reporter in America. and when he finds you are not the real article he may order you thrown off the train."

"I'll take my chances," said Gus.

So I took him along and before we were half way to New York Mr. Von der Ahe was questioning me about Thomas and insinuating that he was not a baseball reporter but a base and ingenious interloper.

I stood by Thomas, however, stood by him for the trip to New York and for a weeks' board at the Grand Central, and at its conclusion Thomas, to my great relief, got a job as reporter on the New York World and quit our party, after shaking hands with Mr. Von der Ahe and every one else and thanking them for their kindness.

And so if it had not been for the generosity of the genial German the man who afterwards wrote "In Mizzoura," "Arizona' and other now famous plays, might never have been heard of. But this was only one of the generous things Von der Ahe did in the heydey of his power.

I shall never forget this series for the World's flag in New York. The people of the metropolis believed their Giants invincible and laughed at the light and slim-waisted St. Louis players who then took the field on the Polo Grounds in search of world honors.

This first game took place on October 17, 1888 and Tim Keefe pitched for the New Yorks and Silver King for St. Louis.

New York won, but only by a scratch and by the close score of 2 to 1.

In the second game played, on October 17, the pitchers were Elton Chamberlain for St. Louis and Mickey Welch for New York. This time St. Louis won, shutting New York out, the score being 3 to 0.

In this game the Browns played with all their best speed and vigor. But perhaps it would have been as well for them to have lost this game, for the players of the St. Louis team never quite recovered from the effect of the treatment they received on their return that evening to the Grand Central.

The great crowd of thoroughbreds who had accompanied the St. Louis players to New York, at the conclusion of the game took the boys into the great bar room and there in goblets of champagne drank to their health and their royal victory.

The players responded, and so nobly that they failed to win another game of the series in New York and the East, and it was not until their return to St. Louis that they were victorious in another contest. The St. Louis Club won four games to New York's six, and but for the New York incident might have won the series.

In the jubilation over the first victory of the St. Louis team in New York, Mr. Von der Ahe not only took part but besides buying wine, he ordered each player in the team to buy a suit of clothes in New York and send the bill to him, and every man who accompanied him on the trip was ordered to visit the New York tailors, dress up and send in their bills to the Brown's president.

In the prosperous days of the St. Louis Browns it was the custom of the American Association, at the close of each season, for the owner of the club winning the championship to give a banquet to the members of the organization. To this banquet all the leading baseball writers of the country were invited.

Several times it fell to Mr. Von der Ahe to be the host and on these occasions he did himself proud, engaging the finest banquet halls at the best hotels and furnishing a meal and its trimmings fit for a king.

Each one of these banquets out-did its predecessor and Mr. Von der Ahe's liberality and lavishness was wondered at and favorably commented on.

I think it but right here to also relate a little story showing the gameness of Mr. Von der Ahe and the sort of true sportsman he was. The incident took place in the Fall of 1886.

The St. Louis Browns had won the championship of the American Association and the Chicago White Stockings, of which club A. G. Spalding was then the president and Anson the captain and manager, had captured the National League flag. These two clubs had also captured the pennants, their respective leagues the season before and in the play off games for the World's Championship, at the close of the 1885 season, the contest, resulted in a tie, each club capturing three games and one of the contests being declared a draw.

The Chicagoans claimed to have been badly treated in this series and when it came to the arranging of another series at the close of the following season, Spalding and Anson demurred and talked as though they would have nothing to do with the St. Louis people.

When the latter broached the subject of a World's series in the Fall of 1886, Spalding and Anson assumed a haughty air, claiming to have been robbed of the series of the year previous. They also claimed great superiority for their team and boasted that their nine could always beat that which hailed from the Mound City. Then, after making these assertions, they declared that they would play the games only on one condition, and that was that the winning club should take every penny of the gate receipts, grandstand and all.

The proposition was one that would have staggered the manager of a winning team of to-day, but Mr. Von der Ahe, with a smile that was childlike and bland, told Messrs. Anson and Spalding that their proposition suited him exactly and that his team would meet theirs on their exact terms.

The games were played, the first three at Chicago and the last three at St. Louis and the St. Louis team captured four out of the six games and with them a king's ransom.

Out of the six games the Chicagos did not receive a penny and their only gain was the experience taught them by the plucky Mr. Von der Ahe and the wonderful gameness of his players.

I mention these incidents to prove the royal and game fellow Mr. Von der Ahe was in the halcyon days days of his career.

It was in those days, too, that Mr. Von der Ahe ordered built the life-sized statue of himself which now adorns the lot he owns in Bellefontaine Cemetery. It is a magnificent statue, cost a fortune, and when Chries dies it will mark for centuries to come the resting place of one who did as much for baseball in St. Louis and the country at large as any man ever associated with the game and whose departure from it was greatly regretted by those who knew him best and who had followed the fortunes of himself and club for years.

STANLEY ROBISON—No two men that ever lived have done more to build up the national game and to increase its areas than the brothers, Stanley and Frank De Hass Robison. These two gentlemen were friends and supporters of the national game when love and sentiment were the only inducements and when to back a club meant to dig down in the pockets at the close of each season to meet the deficit which was then always in evidence.

When boys in the early seventies, the Robison brothers, who then lived in Cleveland, went out to see the famous Forest City team, one of the first of the early and great professional teams, and the interest awakened then grew as they advanced in years, so that in 1889 the Robison brothers bought the controlling interest in the Cleveland National League Club and took complete charge of the baseball field in the Forest City.

That the Robisons were broad, liberal and able men was proven their first year in the National League when they placed in the field a team of great players that in individual strength has perhaps never been beaten.

This team included such great players as Zimmer, O'Connor and Criger, catchers;

Cuppy, Young, Powell, Wilson and Frasier, pitchers; Pat Tebeau and Jack O'Connor, first base; Childs and Tebeau, second; Wallace, third; McKeon, short field and Blake, Frank Burkett, Heidrick and McAleer in the outfield. No team of the class of this one was ever put in the field in a single year and its strength shows the sort of live, hustling men the Robison brothers were. This great team remained almost intact for ten years and in that time it made all comers play ball.

In 1895 and 1896 it contested with Baltimore for the Temple Cup, the championship emblem of those years. In 1895 it won four out of the five games played with Baltimore but in the following year, facing the same club for the same emblem, it lost all four games to the Orioles.

It was in 1899, or just ten years after they had played Cleveland in the National League, that the Robison brothers transferred their franchise and players to St. Louis. Since then the Cardinal team has always been a fighting member of the National League, although it has never finished better than fourth. This, however, has not been due to any failing on the part of the Robison's for they have given their manager a free rein and have spared neither time nor expense in their attempt to build up a first class team in the National League.

Their liberality has been proven on more than one occasion. In the year 1900 they purchased the release of McGraw, Robison and Keister from the champion Baltimore team, outbidding every club in America for the services of these great players.

In the Fall of 1908 Mr. Robison outbid every club in the National League for the services of Roger Bresnahan, who was then the great and popular catcher of the New York Giants.

Recently he has also given an evidence of his liberality, notably in the paying of a heavy sum for Pitcher Zmich, whose services were sought by half a dozen other National League managers.

Frank DeHass Robison passed away at Cleveland in 1908. Since his death his brother, Stanley, has been in complete control of the St. Louis National League team and its properties. Frank De Hass Robison in his day was one of the most intelligent, aggressive and public spirited of the National League leaders. In the council of the National Association he was always a marked figure, being noted for his great resourcefulness, his ability to meet all situations, his keenness and his courage. When he died he was one of the leading citizens of Cleveland, being for a long while at the head of the street car interests there. When he died nearly all of his properties were left to his brother Stanley, who is abundantly able to care for them. Stanley Robison is one of the quiet, earnest and effective directors of the National League, a thorough sportsman, honest and square in all his dealings and perhaps the most popular and best liked of all the great baseball leaders.

BENJAMIN F. SHIBE—One of the best beloved men in baseball is Benjamin Franklin Shibe, owner of the Athletic Club, the team which represents Philadelphia so well in the American Association. Kindly, easy going, Mr. Shibe, chief owner of the Philadelphia Athletics, is a millionaire.

He has been a maker of baseballs for many years in conjunction with A. J. Reach and A. G. Spalding Bros.

He had no idea of becoming a magnate until Johnson, Comiskey and Connie Mack began to talk business with him.

Uncle Ben, as he is familiarly called, was not in the best health at the time and he feared that his duties as a club owner would involve too great a strain. But now-days, hale and hearty, the old fellow will tell you that the ownership of a big ball club, especially a winner, is the greatest thing in the world to build up your constitution.

Mr. Shibe has made a pot of money out of the Athletics. Two years ago he decided to build a new ball park in Philadelphia and spent $500,000, with the result that Shibe Park is one of the greatest sporting arenas in America.

CHARLES W. SOMERS—There is no finer character and no better thought of man in major league baseball than Charles W. Somers, president of the American League and principal owner of the Cleveland Club. He is a millionaire coal merchant, whose money in a large measure helped Johnson and Comiskey to expand the American League circuit. When funds were needed to put clubs in Cleveland and Boston Mr. Somer's was there with the coin, and it is a fact that he stood ready to finance the club placed in New York if Frank J. Farrell had not been discovered. Mr. Somers' partner,

John F. Kilfoyle, is a Cleveland real estate man who has plenty of money and is for the American League to a finish. Mr. Somers is one of the gamest men in baseball. He is determined to put a winning team in Cleveland next season if money can land the talent. He has a big string of scouts working through the minor leagues, and is paying fabulous prices for his new players. Sam Kennedy, who discovered Krause, Baker, Barry and Eddie Collins for the Athletics, is the chief of the Cleveland scouts. He landed Fanwell down in Virginia. Bob Gilks, Bill Bernhard of Nashville and Addie Joss are also looking over young players for Somers. The Cleveland Club paid $7,000 for Jackson, the New Orleans outfielder, and will never stop paying out money to get a first class winning team together.

JOHN I TAYLOR—A thorough sportsman is at the head of the Boston club of the American League.

That team is owned by General Charles H. Taylor, proprietor of the Boston Globe, and his son, John I. Taylor, who is president of the club. General Taylor paid more than $100,000 for the franchise and players several years ago, and has received this outlay three or four times over.

Young Taylor controls the club stock in his own name and has displayed much skill in the development of a fast team. He has picked up some star players himself, and is one of the best judges of talent in the business.

DANIEL O'CONNELL TRACY.
The above is a likeness of Daniel O'Connell Tracy, now a sedate jurist of St. Louis, who, away back in the sixties was a member of the famous Empire Baseball Club of St. Louis. Although an old man Tracy never misses a game at St. Louis major league parks.

THE NATIONAL GAME.

THE LEAGUE HEADS.

LINES ABOUT THE MEN WHO ARE AT THE HEAD OF THE RIVAL BASEBALL ORGANIZATIONS.

Now comes mention of the men who are at the head and who are the secretaries of the rival baseball bodies and organizations, the men who really control the affairs of the major league and on whose shoulders rest the task of keeping the game clean, brilliant and interesting.

JOHN H. FARRELL—John H. Farrell, the secretary of the National Association of Professional Baseball Leagues, has done a great deal for baseball in the way of building up and helping to keep afloat many minor league organizations.

Mr. Farrell was born about 45 years ago at Auburn, N. Y. In the early eighties Farrell had become a skilled newspaper telegraph operator and while representing the Associated Press in his native city, found time to play with and manage local teams. His fame at this time was equally divided between baseball and telegraphy. In working hours everybody wanted to sneak past the city editor's room in the Auburn Daily Advertiser's office to peep into the telegraph room while John Farrell "took messages right out of the air." Hence it may be said that he was one of the first operators to take messages hot from the wire direct to typewriter. His most famous feat was the taking of the Presidential message of Grover Cleveland without a single mistake, an accomplishment unheard of to-day, because such long documents now come in "advance copy" to be released by wire.

In play hours everybody went out to the "game" because they wanted to see John Farrell play third base.

It was as a newspaper man that Farrell saw the tremendous possibilities in the field of professional baseball, and it was he that talked up and then built up the National Association of Professional Baseball Leagues.

In the majors the National Commission is the tribunal that governs the policy and conduct of the two big leagues. In the minors all disputes not affecting a major league team and all the duties similar to those of the National Commission are exercised by Farrell as Chairman of the National Board of Arbitration. The wonderful manner in which he has acquitted himself of these duties demonstrates his unusual talent in dealing with men. Justice, backed up by determination has brought him many victories where men of lesser courage would have failed. Those who know Farrell take his word at face value every time. What he says is truth and what he promises he does.

JOHN HAROLD HEYDLER—John Harold Heydler, the present popular and efficient secretary of the National League, has done more than his share in building up and increasing the areas in so far as the National game is concerned.

Mr. Heydler was born in Lafargeville, N. Y., July 10, 1869.

His father was a clergyman and he was intended for the ministry, but preferred the printing business, and worked on the "Union" and "Advertiser," of Rochester, N. Y.

In 1889 he was in the government service at Washington and while in that city became much interested in baseball. He afterwards showed his versatility by being a baseball correspondent, and was

twelve years with the "Washington Star," and served a while as sporting editor of the "Washington Post."

He was a substitute umpire in the National League from 1894 to 1898, and a regular umpire in 1898.

He was highly esteemed by Mr. N. E. Young, the predecessor of Harry Pulliam, as National League President, and was so well thought of by Mr. Pulliam that he was appointed his private secretary and three years later was elected Secretary-Treasurer of the National League, positions that he filled to the satisfaction of all and which he is filling to this day.

BAN B. JOHNSON—There are many who consider Bancroft B. Johnson th "biggest" man in baseball.

He is not only considered the biggest physically but mentally, being at the head of the youngest major league organization and a member of the National Commission.

Since the American League invaded the major league field Mr. Johnson has always been its leader and in the various controversies that have often taken place between members of the two major organizations, Mr. Johnson, as the representative of the American League, has always held his own easily.

He is a fine representative of the game and thoroughly conversant with all its curves and tangents, having been closely associated with the National Sport for nearly a quarter of a century.

In the eighties Cincinnati had three great baseball writers: O. P. Caylor of the Cincinnati Enquirer; Ren Mulford of the Cincinnati Times-Star and Ban Johnson of the Cincinnati Commercial Gazette.

They were all fine writers and all enthusiastic supporters of the game.

They were small boys in 1869 when Cincinnati was having her fill of professional baseball and when the club of that city was beating all others.

Perhaps it was the fever of 1869 that got into the blood of these three writers but one thing is certain and that is they were loud champions of the sport through all their lives and no one of the three did more to increase its areas and build up baseball in all directions than the now president of the American League.

While reporting the games for the Cincinnati Reds in Cincinnati between 1892 and 1894, when Charles A. Comiskey was the commander of that team, there sprung up between Johnson and Comiskey a warm friendship that resulted a little later in Comiskey and Johnson forming the Western League with Comiskey at the head of a team in St. Paul and Johnson as the president of the whole organization. This same friendship resulted in these two joining together and forming with others the American League, the only actual rival the National League has ever had.

The plans for the formation of this Western Baseball Association and the major league which subsequently took its

THE NATIONAL GAME.

place, were laid by Johnson and Comiskey in the early nineties in Cincinnati. At this time these two spent many evenings at the Ten Minute Club in Redland, where the members made a practice of calling a waiter at the expiration of ten minute intervals. It was there that Johnson and Comiskey hatched a plan to organize the Western League, which was later expanded into the present powerful American League, of which Johnson is the recognized leader and Comiskey the owner of the Chicago White Sox, is the backbone.

It is said that Ban Johnson draws a salary of $20,000 a year now as the chief executive of the American League and is signed up to a contract that has seven years to run. He is the possessor of an iron will. When he declared a year ago that John M. Ward could not be elected president of the National League without a baseball war the magnates of both major leagues knew that Ban meant what he said, and he was allowed to have his way. Ward was set aside and Thomas J. Lynch was elected president of the National League to take the place of Harry Pulliam.

This election of Lynch and defeat of Ward was almost wholly due to the firm stand taken by Johnson.

A man of great intelligence and kindly spirit, Ban Johnson commands the respect of the entire baseball world and will hold a high place in the hearts of both patrons and players as long as the game lives.

WILLIAM H. LOCKE—William H. Locke, or "Billy," as he is well known, is Secretary of the Pittsburg club since 1903, succeeding Harry Pulliam, the National League President of the Pittsburg club. He is also a stock holder and a member of the Board of Directors of the Pittsburg club. He was born in Pittsburg some 36 years ago and inherited his father's taste for the newspaper biz. Locke began his journalistic career on the Pittsburg Press in 1890 and afterwards drifted into the sporting department of the paper, becoming assistant sporting editor in 1903. Mr. Locke is a 32d degree Mason and a member of the Mystic Shrine. He is deservedly popular and the faith shown in him by his employer is displayed by the fact that the business affairs of the club at home and abroad are almost entirely in his hands.

THOMAS J. LYNCH—Thomas J. Lynch, president of the National League, is a fine, sterling character.

He is a thorough student of the game and is familiar with all its points. Mr. Lynch is a native of New Britain, Conn., and began his professional career as an umpire in the New England League in 1884.

His work in that league attracted attention from the beginning and before the season was ended he was offered a position in the National League as umpire, an offer which he accepted. In the major league as an umpire he was a success from the start and he held his own as an umpire in that body for eight years, earning a reputation for absolute honesty. In 1904 he was chosen umpire for all the games of the first of the Temple Cup

series between New York and Brooklyn and at the close of the series he became known as the "king of umpires." For that series alone he received $800. Since leaving the league he has been a theatrical manager in his home town, New Britain. He is an austere-looking man of about 50 with a short-cropped mustache and piercing eyes. His salary is $10,000. A United States senator receives only three-fourths as much.

The new president is a born "fan." Some claim to have it direct from the cradleside that his first spoken words were what sounded mightily like "play ball."

Before the days of the mitt he broke several of his youthful fingers catching barehanded back on the vacant lots of New Britain. When the latter team was tied by its hated rivals, the Hartfords, Lynch was appealed to and agreed to become bench manager for a week or two. Thus he spent his vacation, with the result that his home team took thirteen games in a row. He was now in his element, telling each man who went to the bat when to strike, when to sacrifice and when to bunt—how to play "inside ball." But his discipline became so rigid that some of the players got to sulking, with the result that they lost three games running. Then Lynch quit them in disgust.

To keep his candidacy quiet the league magnates who wanted to elect him their president in December, 1909, brought him to New York by a telegram which sounded like theatrical business. Suspecting a broken contract, he arrived in the metropolis as mad as a hornet, and the magnate who met him nearly had his head taken off before he could break to the surprised Mr. Lynch that he was wanted to head the National League.

N. E. YOUNG—This book would not be complete without a reference to Nicholas E. Young of Washington, D. C. Mr. Young was the president of the National League from 1885 to 1902. He also served as secretary and treasurer of the National League from its organization in 1876 to 1903, inclusive, or twenty-seven years in all. Mr. Young also served as secretary of the original National Association of Professional Baseball Players from 1871 to 1875, inclusive, or five years in all. In other words he was an official of the great baseball leagues for a continuous period of thirty-two years. There were only three presidents of the National League before Mr. Young, the honorable Morgan Bulkeley of Hartford, Conn., who served in 1876; William Hulbert of Chicago, who was president from 1877 to 1882, and A. G. Mills of New York, who officiated in 1883 and 1884. Mr. Young, in fact, was the most prominent baseball official during the early and the later successful years of the National League. He was a great favorite with both club owners and players and all over the league circuit in recent years he was known as "Uncle Nick." Mr. Young is still alive and well, occupying a government position in Washington and is a regular attendant at the American League games played in that city. No man ever connected with the game has had a longer and more respected career than Mr. Young.

305

THE NATIONAL GAME.

THE DEBUT OF FAMOUS OLD CY.

STANLEY ROBISON RECALLS CY YOUNG'S FIRST GAME WITH OLIVER PATRICK TEBEAU'S CLEVELAND SPIDERS.

Cy Young, the veteran pitcher, began his career in Cleveland, and Stanley Robison late president of the St. Louis National League Club, was the man who discovered Young. At the time Robison was owner of the Cleveland franchise, and the Spiders, under Pat Tebeau, were large grapes in the major league vineyard.

It happened that Patsy Tebeau was short on pitchers way back about 1390. In those day they did not have scouts combing the country for talent, and the "tipsters" on blooming talent were usually commercial travelers.

Robison was at the time looking over some of his railroad property at Fort Wayne, Ind., and he was lapping up a few "elixirs of mirth," when he happened to open up his vocal chords on baseball. There was a comercial traveler at the bar, who liked baseball, to say nothing of having a fondness for the "elixir" stuff.

Stanley invited him to have a jolt, and also to discuss baseball. "Rather odd," remarked Robison, "that it is so hard to get a good baseball pitcher nowadays I'm looking for a man for my Cleveland club. I've offered enough real money to choke a manhole to get a fellow from one of the other clubs; but, say, I can't make the deal."

"Have another, and I'll give you the best little three-star special you've ever heard tell of since they named you after Matt Quay," returned the commercial traveler.

After the commercial traveler and M. Stanley had inhaled their mirth water the man of satchels and grips opened the conversation.

"Say, old sport," said the commercial traveler, "you're looking for a pitcher. As I understand the vernacular, you are in quest of someone who can hurl an elusive leather-covered sphere, guaranteed to weigh in ringside at five ounces, and to be of 9-inch circumference, no more or no less, somewhere near a little disk they foolishly refer to as the home plate. Get me?

"Now, my friend, take my tip, pack your grip and go up to Canton. They've got a big kid up there that can do anything with a baseball except eat it. Say, he's got so much speed that he burns chunks of holes in the atmosphere. He's the shoot-'em-in-Pete of that reservation.

"Watched him streak 'em over last Sunday, and he struck out a flock of baseball players. I think he fanned a hundred or two hundred. I didn't keep count. He made them describe figure 'eights,' stand on their beams and wigwag for help. You get your grip, if you want a pitcher, streak it to Canton, and don't let anyone tout you off."

Robison did as he was bade, and when he arrived at Canton he went out to the ball yard. There was a big, lop-sided yap on the mound. He looked as though nature chiseled him out to pitch hay, in-

stead of a poor, little inoffensive baseball, and Robison had to laugh when he beheld the world-renowned bearcat twirler that his friend had tipped him off to.

The big boy in the box showed a lot of steam, and Robison's desire to laugh was turned to amazement. He'd never beheld anyone toss a ball with just such speed and precision and with so many curlicues on it. After the game Robison called the young hay miner aside and offered him a job at a figure which made the youth open his mouth.

Robison slipped him transportation to Cleveland, with instructions to find his way out to the ball yard and call on Pat Tebeau, admonishing him to be careful not to get run over by any street cars, as he (Robison) owned the lines and didn't want any damage suits.

The lop-sided boy found his way to the ball yard, asked for Mr. Teabow, blushed like a June bride and told him what he came for.

Tebeau called Zimmer and a few of his old scouts about him, and they openly laughed at the unusual looking boy, who had the nerve to say that he might be a baseball pitcher fit for major league company.

Chicago was in Cleveland. Old fans will recall those dreaded White Stockings, with Anson at their head; and such stars as Ned Williamson, Tommy Burns, Fred Pfeffer, Dalrymple, Jimmy Ryan and that sort on the roster.

Those old boys used to give great pitchers that earthquake feeling about the knees when they dragged up their hundred-pound batons to thump the bitumen out of anything that came near the plate.

Tebeau thought it would be a good joke to pitch the young man against these sluggers and see the effect. He told the boy he wanted him to pitch. Then they dug up a uniform that fitted the lad like a 14 1-2 collar would incase the neck of Frank Gotch.

Anson and his bunch were as fierce baseball pirates as ever scuttled a ship, but they had to laugh at the lad who was to aim the pill at them. They roared when they saw him go into the box.

But something happened. The mere boy struck out Adrian C. Anson, world's wonder with the bat; then he fanned Fred Pfeffer, the prince of second sackers, and slipped three across that Williamson missed entirely.

Then those Chicago sluggers began to take notice. Pat Tebeau saw that the boy he mistook for a clown was a real jewel in the rough. The boy won that game. He made the White Stockings look like a young simian trying to shave. That night the young lad's name was on every tongue. He was Cy Young, farmer, who became a famous baseball pitcher in one day, and who has been making good ever since.

Young is a farmer yet. He cultivates his broad acres in Ohio and is well off.

THE NATIONAL GAME.

GREAT PRICES FOR BALL PLAYERS.

THE TOP PRICE OF $20,000 PAID CHICAGO BY BOSTON FOR MICHAEL J. KELLY WAS OUTDONE THIS 1911 YEAR WHEN PITTSBURG GAVE $22,500 FOR THE RELEASE OF PITCHER MARTY O'TOOLE OF THE ST. PAUL AMERICAN ASSOCIATION CLUB.

That baseball is a profession worth learning especially where the aspirant is fitted by will and nature to shine in that sphere, is proven by the high salaries paid high-class professional players.

And not only are high salaries paid players, but immense sums are paid for the purchases of releases of players.

When long ago Boston paid $20,000 for the release of Michael J. Kelly, it was thought that the top line had been reached in that direction, but this year even that figure has been excelled.

On July 24, 1911, it was announced that the Pittsburg National League Club had paid $22,500 for the release of "Marty" O'Toole, the young pitcher of the St. Paul Club of the American Association.

This makes O'Toole one of the most talked of ball players of the day.

In this 1911 season, when O'Toole established his league record for strikeouts and followed it up with equally sensational twirling, there were two baseball men who were ready to kick themselves. This pair was John I. Taylor of the Boston Red Sox and Clarke Griffth of the Cincinnati Reds. O'Toole was with the Reds and the Red Sox, but his career with each was shortlived. Clark Griffith tried him out and decided he couldn't be bothered with the young pitcher. He was sent to the Brockton club and Boston drafted him and he never had as much as a trial with the big leaguers. Taylor turned him over to Manager Mike Kelley of the St. Paul team a year ago last Spring as the windup of the trade that brought Hall and Karger to Boston.

O'Toole, owing to lack of confidence in himself, failed to get into the win column as often as he should have liked, and after "blowing up" in several games he asked Manager Kelley to send him to some minor league club, where he could work in his regular turn, and where he might overcome his nervousness. Accordingly. Kelly sent him to the Sioux City Club of the Western League.

After joining that club the red-haired athlete experienced but little trouble in striking his gait, and it was less than two weeks after he struck out 18 batters, thus establishing a record. He won game after game for Sioux City and he is credited with winning the pennant for that organization.

Manager Kelley had sold him with an optional clause in that "bill of sale" and the opening of the 1911 season found him back with the Saints. He started in to pitch in wonderful form and has kept this up until today he is considered one of the "finds" of a decade.

O'Toole was born at South Framingham, Mass., and received his early training in camps in the little Massachusetts fold. When 15 years old he was offered a position on the Denison Manufacturing team of South Framingham. He pitched for the tag company's team for four years and finally broke into professional ball.

He is 21 years old and is a youngster of exceptionally good habits. He uses slippery elm instead of tobacco to moisten his spitball and advocates the use of the saliva furnishing substitute.

O'Toole is not to be delivered to Pittsburg until the close of the 1911 season in the American Association.

Some of the big prices paid in baseball may well be believed, even though the men for whom the money was passed did not make good. Here are a few notables of history who really cost their managers big money:

Michael J. Kelly, Chicago National League Club, bought by Boston National League Club, $20,000.

"Lefty" Russell, Baltimore, Eastern League, bought by the Philadelphia Club, American League, $12,000.

"Rube" Marquard of Indianapolis American Association, bought by the New York Club, National League, $11,000.

"Cy" Seymour, Cincinnati Club, National League, bought by the New York Club, National League, $10,000.

"Spike" Shannon, St. Louis Club, National League, bought by the New York Club, National League, $10,000.

Russell Blackburne, Providence Club, Eastern League, bought by the Chicago Club, American League, $7,500.

Jack Thoney, Toronto Club, Eastern League, bought by the Boston Club, American League, $7,500.

"Chief" Meyers, Indianapolis Club, American Association, bought by the New York Club, National League, $6,000.

It may be noted that out of the entire outfit Meyers and Seymour were the only ones to unquestionably make good. Marquard has improved this year to a point where McGraw can see his way to get back his investment. But he is still far from a convincing pitcher.

It may be stated, as a general proposition, that the high prices paid for minor league baseball players are not justified by subsequent performances. Nearly all the real stars of the game today were obtained for sums less than $2,500.

THE HISTORIC LEGION.

THIS IS A LIST OF THE CLUBS WINNING BASEBALL CHAMPIONSHIPS FROM 1871 UNTIL 1883, THE YEAR BEFORE THE FIRST GAMES FOR THE WORLD'S CHAMPIONSHIP WERE PLAYED.

The following is a list of teams which won baseball championships from 1871 to 1883, or before the first games for the World's Championship were played:

Position	Athletics 1871	Bostons 1872	Bostons. 1873	Bostons 1874
Pitcher	McBride	Spalding	Spalding	Spalding.
Catcher	Malone	McVey	White	White.
First Base	Fisler	Gould	Manning	O'Rourke.
Second Base	Reach	Barnes	Barnes	Barnes.
Third Base	Meyerle	Schafer	Schafer	Schafer.
Short-Stop	Radcliffe	G. Wright	G. Wright	G. Wright.
Left Field	Cuthbert	Leonard	Leonard	Leonard.
Center Field	Sensenderfer	H. Wright	H. Wright	H. Wright.
Right Field	Huebell	F. Rogers	Sweasy	McVey.
Substitute	Bechtel			Hall.
Substitute	Pratt	Birdsall	Birdsall	Beals.

Position	Bostons 1875	Chicagos 1876	Bostons 1877	Bostons 1878
Pitcher	Spalding	Spalding	Bond	Bond.
Catcher	White	White	Brown	Snyder.
First Base	McVey	McVey	White	Morrill.
Second Base	Barnes	Barnes	Wright	Burdock.
Third Base	Schafer	Anson	Morrill	Sutton.
Short-Stop	G. Wright	Peters	Sutton	G. Wright.
Left Field	Leonard	Glenn	Leonard	Leonard.
Center Field	O'Rourke	Hines	O'Rourke	O'Rourke.
Right Field	Manning	Addy	Murnane	Manning.
Substitute	Beals			
Substitute	H. Wright	Bielaski	Schafer	Schafer.
Substitute	Heiffert			

Position	Providence 1879	Chicago 1880	Chicago 1881	Chicago 1882
Pitcher	Ward	Corcoran	Corcoran	Corcoran.
Pitcher	Matthews	Goldsmith	Goldsmith	Goldsmith.
Catcher	Gross.			
Catcher	Brown	Flint	Flint	Flint.
First Base	Start.			
First Base	O'Rourke	Anson	Anson	Anson.
Second Base	McGeary	Quest	Quest	Quest & Burns.
Third Base	Hague	Wiliamsonn	Williamson	Williamson.
Short-Stop	G. Wright	Burns	Burns	Burns & Kelly.
Left Field	York	Dalrymple	Dalrymple	Dalrymple.
Center Field	Hines	Gore	Gore	Gore.
Right Field	O'Rourke	Kelly	Kelly	Nicol.
Substitute				Nicol.

Position	Boston 1883	Position	Boston 1883	Position	Boston 1883
Pitcher	Whitney.	First Base	Morrill.	Left Field	Hornung.
Pitcher	Buffington.	Second Base	Burdock.	Center Field	Radford.
Catcher	Hackett.	Third Base	Sutton.	Right Field	C. Smith.
Catcher	Hines.	Short-Stop	Wise.		

THE NATIONAL GAME.

THE WORLD CHAMPIONS.

THE MEN WHO HAVE PLAYED IN GAMES FOR THE WORLD'S CHAMPIONSHIP SINCE THE FIRST GAMES OF THAT SORT BETWEEN THE PROVIDENCE LEAGUE CHAMPIONS OF THE AMERICAN ASSOCIATION IN 1884 AND UP TO THE 1909 SEASON.

This is a list of the players who have taken part in World's Championship games since the first series of that sort was played in 1884. The season of 1888, 1899, 1900, 1901, 1902 and 1904 are left out because no games for the world's championship were played those years:

1884. PROVIDENCE.	1884. METROPOLITANS.	1885 CHICAGO.	1885 ST. LOUIS.
Start, 1b.	Orr, 1b.	Anson, 1b.	Comiskey, 1b.
Farrell, 2b.	Troy, 2b.	Pfeffer, 2b.	Robinson, 2b.
Denny, 3b.	Esterbrook, 3b.	Williamson, 3b.	Latham, 3b.
Irwin, ss.	Nelson, ss.	Burns, ss.	Gleason, ss.
Carroll, lf.	Kennedy, rf.	Dalrymple, lf.	Welch, cf.
Hines, cf.	Roseman, cf.	Gore, cf.	Nicol, rf.
Radford, rf.	Brady, lf.	Kelly, rf.	O'Neill, lf.
Gilligan, c.	Holbert, c.	Sunday, rf.	Bushong, c.
Nava, c.	Reipschlager, c.	Flint, c.	Caruthers, p.
Radbourne, p.	Keefe, p.	Clarkson, p.	Foutz, p.
Sweeney, p.	Lynch, p.	McCormick, p.	

1886. ST. LOUIS.	1886. CHICAGO.	1887. DETROIT.	1887. ST. LOUIS.
Comiskey, 1b.	Anson, 1b.	Ganzel, 1b. & c.	Comiskey, 1b.
Robinson, 2b.	Pfeffer, 2b.	Brouthers, 1b.	Robinson, 2b.
Latham, 3b.	Burns, 3b.	Dunlap, 2b.	Latham, 3b.
Gleason, ss.	Williamson, ss.	White, 3b.	Gleason, ss.
Welch, cf.	Dalrymple, lf.	Rowe, ss.	O'Neill, lf.
Foutz, rf. & p.	Gore, cf.	Thompson, rf.	Welch, cf.
O'Neill, lf.	Ryan, lf.	Hanlon, cf.	Foutz, rf. & p.
Bushong, c.	Flint, c.	Richardson, lf.	Bushong, c.
Caruthers, p	Kelly, c.	Twitchell, f.	Boyle, c.
Hudson, p.	Clarkson, p.	Bennett, c.	Caruthers, p.
	McCormick, p.	Getzein, p.	King, p.
		Baldwin, p.	
		Conway, p.	

1888. NEW YORK.	1888. ST. LOUIS.	1889. NEW YORK.	1889. BROOKLYN.
Connor, 1b.	Comiskey, 1b.	Connnor, 1b.	Foutz, 1b.
Richardson, 2b.	Robinson, 2b.	Richardson, 2b.	Collins, 2b.
Whitney, 3b.	Latham, 3b.	Whitney, 3b.	Pinckney, 3b.
Ward, ss.	White, ss.	Ward, ss.	Smith, ss.
O'Rourke, lf.	O'Rourke, lf.	O'Rourke, lf.	O'Brien, lf.
Slattery, cf.	Lyons, cf.	Gore, cf.	Corkhill, cf.
Tiernan, rf.	McCarthy, rf.	Tiernan, rf.	Brown, rf.
Ewing, c.	Milligan, c.	Ewing, c.	Bushong, c.
Brown, c.	King, p.	Brown, c.	Visner, c.
Murphy, c.	Chamberlain, p.	Keefe, p.	Clark, c.
Welch, p.		Welch, p.	Terry, p.
Crane, p.		Crane, p.	Caruthers, p.
Keefe, p.		O'Day, p.	Lovett, p.
George, p.		Hughes, p.	

1890. BROOKLYN.	1890. LOUISVILLE.	1892. BOSTON.	1892. CLEVELAND.
Foutz, 1b.	Taylor, 1b.	Tucker, 1b.	Virtue, 1b.
Collins, 2b.	Shinnock, 2b.	Quinn, 2b.	Childs, 2b.
Pinckney, 3b.	Raymond, 3b.	Nash, 3b.	Tebeau, 3b.
Smith, ss.	Tomney, ss.	Long, ss.	McKeon, ss.
O'Brien, lf.	Hamburg, lf.	Lowe, lf.	Burkett, lf.
Corkhill, cf.	Weaver, cf.	Duffy, cf.	McAleer, cf.
Burns, rf.	Wolf, rf.	McCarthy, rf.	O'Connor, rf.
Donovan, rf.	Ryan, c.	Kelly, c.	Zimmer, c.
Daly, c.	Weckbaker, c.	Ganzel, c.	Young, p.
Bushong, c.	Stratton, p.	Bennett, c.	Cuppy, p.
Clark, c.	Ehret, p.	Nichols, p.	Clarkson, p.
Lovett, p.	Dailey, p.	Stivetts, p.	
Caruthers, p.	Meekin, p.	Staley, p.	
Terry, p.			
Hughes, p.			

1894.
NEW YORK.
Doyle, 1b.
Ward, 2b.
Davis, 3b.
Fuller, ss.
Burke, lf.
Van Haltren, cf.
Tiernan, rf.
Farrell, c.
Rusie, p.
Meekin, p.

1894.
BALTIMORE.
Brouthers, 1b.
Reitz, 2b.
McGraw, 3b.
Jennings, ss.
Kelley, lf.
Brodie, cf.
Keeler, rf.
Bonner, rf.
Robinson, c.
Gleason, p.
Esper, p.
Hawke, p.
Hemming, p.

1895.
CLEVELAND.
Tebeau, 1b.
Childs, 2b.
McGarr, 3b.
McKean, ss.
Burkett, lf.
McAleer, cf.
Blake, rf.
Zimmer, c.
Young, p.
Cuppy, p.

1895
BALTIMORE.
Carey, 1b.
Gleason, 2b.
McGraw, 3b.
Jennings, ss.
Kelley, lf.
Brodie, cf.
Keeler, rf.
Robinson, c.
Clarke, c.
Hoffer, p.
McMahon, p.
Esper, p.

1896.
BALTIMORE.
Doyle, 1b.
Reitz, 2b.
McGraw, 3b.
Jennings, ss.
Kelley, lf.
Brodie, cf.
Keeler, rf.
Robinson, c.
Clarke, c.
Corbett, p.
Hoffer, p.

1896
CLEVELAND.
Tebeau, 1b.
Childs, 2b.
McGarr, 3b.
McKean, ss.
Burkett, lf.
McAleer, cf.
Blake, rf.
Zimmer, c.
Chamberlain, p.
Young, p.
Cuppy, p.
Wallace, p.

1897.
BALTIMORE.
Doyle, 1b.
Reitz, 2b.
McGraw, 3b.
Jennings, ss.
Kelley, lf.
Stenzel, cf.
Keeler, rf.
Robinson, c.
Bowerman, c.
Nops, p.
Corbett, p.
Hoffer, p.

1897.
BOSTON.
Tenney, 1b.
Lowe, 2b.
Collins, 3b.
Long, ss.
Duffy, lf.
Hamilton, cf.
Stahl, rf.
Bergen, c.
Ganzel, c.
Klobedanz, p.
Nichols, p.
Hickman, p.
Stivetts, p.

1903.
BOSTON AMERICANS.
La Chance, 1b.
Ferris, 2b.
Collins, 3b.
Parent, ss.
Dougherty, lf.
Stahl, cf.
Freeman, rf.
Criger, c.
Farrell, c.
Young, p.
Dineen, p.
Hughes, p.

1903.
PITTSBURG NATIONALS.
Bransfield, 1b.
Ritchey, 2b.
Leach, 3b.
Wagner, ss.
Clarke, lf.
Beaumont, cf.
Sebring, rf.
Phelps, c.
Smith, c.
Phillippe, p.
Leever, p.
Vail, p.
Kennedy, p.
Thompson, p.

1905.
NEW YORK NATIONALS.
McGann, 1b.
Gilbert, 2b.
Devlin, 3b.
Dahlen, ss.
Mertes, lf.
Donlin, cf.
Browne, rf.
Bresnahan, c.
Mathewson, p.
McGinnity, p.
Ames, p.

1905.
PHILADELPHIA. AMERICANS.
Davis, 1b.
Murphy, 2b.
Lave Cross, 3b.
Monte Cross, ss.
Hartsel, lf.
Lord, cf.
Seybold, rf.
Schreckengost, c.
Powers, c.
Plank, p.
Bender, p.
Coakley, p.

1906.
CHICAGO AMERICANS.
Donohue, 1b.
Isbell, 2b.
Rohe, 3b.
Tannehill, ss.
Davis, ss.
Dougherty, lf.
Jones, cf.
Hahn, rf.
Sullivan, c.
White, p.
Owen, p.
Walsh, p.
Altrock, p.

1906.
CHICAGO NATIONALS.
Chance, 1b.
Evers, 2b.
Steinfeldt, 3b.
Tinker, ss.
Sheckard, lf.
Hofman, cf.
Schulte, rf.
Kling, c.
Brown, p.
Reulbach, p.
Pfeister, p.
Overall, p.

1907.
CHICAGO NATIONALS.
Chance, 1b.
Howard, 1b.
Evers, 2b.
Steinfeldt, 3b.
Tinker, ss.
Sheckard, lf.
Slagle, cf.
Schulte, rf.
Hofman, cf.
Kling, c.
Brown, p.
Reulbach, p.
Pfeister, p.
Overall, p.

1907.
DETROIT AMERICANS.
Rossman,' 1b.
Schaefer, 2b.
Coughlin, 3b.
O'Leary, ss.
D. Jones, ss.
Crawford, cf.
Cobb, rf.
Schmidt, c.
Payne, c.
Archer, c.
Killian, p.
Mullin, p.
Donovan, p.
Siever, p.

1908
CHICAGO NATIONALS.
Chance, 1b.
Howard, 1b.
Evers, 2b.
Steinfeldt, 3b.
Tinker, ss.
Sheckard, lf.
Hofman, cf.
Schulte, rf.
Kling, c.
Brown, p.

1908
DETROIT AMERICANS.
Rossman, 1b.
Downs, 2b.
Schaefer, 2b.& 3b.
Coughlin, 3b.
O'Leary, ss.
McIntyre, lf.
Crawford, cf.
Cobb, rf.
D. Jones, rf.
Schmidt, c.

1909.
PITTSBURG NATIONALS.
Abstein, 1b.
Miller, 2b.
Byrne, 3b.
Leach, 3b. & cf.
Wagner, ss.
Clarke, lf.
Hyatt, cf.
Wilson, rf.
Gibson, c.
Adams, p.

1909.
DETROIT AMERICANS.
Tom Jones, 1b.
Delehanty, 2b.
Moriarity, 3b.
O'Leary, 3b.
Bush, ss.
McIntyre, lf.
D. Jones, cf.
Crawford, rf. & 1b.
Cobb, cf.
Schmidt, c.

Reulbach, p.
Pfeister, p.
Overall, p.

Thomas, c.
Killian, p.
Summers, p.
Donovan, p.
Mullin, p.
Winters, p.

Camnitz, p.
Willis, p.
Maddox, p.
Leifield, p.
Phillippe, p.
O'Connor, c.
Abbatichio, utility.

Stanage, c.
Mullin, p.
Donovan, p.
Summers, p.
Works, p.
Willett, p.

1910
PHILADELPHIA
AMERICANS
Davis, 1b.
Collins, 2b.
Baker, 3b.
Barry, ss.
Lord, lf.

Strunk, cf.
Murphy, rf.
Thomas, c.
Lapp, c.
Bender, p.
Coombs, p.

1910
CHICAGO
NATIONALS.
Chance, 1b.
Archer, 1b.
Zimmerman, 2b.
Steinfeldt, 3b.
Tinker, ss.
Sheckard, lf.
Hofman, rf.

Schulte, rf.
Kling, c.
Archer, c.
Brown, p.
McIntire, p.
Overhall, p.
Reulbach, p.
Pfeister, p.
Cole, p.

THE NATIONAL GAME.

THE WORLD'S CHAMPIONSHIP.

A COMPLETE RECORD OF ALL GAMES PLAYED FOR LEADING HONORS IN THE BASEBALL FIELD AT THE CLOSE OF EACH SEASON.

The most interesting feature each year in the baseball line is the series played each fall for the World's Championship between the nines which have won the pennants in the National and American Leagues. The first of these post season games were played by the Metropolitans of New York, winners of the American Association Championship in 1884 and the Providence team, which had captured leading honors in the National League that season. No series was played in 1891.

In 1892 the National League season was divided into two parts, Boston winning the first half and Cleveland the second. In the play-off Boston won.

There were no games in 1893, and in 1894 a new series was inaugurated—the Temple Cup series—for contest between the two leading clubs in the National League. This series continued up to 1898, when it was discontinued, and no further post season championship games were held until 1903, when the National and American League winners—Pittsburg and Boston—met.

In 1904 no games were played, but in 1905 they were resumed under the auspices of the National Commission, under whose supervision they have since been held. The following is the record of World's Championship games played up to date:

Year.	Clubs.	Organization.	Games Won.
1884	Providence—National	League	3
1884	Metropolitan—American	Association	0
1885	Chicago—National	League	3
1885	St. Louis—American	Association	3
1886	St. Louis—American	Association	4
1886	Chicago—National	League	2
1887	Detroit—National	League	1
1887	St. Louis—American	Association	4
1888	New York—National	League	6
1888	St. Louis—American	Association	4
1889	New York—National	League	6
1889	Brooklyn—American	Association	3
1890	Brooklyn—National	League	3
1890	Louisville—American	Association	3
1892	Boston—National	League	5
1892	Cleveland—National	League	0
1894	New York—National	League	4
1894	Baltimore—National	League	0
1895	Cleveland—National	League	4

Year.	Clubs.	Organization.	Games Won.
1895	Baltimore—National	League	1
1896	Baltimore—National	League	4
1896	Cleveland—National	League	0
1897	Baltimore—National	League	4
1897	Boston—National	League	5
1903	Boston—American	League	5
1903	Pittsburg—National	League	3
1905	New York—National	League	4
1905	Athletics—American	League	1
1906	Chicago—American	League	4
1906	Chicago—National	League	2
1907	Chicago—National	League	4
1907	Detroit—American	League	*0
1908	Chicago—National	League	4
1908	Detroit—American	League	1
1909	Pittsburg—National	League	4
1909	Detroit—American	League	3

*One game drawn.

THE FIRST WORLD'S CHAMPIONSHIP.

The first games played for the World's Championship were played in 1884.

The Providence team that year had captured the National League flag and the Metropolitans had taken the championship of the American Association.

The Providence that year were captained and coached by Arthur Irwin, the greatest short fielder of his day and a left-handed batsman of no mean caliber.

He had with him this 1884 season, two of the greatest pitchers ever known to the National game, Charles Sweeny being the one and Charles Radbourne the other. The American Association had no pitchers to match these two, either in speed or skill and this was proven easily when the games were played, the Metropolitans

scoring but three runs in the only three games played.

The Metropolitans were managed by James Mutrie and captained by William Holbert, one of the best catchers of his day. They had a fine pitcher, too, in Tim Keefe, but when the games were commenced on the Polo Grounds in New York, it was easily seen that they were no match for their League rivals. Compared to the magnificent crowds which turned out at Pittsburg and Detroit last year to witness the World's Championship games between Pittsburg and Detroit, but little interest was taken in these initial contests between the Providence and the Metropolitan teams and the last game of 1904 series was witnessed by only a little over 2,000 spectators. The record that year was:

RECORD OF 1884.

Date.	Contesting Clubs.	Where Played.	Score.
October 23.	Providence vs. Metropolitans—At Polo Grounds, New York		6—0
October 24.	Providence vs. Metropolitans—At Polo Grounds, New York		3—1
October 25.	Providence vs. Metropolitans—At Polo Grounds, New York		12—2

Total runs—Providence, 21; Metropolitans, 3.

WHEN BROWNS MET WHITES.

While the games between the Providence and Metropolitan Clubs in 1884 were hastily arranged and but little attention was paid to them, all hands stood up and took notice when in 1885 the first of the regularly arranged games for the championship of the world took place. This time the St. Louis Browns, winners of the American Association flag in 1885, faced the Chicago White Stockings, winners of the National League pennant of that year.

This time a prize of $1,000 was put up, each club contributing $500, with the understanding that the winning club should take the $1,000 and sixty per cent of the gate receipts. In the contest at St. Louis, on Ocober 15, the umpire awarded the game to the home team and that left the series a tie and each club took down $500 of the capital prize and divided the gate receipts evenly. The figures this year were:

RECORD OF 1885.

Date.	Contesting Clubs.	Where Played.	Score.
October 14.	St. Louis vs. Chicago	At Chicago*	5—5
October 15.	Chicago vs. St. Louis	At St. Louis*	5—4
October 16.	St. Louis vs. Chicago	At St. Louis	2—4
October 17.	St. Louis vs. Chicago	At St. Louis	3—2
October 22.	Chicago vs. St. Louis	At Pittsburg**	9—2
October 23.	Chicago vs. St. Louis	At Cincinnati	9—2
October 24.	St. Louis vs. Chicago	At Cincinnati	13—4

Total games won—Chicago, 3; St. Louis, 3; drawn, 1. Total runs scored—Chicago, 43; St, Louis, 41. *Eight innings. **Six innings, (forfeited.) ***Seven innings.

WHEN THE BROWNS TOOK ALL THE MONEY.

In the following year Chicago and St. Louis again captured leading honors in their respective organizations and again were competitors in the post season's series for the World's Championship. The Chicagos, angry at the way they had been treated in 1885, refused to play the St. Louis Club unless the gate receipts, grand stand and all were given to the winning club. This proposition suited the St. Louis manager and leader, and the series was one of the most exciting ever played. The Chicago Club at this time contained such famous players as Flint, Clarkson, Anson, Pfeffer, Burns, Williamson, Ryan, Dalrymple and Gore, and the St. Louis, pitchers like Caruthers, Foutz, Hudson and McCormick and catchers and players like Bushong, Comiskey, Robison, Latham, W. Gleason, O'Neill, Welch and Nicol.

In this season the figures at the finish were:

RECORD OF 1886.

Date.	Contesting Clubs.	Where Played.	Score.
October 18.	Chicago vs. St. Louis	At Chicago	6—0
October 19.	St. Louis vs. Chicago	At Chicago*	12—0
October 20.	Chicago vs. St. Louis	At Chicago**	11—4
October 21.	St. Louis vs. Chicago	At St. Louis	8—5
October 22.	St. Louis vs. Chicago	At St. Louis***	10—3
October 23.	St. Louis vs. Chicago	At St. Louis	4—3

Total runs—St. Louis, 25; Chicago, 29. *Six innings. **Seven innings. ***Eight innings.

WHEN ST. LOUIS MET DETROIT.

This series between Chicago and St. Louis created great excitement and enthusiasm throughout the baseball world and the baseball loving public of America were clamoring for a peek at the games.

It was claimed that Chicago and St. Louis were having a monopoly of the fun and the suggestion was made that the circuit of cities in which the world's series of games were to be played be enlarged.

So in 1887, when Detroit won the National League pennant and St. Louis again captured the American Association flag, the number of post season games was increased from six to fifteen, and the circuit was enlarged so as to take in nearly all the great baseball cities. The full record of these games is given below:

RECORD OF 1887.

Club.	Contesting Clubs.	Where Played.	Score.
October 10.	Detroit vs. St. Louis	At St. Louis	6—1
October 11.	Detroit vs. St. Louis	At St. Louis	5—3
October 12.	Detroit vs. St. Louis	At Detroit	*2—1
October 13.	Detroit vs. St. Louis	At Pittsburg	8—0
October 14.	St. Louis vs. Detroit	At Brooklyn	5—2
October 15.	Detroit vs. St. Louis	At New York	9—0
October 17.	Detroit vs. St. Louis	At Philadelphia	3—1
October 18.	Detroit vs. St. Louis	At Boston	9—2
October 19.	Detroit vs. St. Louis	At Philadelphia	4—2
October 20.	St. Louis vs. Detroit	At Washington	11—4
October 21.	Detroit vs. St. Louis	At Baltimore	13—3
October 22.	Detroit vs. St. Louis	At Baltimore	13—3
October 24.	Detroit vs. St. Louis	At Detroit	6—3
October 25.	Detroit vs. St. Louis	At Chicago	4—3
October 26.	St. Louis vs. Detroit	At St. Louis	9—2

Total runs—Detroit, 79; St. Louis, 51.

*Thirteen innings.

THE NATIONAL GAME.

WHEN NEW YORK BEAT ST. LOUIS

In 1888 the New York Club, then known as the New York Giants, and which had such great players as Ewing, Keefe, Connor, Ward and Tiernan in its ranks, captured the National League championship and the St. Louis Browns took the American Association pennant for the fourth time. So Giants and Browns came together this time in the post season series and the Giants won six out of the four games played. St. Louis might have captured the world's flag a second time and perhaps would have done so had not its players celebrated in tankards of wine its first victory and shut out of New York in the Metropolis, the score being 3 to 0, and October 17, 1888, being the day and date. Keefe and Welch for New York, and King and Chamberlain for St. Louis, were the pitchers in this memorable series.

To Keefe went the bulk of the honors, for he won all his games and came out of the series with a record of 1,000. The full record of games played in this series was:

RECORD OF 1888.

Date.	Contesting Clubs.	Where Played.	Pitchers.	Score.:
October 16.	New York vs. St. Louis	New York—Keefe-King		2—1
October 17.	St. Louis vs. New York	New York—Chamberlain-Welch		3—0
October 18.	New York vs. St. Louis	New York—Keefe-King		4—2
October 19.	New York vs. St. Louis	Brooklyn—Crane-Chamberlain		6—3
October 20.	New York vs. St. Louis	New York—Keefe-King		6—4
October 22.	New York vs. St. Louis	Philadelphia—Welch-Chamberlain		12—5
October 24.	St. Louis vs. New York	St. Louis—King-Crane		7—5
October 25.	New York vs. St. Louis	St. Louis—Keefe-Chamberlain		11—3
October 26.	St. Louis vs. New York	St. Louis—King-George		14-11
October 27.	St. Louis vs. New York	St. Louis—Chamberlain-Titcomb		18—7

Total runs—New York, 64; St. Louis, 61.

WHEN NEW YORK TROUNCED BROOKLYN.

Brooklyn played its sister city, New York, for the World's Championship in 1889 and the Giants again came out on top, taking six games out of the nine played. In this series Henry O'Day, now a National League umpire, carried off the pitching honors, winning both his games by close scores. Crane, too, did great work in the box for the Giants. The attendance fell off and the crowds were not nearly so large as those which had witnessed the games the previous year between St. Louis and New York. The figures of the post series this year were:

RECORD OF 1889.

Date.	Contesting Clubs.	Where Played.	Pitchers.	Scores.
October 18.	Brooklyn vs. New York	New York—Terry-Keefe		12-10
October 19.	New York vs. Brooklyn	Brooklyn—Crane-Caruthers		6—2
October 22.	Brooklyn vs. New York	New York—Hughes-Caruthers		8—7
October 23.	Brooklyn vs. New York	Brooklyn—Terry-Crane		10—7
October 24.	New York vs. Brooklyn	Brooklyn—Crane-Caruthers		11—3
October 25.	New York vs. Brooklyn	New York—O'Day-Terry		2—1
October 26.	New York vs. Brooklyn	New York—Keefe-Lovett		11—7
October 28.	New York vs. Brooklyn	Brooklyn—Crane-Foutz		16—2
October 29.	New York vs. Brooklyn	Brooklyn—O'Day-Terry		3—2

The game of October 25 required 11 innings.

WHEN LOUISVILLE AND BROOKLYN TIED.

In the Brotherhood year 1890 Boston won the Players' League championship with a percentage of .628, Brooklyn took the National League flag with a record of .667, and Louisville took the American Association pennant also with a record of .667.

All through the country when it came to the arranging for the post season games, baseball enthusiasts called for a three-cornered fight, but the Brooklyns and Louisvilles refused to have anything to do with the Boston Players' team and the series was again a two-handed affair. Out of the seven games played, each team captured three and one was declared a draw. Deciding games would have been played, but a cold wave came along and put a period to the sport for the time being. The figures were:

THE RECORD FOR 1890.

Date.	Contesting Clubs.	Where Played.	Score.
October 17.	Brooklyn vs. Louisville	At Louisville	9—0
October 18.	Brooklyn vs. Louisville	At Louisville	5—3
October 20.	Brooklyn vs. Louisville	At Louisville	7—7
October 21.	Louisville vs. Brooklyn	At Louisville	5—4
October 25.	Brooklyn vs. Louisville	At Brooklyn	7—2
October 27.	Louisville vs. Brooklyn	At Brooklyn	9—8
October 28.	Louisville vs. Brooklyn	At Brooklyn	6—2

Games Won—Louisville, 3; Brooklyn, 3. Games Lost—Louisville, 3; Brooklyn, 3. Games Drawn—one. Total Runs—Brooklyn, 42; Louisville, 32.

Nothing in a post-season way happened in 1891 but in 1892 there was the double season championship of the new 12-club National League, one season ending in July and the other in October.

Boston won the first series and Cleveland the second. In the play-off the games came out in this way:

THE NATIONAL GAME.

Date.	Contesting Clubs.	Where Played.	Score.
October 17.	Boston vs. Cleveland	At Cleveland (11 innings)	0—0
October 18.	Boston vs. Cleveland	At Cleveland	4—3
October 19.	Boston vs. Cleveland	At Cleveland	3—2
October 21.	Boston vs. Cleveland	At Boston	4—0
October 22.	Boston vs. Cleveland	At Boston	12—7
October 23.	Boston vs. Cleveland	At Boston	8—3

Boston victories, 5; drawn, 1.

THEN CAME THE TEMPLE CUP.

In 1893 at the meeting of the National League, Mr. W. C. Temple presented a magnificent cup to the members of that body.

It was called the Temple Cup and was put up as a trophy to be competed for at the close of each season by the two clubs of the National League, which finished first and second in that body. The series was fixed at five games, the club winning three out of five to take the cup.

Here is the four years' record of the contests for the Temple Cup series, from 1894 to 1897, inclusive:

SERIES OF 1894.

Date.	Contesting Clubs.	Where Played.	Pitchers.	Score.
October 4.	New York vs. Baltimore	At Baltimore—Rusie-Esper	4—1
October 5.	New York vs. Baltimore	At Baltimore—Meekin-Gleason	9—6
October 6.	New York vs. Baltimore	At Baltimore—Rusie-Hemming	4—1
October 8.	New York vs. Baltimore	At New York—Meekin-Hawk	16—3

SERIES OF 1895.

Date.	Contesting Clubs.	Where Played.	Pitchers.	Score.
October 2.	Cleveland vs. Baltimore	At Cleveland—Young-McMahon	5—4
October 3.	Cleveland vs. Baltimore	At Cleveland—Cuppy-Hoffer	7—2
October 5.	Cleveland vs. Baltimore	At Cleveland—Young-McMahon	7—1
October 7.	Baltimore vs. Cleveland	At Baltimore—Esper-Cuppy	5—0
October 8.	Cleveland vs. Baltimore	At Cleveland—Young-Hoffer	5—2

SERIES OF 1896.

Date.	Contesting Clubs.	Where Played.	Pitchers.	Score.
October 2.	Baltimore vs. Cleveland	At Baltimore—Hoffer-Young	7—1
October 3.	Baltimore vs. Cleveland	At Baltimore—Corbett-Wallace	7—2
October 5.	Baltimore vs. Cleveland	At Baltimore—Hoffer-Cuppy	6—2
October 8.	Baltimore vs. Cleveland	At Cleveland—Corbett-Cuppy	5—0

SERIES OF 1897.

Date.	Contesting Clubs.	Where Played.	Pitchers.	Score.
October 4.	Boston vs. Baltimore	At Baltimore—Nichols-Nops	13—12
October 5.	Baltimore vs. Boston	At Boston—Corbett-Klobendanz	13—11
October 6.	Baltimore vs. Boston	At Boston—Hoffer-Klobedanz	8—3
October 9.	Baltimore vs. Boston	At Boston—Nops-Stivetts	12—11
October 11.	Baltimore vs. Boston	At Boston—Hoffer-Hickman	9—3

The Temple Cup series ended in 1897, when the National League returned the cup to the donor with thanks, the League finding the series not advantageous to the welfare of the game that year. New York won the cup in 1894, Cleveland in 1895, and Baltimore in 1896 and 1897. No world's series of games was played from 1897 until 1903, the struggle of the American League to obtain a foothold in New York preventing any arrangement of the kind.

WHEN NATIONAL FIRST MET AMERICAN LEAGUE.

It was in the fall of 1903 that the first great series of games between the champion clubs of the National League and the American League took place. The Bostons won the Association flag that year and the Pittsburgs were the League champions.

The first three games were played in Boston and the Pittsburgs seemed to lead their rivals so easily that it was thought they would win the world's flag by a wide margin.

But the Boston boys came strong at the finish, winning all four of the last games played and taking the world's pennant of 1903 by these figures:

RECORD OF 1903.

Date.	Contesting Clubs.	Where Played.	Pitchers.	Score.
October 1.	Pittsburg vs. Boston	At Boston—Phillippe-Young	7—3
October 2.	Boston vs. Pittsburg	At Boston—Dineen-Leever	3—0
October 3.	Pittsburg vs. Boston	At Boston—Phillippe-Hughes	4—2
October 5.	Pittsburg vs. Boston	At Pittsburg—Phillippe-Dineen	5—4
October 7.	Boston vs. Pittsburg	At Boston—Young-Kennedy	11—2
October 8.	Boston vs. Pittsburg	At Pittsburg—Dineen-Leever	6—3
October 9.	Boston vs. Pittsburg	At Pittsburg—Young-Phillippe	7—3
October 12.	Boston vs. Pittsburg	At Boston—Dineen-Phillippe	3—0

1904 AND OFF YEARS.

In 1904, at the close of the season, the New York National League Champions refused to meet the Bostons, the winners of the American League pennant that year and so there was no post-season series and the title of World's Champions went to Boston by default.

Up to this time the record of world's championship series had been as follows:

1884 Providence, N. L.................... 3 games		1887 St. Louis, A. A..................... 5 games
1884 Metropolitan, A. A................... 0 games		1888 New York, N. L.................... 6 games
1885 Chicago, N. L..................... 3 games		1888 St. Louis, A. A.................... 4 games
1885 St. Louis, A. A..................... 3 games		1889 New York, N. L.................... 6 games
1886 Chicago, N. L..................... 3 games		1889 Brooklyn, A. A.................... 3 games
1886 St. Louis, A. A.................... 4 games		1903 Boston, A. L.................... 5 games
1887 Detroit, N. L....................10 games		1903 Pittsourg, N. L..................... 3 games

THEN SPECIAL RULES TO GOVERN.

There was great feeling in baseball circles the country over at the refusal of the New Yorks to meet the Bostons in a world's series in 1904 and that fiasco in the winter of 1904-05, led to the joint adoption by the two major leagues of special rules to govern future world's championship series, making the playing of the same compulsory and placing the entire control thereof in the hands of the National Commission. Under these rules the contesting clubs were bonded in the sum of $10,000 each for the faithful performance of all written rules and all conditions laid down by the National Commission. The other rules were in the main as follows:

The series is to consist of seven games, three for each ground of the contesting club, the choice of the first three games to be determined by lot and the place of the seventh game by the Commission.

Two umpires for each game, one from each league. The winning club is to receive a championship pennant, and each player of the winning team a gold button suitably inscribed.

The players of the two clubs to receive 25 per cent of the gross receipts of the first four games; 75 per cent of this amount to go to the winner of the pennant and 25 per cent to the loser. The National Commission to receive 10 per cent of the gross receipts from all of the games, and after this amount and that of the players have been deducted, the rest is to be divided equally between the two clubs.

Each of the clubs participating in the games to guarantee to the National Commission that it will play all of the games called for and will not exercise any arbitrary right to withdraw before the series has been completed or the championship determined.

NEW YORK AND ATHLETIC SERIES.

In 1905 the New Yorks, representing the National League and the Athletics of Philadelphia, were the representatives in the world's series, the first game of which was played in Philadelphia. Among the many present at this game were Chairman Herrmann and Messrs. Pulliam and Johnson, members, and Mr. John Bruce, secretary of the National Commission, under whose sole jurisdiction the series was placed. In addition there were present many major and minor league magnates and managers, and a host of rooters from New York, Boston, Pittsburg, Washington, and a number of towns contiguous to Philadelphia.

The New Yorks won by superior, allround play. They ran bases with impunity, fielded sharply, and hit Plank opportunely in every inning. Mathewson

was invincible, he shutting the Athletics out with four hits, only one man getting as far as third base. New York scored two runs in the sixth inning on Bresnahan's force hit, a steal, Donlin's single, McGann's base on balls, and Mertes' double. In the ninth they got one more on Gilbert's single, Mathewson's sacrifice and Bresnahan's single.

This victory of the New Yorks in Philadelphia discouraged the admirers of the latter club greatly, but their hopes were revived when the Athletics on the very next day turned the tables on their opponents, winning out by the exact score by which they were beaten in the initial contest. But in the full series New York won out by winning three out of the five games played. The scores in this series were:

RECORD OF 1905.

Date.	Contesting Clubs.	Where Played.	Pitchers.	Score.
October 9.	New York vs. Athletics..............At	Philadelphia—Matthewson-Plank........	3—0
October 10.	Athletics vs. New York..............At	New York—Bender-McGinnity-Ames....	3—0
October 12.	New York vs. Athletics.............;......At	Philadelphia—Matthewson-Coakley......	9—0
October 13.	New York vs. Athletics..............At	New York—McGinnity-Plank............	1—0
October 14.	New York vs. Athletics..............At	New York—Matthewson-Bender.........	2—0

WHEN TWO CHICAGO CLUBS MET.

In 1906 the two Chicago Clubs battled for the World's Championship. It was a great battle, perhaps the best ever fought and only the skill and generalship of Comiskey won for the Chicago White Stockings of the American League over the Chicago Cubs, the head liners of the National.

There were six games played and out of them the White Stockings won four to the Cubs two.

In this famous series Walsh and Reulbach carried off the pitching honors, the former proving most effective and almost invincible at all stages.

The fielding averages at the close of this series showed that in fielding the National Leaguers excelled their rivals in nearly every position, but in all other departments the American Leaguers came out on top. The record was:

RECORD OF 1906.

Date.	Contesting Clubs.	Where Played.	Pitchers.	Score.
October 9.	Chicago A. L. vs. Chicago N. L....At	Chicago—Altrock-Brown..................	2—1
October 10.	Chicago N. L. vs. Chicago A. L....At	Chicago—Reulbach-White-Owen.........	7—1
October 11.	Chicago A. L. vs. Chicago N. L....At	Chicago—Walsh-Pfeister-Gissler........	3—0
October 12.	Chicago N. L. vs. Chicago A. L....At	Chicago—Brown-Altrock..................	1—0
October 13.	Chicago A. L. vs. Chicago N. L....At	Chicago—Walsh-White-Pfeister-Overall.	8—6
October 14.	Chicago A. L. vs. Chicago N. L....At	Chicago—White-Brown-Overall..........	8—3

THE NATIONAL GAME.

This series excelled from a financial standpoint even the series of 1905. In the six games played in this series of 1906 the attendance and receipts was as follows:

	Attendance.	Receipts.
Game No. 1. National League Park	12,693	13,899.00
Game No. 2. American League Park	12,692	13,910.00
Game No. 3, National League Park	13,667	14,056.50
Game No. 4. American League Park	18,384	19,989.50
Game No. 5. National League Park	23,267	23,834.00
Game No. 6. American League Park	19,249	20,861.00
	99,855	$106,550.00

In the division of this large amount of gate money the distribution was made in this way:

DISTRIBUTION.

National Commission	$ 10,655.00
Chicago American League Players, voucher 241	25,051.28
Chicago National League Players, voucher 242	8,350.42
Chicago National League Club, voucher 249	31,246.65
Chicago American League Club, voucher 248	31,246.65

WHEN CHICAGO WALLOPED DETROIT.

In 1907 the Detroit and Chicago Clubs were the representatives in the World's Championship games played that year. The Detroits had won the American League pennant after a fearful struggle and the Chicagos had had nearly a walk over for the National League flag. The great feature of this series was its one sidedness, the Chicagos winning four out of the five games played, tying the other and outbatting and outfielding the American League champions. The great playing of Evers, Pfeister, Reulbach and Brown of the Chicago team was the best feature of these games. The full record was:

RECORD OF 1907.

Date.	Contesting Clubs.	Where Played.	Pitchers.	Score.
Oct. 8.	Detroit-Chicago	Chicago—	Donovan-Reulbach and Overall	3—3
Oct. 9.	Detroit-Chicago	Chicago—	Pfeister-Mullin	3—1
Oct 10.	Chicago-Detroit	Chicago—	Reulbach-Sievers and Killian	5—1
Oct. 11.	Chicago-Detroit	Detroit—	Overall-Donovan	6—1
Oct. 12.	Chicago-Detroit	Detroit—	Brown-Mullin	2—0

In 1907, before the World's Championship games were played, the National Commission and Mr. B. B. Johnson, representing the American League, proposed an amendment to paragraph 2, section 17, that said section should thereafter read as follows:

"Second— Sixty per cent of the balance from the first four games shall form a pool for the players of the two teams, to be divided sixty per cent to the winner, and forty per cent to the loser of the contest."

This 1907 was one of the best paying series of post-season games and the players benefitted handsomely from the big gate receipts.

This change was unanimously agreed to by all of the clubs representing both the National and American Leagues and the gate receipts of the 1907 series were divided in obedience to this rule.

The prices of admission were also fixed by the Commission as follows:

At Chicago—General admission, $1.00; grand stand (on account of large seating capacity), $1.50; box seats, $2.00.

At Detroit—General admission, $1.00; grand stand in view of limited seating capacity), $2.00; box seats, $2.50.

The full attendance and receipts at this series was:

	Attendance.	Receipts.
Game No. 1, Detroit American League Park	24,277	$29,162.50
Game No. 2, Chicago National League Park	21,901	26,430.00
Game No. 3, Chicago National League Park	16,212	16,212.50
Game No. 4, Detroit American League Park	11,306	17,825.50
Game No. 5, Detroit American League Park	7,370	12,638.50
Total	78,068	$101,728.50

National Commission	$ 10,172.86
Chicago National League players, voucher 373	32,960.03
Detroit American League players, voucher 374	21,973.30
Chicago National League Club, voucher 375	18,311.13
Detroit American League Club, voucher 375	18,311.13
Total	$101,728.50

This large amount was divided almost equally by the players on the one side and the club owners and the National Commission on the other. The exact distribution was as follows:

For the 1907 series the National Commission appointed as official scorers, Mr. A. J. Flanner, of the Sporting News of St. Louis and Mr. Francis C. Richter, of the Sporting Life, of Philadelphia. The official umpires were Henry O'Day, of the National League and John F. Sheridan, of the American League. In this post-season series, the most important ever played, the batting record given below shows just what players took part in these great games and just the kind of hitting they did:

CHICAGO PLAYERS.

Player.	G.	AB.	R.	H.	SH.	SB.	Pct.
Steinfeldt	5	17	2	8	1	1	.470
Evers	5	20	2	7	1	3	.350
Slagle	5	22	3	6	0	6	.273
Schulte	5	20	3	5	0	1	.250
Sheckard	5	21	0	5	1	1	.238
Chance	4	14	3	3	0	3	.214
Kling	5	19	2	4	1	0	.210
Overall	2	5	0	1	2	0	.200
Reulbach	2	5	0	1	0	0	.200
Tinker	5	13	4	2	2	2	.154
Zimmerman	1	1	0	0	0	0	.000
Pfiester	1	2	0	0	1	0	.000
Brown	1	3	0	0	0	0	.000
Howard	2	5	0	1	0	1	.200

DETROIT PLAYERS.

Player.	G.	AB.	R.	H.	SH.	SB.	Pct.
Killian	1	2	1	1	0	0	.500
Rossman	5	20	1	8	0	2	.400
Jones	5	17	1	6	1	3	.353
Payne	2	4	0	1	0	0	.250
Coughlin	5	20	0	5	0	1	.250
Crawford	5	21	1	5	0	0	.238
Cobb	5	20	1	4	0	0	.200
Schmidt	3	12	0	2	0	0	.166
Schaefer	5	21	1	3	1	1	.143
O'Leary	5	18	0	1	1	0	.055
Donovan	2	8	0	0	0	0	.000
Mullin	2	6	0	0	0	0	.000
Sievers	1	1	0	0	0	0	.000
Archer	1	1	3	0	0	0	.000

TEAM BATTING.

In this 1907 series the pitching averages show no overshadowing performance for any one pitcher as was the case in the two preceding World's Championship Series.

The Detroit Club used all of such of its pitchers as were in condition, while the Chicago Club held back only two, using four pitchers with equal success. Following were the figures:

Pitchers.	W.	L.	Tie.	Pct.	H.H.	B.S.	H.P.B.	S.O.	W.P.
Overall	1	0	1	1,000	14	4	0	10	0
Pfiester	1	0	0	1,000	9	1	1	3	0
Reulbach	1	0	0	1,000	6	3	0	4	0
Brown	1	0	0	1,000	7	1	0	4	0
Donovan	0	1	1	.000	17	5	3	16	0
Mullin	0	2	0	.000	7	0	0	1	0
Sievers	0	1	0	.000	16	5	1	7	0
Killian	0	0	0	.000	3	1	0	1	0

In the first game, October 8th, Reulbach relieved Overall after the ninth inning, with the score tied, and pitched three innings without altering the result.
Killian relieved Sievers in the fifth inning of the game of October 10th, which is charged as a defeat to Sievers.
In the remaining games each club worked but one pitcher.

THE RECORD OF 1908.

The record of 1908 came very near being a repetition of the record of 1907. In 1908 the Chicago Cubs, representing the National League and the Detroit Tigers, representing the American League, were again the competing teams. In 1907 Chicago won six games straight from Detroit, and this year later they captured four out of the five games played. The full 1908 record was:

Date.	Contesting Clubs.	Where Played. Pitchers.	Score
Oct. 10.	Chicago-Detroit	Detroit—Brown-Killian and Summers	10—6
Oct. 11.	Chicago-Detroit	Chicago—Overall-Donovan	6—1
Oct. 12.	Detroit-Chicago	Chicago—Mullin-Reulbach	8—3
Oct. 13.	Chicago-Detroit	Detroit—Brown-Summers	3—0
Oct. 14.	Chicago-Detroit	Detroit—Overall-Donovan	2—0

ATTENDANCE AND RECEIPTS.

The attendance and receipts in this series was as follows:

	Attendance.	Total Receipts.	Player's Share.	Clubs' Share.	National Commission
First game, at Detroit	10,812	$16,473.00	$ 8,895.42	$ 5,930.28	$1,647.30
Second game, at Chicago	17,760	26,927.00	14,540.58	9,693.72	2,692.70
Third game, at Chicago	14,543	22,767.00	12,294.18	8,196.12	2,276.70
Fourth game, at Detroit	12,907	19,231.00	10,384.74	6,923.16	1,923.10
Fifth game, at Detroit	6,210	9,577.50	....	8,619.75	957.75
Total	62,232	$94,975.00	$46,114.92	$39,363.03	$9,497.55

THE RECORD OF 1909.

In the Fall of 1909 the Pittsburg Club of the National League having won the championship of its organization in the World's Championship Series, played that Fall, faced the Detroits, who for the third successive time had taken the American League flag. This series was by long odds the most successful from a playing as well as a gate receipt standpoint, ever played. The gross receipts were $8,000, better than the next best in this line, the

Cubs-Sox clash of 1906, while the players got $12,000 more than the best preceding split, which was that of the Detroit-Chicago games of 1907. These records might easily have been bettered had Detroit greater reserved seat accomodation, or had Pittsburg's magnificent stand, supposed to be equal to the emergency, been of capacity to meet all demands on it Of the seven games played, Pittsburg won four to Detroits three. The record was:

Date.	Contesting Clubs.	Where Played. Pitchers.	Score.
Oct. 8.	Pittsburg-Detroit	Pittsburg—Adams-Mullen	4—1
Oct. 9.	Detroit-Pittsburg	Pittsburg—Donovan-Willis	7—2
Oct. 11.	Pittsburg-Detroit	Detroit—Maddox-Summers	8—6
Oct. 12.	Detroit-Pittsburg	Detroit—Mullin-Leifield	5—0
Oct. 13.	Pittsburg-Detroit	Pittsburg—Adams-Summers	8—4
Oct. 14.	Detroit-Pittsburg	Detroit—Mullin-Willis	5—4
Oct. 16.	Pittsburg-Detroit	Detroit—Adams-Donovan-Mullin	8—0

THE RECORD OF 1910.

The series of 1910 was between the Chicago Cubs of the National League and the Athletics of Philadelphia of the American League. Contrary to expectation the games were wonderfully one-sided and a great surprise was given the National League men, the American Leaguers not only winning four out of the only five games played, but excelling

their rivals in all departments of the game.

Before the games were played, Evers, Chicago's great second baseman, fractured an ankle and Oldring, the Athletics' star fielder, was injured. This prevented these two great players from taking part in the games. The complete record of this 1910 series was as follows:

Date.	Contesting Clubs.	Where Played. Pitchers.	Score.
Oct. 17.	Athletics-Chicago	Philadelphia—Bender-Overall-McIntire	4—1
Oct. 18.	Athletics-Chicago	Philadelphia—Coombs-Brown	9—3
Oct. 20.	Athletics-Chicago	Chicago—Coombs-Reulbc'h-M'I'tire-Pfeister	12—5
Oct. 22.	Chicago-Athletics	Chicago—Bender-Cole-Brown	4—3
Oct. 23.	Athletics-Chicago	Chicago—Coombs-Brown	7—2

OFFICIAL INDIVIDUAL FIELDING AVERAGES.

The following are the individual fielding averages made by the players of the Chicago and Athletic teams in their 1910 World's Championship series:

Catchers.

Player.	G.	PO.	A.	E.	Pct.
Lapp	1	4	2	0	1.000
Kling	3	11	7	0	1.000
Archer	2	18	3	0	1.000
Thomas	4	27	8	1	.972

Pitchers.

Player.	G.	PO.	A.	E.	Pct.
Bender	2	1	2	0	1.000
Reulbach	1	0	1	0	1.000
Pfiester	1	0	1	0	1.000
Cole	1	1	3	0	1.000
Brown	3	0	10	1	.909
Coombs	3	1	4	2	.714
McIntire	2	0	2	1	.666
Overall	1	0	0	0	.000

First Basemen.

Player.	G.	PO.	A.	E.	Pct.
Chance	5	51	4	0	1.000
Archer	1	9	0	0	1.000
Davis	5	43	1	3	.936

Second Basemen.

Player.	G.	PO.	A.	E.	Pct.
Collins	5	17	17	1	.972
Zimmerman	5	10	18	1	.966

Third Basemen.

Player.	G.	PO.	A.	E.	Pct.
Steinfeldt	5	2	12	2	.875
Baker	5	9	11	3	.869

Shortstops.

Player.	G.	PO.	A.	E.	Pct.
Barry	5	8	12	0	1.000
Tinker	5	11	14	2	.926

Outfielders.

Player.	G.	PO.	A.	E.	Pct.
Lord, lf.	5	8	0	0	1.000
Murphy, rf.	5	6	2	0	1.000
Strunk, cf.	4	10	0	1	.909
Sheckard, lf.	5	8	2	1	.909
Hofman, cf.	5	7	0	1	.875
Schulte, rf.	5	4	0	1	.800
Chicago team fielding					.954
Athletic team fielding					.945

INDIVIDUAL OFFICAL BATTING AVERAGES.

Chicago Players.

Player.	G.	AB.	R.	H.	SB.	S.	Pct
Schulte	5	17	3	6	0	2	.353
Chance	5	17	1	6	0	0	.353
Tinker	5	18	2	6	1	0	.333
Sheckard	5	14	5	4	1	0	.286
Hofman	5	15	2	4	0	2	.267
Zimmerman	5	17	0	4	1	2	.235
Archer	3	11	1	2	0	0	.182
Steinfeldt	5	20	0	2	0	0	.100
Kling	5	13	0	1	0	0	.077
Overall	1	1	0	0	0	0	.000
McIntire	2	1	0	0	0	0	.000
Brown	3	7	0	0	0	0	.000
Richie	1	0	0	0	0	0	.000
Reulbach	1	0	0	0	0	0	.000
Pfiester	1	2	0	0	0	0	.000
Beaumont	3	2	1	0	0	0	.000
Cole	1	2	0	0	0	0	.000
Needham	1	1	0	0	0	0	.000
Chicago team batting							221

Athletic Players.

Player.	G.	AB.	R.	H.	SB.	S.	Pct
Collins	5	21	5	9	4	1	.429
Baker	5	22	6	9	0	0	.409
Coombs	3	13	0	5	0	0	.385
Davis	5	17	5	6	0	2	.353
Murphy	5	20	6	7	0	2	.350
Strunk	4	18	2	5	0	0	.278
Thomas	4	12	2	3	0	0	.250
Lapp	1	4	0	1	0	0	.250
Barry	5	17	3	4	0	2	.235
Hartzel	1	5	2	1	2	0	.200
Lord	5	22	3	4	0	1	.182
Athletic team batting							317

OFFICIAL PITCHING RECORDS.

Pitcher,	G.	W.	L.	T.	Pct.	R.	H.	B.	P.	O.	P.
Coombs 3	3	0	0	1.000	10	23	14	0	17	0	
Bender 2	1	1	0	.500	5	12	4	0	14	0	
Brown 3	1	2	0	.333	16	23	27	0	14	1	
McIntire ...2	0	1	0	.000	4	4	3	1	3	0	
Pfiester 1	0	0	0	.000	5	9	1	0	1	0	
Cole 1	0	0	0	.000	3	10	3	1	5	0	
Overall 1	0	0	0	.000	3	6	1	0	1	0	
Richie 1	0	0	0	.000	0	1	0	0	0	0	
Reulbach ..1	0	0	0	.000	3	3	2	0	0	0	

ATTENDANCE FIGURES.

First Game at Philadelphia.

Attendance	26,891
Total receipts	$37,424.50
Players' division	20,269.23
Club-owners' share	13,472.80
National Commission	3,742.50

Second Game at Philadelphia.

Attendance	24,597
Total receipts	$35,137.00
Player's division	18,973.98
Club-owner's share	12,649.32
National Commission	3,513.70

Third Game at Chicago.

Attendance	23,210
Total receipts	$36,771.50
Player's share	19,845.81
Club-owner's share	13,250.54
National Commission	3,675.15

Fourth Game at Chicago.

Attendance	19,150
Total receipts	$27,550.50
Player's share	14,877.27
Club-owner's share	9,918.18
National Commission	2,755.08

Fifth Game at Chicago.

Attendance	27,371
Total receipts	$37,116.50
Player's share	20,042.91
Club-owner's share	13,361.94
National Commission	3,711.65

THE NATIONAL GAME.

THE WORLD'S CHAMPIONSHIP.
CHARLES A. COMISKEY, PRESIDENT OF THE CHICAGO WHITE SOX, COMPARES THE WORLD'S CHAMPION TEAMS OF THE PRESENT DAY TO THE WORLD'S CHAMPION TEAMS OF TWENTY-FIVE YEARS AGO.

CHARLES A. COMISKEY.
President and Owner of the Chicago White Sox.

"What do you think of them?"

It was Charles A. Comiskey, president and owner of the Chicago White Sox of 1910 that asked the question.

"Are they any better than we were?"

"No, nor as good."

It was at the opening game in the National League Park at Chicago of the 1910 World's series that Comiskey put this question.

His query and my reply set me to

thinking.

It was just twenty-five years before that Comiskey and I had had business in this same enclosure.

Then he was commander of the "Four Time Winner" St. Louis Browns, and his men were assembled to cross bats for the Championship of the World with the Chicago White Stockings, that heroic legion, who led by Captain Anson, were for many a year cock-of-the-walk in the big baseball world.

I was there to score the game and to report the proceedings for the Globe-Democrat.

Now, twenty-five years after, we were in the old park again, Comiskey, gray as a badger, but of stalwart frame and ruddy complexion, and still looking the strong and sturdy athlete and me a baseball writer as of yore.

"What do you think of them?"

He meant to ask me how I thought the Athletics of Philadelphia and the Chicago Cubs of the 1910 year compared with the Chicago White Stockings and the St. Louis Browns, who fought for the World's pennant on this same field in 1885.

"Honestly now, is this Chicago team any better than Anson's old nine and have the Athletics an edge on my team?"

It would not have done in that great Chicago crowd to have answered this question save in a whisper. For me to have replied to the question honestly might have brought on a small sized riot and so I sat and gazed at the teams before me; gazed and wondered and then after a long pause said in a low voice:

"If they are better I would like you to show me just where?"

Twenty-five years is a long while especially in the world of baseball. Twenty-five years ago the game was just being developed.

The National League and the American Association, then the two major leagues, were just rounding into form.

The minor leagues then in the field were scarce worth while and all the great players, perforce of circumstance, were enrolled under the banner of one or the other of these major league organizations.

The Chicago White Stockings of 1885 were far and away the best club of that year in the National League.

In their entire season they had won eighty-seven games and lost but twenty-five. They had taken first honors with scarcely the semblance of a struggle. Their superiority as players over the men composing the other seven teams in the National League that year shone out as prominently as great knots on a white pine board.

As the Chicago White Stockings outclassed all other teams in the National League in 1885 so did the St. Louis Browns of 1885 easily excel all their rivals in the American Association that year. Of the one hundred and twelve games they played that year they won seventy-nine and lost only thirty-three. It was this team in fact that won the championship of the American Association in 1885, 1886, 1887 and 1888 and which in 1885 and 1886 captured the World's pennant.

And the question Comiskey asked was as to how these two teams of the long ago compared with the teams that were now on this same old field in this 1910 year, the world-famed and often World's Champion Chicago Cubs and the Athletics of Philadelphia, three-time winners of the American League pennant. And it was to Comiskey's question that I replied:

"If they are better I should like you to show me just where."

I do not mean by this that there were as many great players twenty-five years ago as there are now. I simply say that when it comes to drawing a comparison between the old and heroic legion of baseball, the Chicago White Stockings led by Anson in 1885, and the St. Louis Browns led by Comiskey that same year, and these two teams placed in the balance on the one scale and the Chicago Cubs and the Athletics of Philadelphia of the 1910 year in the other that the teams of today as I saw them at Chicago do not out weigh the teams of twenty-five years ago a single penny weight.

In fact, taking them man for man and weighing them in the scale, I do not know but, what the old fellows would at many a point out weigh the others.

After the Athletics had beaten the Chicagos in the deciding game for the World's Championship at Chicago, Comiskey said:

"The Athletics will be Champions of the World for a long while. Each decade brings some great team to the front, some team that out classes all the others and that shows the way until the break comes and then it must step aside and give way to a younger and better organization, for youth must be served.

"It is the same story in all forms of athletic exercise. Hanlan was the greatest oarsman for nearly a quarter of a century. For ten years Sullivan was invincible as a pugilist and for ten years afterwards Jeffries had no superior. In baseball the Cincinnati Reds were the greatest players of the decade which commenced with 1869 and when they fell away the Chicago White Stockings, with Anson as their head, and the St. Louis Browns, with Comiskey showing the way, came to the front and held their own until the New York Giants and the Chicago Cubs came along and pushed them out of their place at the head of the column.

"Now the Chicago Cubs have been relegated to the rear and this Athletic team has jumped into their old and proud position. It is a team composed mostly of young, speedy and stalwart players, men who are likely to remain at the top in their profession for many a day. But great as is this Athletic team it is perhaps no speedier or better than other of the teams that battled on this same field twenty-five years ago for World's honors."

It was this statement from the old Roman that set me to drawing the comparison between the old champion teams and the new and to taking a stand that will be challenged by many of the baseball writers of the present day who believe that the great game has made wonderful strides in the last quarter of a century, a belief I do not share in for reasons that will appear obvious to all before I have fairly finished this article.

In comparing the old teams with the new I will leave nothing undone considering the uniforms, the condition, the general appearance, the speed, the skill and the quick wit of every man concerned, and to begin will start off with the uniforms.

When the St. Louis Browns led by Charles Comiskey and the Chicago White Stockings led by Captain Adrian C. Anson, appeared on the Chicago field in October, 1885, to battle for World's honors, they were a thing of beauty and a joy forever. The St. Louis team appeared in jackets and trousers made of the finest white cricket flannel, with brown caps and stockings. Their uniforms were spick and span and white and new and immaculate in their neatness and cleanliness.

And when it came to bright and handsome raiment this splendidly dressed St. Louis team had none the best of its Chicago rival save that in pure whiteness the latter excelled a trifle, its stockings being like its shirt and trousers as white and chaste as pure milk.

What a contrast indeed between the beautiful uniforms worn then to the faded and soiled uniforms worn by the Athletics and the Cubs in this their opening game at Chicago in this 1910 year.

In the management of a baseball team cleanliness of uniforms should be one of the cardinal virtues and filthy uniforms should be considered as a lack of order and discipline on the part of the offending player or players.

In the matter of uniforms indeed the old players out weighed the new a thousand fold and here you must score the first tally for the veterans. And now breaking away from the question of uniforms and considering the condition of the men.

The St. Louis Browns of 1885 were perhaps the finest looking set of athletes that ever took the field but they had wasp-like waists and were almost slender in build compared to the stalwarts that Anson placed in the field that year. In fact in magnificent appearance, condition and general build the Chicago Cubs of 1910 do not begin to compare with Anson's old heroic legion of 1885. In fact the 1910 team of Chicago Cubs was to me a disappointment in many ways.

Chance may be the peerless leader, and Kling a great assistant, but they compare in no way as coaches to the old Marshalltown infant, nor can they ever hope to match the quick wit, the speedy action or the wonderful headwork of those old kings of the Chicago Club, Mike Kelly, Ed. Williamson and Fred Pfeffer.

Nor is there a coach on either of the present day champion teams to compare with Comiskey, Latham, Gleason or Welch of the old Browns.

On the coaching lines, therefore, I give the old players the edge over the present day men.

And now as to the different playing positions. Two men did nearly all the catching in the games of last October, Kling for Chicago and Thomas for the Athletics. Kling caught three of the five games for Chicago and Archer the other two. Thomas caught four games for the Athletics and Lapp one.

In the olden games Flint did all the catching for Chicago and Bushong nearly all the receiving for St. Louis. And no catcher on either Chicago or Athletic team last October did speedier or better work than did Flint and Bushong for the old teams.

In the World's Championship games twenty-five years ago Clarkson and McCormick were the only pitchers the Chicago Club could boast of and Caruthers and Foutz were the only pitching material on the St. Louis team.

In terrific speed, magnificent command of the ball, in strategy and in all the points that go to make a great pitcher these four twirlers of 1885 were just as great and effective in their way as any of the boxmen who officiated in the World's Championship games at Chicago last October.

Comiskey and Anson were the first basemen of the 1885 teams. If there were better first basemen in the last October games than these two were in their prime I failed to see them.

Collins of the Athletics and Zimmerman of the Chicagos, who covered second base in the last October games are both fine players, but not a bit finer than were Fred Pfeffer of the Chicagos in 1885 and Billy Robinson of the St. Louis Browns of that year.

And at third base I do not believe that Baker and Steinfeldt, the men of today, have the edge on Williamson and Latham respectively, the third basemen of the Chicago and St. Louis clubs in 1885.

Neither do Barry or Tinker, the present day shortstops, excel Gleason and Burns, the shortstops of the 1885 competing teams. Nor do I believe that Lord, Murphy, Strunk, Sheckard, Hoffman or Schulte, outfielders of the Chicago-Athletic teams of today are any faster, if even as fast as were Dalrymple, Gore, Kelly, Sunday, Welch, Nicol and O'Neill of the old Chicago and St. Louis champion teams.

Now I say all this after having seen all four of the teams in actual encounter. And I do not make comparison favorable to one and odious to the other because I am an old-timer myself and naturally prejudiced in that direction but I make the assertion boldly and because I have good eyes and have seen all sides of the question.

And I make the statement too, to prove to the professional players that there is still great room for improvement, especially on the coaching lines, in the matter of uniforms and in the work of thinking quickly and acting on the spur of the moment.

I make it too to prove that great and wonderful as have been the strides in baseball in the past few years there is still plenty of room for all to forge ahead and to improve the game in directions where in recent years it seemed to have been going backward and this applies especially to the matter of uniforms and to the general appearance of teams on the field.

If this article will only serve as an incentive to managers and players to improve the sport if only in this one direction why even then it will have solved its mission.

THE NATIONAL GAME.

THE BASEBALL WRITERS.

LINES ABOUT THE MEN WHO REPORT THE GAME AND SPREAD ITS STANDARD AND INFLUENCE IN ALL DIRECTIONS.

After the baseball presidents, it is perhaps right and proper that I should tell of the men who have helped build up the game, who helped players, managers, presidents and all to widen its areas and make it the great pastime it is today.

I believe the first credit of building up the game should be given to the early baseball writers like Henry Chadwick of Brooklyn, William Macdonald Spink of St. Louis, Louis Meacham of Chicago, O. P. Caylor of Cincinnati and others like them, for they not only wrote of the game but they organized baseball teams and helped build up the sport in all directions. First and foremost of these builders-up of the game was Henry Chadwick, who was really the first to write baseball for the New York press and who at the time of his death was known as "The Father of the Game."

Up to this time no record whatever has been kept of the men who have written about baseball and who more than any others have helped to bring the game into the prominence it now enjoys.

Many a good fellow has come into the world and with pen and brain written of the sport and made the world all the better and brighter for his coming.

And many of these same good fellows have passed away without any record having been kept of their coming or going. I am in my poor way going to try and remedy this sort of thing and in the pages of this book to-day and to-morrow the life work of the baseball writers will have recognition and record. And in saying this I make no distinction. Every one of the fraternity look alike to me. I love them all and in all the profession I do not believe I have ever had an enemy. And in this book I have endeavored to treat one and all alike. Time and again I have written this man and that for portraits of themselves and sketches of their careers. Some have been too busy to reply to my poor letters and, as a result, they are not given the prominence in this work that others are given who responded to my appeals. I mean to say that I wanted to treat one and all alike and that I have done so as far as lay in my power. I make this brief statement so that one and all will understand that my intention has been to give every one of the fraternity an equal representation. The old time baseball reporters were all my personal friends and they will forgive any short comings that may be in evidence in this work. The others should bear with me and believe that if I have erred in the treatment of any one of them the error was one of accident and not of heart.

It is only right and proper that in this work a tribute should be paid to the early and to the present writers of the game, the men who helped bring baseball from the prairies into the enclosure and made the pastime a profession as well as a sport, and the men who with pen and brain are today booming baseball.

Foremost of these writers in the olden time were Henry Chadwick of the New York Clipper in the Far East and William Macdonald Spink of the St. Louis Globe-Democrat of the West.

At one time they were the only two writing about the game in their respective cities.

After them came J. B. McCormick and O. P. Caylor of the Cincinnati Enquirer; Louis Meacham, Harry Palmer and Frank Brunell of the Chicago Tribune; Jacob Morse of the Boston Herald; Tim Murnane of the Boston Globe; Alfred H. Wright of the New York Clipper; William M. Rankin of the New York Clipper, and his brother, June Rankin of the New York Herald.

The third crop of writers included Frank Wright and Harry Weldon of the Cincinnati Enquirer, Jim Nolan and Dave Reid of the Missouri Republican, Ben Armstrong of the Sporting News, Francis C. Richter of the Sporting Life, Ban Johnson of the Cincinnati Commercial-Gazette, Ren Mulford of the Cincinnati Times-Star, Peter J. Donahue, or as he was best known, "P. Jay" of the New York World; Edward Sheridan of the Chicago Tribune, Tim Murnane of the Boston Herald, Charley Crane of the New York Press, Lyndon Smith of the New York World, Jim Kennedy of the New York Times, Sam Austin of the New York Herald, George Stackhouse of the New York Tribune, John Mandigo of the New York Sun, Charles F. Mathison of the Detroit Free Press, Harry Pulliam of the Louisville Commercial, Hugh Keough and Joe Murphy of the Chicago Tribune, J. B. Sheridan and Richard Collins of the St. Louis Republic, Charles Dryden and L. E. Sanborn of the Chicago Tribune, Harold Lanigan of the St. Louis Times, his brother Ernest Lanigan of the New York Press, W. H. Hicks, Jr., of the New York Journal; C. P. McDonald of the Chicago Tribune, Hugh Fullerton of the Chicago Examiner, T. P. Magilligan of the San Francisco Globe, Eddie Wray of the St. Louis Post-Dispatch, Willie Murphy of the St. Louis Star, Myron Townsend of the Cincinnati Times-Star, William B. Hanna of the New York Sun, J. J. Karpf of the New York Evening Mail, John R. Robinson of the Boston Traveler, A. H. C. Mitchell of the Boston American, O. W. Brown of the Boston Traveler, Ray Ziegler of the Philadelphia Record, J. Ed Grillo of the Washington Post, J. M. Cummings of the Sporting News, A. R. Cratty of the Pittsburg Leader, James J. Long of the Pittsburg Sun, Ralph S. Davis of the Pittsburg Press, C. B. Power of the Pittsburg Dispatch, C. H. Zuber of the Cincinnati News, Jack Ryder of the Cincinnati Enquirer, Edward F. Bang of the Cleveland Plain-Dealer, Paul H. Bruske of the Detroit Times, W. A. Phelon of the Cincinnati Post, George C. Rice of the Chicago News, Charles A. Hughes of the Chicago Record-Herald, E. G. Westlake of the Chicago Post, James C. Gilruth of the Chicago News, Will McKay of the Cleveland Leader, Gym Bagley of the New York Evening World, Harry Niemeyer of the New York Globe and Joe Campbell of the St. Louis Chronicle and the Washington Post.

Sam Crane and Tim Murnane, the former of New York and the latter of Boston, are the only simon pure baseball players who make use of the pen as a

324

steady diet to earn their livelihood. These boys are in baseball for life and it seems they enjoy their vocations more and more as the years roll on.

Many a player has taken a dab at the newspaper end. It would not be surprising if Addie Joss would be in for keeps so soon as his ball playing days are over, as he does more than any other player in that line during the off season.

Umpire Billy Evans is a first-class baseball critic and it seems that Fred Tenney made as much of a hit in New York, when the club was South, as he did when he wrote for the Boston papers when a member of the Boston Club.

Roy Thomas, formerly of the Phillies and the Pittsburgs, also did much in this line while his club was on the road. So did Johnny Evers, the great little second baseman of the Chicago Cubs.

Horace Fogel is another newspaperman who has jumped into prominence in baseball by his assumption of the position of president of the Philadelphia National League Club.

John Heydler, secretary of the National League was more printer than writer, although he has had ample newspaper experience; Secretary Frank Hough of the Athletics, is sporting editor of the Philadelphia Enquirer, and Director "Butch" Jones was connected with the Associated Press of that city for a long time; President Tom Noyes of the Washington Club is the head man of the Washington Star; Charley Murphy owes the fact that he is the president of the Chicago National League Club to his former newspaper entanglement.

Secretary Barnard of the Cleveland Club used to write baseball when he was in Columbus.

Secretary Will Locke of the Pittsburg Club was formerly sporting editor of the Pittsburg Press.

Sid Mercer of the New York Globe was once secretary of the St. Louis Americans, and J. Ed Grillo, sporting editor of the Washington Post, preceded Joe O'Brien as president of the American Association.

Charles Powers, a well-known Pittsburg newspaper man, was one of the few who dared brave the trials of the position of umpire, along with John Heydler.

William G. Evans of the American League umpire staff, was a newspaper man before he assumed his present position, but is now in baseball to stay and is one of the best liked umpires in the country.

A man who is doing as much as any other writer living to build up baseball the country over is Jacob C. Morse, the editor of the Boston Baseball Magazine.

And now breaking away from a story of all the past and present, I will now start out to give brief sketches of the men now writing of baseball in the various major league cities, their names being given in alphabetical order:

TOM AKERS — Tommy Akers is the sporting editor of the Atlanta, Ga., Journal, one of the most widely read papers of the South. Akers has been writing baseball for many years and is recognized in the Southern League circuit as one of the fairest and most friendly of baseball authorities. Akers, besides handing out well written matter about the game, has also won for himself an international reputation as a baseball poet.

TOM ANDREWS—Tom Andrews is the sporting editor of the Milwaukee Wisconsin and up North is held in high esteem wherever sporting matters are discussed. Mr. Andrews is one of the biggest boosters the American Association can boast of. Tom is an old-timer, though still in his thirties, and has been writing about baseball, football, racing and, last but not least, pugilism. They say that it was Andrews who first discovered that there was championship material in Battling Nelson, the boy who defeated Gans for the world's championship a few years ago, but who later lost out to Adolph Wolgast, Andrews, besides editing the great sport page of his paper is the publisher of one of the most complete and correct sporting guides issued in America. Andrews is one of the popular sporting writers of America. He attends all the big championship games, baseball meetings and other conventions wherein sports are concerned.

SAM AUSTIN—Sam Austin, now the able and famous sporting editor of the Police Gazette, was in his day one of New York's best and most popular baseball writers. When tne New York Giants and Charlie Comiskey's St. Louis Browns, in the eighties, were playing games in New York for the World's Championship, Austin was reporting the events for the New York Herald and in fine, descriptive and bright and interesting work, no writer of his day excelled him. He was the friend and companion of that bright galaxy of baseball writers that flourished in New York in the eighties, the list including such stars as Chadwick, Mandigo, Stackhouse, Goodfriend, Lyndon Smith, Jim Sullivan, Donahue and other royal fellows like them.

O. W. BROWN—O. W. Brown is the baseball editor of the Boston Traveler. He was one of the baseball writers who, in 1908-09 declared themselves against the spit ball way of pitching. Mr. Brown is a fine writer and stands near the top in his profession.

FRANK BRUNELL—Frank Brunell, now the wealthy and influential owner of tne Chicago Daily Racing Form, was in his day one of the best of the great array of baseball writers. He commenced writing baseball for the Cleveland Plain Dealer and wound up his career as a baseball writer in Chicago on the Tribune. Brunell was the secretary of the Brotherhood League, and quit the game when that august body tossed up the sponge. In his day the game had no abler representative in the newspaper line than this same Frank Brunell.

PAUL HALE BRUSKE—Paul Hale Bruske, sporting editor for several years of the Detroit News-Tribune and until the spring of 1910 occupant of a similar position on the Detroit Times, is a native Michigander and has never toiled in a fixed spot outside the commonwealth in which he first saw light.

Born in Charlotte, his boyhood was spent in Saginaw and his collegiate education secured at Alma, of which his father is president. In collegiate athletics Mr. Bruske specialized in tennis and baseball, winning his championship in the former sport during his final four years of competition, and playing regularly in the infield on the baseball club of which he was captain in his senior year,

THE NATIONAL GAME.

Entering newspaper work on his graduation from school, Mr. Bruske worked as a member of the staff of the Lansing State Republican, the Grand Rapids Herald and the Grand Rapids Free Press. In Grand Rapids he secured a baptism in sporting reporting, being assigned to cover the games for Tom Loftus' Western League Club, which contained at the time such stars as Rube Waddell, Sam Crawford, Charlie Buelow, Ollie Pickering and Jake Beckley.

From 1900 on, Mr. Bruske reported sport in Detroit. The green sport section of the Detroit News-Tribune, the first color supplement in Michigan, was his work. Entering the afternoon field shortly after he had become a benedict, Mr. Bruske assumed the sport desk of the Detroit Times, which he left but recently to enter the field of motor advertising with the E-M-F Company. His first work in the new field was the management of the "Under Three Flags" trip of the Flanders "20," which started at Quebec, June 6 and finished at Mexico City August 3, after the most remarkable journey ever placed to the credit of a car of its power.

During his work in baseball reporting, Mr. Bruske was on particularly intimate terms with the members of Detroit's three-time American League champion club, his departure from the field being made the occasion of a floral expression of regret and esteem. Mr. Bruske still retains one newspaper connection, his position as Detroit correspondent of Sporting Life.

O. P. CAYLOR—It seems strange to me sitting here and writing a story of O. P. Caylor, for many a day the baseball editor of the Cincinnati Enquirer.

For we two were great rivals in our day and often berated each other with the editorial tripod.

Our natures ran apart. I was a careless devil of a lad, willing to play on Sunday or on any other day of the week or to bet my last dollar on the result of a game.

Caylor was a sedate, dignified sort of a chap, a man of few words, but an earnest, effective and enthusiastic champion of the game.

And so it came that we often disagreed, but when it came to the organizing of teams, to the placing of them in the field and to the writing of the contests after they had been disposed of, I found no better friend and helper than Caylor. And so in the early eighties, after William Spink had quit active service, I took up the gauntlet and no one in the West at this time did more in helping me build up the game in this direction than Caylor.

It was he who in 1880 organized a team over in the Queen City, which he called the Cincinnati Reds, a team which he brought here to play a nine which I had gotten together and which I had christened the St. Louis Browns.

It was this series of games gotten up by Caylor and myself that led to the subsequent organization of the American Association, and to the later appearance in the field of the invincible four-time winner St. Louis Browns.

It was Caylor and I that set on foot the organization of the first American Association, and its first season he was the honored secretary of the Cincinnati

Club, which captured the first championship of the new organization.

The Cincinnati team of that year included Charles Fulmer, manager; Charles N. Snyder, field captain and catcher; Phil Powers, catcher; William H. White and Henry McCormick, pitchers; Dan Stearns, first base; John A. McPhee, second base; W. W. Carpenter, third base; Charles Fulmer, short stop; Joe Sommers, left field; J. Macullar, center and Harry Wheeler, right.

It was Caylor who selected this team and who saw that it was gotten into championship form.

Mr. Caylor was the baseball editor of the Cincinnati Enquirer and the recognized authority in that section on baseball for nearly twenty years.

When he left Cincinnati it was to go to New York City, where he continued his labors as a baseball writer up to the time of his death.

Caylor was never popular with the players, seldom associating with them, but he was looked on by them as one of the most fearless and wide open critics of the game and as one who dealt out his opinions without fear or favor.

As a hard working writer of the game and its affairs, he contributed as much pleasure to those who love that sort of literature as any other man I know of and as a builder up of the game in Cincinnati he had no actual rival.

His hands were always clean, his reputation for honesty the best and he stood out always for that which was the highest and most glorious in this particular realm of sport.

HENRY CHADWICK—In 1870 when I made my first visit to New York I found the metropolitan daily press paying but little attention to baseball. The daily press papers had up to that time devoted but little space to the affairs of the National Game. The term sporting editor or baseball editor was a thing unknown.

Coming to the Capitoline Grounds when a game was to be played was an elderly gentleman, a little above the medium height, who created some comment always by carrying a large score book under his arm and being pointed out as the only man who knew how to score the game in all its details, and, according to the very latest and up to date methods.

This elderly gentleman was Henry Chadwick, subsequently known the country over as "The Father of Baseball."

The men who then knew how to keep the regular box score could be counted on the fingers of the one hand.

Henry Chadwick, who then reported the games for the Brooklyn Eagle; Al. Wright, who worked for the New York Clipper; J. B McCormick of the Cincinnati Enquirer; William Macdonald Spink of the St. Louis Globe-Democrat, Louis Meacham of the Chicago Tribune, Alfred H. Wright of the Philadelphia Sunday Mercury and George T. Lanigan of the Philadelphia Record, were about the only journalists then in America who knew the game well enough to work out a box score of it.

The box score was really the child of Chadwick. The man who later became the dean of baseball writers of America was in his eighty-fourth year when on April 2, 1908, he passed away at his home in Brooklyn.

He had come to this country from Eng-

326

land when a lad of 13, so that he had spent all of his manhood on this side. He brought with him from the mother country a love of outdoor sport that was born in him and in 1856 when he went to work as a reporter on the New York Times he broke away often from the regular routine to attend some outdoor sport and to smuggle some reference to it into the columns of his newspaper. His skill as a writer on sporting topics attracted the attention of Frank Queen, who then owned the New York Clipper, then the leading authority on all sports and the result was the engagement by the Clipper in 1858 of Mr. Chadwick to write baseball and cricket, something he did for that publication for thirty years afterwards.

But while engaged on the Clipper from 1858 to 1888 Mr. Chadwick frequently reported the games for the daily newspapers, being often a contributor to the New York Herald and the New York Sun.

When he quit the Clipper in 1888 and moved across the river Mr. Chadwick went to work for the Brooklyn Eagle, and he was with that newspaper almost to the day of his death. While with the Eagle he also acted as a free lance writing letters early and often for the Sporting News, the Sporting Life and other baseball journals.

Mr. Chadwick was essentially a home person. I can never remember seeing him away from his home at New York or Brooklyn. When I started the Sporting News in 1884 Mr. Chadwick frequently wrote me, but I always imagined that he had it in for me and for this reason:

Soon after we tried to put baseball on a professional footing in this section we discovered that we could not make the game pay without the Sunday games. Simply for the reason that necessity compelled it I favored the Sunday games.

The proposition was abhorrent to Mr. Chadwick. Brought up in the shadow of the Episcopal Church, Mr. Chadwick had been taught to observe the Sabbath day and to keep it holy and he could not for a moment condone so grave an offense as playing baseball on Sunday. This at least was his position when I tried with others in 1882 to place the first American Association on a paying basis with the aid of the Sunday games.

Ten years later I met Mr. Chadwick one Sunday on the old Ridgewood grounds at Brooklyn. He had come out with others to see the game. I said nothing, but marveled at the appearance of the old gentleman at such a time and place and wondered what had brought about his change of heart. Perhaps, like me, he had bowed to necessity.

That Mr. Chadwick had fairly earned the title of "Father of Baseball" can be easily proven. In the interest of the game he did wonderful work with his pen. Nearly fifty years ago or to be more exact in 1860 he edited Beadle's "Dime Baseball Player." From 1868 to 1880 he was the editor of DeWitt's "Baseball Guide." At about the same period he found time to write "The Art of Batting and Running," the "American Boys' Book of Sports," and many works of the same kind.

In 1881 he became the editor of "Spalding's Official Baseball Guide" and he held that office up to the time of his death. He had written of baseball, championed its cause and helped build it up for a period of fifty-five years. What other baseball writer we should like to know will ever equal this wonderful record:

As I have already stated Mr. Chadwick passed away on April 20, 1908, and on April 20, 1909, the monument erected in his honor in Greenwood Cemetery, Brooklyn, was unveiled in the presence of thirty persons. Among these were Miss Caylor, a daughter of O. P. Caylor, at one time a famous baseball writer and the unveiling of the tribute to the "Father of the Game" was performed by this young lady.

At the unveiling Mr. William Hudson, an old friend of Mr. Chadwick, said:

"To hold up an ideal and to adhere to it with a fidelity that knows no lessening of grip, is to pursue the pathway of progress and to be useful to your day and generation.

"This, it seems to me, to be the pertinent reflection as we gather about this sculptured stone you have erected to the memory of Henry Chadwick.

"You have inscribed on the shaft that he was the father of baseball. From the beginning of the days of baseball to the end of his own days, Henry Chadwick stood in the light of a loving father who never evaded the responsibilities of parentage.

"I do not mean that he was such father because he invented the game or made it. Nor do I believe that you who have erected this monument mean that he was its inventor. Fifty years ago the game was a development. And fifty years from now it will yet be a development.

"Many minds have had their share in this labor. It is by no means the work of one mind or of one pair of hands. But in looking back over his career of more than half a century in the light of forty years of intimate acquaintance with him, that insistence, that doughty battle he waged with tongue and pen for a clean game, honorably played, looms up to me as the great achievement of his life.

"From that day, when crossing a Hoboken field to a game of cricket he stopped to watch some boys at play at rounders and had that vision of an improved game, glorified in the baseball of our day until he laid down his pen for the last time, our departed friend ever held true to that ideal of a clean game, honorably played, in which the manly qualities should be uppermost in a strife that should see no abatement of endeavor.

"This monument has been erected by many baseball leagues, and in doing so, they make acknowledgement of all this. As the veil is drawn from its face, they pay this tribute to one man's devotion to an ideal—to one who early assumed this watchful attitude of an affectionate parent, who chided and corrected, praised and inspired—a parent's work. You do well to write on this stone, "The Father of Baseball.""

The committee which had charge of the building of the monument over the grave of Mr. Chadwick consisted of, Chas. Ebbets of Brooklyn, Charles Murphy, of Chicago, and George B. Dovey, of Boston.

The monument has been erected on a beautiful plot suitable for three graves, near the Ninth Avenue Twentieth street entrance to Greenwood cemetery.

The location was especially selected by Mr. Chadwick and the plot was presented to the veteran baseball writer by his lifelong friend, A. G. Spalding.

Pat Powers, President of the Eastern League, suggested that a monument should be erected in memory of Mr. Chadwick and as a result, Mr. Spalding, Pat Powers and other baseball admirers of the departed writer, contributed the amount necessary to build the monument.

Henry Chadwick, known throughout America as the "Father of Baseball," died on April 20, 1908, at his home in Brooklyn, New York. He was born in Jessamine Cottage, St. Thomas Exeter, England, on October 26, 1824. So he died in his eighty-fourth year and after devoting more than fifty years to writing up happenings on home and foreign baseball diamonds.

ALFRED R. CRATTY—Alfred R. Cratty, Pittsburg correspondent of the Sporting Life, began baseball writing in 1885, being the originator of the baseball and sporting department of the Pittsburg Chronicle Telegraph. He held down this desk for twenty-three years, leaving in September, 1906, to enter a medical college. He began to represent the Sport-

JOHN CREMER
Of the Detroit Journal.

in Muskegon, Michigan, and perhaps when Andrew Carnegie lost out as a mill hand, the world of letters gained in the acquisition of Jack. Though only 30 years old Mr. Cremer, admits being identified with journalism for fifteen seasons. Besides looking after the heavy baseball work on the Detroit Journal, Cremer is in charge of the political policies of his paper. Between baseball, ballooning, and politics, Cremer is kept unusually busy.

JOSEPH CUMMINGS — Joe Cummings has been the editor of the St. Louis Sporting News for a year or more. Cummings is one of the veteran sporting writers, having been associated for years with the big metropolitan dailies of Baltimore. He has also for years been a regular contributor to the Sporting News, Sporting Life and several other publications devoted exclusively to the great national game. Away back around 1892 to 1897, when the famous Baltimore Orioles were leading them all, Cummings, or "Little Joe," as Hanlon and his band called him, traveled with the ball club all the time. He saw such ball players as Keeler, Donlin, Jennings, Doyle, McGraw and Joe Kelly play their first baseball. Then Cummings has studied the politics of baseball very closely. For years and years he has attended all the important league meetings, and, of course, he has been one of the most important authorities on hand at all the big championship battles. The owners of the St. Louis Sporting News could not possibly have selected a more competent writer to succeed Joe Flanner, who had for fifteen years been its editor. Among the newspaper fraternity Mr. Cummings stands very high and where Baltimore lost its greatest light in the

ALFRED R. CRATTY
Of the Pittsburg Chronicle Telegraph.

ing Life in Pittsburg in 1886 and hopes to round out a quarter century on the Sporting Life staff. During four summers past he has been a baseball and sporting writer on the Pittsburg Press. He was on the road with the old Pittsburg nine as their correspondent for eight years. He enjoys an acquaintance with the old boys of the late nineties and since and to them he is known as one of the cleverest and best fellows ever associated with the game.

JOHN CREMER—John Cremer, who in the world of baseball letters is best known as "Jack" Cremer, is one newspaper man who is muchly adverse to publicity. It may not be generally known, but Cremer like the great John L. Sullivan, was once a rolling mill man. Just how Cremer set out as a mill hand has never been clearly explained. However, he wound up finally

JOSEPH M. CUMMINGS
Of the St. Louis Sporting News.

journalistic field St. Louis has gained and the entire country as well.

RALPH S. DAVIS—Ralph S. Davis, born at Blairsville, Pa., in 1892. He was educated at Washington and Jefferson college

RALPH S. DAVIS
Of the Pittsburg Express.

in that city. He joined the reportorial staff of the Pittsburg Press in 1900, and

in 1903 he was made sporting editor, succeeding W. H. Locke, who became secretary of the Pittsburg Baseball Club when Harry C. Pulliam left that position to assume the presidency of the National League. He has been on the Press staff continuously ever since. He has always fought for clean baseball, and the carrying out of the policies inaugurated in the National League by Mr. Pulliam.

DAVID J. DAVIES—D. J. Davies is one of the busy sporting writers of that well-known city of Pittsburg, which is located in the far western end of Pennsylvania. Davies, confesses to being all of 30, and of Welsh extraction, and admits being engaged in the newspaper business for a dozen or more seasons. He is now the

DAVID J. DAVIES
Of the Pittsburg Dispatch.

worthy sporting editor of that most popular of Pittsburg journals, the Pittsburg Dispatch, and has reveled in the joy appertaining to that berth for a year. Prior to this ascension he was city editor, New York correspondent, assistant night editor, police reporter, and in fact he worked in every department of a newspaper. He has been employed on the Dispatch a long time and naturally has prospered sufficiently to take unto himself a wife, two daughters being the result of this step. Davies is a hustling, brilliant, aggressive sort of a scribe and is one of the real boosters of the great Pittsburg Pirates.

P. J. DONAHUE—For many a day P. J. Donahue, or "P. Jay," as he was best known, was one of the best known and most famous sporting writers. "P. Jay" died before his time and when he was called away he had won for himself the name of being the real, live, sporting "thought" in big New York. He was for years an employe of the New York World.

LOUIS A. DOUGHER — Louis A. Dougher is the popular sporting editor of the Boston Traveler. Mr. Dougher understands the game and gives very interesting accounts of the games in and around Boston.

PAUL W. EATON—Paul W. Eaton, who of late years has been having his regular mail addressed in care of the house of Uncle Sam, Washington, D. C., is one of what I would call, 'the finer lights of baseball." That is to say, Eaton, while not regularly engaged in the dear old game's history for some time past, has given whatever spare time he had to writing intelligently about the sport. His stories to the Sporting Life, and other publications devoted to matters of baseball, have for years been read with interest. Mr. Eaton, writes baseball, as I

city in 1900 he became desirous of having a league baseball club and he was made official scorer. He was then the only one in Dunkirk, who could make out a box score. It was in that league the W. N. Y. and P., that year, that such famous baseball men as Johnny McGraw, Jack Doyle, Bill Armour, Jack Menefee, Jack Shearon, Nig Cuppy, Alex Jones and others, first broke in. Dunkirk, however, could not support a team and the league carried it for the last month, the outfit being on the road all the time, just as did the Cleveland Misfits later on. Later on Edwards wrote sports of all kinds for the Dunkirk Evening Observer. Finally, he landed in Cleveland in 1898 as sporting editor of the Recorder, a paper that was then quite popular, being the first morning paper in Cleveland. Being angered at the veteran baseball writers of Cleveland the following Spring, Frank DeHass Robinson made Edwards the official scorer

PAUL W. EATON.
Sporting Writer of Washington, D. C.

HENRY P. EDWARDS
Of the Cleveland Plain Dealer.

said from the higher plane. He delves deeply into the history of the game, the characteristics of the players, the changes in rules and "uplift" of the game. For thirty years, the name of Paul W. Eaton, has been known in baseball. Mr. Eaton, as is well known, is the author of "The Treasure," an historical novel, dealing with the war of 1812, whch was published by R. F. Fenns & Co., of New York, in 1909. Mr. Eaton, while resting, is forced to grind out heavy thought matter for a thousand newspapers on things which concern the Government—which means all of us.

HENRY P. EDWARDS—Henry P. Edwards is the able baseball writer of the Cleveland Plain Dealer. Mr. Edwards was born in Dunkirk, N. Y., and his first baseball experience was gleaned when in that

for the famous Misfits, who, however, played but about twenty or thirty games at home.

About that time, however, the Recorder began to get in the class with the baseball team and slide. The editorial staff was cut in two and then again and H. P. E. was made managing editor, a mere nominal title, however, as there practically was no editorial force remaining. He stuck it out for a year or so, however, and then became editor of the American Sportsman, a weekly devoted to the interests of the light harness horse. He was thus employed for three months when the position of sporting editor of the Plaindealer was offered him. That was July 28, 1901, and he has filled the chair successfully for the last nine years.

Edwards was nominated twice for the

Ohio and Pennsylvania League presidency. There was a dead lock each time and on each occasion, when the tie was broken, the other fellow—Charles Morton, the old time player and manager, won out.

For the last two years Edward has been a member of the committee named by the Baseball Writers Association to represent the association at the meetings of the joint rules committee of the two big leagues. In fact, the present scoring rules are the direct result of the labors of Jack Ryder, Ed Grillo, Si Sanborn, Sid Mercer and Edwards. With Ryder and Sanborn, Edwards also had a hand in the formulation of the constitution of the Baseball Writers' Association.

FRANK X. FINNEGAN—Frank X. Finnegan is one of the deans of the Baseball Writers League of America. He has been drawing pay as an illuminator of things sportorial for twenty seasons, despite the fact that he is still rather a young fellow. Finnegan has done most of his writing on the Hearst newspapers, being located in Chicago the best part of his career. He began his career when but a mere child as cub reporter on the old Chicago Chronicle. He remained with this paper for many years and held down almost every assignment on the paper. Several years ago, when the Chronicle went out of business the famous Francis Xavier was signed up by William R. Hearst, who had just incorporated the Chicago American. Mr. Finnegan's jovial disposition, his pure Irish wit and above all his perfect style soon won for him a great reputation. He wrote equally well on political science, religion, the drama, and besides drifted into poetry. Several years ago he became a close companion of George Ade, the world-famous humorist and dramatist, also a Chicago boy. Mr. Finnegan, so it is said, collaborated with George Ade in writing that most successful musical comedy, "The Sultan of Zulu." Mr. Finnegan is regarded as one of the most versatile literary lights Chicago has ever turned out.

JOSEPH FLANNER—There never was a better booster of the national game than "Joe" Flanner, who nearly a score of years ago became the editor of the Sporting News and remained in that position until 1909. Mr. Flanner left St. Louis to go to Chicago to fill the position of secretary to President Ban Johnson of the American League and to become the official statistican of that body. In good, sound common sense, in being a deep student as well as perfect master of the game, no baseball writer living has the edge on "Joe" Flanner. In wide acquaintance with players and officials no one can begin to compete with him. Mr. Flanner is one of the honest and conscientious writers of the game. He is perhaps too conservative in his work but that is because he believes in strict discipline and the carrying out of order and good conduct in all departments of the sport. Kindly and considerate of all men Mr. Flanner numbers his friends by the hundreds.

Mr. Flanner, with Francis C. Richtler, editor of the Sporting Life of Philadelphia, was for several years appointed as official scorer of the World's Championship games and his work in them was absolutely perfect.

In the Winter of 1910-1911 Mr. Flanner,

who had for some time been working in the office of President Johnson of the American League at Chicago, returned to the Sporting News office in St. Louis and took up his old position as editor of that paper.

He had only been here a short time when the National League and American League baseball men learning that they needed a competent and well-posted and up-to-date baseball man to handle the hundreds of minor league cases which came before them each year, selected Mr. Flanner for the position, paying him a good salary and installing him in the National Commission headquarters at Cincinnati.

Now Mr. Flanner attends each meeting of each minor league and all controversies are first referred to him; placed in shape and then brought before the National Commission.

No baseball man in America has a larger acquaintance among the minor league players than Mr. Flanner so that his selection for the position in question is a peculiarly happy one.

Mr. Flanner came to St. Louis nearly twenty years ago from Topeka, Kas. In the West he had formed a love for the national game and when he arrived here he found St. Louis a fine field for his efforts as a baseball writer and he had no trouble securing a position on the sporting department of the St. Louis Republic. He also worked on the Globe-Democrat and on the Post-Dispatch.

In the early nineties he went to work on the Sporting News and he helped build up that great sporting paper and place it in the proud position it occupies in the baseball world today.

In his long career with the Sporting News Mr. Flanner formed a personal acquaintance with nearly all the prominent players of the present day, not only in the major but in the minor leagues an acquaintance that serves him well in the position he now occupies.

In his day Mr. Flanner helped many a young player climb from the minor to the major leagues. He also helped many a club to many a good player, but he did all this without ostentation and many a player and manager was given a lift without knowing to whom it was they were responsible for the favor.

Some time ago Mr. Flanner's name was mentioned in connection with the presidency of several of the minor leagues. His name on these occasions were used with out his knowledge or consent. He is a man who has never sought office or bored into the lime-light.

A kindly, earnest and consistent gentleman baseball has few better friends than Joe Flanner.

OTTO FLOTO—Otto Floto is the sporting editor of the Denver Post, also the Kansas City Post, papers which are under the same management. Floto is one of the veteran sporting writers of the West and for years had been looked upon as the star of them all west of the Mississippi River. He, while being regarded as a baseball enthusiast, is probably best known as a writer, backer and manager of boxers. With others, he is also engaged in the circus business, and the Floto-Sells shows are known all over America. Otto is a great big, fat, good-natured, intelligent fellow. He's a credit to the newspaper profession.

NICHOLAS J. FLATLEY—Nicholas J. Flatley is the associate editor of the Base-ball Magazine of Boston. He has written many grand stories for that periodical, stories that have won him friends all over the circuit. Mr. Flatley knows the game thoroughly and stands at the top of the profession in Boston and vicinity.

JOHN B. FOSTER—John B. Foster, baseball editor of the New York Telegram, succeeds Henry Chadwick, as editor of Spalding's Official Baseball Guide.

The selection appears to be a most happy one, judging only by the splendid work Mr. Foster has done in the Guide since the death of Father Chadwick.

Mr. Foster was born in Norwalk, Ohio, and when a lad he played baseball with a team of youngsters in his native city.

When sixteen years of age he was the scorer for a semi-professional team in Norwalk. Prior to leaving school ne learn-ed the printers trade and did reportorial work on local newspapers.

After graduation from school Mr. Foster was appointed assistant postmaster of Norwalk, a position which he held until he resigned it to take up active newspaper work in Cleveland. During this period he was correspondent for many news-papers in the East and West, and his experience and success in that capacity paved the way for his entrance into reg-ular newspaper work. While in the ser-vice of the government he became greatly interested in postal work and devoted much time to the study of postal routes and the rapid distribution of mail.

On the Cleveland Press he served as State editor for a term of years report-ing news generally throughout Ohio. He was a member of the city staff of that newspaper, and resigned that position to accept a position on the staff of the Cleve-land Leader. On that newspaper he served as assistant news editor and general writer.

It happened that the sporting editor was ill one afternoon, and Mr. Foster joking-ly remarked that he would attend the baseball game and write a story about it. He was requested to do so, and from that date became a writer on sporting topics, baseball being the most import-ant, and shortly was appointed sporting editor of the Cleveland Leader. Barring a short trip in Europe he was in charge of the sporting department of the Leader until 1896, when he resigned the position to accept one with the New York Even-ing Telegram, in charge of the bicycle de-partment, cycling then being all the mode. Subsequently he was placed in charge of the editorial page of the Evening Tele-gram, and following that was made the editor-in-charge of the sporting depart-ment. He also acted in the capacity of afternoon city editor of the Evening Tele-gram, returning for the second time to the sporting department of that well-known metropolitan newspaper in charge of the news. He has contributed to other newspapers of New York and has held editorial positions upon them. He has also written largely upon general sports and baseball for publications throughout the United States. In addition to that the present editor of the Guide has also been a contributor to many magazines and weekly publications of prominence, and has engaged in correspondence on politi-cal and general news and in literary work.

HUGH FULLERTON — Perhaps the ablest baseball writer in America is Hugh Fullerton, who has charge of that depart-ment of the Chicago Examiner. He is known everywhere as America's most pop-ular contributor of baseball articles to the Boston Baseball Magazine. His work in reporting games for the Examiner has at-tracted attention the country over, being written in a bright, catchy and interest-inw vein. Besides being an able baseball writer Mr. Fullerton is one of the best all-around sporting writers in the busi-ness.

SI. GOODFRIEND—Si. Goodfriend was writing baseball for the New York World when Al. Spalding took the Chicago and All-American teams around the world. Goodfriend went with the band and re-ported the games for his paper. Later he forsook baseball for the stage, and he is now one of the most popular and by the way wealthiest of theatrical manag-ers.

GEORGE M. GRAHAM—George M. Gra-ham is the sporting editor of the Phila-delphia North American. He is most pop-ular with all the players of the Quaker City, writing always in a kindly and good-natured vein.

S. O. GRAULEY—S. O. Grauley has been connected with the sporting depart-ment of The Philadelphia Inquirer for the last twelve years. During that time he has been covering nearly everything

S. O. GRAULEY
Of the Philadelphia Enquirer.

in the sporting line, baseball, boxing, bas-ket ball and trap shooting being his speciality.

He was president of the Suburban Base-ball League in 1904 and also president of the Philadelphia Independent League of Professional baseball clubs in 1907 and 1908.

He was also president of the North

Philadelphia basket ball team of the Philadelphia Basket Ball League from 1903 to
1908. And he is now president of the
DeNeri Club of the Eastern Basket Ball
League of this year. · Mr. Grauley played
ball with the Temple College and Hilton
Athletic Association during 1897, '98 and '99

and umpired independent ball during 1901,
'02, '03 and '04. He has also had some
little experience as a basket ball and football player. With the fans and players
of Philadelphia he stands at the very top
of the baseball ladder.

RICHARD GUY.
Baseball Writer of Pittsburg.

RICHARD GUY—Richard Guy, for many
years baseball editor of the Pittsburg Dispatch and Pittsburg Gazette-Times, is
one of the best known baseball men in

America. He was with the Pittsburg Dispatch for three years and with the Gazette-Times for nine years and in point of
long active service is excelled by few of

the present day writers of the game. He was the president of the P. O. M. during its existence, but when it lost $35,000 the second year he quit. For the past nine years he has managed the Pittsburg Collegians. Lefty George, with the St. Louis Browns; Kirsch, the property of Cleveland, now with Columbus; Eastley, with San Francisco; Shultz, the Pennsylvania pitcher and captain, are some of the prominent pitchers graduated from the club. Guy also picked up several good men now in the majors.

W. B. HANNA—W. B. Hanna, who is the baseball editor of the New York Sun, is a veteran in the business. His stories of the doings of the game are read with much interest. Hanna is one of the most popular sporting writers of Greater New York.

CLAUDE JOHNSON—Mr. Johnson is the veteran sporting editor of the Kansas City Times-Star and is the man who succeeded dear old Jimmy Whitfield, when the latter was called away several years ago. It is almost needless to state that the Times-Star is one of the greatest newspapers in the Western world and that its sport pages are widely read and perfectly edited by little Johnson. He is a real baseball enthusiast and follows the doings of the American Association each season with great interest. Johnson ought to be dancing in the big league.

J. J. KARPF—J. J. Karpf of the New York Evening Mail staff has been chronicling the doings in the baseball world for

J. J. KARPF
Of the New York Evening Mail.

many years. He possesses a sunny disposition and has made thousands of friends among the ball players and enthusiasts.

WILLIAM A. KELSOE—One of the first of St. Louis baseball writers was William A. Kelsoe, now a member of the editorial staff of the Post-Dispatch. Mr. Kelsoe was one of the men who reported that famous game between the St. Louis Browns and the Syracuse Stars on May 1, 1877. In those days the local newspapers placed an embargo on baseball news. And the man who wrote that sort of thing did it through sheer love of the game and then had to beg his way into print. 'Bill" Kelsoe, as we called him in the long ago, was one of the men who wrote the game because he loved it. He was the city editor of the Republic in the early eighties and I was a cub reporter on that newspaper then. It was my ambition in those days to write of the baseball games and to smuggle as much of the stuff into the newspaper as possible. In my essays in this direction I always found a true friend in "Old Bill." He passed my copy early and often, and was so kind and good always that I learned to love him as did the other reporters who followed me. To-day "Old Bill" often goes to the ball games and of the little army of newspaper men that follow the game there are none so universally beloved, so well honored and respected or so well thought of as he.

JAMES C. KENNEDY—For many a year James C. Kennedy, a big hearted and big bodied man, was the baseball and sporting editor of the New York Times. He was a great promoter of sports in the metropolis, and with Tim Hurst, he brought off many a sporting event in Madison Square Garden. "Jim" Kennedy was one of the most popular men in New York and Brooklyn. He died of heart disease one day while riding into New York from Brooklyn on the elevated road.

HUGH F. KEOUGH — Hugh Keough, now the genius in the sporting department of the Chicago Tribune, did his first baseball writing away back in 1884, when he commenced sending baseball stories from Chicago to the Sporting News, the original paper devoted to baseball, and which was launched by the author of this book in St. Louis, that year. Keough was a novice then, but he has developed since so that he is regarded as one of the most talented writers of sport in the world. There are few writers to-day, who have any larger following than this self-same, friendly Keough.

HAROLD W. LANIGAN—Harold W. Lanigan, who is better known to the millions of baseball followers throughout the United States and wherever the greatest game of them all is discussed, as "Harry" Lanigan, is sporting editor of the St. Louis Times. Lanigan is one of the real characters in baseball in America. For twenty or more years he has been identified with out-door sports. He first became a baseball fan in Philadelphia on July 4, 1874, which is just about thirty-six years ago. In his youth, that is to say, in about 1880, he was playing the game around the lots in Philadelphia. He liked the pastime of "Old Cat" and "Rounders" immensely. His parents both of whom were even then known nationally as literary persons sent young Harry to the University of Pennsylvania. Between studies and other things he drifted onto the college team and when seventeen years old he had won quite a name for himself as an athlete, both as a Rugby and a baseball player. About that time Horace Fogel, present owner of the

HAROLD W. LANIGAN,
St. Louis' Great Baseball Wrter.

THE NATIONAL GAME.

Philadelphia National League Baseball Club was sporting editor of one of Philadelphia's greatest newspapers, the Philadelphia Enquirer. Young Lanigan, who had drifted through the University of Pennsylvania in about the usual way of most cut-ups—through the front door and out the rear—held consultation with himself and decided that he was destined to become one of America's real royal literary lights. Fogel took a chance on Lanigan and installed him in his office as copy boy. It wasn't long before Lanigan evinced an inclination to not alone run the office, but he began writing criticisms of the baseball teams. Fogel, declares the little fellow, made a noise like unto one who knew what he was talking about. As a result the kid became baseball editor of Mr. Fogel's paper long before he had reached his majority.

He is a natural born baseball fan and even today they say that he lives, dreams, thinks, talks and writes baseball. He remained with Fogel one season, when he was called to St. Louis by the author of this book to accept the position of managing editor of The Sporting News. The author, his uncle, had heard a great deal about his promising young nephew and when the boy arrived in St. Louis in 1894, it might be said that the uncle was a bit disappointed in meeting up with the aspiring Lanigan, for instead of a grown up young man, he was only a slender lad in knickerbockers. He was given a desk in the office and told to go ahead and grind out some real live baseball gossip. Though the kid was about all in after having experienced many hours of hard travel on the road from Philadelphia, he set to work and turned out several columns of up-to-date baseball. He made an instantaneous hit with his uncle and step by step developed into a competent sporting writer. In 1896, when Howard Pearson and Ed Mockler were the sporting editors of the Globe-Democrat, and a great page it was, Lanigan was coached from the weekly sport paper and gobbled up by the great Joe McCullagh, then editor of the Globe-Democrat. Under the careful watching of this pair of geniuses, Lanigan became known and recognized as an authority on baseball subjects. He remained a member of the Globe-Democrat's great staff until February, 1902, part of which time he held down the position of sporting editor. On St. Patrick's Day, March 17, 1902, John Magner, then managing editor of the Star-Sayings, secured Lanigan from the Globe-Democrat by offering him inducements which he could not well refuse. It was while sporting editor of the Star that Lanigan flashed on the baseball followers of St. Louis the now famous green sheet—also the pink sheet. In those days it was simply a case of: "If you want to get all the up-to-date, correct and cleverly hashed-up sporting news, get Lanigan's green and pink sheet." Lanigan danced along beautifully as sporting editor of the Star until the late winter of 1905. The St. Louis Times was just being launched and Homer Bassford and Eddie Pretorious, the editor and manager respectively of that great newspaper, played a winning hand and stole Lanigan from the Lewis publication. Lanigan opened the first sport page of the Times and ever since has been grinding out daily a mighty interesting sheet of sporting doings. Besides possessing extraordinary ability, a distinctive style and a pointedly positive will of his

own the young man is regarded as one of the best posted writers on matters pugilistic under the name of "Jab." Lanigan is known wherever the art of fisticuffs are known. During the off season he passes the time viewing and incidentally writing about the stage. His criticisms are written in a "a lighter vein" and are just as interesting as his perfect baseball stories ever dared to be. He is one of the charter members of the Sporting Writers' Association, besides being a member of a number of clubs and lodges.

ERNEST LANIGAN—Ernest and Harold Lanigan have done much for the game as baseball writers. Ernest is the baseball editor of the New York Press and Harold is sporting editor of the St. Louis Times. These two Lanigan boys and W. H. Hicks, Jr., the sporting and baseball editor of the New York Journal, are all nephews of mine. The Lanigan boys are sons of George T. Lanigan, one of the most famous newspaper men of his day and of whom I have written in the early pages of this work. When George Lanigan died my sister sent her two boys out from Philadelphia to help me edit the Sporting News. They came to me in short trousers and in the Sporting News office they learned enough about writing of baseball to gain them a high place later among the writers of the game. I do not know how my other nephew, W. H. Hicks, Jr., came to enter the field of baseball journalism, but like all the rest of the family I suppose he came by it naturally. At any rate he is considered one of the top notchers in sporting journalism in New York. At the same place no one holds a higher position among baseball writers and statisticans than Ernest Lanigan, one of the best, most conscientious and ablest and accurate of baseball writers and scorers. At St. Louis, Harold Lanigan is considered by many the leader in the way of accurate and up-to-date baseball reporting.

R. W. LARDNER—R. W. ("Bob") Lardner, is the battery partner of "Cy." Sanborn, of the Chicago Tribune's large sporting staff. Between Lardner and "Old Cyrus," the baseball reading public of the Garden City are handed out sufficient real, rollicking, roaring baseball. Lardner is the junior member of the battery. He's bigger, stronger (physically) noisier and perhaps handsomer than his elderly teammate, Sanborn, but when it comes down to "catching" every day, the probabilities are old Daddy Cy has a few goals on the b.g, blustery Lardner. Lardner began writing baseball for that dear old South Bend (Ind.) Times in the winter of 1905-06. It was a cold winter as will be remembered. The White Sox had also just succeeded in winning the world's highest honors from the Chicago Cubs. Lardner was the live wire correspondent of the South Bend Times during the series. He liked the Cubs, so the story goes, and that's why he is now a resident of Chicago. Before being "waivered" on by the Times, the Chicago Examiner had scouts looking him over, and after the drafting period, Fred Lawrence, of the Examiner league, grabbed him. With Duffy Cornell, H. ("Dream") Fullerton, Charles Dryden and the noted Francis X. Finnegan, Mr. Lardner made up as strong a defensive band as the windy old burg ever saw. After the conclusion of the 1908 baseball season,

R. W. LARDNER
Of the Chicago Tribune.

Mr. Lardner moved down Madison street a few jolts and tied up with the Tribune. He's still there and at press time was turning out his usual amount of live, literary baseball gossip.

FREDERICK C. LIEB—Frederick C. Lieb has justly been called baseball's foremost biographer. His thorough knowledge of the game accounts for the fact that he is the most able biographer the game ever had. He has written some very fine stories of the game, stories that have won him life-long friends in the sporting world.

JOHN MANDIGO—No baseball writer in and around New York in his day was better known than John F. Mandigo, for many years the able sporting writer of the New York Sun. Mandigo was learning the game in New York when the original New York Giants, Ewing, Connor, Keefe, Ward and others were doing business at the Polo grounds.

LOUIS MEACHAM—Louis Meacham, then attached to the staff of the Chicago Tribune, was the first boomer of the game in Chicago.

In the sixties, fifty years ago, Meacham was the only reporter in Chicago to keep a box score and to give a running report of the game played in the Lake City.

When the Chicago White Stockings took the field in 1870 Meacham was their only champion and he stood by them up to the time of his death.

It was the fine work of Meacham in the sixties and early seventies in reporting baseball games for the Chicago Tribune that led to the other newspapers in Chicago devoting some space to the sport

and to the bringing forward of other baseball writers.

And from this humble beginning of Meacham came the building up of the game in all directions in Chicago until to-day every section of the city has its magnificent enclosed grounds.

Meacham, like all the first lot of baseball writers, wrote of the game only out of pure love for it and without any thought of profit or future reward.

When he was not writing sport he was doing regular reportorial duty on the Tribune.

GEORGE EDGAR McLINN—George Edgar McLinn, sporting editor of the Philadelphia Press, was born Nov. 9, 1884. He always intended to be a newspaperman and worked when a kid as a cross-roads correspondent for the Loudonian, a weekly journal at Leesburg, Va. He attended high school and college. He entered the newspaper field in Pittsburg, Pa., as reporter for a Pittsburg news agency. He became a member of the Pittsburg Gazette staff in January, 1906, and continued with that newspaper when it was consolidated with the Times and became the sporting editor of the Pittsburg (Pa.) Gazette-Times in the same year. He left Pittsburg in October 1907 to become a member of the reportorial staff of the Philadelphia Press. He was appointed sporting editor of that newspaper in July, 1908, and has acted in that capacity since. Mr. McLinn is the president of the Pen and Pencil Club, a Philadelphia newspapermen's organization. He is also a member of the Philadelphia Sporting writers' Association and of the Baseball Writers' Association of America.

GEORGE EDGAR McLINN
Of the Philadelphia Press.

A. H. C. MITCHELL—A. H. C. Mitchell is the baseball editor of the Boston American. He is one of the most popular writers in the business.

GEORGE MORELAND—George Moreland, who has been discussing baseball in all its phases in Pittsburg for many, many years, is to-day looked on as the "expert statistician" when it comes to baseball in America. "Moreland's Records" are used by almost every big newspaper in the United States and the reason for this is because of Moreland's positive correctness and fairness in dealing with these ball players. Moreland has been writing baseball for a dozen years or more and is easily one of the .400 hitters in the Sporting Writers' Association.

JACOB C. MORSE—Jacob C. Morse is one of the old-time sporting writers who seems to have weathered the storms of years and so far has managed to bat sufficiently high to keep out of the minors. Mr. Morse's name is known wherever the big game is read or spoken. He admits having been identified with the green diamond for 40 years, and as he is now editor, and part owner of the Boston Baseball Magazine, the reader should place much confidence in whatever he says. Morse and Boston, much like the early history of "Boston and the Tea Party," are inseparable. Jake began newspaper work as a copy boy on the Boston Herald years ago. In 1883, when the Athletics won the pennant up to 1907, he was identified with the Herald. In the winter of 1907 he launched the Baseball Magazine. For 17 years Morse has been the Boston correspondent of Sporting Life. He has a large following among the professional players and is popular with all of them.

GEO. W. MUNSON—Among the builders up of the game in St. Louis no one deserves more credit than George Munson, for years secretary of the St. Louis Browns and who up to the time of his death, two years ago, was the foremost promoter of honorable sports in St. Louis. In St. Louis Mr. Munson was known as the boss secretary of the boss club when Comiskey was its commander and Von der Ahe its commissary general. It was George Munson who planned the first trip of the two greatest professional baseball teams. It was he who took the Chicago White Stockings and the St. Louis Browns, champions of their respective leagues, on their first long tour to the Pacific coast. It was Munson, too, who arranged the itinerary for the great tours which the four-time winner St. Louis Browns made at the close of each of their successful seasons. It was the money of Von der Ahe, the skill and strength of Comiskey, and the brain and pencil of Munson that made these tours the most successful from a financial standpoint the game has ever known. As a press agent for the great baseball teams Munson had no equal. He held a night key to all the newspaper offices in all the great cities. Besides acting as secretary for the four-time champion Browns, Munson was their official scorer. He was a left-hander, and Latham, the wit of the Browns, lovingly christened him "The Old Southpaw." To this day Comiskey, Tip O'Neill and those who are left of the old team refer to their old scorer by that strange title. Thirty years in baseball and during all that time never at outs with a player or manager, or anyone else. That was George Munson's record and it tells better than anything else of the goodness of the man. "He was a good fellow," says one; "He was a thoroughbred," says another. "He was the kindest and best soul ever connected with the game," says a player, and none of them quite hit the mark. Munson loved the game for the good there was in it. When the Baseball Brotherhood was formed in 1890, Ned Williamson, Mike Kelly, Charley Comiskey and all the famous players went with it. They were all Munsons friends; where they went he followed, and he stood by them until the last gun was fired in the baseball war. When the Brotherhood flag went down Munson went with it. It never seemed the same game to him after that, and he turned his attention to other sports. He died in March, 1908, and his body now rests in Calvary Cemetery in the city of St. Louis.

JOSEPH A. MURPHY—Joseph A. Murphy, now famous as a judge of racing, was at one time well and favorably known in baseball circles. He was the baseball and sporting editor of the Globe-Democrat and Chicago Tribune back in the eighties. In 1884 he was St. Louis' one hundred-yard champion. He also pitched a professional game occasionally, helping the St. Louis Browns and the Cincinnati Reds out in a pinch. A fine player and gentleman was Murphy and in the world of racing he is now at the very top.

WILLIAM MURPHY—A pleasant, kindly face, a winning smile always, a hand that seems to stretch out from the heart and a voice that tells of the good fellow and liberal spirit behind it are the things you see and hear when you come face to face with "Billy" Murphy, the able and live sporting editor of the St. Louis Star. Mr. Murphy's father before him played and loved baseball and the son is only following in the footsteps of his father. "Billy" Murphy was born on Goose Hill, June 26, 1875, at Eleventh and Mound streets, St. Louis. Mr. Murphy is a graduate of St. Louis University. He is one of my numerous proteges who have made good. After serving a novitiate with the Sporting News, Mr. Murphy was for four years baseball editor of the Post-Dispatch. For three years he served the Star-Chronicle under John Magner as assistant sporting editor and earned fame as the inaugurator of the famous "Green Sheet." For the past two years Mr. Murphy has been the sporting editor of the Star. No sporting writer in the West is better posted on all sorts of sport than Mr. Murphy and no man writing in that direction has a larger circle of friends.

HERMAN NICKERSON—Sports form a prominent part of the newspapers in the East, more particularly those of Boston. In the "Hub" every branch is represented the heart of the athletic world with Harvard University just across the Charles and each has a wide following. Located in River Dale but a few hours' ride away with Brown at Providence and Dartmouth

WILLIAM MURPHY.
Sporting Editor of the St. Louis Star.

HERMAN NICKERSON
Of the Boston Journal.

at Hanover, N. H., the college athlete takes a prominent place the season around.

Add to these the American and National League seasons, the New England League efforts and the baseball of Young America with one of the best boxing clubs in the country holding weekly shows, while golf from every quarter crowds in and one gets a faint idea of the detail to be cared for in the conduct of a sporting department where competition is keen and knowledge general among a sport-loving public.

Herman Nickerson, sporting editor of the Boston Journal, one of Frank A. Munsey's string of newspapers, has kept that department before the readers of New England where it is accepted as among the best in the East.

As the American League club is the more popular one in Boston, Nickerson follows its work closely from Spring training to the close of the season, travelling with the team, being widely known on the circuit for his fairness and accuracy.

Herman Nickerson broke into the newspaper game as a "cub" on a morning paper known as the Boston News, which lived but a few years. In 1894 he joined the staff of the Boston Journal as a reporter. In 1898 he was appointed dramatic editor and later occupied the financial desk. In 1900 he spent a season on the road with Richards and Canfield, who were producing Hoyt's "A Temperance Town," and the following year he published a weekly newspaper, "The Dramatic Review." In 1902 he became a member of the staff of the Boston Herald, remaining in the service of that paper as head of the copy desk until offered a position on his "first love," the Journal, this time entering the sporting department, handling the

news and making up. In 1907 a change was made in the head of the department and Nickerson was appointed sporting editor.

He was born in Boston May 15, 1870, the son of John Freeman Nickerson and Susan Sophia Robinson. On his father's side he is a direct descendant of William Nickerson, who came to this country in 1620, settling at Chatham, Mass. On his mother's side he is a descendant of Rev. John Robinson, the pastor of the Pilgrims. On August 10, 1892, he married Nellie Gertrude Bosselle. He is a member of the Society of Colonial Wars and the Sons of the American Revolution.

HARRY NIEMEYER—Harry Niemeyer is a native of St. Louis. He has been associated with the newspaper game for fifteen years. He is one of my boys. I was responsible for his entering the game. When a mere child, I might say, Niemeyer was made a member of my staff on the old Post-Dispatch. He showed an inclination to follow the game of sport early. Horse racing, in those days, was outside of baseball, one of the items of sport. The young man was strong for the racing game. In 1898, when the Spaniards made an attempt to hand the great U. S. A. a knock-out, Niemeyer was one of the band of newspaper men who tossed his "pen" out of the window and became a regular. He was a member of the famous Battery A, a military organization of St. Louis for several years. He was one of the biggest, bravest of all the "feather bed" recruits in that most famous war. Battery A did not get much of a chance to distinguish itself in the war.

In those days Missouri was a strong Democratic state. The result was, naturally that old "Mizzoo" was not shown much respect in the big war. Battery A, after being forced to lodge for weeks, months, and almost a year, in unsanitary camps down South, was finally ordered to Porto Rico. This happened just after the battle of Santiago. The Missourians did not complain. Niemeyer was simply a sergeant. One afternoon there was much commotion in the camp of Battery A. Spaniards were marching, 20,000 strong, into the city of Porto Rico where the famous Missouri Battery A was located. Niemeyer, always alert, was the first man to discover the approach of the enemy. Battery A finally became active, due of course to Niemeyer's foresight. I was not able to "attend" this big war, but in that old company were many of my boys. They have since told me of the first "fire" of war. Just about the time when the famous old battery was about ready to shell the hated Spaniards, there arrived a friendly scout on horseback. He blocked the Missouri boys ten minutes before the big battle. "The war is over. In fact, it has been over for four weeks," was the way the message he carried read.

That was the finish of the finish of the famous Battery A, but not of Harry. He returned to St. Louis. He was "peeved," and could not understand just why old Uncle Sam would not allow the battery to fight in Porto Rico. He sat down and wrote in the old, and, by the way, original press club of later days, a book. It was entitled "The History of Battery A. of Missouri." Niemeyer developed into a clever, steady sporting writer. St. Louis became too small for him and he went to New York in 1900. He worked on the

New York World, Sunday Telegraph and later joined the sporting staff of the New York Globe. Sidney Mercer, another St. Louis boy, is present sporting editor of the Globe. Niemeyer is the paragrapher, turf editor and general utility man of the sheet and there is no better in the business.

HARRY NEILY—Harry Neily is the popular sporting editor of the Detroit Times, which position he has held down since January, 1910, when he succeeded Paul Bruske, who looked after the desk for years, but who resigned and went into the automobile business. Before going to Detroit Neily was assistant sporting editor and baseball writer on the Cleveland Plain-Dealer. For three years prior to that he was one of the big guns in the minor newspaper leagues, being sporting editor of the Vindicator of Youngstown, Ohio. Previous to this he had served in various capacities with a multitude of newspapers in various states. He has been engaged in the newspaper business

HARRY NEILY
Of the Detroit Times.

for ten years or more and at odd times picked up the printers' trade, still having his card in the International Typographical Union. He worked a linotype machine on the Pittsburg Post and was a stereotyper once in McKeesport, Pa. When scarcely of age he had the nerve

to lease a plant in Kane, Pa., and conducted the Courier for six months. Neily says the net result of this experience was a ticket home, a balance of thirty-five cents and several thousand dollars' worth of experience. In 1900 and 1901 he made a try at playing semi-professional baseball in Pennsylvania and New York. While Neily was a rank failure as a ball player he developed later into one of our very best discussors of the national game. Neily travels with the baseball team and is well known and highly respected all over the circuit.

MARION F. PARKER—Marion F. Parker is the sporting editor of the St. Louis Globe-Democrat. The mere mention of the fact that Parker is looking after the "averages" of the sport page of such a nationally known paper as the Globe-Democrat should honestly be sufficient. Parker is what the enthusiastic young baseball writer in the Spring would term a regular phonomenom. Parker, like the aspiring youths who each season appear upon the baseball horizon in the training camps, is a "chicken." In fact in point of years he might properly be termed a child. He may be young in years, youthful in appearance, but there is buried within the confines of the five feet, six inches of "human make-up" sufficient regular brain matter, industry and energy to short-circuit any old power house. Parker is probably the last of the regime of McCullagh, Joseph McCullagh, the old editor of the Globe-Democrat.

Away back in the nineties—let us say to be correct—when the author of this work was about ready to step down and out as a sporting editor, this youngster was in the employ of the Globe-Democrat. He was Joe McCullagh's copy boy. McCullagh, though a good-natured, lovable character, was inclined to be a crab while tied down to his desk. Young Parker was unlike the average fresh newspaper kid. McCullagh soon found this out. He used to dance about his office, orate on every subject under the sun; call down every member of his big staff, the entire city and, in fact, every soul of whom he could think. This quiet, studious Parker was usually the famous editor's "audience." Parker, outside of smiling occasionally, gave vent to little comment. McCullagh learned to like him. So the young fellow gradually began to absorb all the finer and higher points of journalism. In the sporting department on the Globe-Democrat in those days there worked such great lights—even to-day—as Howard Pearson. Ed. Mockler, H. W. Lanigan, John Brinsley Sheridan and others. Parker began writing amateur notes, then took up rowing, pugilism, and finally baseball. When Eddie Wray resigned as sporting editor of the paper several years ago, Captain King immediately handed friendly Frank the key to the sport department. He has certainly made good in the position. He is a splendid mixer, a close, keen student of every angle of the sport game, and ofttimes takes part in swimming and field meets in person. Parker is a native of St. Louis and a credit to the city, indeed.

Mr. Parker was one of the original organizers of the Baseball Writers' Association of America and is at present its representative in St. Louis.

He has always taken an active interest

in sport. He was the manager of the original Missouri Athletic Club basket ball team which held the Western Division A. A. U. championship for several years. He was also a member of the Missouri Athletic club when it was first organized. He was the chairman of the committee which conducted an athletic meet at the St. Louis Exposition two years before it was closed, and has been a member of the athletic committee of the Missouri Athletic Club for several years. He was also a member of the rowing committee of the Louisiana Purchase Exposition and the first one who suggested to Secretary Walter B. Stevens that athletics be featured at the big fair. Mr. Parker was one of those who revised the present baseball scoring rules and had the scoring rules placed in charge of the Baseball Writers' Association.

WILLIAM A. PHELON—There is no baseball editor in the country who has hit the nail on the head oftener than William A. Phelon, the baseball editor of the Cincinnati Times-Star. Mr. Phelon has written for Chicago and New York papers and he first came into the limelight when writing baseball for the New York Telegraph. He knows the game thoroughly and in picking the winning team before each season he stands at the head of the list.

CHARLEY POWER—Charley Power, for years the sporting editor of the Pittsburg Leader, has done much for baseball in that part of the country.

Recently Power, formerly prominent in baseball newspaper circles in Pittsburg, who has had a dash of National League umpiring and has been a minor league offcial, has given it all up and receives for his theatrical presswork a figure far exceeding anything he ever received for following baseball. More power to Charley.

W. M. RANKIN—W. M. Rankin was born May 20, 1849, in Greencastle, Pa. His father, the late Andrew N. Rankin, was a lawyer and inventor. In 1856 he became the editor and proprietor of the Franklin Repository of Chambersburg, Pa., and the subject of this sketch attended the public schools in that place until he reached the age of 14 years, when he took a course at the Chambersburg Academy. While attending that school his father, at the solicitation of the late and Honorable Thaddeus Stevens, came to New York and became the general business agent for an organization for sending teachers South to educate the ex-slaves. During the latter part of March, 1865, Mr. Rankin took up a residence in Brooklyn, N. Y., and at once removed his family to that city. In 1866 young William was taken into his father's office and remained there until August 27, 1867, when he went to learn the trade of job printing. In the spring of 1868 Mr. Rankin had removed to Rockland County, N. Y., and in the summer of 1870 the subject of this sketch began writing up baseball for the Rockland County Journal of Nyack, N. Y. He continued at that work until the Fall of 1873, when he went back to his trade. While at Nyack Mr. Rankin met and married an estimable young lady with an even temperament and cheerful disposition which has enabled her to bear the trials and vicissitudes of life with remarkable patience. Mr. Rankin continued at his trade until the Spring of 1876, when he was engaged to do the base-

ball work on the Daily Witness. He was appointed official scorer of the Mutual Club by President William H. Cammeyer, and during that Summer he also did the baseball work for the Tribune, the Times and the World. Later he was connected with the Mail and Express, The Sporting World, The Evening Sun and the New York Clipper. He has also done special work for many weekly and monthly papers and at various times has been the New York correspondent for the Boston Herald and Globe, the Brooklyn Citizen, Baltimore American, Free Press and Evening Journal of Detroit, the Sporting News, the United, New England, Northwestern and Associated presses and the New York Press Association. During the seasons of 1883 and 1884 he was the official scorer of the Brooklyn Club. He has written brief histories of the National Game, the Metropolitan, Brooklyn and Chelsea Clubs. Also a complete history of the New York Club, that appeared in the New York Press during the Summer of 1905.

While living at Nyack, Mr. Rankin organized the Tidal Wave Baseball Club, caught for the nine, captained and managed it and during its three years' existance that team lost only one series—two out of three. That was to the Sunnysides of Sing Sing, a semi-professional team. Under Mr. Rankin's three years' management, the team won forty games and lost five.

Will Rankin and his brother, June Rankin, in New York for the past thirty years have been known as the best boosters of the game in that section. They were never known to knock a player but were always trying to help some poor fellow along. They will be known forever as the two best friends the game has ever had in the Eastern metropolis.

GEORGE C. RICE — George C. Rice of the Chicago Journal has been writing baseball since the start of the big baseball war between the National and American Leagues. He broke into the game in the winter of 1900-1901 and has been on the job ever since, travelling around the country with first the Cubs and then the White Sox and there is no one war correspondent in the game now that has travelled longer than he has without an interruption until this Summer.

For ten seasons he travelled as a representative of the Chicago Daily News but in the middle of the season of 1910 he went over to the Chicago Daily Journal and has quit the road with the exception of taking in the big world's series and other meetings of great importance.

Rice is a native of Wisconsin and entered newspaper work as a college correspondent. He was a student at Lake Forest College and started in the newspaper work with the old Chicago Chronicle in 1895. Since that time he has worked on several Chicago papers but his longest time was with the Daily News, where he worked for just ten years and travelled all over the United States as their baseball expert. He is known from one end of the country to the other as an impartial writer and is said to be one of the most popular newspaper men with ball players and magnates that has ever written baseball. He is a contributor to many of the magazines of the country on his favorite topic of baseball and his articles are much sought for by the publishers.

GEORGE C. RICE
Of the Chicago Journal.

FRANK W. ROSTOCK
Of the Cincinnati Post.

GRANTLAND RICE—Grantland Rice is the sporting editor of the Nashville Tennessean, one of the best papers printed in the South. Mr. Rice is one of the best friends the baseball players ever had. He has been hammering out boosts and beautiful poetry about the happenings of the game for fifteen years or more. He is a native of Nashville and is a typical Southern gentleman. He comes from one of the most blue-blooded of Southern families and comes natural by his talent as a writer. He began his career in journalism right in Nashville, and, by the way, on the Tennessean, the paper of which he is now sporting editor. Three years ago he was drafted by the big league and jumped Nashville for Cleveland, Ohio. Here he held down the big desk on the Plain-Dealer and his crisp, bright style and poetic gingles were most widely read all over the American League circuit. Rice was never enamored of the North, he loved the Sunny Southern Skies and its thousand of friendly souls. He returned to Nashville about a year ago and today is one of the best boosters the Southern League has.

JOHN R. ROBINSON—John R. Robinson who is one of the live wires in the Boston newspaper field, has been engaged in the business for fifteen years. Robinson is one of the "breeziest" writers to be found in the East. He began writing in Cleveland on the Plaindealer. Three years ago he migrated to Boston, where he held down the sporting desk of the Traveler until the Fall of 1908, when he resigned to become manager of Battling Nelson, the prize fighter.

FRANK W. ROSTOCK — Frank W. Rostock's career as a baseball writer commenced in Akron, Ohio in 1902, where he had charge of the sport page of the Akron Press. In the Fall of that year he was transferred to the Cleveland Press, where he acted in the capacity of assistant sporting editor. The Cleveland Plain Dealer then offered him a better opportunity which was accepted. Later he was re-engaged by the Cleveland Press and then transferred to Cincinnati, where he has been baseball editor of the Post for the past three years, writing under the nom-de-plume "Ros."

I. E. SANBORN—I. E. Sanborn is one of Chicago's recognized baseball authorities. Sanborn is, of course, a veteran, as his tales of just how the game is being played, how it should be played and how it will be played when we are dead and gone, have been one of the pretty features of the sport pages of the Chicago Tribune for years. Sanborn is like a majority of the good baseball experts—a real, right royal, ranting fan himself. He is what the inside ones would call a "wise baseball mogul." He is a liberal contributor to magazines, baseball guides and leading newspapers. Sanborn was recruited from the minor leagues in 1890. He had been issuing noisy baseball screams as chief authority on all matters pertaining to sports on the Springfield (Mass.) Union. The Tribune of Chicago purchased him outright, and so far he has been batting beautifully each season and fielding in big league form for that newspaper.

ALLAN SANGREE—Allan Sangree is one of the most popular baseball writers and contributes many interesting articles to the general magazines. His many friends are ever interested in his stories.

JOHN B. SHERIDAN—Dean of the St. Louis corps of baseball writers now in active harness is John B. Sheridan of the St. Louis Republic. Sheridan as an all around sporting writer is perhaps the best man in his line in America. He is not only a natural writer and a lover of sports, but he is also a splendidly educated gentleman and when not writing of sport for the Republic he is frequently engaged in the getting up of editorial copy, dramatic criticism or doing anything that happens along in the newspaper line, for there is no task beyond his vision and capacity. Sheridan is a natural lover of sport. You can see that in the fine eye, the bright face and the clear cut forehead. And Sheridan's sympathies are always with the player and the one who essays to conquer in any line of sport or pastime. His writing, therefore, is always sympathetic, but he can be aggressive if need be and he has written at times with a biting sarcasm that has cut the poor fellow aimed at to the marrow. Sheridan is an Irishman who learned cricket first, then racing and then baseball. He knows no letter perfect in them all. Before coming to St. Louis he wrote for the best newspapers in San Francisco and here at home he has been with the Globe-Democrat, the Post-Dispatch and now with the Republic.

E. B. SKEELE—E. B. Skeele was one of the earliest of St. Louis baseball reporters in the seventies. He was one of the first men to write sport and baseball for the Missouri Republican and he was one of the men who reported the famous game played at Sportsman Park between the first St. Louis Browns and Syracuse Stars, mention of which is made elsewhere in this book.

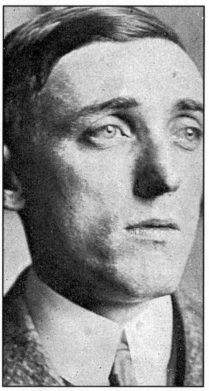

JOSEPH S. SMITH
Of the Detroit Evening Journal.

JOSEPH S. SMITH—Joseph S. Smith, now sporting editor of the Detroit Evening Journal and local representative in Detroit of the Baseball Writers Association of America, is one of the brightest and best baseball writers in the business. He has been writing sport in Detroit for eight and a half years, starting out originally as assistant sporting editor of the Detroit Free Press.

For the past seven years he has been sporting editor of the Detroit Journal. He has always been an advocate of clean sports and a booster for baseball. For two years he was president of the Detroit City League. This was five years ago and since then he has had the satisfaction of seeing many of the City League players develop into good ball players.

Mr. Smith will be 28 years old this October. He was born and bred in Detroit and was one of the original organizers in New York of the Baseball Writers' Association. He started out under Joe S. Jackson, now of the Washington Post.

ALFRED H. SPINK—Like his brother, William McDonald Spink, "the first of St. Louis sporting writers," Al. Spink, the author of this book, was born in Quebec, Canada, and educated at the Quebec High School.

He and his brother, William, played on the High School cricket eleven and then and there became enamored of outdoor sports.

The great book at the high school then was "Tom Brown's School Days at Rugby."

In it the great story was the description given by Tom Hughes of the fight between Tom Brown and "Slogger" Williams.

It taught the school boys that there was nothing so fair as a game at fisticuffs and down the hill from the high school there was a platform on which was settled with the fists all real differences that came up. Manliness and fair play came from this practice and with it a wish to excel in all manly sports. So it came that the Spink boys early became enamored of cricket and boxing and when these two brothers left Canada they carried this love of sport with them.

William Spink came to St. Louis from Quebec when a mere lad to take charge of the Western Union telegraph office. He was even then the fastest receiver in that company. Soon after William Spink located here his brother Alfred came on and joined him.

That was back in the sixties. Since then Mr. Spink has done special or regular newspaper work for nearly all the leading newspapers of America. He was sporting editor of the Globe-Democrat, the Missouri Republican and the Post-Dispatch, all of St. Louis. For them he did all around sport work, but mostly baseball. In the early days of the game he organized many baseball leagues and in his time he was president of the first Western League, the first Inter-State League, and the first St. Louis College and Business Men's League. In 1884, while acting as secretary of the St. Louis Union team, he established The Sporting News, now the great baseball paper. A year or two later he was the secretary of the St. Louis Browns. He was one of St. Louis' early players and he was the president of the Standard Baseball Club, with whom he played in the early seventies

Ten years ago he promoted the ST. LOUIS WORLD, a daily newspaper, which is still being published in St. Louis. It would, in fact, take more space than this book allows to tell of the many things he has started during his career, and this history of the National game is only one of them. Some future historian will perhaps tell the rest.

WILLIAM MACDONALD SPINK—William Macdonald Spink for twenty years the sporting and telegraph editor of the St. Louis Globe-Democrat, was the first of the baseball writers and boomers of the game in the West.

While Mr. Chadwick was building up the game and writing about it in the East, Mr. Spink was at work doing the same thing for it in the West.

"Billy" Spink, for that was the name he was known by in the sporting world from Portland, Maine, to the Pacific Slope, like Chadwick, was born under the British flag and, like Chadwick, he played cricket before he went to baseball.

"Billy" Spink was the son of William Spink of the Legislative Assembly of Quebec, Canada. He was born there and educated in the Quebec High School He was not out of his teens when he became an expert telegraph operator At fourteen he was placed at the head of the telegraph office in the Legislative Assembly at Quebec. He was at that time one of the only "sound" operators in Quebec.

A year later when he was but fifteen, he arrived in St. Louis and six weeks after his arrival he was placed in charge of the night office of the Western Union. He was such an expert receiver and sender that often alone and unaided, he attended to all the work that offered. All of this was in the early sixties.

In Quebec the boy had learned to play at cricket, and when he reached this side the inborn love of sport looked for something else and found it in the baseball games that were then being played on the prairie in North, South and West St. Louis.

This boy had the blood of a Scotchman in his veins, was sturdy and athletic and soon learned to play the game as well as the next. He played all the positions on a team and played them well.

He was one of the first players in the sixties who played close to the batsman and caught the speediest pitching without the aid of mask, gloves or chest protector.

He did his first playing with the "Night Owls" of Cincinnati, a club made up of telegraph operators. He also played with the Mutuals of Chicago and with the Actives of St. Louis.

When in the sixties the Western Union operators went on strike, "Billy" Spink was the secretary of the Union, and when they lost their strike he abandoned the key and swore he would never again work for the Western Union Company, an oath he kept until the time of his death.

When he quit the Western Union he went to Cincinnati and accepted a position as reporter on the Cincinnati Gazette. It was while employed there that he became associated with the leading baseball players of the day for Cincinnati in the sixties, was a hot-bed of baseball. And it was while associated with them that "Billy" commenced writing of the National game.

It has often been claimed that he was the man who first called the famous Cincinnati team of 1869 the Cincinnati Reds.

This may not have been so, but I know for an actual fact that he was the first to call the St. Louis League team the St. Louis Browns and the first to call the Chicago League team the Chicago White Stockings.

In the sixties, when he came to St. Louis, Mr. Spink went to the Missouri Democrat, later to the Dispatch, and when the Globe and Democrat were consolidated, he went to work for that newspaper as its telegraph editor.

His duties on that paper were onerous, but Mr. Spink performed them with the greatest of ease and facility. His work was done in the night and he spent his spare hours in the day playing baseball or watching the games.

One day he asked the editor of his paper leave to insert baseball and other sporting items in the Globe-Democrat. Mr. Spink offered to do this work as a labor of love, and his offer was accepted.

Nightly after that when work at his telegraph desk lagged, he wrote of baseball, cricket, billiards, pugilism, the turf and other sporting events of the day. He worked so hard and put in such long hours that soon the pace told and just to rest "the boy up," "Mack," then the Globe-Democrat's great editor, used to send "Billy" away to report the important sporting events.

And so it came that in those early days when great billiardists like Cyrille or Joe Dion and John McDevitt, great oarsmen like Edward Hanlan and Evan Morris, great race horses like Tenbroeck and Mollie McCarthy, great baseball teams like the Cincinnati Reds and the Chicago White Stockings were engaged in some great contest, "Billy" Spink was always there to report the proceedings for the Globe-Democrat.

This experience made him a master in the line of reporting all sorts of sport. He could write equally well about all the sports and pastimes of the day. He knew cricket, he was letter perfect in billiards and baseball he knew every race horse and knew the pacing and trotting records by heart.

He wrote the articles of agreement for the early prize fighters like McCoole, Allen, Coburn, Hogan, O"'B'a'l'dwin, Wormald, Goss and that crowd, knew all of them well and reported their fights better than any man of that day.

When McCoole and Allen fought for the world's championship up and down the river and when Allen and Gallagher and Allen and Hogan did the same thing, "Billy" Spink carried his pocket telegraph instrument with him, climbed telegraph poles and was generally the first to get the news to his paper.

"Billy" Spink was, in fact, the best all around sporting writer of his day, if not the best all around sporting editor that ever lived.

Naturally he was the friend of all who loved sports and pastimes and naturally he gave all enterprises that meant the building up of sport a friendly hand.

And so it came that his writings led to the early embarkation of St. Louis in the professional baseball world and when the first National League Club was established here in 1875, Billy Spink was its official scorer and only newspaper champion.

George McManus, now the manager of the Empire Theater in Brooklyn, was the manager of the first St. Louis Browns, and he tells a funny story of "Billy" Spink in connection with the first tour of that team.

"We took 'Billy' with us," says George, "to score the game, for he was the only man that knew how to score, but at the same time we took him along just to get him away from the telegraph desk and give him a needed rest.

"The boy had been doing night work so long he could not sleep in the night, and generally sat up around the hotel until daylight.

" 'Billy' was a stubborn lad and had a mind of his own that got him in trouble one night in Rochester, N. Y.

"They had a law there then, a sort of curfew, which prohibited any one from walking or being seen on the streets after midnight.

"It was after that hour when 'Billy,' seated in front of his hotel at Rochester, was accosted by a policeman with a club.

"You'll have to go in," said the officer to 'Billy. "Its against the law for any man to sit out here after 12 o'clock at night."

"You don't tell me," said 'Billy' "and the officer backed up and walked off.

"An hour later the same officer came around again and, seeing 'Billy' in the same old place, puffing away at a cigar and as wide awake as ever, walked into the hotel and called the attention of the clerk to the law's infraction.

Then the clerk approached "Billy" and told him of the curfew law in Rochester.

"That's all right," said 'Billy,' "and perhaps its a good law, but in so far as I'm concerned you'll have to repeal it, for I havent been to sleep before daylight in seventeen years and all the people in Rochester can't put me to sleep before that time."

Then the officer and hotel clerk conferred again, concluded to let "Billy" have his way, and he sat there smoking until night's candles had burned out and a blazing sun had turned the dark sky into daylight.

In the early days "Billy" Spink championed the Empires and the St. Louis Reds. He was their friend even after the professional teams had come in.

As late as 1875 no names were given the baseball parks. The main play ground then, located on Grand avenue, the ground now occupied by the St. Louis Browns, was only referred to as "the baseball park."

The Red's grounds, at Compton avenue and the Missouri Pacific Railway tracks, was only referred to as the grounds near the Pacific Railway. Billy Spink soon made the parks easily known by calling one the Grand Avenue and the other the Compton Avenue Park.

When in the late seventies the Sportsman Park and Club was organized and took possession of the Grand Avenue grounds, "Billy" named the place Sportsman's Park, a name that has clung to it ever since.

When the Union Association came to St. Louis in 1884, "Billy" named the grounds at Cass and Jefferson avenues, Union Park, and by that name it was always known.

"Billy" championed the St. Louis Union

team of 1884, their only season in St. Louis, and he passed away that year.

His funeral was one of the largest ever seen in St. Louis, for his friends in all walks of life were legion, and he was known and beloved in all ends of the City of St. Louis.

GEORGE STACKHOUSE—George Stackhouse was for years the baseball editor of the New York Tribune. He was at the top of the profession when he passed away a few years ago.

JAMES E. SULLIVAN—No man living has done more to spread the gospel of baseball, to increase its areas and to build it up than James E. Sullivan, president of the American Sports Publishing Company of New York.

Mr. Sullivan commenced the good work away back in 1878, and is at it yet. And in these thirty-two years he has put more baseball literature in circulation than any other man connected with the game.

Mr. Sullivan's life has been such a busy one that it reads like a romance. He entered the publishing house of Frank Leslie in 1878, and has been connected continuously with the publishing business since then, and also as athletic editor of various New York papers; was a competing athlete, one of the organizers of the Amateur Athletic Union of the United States; has been actively on its board of governors since its organization until the present time, and president for two successive terms; has attended every championship meeting in America since 1879, and has officiated in some capacity in connection with American amateur championship track and field games for nearly twenty-five years; assistant American director Olympic Games, Paris, 1900; director Pan-American Exposition athletic department, 1901; chief department physical culture Louisiana Purchase Exposition, St. Louis, 1904; secretary American Committee Olympic Games at Athens, 1906; honorary director of athletics at Jamestown Exposition, 1907; secretary American Committee Olympic Games at London, 1908; member of the Pastime A. C., New York; honorary member Missouri A. C., St. Louis; honorary member Olympic A. C., San Francisco; ex-president Pastime A. C., New Jersey A. C., Knickerbocker A. C.; president Metropolitan Association of the A. A. U. for fifteen years; president Outdoor Recreation League; with Dr. Luther H. Gulick organized the Public Schools League of New York, and is now chairman of its games committee and member executive committee; was a pioneer in playground work and one of the organizers of the Outdoor Recreation League of New York; appointed by President Roosevelt as special commissioner to the Olympic Games at Athens, 1906, and decorated by King George I. of the Hellenes (Greece) for his service in connection with the Olympic Games; appointed special commissioner by President Roosevelt to the Olympic Games at London, 1908; appointed by Mayor McClellan, 1908, as member of the Board of Education of Greater New York.

R. P. THOMPSON—R. P. Thompson was the sporting editor of the St. Louis Times in the seventies. He was an enthusiastic champion of outdoor sports, and his hobby was baseball and the turf. He is still alive and is often seen at the local baseball parks.

AL. E. WATTS
Of the Boston Traveler.

WILLIAM G. WEART
Of the Philadelphia Evening Telegraph.

AL. E. WATTS—Mr. Watts is sporting editor of the Boston Traveler and he has been holding down this desk for five years. He is a keen student of sporting matters, his hobby's being base ball and foot ball. He is popular with the base ball players and followers of the game as well. He began newspaper work as member of the Worcester Spy, one of the oldest papers in the country, but which ceased publication in May, 1904. Before graduating into the important department of sports he went the usual route of all good newspaper men.

WILLIAM G. WEART—William G. Weart was born at Independence, Iowa, September 15, 1872, and has lived in Philadelphia since 1879. He started work on the Philadelphia Times in June, 1891, and became baseball editor of that paper the following spring. He remained in that position until 1896, when he became baseball editor of the Philadelphia Press and held that position until he joined the staff of the Philadelphia Evening Times in July, 1908. He remained on the Evening Times until January, 1909, and then accepted the position of baseball editor of the Evening Telegraph, which position he still holds. He was elected secretary of the Baseball Writer's Association of America in December, 1908, and was re-elected in 1909. He has been official scorer of the Philadelphia Nationals and Philadelphia Americans several times, and has also done considerable political reporting and out of town work for the papers with which he was connected. When the National League magnates met with great secrecy at the Hollenden House, Cleveland, decided upon the terms for the cutting down the list of clubs from twelve to eight, he pulled off the "scoop" which

smoked out the club owners and started a mystery as to how the story was secured, which was not revealed for many years. Weart is a jovial, good fellow, and is popular with all the major league players.

HARRY WELDON—Following O. P. Caylor as baseball and sporting editor of the Cincinnati Enquirer, came Harry Weldon, for years one of the best known and best beloved of the fraternity. Weldon was big, stout, able, generous and good natured, and while his friends were legion, he had not an enemy in the world. Once he halted in his journalistic career to become secretary of the St. Louis Browns, but after a single season with them he returned to the Enquirer. When Weldon passed away there were sighs and tears all along the line.

JAMES WHITFIELD—Jimmy Whitfield, whom many of the old time baseball fans will remember was up to his death recognized as one of the cleverest, most conscientious and best beloved of sporting writers. For years and years, Whitfield was the sporting editor of the Kansas City Times-Star. Besides looking after the interests of his paper he was interested in the promotion of athletic sports in the Kaw City. He was associated with me when the old Western League was organized many years ago. Later he was elected president of this organization which position he filled to perfection.

L. F. WOOSTER—L. F. Wooster, one of the foremost baseball writers, began his newspaper career from the bottom of the ladder, starting as copy boy twenty-one years ago for the Brooklyn Times. Later he was taken in as a reporter on the sporting staff and after a few years he was elevated to the position of sporting editor. In all this time he was connected with the one paper. The turf seemed to be his specialty. Mr. Wooster was one of the very first reporters of bowling news and the Times was the first paper in the United States to publish bowling news and bowling scores, likewise baseball.

EDDIE WRAY—Eddie Wray, sporting and baseball editor of the St. Louis Post-Dispath, is one of the finest and best characters connected with the National game. His pen is always steeped in the milk of human kindness and he is never as happy as when giving some young player a friendly boost. Wray's work is arduous having to fill many columns in the Post-Dispatch every day with much interesting matter. But he is always equal to the task.

Wray is a native of St. Louis, and his family have resided in the old western town for one hundred years or more. He comes fom the old Lincoln school neighborhood, where he first learned to make "pot-hooks" and write his name.

ALFRED H. WRIGHT—While Chadwick was at work building up the game in New York and Meacham, Spink and others were employed in introducing it to the people of the West, Alfred H. Wright was at work with pen and pencil fostering and introducing the game to the people of Philadelphia.

I have mentioned him as one of the few who knew how to score the game in the sixties, according to the tabulated record in use by all well posted baseball reporters of today.

Like Chadwick, Spink, Caylor and the rest of the early baseball scribes, Wright's work as a baseball writer was wholly a labor of love.

He was born at Cedar Grove, New Jersey, but received his early education at the Central High School in Philadelphia.

Wright's father was a prominent publisher and book seller, and the boy found time to play at "Old Cat" or town ball, and is said to have been the first to introduce that sort of thing to Philadelphia. That was in 1858, and that the game caught on rapidly was proven when two years later the Athletic Club of Philadelphia was organized.

In 1858 Mr. Wright was so enamored of baseball that he went to New York and for ten years he played with the leading teams representing that city on the diamond.

Ten years later, in 1868, he returned to Philadelphia and went to work there writing baseball for the Sunday Mercury. He made that newspaper in the ten years following the leading baseball paper of Philadelphia and secured such a fine reputation as a baseball writer that he was employed by Mr. Frank Queen to take the place of Mr. Chadwick on the New York Clipper, a position he held until illness drove him from active service.

Mr. Wright was the first reporter of his day to compile the National League averages in the initial year of that organizaticn. He was also the first to suggest that the championship go to the club which won the largest percentage of games.

For eleven years Mr. Wright was the official scorer of the Athletic Club of Philadelphia, accompanying them on all their trips and even going with them to England in 1874.

He was also the manager of the Athletics in 1876 and also the manager of the co-operative team known as the Athletics in 1878.

From the opening to the close of his career, Al. Wright was early and late employed in the furthering and building up of the game he had loved and followed from his early boyhood days.

ABE YAGER—Abe Yager of the Brooklyn Eagle, is one of the boys that grew up in the newspaper game and who has gained quite a reputation in the sport-

A. YAGER
Of the Brooklyn Eagle.

ing department of this large Eastern paper. Besides being on the staff of the Eagle, Mr. Yager has at different times contributed a weekly letter to the Sporting News. He is one of the authorities on baseball in greater New York.

MARION F. PARKER.
Sporting Editor of the St. Louis Globe-Democrat.

THE NATIONAL GAME.

THE BASEBALL WRITERS' ACCOCIATION.
WILLIAM G. WEART, PHILADELPHIA'S FAMOUS BASEBALL EDITOR, TELLS OF THE FIRST MEETING OF THE SCRIBES AND OF THE ORGANIZATION OF THEIR PRESENT BODY.

BY WILLIAM G. WEART.

It was at the session of the Baseball Writers' Association of America at the Waldorf-Astoria Hotel, New York, in December, 1909, that T. H. Murnane of Boston, paid the organization its biggest compliment.

"I desire," said Mr. Murnane, "to congratulate this association.

"It is the first time that an organization of baseball writers has ever held an annual meeting."

Several times in the past the baseball writers of the major league cities formed an organization, but not one of them ever got out of-even if into-its swaddling clothes. Something always happened to chill the enthusiasm of the members and usually Tim Murnane and Jake Morse, then of the Boston Herald, formed something like a "Last Man's Club" whenever an effort was made to hold a second meeting.

The present association of baseball writers has now been in existence nearly three years and it is a very lusty infant. The idea of forming an organization originated with Joseph M. McCready of Philadelphia, about four years ago and he did missionary work among the correspondents of out of town newspapers who visited Philadelphia with the major league clubs. The idea took hold and careful sounding of the magnates and league presidents showed that they would do all that they could to further such a movement.

The primary reason for an organization was the overcrowding of the scorers' boxes and in some cities it was almost impossible for out of town correspondents to find seats. No one cared to assume the authority to request interlopers to keep out of the space reserved for the newspaper men and it was seen that something had to be done to abate the nuisance. In the Summer of 1908, a number of traveling correspondents held a meeting in the office of President Pulliam of the National League in New York. Many of the New York baseball writers were also present. The seed was then sown for the present organization. .

The first big meeting was held at Detroit during the World's Series between Detroit and Chicago in the Fall of 1908. An incident during the play off of the memorable tie between the New York Giants and the Chicago Cubs at the Polo Grounds a few days previous had shown the reporters that it was absolutely necessary for them to organize. This was in the overcrowding of the press box when a number of actors and others pre-empted the seats and refused to give them up. One of those who had a very trying experience was Hugh Fullerton of Chicago, who was forced to sit on the edge of the box with his feet dangling outside while he dashed off copy for his operator. The incident was still fresh in the minds of the reporters when they gathered at Detroit and held a meeting at the Hotel Pontchartrain.

Twenty-two writers were in attendance. Joseph S. Jackson of the Detroit Free Press, was made temporary president; I. E. Sanborn of the Chicago Tribune was made temporary secretary, and T. H. Murnane made temporary treasurer.

It was decided to call the organization The Baseball Writers' Association of America and the wisdom of having some cash to start things going was quickly seen. Mr. Murnane was appointed to pass the hat and collect $1 from each person present. Tim did so and when he counted up he found that the total amount was $21.80. Some one had "crossed" the temporary treasurer by dropping three quarters and a nickel into the hat instead of a dollar and the laugh was on Tim, who thought that he was getting off lucky because none of the quarters were Canadian.

After a general discussion it was decided that the objects of the association should be to control the scorers' boxes at the various major league parks and to secure better scoring rules. President Jackson appointed Henry P. Edwards of the Cleveland Plain Dealer, H. S. Fullerton of the Chicago Examiner and the writer, then of the Philadelphia Times, a committee on constitution. Dan T. Murray and H. E. Keough of Chicago, both of whom were charter members of the Turf Writers' Association outlined the constitution of that association.

Those who were present at this meeting were: Ed F. Bang of Cleveland, J. A. Cruisenberry of St. Louis, H. P. Edwards of Cleveland, A. J. Flanner of St. Louis, H. S. Fullerton of Chicago, C. A. Hughes of Chicago, J. S. Jackson of Detroit, H. E. Keough of Chicago, H. W. Lanigan of St. Louis, J. W. McConaghy of New York, M. A. McLean of Chicago, Sid Mercer of New York, G. L. Moreland of Pittsburg, T. H. Murnane of Boston, W. G. Murphy of St. Louis, W. A. Phelon, Jr., of Chicago, Jack Ryder of Cincinnati, I. E. Sanborn of Chicago, P. H. Shannon of Boston, J. B. Sheridan of St. Louis, J. S. Smith of Detroit, C. H. Zuber of Cincinnati and W. G. Weart of Philadelphia.

A permanent organization was effected at New York in December, 1908, during the meetings of the National League and the American League. Nearly forty newspaper men gathered in one of the rooms of the Waldorf-Astoria. The first matter brought up was the report of the Committee on Constitution. The report had been hurriedly prepared as two members of the committee and Mr. Sanborn, who acted for Mr. Fullerton, had been able to hold a meeting only a few hours before. The constitution was finally adopted and the temporary organization of President Jackson and Treasurer Murnane was made permanent. Jack Ryder of Cincinnati, was elected vice-president and at Mr. Sanborn's suggestion it was decided to elect an easterner as secretary, the writer being chosen for the position. The following directors were elected: John B. Foster of the New York Evening Telegram, I. E. Sanborn of the Chicago Tribune and Paul Shannon of the Boston Post.

Only two changes have been made in the officers from that time to this. It being found that the transaction of the business of the association was confused by the secretary and the treasurer, being in different cities, at Mr. Murnane's suggestion, the two offices were combined at the meeting held in New York last December, the writer being elected. It was then decided to add another member to the Board of Directors, the suggestion that a western man should be chosen was approved and Ed F. Bang of Cleveland, was elected.

Going back to the meeting in 1909, J. Ed Grillo of Washington, Sid Mercer of New York and H. P. Edwards of Cleveland, were elected as the committee on scoring rules.

President Jackson then appointed I. E. Sanborn of Chicago, E. J. Lanigan of New York and Elmer Bates of Cleveland, as the auditing committee.

A committee of which Jack Ryder was chairman, was appointed to notify the two major leagues then in session that an organization had been perfected and to explain the objects of the association. Mr. Ryder acted as spokesman for the committee, which was given a very cordial reception by both of the leagues and President Johnson of the American League and President Pulliam of the National League, after some complimentary remarks from the club owners, pledged themselves to do all that they could to aid the Baseball Writers' Association. This pledge has been faithfully kept to this day.

The following local representatives were appointed: Boston—Walter S. Barnes; Brooklyn—Abe Yager; Chicago—I. E. Sanborn; Cincinnati—J. C. Hamilton; Cleveland—Ed F. Bang; Detroit—J. S. Smith; New York—Sid Mercer; Philadelphia—J. M. McCready; Pittsburg—John Gruber; St. Louis—M. F. Parker; Washington—J. Ed Grillo.

Among those present at the meeting, in addition to those named, were: William J. Granger, Brooklyn; E. B. Coate, Brooklyn; A. Yager, Brooklyn; G. O. Tilden, New York; W. B. Hanna, New York; P. T. Knox, New York; R. M. Zeigler, Philadelphia; J. C. Isaminger, Philadelphia; G. E. McLinn, Philadelphia; G. W. Axels, Chicago; Bozeman Bulger, New York; Will McKay, Cleveland; Elmer Bates, Cleveland; Herman Nickerson, Boston.

Thanks to the work of the officers and the committees and the hearty co-operation of all the members, the association has been more successful than its organizers could have dreamed of. The objects of the organization were kept faithfully in mind and so great has been the appreciation of the members in the results attained that organizations have been formed on similar lines in many of the minor league circuits.

It was found impossible to affiliate with the minor league associations, but the parent body has always been ready to do all that it could to assist the others.

At the next meeting of the organization held in February, 1909, owing to the absence of two members of the committee on scoring rules. Messrs. Ryder and Jackson assisted Mr. Edwards in preparing a number of changes in the scoring code, which were adopted by the Joint Rules committees of the major leagues. The committee, together with Mr. Nickerson of Boston, who co-operated with Messrs. Edwards and Ryder at Pittsburg, in January, 1910, performed their work so well that this year only one suggestion for any changes in the scoring rules was heard, this being as regards a play which occasionally comes up.

During the first year of the association 125 writers joined. Those who were eligible but who declined to join that year quickly saw the advantages of an organization and last year, 1910, the membership reached 166.

The method of distributing the press tickets for the games of the World's Series being found to have caused dissatisfaction, at the request of the association the National Commission last Fall turned the scorers' boxes for the inter-league contests over to the association. The secretary was empowered to receive applications for press tickets and President Jackson appointed Joseph M. McCready to have charge of the press arrangements at Philadelphia and Frank M. Hutchinson, Jr., at Chicago.

Two deaths have occured in the association's membership. Strangely enough each man was killed in an automobile accident. Henry L. Buckley of the Philadelphia Press, was killed in 1909 while carrying a message from President Taft to the Seattle Exposition, and in 1910 George A. MacDonald, of Chicago, was killed while riding in an automobile with a player of the Chicago National League Club.

The association played a part in the erection of a memorial to Henry Chadwick, the "Father of Baseball," at Brooklyn and each year it decorates the grave of Henry C. Pulliam, the late president of the National League.

The present local representatives are: Brooklyn—Abe Yager, Chicago— W. L. Veeck, Cincinnati—Frank W. Rostock, Cleveland—Ed F. Bang, Detroit—Joseph S. Smith, New York—John B. Foster, Philadelphia—Joseph M. McCready, Pittsburg, John H. Gruber, St. Louis—Marion F. Parker, Washington—J. Ed Grillo, Boston—Herman Nickerson.

JAMES R. PRICE.
Sporting Editor of the New York Press in 1911.

JACOB C. MORSE.

Jacob C. Morse is the editor of a monthly magazine devoted entirely to baseball, known as The Baseball Magazine. This work is published in Boston, Mass., where Mr. Morse has been engaged in illuminating the beauties of baseball for a thousand years or more.

FRANCIS C. RICHTER.
Editor of the Sporting Life of Philadelphia.

CONNIE MACK.
Manager of the Champion Athletics of Philadelphia in 1910.

THE NATIONAL GAME.

BASEBALL WRITERS PROMINENT IN THEIR DAY.

WILLIAM M. RANKIN, DEAN OF NEW YORK'S BASEBALL WRITERS, CONTRIBUTES THESE LINES TO THE NATIONAL GAME.

BY W. M. RANKIN.

On January 27,1911, I received these lines relating to baseball writers prominent in their day from Mr. William M. Rankin, dean of New York corps of baseball writers. I give these lines just as they were sent to me changing no dates, nor the wording, for Mr. Rankin, being my senior both in years and regular service I take it that his records are naturally more correct than mine. They form a chapter in this book that will be of value for all time and for his pains in getting up and sending me this matter I feel deeply grateful as should all others who have the game's real interest at heart and who want to see its records preserved for all time. Mr. Rankin's lines read in this way:

The first man to write up baseball for the newspapers was Mr. William Cauldwell, editor and proprietor of the old New York Mercury. He began in April, 1853.

The New York Clipper at the time also printed baseball, but the games were furnished to it by the secretaries of the clubs. In 1856, W. H. Bray, a cricket reporter, was engaged by Mr. Queen to do the baseball and cricket work for the Clipper.

On September 1, 1856, Mr. William Porter issued the first number of Porter's Spirit of the Times. He engaged an English cricket reporter to do the cricket and baseball work on his paper. These three papers were the only ones which made a specialty of baseball games.

In the Spring of 1858 Mr. Cauldwell was compelled to give up the outside work for the Mercury, which he had been doing ever since the paper was started, and take full charge of the business end. He then engaged Mr. Chadwick, who had been doing the cricket work for the New York Times and a Brooklyn paper, to do the baseball and cricket work for the Mercury.

In May of that year Mr. Queen took W. H. Bray into the business office, and on the latter's recommendation Mr. Chadwick was engaged by Mr. Queen to do the baseball and cricket work for the Clipper. His first effort in baseball was the opening game of the Fashion Course series, played July 13, 1858, at Flushing, L. I.

With the Fashion Course games all the New York and Brooklyn papers began to recognize baseball and make a specialty of it. Prior to this the bare result of a game was given, merely a dinner was on the board. Then a "write up" followed.

At one time I had a complete list of all the baseball writers from 1858 to 1880, but it has been mislaid or lost, therefore, I will give as many as I can recall.

Between 1858 and 1876 the following were more or less noted writers of their day: Charles A. Peverelly, who wrote the first history of baseball; Henry G. Crickmore, afterwards a noted authority on horse racing; Michael J. Kelly, who introduced the short-hand system of scoring and the box scores, and the first editor of De Witt's Guide, and for nearly ten years the baseball reporter of the New York Herald; Wm. T. Picott, David A. Sutton, John Carpenter and Messrs. Mahlen, Rivers, Brodie, Hudson, Mitchell, Lewis, Snyder, Monpere, Brasear, Coyle, Marty Malone, W. M. and A. B. (June) Rankin, Carl Joy and others.

Mr. Chadwick was the only one who remained in the game from the time he began writing baseball in 1858, until he died in April, 1909, over fifty years. The above names do not complete the list by any means, but I cannot recall the others.

At no time after the Fashion Course games in 1858, were there less than half a dozen baseball writers in and around New York City.

I do not know when J. B. McCormick began writing baseball, but O. P. Caylor began on the Cincinnati Enquirer in November, 1874.

Alfred H. Wright began his baseball writing on the Philadelphia Sunday Mercury in 1868. It was he who introduced the checker-board arrangement now in use showing the standing of the clubs with the percentage of victories and defeats, which was first adopted by the old American Association and later by the National League.

David L. Reid took up baseball writing about the same time Wright did, and it was D. L. Reid who introduced the present system of batting and fielding averages.

W. M. Rankin began writing up baseball for the Rockland County (N. Y.) Journal in 1870.

Edward F. Stevens began writing up baseball on the Boston Herald in 1872.

A. B. (June) Rankin, started his baseball work on the New York Sunday Mercury in the Summer of 1875, and on the New York Herald in 1876.

J. C. Morse started his baseball work on the Boston Globe in 1883.

Harry Palmer began writing baseball stories from a Philadelphia weekly in 1886.

Frank Brunell's baseball work began on the Cleveland Herald in 1883.

Tim Murnane succeeded W. T. Harris on the Boston Globe in 1888.

Harry Weldon began his baseball work on the Cincinnati Enquirer in 1882.

I have records to prove every statement I make.

The short-hand system of scoring, with the box scores, was invented by Michael J. Kelly of the New York Herald, the former in 1861, and the latter in 1868.

You say that Sam Crane and Tim Murnane are the only simon pure baseball players who make use of the pen," etc. If you mean only professional, how about Charles Powers, of Pittsburg? If you mean men who played ball before becoming writers of the game, you overlook quite a bunch of them.

You say you fell out with Mr. Chadwick at first on the Sunday game question. You say the idea of playing games on Sunday was abhorrent to him at first, but that he later came around to your way of thinking. Mr. Chadwick was the official scorer of the Brooklyn Club during the four seasons its team played at Ridgewood Park on Sundays and did not hesitate to take his pay for scoring the games played there. Furthermore he was one of the eight to share in the benefit game at Ridgewood Park, played on a Sunday. He signed the pay roll with each of the other seven men and I have it today.

You also say: "Mr. Chadwick's skill as a writer on sporting topics attracted the attention of Frank Queen, etc." Mr. Chadwick had been writing up only cricket for several morning newspapers, and was introduced to Mr. Queen by W. H. Bray, the cricket and baseball reporter of the Clipper, when the latter was taken into the business office by Mr. Queen. In April 1858, Mr. Cauldwell, who had to take up the inside work on the Mercury, engaged Mr. Chadwick to do the baseball and cricket for his paper. Mr. Bray knew this and so informed Mr. Queen when the latter asked him if he knew any one he could recommend to succeed him (Bray) when he entered the business office.

You also say: "But while engaged on the Clipper from 1858 to 1888," etc. Mr. Chadwick retired from the Clipper in the Spring of 1867 to become the editor of the Ball Players' Chronicle, which died in June or July, 1868. Mr. Chadwick was re-engaged by Mr. Queen in the Spring of 1869 and continued with the paper until the Spring of 1886 when he resigned to join the editorial staff of Outing.

And now I will give you a few sketches of baseball writers that I knew and that were prominent in their day.

Alfred H. Wright—Mr. Wright's baseball journalistic career began on the Philadelphia Sunday Mercury in 1886, as an assistant to Charles H. Graffen, who had been writing baseball from the time it had been introduced in Philadelphia by the members of the Winona Club, May 18, 1860. Mr. Wright continued with the Mercury until January 1, 1879, when he came to New York to take charge of the baseball work on the New York Clipper. He was the first to use the checker-board arrangement showing the standing of the clubs, and suggested the plan of deciding the championship by the greatest percentage of victories to games played, which was first adopted by the old American Association and later by the National League. Mr. Wright was for several years secretary of the Athletic Club of Philadelphia, and accompanied the Athletic and Boston teams to Great Britain in 1874. He was a fluent writer and one of the best statisticians ever connected with the game.

David L. Reid—There were few newspaper men, if any, who were more prominently and actively identified with the National Game from the inception of professionalism up to his retirement, than was David L. Reid. For some years he was the editor of sports on the Philadelphia Sunday Dispatch, and his brilliant pen wielded an authoritative influence in the destinies of the national game. In 1875 Mr. Reid went to St. Louis where he served with distinction on the Republican, Post-Dispatch, Spectator and Critic. For several years he was secretary of the St. Louis Club, owned by Chris Von der Ahe.

Harry F. Boynton—Mr. Boynton was for many years connected with the Chicago Times. He began writing on baseball as far back as 1869, and made a number of trips with the old White Stocking team of that city.

Louis Meacham—In the Summer of 1870, Louis Meacham was one of the best-known baseball writers in the country. It is hardly possible to say how much he did toward furthering the national game at the

Garden City, where his well-earned reputation as a journalist and his genial deportment made him exceedingly popular.

Edward F. Stevens—Big Ed Stevens was for many years the baseball editor of the Boston Herald. He began to write up baseball in 1872 and he made that department of the Herald one of the best in the country. He was a vigorous writer, who gave facts and made no pretensions to brilliancy. He was so long identified with baseball he was known everywhere. In 1887-88 he was secretary of the New England League.

Oliver Perry Caylor—No one in any way interested in baseball during the first fifty years of the existence of the National League will ever forget O. P. Caylor. Baseball suffered a severe loss when he passed away, and he "died with his boots on," as it were. For only a few days before his death he furnished the New York Herald with his usual weekly letter, caustic, entertaining and written in a style peculiarly his own. He was one of the most fearless and independent writers ever known to the game. Undoubtedly he was one of the most brilliant of baseball specialists. The manner in which he arraigned the Players' League during the troublesome days of the season of 1890 showed him to be a master of satire and pithy expression. O. P. was regularly engaged on the staff of the Cincinnati Enquirer in 1874, and he soon electrified the whole baseball world with his brilliant Cayloresque manner of writing about the game and the events which surrounded it.

A. B. (June) Rankin—June began his baseball work on the old New York Sunday Mercury in 1875. In the Spring of 1876 he was engaged by the New York Herald to do the baseball work on that paper, and continued with the latter until the Fall of 1889. He was the official scorer of the old Metropolitan Club of New York from its inception in 1880, until the close of the season of 1883. He was also the official scorer of the New York Club from 1883 to 1889, inclusive. He was a bright and ready writer, and for years, while he had entire control of the Herald's baseball, made it interesting and reliable. June Rankin was a delegate to the National Association when it was formed in 1877. Some years ago June retired from baseball and entered the golf field where he soon became as well-known an authority on it, as he had been while connected with baseball.

Thomas S. Fullwood—"Tom" Fullwood was one of the best known baseball writers in the west for upward of twenty years beginning with 1876. "I began my journalistic work," he once told the writer, "as a printer's devil." He then passed through the various branches of the mechanical work until he graduated as a writer of sports in 1876. He was a versatile writer, although inclined to be facetious. Personally he was very popular with everybody with whom he came in contact.

Henry H. Diddlebock—Mr. Diddlebock was more familiarly known as Harry, and baseball was his hobby. He began writing baseball on the Philadelphia Item in 1876, and in 1887 he was on Philadelphia Press. In 1880 he joined the staff of the Times of the Quaker City and in 1889 became the editor of sports on the Philadelphia Enquirer. He did a great deal toward keeping baseball alive in the Quaker City during the seasons of 1877-78-79, when at times he managed teams under the names of Athletic and Philadelphia Clubs. He helped to organize the Eastern League in the winter of 1883-84 and was elected its president and secretary, which positions he held for several years.

Harry M. Weldon—Harry Weldon was well and much beloved in all branches of the sporting world. He was one of the most brilliant and entertaining writers on sporting subjects that ever put a pen on paper. He joined the staff of the Cincinnati Enquirer in 1880, and two years later took charge of that sporting and baseball departments of that journal. In addition to his newspaper duties he served as official scorer of the Cincinnati Unions in 1884 and in 1886 he was secretary of the St. Louis Browns.

James C. Kennedy.— Big Jim Kennedy was a few years ago one of the best known and best liked men in sporting circles. Prosperity never raised him beyond the pace of man. He never forgot a favor any one did for him. We meet few in the every day walks of life like Big Jim Kennedy For about eight or ten years Jim did the baseball work on the New York Times. He began his work during the late Summer of 1882 at the Polo Grounds, and soon thereafter began writing bright and newsy matter. In the Fall of 1887 he and P. J. Donohue, with the assistance of Messrs. John B. Day and James Mutrie, started the New York Sporting Times. "Billy" O'Brien induced "Jim" Kennedy to forsake baseball for the "squared" circle, and Jim never regretted the move, as prosperity followed after the change was made.

Harry C Palmer was another bright luminary that came in 1882 to enlighten the people in the baseball world, and how well he succeeded is a matter of history. He was a most fluent and graceful writer being especially strong on descriptive work and was counted among the ablest of the baseball journalists.

George E. Stackhouse—"Stack," as he was familiarly called, was a gentleman from the soles of his feet to the crown of his head. He was a Kentuckian by birth and came to New York during the Winter of 1879-80. He had an uncle on the editorial staff of the Tribune who obtained a position for him on that paper. He was there several years before he started his baseball work in the Spring of 1883. He was a free writer and a good news-gatherer. George did not confine himself to baseball, as he did horse racing, foot ball, bowling and amateur athletic work. He was undoubtedly the most popular newspaper man that was ever connected with local baseball matters.

Harry McAuliffe—When Harry started his baseball work in 1883, he was known as Harry Plummer, but he dropped that nom when he took up horse racing. Harry was a whole-souled, genial little fellow and was sadly missed by the "boys" when he was "drafted" for the ponies. He was not the first baseball writer to forsake the ball field for the race track. For some years after leaving baseball he was an assistant to H. G. Crickmore and later was on the staff of the sporting department of the New York Herald.

Frank H. Brunell, J. C. Morse and Horace Fogel were also of the 1883 crop of baseball writers. Mr. Brunell made his

start with the old Cleveland Herald in 1883, and was appointed official scorer of the Cleveland and National League Club the same season. He expressed his views about the game fearlessly and conscientiously, denouncing the wits in a manner that carried right and his opinion commanded respect. In 1884 he and O. P. Caylor fought the old Union Association tooth and nail, and five years later Mr. Brunell assumed the advocacy of the Brotherhood cause, while Mr. Caylor espoused the old National League and the pithy combat in their respective journals between the two were greatly enjoyable to their readers during those troublesome days of the Players' League period. It was of the liveliest nature, keenly ironical, cutting and full of scornful utterances, for each could command a flow of diction with a thorough art of using it.

Horace S. Fogel may have built air castles when he started to write up baseball for the Philadelphia Press in 1883, but he can hardly be accused of then laying the foundation for the presidency of the Philadelphia Club. Such things are frequently seen in visions, while the pipe burns, but—well, Horace plodded on through all the narrow and winding paths of the game until he finally reached the summit of the club, footsore and weary, but satisfied with his journey. If he does as well in his new berth as he did during the many years before he reached it he will do himself proud.

Frank Hough, P. J. Donohue, C. F. Mathison and W. D. Sullivan, were some of the bright and brilliant stars that began to twinkle in the baseball firmament in 1884.

Frank Hough is the only one of the quartet who is still actively engaged in baseball, and the game has much to feel proud over by his acquisition to its ranks. Messrs. Sullivan and Mathison have turned their talents to other channels in the newspaper line, while P. J. Donohue has passed beyond the "Great Divide." Mr. Hough is deeply interested in herding and caring for the "White Elephants" on the plains of Schibe. The "old sport" saw a good thing coming his way, and, instead of "passing it along," he gathered it in, and when the grand-children are grouped around his knees on the long, cold wintry nights, he will not have to go out in the storm to gather wood to keep them warm.

John H. Mandigo, Alfred R. Cratty, Philip F. Nash and others came into the baseball limelight in 1885. John Mandigo was one of the largest- hearted and the most whole-souled person it was ever my good fortune to meet, and he was not only one of the best news-gatherers hereabouts, but had the knack of knowing how to cull out the good from the bad and he always had the best page of sporting matter printed in New York, and he didn't have to tell the people so either. Mr. Mandigo started at the bottom rung and by his own energy and ability worked himself to the top of the ladder, and his paper and all of his friends were proud of him.

J. C. Morse's initiary baseball work was on the Boston Globe, but shifted his scene of base to the Herald of that city, where he gained his greatest renown. As a writer of the national game, he has shown independence and ability, proving himself a man who has the best interests of the game at heart, though tempered with an earnest desire to treat all connected with it with absolute fairness. For years he has been secretary of the New England league and is well known all over the country.

Wm. T. Harris and Edward S. Sheridan, two able and clever writers, entered the baseball vineyard in 1886, and were soon enrolled with the faithful and producing workers. Mr. Harris started his green diamond lore on the Boston Globe in 1886, and continued with that paper until April, 1888, when he came to New York to do the baseball work on the New York Press. Mr. Harris was succeeded on the Globe by John J. Drohan and Timothy Hayes Murnane. The latter is still doing the baseball work on the Boston Globe.

Chas. J. Merrill, Simon Goodfriend and Walter O. Eschwege also began their baseball work in 1888. The former had full charge of the work on the New York Evening World. "Si" Goodfriend started by writing "quibs" for the New York Evening Sun, but a year later he made "quite a spread" with his stories of the New York Nationals, and they were exceedingly interesting too. Walter Eschwege did the Brooklyn games for the New York Press. "Doc" McDonough was another 1888 baseball debutant.

George H. Dickinson and Langdon Smith were added to the baseball reportorial family in 1889, and both were writers of rare ability.

Then followed Joseph Villa, Robert Curtis, Samuel N. Crane, George O. Tidden, Jacob and Samuel Karpf and a host of others too numerous to mention.

JEREMIAH FRUIN.
The father of real baseball in St. Louis.

Tall and straight as an arrow, standing over six feet in height, is Jeremiah Fruin, the father of baseball in St. Louis.

Mr. Fruin is at the head of the Fruin-Colnon Construction Company, works out in the open every day in the week, is as active as most men at 50, and yet in July next he will have completed his 80th year.

Mr. Fruin is a fine specimen of the ad-vantages of outdoor sport and especially of baseball.

"Yes," said Mr. Fruin to me as I sat on the broad porch of his grand old home in Arloe, "I have heard it said that I was the first to introduce baseball into St. Louis.

"But I make no such claim. I know there was some such game here before I arrived in the year 1862. But it was perhaps not the real simon pure article.

"I came to St. Louis direct from the cradle of baseball. I came from Brooklyn where at that time there were two great baseball teams at play—the Atlantics and the Excelsiors.

"The Excelsiors were the swell team and the Atlantics were a rough and ready set made up almost exclusively of Irish-American players. They could fight as well as play baseball. I played with the Excelsiors first and then with the Atlantics.

"The great players of the later famous Atlantic team were then just budding into manhood. Start, Pearce, Crane, Charley Smith, Chapman, O'Brien, Pidgeon and others of them were just beginning to be recognized as great players.

"Having played with them I had learned to catch the ball by giving to it as it was thrown, with the hands low down or high up as the occasion demanded.

"I had, of course, learned the rules of play that were in vogue then. I was able on my arrival in St. Louis, therefore, to give the boys I found playing out on Gamble Lawn a few lessons on the improved Eastern method.

"I played my first game as near as I can recollect with the Empires of St. Louis on May 10, 1862, the Unions being our opponents. I covered second base for the Empires. Two years later I was made captain of the Empires and I remained captain of the team for four successive years.

"When I went to the nine I found it composed of a rough and ready set who were ready at any time to call a halt in the regular proceedings to engage in a game of fisticuffs. But I quickly put a stop to that sort of thing and taught the men that the game could be carried on in a gentlemanly and sportsman's-like manner.

"The game at this time resembled much the game as it is played to-day except that the player was out where the fielder caught the ball on the fly or first bound. There were few catchers then who had the nerve to stand up close to the bat. Most of the catchers stood fifty feet or more behind the home plate and even then often threw men out on the bases.

"Many of the great players who were then playing baseball with me are now a power in the business world.

"The first battery of the Unions was made up of Bob Lucas, pitcher, and Charles H. Turner, catcher. When Turner let a ball get by him Bob cursed the little 'Red Head.'"

"Gerald Fitzgibbon was the pitcher for the Empires. He is still alive and in the contracting business here and so is John W. O'Connell, now a wealthy painter in St. Louis, who used to handle the speedy underhand pitching.

"E. C. Simmons, now at the head of the Simmons Hardware Company was I think the first captain of the Unions. But he was so overbearing and arbitrary that his players fell out with him and he went in another direction and started a team of his own.

"Charley Cabanne, Supreme Court Judge Shepard Barclay, Rufus Lackland, J. B. C. Lucas and other later prominent men of St. Louis were then playing baseball with the rest of us on Gamble Lawn. No, I do not claim to have been the first to introduce baseball to St. Louis, but I was perhaps the first to show the boys how to catch the ball easily rather than by fighting it, how to trap the ball, to make a double play and that sort of thing. Do I love baseball yet? Why, certainly. One who has ever played the game in real earnest will never lose his love for it."

THE FUNNY AND THE SAD SIDE SIDE OF THE GAME.

STORIES ABOUT THE LUDICROUS AND PATHETIC SIDE OF THE SPORT
PICKED UP IN MANY DIRECTIONS AND ALL TOLD IN AN IN-
TERESTING WAY.

Who Has Recited "Casey at the Bat" Over   a Thousand Times.

"A little nonsense now and then,
Is relished by the best of men."
And so it is doubtless well to add a little jest and spice to this work by giving
some space in it to the odd and funny
side of the game.

In fact the baseball world has always
had its humorous side and scores of fun-

ny stories are told of strange and ludicrous incidents that have happened on the field. It also has its pathetic strain.

Many of these stories have been gathered from this direction and that and they are given here just as they were told by the various players and writers.

And with these humorous stories are also given leading rhymes of the game, notably the best baseball poem that was ever written, entitled "Casey at the Bat"

"CASEY AT THE BAT."

The outlook wasn't brilliant for the Mudville nine that day;
The score stood four to two with but one inning more to play.
And then when Cooney died at first, and Barrows did the same,
A sickly silence fell upon the patrons of the game.

A straggling few got up to go in deep despair. The rest
Clung to the hope which springs eternal in the human breast;
They thought if only Casey could get a whack at that—
We'd put even money now with Casey at the bat.

But Flynn preceded Casey, as did also Jimmy Blake,
And the former was a lulu and the latter was a cake;
So upon that stricken multitude grim melancholy sat.
For there seemed but little chance of Casey's getting to the bat.

But Flynn let drive a single, to the wonderment of all.
And Blake, the much despised, tore the cover off the ball.
And when the dust had lifted, and the men saw what had occurred,
There was Johnnie safe at second, and Flynn a-hugging third.

Then from 5,000 throats and more there rose a lusty yell;
It rumbled through the valley; it rattled in the dell;
It knocked upon the mountains and recoiled upon the flat,
For Casey, mighty Casey, was advancing to the bat.

There was ease in Casey's manner as he stepped into his place;
There was pride in Casey's bearing and a smile on Casey's face.
And when responding to the cheers ,he lightly doffed his hat.
No stranger in the crowd could doubt 'twas Casey at the bat.

Ten thousand eyes were on him as he rubbed his hands with dirt;
Five thousand tongues applauded when he wiped them on his shirt.

"CASEY'S REVENGE."

There were saddened hearts in Mudville for a week or even more;
There were muttered oaths and curses— every fan in town was sore.
"Just think," said one, "How soft it looked with Casey at the bat,
And to think he'd go and spring a bush league trick like that."

and the sequel to that, "Casey's Revenge."

"Casey at the Bat" was written by Ernest Thayer, of Worcester, Mass. He was a schoolmate of William R. Hearst at Harvard and wrote the poem in San Francisco. The poem has been recited on the stage by the famous comedian, De Wolf Hopper, thousands of times.

"Casey's Revenge" was written by Grantland Rice, a Nashville newspaper man, famous in the south as a poet and baseball writer. Here are the stories:

Then while the writhing pitcher ground the ball into his hip,
Defiance gleamed in Casey's eye, a sneer curled Casey's lip.

And now the leather-covered sphere came hurling through the air,
And Casey stood a-watching it in haughty grandeur there.
Close by the sturdy batsman the ball unheeded sped—
"That ain't my style," said Casey. "Strike one!" the umpire said.

From the benches black with people, there went up a muffled roar.
Like the beating of the storm-waves on a stern and distant shore.
"Kill him! Kill the umpire!" shouted some one in the stand;
And it's likely they'd have killed him had not Casey raised his hand.

With a smile of Christian charity great Casey's visage shone;
He stilled the rising tumult; he bade the game go on;
He signalled to the pitcher and once more the spheroid flew;
But Casey still ignored it and the umpire said: "Strike two!"

"Fraud!" cried the maddened thousands, and the echo answered fraud.
But one scorful look from Casey and the audience was awed.
They saw his face grow stern and cold, they saw his muscles strain,
And they knew that Casey wouldn't let that ball go by again.

The sneer is gone from Casey's lip, his teeth are clinched in hate;
He pounds with cruel violence his bat upon the plate.
And now the pitcher holds the ball and now he lets it go,
And now the air is shattered by the force of Casey's blow.

Oh! somewhere in this favored land the sun is shining bright;
The band is playing somewhere and somewhere hearts are light,
And somewhere men are laughing and somewhere children shout;
But there is no joy in Mudville—mighty Casey had struck out.

All his past fame was forgotten—he was now a hopeless "shine"—
They called him "Strike-out Casey" from the mayor down the line;
And as he came to bat each day his bosom heaved a sigh,
While a look of hopeless fury shone in mighty Casey's eye.

He pondered in the days gone by that
  he had been their king;
That when he strolled up to the plate
  they made the welkin ring;
But now his nerve had vanished—for when
  he heard them hoot,
He "fanned" or "popped out" daily, like
  some minor league recruit.

He soon began to sulk and loaf—his batting eye went lame;
No home runs on the score card now were
  chalked against his name;
The fans without exception gave the
  manager no peace,
For one and all kept clamoring for Casey's
  quick release.

The Mudville squad began to slump—the
  team was in the air;
Their playing went from bad to worse—
  nobody seemed to care;
"Back to the woods with Casey!" was the
  cry from Rooters' Row—
"Get some one who can hit the ball and
  let that big dub go!"

The lane is long, some one has said, that
  never turns again,
And fate, though fickle, often gives another chance to men;
And Casey smiled—his rugged face no
  longer wore a frown—
The pitcher who had started all the
  trouble came to town.

All Mudville had assembled—ten thousand
  fans had come
To see the twirler who had put big Casey
  on the bum;
And when he stepped into the box the
  multitude went wild;
He doffed his cap in proud disdain—but
  Casey only smiled.

"Play ball!" the umpire's voice rang out—
  and then the game began;
But in that throng of thousands there
  was not a single fan
Who thought that Mudville had a chance,
  and with the setting sun
Their hopes sank low—the rival team was
  leading, "four to one."

The last half of the ninth came round,
  with no change in the score,
But when the first man up hit safe the
  crowd began to roar;
The din increased—the echo of ten thous-
  and shouts was heard
When the pitcher hit the second and gave
  "four balls" to the third.

Three men on base—nobody out— three
  runs to tie the game!
A triple meant the highest niche in Mudville's hall of fame;
But here the rally ended and the gloom
  was deep as night,
When the fourth one "fouled to catcher"
  and the fifth "flew out to right!"

A dismal groan in chorus came—a scowl
  was on each face—
When Casey walked up, bat in hand, and
  slowly took his place;
His bloodshot eyes in fury gleamed—his
  teeth were clinched in hate,
He gave his cap a vicious hook and
  pounded on the plate.

But fame is fleeting as the winds and
  glory fades away;
There were no wild and wooly cheers—
  no glad acclaim this day;
They hissed and groaned and hooted as
  they clamored, "Strike him out!"
But Casey gave no outward sign that he
  had heard this shout.

The pitcher smiled and cut one loose—
  across the plate it sped—
Another hiss—another groan—"Strike one!"
  the umpire said.
Zip! Like a shot the second curve broke
  just below his knee—
"Strike two!" the umpire roared aloud—
  but Casey made no plea.

No roasting for the umpire now—his was
  an easy lot;
But here the pitcher whirls again—was
  that a rifle shot?
A whack—a crack—and out through space
  the leather pellet flew—
A blow against the distant sky—a speck
  against the blue.

Above the fence in center field in rapid,
  whirling flight
The sphere sailed on—the blot grew dim
  and then was lost to sight,
Ten thousand hats were thrown in air—
  ten thousand threw a fit—
But no one ever found the ball that mighty
  Casey hit.

Oh, somewhere in this favored land dark
  clouds may hide the sun,
And somewhere bands no longer play and
  children have no fun,
And somewhere over blighted lives there
  hangs a heavy pall;
But Mudville hearts are happy now—for
  Casey hit the ball.

THE MOST REMARKABLE THING THAT EVER HAPPENED ON THE BALL FIELD.

The most remarkable thing that ever
happened on a ball field is, by common
consent, the batting streak which Ed Delehanty, left fielder for the Phillies, showed
in a game with the Chicago nine out on
the West Side grounds in Chicago in '97.
"Adonis Bill" Terry was pitching for
Chicago. Altogether the Philadelphians
made just eight hits off Terry, and of
the eight Delehanty made no less than
five out of five times at bat.
The first time up Delehanty lined out
a home run to the left field bleachers.
The second he hit for four bases to
right field.
On his third effort he sent a sizzling
liner out into "Bullhead" Dahlen's territory.
Dahlen got under and stuck up his
hands but the ball was going so fast that
it almost amputated both of his fins.
Delehanty got to first on it.
The fourth time to bat Delehanty sent
one right straight for center and cantered
clear around to home without trouble.
When he walked to the plate for the fifth
time the fans were crazy with excitement.
"Another home run, Del," they shouted,
and by way of humoring the crowd Big
Bill Lange went out between the two
clubhouses in center and waved his hands
derisively.
Delehanty hit the first ball that was
pitched. It went sailing out into left,

hit the roof om the club house on that side, and bounded off on the roof of the other. Meanwhile Del walked leisurely around the bases and scored his fourth home run.

A STORY OF WHEN COMISKEY LED THE FOUR TIME WINNERS.

In this book I have told the story of the first game in which Comiskey played in old Sportsmans Park at St. Louis.

He was then the first baseman of the Dubuque Rabbits.

From the Rabbits he was graduated to the St. Louis Browns, the joke team of 1882, from which Comiskey built up the great Four-time Winner Team—the nine that won American Association and then World's Championships and that made the word St. Louis a thing to fear, to respect and to conjure by in the world of baseball.

Was it easy work transforming the joke team into a great stone wall?

Is the top of any profession reached easily in these days of rivalry and competition where he who tarries in any line is damned and where the bravest heart often breaks in the struggle?

So in Comiskey's battle for the top there were often strenuous, heart-breaking times and then other incidents often ludicrous but pleasant now to look back upon.

The Old Roman perhaps thought then as others have thought before, "And all these troubles shall serve for sweet discourse in time to come," for he took all things good naturedly.

The real material in the early eighties was as scarce as chickens' teeth.

And the followers of the game were a rabid lot, ready to go into ecstacies when the team won or to lynch the whole nine when it lost.

The Young Commander was praised lavishly and fondly when victory perched on the banner of his nine, but when defeat came he was made the target of the meanest sharpshooter.

So it behooved him to look about and to seek on all sides material with which to strengthen any weak spot that developed.

He was assisted in his search generally by Tom, Dick and Harry, who had some axe to grind or, perhaps, wanted a job for some relative.

It was General Grant who said that while in command of the Federal forces he never made a move but that some young war correspondent told him later of how he could have improved on it.

As a general, too, Comiskey lacked nothing in the way of advisers, and he was often held up by some enthusiast with a plan to strengthen the team and to better its standing.

One bright day in June a steady patron of the game called on Comiskey.

"I have a cousin," he said, "Andrew Jackson Jones by name. He lives on a farm near Joplin, but he often comes to town to play at short for the Joplin Blues. I want you to give him a trial, Charley. I'll bet the hair off my head he makes good—and if he don't, why you can kick a hole right through the thickest part of me."

"You've seen some players," said Comiskey, with that same old smile; "oh, yes, you've seen more than some and then

some more, and you're over 7. You ought to know. Now, if you think this Joplin terror is the goods, I'll give him a whirl at it."

It was late in July before Andrew Jackson Jones and his grip came through the old gate at Sportsman's Park.

He was looking for the young Commander.

They were near of a height when they met—Comiskey, tall, straight as an arrow and six feet in height, and Andrew Jackson Jones just as tall, but a trifle more stalwart than the captain.

"Yes, I'll let you take a crack at it," the captain said, "come over to the dressing room and I'll fix you up for a uniform."

The Brewery team were the Browns' opponents that day.

The Brewery team was the nine that hailed from Pittsburg and that was called the Brewery because it never went on the field without the contents of at least part of a brewery stowed beneath its belt.

But the Brewery team had in its ranks some awful hitters.

That is they were sometimes awful and on this particular occasion each man of the lot acted as though suffering from delirium tremens, for the way they hit the ball was something uncanny and fearful.

It may have been a job on Andrew Jackson Jones.

But Shappert, who was pitching for the Browns, sent them in just to the Brewers' liking, and nearly every smash they made saw the ball whirling at frightful speed in the direction of Andrew Jackson Jones.

True to his name the farmer boy from near Joplin faced the music bravely and honestly.

Often and often the whirling sphere hit him on the feet, ricocheted up his knees and caromed on his epigastrium.

His body and hands were alike blistered before it was all over, and when the game was done he came over to the captain, shook him by the hand and said:

"I done the best I knew how. I don't know just what you think of me and my playing. But I ain't no hog. I know when I've had enough. All the same captain, I'm much obliged to you just for the chance you gave me to make a d—— fool of myself."

The shades of night were falling when there passed down Grand avenue that night a limping and raw six-footer carrying a grip. It was Andrew Jackson Jones going back to the farm near Joplin.

The July sun faded, August came and went; the leaves began to fall and autumn's tint was in evidence when the Browns bade farewell to their Young Commander.

Some went west, others east and still others in other directions.

Comiskey, who, with his young wife, lived in a little cottage adjoining the baseball grounds, settled down in St. Louis

But in spite of Delehanty's marvelous record of four home runs and a single out of five times at bat his team lost the game by a score of 8 to 6.

for the winter and dreamed of the Summer days and of the Andrew Jackson Jones and other strange incidents that had developed during their first year in St. Louis.

Then Christmas drew near and the Young Commander and his wife were planning some fun for their only boy, when an expressman drew up in front of their cottage.

He had a box for them, he said.

No; he didn't know what was in it.

But it was something alive and it had come all the way from Joplin.

There was a letter, too, with the box and the expressman handed it to Comiskey.

The Young Commander opened the homely looking thing and read:

"On the Farm, Near Joplin, Dec. 20, 1882: Dear Cap—I wuz thinking today of you in St. Louis. I wuz a-thinkin' of the chanct you gave me to be a ball player. I wuz a-thinkin of what a consarned fool I wuz. And then I wuz thinkin' of how good and kind you wuz to me after causin' you all that trouble. And then some one told me that ball players don't have much in winter that's good to eat. And then it was I thought I'd remember you with a Christmas present and as I've got plenty, I'm a-sendin' you a nice little shoat and a nice little sheep and you can eat them at Christmas, and when you're a-eatin' the little hog you can just think of the fellow you give a chance too and that told you he wa'ant no hog, but knew when he had enuf. And if you and your wife and the boy ever get as far as Joplin just run out to my farm and I'll show you something that beats ball playin' to all creation.

Well, good-bye. A Merry Christmas and a Happy New Year for you and the missus. Your friend.

ANDREW JACKSON JONES.

A STORY OF THE DAY BUCK EWING'S BROTHER JOHN DIED OF A BROKEN HEART.

Perhaps the saddest story that ever came out of old Sportsman's Park in St. Louis was this one.

The incident occured in the early eighties when the St. Louis Browns management was hard pressed for players. One day in despair Comiskey asked Chris Von Der Ahe, who then owned the St. Louis Club, to go to Cincinnati and see whether or not money would induce him to come to the Browns.

To Cincinnati Chris went.

"I want you for catcher," said Vondy to "Buck." "'Commy' wants you too. Will you come?"

"For how much?" said the bread and butter man.

"Oh, I don't know," said Chris. "What do you think?"

"I'll go," said "Buck," for six thousand dollars"—an unheard of salary at that time.

"Six thousand!" said Chris; "six thousand! Are you a whole team? Won't 1 need anyone else if I hire you? That's more than I'm paying all the rest put together."

Chris gave up all thought of hiring "Buck," but the big catcher had a brother—John Ewing—who was a great player. Why couldn't Chris take him?

John Ewing's figures were the right mark and he was brought to St. Louis and heralded as the spit of his great brother, a fielder of the first class and a great batsman.

It would be sacrilege to talk of the boy now save in kindness.

He was a finely featured lad, kind, gentle and good as a woman, but lacking the devil and spirit that is needed to make a great player.

When the Young Commander one day in the gentlest of tones told young John Ewing that he would not do and that his services were no longer required, he did something he would not have done for all the world had he known of that which was to follow.

For long before the winter snow had covered the ground they dug a grave for the grand young fellow who they often said afterward had died of a broken heart—broken by a failure that might have been a victory but for the great things that were said of and expected of him before his real beginning.

HOW FRED DUNLAP, ONCE THE RICHEST PLAYER, DIED IN THE PHILADELPHIA ALMS HOUSE.

Of the great players of the olden time Fred Dunlap was considered by many the greatest.

And besides being the greatest player he was perhaps the thriftiest and in all probability earned more salary while at the height of his fame than any other professional player living.

Dunlap was playing at second base for Cleveland in 1883 when Henry V. Lucas, then a young St. Louis millionaire, went out hunting for players for the St. Louis Union Club.

About the first man he met was Dunlap and he asked him to become the captain and second baseman of the St. Louis Unions.

Dunlap laughed at the proposition. There was not money enough in the world to induce him to take such a step.

Lucas pulled a roll of bills out of his pocket. Dunlap in all his life had never seen so large a roll.

"How much can you earn a year playing ball?" asked Lucas.

"Seventeen hundred and fifty," said Dunlap, which was about the top salary at that time.

"Well, here's your seventeen hundred and fifty," said Lucas, "and as much more as you want."

Dunlap's eyes commenced to glisten, but he was silent as a clam.

"There's fifty thousand in this roll," said Lucas, "and you can have any part of it if you will sign this contract."

Dunlap looked at the contract. It called for his services for two years at a salary of $5,000 a year.

"That means ten thousand for the two years, doesn't it?" queried Dunlap.

"Yes," replied Lucas.

"But some say you wont last two years," said Dunlap, "and then where would I be."

"So you get the ten thousand it doesn't matter much to you whether we last or not, does it?" queried Lucas.

"No," said Dunlap.

"Then," said Lucas pulling ten one thousand dollar bills out of his roll, "here's your money and you put your name right here."

Dunlap counted the money twice, looked at each bill carefully to make sure it was the real goods, pocketed the roll and then signed the contract.

And although paid in advance, he served on the baseball field for the two years following as no baseball president had ever been served before. Indeed his work was so royal and true that Dunlap, during the balance of his career, was able to command the top salary. He was paid tremendous sums by Detroit and Pittsburg.

I last met Dunlap in Philadelphia in the winter of 1896. He had then quit the major league and laughed at the idea of playing with the minors.

He told me of the wonderful sums he had made playing baseball and of the way he had taken care of his money. He carried a bank book with him which showed that his check was good for over $100,000 and beside that he owned some valuable business property in Philadelphia.

One night a year or two later there came a telephone message to the newspaper offices in Philadelphia that a man named Fred Dunlap, supposed to have at one time been a great baseball player had died in the Alms House and was to be buried the next day in the Potters' Field.

A sporting editor of Philadelphia who had known Dunlap for years and who could not believe he was the man who had died in the Alms House went out there to investigate. To his great surprise he found that it was Dunlap sure enough and discovering too, that he had died there without friends or money, he had the body taken to an undertakers and found him a grave in a well-known cemetery.

"But," said this old sporting editor to me a little later, "there were not enough of us there to carry Fred's body to the grave and we had to call on the hack drivers to give us a lift in that direction. And to this day no one in Philadelphia knows what ever became of the great lot of money that Fred had earned and at one time had on deposit in a Philadelphia bank. He had never married and as far as we could learn when he died he had no living relative. The story of his strange and sudden fall and death in the Alms House at Philadelphia is still talked about by the veteran players of the Quaker City."

HOW FRIENDLY NAIL ON A FENCE GAVE MINNEAPOLIS THE GAME.

Frank Isbell, late first baseman of the Chicago White Sox, tells of how one day a friendly nail won a game for Minneapolis.

"In 1898 I was pitching for St. Paul," said Isbell.

"We were not allowed to play Sunday games inside the corporation limits and so a little park had been fitted up outside for Sunday play. The park was extremely small. The field was so short that a fence twelve or fifteen feet high had been built behind it to keep the balls from going out of bounds.

"As a consequence of the small field it was almost impossible to hit out better than a two bagger, for the ball would roll back into the infield.

"One Sunday we were playing Minneapolis. I was pitching for St. Paul. Minneapolis was at bat in the last half of the ninth inning and we were two runs ahead.

"There were two men out and two men on bases. The next man at bat lined out a high fly. It struck the high center field fence about twelve feet from the ground and everybody was certain we had the game won.

"But we didn't. The ball struck the fence—and stayed there. It struck directly on the sharp end of a wire nail, and before we could get a step ladder and climb up after it the Minneapolis nine had its three runs in and the game was over."

HOW JIMMY RYAN EASILY MADE THE VERY LONGEST HIT ON RECORD.

The longest hit on record was one which carried the ball from Staten Island to Liverpool, though all the wide Atlantic rolled between.

Chicago was playing New York one day in '90.

The One Hundred and Tenth street park of the New York team had been ruined by the opening of a street and a temporary park had been built in Staten Island, right on the shore of the bay.

The center field, in fact, was built out on boards over the water, and the man who fell out of the center field bleachers had nothing before him but an ignominious death in the ocean.

With the score a tie in the last inning Jimmy Ryan came to bat. He hit the ball a ponderous swipe and it went sailing over the center field fence into the vastly deep.

Ryan's hit and his ensuing home run were forgotten when one day, a month later, he got a letter and a small package by mail from Liverpool.

The writer said he had sailed for Europe the day of the ball game and had been struck by the ball as he stood on the deck of the liner.

After he got to Liverpool he read an account of the game in the New York papers and concluded that he had found the missing ball.

Jimmy still has the much traveled sphere to show as proof of his holding the record on long hits.

WHY VON DER AHE WOULD NOT ALLOW HIS PLAYERS TO WEAR POCKETS IN UNIFORMS.

Way back in '89 Cincinnati was playing one afternoon with Chris Von Der Ahe's St. Louis aggregation on the St. Louis grounds.

Cincinnati had a man on first base and two out, and needed two runs to win.

Cliff Carroll was playing center field for the St. Louis nine.

The Cincinnati batter hit a slow grounder to center and Carroll ran up to gather it in.

The situation was ticklish and Carroll prepared to field the ball carefully. He squatted down to meet it and got his hands in position. Just before it reached him the ball hit a clump of dirt and bounded high.

Carroll grabbed for it with both hands, just as it hit him in the chest.

Somehow in the struggle the ball was wedged into the pocket of Carroll's uniform shirt. It got in there, and Cliff had a terrible time trying to get it out.

The runner stopped at second long enough to see that something was the matter. Then he started for third, with Carroll running fast after him still digging away at his shirt pocket.

From third the runner started home.

HOW JIM McALEER MADE A HIT THAT BROUGHT UP A QUEER QUESTION

In Boston the left field fence backs on a railroad track.

As a consequence a lot of empty tin cans and other debris are often found about the bottom of the fence.

Cleveland was playing the Boston nine. Jim McAleer came to bat for the Ohio city. He knocked a long liner to left field and the ball rolled up under the fence and straight into an empty tomato can.

Hugh Duffy was fielding the left garden for the Beaneaters. He grabbed the can and tried wildly to dig the ball out.

Carroll still close behind him and still unable to separate himself from the ball.

The result was that the runner got home safely and Cincinnati won the game.

Von Der Ahe almost had a fit. He fined Carroll fifty for putting the ball in his pocket and made a rule that thereafter no pockets of any kind should be allowed in the uniforms of his team.

Meanwhile McAleer was running to second. Finally, growing desperate, Duffy threw can and all over to third base, from which McAleer had just started for home.

The third baseman hurled the can inclosing the ball to the catcher and the latter touched the runner out with it.

There was a loud protest from the Cleveland nine and the umpire finally decided that McAleer was safe and the run must count, because the rules provide that the runner must be touched by the ball.

A STORY OF THE DAY ELMER FOSTER CAUGHT A SPARROW IN CHICAGO'S LEFT FIELD.

Elmer Foster must always be borne in mind when one is relating the wonders of baseball.

Late in the afternoon, as fans will remember, the shadow of the grand stand falls over the field at the West Side Park in Chicago and makes it impossible for the outfielders to see a hit ball until it has traveled beyond the shadow.

Back in '94 one of the Eastern teams was playing in Chicago on the West Side, with Foster in center field. The man at the bat made a terrific swipe at the ball and hit it. The shadow was deep over the infield and Foster could not see the ball.

He started to run out into far center, so as to be prepared.

As a matter of fact the ball was only a bunt. The shortstop caught it and threw the batter out at first. But Foster kept on running—running like mad.

"Look at Foster," yelled the crowd in the bleachers. "What does he think he is after?"

Foster ran at the top of his speed almost to the center field fence. Then he jumped high up into the air, threw up his left hand, and came down to the ground with—an English sparrow tightly clutched in his fist.

"BULLHEAD" DAHLEN'S HIT THAT KILLED A BULL PUP ON THE POLO GROUNDS.

The score was 3 to 1 in favor of New York.

It was the ninth inning and Chicago had two men out.

The game was being played on the Polo Grounds in New York.

As you will remember there was a fence about the outfield of the Polo Grounds and just outside the fence the carriages used to be drawn up, so that their occupants could watch the game.

On this particular day in '96 Digby Bell, the actor, was sitting in his high trap, in the midst of the crowd. On the seat beside him sat an English bulldog.

As above related Chicago was "in,"

there were two men out, two men on bases, the score was 3 to 1 in favor of New York, and it was the last half of the ninth inning.

"Bullhead" Dahlen came to bat.

The first two balls that were pitched the umpire called as strikes. The third ball "Bullhead" hit a mighty wallop.

It sailed far out over the fence and struck Digby Bell's bulldog fairly on the head.

When the excitement cleared away it was discovered that Dahlen had chased home the two winning runs, while Digby Bell was mourning the accidental and unexpected death of an imported canine.

THE NATIONAL GAME.

THE MAJOR LEAGUE UMPIRES.

JUST A FEW WORDS ABOUT THE GENTLEMEN WHO CONDUCT THE GAME ON THE FIELD AND WHO INTERPRET THE RULES.

Wm. Evans. "Silk" O'Loughlin. Wm. Klem. James E. Johnstone.
American League. National League.

The following is a list of the umpires who officiated in the American and National Leagues during the season of 1910:

NATIONAL LEAGUE.	AMERICAN LEAGUE.
O'Day.	Sheridan.
Johnstone.	Evans.
Emslie.	O'Loughlin.
Rigler.	Connolly.
Klem.	Dineen.
Kane.	Egan.
Brennan.	Perrine.
Eason.	Colliflower.

The above named gentlemen are the experts who are engaged by the presidents of both big leagues and whose installation as officials of the American and National Leagues are indorsed by every club owner in both the major organizations.

This work on the history of the national game would indeed be an incomplete volume should the author have neglected to say a few words about the much maligned or much discussed arbitrator. The duties of the umpire are clearly set down in the rule book. The following is a paragraph which, of course, was framed by the owners of the ball clubs:

UMPIRE'S AUTHORITY.

"Under no circumstance shall a captain or player dispute the accuracy of an umpire's judgment and decision on a play. If the captain thinks the umpire has erred in interpretation of the rules he may appeal to the umpire, but no other player is privileged to do so."

During the past season of 1919 there has

369

been heard on all sides much complaint as to the incompetency of some of the umpires. This has been the case particularly in the National League. The second division clubs—who are, of course, always playing in hard luck and, of course, getting the worst of the breaks, so they claim, from the umpire, have made the most noise.

On February 16, 1905, the National Commission adopted rules and regulations for the governing of the contests each year for the professional baseball championship of the world.

These rules and regulations were first adopted by the National and American Leagues and then were approved by the National Commission. In them these rules relating to the number of umpires in each World's Championship game and the manner of their selection and compensation appear and they read as follows:

THE UMPIRES.

Sec. 11. There shall be two umpires, who shall be invested with the authority and discretion that the playing rules confer, and they shall observe the same general instructions with reference to maintaining order and discipline upon the ball field during these contests that govern them in the performance of their duties in all other games in their respective leagues.

UMPIRES—HOW SELECTED.

Sec. 12. The President of the National League and the President of the American League shall each select one umpire from their respective leagues, and the umpires so chosen shall be assigned to duty and be subject to the orders of the Chairman of the National Commission.

Sec. 13. The compensation of the umpires shall be fixed by the National Commission.

Subsequently it was agreed to use four umpires in each game instead of two. From the time of the passage of these rules in 1905 it has been the custom at the close of each season to pick the best umpires in the country from the two major leagues to umpire the World's Championship contests.

And so by common consent the men who have officiated in these games have been considered the greatest umpires we have ever had.

So a list of the men who have umpired in the World's Championship games since that sort of rule was inaugurated is given below:

1905—New York vs. Athletics, Jack Sheridan and Henry O'Day.

1906—Chicago National League vs. Chicago American League, James E. Johnstone and Frank Laughlin.

1907—Chicago vs. Detroit, Henry O'Day and John F. Sheridan.

1908—Chicago vs. Detroit, O'Day, Sheridan, Klem and Connolly.

1909—Pittsburg vs. Detroit, William Evans, "Silk" O'Laughlin, William Klem and James Johnstone.

1910—Athletics of Philadelphia vs. Chicago National League team, O'Day, Sheridan, Rigler and Connolly.

But beside the men whose names appear above as having officiated as umpires in World's Championship games since the National Game came into prominence there have been many famous umpires.

In the first great series of baseball games that in which the famous Cincinnati Reds and the Chicago White Stockings took part, the first really great series of games played in Chicago, Robert Ferguson, the catcher of the then famous Atlantics of Brooklyn, was the umpire.

Ferguson had been brought all the way from New York to Chicago to umpire this series. Up to this time—the Summer of 1870—there was no regular corps of umpires. It was the custom simply to pick a player from some other leading club to fill the position and generally some noted catcher was taken. And this was how it happened that Robert Ferguson, the famous catcher of the Atlantics of Brooklyn came to umpire the never-to-be-forgotten game played between the first Chicago White Stockings and the Cincinnati Red Stockings at Dexter Park, Chicago, on October 13, 1870, in the presence of a crowd estimated by many to number fifteen thousand persons.

In later years when President Nic Young selected his first regular corps of umpires for the National League he placed Robert Ferguson at the head of his staff and the old Atlantic player held his own in the position until only a year or two before his death.

Contemporaneous with Ferguson as an umpire in the eighties and nineties were Honest John Kelly, John Gaffney, Charles Daniels and the present dean of the National League staff, Robert Emslie.

Following these great umpires came another army which included such later famous umpires as Henry O'Day, the present veteran of the National League staff; Tim Hurst, Tom Lynch, Jack Sheridan, Billy McLean, Herman Doescher, Tom Connolly, Joe Cantillon, Fred Perine, Jack Kerins, Bill Evans, Johnstone, Rigler, Kiem, Kane, Brennan, Eason, O'Laughlin, Dineen, Eagan and Colliflower.

Henry O'Day, better known as Hank O'Day, now the veteran of the National League staff of umpires, is a Chicago boy. His father was superintendent of a public school on the far west side of Chicago away back in the sixties. On the prairies surrounding this school house, the three O'Day boys, Dan, Jim and Hank, learned to play baseball. They were all pitchers, Dan and Hank right handers and Jim a left. Hank was the best pitcher of the three and he rose to the top of his profession, being the star twirler of the New York Giants in 1889 when they met and defeated Brooklyn of the American Association in the race for that year's World's Championship.

As fine a critic as Ted Sullivan places O'Day in the lead in so far as still being the greatest umpire is concerned. Writing of O'Day recently Sullivan had this to say:

"The umpire with a butterfly individuality or a ribbon counter disposition, will never do as an umpire, though his brain is an encyclopedia of all the rules of the game. There is a hidden friction between player and umpire and the official in all his work must be decisive and earnest in his verdict. Does any patron of the game imagine that every umpire in the country would make the decision, Hank O'Day did on the Polo Grounds in the final game between the Chicago Cubs and the New York Giants in 1908, under the conditions in which the game terminated? I think not. There was a game that New

370.

York won practically, yet lost technically, according to straight baseball rules.

"If O'Day had made that decision in Chicago, in defiance of the protests of nine ball players of the Giants, nothing would be thought of his courage. But to make a decision that he knew was honest and right in defiance of a menacing, bedlam-loosed crowd of 25,000 took temerity and marked him a man who stood unflinchingly by the honesty of his convictions. It furthermore showed that he possessed the blood of a race that never turned its back to an enemy nor its face from a foe.

"I don't want it understood that other umpires would not make the same decision under the same circumstances—not at all. I know of three others who would. One is Jack Sheridan and the other two are O'Loughlin and Tim Hurst. I have known Sheridan for 16 years and I have seen him more than once under fire from the tough ball player and howling mob. Never did he flinch, nor skulk from doing his duty. This is my tribute to one of the gamest and greatest umpires who ever walked on a ball field."

I might add to what Sullivan has said about O'Day, but I think he has covered the ground fully. I say I might add because I knew and played baseball with all the O'Day boys in the olden time. With-out mask or gloves I caught the pitching of all three, but when I did this Dan and Jim were real pitchers, while Hank was only a youngster just beginning to come into his own. But the O'Day boys were all fine, brave fellows and Hank, the last of the family, is perhaps the bravest and best of the lot.

It used to be said that Tim Hurst was the best wit of all the old galaxy of umpires and many a good story he has told at his own expense.

"I have been asked to tell of the hardest decision that I ever made," said Tim one day. "The most important, I think, occured several years ago during a game between Cleveland and Baltimore at Cleveland. It was the ninth inning, and the score was tied. Childs was on second base for Cleveland, with but one out, and Pat Tebeau was at the bat. Hoffer was pitching for Baltimore and Robinson was catching. Hoffer was using a dinky out-curve that broke some distance from the plate and Tebeau was having great trouble in meeting it squarely. On several occasions he walked out of the box to hit the ball and I had repeatedly warned him about it.

"Finally when Childs reached second, Tebeau saw an outcurve coming and ran ten feet out of the box to hit it. He met the ball squarely before it "broke" and drove it to the center-field fence for two bases. Childs easily scored, making the game 3 to 2 in favor of Cleveland.

"The crowd was whooping and yelling over the victory. Robinson ran up to me and called my attention to the fact that Tebeau had run out of the batter's box. I knew he was right, and during the tumult I called Tebeau out and sent Childs back to second. The crowd was absolutely stunned.

Tebeau came running in from second with tears in his eyes. 'You didn't call me out for that?' inquired Patsy.

"Sure, I did. You know that you stepped out of the box, and you are only getting what is coming to you.'

" 'Well, I might have stepped out a few

feet,' he wailed. 'But you ought not to give a decision like that in the presence of this home crowd.'

"That tied up the game and it went along until the twelfth inning, when Baltimore won. You can imagine that I was a very popular guy in Cleveland that night. But just to show you how they forgot those things, when I went back there as an umpire in the American League I was given an ovation."

During the heat of battle the umpires' friends are often in the minority. A little happening that was staged at Chicago several years ago clearly proves this assertion. Joe Cantillon, now the manager of the Minneapolis Club, champions of 1910 of the American Association was umpiring in the American League at the time. Joe appeared at the ball park one day accompanied by two men. The man in charge of the gate was a new employe, and he refused to pass in the two Chicagoans.

"I have orders not to let anyone through the turnstile without a pass, Mr. Cantillon. I am sorry; but you will have to see Mr. Comiskey," was the gateman's none too cheerful greeting.

"Tell Comiskey that I have two friends with me and I would like to pass them into the game," requested the offended ump.

The gatekeeper wrote out the request and gave it to one of the attendants to be taken to Owner Comiskey of the White Sox.

The note read as follows, "Umpire Cantillon has two friends with him and wants to get them into the game."

It seems the day before Cantillon had a very tough game to umpire, in which several close decisions went against the home team, preventing Chicago from scoring a possible victory. While still a trifle sore over the outcome of the game, Comiskey couldn't let a chance slip by to have a little fun at Cantillon's expense. Sitting down at his desk he scribbled off this reply, "If there are two men in Chicago brave enough to pose as an umpire's friend, especially Cantillon's, pass them in and give 'em box seats."

Cantillon wasn't any too pleased with the answer at the time; but in after years he managed to get many a hearty laugh out of the situation.

Civil War veterans may boast of Grant and Lee, Spanish War veterans may praise Dewey and Schley, but American League umpires consider the veteran Jack Sheridan a greater hero than any of them.

For twenty-six years Sheridan has been before the American public as umpire. He started when the position was not nearly so easy and safe as it is today. The veteran has been the central figure in many a memorable diamond battle, has seen youngsters come and go; but is still at his post performing valuable service, and evidently is destined to go on forever.

Sheridan's career as umpire, which has been a most brilliant one, was launched in a unique way. Back in the '80s he was a ball player of ability. His work attracted the attention of a manager in the Southern League, who secured him to strengthen his club, which was weak only at second base, the very position in which Sheridan was regarded as a star.

The club was playing better than the average ball before Sheridan joined the team; but the manager regarded the pennant as a certainty with Jack in the line-up. Sheridan's arrival was hailed with great joy, as wonderful advance notices had been printed about him. His debut was marked by overwhelming defeat of the home team, although he played high-class ball. The second day also resulted in defeat, and, try as they might, the players seemed unable to win, no matter how well they performed. Finally, after the team had lost twenty-two straight games, Sheridan, who was looked on as the hoodoo, drew his release because of injury to his throwing arm. The day following his release the team started to win, and managed to finish second in the race, by a wonderful fag-end spurt.

Sheridan was shy on money, and, realizing that he had lost his arm could no longer earn any money playing ball, set about to beat his way back to his home in San Francisco. He stopped off at Nashville to see a game, and, as luck would have it, the regular umpire failed to show up. Some of the players noted Jack's presence and he was requested to work. He did so well in his initial effort that a regular position was offered him and accepted. Sheridan made his start as umpire in 1884, and is still at it, as king of them all.

Among umpires, players, and even fans, any announcement relative to Sheridan's retirement is treated as a joke. Five years ago Sheridan really did intend to get out of the game, announced his retirement, and then, for obvious reasons, failed to make good. Each year some newspaper man, more to have a little fun at Jack's expense than anything else, issues a fake announcement of Sheridan's determination to forsake the diamond for good.

At the time Sheridan really did intend to resign he was so situated that he decided he could put his ability to better advantage in another line. In all sincerity he announced his retirement, and went so far as to make a farewell speech at Detroit. In his oration he thanked the fans for the great courtesy they had always shown him, and wound up sarcastically by saying that he was sorry he couldn't accept an urgent invitation to go under the grandstand and get his block knocked off.

While many of the fans had at various times been sore at Jack over decisions that worked to the detriment of the home team, all of them regretted his determination to quit.

"Forget it and come back in the Spring!" was the almost unanimous reply to Jack's speech.

Everything moved along nicely until about the eighth inning that day, when Jack gave a close one against the home boys. There was only a mild protest from the players, but a fan in the bleachers set the crowd, players and Sheridan himself to laughing, when, in a high tenor voice that carried all over the grounds, he sang:

"We don't care if you never come back! Just take your clothes and go!"

In the Winter Sheridan is connected with an undertaking firm at San Jose, California, he and his brother-in-law being partners. One day last Summer some kind friend asked Jack why he didn't stick to undertaking the year round, to which he replied that he would only he could make more money handling "stiffs" on the diamond in the Summer.

Perhaps no umpire who ever broke into the major league let the position worry him more than Jack McCarthy, who was a member of the American League staff in 1905. Although he managed to lose something like thirty-eight pounds during the summer, McCarthy was too game to pass the job up for the simple life, and last year umpired with success in the Pacific Coast League.

In no city did McCarthy bump into more trouble than in Cleveland. The harder he tried to meet with favor in the Forest City, the more trouble he got into. McCarthy now gets lots of amusement in telling how he missed one play five times on the same man. At the time, however, the affair was anything but a joke to him.

American League umpires still relate how McCarthy, when the conductor on a train announced that Cleveland was next stop, would close his eyes tight and request the porter to inform him when the train had passed safely through the city. He just couldn't bear the sight of the old place, and insisted that his one great regret was that he couldn't hold his breath while going through the burg, so he wouldn't have to take any of the air into his lungs.

The worries of the position affected McCarthy's appetite, which of course accounts for his great loss in weight during his six month sojourn in the big league. Often his breakdown consisted of nothing but a bromo selzer, sometimes two.

Finally in mid-season he began failing so badly that it became evident to him that he would have to do something to improve his physical condition. Walking into a prominent Chicago drug store, he explained his trouble to one of the pharmacists, who recommended a remedy strongly. McCarthy agreed to take a chance on it. The medicine, it seems, was very powerful, only a very few drops to be taken in a tumblerful of water. While wrapping the bottle up the druggist explained this to McCarthy and told him to use care in taking it. McCarthy was suffering from a severe case of blues at the time, and without thinking replied: "I really don't care if it kills me."

The druggist was so taken by surprise that he feared McCarthy might possibly intend to commit suicide, and refused to sell the medicine.

It was not until Jack Sheridan, who was working with McCarthy at the time, and happened to know the druggist, swore that McCarthy had no such intention, that he was able to get the medicine.

Like the veteran Hank O'Day, Jack Sheridan in his day was once a great baseball player.

Jack, so the old-timers say, looked like the real thing in the baseball line until his arm gave way and compelled him to take up umpiring as a livelihood.

It was a mighty good thing for baseball that Sheridan had to quit playing because of a lame arm, for umpires of his ability are few and far between.

The dean of the American League staff has worked in most of the prominent organizations in the country, and is the highest salaried arbitrator in the business. Sheridan enjoys the unique distinction of having worked in nearly every big series of importance. During his entire career he has never missed a single engagement, and has never been late for a game.

That's certainly a record of which any one may well feel proud.

On the ball field, Sheridan is the master of the situation at all times, but he rules in a way that wins for him the respect of the players rather than their antagonism.

He is never looking for trouble, but always trying to avoid it.

When trouble presents itself, however, he is equal to the emergency, and always comes out on the top of the heap.

Sheridan is forty-five years of age, and has been umpiring for twenty-four years, a greater portion of that time having been spent in the major leagues.

He is the one original man left on the American League staff, and will have a berth just as long as he desires to call balls and strikes, unless he should suddenly lose his sight.

Tom Lynch, the present head of the National League, was in his day considered the greatest umpire in the business.

Writing of Lynch as he appeared on the field at Washington, the veteran Ted Sullivan, recently had this to say:

"When I was in the National League as manager of the 1888 Washington Baseball Club, a certain man entered the service of that body as an umpire. His manner, dignity and courtesy impressed every one whom he met. His personality dominated the whole field. When he made a decision there was such a positiveness about his manner that few questioned it. We never saw him around the hotels at night where the players stopped and they didn't get a glimpse of him until the next afternoon when he walked on the field to resume his work. I thought if I ever should write an article on how an umpire should deport himself during the playing season that I would set Lynch up as the model umpire for this as I knew him he certainly was."

Like all other professions umpiring has its trials and tribulations; but the life of the arbitrator also has its many bright sides. The double umpire system has greatly lightened the burden of the position, and incidentally has given much more satisfaction to the public. The support always given to the umpires in the major leagues by President Lynch and Johnson makes the judge of play feel secure in all his rulings.

Ask any umpire, however, what he likes best about his position, and without the slightest hesitation he will tell you the fat salary checks that comes to him every two weeks.

"THE UMPIRE."

By F. X. Mooney.

(With apologies to Kipling.)

A Fool there was and he thought that he,
Even as you and I,
Would really and truly like to be
Out on the field where all could see,
Calling the plays for a great big fee,
Even as you and I.

Oh, the time they waste and the strength
they waste,
And the work of their heart and hand,
They don't think of the awful life's that
led
By an umpire, though he be clothed and
fed,
They never can understand.

But he wouldn't give in, for he's made up
his mind,
So a juicy contract he quickly signed
And he soon got down to the daily grind,
His face became careworn and lined,
No cause to wonder why.

Oh, the years they waste and the tears
they waste,
And the work of their head and hand,
When they think they have called what
the fans will like,
Then find that a "ball" should have been
a strike,
'Tis hard to understand.

A smile appeared on his gloomy face,
His spirits soared like a bird,
When at last he landed a big league place,
He rendered decisions with airy grace,
Till one day they gave him an awful
chase,
For missing a play at third.

Now it isn't the shame and it isn't the
blame,
That sears like a white-hot brand,
It's coming to know all the things they
have said,
That they think you should see with the
back of your head.
Will the Fans never understand?

THE LATEST DEATH LIST.

IT INCLUDES THE NAMES OF PRESIDENT ROBISON OF THE ST. LOUIS NATIONAL LEAGUE CLUB AND PRESIDENT DOVEY OF THE BOSTON NATIONAL LEAGUE CLUB.

Since the first appearance of The National Game a year ago death has entered the ranks of the game and stricken down more than one shining mark.

Among the names added to the death list in this time are those of President Robison of the St. Louis National League Club and President Dovey of the Boston National League Club.

Adrian Joss better known to followers of the game as "Addie" Joss the great pitcher of the Cleveland American League team passed away at his home in Toledo, Ohio at 1:45 a. m. April 14, 1911.

Joss was not only a pitcher of great attainments, he was also talented along various lines. He was fast securing an enviable reputation as a writer and would have no doubt left himself a name in any line which he might have cared to enter.

He was a man of exceptionally good education and of refined tastes. A great lover of grand opera and the drama, he seldom accompanied his team-mates when attending burlesques or musical comedies.

On January 2, 1910, Samuel Wise, for years one of the greatest professionals living and who had played at short field and at second base for the Boston and other major league teams died at his home at Akron, Ohio. He had commenced his professional career with the team of that city.

On March 13, 1910 Col. John I. Rogers one of the principal owners of the Philadelphia National League Club died suddenly at Denver, Colorado.

March 14, 1910 Michall P. Hines, once famous as the catcher of the Boston National League Club died at New Bedford, Mass.

Alan T. Storke, once a member of the St. Louis and Pittsburg National League Clubs died at Newton, Mass. on March 18, 1910.

Thomas J. Loftus, well known as manager of major league clubs died at Dubuque, Ia., April 16, 1910.

Charles Esper, who pitched in his day for the Philadelphia, St. Louis and Baltimore clubs died at Philadelphia, Sept. 1, 1910.

Sept. 5, 1910 Jack Nelson, the famous old short fielder of the New York Metropolitions died in Brooklyn of heart failure.

Henry V. Lucas, president of the old Union Association died in St. Louis on Nov. 15, 1910.

MONUMENT ERECTED OVER GRAVE OF HENRY CHADWICK, "THE FATHER OF BASEBALL," IN GREENWOOD CEMETERY, BROOKLYN, NEW YORK.

IN MEMORIAM.

—

HARRY C. PULLIAM.

Monday, October 17, 1910, was the day scheduled for the playing of the first game of the "World's Series" for that year

In the Fall of 1909, the National Commission established an annual memorial as a tribute of organized baseball to the late Harry C. Pulliam, as follows:

This series is the fifth one played under the auspices of the National Commission. A year makes changes indeed. Harry C. Pulliam, one of the originators of these series, has passed away. His counsel in this body will be heard no more. Organized baseball never had a more zealous and devoted sponsor. In order, therefore, that his memory may forver remain green, it is directed by the National Commission that a memorial card be printed, and that on the day scheduled for the first game of the World's Series in each year, the same be distributed to all of the eligible players of the contesting clubs, the official umpires, scorers and business representatives, as well as to the owners of the contending clubs and the press; and that on the same day in each year there be placed on the grave of Harry C. Pulliam, at Louisville, Ky., a floral wreath, as a token of the esteem in which he was held by every one connected with organized baseball.

By order of the National Commission.

> B. B. JOHNSON.
> THOMAS J. LYNCH,
> AUG. HERRMANN, Chairman,
> JOHN E. BRUCE, Secretary.

Philadelphia, Pa., October 17, 1910.

Pulliam Memorial Cards were distributed before the initial game of the "World's Series" of 1909 and also of 1910.

LAST RESTING PLACE OF HARRY C. PULLIAM AT LOUISVILLE KY., AS IT APPEARED OCTOBER 17, 1910.

DANNY MURPHY.
The Hard Hitting Right Fielder of the World's Champion Athletics of Philadelphia in 1911.

ROBERT HOGAN.
The Pitcher of the Standards of St. Louis, When They Beat the St. Louis Browns in the Opening Game of the Season on April 2, 1882.

THE AMERICAN ASSOCIATION.

NO BASEBALL LEAGUE NOW IN EXISTENCE HAS MADE MORE RAPID STRIDES THAN THIS ONE IN THE LAST FIVE YEARS.

The American Association is fast coming to the front and will soon take rank with the two major baseball leagues, the National and the American.

The full roster of the American Association today reads as follows:

AMERICAN ASSOCIATION.

President—T. M. Chivington, 1414 Fisher Building, Chicago, Ill.

1911 season—April 12- October 1.

MINNEAPOLIS CLUB — Minneapolis, Minn.; M. E. Cantillon, President; Joseph Cantillon, Manager.

TOLEDO CLUB—Toledo, Ohio; William R. Armour, President; Harry Hinchman, Manager.

COLUMBUS CLUB—Columbus, Ohio; E. M. Schoenborn, President; William E. Friel, Manager.

ST. PAUL CLUB—St. Paul, Minn.; George E. Lennon, President; M. J. Kelley, Manager.

KANSAS CITY CLUB—Kansas City, Mo.; George Tebeau , President; Daniel Shay, Manager.

MILWAUKEE CLUB—Milwaukee, Wis.; Charles S. Havenor, President; James J. Barrett, Manager.

INDIANAPOLIS CLUB — Indianapolis Ind.; Wm. H. Watkins, President; James T. Burke, Manager.

LOUISVILLE CLUB—Louisville, Ky.; William Grayson, Jr., President; George E. Howard, Manager.

Here are a few sketches of the men at the head of the American Association.

THOMAS M. CHIVINGTON—Thomas M. Chivington, the present head of the American Association, has had but five years' actual experience in professional baseball, but he has been a student and critic of the national sport for many years as a semiprofessional player, writer and scorer. He was born in Nebraska, and on the paternal side comes from a family of ministers. He attended the public schools in his native state, and began his business career as a junior clerk in the general offices of the Burlington Railroad in Chicago, when but a boy. He developed a tendency to wander early, and in the nine years of his railroad work he covered most of the states of the central west. At one time he was commercial agent of the Cotton Belt road in Sherman, Texas, and the same year represented the Lehigh Valley road in Minneapolis and the northwest. In 1903 he gave up railroading and Colorado attracted him. There he was a deputy coroner in Denver for a time. He also tried cow punching in Southern Colorado and New Mexico. Returning to Denver he took up newspaper work with the Denver Republican and finally returned east where he continued his newspaper work with Chicago, Milwaukee and Louisville papers for some years. Incidentally he became interested in horse racing and was associate judge at Harlem, Worth and the Indiana tracks near Chicago for several seasons. It was only when the decline of horse racing began that he devoted his entire attention to newspaper work. It was when he was sporting editor of the Louisville Herald that George Tebeau, then owner of the Louisville Baseball Club, induced him to take entire charge of the property, both as to the financial and playing end.

In 1907 his team, with Dick Cooley as field leader, finished at the .500 mark. In 1908, with Jimmy Burke as team leader, he finished second, having been nosed out of the pennant the last three days of the season. In 1909, with still another captain, Heinie Peitz, he won the pennant, after one of the most remarkable races in the history of the American Association. When the time came for the election of a president for the organization for 1910, Mr. Chivington was favored by a majority of the club owners, and his successful administration of the affairs of the league brought about his unanimous re-election for 1911.

WILLIAM GRAYSON, JR.—William Grayson, Jr., president and owner of the Louisville Club of the American Association, was born in St. Louis thirty-two years ago. He was formerly with the Grayson-McLeod Lumber Company of St. Louis. Mr. Grayson, from his early youth, was a follower of the national game. When a student at the University of Michigan College at Ann Arbor, Michigan, Mr. Grayson played at shortfield for the college team and made a reputation for himself there as a fine fielder and batsman. In recent years he has been a staunch follower of the St. Louis Browns and it was while attending the games at Sportsman's Park in St. Louis, that he was offered the Louisville Club. He bought that team, lock, stock and barrel on July 15, 1909, and that year his nine won the pennant of the American Association. The following year, 1910, it finished last and Mr. Grayson says that this 1911 year, just for a change, it will finish on top again. A live, hustling young man, fond of the game and one of the real champions, Mr. Grayson is just the man to help the other American Association officials to build up that body until it stands the equal of any other baseball organization on earth.

W. R. ARMOUR—W. R. Armour, president of the Toledo Baseball Club, is one of the veterans of the national game. Mr. Armour started playing professional baseball in 1880 with Bradford, Pa., as right fielder. He was there from 1890 to 1891. He was with Toledo in 1892 in the Western League. In 1893 he was with Kansas City in the Western League. He was signed with Buffalo in 1894, but did not go out owing to a bad coasting accident. In 1895 he was with Montgomery in the Southern League. In 1896 he was with Patterson, N. J., in the Atlantic League. In 1897 he purchased an interest in the Dayton Ohio Club in the Inter State League, retiring as a player to take up the managing end of the game. He was located there for five years, winning three championships and second in five years. In 1902 he took charge of the Cleveland American League Club, finishing third and fourth in the three years that he was there. From there he went to Detroit for two years, finishing third and sixth. In the Fall of 1906 he purchased the Toledo Club and he has been there ever since. He has the most complete baseball plant of modern times.

MICHAEL E. CANTILLON—Michael E. Cantillon, president of the Minneapolis Baseball and Athletic Association, commenced his baseball career as an amateur player on the Janesville, Wis., and St. Cloud, Minn., teams. He afterwards played professional ball at Green Bay, Wis., and at Iron Mountain, Michigan.

Six years ago he purchased the Des Moines Club in the Western League, and after winning two pennants, bought the Minneapolis Club, immediately placing a first division team in that city. Last year he had one of the best balanced teams that ever represented a minor league city, winning the pennant by a large margin. In his efforts to give his patrons the best there is in baseball, he is ably assisted by his brother, Joe Cantillon, who has full management of the players of the Minneapolis Club.

EDWARD M. SCHOENBORN—Edward M. Schoenborn, president of the Columbus Club of the American Association, is one of the livest men in baseball. He was born in St. Louis, but went to Columbus eighteen years ago. He is in the wholesale and retail cigar business and has the finest retail stores in his part of the country. He conducts the cigar stands in all of the leading hotels of Columbus. Ten years ago when it was impossible to raise money enough to keep a baseball club in Columbus and when the city had been pronounced by baseball men throughout the country, a baseball graveyard, the late President Bryce appealed to Mr. Schoenborn to join with him in keeping the city on the map. Mr. Schoenborn immediately put his money into the venture and made every effort to make the game a success. He was elected secretary of the club and how well the game succeeded is a matter of history of the Columbus Club. Upon the death of Mr. Bryce, two years ago, Mr. Schoenborn was elected president and was reelected at the last annual meeting in November.

GEORGE E. LENNON—George E. Lennon, president of the St. Paul Club of the American Association, is one of the real gentlemen sportsmen of the Northwest. Mr. Lennon represents the highest and best line of the national game and is a universal favorite with his fellow members of the American Association.

Sketches of the veteran William H. Watkins, the owner of the Indianapolis Club of the American Association; of George Tebeau, president and owner of the Kansas City Club, and the wealthiest and most influential member of this association and of Charles S. Havenor, the big-hearted owner of the Milwaukee Club, will be found in another part of this book.

JACK RYAN.

HOTEL CLERK KNOWN BY EVERY PROFESSIONAL BASEBALL PLAYER AS THE GREATEST WIT AND BEST BOOSTER OF THE GAME LIVING.

Jack Ryan, of St. Louis, hotel clerk, baseball fan and story teller extraordinary, has, perhaps, the largest following among professional baseball players of any man living.

A hundred years from now when some one asks who was the most popular citizen of St. Louis at the commencement of the present century, the records will show that honor belongs to Jack Ryan, late chief clerk of the Planters' House. You often hear it said that this man and the other has more friends and is more popular than any other person.

But this sort of talk is generally haphazard and amounts to little.

In the case of Jack Ryan there are figures to prove the truth of the assertion that he is by long odds the most popular and best known man in St. Louis. These figures were obtained in a genuine contest carried by the St. Louis Republic in July, 1906. The Republic at that time inaugurated a big voting contest. Prizes were offered aggregating $26,541.10. The contest was to decide who was the most popular and best man in the State of Missouri.

It was a contest carried on openly and above board and among the contestants were many of the best known men and women in the state. Members of the clergy of the legal and other professions, mechanics and men of all sorts took part in the contest. And when the summing up came it was found that Jack Ryan had more votes than any man of them. When the vote was announced on July 15, 1906, Jack Ryan was declared the winner and the number of votes alloted him were 916,962. His nearest competitor was A. E. Bassett of Alton, who polled 512,799 votes. Ethan Harris of St. Louis, came next with 242,629 votes. Mr. Ryan won out, it will be seen, by over 400,000 votes.

Jack Ryan, to whom the title of being the most popular and best known man in St. Louis, Mo., was born in this city on June 25, 1871. His parents then resided at 2319 Division street. From that home, Jack as soon as he was able, attended St. Bridget's School and later became a scholar at the Hamilton Public School. His education there and his native wit, has made him a match for any one in his battle of life and he has been wonderfully successful in the hotel business. At 15 he commenced his career in this line at Hotel Richelieu at 13th street and Washington avenue.

In 1868 he was graduated from there to the Southern Hotel, where he became captain of the bell boys. He was promoted from there to the position of chief clerk and he made so many friends in this latter position that he received a call from the owner of the Holland House in New York. He was at the Holland for several seasons and only came back to St. Louis to return to his old place at the Southern. He was at the Southern until about a year ago when he was called to the Planters' Besides being popular and well known at home, Jack Ryan holds the esteem and friendship of nearly every professional baseball and theatrical man in America. His kindly manner, his ready wit and his good treatment of all-comers has made him the most valuable hotel clerk in America.

JOHN E. BRUCE.

LINES ABOUT THE POPULAR AND UNIVERSALLY BELOVED SECRETARY AND TREASURER OF THE NATIONAL COMMISSION SINCE ITS ORGANIZATION.

John E. Bruce,* the secretary and treasurer of the National Commission ever since its organization was born in Cleveland, Ohio., October 1, 1856. He graduated from Western Reserve College, Hudson, Ohio, now Western Reserve University, Cleveland, Ohio, in the class of 1876. Teaching for two years in the High School of Hudson, he studied law in his spare moments and in the Fall of 1878 he went to Cincinnati to finish his studies, and was admitted to the bar in the Spring of 1879. While getting a start at the law, he was the night agent of the Associated Press for five years and did educational editorial work on the Cincinnati Commercial, the latter work continuing for nearly twelve years. During the Brotherhood times he was the attorney for Messrs. Prince and Al. Johnson in the Cincinnati Club matters and through that work, as well as his newspaper connections, became intimately associated with President Johnson of the American League, who was also then on the Cincinnati Commercial. His connection thereafter with Mr. Johnson in the old Western Association, American Association and American League is well known. Mr. Bruce is a part owner and director of the St. Louis Browns.

Mr. Bruce is a member of the law firm of Bruce and Bruce, consisting of father and son. He was first Assistant United States Attorney of Southern Ohio, under both Cleveland administrations, and is connected as officer and director with several leading business corporations of Cincinnati. During the year 1910 he handled and fully accounted for as treasurer of the National Commission, the sum of $666,929.65.

FRANCIS C. RICHTER.

FOUNDER, EDITOR-IN-CHIEF, AND VICE PRESIDENT OF "THE SPORTING LIFE," THE GREAT BASEBALL PAPER OF PHILADELPHIA.
From "Sporting Life's" 25th Anniversary Number, March 14, 1908.

Editor and founder of "Sporting Life," Francis C. Richter is a Philadelphian to the manor born. Here he first saw the light of day in January, 1854; here he was reared and educated; here he served his journalistic apprenticeship, and here he has passed his whole life. In his youth he was devoted to all branches of athletic sports. His chief delight, however, was baseball, which he played for many years as an amateur. In these years he conceived a fondness amounting to a passion for baseball, which has never waned: which has, in fact, grown stronger with the passing years, finding him today absorbed in, and enthused over, the great game as in the first flush of youth. Mr. Richter's journalistic debut was made with the old "Day" in 1872, and he served that paper in all capacities from reporter to managing editor. The political upheaval inaugurated by the famous "Committee of One Hundred" ended the existence of "The Day" in 1880 and Mr. Richter then became connected with the "Sunday World." During this period Mr. Richter lent valuable assistance toward the revival of baseball in Philadelphia, which culminated in the organization of the old American Association in 1882, the admission thereto of a newly-organized Athletic Club, and the admission of the new Philadelphia Club to the old National League in 1883. The season of 1882 convinced Mr. Richter that his beloved game of baseball was due for a new lease of life and in the Spring of 1883 he started "Sporting Life" in partnership with Mr. Thomas S. Dando, who was one of the leading printers of Philadelphia, a crack amateur baseball player and pigeon shot, and a splendid all-around sportsman as well as a first-class business man. The first number of "Sporting Life" was issued on April 15, 1883, and it never missed a week from that time to the present. Moreover, from the start to the present time, Mr. Dando has been business head and Mr. Richter editor-in-chief of "Sporting Life"— a unique thing in the history of sporting journalism. The paper was a huge success from the start, has remained uninterruptedly successful for twenty-five years and is today more popular, more influential and more widely read than at any period in its long and eventful career—another unprecedented record in sporting journalism. "Sporting Life" has always been and is still, the recognized authority of baseball and its editorial opinions on all topics connected with the sport are eagerly read and received with at least respectful attention. Editor Richter's pen has unquestionably rendered great service to the national game, and has always been consistently and insistently for decency and honesty in sport. He has, moreover, been uniformly loyal to organized ball, fair to clubs and players, and impartial to a degree. His policy is tersely expressed in the motto of "Sporting Life's" editorial page—"Devoted to Baseball Men and Measures, With Malice Toward None and Charity for All." This policy, undeviatingly adhered to, has won well-deserved popularity for "Sporting Life" and its editor, and commanded the respect and support of all baseball parties and partisans.

THE CHICAGO WHITE SOX IN ROYAL GORGE ON THE DENVER AND RIO GRANDE RAILWAY, AND WHILE ON THEIR 1910 TRAINING TRIP IN CALIFORNIA.

THE FIRST MASK.

THE QUESTION AS TO JUST WHEN T CAME INTO BEING AND WHO WAS
THE FIRST TO WEAR IT IN AN ACTUAL GAME IS SOLVED BY
ONE WHO APPEARS TO KNOW WHAT HE SAYS.

BY WARREN R. BRIGGS.

"Those old-timers must have had a lot of nerve, catching without a mask. I know it's more than I'd ever care to tackle," you will often hear a fan of the present day remark. Perhaps it did require a lot of nerve for the first fellows who tried it, but I know that in my early days as a ball tosser it was considered nothing at all out of the ordinary, and it was looked on as a part of the catcher's regular curriculum that he have a broken nose or a battered countenance as a result of being in the way of a foul tip or something of the kind. Of course, it must be borne in mind that the twirlers of those days did not have the assortments of curces and benders that are served up at the present time. It was a matter of straight balls, more or less swift, and the man behind the bat had ample opportunity to judge them, and to get his face out of the way, lest he bo injured. It was the introduction of the curve ball that was responsible for the invention of the mask, an invention which has enabled the game to reach the perfection it has now attained. Picture, if you can, Ossie Schreck, trying to catch Rube Waddell; Bresnahan, Mathewson; or Sullivan, Walsh, without some protection for the face. Think of the havoc the fouled spitters and shoots would raise. Why, a catcher that lasted a week, to say nothing of a whole season, would be an oddity.

The story of the introduction of any one of the many necessary features that now go to make up the battle regalia of the ball player, is at times interesting to lovers of our national game, wherefore I offer the story of the invention of the mask, a piece of history but little known, and, which I trust, will be appreciated as an authentic addition to baseball's story.

In the year 1896, in a story in the New York Sun, Howard K. Thatcher, a practising physician of Dexter, Me., wrote as follows:

"I entered Harvard University in 1874 and in that year played on the ball team always catching. Henry Hooper, now a successful merchant of Boston, used to pitch for me, and he always delivered the ball overhand. He was very swift, and I always stood as near the bat as the catchers do now, though I had no protection for the face. I could dodge pretty well, and as curves were unknown, I could judge the ball to a nicety.

In the Winter of 1875, Ernst, a student at the university, thought he would try a new wrinkle, and started in practising the underhand throw, and discovered that the ball would curve. I had to catch for him, too, and I set about thinking how I could protect my face. I used to wear a rubber band over my mouth, but I decided that this was not enough protection for me. When we played our first game in the Spring of 1876, I put on a mask which I had made from heavy wire. The edges were wound with leather, and I had a strap on the chin and another at the forehead. My chum, Fred Thayer, helped me to make it, and I confess it was a queer-looking thing.

"It was ridiculed the first time I wore the mask, partly because it was a new thing, and partly because the people considered that a catcher did not need any protection for his face. I threw the mask away, but Thayer took it up and had it patented, but received no royalty. Dealers in baseball goods knew a good thing when they saw it, and they commenced to manufacture masks and put them on the market. Thayer promptly brought suit against them, and won every case taken into court."

About a month after this story appeared, a denial was sent in by James A. Tyng, who was at the time a resident of Bar Harbor, Me. The writer spoke as follows:

"I have just received a copy of the Sun of June 30, which contains a short account of the discovery and use of the baseball mask. Your correspondent who furnishes you with the 'facts,' is about as far from the center of truth as he is from the center of civilization. I am experiencing myself the delights of the Maine atmosphere and realize its efficacy in the promotion of health, but I never supposed it had an equally stimulating effect on the imaginative faculties, until the news, furnished by your correspondent in Dexter, Me., and printed in your truthful paper, was first called to my attention.

"I have not time to follow your correspondent through all his airy flights. Perhaps after a two months' stay in this invigorating country, I may become something of a prevaricator myself, and so before I am deflected from the path of truth I will give you an account of how the mask really and actually did come into use.

"Your correspondent is not very far off in his dates. The first public appearance of the mask was in the Spring of 1877, not 1876, as he places it.

"I was at the time a member of the Harvard nine, and Thayer, who was then captain of the nine, wanted me to fill the position of catcher. To this my family were opposed, on account of the danger, and I suggested to him the idea of having a mask made that would protect my face. He followed my suggestion and a wiremaker in Boston made me a mask, which, although heavy and clumsy, compared to the one now in use, answered the purpose for which it was intended, and this mask was worn by me in the three remaining years that I played and caught on the nine.

"Thayer took out a patent on the invention, and, I believe, made quite a large sum of money out of it. This latter statement, however, is entirely on hearsay, as neither the poor wiremaker, nor the original suggestor of the idea of such a protector for the catcher, have ever seen any of the fruits of their ingenuity."

I was much interested in these items, as I knew both of the gentlemen engaged in the controversy. From my own actual knowledge I was aware that the pair of them needed a little correction, and consequently I ventured to address a letter to the editor of the Sun, stating my opinions on the subject, and this appeared in the issue of July 7. In the letter I showed the facts as I knew them, and I believe that it would not be out of place to repeat the letter here. It ran as follows:

"In the Spring of 1875 I returned from my studies in Europe, and resumed my position as catcher for the Boston nine of Boston at that time catching Beals, Hooper and occasionally Ernst. During the early Summer of that year the Beacons played several games with the Harvards, and I heard rumors at Cambridge

of a face protector or mask that Fred Thayer captain and third baseman of the Harvard nine, was getting up, and which Thatcher, who was catching for Harvard at that time was to use. Naturally I was interested in the new-fangled protector and went to Thayer's room some time during the Summer or Fall of '75, saw a working model of the device, and, if I remembered rightly, made some suggestions concerning it. Soon after this, either in the Fall of 1875 or in the Spring of 1876, I procured one of these masks, of whom I cannot remember, but I think through Thayer, and used it a little during the early games of 1876. I left Boston on the 5th of July, 1876, and came to this city, where I have resided ever since. I brought with me at that time the mask to which I have referred, and have it in my possession today, a relic of the past and, I believe, one of the first things of its kind ever used. Later I saw Tyng using the same thing, but as I left Boston a year before the date he mentions, and as I saw a model of the device some months before in Thayer's room, I do not think there can be any doubt about the accuracy of my statements.

I had always supposed that the invention was wholly Thayers and am still inclined to believe he should have all the credit of it. Be this as it may I know I had and used a mask, that is now in my possession, in Boston in the Spring of 1876."

This letter was written some thirteen years ago, and the old "face-cage" alluded to, is still at hand looking just the same as ever. It is in a very good state of preservation, in fact, it could if it were necessary be used in a game at the present time. This old relic, while it would look very peculiar if placed side by side with one of the perfect protective devices that the backstops use these days, was none the less a complete protection and fully answered all the necessary requirements.

As regards who wore the first mask Thatcher or Tyng, there may be some doubt, though I believe that the evidence is all in favor of the former. There is one thing that cannot be questioned—the first mask was the invention of the captain of the Harvard team of 1875—Fred Thayer.

THE NATIONAL GAME.

PROFESSIONALS WHO HAVE RISEN IN LIFE.

BASEBALL PLAYERS WHO HAVE BECOME GREAT AND FAMOUS IN MANY OTHER LINES AND CUT A PROMINENT FIGURE IN THE BUSINESS AND POLITICAL WORLD.

GOV. JOHN K. TENER.
New Chief Executive of Pennsylvania But Once The Crack Pitcher of The Chicago White Stockings.

From certain quarters at a certain time, there came repeated sneers at the candidacy of A. G. Spalding for the United States Senatorship on the ground that he was "only a baseball player;" that a ball player could not possibly contain senatorial timber; that a man who was interested in many athletic sports could not be interested in government, etc., etc., ad nauseam.

It happens to be a fact of baseball history that when Abraham Lincoln was notified of his nomination to be the Republican candidate for President of the United States the committee appointed by the Chicago Convention to convey the news to him at Springfield, found him on a big suburban lot of that city in his shirt sleeves bat in hand, engaged in a game of baseball; and the authentic story of that incident adds that Mr. Lincoln, intensely interested in the matter at hand, sent word to the committee, awaiting him at the hotel that he would join them as soon as he had made just one more hit.

And so I might go on forever proving that out of the ranks of the men who played the national game have come heroes who have shone in other directions and who gained their first lessons in the art of shining out on the green sward and under the summer sun.

Many men, in fact, who played baseball on the professional and semi-professional baseball teams in the olden days have become eminent in public life.

At his home town of Dalton, Mass., United States Senator W. Murray Crane manages a team of paid ball players as his ideal form of recreation.

Whenever he feels inclined—which is quite frequently, by the way—he orders up a game of baseball almost as one would call for a siphon of vichy.

Mr. Justice William H. Moody of the United States Supreme Court an ex-president of the New England League, has lavished both time and money on the team in his home city of Haverhill, Mass.

Senator Morgan G. Bulkeley of Connecticut was responsible for the existence of the famous old Hartford professional team, which was the successor of the old-time Mansfields of Middletown, Ohio., a semi-professional organization founded by Benjamin Douglas, son of a former governor of the Nutmeg State.

Those who have long memories recall the time when Charles F. Murphy, Tammany chief since 1902, was an exponent of the semi-professional phase of the game, with a strong tendency to lapse into a full-fledged salaried player.

Ex-Mayor Thompson of Detroit was president of a National League club.

The late Senator Arthur Pue Gorman of Maryland, who served as Senate page for fourteen years, between the ages of 13 and 27, was a salaried member of the old Olympics of Washington until he became a revenue collector of the Fifth District of Maryland in 1866.

Harold McClure, who caught for John M. Ward in the 70s, is now a district judge.

Addison Gumbert, a member of the Chicago team when John K. Tener belonged to that organization, was elected sheriff of Allegheny County, Pa., and is slated for higher preferment.

Harry M. Taylor, district judge on the Western Circuit of New York State, played first base in the Louisville and Baltimore clubs. He is a trustee of Cornell University.

William J. Mills, the new governor of New Mexico, played semi-professional ball with the Norwich (Conn.) club, organized in 1866 to compete with the famous Charter Oaks of Hartford, who had not lost a game during the season. Mills, then a lad of 17, and still another pioneer with a curve of his own devising, pitched a game the Charter Oaks could not bat, and the victory went to the Norwich team. Instead of entering the professional ranks, Mills went back to Yale. When he was practicing law in New Haven he was elected to the lower house of the Connecticut Legislature and later to the State Senate. In 1898 he became chief justice of the Supreme Court of New Mexico and governor this year.

John M. Ward, once famous as captain and manager of the New York Giants, is now a prominent attorney, with offices in that city.

Supreme Court Judge, Shepard A. Barclay of Missouri, in the early days of baseball in St. Louis, was one of the greatest pitchers the game could boast of.

John K. Tener, now Governor of Pennsylvania, was one of the pitchers of the Chicago Club in 1888, and he made the world's tour with that team that year at the same time officiating as treasurer of the organization. Mr. Tener is now the Republican Governor of Pennsylvania. In fact, Mr. Tener has climbed higher than any other baseball player.

Mr. Tener was the greatest ball player longitudinally, in the history of the game. He is even taller than Larry McLean now of Cincinnati.

The Gigantic Tener joined Anson's team late in 1888, and at once showed considerable class as a hurler. In 1889 he pitched finely, batted .275, and played first base in the final games of the season, after Anson had been disabled by a collision with "Pop" Schriver.

Next season found Tener with the Pittsburg Brotherhood team.

By this time he had grown interested in business life and politics. He reluctantly gave up the game and set out to elevate himself via Charleroi, Pa. How well he has succeeded, the vote of Pennslyvania in 1910 eloquently tells. Mr. Tener is one of the biggest Elks in the country and of recent years, has been a congressman. Elking and Congressing, however, never took away his love for baseball, and he has played a great number of games each season, his good right arm seeming to have lost but little of its skill. Who will be the first big league player to occupy the presidential chair? Mr. Tener has shown that a ball player can become a governor; what ambitious pitcher, catcher or shortstop will climb still higher in the future?

Although Capt. "Pop" Anson claims to have been the discoverer of the clever Tener, it is probable that that once great player would not have long remained undiscovered. Happening in Pittsburg one afternoon with time on his hands, the giant Chicago player went out to the ball grounds to see a game between two amateur teams. He had scarcely taken his seat when his attention was captured by the extraordinary performance of the man who was pitching. Experienced as he was in such matters, it was a revelation to him.

The pitcher, was young and of unusual stature—taller even than Captain Anson, who measures 6 feet 2 in his stocking feet—and his muscular development was proportionately beyond the average. He stood straight as an Indian and quite as motionless while the ball was out of his hands. The moment he came into possession of it, however, he underwent a remarkable transformation and became a marvel of activity. Raising his long arms high above his head, he executed a series of movements that would have qualified him for a master in calisthenics, and when finally he let go of the sphere it spread through the air with a curve that was easily perceptible, an arc that made it almost impossible to interrupt it with the bat.

After the game the captain made himself known to the young man and proceeded to catechise him.

"Who are you?" he asked as a starter.

"John K. Tener," was the reply, given with manifest diffidence.

"Ever play with a professional team?"

"Not regularly."

"Where did you get on to that curve?"

"Invented it."

Further investigation brought out the fact that Tener was a bookkeeper in a steel concern, and a very good one.

He was in receipt of a fair salary and seemed to be satisfied with his prospects.

"No man who can negotiate that twirl need sit on a high stool and make figures for a living," observed the captain sagely, after he had learned all this.

Tener admitted laughingly that he had dreamed of softer snaps, but was satisfied on the whole with what he had in hand.

"I want you on my team," said "Pop" in his best business manner. "I'll give you——" then he put his mouth close to the young fellow's ear and whispered.

Within a week John K. Tener was enrolled as a member of the Chicago team, and his highly specialized curves were soon making records for that company of giants, both in a physical and a baseball sense.

Soon after Tener signed with Capt. Anson, the round-the-world tour was organized and on account of his knowledge of bookkeeping the new man was made secretary and treasurer of the expedition. In those early days he was a sedate and rather dignified young man, with a tendency to self-improvement and a distaste for all forms of amusements that were merely trivial.

Apropos of Capt. Anson's "discoveries," several of whom became eminent in public life after retiring from the diamond, it may be added that "Pop" himself, who was once a public man, politically, was a "discovery."

His discoverer was Albert G. Spalding, and it was due to the latter's prompt recognition of the captain's baseball ability that the big Iowan made his professional debut with the Forest Citys of Rockfort. Spalding—who had been playing professional ball for a year or so—went with the Rockford team to play a series of match games with the amateur club of Marshalltown, Ia., and it was then that these two men so long associated in the game first met.

At that meeting Spalding—then a lad of 18 or thereabouts—was so impressed by the other boy's clever batting and general efficiency that he advised the Rockford management to secure him. When Anson went into the Rockford Club Spalding had gone to Boston, but they were brought together again five years later in Chicago. Anson, too, on his retirement from baseball, went into politics and was elected and served a term as city clerk of Chicago.

And the gospel, too, has drawn occasionally on the ranks of the national game for men to fight its battles.

Take William A. Sunday for example. He was once the speediest player on the old Chicago White Stockings. And from that position he was transformed into a powerful expounder of the Gospel, and he is now known all over the land as an evangelist of remarkable ability, He was "discovered" by the merest accident. At a fireman's tournament held at Ames, Ia., Capt. Adrian C. Anson, then in the full flower of his glory as manager of Chicago's pennant-snatching team, happened to be present as an invited guest, and he was so impressed by the speed shown by Sunday on that occasion that he sent for him and interrogated him as follows:

"Haven't I seen you somewhere before today?"

"I used to drive the undertaker's wagon in Marshalltown," Sunday admitted.

"When you were visiting your father last Summer you might have seen me."

"If I did I guess I didn't see you making any great speed," the captain remarked, dryly.

"Probably not, under the circumstances," Sunday agreed soberly.

"How would you like to come to Chicago and play ball on my team?" Anson asked bluntly.

"I won't play ball on Sunday for any man," Sunday declared stoutly.

Before they parted it was arranged that Sunday should go to Chicago and have a try-out. The first thirteen times he went to the bat after he began playing with the Chicagoes he was struck out, but Anson was confident he would make a star player, and he hung on to him. Afterward Sunday became the fastest man on his feet in the profession.

When Sunday's bona fide call came, he dropped his bat and took his place with all the dignity and ease of a born theologian. He does not, like Dr. Bustard claim to have been called to two professions, but is inclined to regard his experience in the professional baseball ranks as a valuable preparation for his work as an evangelist—an opportunity to acquire firmness of character and a deep insight into men and their motives.

W. W. Bustard, in the late '90s, was one of the star pitchers of the Boston National League team. From the stump to the pulpit is not an appalling leap, far less sensational in its nature than a jump from the professional ranks of baseball into the ministry. At least two professional players have made the latter plunge and both of them have come as far to the front in the novel experiment as ever they stood in the old ranks. One of them is Rev. Dr. W. W. Bustard, a dozen years ago a star pitcher on the Boston National team, and today the pastor of the Euclid Avenue Baptist Church in

which John D. Rockefeller worships when he is at his Cleveland home.

"I have been called twice," Dr. Bustard declares, with a humorous twinkle in his keen eyes. "First I had a distinct call to become a ball player—a pitcher. It was too insistent to be disregarded and I responded to it. I became a pitcher, a good one, I think. Any man who can pitch a one-hit game may call himself a good player if he wishes, and that is what I did with the Bostons. Then the call to preach the Gospel came, and it was as imperative as the other had been—perhaps more so. I responded to that—I should have been a coward if I hadn't.

"To score you must be ready to take chances. I've seen players who could get to first, steal second and third and then stick. They seemed wedded to third. They couldn't score without being forced in. They weren't ready to grasp the opportunity."

That was not the sort of player Dr. Bustard was. When his opportunity came he seized it with both hands, and he has scored.

St. Louis has one notable addition to the list of baseball men who have risen to high rank in life. This addition is the Hon. John Thomas Hunt, who represented the Eleventh Missouri District, St. Louis City, in Congress for two years. Mr. Hunt managed and helped build up amateur baseball teams in St. Louis in the early days of the game here. In the eighties he commenced umpiring both amateur and professional games and he had the reputation of being the best man in the position in these parts. He was so successful indeed that he won hundreds of friends, who to reward him for his honest work on the ball field and in his business life returned him twice to Congress from one of the most important districts in the country. In Congress Mr. Hunt became famous as the best champion labor had ever had in the House of Representatives. It was he, in fact, that forced the passage of the only labor bill that ever got through both houses. Mr. Hunt was born in St. Louis in 1860 and was educated in the public schools of this city. He is a stone cutter by trade and has been in charge of building of some of the finest church edifices in St. Louis. He is now at work superintending the building of the Jefferson Memorial Building in Forest Park. As an umpire he became known as "Honest John" Hunt and that name has clung to him through life.

JUDGE JAS. J. SPAULDING.
Captain of the Old Empires of St. Louis in the Sixties.

THE NATIONAL GAME.

HOW TO PLAY BASEBALL.

NO ONE HAS TOLD THE STORY OF HOW TO DO THAT BETTER THAN TIM MURNANE, WHO HAD THE AID OF MANY GREAT PROFESSIONALS IN ANSWERING THE QUESTION.

TIM MURNANE.

No one has told the story of "How To Play Baseball" better than Tim Murnane, the veteran baseball editor of the Boston Globe.

In a book bearing that title which was published several years ago by the American Sports Publishing Company and which was edited by Mr. Murnane, he solved the proposition in such a clear way that I take pleasure in republishing the lines in this book just as Mr. Murnane gave them years ago.

INTRODUCTION—BY T. H. MURNANE.

To teach the youth how to play our national game of baseball is the object of this book.

The amateur player will find much to interest him, and even the leading professionals can pick up valuable points by perusing the instructions offered by the genuine stars of the game.

There has been no effort to pad the advice given, but every line is full of meat for the ball player who is anxious to become proficient in some one of the nine positions on a team, as well as to hit the ball and run the bases, perchance later on become a member of some champion aggregation which has pulled off the honors by heady work and team play.

It would be a rare thing to find an American youth past the age of ten who is not familiar with the simple rules of the game, and therefore the idea will be to teach those who are posted on the rules and have more or less faced the music in some sort of game.

HOW TO BECOME A GOOD CATCHER. BY WILLIAM SULLIVAN.

Parrying the question as to what is the first attribute of a good catcher, I would say that he must first be able to catch and throw. But that is only the mechanical basis for work in a position which many spectators think is largely a mechanical one, a sinecure because of the chest protector, mask and large padded mit. Yet more signs and signals are used or understood by the catcher on a baseball team than by all the other members of the team combined.

This statement is true, not because the position is more scientific, but because it is essential that the intended moves of the pitcher or the intended throws to bases be kept a secret from the opposition as far as possible. Every throw of the pitcher to the batsman is prefaced by a signal from the catcher telling what kind of a ball to send, except in a few cases where the pitchers give their own signals. Every throw to the bases in an attempt to catch the runner napping is called for by a sign from the baseman to the catcher. Only when a runner tries to steal is no sign given, and then all are watching the play and know what is expected.

Thus the catcher has to watch the pitcher and the baseman in addition to the purely mechanical work of his position. This is to say nothing of the value of old and experienced men in steadying young pitchers and in indicating to them what balls to try on batsmen with whose weakness they are familiar. Headwork and coolness count as much behind the bat as anywhere except in the pitchers' box.

My method of steadying a pitcher is to first try to slow him up and let him get his bearings again. Walk down with the ball and hand it to him, say something encouraging or offer advice if he seems to need any. Stop to fasten your chest protector, adjust your mask, or tie your shoe, anything to gain time if the situation is critical and the pitcher's wildness only temporary. If the pitcher, however, shows a continued tendency to throw the ball a little wide of the plate move to the other side, and in aiming for you he will send the ball over the pan. Often these things will help out not a little.

In signaling with my pitchers I usually give the signals, although often the pitcher with two strikes on the batsman will want to try a certain ball or has an idea on the subject. But after working several games with the same pitcher you know pretty well what he prefers to offer, and there is seldom a change of signals. With Griffith I never use signals at all, except when men are on bases. He does not use extreme speed and has such excellent control it is easy to catch him. On the third strike I like to know where the ball is coming to avoid a passed ball, and of course with men on bases I must know so as to be ready for a throw on an attempted steal.

It is when men are on bases that the pitcher and catcher are put to the severest strain. The pitcher is offering the very best ball in his category, and the catcher is at high tension to prevent stolen bases. Often a pitcher with a slow delivery will handicap his catcher into wild throws, but on the White Stockings none of the pitchers are bad in that respect. With men on base you must set yourself for a throw on every ball pitched, for the base runner may attempt to steal at any time. If the runner is on first and likely to steal second, or the shortstop or second basemen signal for a throw to the middle bag to catch a runner napping, instinctively you pull back the right foot as the ball is on its way. Thus you are poised for the throw and the ball strikes your mitt and is away again without any loss of time. If the throw is to third the left foot comes back so you can throw past the batsman. Few people have any idea how a clever batsman can hamper a catcher who is forced to get his throws away with a quick snap. I formerly played shortstop and can throw much better from second to the plate than from the plate to second.

Many spectators wonder why, with men on bases, the pitcher does not put the first ball over the plate and trust to luck in forcing the man out at second. Often this is due to the catcher. Sometimes when I am sure of my pitcher, and know he has control, I signal him to waste the first two balls in an attempt to coax the man on first base to try to steal second. Then with the ball coming where the batsman cannot well hit it, I am ready for the throw. Signals from the basemen to the catcher for throws to the bag do not catch a runner very often, but they are worth trying, and moreover hold the runner closer to the bag and are invaluable for that reason, because a fraction of a second often determines the difference between a put-out and safety to the runner. The catcher and baseman must work together and a catcher will not throw without a signal.

The pitcher usually determines for himself when to throw the ball to base to catch a runner, and when to deliver it to the plate. Some catchers signal on these occasions, but I have tried it and found that it is likely to cause confusion. So many different players are concerned that one may be off balance or out of his position when the ball is delivered or hit in his direction.

Manager Frank Selee was accustomed to call his players together to discuss any such play or if a new one is presented he calls for the opinion of his men as to how the play should be met. Thus there is an exchange of ideas, and without signals they know just what each man is expected to do if such a condition arises again. I think it a good idea. Such knowledge is almost as valuable to a catcher as to the other players, for there is no telling when he will be brought into the play by some one's dash for the plate.

There is much to be said in throwing to bases. Of course the throws should be low to enable the basemen to tag the runner without changing his position, but the catcher throws in such a hurry that he is satisfied to get the ball to the baseman any old way, so it is on time. Naturally his speed in throwing it and the manner in which it goes to the baseman determines the difference between a good and a poor catcher. But all these latter considerations revert to the original proposition that a catcher must be able to catch and throw. Then comes the science of the game.

HOW TO BECOME A GOOD PITCHER. BY CY YOUNG.

"Command of the ball is the first essential to success in pitching. A good, fast, overhand ball, kept high, is the one I depend on mostly when anxious to get an out.

"I take the ball with the two forefingers and thumb for all styles of work, as it gives me the best control.

"Straight balls over the corners will often proves more effective than the widest curves. This style is of little use, however, unless the umpire is a good judge of corner work.

"When in good shape I use a jump ball considerably. It comes with extra speed and if worked well into the batsman is perhaps the most difficult ball to hit safe.

"The ball should be kept high when the batsman is out for a sacrifice, and a clever slow ball with a change of pace is very effective when you want to see the batsman send up a weak fly. The underhand ball with a raise I use but very little, as it has a tendency to lame the arm and must be curved as well as raised to be effective.

"Many pitchers are effective until men get on bases, when they must shorten their swing. Therefore, a pitcher should have two distinct movements. In his preliminary swing, holding men close to the bases is one of the important features of the game.

"A pitcher should throw seldom to the bases unless with a fair chance of getting the man. Too much throwing will affect his command over the ball and lose the lines he has on the man at the bat.

"There is a vast difference in pitching to right and left handed batsmen, and I think the left hander the more annoying for a right hand pitcher. I work a left hand man with close curves about waist high, with a curve on the out corner of the plate. As most of the left handers are "choppers," they are ever ready for speed, and bothered more with curves and a change of pace.

"It is a very good plan to keep your batter in the hole, or at least not get where you must put every ball over the plate.

"In the every day run of games, it is not a bad idea to remember that seven other men are behind you on the field, ready to handle the ball if it comes their way, and with plenty of room. I believe in putting the ball over the plate for hitting, trusting to the fielders, in this way saving your arm, for, after all, a pitcher amounts to but very little unless his pitching arm is strong.

"Pitchers should practice getting back into position after delivering the ball to the bat, for nothing looks worse than to see a weak grounder go bounding through the box with the pitcher out of form, after losing his balance.

"I always size up my batter and, if a new man, try first to drive him away from the plate. If he refuses to pull away, I know that I have a cool, determined batsman, and the chances are a good one. If I find a batter coming forward to meet the ball, I cut the curves and work both high and low straight balls, being careful not to line one about waist high, and yet with a batsman anchored in one position a waist ball close in is a most difficult ball to meet square.

"The preliminary swing is everything to a pitcher. By putting your shoulder and back muscles into your delivery, you will save the arm and be able to keep up

speed. A fast straight ball kept high, an out curve, a change of pace and the in-shoot are all the balls I find use for, and I would advise pitchers to get perfect control of those four styles before using any other variety, for, as I said before, control is everything.

"The successful pitcher, too, is the one who can stand a bad deal from the umpire and not grow worried, and often lose control of the ball. Try and keep a cool head for a game is never lost until the last man is out, and endeavor to keep your opponents' score down, with the hope that your own team may rally and win out after an uphill fight.

"I always start off the season with light work and get my arm into condition before taking and long chances with speed."

HOW TO PLAY FIRST BASE BY HUGH JENNINGS.

First base is one of the most difficult positions on a ball field to play properly. Catching a thrown ball while keeping one foot on the base is but the preliminary work to what is called for at the first corner.

A first baseman must have natural talent for taking all kinds of pickups. He should be a sure catch with either hand gloved or ungloved. He must not be afraid of a runner coming into the bag, and should be able to judge a high throw after a jump as well as a line one into the big mitt. I go out and meet the throw, as it often gives an out where the man would otherwise be safe. Then, too, I think it encourages the player throwing the ball.

With a base runner at first I play in the inside of the base, and when looking for a bunt or sacrifice move in with the pitch. With men at first and second play well back of the base for a fast ground hit but keep in touch with the catcher, who can often see a man taking long chances away from the base. Throws from the catcher must be tipped out ahead and the play made very fast, the baseman taking the ball on the run and blocking off the runner.

I believe in giving the runner a clean path to get back to the base, but am not particular about playing the ball easy on the man. As everything must be done quickly, basemen are likely to be considered rough.

It requires a heap of practice to take the ball on the swing and put it on the runner. I do not believe in the pitcher throwing continually to first, as he is more apt to get his man by picking the time and doing his work well.

When scores are close a first baseman must often take long chances, and with a clever man in the box clever plays are pulled off. Heading men off at second and third on clever bunts is impossible, but when the balls are hit lightly or at times freely the first baseman can take the ball on the move-in and by accurate throwing get his man at second.

After taking a throw the baseman should get into a throwing position at once, as a second lost may give a clever base runner a big lead for another base where the score is close and the player taking desperate chances.

The first baseman should go for every fly ball within reach to the left of the second baseman's territory, especially the balls going up between the pitcher and himself.

Keeping the foot against the base and judging to a nicety how far you can reach requires long practice. A player should never make the mistake of remaining on the base on a throw too wide to handle; rather take a chance and go after the ball and find the base later. The runner coming for the ball will often decide what chances you are to take.

When balls are thrown low try and block the ball at least. For this reason it is well to practice making your long break pickups well in front, so that you may block the ball, even if you fail to get it into your hands.

A first baseman should be a good fielder of ground balls, and with the bases clear should depend on the pitcher covering the base on every ball hit to his left.

I play well back of the line and go for every grounder that goes to my left, as well as those to my right, when I think they are out of the second baseman's reach. With a ground-covering second baseman it's a sharp drive that can get through when the first baseman plays well back and capable of making all his plays on the run. It is well to toss the ball to the base well ahead of the pitcher, so that he can take it crossing the base. A ball tossed is much easier to handle than a ball thrown.

A baseman should have absolute confidence in the pitcher covering the base, even when the ball is hit slowly out of his reach. The play at all times is for the first baseman to get the ground balls depending on the pitcher to cover the base.

HOW TO PLAY SECOND BASE BY NAPOLEON LAJOIE.

Unless able to cover a lot of ground and take balls on either side, under full head way, a player should never try to become a second baseman.

Men with long arms make the best second basemen, as they are often able to make stops without slacking their speed and toss the ball to a base for an out.

I play a deep field and change my distance from the base according to the style of pitching I am backing up. If a weak fielding pitcher, who will allow medium hit balls to go through the box I play closer to second. Then again you must size up the man at the bat and know the style of ball the pitcher is to feed him. It is always best to go in and meet the ball and smother it if you find it coming with a shoot. I never make up my mind how to take the ball until it is very close, for it may take a jump if you set yourself for the regulation bound.

It pays to keep on your feet, although at times the spectators have an idea that the man rolling about in the dust is doing the most effective work.

I always have a perfect understanding with the shortstop and catcher, as to who will cover the base, and play a bit closer when out for a double play. It is not a bad idea to take your cue from the second baseman after he sends you a ball for a force-out. If there is no chance for a double you should hold the ball A tip to let the ball go will help, as you feel there is a good chance to get the man. In turning to throw, step in front of the base and throw regardless of the man coming down, as he will generally look out for himself, and is not anxious to get hit with the ball.

A second baseman should go for short flies, and depend on the outfielders for the coaching, as they are in a better position to judge the ball.

The second baseman should go in for the short throw with the catcher sending the ball down for a man and a runner at third. This play requires practice and a good throwing catcher. When running down a man between bases go after him on the jump, and get him under full headway before throwing the ball.

I instinctively start for the second base as soon as I see the ball is hit to the right of me. It pays to be at the bag in

time to help the throw from short or third, for a fraction of a second will lose a double play, and nothing is more effective than a fast double play on a ground hit. When taking throws from the catcher to get a base-runner coming from first, stand to the left of the base if the throw will allow, as nine out of ten runners will try to go back of the base. Fall back with the ball, as the runner often do phenomenal stunts in getting away from being touched.

Underhand throwing is very essential, as you have many short throws to make and no time to straighten up for a full swing.

Second base gives a player an opportunity to show up better than any other position, as it is truly styled "the key to the infield," and I believe a player will last longer in the game in this position than any other, if he is a natural and not a made ball player.

All the fine team plays of the game are made by first signaling. With a man at third and second, the latter will usually take big ground, especially when his run would win a game. A throw from the catcher could generally be a cue for a clever base-runner to go on to third, but in this case he is blocked off by another runner, so that his chances are all in returning to the base. I see the opportunity and tip the catcher to throw the next ball straight to the bag and as soon as the ball is sent in by the pitcher I am on my way to the base to head off the runner. Finding that he is cut off the runner will start for third base and I have no trouble in getting the man nearest home. The pitcher must be in on the play, and keep the ball wide of the batsman.

HOW TO PLAY THIRD BASE BY JAMES COLLINS.

First of all a third baseman must be a good thrower. Next he must have the knack of taking a ball between bounds and thirdly he must be ever on the alert and fearless, for no man has the hot shot to handle as the third baseman.

A clever batsman that can bunt and hit out will keep you guessing at third base. I play quite deep on all and come with the pitch, if I see any signs of bunting, unless I have been tipped off by the catcher to keep back for a hard drive.

I always cross in front of the shortstop for the slow grounders as I can get to them first. I usually take a wide ball with one hand, as it gives a better chance to get into position to throw.

A player should have his mind made up before the ball is pitched as to which base he will throw to. In fact, a player should never take his mind off the game.

Slow grounders to my right I take with one hand and throw first without getting into position, as deliberate work will lose the man.

Trapping the ball is the most scientific department of base ball, and no player has more difficult work in this line than the third baseman. A very slow runner will sometimes allow you to play an ugly grounder on a long bound, taking chances that it jumps and gets by. The best way to play all kinds of ground balls is to be on the move and trap them just as the ball is about to come from the ground, being well over the ball, with the side of the hands close together in a such a

position that the ball will have no chance to come up and can be scooped, when not held, the first time.

I believe in giving the runner a fair show to reach third and never block a player off, unless I have the ball. I never force a runner outside his proper latitude, as there is great danger of injuring a base-runner making close connections for home. I think a player will last longer and be of more value to his club who plays the game without an idea of putting his fellow player out of business. This has been my rule and I have yet to find a player attempting to do me an injury. A player's reputation counts, and a player injured is an expensive adjunct to a ball team.

Base-runners come into third feet first, head first and throwing twisters, as it is usually a close call and players seldom attempt to steal runs unless runs are scarce and desperate chances are called for. Mindful of this a baseman is often apt to drop a finely thrown ball. I should say, first to be sure of the ball and be careful to hold it after colliding with the runner.

With a chance for a force-out at second the ball should be thrown for the bag at a medium pace, trusting the second baseman to get there. When trying for a double play with a fast man at the bat it is well to put extra steam on the throw to second.

I want to know the kind of ball the pitcher is about to deliver; that is, whether a curve or a straight ball, as it improves one's ground covering at least twenty-five per cent.

Third basemen should be about as careful as the pitchers in starting out in the spring, for a lame arm is a hard thing to get rid of and without the arm in the pink of condition a third baseman will carry a big handicap.

HOW TO PLAY SHORTSTOP BY HERMAN LONG.

The shortstop should be a first-class thrower from long and short distances, and from most any kind of a position. I play the position very deep, well to the right for a left handed batter, figuring that the third baseman will come across for the slow grounders. I always watch closely the signs given by the pitcher and catcher, as it enables me to cover more ground. An out-curve to a right handed batter means the ball will go to the right of second base, while a straight ball is likely to come fast to short short or third base.

Taking a ball on the run near or past second base should be done with one hand, and the throw to first made carefully, as the ball will raise when thrown on the run and it is out of the question to steady yourself.

A grounder coming with extra speed should be played carefully, while a slow grounder must be handled on the run and chances taken on a pickup between bounds.

I pay little attention to keeping my heels together on a ground ball, depending wholly on my hands as the outfielders will prevent an extra base should the ball break through.

I watch the catcher for signals as to when he intends to have me cover second for a thrown ball, but one should be careful about leaving the position before the ball is on the way to the plate, in this way preventing the batsman from knowing who will leave a place open for a grounded ball.

I want the catcher to throw the ball at the base taking chances on having it taken care of by either the second baseman or shortstop.

The shortstop should always cut right for second base on every ball hit to the left of the pitcher, and should cover the base on the throwdown from the catcher with a man on first and third base, as the second baseman will be in a better position to return a short throw to the plate if the man starts for home.

Shortstops run the greatest risks of being injured by covering second base on a throw from the catcher to get a runner trying for a base. The shortstop has very little chance to block the man off and must make the play by swinging the ball low and while going back, as the runner is sure to go wide of the base. Never go after a man the second time, for the umpire is usually in sympathy with the fielder who handles the ball in good style. This is a feature of shortstop work that requires a great deal of constant practice and a heap of nerve for once a fielder is shy of the runner he will make a poor man to throw to.

A weak third baseman is a big handicap to a shortstop. I go for every fly hit to the short outfield, as you never know just how much ground you can cover when you start. The outfielders knowing that you are after everything will help you by calling out, as a shortstop cannot afford to take his eye off the ball long enough to see if another fielder is headed for the same place.

I go to meet the throw from a long hit, as time is gained by handling the ball twice when the throw is too far to line the ball home. In throwing to the plate the ball should always be sent low, as extra speed will cause it to rise; while, should the throw be short, if it is on a line, it may answer the same purpose and get the runner.

I never could get too much good lively practice in fielding, and believe in fast preliminary work by the infield before a game and a chance to measure the distance to first by a throw when there is time as the game proceeds.

A shortstop must practice underhand throwing, as no other position is called on for the variety of throwing as is the shortstop. My advice is practice, practice, practice.

HOW TO PLAY THE INFIELD BY CHARLES A. COMISKEY.

Only players with a natural aptitude for baseball can become successful infielders. A good mechanical player, who can hit at a fair clip, may make good and hold a position in the outfield, but when he comes into the diamond he must be a quick thinker, a fast fielder and a natural player as well.

I wonder how many baseball fans have thought of the build of these infielders and the part that plays in determining a man's qualification for a certain position. For instance, the first baseman must be a tall, rangy fellow, who can cover ground. but more especially one who has a reach to catch throws a trifle wild. Then again height and reach are valuable in stepping forward to meet thrown balls Many a first baseman who understands his position robs batsmen of hits merely by stretching out and meeting the ball. In the course of a season this one or two feet advantage will mean a score or more less base hits. Now the second baseman and shortstop, on the other hand, the latter especially, should be short, chunky men, something of the dachshund order, for they have to gather the ball in from all positions while on the go, so the lower they are to the ground the better. Most of the great third basemen are small men or men of medium height, but it is not so essential there.

In playing the bags many managers have different ideas, but I have my own, and in regard to first base, the position I played on the old St. Louis team my opinions are set. I am a great believer in playing deep and depending on the pitcher to cover the bag in many instances. I always played my position ten or fifteen feet deeper than the other first basemen, and the pitchers had to get over to cover the bag. They could not be sluggish and try to show me up. If I saw the pitcher was loafing on me I fielded the ball and then threw to first whether anyone was there or not Then the crowd saw who was to blame, and pretty soon the pitchers got in the habit of running over rapidly rather than be roasted. But generally a baseman has no trouble, for when a pitcher sees his first baseman cutting off hits into right field, he is glad to do his part. Often I have worked plays where the second baseman ran over to receive my put out At the same time I always played the foul line safe, for a hit along the foul lines is the most damaging of any. It is nearly always good for two bases, and often for three, for the fielders are away off and have a long run to field the ball. The same principle holds good at third. As a general rule, I would say the first baseman should field the ball whenever possible and leave his pitcher to cover first.

The same idea of playing deep I would apply to second and short, as it gives better opportunity to cover ground and it is much easier to run in on a slow ball than to run out on a short fly. I also favor playing the shortstop and second baseman pretty wide of second base to allow the first and third basemen to watch the foul lines. Any ball the pitcher cannot stop is pretty likely to clip through to center anyway. The third baseman need hardly play as deep as the first baseman, because his is a long throw to first and there is always the danger of bunts. So much for the fielding of the positions.

Then comes in the science of team play—what man shall cover second, and whether to play for the batter or baserunner. No set rule can be laid for much of this, and it is here the instinct of a ball player shows itself and the difference between good and bad players is shown. My general rule is to play for the batter unless the score is very close. In other words, do not try so much to recover from harm already done as to prevent more harm. So unless the score is very close and it is near the end of a game, I never pull in my infielders for a possible play at

the plate, but rather play for the base runner. The same applies on a single to the outfield. Forward the ball to second, and keep the runner at first rather than try for a doubtful out at the plate. Of course, situations alter any such rule, and circumstances may force an infield play close in, although the batter's chances of cutting it through are greater. Whether the shortstop or second baseman shall cover second is a question determined by team signals and is frequently changed. Often an opposing base runner will make a bluff to steal second, so his batter may see which man is slated to cover the bag. The batter then tries to cut the ball through the prospective opening. This is part of the science of the game.

With one man on base, the play on a ball hit to second or short is naturally to second base, with a chance for a double play. But on balls hit to third, or first, the play is generally to first. With a man on first and third, unless the hit be very short, the play is to first or second, allowing the runner to score, for the chances are he has a good lead and cannot be caught anyway.

With two out the play is always for the batsmen, except in the case of an easy force-out, for any run crossing the plate on third out does not count.

I am a great believer in a safe ball but at that it is the knowledge when to make a daring play or turn a clever trick that makes the great ball players and the winning teams, and I think our old St. Louis Browns knew about as well as anybody. Of course, having been a first baseman I'm a crank on the subject of first base play. When I began it was the jumping-off place. It was from first base to the bench, but I regard it as one of the most important positions, and I always want a good first baseman on my team.

HOW TO PLAY THE OUTFIELD BY FRED CLARKE.

I stand perfectly natural, ready to go in any direction, with my spikes having a good hold, for the least slip or late start will often make a difference of from one foot to two yards, and a ball can be lost on a loss of two inches. Therefore I say there is everything in a quick and a sure start, when the ball is hit.

Then, too, every outfielder should be ready to back up, the center fielder having more than the others in that line, as he is called on to back up both the left and right fielders as well as the balls that come out from the catcher's wild throwing to second. By keeping track of the batsman you can tell pretty well how to play. Some are short hitters, while others are both long and short hitters. In the latter case I play deep for the man, unless the score is close and there is a man on second who may try to score; then I come in close, with the idea of throwing to the plate if the ball is a grounder.

When throwing, always keep the ball low, and to the home plate a good fast bound is often the best way, as the chances are that it will not go over the catcher's head, as a fast line ball sent high is likely to rise.

It is well to get the ball away from the outfield as soon as possible, as clever base runners will get a good start on a low return of the ball, and finding himself

hurried and surprised the fielder is more apt to throw wild.

Outfielders should practice handling grounders in the outfield. Infield practice is beneficial for this work. I prefer to go in to meet the ball and smother it rather than play it sure, as outfields are usually rough and the ball may take unlooked-for bounds and get by, when every one on the bases will have a free run home. Often the outfielder is blamed where he is not at fault, as the grounds make the trouble.

A line drive to the left field will raise, and must be watched carefully. Balls that drop grow heavy and when taken on the dead run well in front a fielder must not be too particular about keeping his feet.

An outfielder should hold any ball that he can get his hands on. When very low he must take chances of soiling his uniform; when high he should give with the ball, and when over the head take them in the most natural way; but keep your eye on the ball, the exception being a tremendous drive far over your head, when better time can be made by turning around and going down the field after timing the direction of the ball, and when well under the spot you look for it to drop turn and take the ball. This kind of work can be satisfactorily accomplished by long practice and then only a natural ball player can expect to become the real thing.

I usually play my man without regard to the signals of the pitcher, unless where I am tipped off that a slow ball is to be sent in, when I fall back and go closer to the foul line where the ball ground will allow.

Balls to the left and right fields are likely to curve more than to center. A good fielder can, with a little practice, play one about as well as the other. The left and center fielders have more throws to make to the home plate and should therefore be good hard throwers, who can get the ball in play on the run.

I am one who fully believes in getting the arm in good shape in the spring before taking any chances with long distance throwing. It is well to practice the different distances from the outfield to the bases, for you will often be hurried and must take a chance without being too particular.

After you once start, never let up, for you never can quite tell how much ground you can cover for a ball, especially a weak fly out of reach of the infield. Once sure of the ball, call out you have it, and the first man that calls give him the right of way. He knowing that he has a clear field will hustle to the last without fear of a collision. It is just as much of a trick to play the outfield as any other position.

HOW TO SCORE A GAME BY T. H. MURNANE.

Give the batsman the benefit of all doubts, for a slow bounding ball is the most difficult to handle.

A scorer should never take his eyes off a play, and when in doubt as to who handled the ball he should seek for the information from the players.

I find no trouble in agreeing with scorers who have played the game, but have found those who learned to score by book and observation hard on players, and ever anxious to credit errors, even when difficult plays were missed.

Outfielders should never be credited with an error unless when they get two hands on the ball. As they use gloves, there should be no excuse for muffing line drives. When the outfields are rough, considerable leeway should be given when scoring errors on ground balls that pass the fielders while coming in fast to get the ball for a throw to the bases.

Never give an error where a fielder misses a short pick-up, as all balls are supposed to carry the distance aimed at and when they go low or wide the error must go to the player who threw the ball. Where two or more players get mixed up over a slow ground ball, it should go as a base hit, the same as a ball that drops between two fielders.

The pitcher and third baseman are entitled to great leeway as they are close to the batsmen and must face hot shot with little time to figure out the bounds.

Players should not be given errors when they miss a slow ground hit while trying to make a running one-hand play. This is taking chances and should be encouraged.

Infielders playing deep and taking chances should be dealt with leniently, and the same rule should apply to infielders covering bases for a throw, when they drop the ball in a collision with the base runner.

INDIANAPOLIS TEAM, CHAMPIONS AMERICAN ASSOCIATION IN 1908.

THE NATIONAL GAME.

BREITENSTEIN, GRAND OLD MAN OF THE MINORS.

THE ST. LOUIS BOY, WHO ONE DAY PITCHED GREAT BALL FOR THE BROWNS, NOW A SOUTHERN LEAGUE PITCHER AND HOLDS RECORD SIMILAR TO CY YOUNG'S.

They call Cy Young of the Cleveland Americans the most remarkable ball player of the age. I don't think he is. How about Theodore Breitenstein of New Orleans?

Cy Young is a remarkable player. He has been pitching for over 21 years, the greater part of that time in fast company. Old Man's Breitenstein's record as a pitcher is greater by far, to my notion.

Breit, like Cy Young, has been pitching for 21 years. But that's as far as the analogy goes.

Cy Young has never been a has-been. He's pitched practically the same kind of ball—good ball—all these 21 years. He has always taken care of himself, the best of care. Breit has been down-and-out, through, very likely, failure always to take care of himself as Cy Young has.

Theodore Breitenstein was a dead one everybody agreed when the Memphis team of the Southern League signed him in 1902. In his palmy days, he had been worth the $10,000 Cincinnati had paid St. Louis for him, but he had been going

back. He played the last of 1901 in the outfield for St. Paul. He was only a fair outfielder and he was no pitcher at all. He had blown up, the wiseacres said.

Breit turned over a new leaf in the Southern League. He came back, and stayed back until 1907, when, having been taken to New Orleans by Charley Frank, he lost nine of 13 games. He had started to go back again; he had let up on taking care of himself.

It was the outfield for him, his kind friends decided again. But Mister Breitenstein took another brace. The very next year he came back and won 17 out of 23 games. He has stayed back ever since. In 1910, his 21st year on the slab, he lost but 9 of 28 games. This, the pitcher, who in 1901, had lost every one of the measly three games he had been permitted to pitch for St. Louis.

As a sidelight, let me point out that Breit has four no-hit games to his credit in major and bush leagues and that he has pitched more one and two hit games than any other pitcher in any company.

THE OLD PLAYERS.

WHERE A GREAT MANY OF THE PLAYERS WHO WON FAME ON PROFESSIONAL DIAMONDS IN THE DAYS LONG AGO ARE NOW LOCATED.

What has become of the old-time ball players?

Where do they go and what do they do after advancing years and stiffened muscles make them fade from the green sward?

Adrian C. Anson, well and hardy and still a "colt" physically, is in Chicago taking things easily.

James O'Rourke is practicing law in Bridgeport, Conn.

John Montgomery Ward is now a shining member of the New York bar.

Mickey Welch is proprietor of a hotel in Troy.

Tim Keefe is a drummer.

Roger O'Connor is the owner of the Springfield, Mass., club.

Arthur Whitney and John Morrill are drummers for rival sporting goods manufacturers.

Sam Crane writes baseball for a New York newspaper.

George Gore and Charley Jones are on the New York police force.

Joe Hart runs a hotel in Providence.

Jerry Denny has a gentlemen's furnishing goods store in Derby, Conn.

Paul Hines does contracting work in Washington.

Joe Hornung is an assistant ground keeper at the Polo grounds, New York.

Buffington is in the coal business in Fall River, Mass., where also his old catcher, Dr. Gunning, is practicing medicine.

John Manning is ground keeper in Boston. George Wood and Billy Purcell are bookmakers. Dr. Bushong was a prosperous dentist in Brooklyn.

Charley Comiskey is president of the American League Club at Chicago.

Tip O'Neil is "lumbering" in Canada.

The two Gleasons—not Billy of Detroit—are both in the St. Louis Fire Department.

Jake Virtue has charge of the press box at the Athletic grounds.

Jake Rowe was in business in Buffalo, but died this Spring and was buried in St. Louis.

Ed Hanlon is a rich man in Baltimore.

George Meyers is a wealthy real estate operator in Buffalo.

Fred Pfeffer is in business in Chicago.

Ed Dalrymple is in the tobacco business in Denver.

Ed Swartwood has a saloon in Allegheny City, Pa.

Harry Stovey, the greatest base runner the game has ever seen, has a hotel in Clinton, Mass.

Cub Stricker sticks to his milk route and still plays with clubs around Philadelphia.

George Washington Bradley and Buck Weaver are both Philadelphia policemen.

Jack O'Brien was a pressman in Philadelphia until December, 1910, when he died.

Lon Knight is a traveling salesman.

Billy Holbert is a stereotyper and employed on a Philadelphia paper.

Charley Bennett, minus both legs, has a cigar store in Detroit.

Guy Hecker is in business in Oil City.

Pete Browning was proprietor of a saloon in Louisville, Ky., until he died.

Hick Carpenter lives in Cincinnati, where he is in business.

Billy Sunday, the famous base runner, is an evangelist.

Will and Jim White, the famous players, are in the optical business in Buffalo.

John Corkhill and Charlie Fulmer, after getting through with their Cincinnati engagement, both returned to Philadelphia, and the latter was subsequently elected a magistrate.

Bid McPhee was manager of the Cincinnati Club until the latter part of last season.

Charley Snyder has a government position in Washington.

Eddie Cuthbert died in St. Louis and Chief Roseman is a New York fireman.

Charley Jones is a resident of New York City.

Arlie Latham is the coach of the New York National League team.

Bobby Caruthers was umpiring last Summer in the Illinois-Iowa League.

George Wright is living happy and making money in Boston.

Al Reach is a millionaire in Philadelphia.

Jimmy Peoples is living in New York City.

Dick McBride is still alive and well in Philadelphia.

THE SOUTHERN LEAGUE.

IT HAS COME TO THE FRONT LIKE A THOROUGHBRED AND IS NOW ONE OF THE MOST PROSPEROUS ORGANIZATIONS IN THE COUNTRY.

It was only a few years ago that Ted Sullivan went to the Sunny Southland and organized the first baseball organization that ever amounted to much in that country.

The Southern League circuit now includes Atlanta, Birmingham, Chattanooga, Memphis, Montgomery, Mobile, Nashville and New Orleans.

The big jump that baseball has taken in the South cannot be better exploited than by citing the case of Atlanta, Ga.

In 1901 Atlanta's franchise was turned down as a gift—figured as less than nothing by the citizens of the Georgia metropolis. In 1902 Owner Peters of the Selma transferred his franchise over and sold a half interest to Ab Powell for $2,000. So in one year the franchise had moved up from nothing to $4,000. In 1903 Powell bought out Peters' share for $2,500. In 1904 the same owner sold out his interest to the Georgia Street Railway Company for $20,000. This company has erected a ball park and stands that cost above $40,000. If you offered $75,000 today for the entire plant it would be treated as a joke. So from strictly zero in 1901 to $75,000 in 1911 shows in a measure that the game around Atlanta has been taking a few strides of considerable note.

And the same holds true all over the circuit. Where games were played in 1901 before a few hundred people, with rambling structures more upon the order of stables for grandstands, thousands today are filling up-to-date parks that cost young fortunes. Over $40,000 was spent in the park at

Atlanta; nearly $50,000 in New Orleans; Nashville has built a new set of stands and her owners have purchased the playing field. Chattanooga is just completing a modern plant that will range well up into the thousands, while Rick Woodward, a young millionare and keen sportsman of Birmingham, has recently bought that franchise and is planning the erection of a new home for the Barons and their supporters.

Memphis has built a new and commodious set of stands—in fact across the circuit now every modern accomodation has been prepared for the fan flock that has grown from year to year and will continue to grow as the game moves along and the cities increase in population.

For it begins to look as if the circuit had at last settled upon its best membership.

After Atlanta had supplanted Selma and Montgomery secured Chattanooga's franchise, the two weak spots of the league were recognized as Shreveport and Little Rock. Both were game towns, ready to meet all emergencies and fair base ball centers, but the main trouble was that both were off the beaten track and neither was large enough to make up the difference the extra amount of mileage meant. Shreveport was the first to go. The Louisiana township gave way to Mobile, Ala. With the passing of Shreveport, the exit of Little Rock was only a matter of brief time. The Arkansas metropolis at last gave way before Chattanooga and the circuit for the first time since 1901 looks to be settled for a good many years ahead.

WHY DICK COOLEY NEVER HAD ANYTHING TO SAY TO THE UMPIRE.

BEING A YARN INVOLVING JOE CANTILLON WHEN HE CALLED PLAYS IN THE OLD DAYS IN THE NATIONAL LEAGUE.

Dick Cooley, owner of the Salt Lake baseball club, has little sympathy with umpire baiters, although when Dick was in the big leagues he had quite a reputation as one of the worst foes the umpires met on the diamond.

But Dick excuses his faults in this respect on the ground that the umpires of those days were much more tantalizing than the arbiters of the present.

No more bitter feud existed in the big leagues than that between Umpire Joe Cantillon and Dick Cooley. For years they never spoke civilly to each other. Dick tells the story of the final break between Cantillon and himself.

"Cantillon was a good umpire," said

Dick, "but for some reason we were always at outs. Joe didn't like me and I had no use for him. However, we got along passably fair until one day in Chicago when Cantillon played the meanest trick on me that I have ever known an umpire to be guilty of. I suppose the laugh is on me, but at any rate I never got over it, and Cantillon and I have never spoken since.

"I was playing with Boston against Anson's Chicago team. Bill Lange, one of the greatest outfielders who ever lived, was playing center for Anson. I was at bat and caught one squarely on the end and drove the ball on a line to deep center. As I was rounding first, I saw the ball going over Lange's head. I figured it was good for the circuit, so I tore around as hard as I could.

"As I was nearing third I heard Cantillon yell, 'Touch third, you or I'll call you out.' I touched the sack and tore for home. When I was getting near the plate I saw Cantillon running, apparently to make a close decision at the plate. As he came up he yelled, 'Slide!' I slid. Then Cantillon bawled, 'You're out.'

"I jumped up and shouted, 'What; where's the ball?' 'Bill Lange caught it,' said the ump.

"I then found out that while I was running with my head down, confident that I could get around safely, Bill Lange had made a wonderful running and jumping one-hand catch of the ball away back against the fence in deep center and that Cantillon kept me going merely to make a monkey out of me.

"After that we never spoke."

THE McNEARY BROTHERS

HOW THOMAS, JOHN AND FRANK BUILT UP BASEBALL IN ST. LOUIS AND HOW THEY WERE THE FIRST TO SEND A TEAM AWAY ON TOUR FROM THIS CITY.

The McNeary brothers, Thomas, John and Frank, were about the first real builders up of the game of baseball in St. Louis.

Thomas is dead, but John and Frank are still alive and well-to-do business men in St. Louis.

Early in the sixties Thomas McNeary leased a piece of ground at Compton avenue and the Missouri Pacific Railway tracks. He fitted it up for baseball purposes, covering the field with a coat of blue grass and making its surface as level as a billiard table.

Upon this field he placed a team which he called the St. Louis Reds and they played so well that soon the field became known as Red Stocking Park and later Compton Avenue Park.

On this field McNeary gathered in such later famous players as Jimmy Galvin, the great pitcher, Tom Dolan and Tom Sullivan, catchers; Charley Houtz, Arthur Croft, Packie Dillon and Ed Gault, first basemen; Charlie Sweasy, Tom Loftus and Hugh McDonald, second basemen; Danny Morgan, Harry McCaffery and Henry Oberbeck, third basemen; Arthur Redmond and Johnnie Peters, short fielders and John T. Magner, Jack Maher, George Seward and other later great outfielders.

When Tom McNeary died the work of carrying on the park and conducting the team fell on the shoulders of John and Frank McNeary and they did the work well.

The two are now retired business men in St. Louis, living on the sunny side of Easy street and attending the local professional games whenever there is one on tap.

THE GAME IN ENGLAND.

BASEBALL INCREASING ITS AREAS, AND IN RECENT YEARS IT HAS GAINED QUITE A FOOTHOLD IN ENGLAND.

Base ball has taken a firm hold in England it having been introduced there by Newton Crane at one time a well known St. Louis lawyer of the firm of Pattison and Crane.

In the spring of 1911 the base ball season in London was opened by B. Newton Crane now the honorary president of the Baseball Association and now one of the best known American born lawyers in England. Before a good sized crowd he tossed the ball into the Crystal palace grounds and the annual schedule began. Six teams have been formed and play every Saturday in and about London. Baseball is kept alive in England by a few American enthusiasts and by the American colony, which contributes generously towards any deficit that arises.

THE NATIONAL GAME.

JOHN C. CHAPMAN.

THE VETERAN FIELDER OF THE OLD ATLANTICS OF BROOKLYN, STILL HALE AND HEARTY AND HE SPINS A YARN FOR THIS ISSUE OF THE NATIONAL GAME.

John C. Chapman, once famous as the left-fielder of the old Atlantics of Brooklyn, is about the last of the Mohicans.

"Jack" Chapman at least is the only one of the old Atlantics, who now shows up at league meetings when the big base-ball men gather in convention in New York City.

"Jack still lives in Brooklyn, but he spends a great deal of his time on the road traveling for a big New York house.

Despite the fact that he is out of the game, "Jack" Chapman is as great a baseball fan now as he ever was, and he is sought for wherever he goes for talks on the national sport, past present and future. And there isn't a man with great-er fund of reminiscences of the game living today.

"I have read quite a number of stories of late reminiscent of old baseball days, and especially about the Atlantics, but most of them have been somewhat garbled, probably through the wear and tear of time," he said, in course of a fanning bee the other day. "Many things have come under my observation during the long period I have been in the game, and I am free to admit that I have never for a minute lost my love for the sport.

"As a rule, ball players have been very fortunate in escaping accidents when trav-eling. While a few have been injured, there have been some very narrow es-capes from loss of life and injury. In 1868 the first long trip west of the Atlantic Club of Brooklyn was taken. They visited Louisville, Ky., and played what was then known as the Eagle Club, of that city. The next day was an open date and the Atlantics remained over and visited the places of interest in the Falls City. They had about decided to go by boat to Cin-cinnati that night on the large steamer Patrick Rogers. The manager and secre-tary were on their way to the office of the steamboat company to purchase their tickets, when a committee of the leading business men of Louisville met them and persuaded them to have the team remain over, as they had arranged to tender them a banquet and good time that evening.

"The Brooklyn boys were treated hand-somely that night by their Kentucky friends. The next morning the Atlantics left by early train for Cincinnati and that same night the boat Patrick Rogers was burned and many lives were lost, quite a number being drowned in the Ohio River or burned to death. The Atlantic boys first heard of the terrible calamity just before reaching Cincinnati and all declared it was old Atlantic luck again. They were congratulated on their fortun-ate escape by Manager Harry Wright and his men when they reached the Cincinnati ball grounds that day where they met with a great reception from President Champion, Secretary John P. Joyce and the immense crowd that was present.

"On the first long trip of the Atlantics in 1868, they played at Albany, Troy, Utica, Syracuse, Rochester, Buffalo, Cleveland, Toledo, Detroit, Chicago, Rockford, Free-port, Springfield, St. Louis, Indianapolis, Louisville, Cincinnati, Pittsburg and other cities, winning all games but one and that was lost to the Niagara Club, of Buffalo. This Atlantic trip had a great deal to do with building up the game in the West and through New York State. It was the means of a large number of clubs being organized and the game increased rapidly in popularity.

"After playing the Central City Club at Syracuse, the Atlantics left that city on the Western bound train for Buffalo, hav-ing the last car for themselves and their friends. The total number in the party as far as Buffalo was over fifty. When the train was about thirty miles out of Syracuse, the conductor rushed into the players' car saying:

"'Boys, I might have to call on you for help as there are four big toughs coming through the train insulting the passengers and my helpers.'

"He left and returning in a few seconds said: 'Here they come, boys, watch out.'

"In the first seats of the car were sev-eral friends of the Atlantics who were considered very clever with their 'dukes' in those days. Among them were John J. Dwyer, Mike Henry and another good fellow called 'Honest Crowd Smith,' a re-tired butcher. Smith was the first man tackled by the largest of the toughs and 'Honest' landed on the loafer good and hard, knocked him down and jumped on him, while Henry and Dwyer worked on two of the others until they were almost helpless. The intruders saw that they had struck a large sized snag and tried to make their escape through the car to the rear platform. They were met by the rear guard of the Atlantics and received an-other good thrashing. When finally the conductor told the boys that the toughs had received punishment enough the train was stopped and the intruders kicked off the car, much to the delight of the pas-sengers and trainmen who congratulated the Brooklyn boys on their good work. The four bullies pulled themselves to-gether and took to the woods in very bad condition.

"The following day the Atlantics played the Niagara Club at Buffalo and each member of the team pas presented with a large horseshoe of flowers before the game from some unknown person who was on the train during the trouble with the toughs. While the boys appreciated the gifts they voted them bad luck that day, as the game was lost to the Niagaras be-fore the largest attendance ever gathered together in Buffalo up to that time. It was the only game lost by the Atlantics on that long trip. The team at that time was made up of: Mills, catcher; Zettlein, pitcher; Start, first base; Smith, second base; Ferguson, third base; Pierce, short-stop; Chapman, left-field; Crane, center-field, and Pratt, right-field.

"The players and their friends enjoyed good health until they reached St. Louis,

THE NATIONAL GAME.

when several of them were knocked out for a while by drinking too much of the muddy Mississippi water. It was suggested by some would-be doctors in the party that the players drink some of the Western whisky or beer for which St. Louis is noted, but it would not work, as a majority of the team were young men of very temperate habits. However, with a little nursing they were brought around in fairly good condition for the games. They defeated the Empires and the Unions of that city by large scores.

All along the line the team was treated royally and entertained handsomely and the trip was a big success financially.

"During the 60s the Atlantic Club visited several cities in the East, among them Philadelphia, Washington and Boston. In Washington they played on the White House lot in the rear of the President's mansion, which was then the regular ball field. The Washington team was a good one and included some able men, among them Arthur P. Gorman, late Senator from Maryland.

"On their first visit to Boston the Atlantics played a series of games with the Tri Mountains, Lowells of Boston and Harvards. The games were played on the Boston common on the most level part nearest to what is known now as the Public Garden. The left-fielder had about the hardest position to field and he was compelled to chase the ball up a hill. The Tri Mountain fielder had a big day's work, as he was on the hunt for the ball most of the game. The Atlantics won by an immense score. Those of the team still living have never forgotten the hospitable treatment accorded them by their friends during that first visit to the city of culture

"The Atlantics and the Athletics of Philadelphia played some very exciting games together and always attracted very large crowds. In the sixties at one of the games in Philadelphia played on the grounds at Seventeenth street and Columbia avenue, the attendance was enormous. The mass of people outside broke down the fences and rushed on the field, putting an end to the contest that afternoon. A meeting of the two clubs was held that evening at the old American House, when a committee from each club was named and an agreement was made that the clubs should play the following week and the Athletics would put up a 14 foot board fence around their grounds and charge an admission of $1, the Atlantics to receive 50 per cent of the gross receipts.

"The Atlantics lived up to their part of the agreement, returning to Philadelphia and playing the game in the presence of a large attendance, which is saying a great deal for that city is known now as a better money maker at a 25 cent admission. After the game the committees met to make a settlement. The Athletics presented several bills of expense, claiming the Atlantics should pay half of their share of the receipts. This the Brooklyn men very properly refused to do and they declined to take any part of the money on such conditions. The Athletics, however, squared up matters with the Brooklyn boys by visiting the Capitoline grounds in that city later in the season. The

game was played on the Fourth of July, the Athletics agreeing to let the entire receipts go to the home club with one exception of the ground proprietor's share.

"As it turned out, the game paid the Atlantic players well, each one receiving nearly $300 for his share and best of all the Atlantics won the game. The Brooklyn boys were always royally entertained by their friends of the Athletic and Keystone clubs when visiting the City of Brotherly Love.

"The Haymakers of Lansingburg, now Troy, N. Y., on their first visit to New York and Brooklyn, to play the Atlantics and Mutuals, put up at the Grand Central Hotel in Manhattan. On their first day in Gotham they started out early in the morning dressed in their new baseball uniforms, causing a great deal of amusement among the people on Broadway. Despite their verdancy, the Haymakers had a strong team and they made the older clubs hustle to defeat them.

"In 1875 St. Louis had its first big team of professionals, with James H. Lucas, Charles A. Fowle, William Macdonald Spink, Orrick Bishop, Charles H. Turner, Charles C. Maffit, George McManus and other prominent business men of that city at its head. In the Fall of that year, William A. Hurlburt, of the Chicago Club; Charles E. Chase, of the Louisville Club, and Charles A. Fowle, of the St. Louis Club, after many meetings and much scheming, decided on the formation of the National League of Professional Baseball Players. The first meeting of the four Western clubs—Cincinnati, Chicago, Louisville and St. Louis—was held at the Louisville Hotel, and they adjourned to meet in New York the following February, when the Eastern end of the league was made up for their first season in 1876. The three gentleman above named were really the originators of the National League. Charles E. Chase is still living and is a wealthy resident of Louisville, where he is greatly respected.

"In 1877 the Louisville Club played their last game of a long trip to Pittsburg, and several Colonels, being married men, were very anxious to get back to Louisville as soon after the game as possible. They waited on their manager and asked him if they could hurry the game through so as to catch the 6:10 train which reached Louisville very early the following morning. The manager informed them that they must not hurry, but insisted on their playing hard ball and winning the game if possible. He promised them, if successful, they would receive a couple of boxes of the finest cigars that could be found in the City of Smoke. The boys felt sore all through. Still they worked hard and won the game. They received the two boxes of cigars, but were too late for the train and were compelled to go on the 8:30 which reached Louisville a few hours late.

"The 6:10 train they were so anxious to catch was in a bad smashup and the Louisville sleeper was almost a total wreck. Several passengers were killed or injured. When the players learned the terrible news at the station just before reaching the scene of the disaster they were wild with joy to think they had had such a close call. They awoke their man-

402

ager and made him get out of his bunk, whereupon they danced around him like a lot of happy schoolboys and thanked him for their good luck. There was no more sleep for the team that night.

"When the Troy and Buffalo clubs were members of the Eastern League. Buffalo played Troy at West Troy, July 3, 1893. The visiting clubs always stopped in Troy proper, and rode over to the ball ground in a large wagon drawn by four horses. They were compelled to cross the tracks of the Delaware and Hudson Railroad in West Troy. Returning from the game of the above date, the players were singing, as they usually did after winning and nothing was heard of an approaching train until the driver saw it almost upon them: He gave the horses a clip with his whip and they dashed forward, just clearing the tracks as the Saratoga 'flyer' shot by, at a speed of sixty miles an hour. Several of the players jumped from the wagon and were severely hurt. It was a narrow escape from death, and it was many hours before the Bisons recovered from the shock.

"In the early Spring of 1890 the new Louisville team, champions of the American Association, were all in the Buckingham Theater, in Louisville, on the evening of the terrible cyclone, the path of which was only three squares from the playhouse. It was the most destructive tornado that ever visited that section of the country. Over 100 lives were lost, and the damage to property was enormous. Had the old Buckingham been in its path, it would surely have been demolished and that Louisville ball team buried or blown into the Ohio River.

"The following morning a bright little fellow, about 14 years old, and lame, called at the hotel and persuaded the manager of the club to engage him as a mascot, saying that he was at the Buckingham the evening previous with the ball team and he thought his presence was good luck and saved them from all danger. He was positive they would surely win the championship if he could act as mascot during the season. He was engaged, and after a series of practice games he informed the manager. 'They will land the pennant sure; watch them,' and he christened them the 'Cyclones of Kentucky.' He proved to be a real mascot, and Louisville did win out. They played Brooklyn, winners of the National League pennant, a tie for the world's championship that Fall. The deciding game was not played, owing to the cold and disagreeable weather. The 'Cyclone Mascot' of 1890 is now the treasurer of one of the largest theaters in New York City, and is very popular with the theatrical profession.

"Most ball players are very superstitious and the Louisville Club had a bunch of them in 1890. While visiting St. Louis to play a series of games, the first day going out to the ball grounds, the 'bus overtook a long funeral on Grand avenue going in the direction of the ball park. The driver of the wagon was told to hurry and get ahead of the funeral or they would lose the game, sure. He tried his best, but when half way up the line one of his horses fell and was so severely injured that he could not proceed. As the

ball ground was only four squares away the players started on a run, but before they reached the park the hearse had passed. Louisville lost the game that afternoon by a score of 10 to 0, and the cry was, 'I told you so.' Chris Von der Ahe was happy that evening, but it was a different story the next two days.

"In 1887 the Buffalo and Syracuse clubs were playing a game at Syracuse. No runs had been scored up to the eleventh inning. Buffalo had the last turn at bat and with two men out John Fanning, one of the pitchers, with two strikes called on him, lined out the next ball to right field. It shot through a chicken hole in the fence and Fanning made a circuit of the bases winning the game for Buffalo, 1 to 0.

"One of the greatest games ever played with the largest attendance in Brooklyn was the Atlantic-Cincinnati game on the Capitoline ground on June 14, 1870. It created more excitement than any game that was ever played in this city. The Atlantic players divided their share of the receipts, each man receiving $364 for his work that afternoon. It was the first time an admission fee of 50 cents was charged at the Capitoline Grounds. The Cincinnati Club insisted on the increase of price, while the Atlantics were much opposed to it. Sooner that not play the game the Brooklyn team agreed to the Cincinnati figure. The Red Stockings share of the receipts went into the club treasury. The Atlantic players always took care of their end of the money.

"The Cincinnatis had not lost a game from the Fall of 1868 up to the time they met the Atlantics, going through the season of 1869 without a defeat. The Atlantics were the last to defeat them in 1868 and the first in 1870, and in this later game the Atlantics were victorious by the score of 8 to 7 in an eleven inning game.

"At the end of the ninth inning of that memorable game the score was a tie and the players left the field thinking the game would be called and played off the following day, as it was an open date. The Cincinnati players, with the exception of Harry Wright, were in their coach and the Atlantic players, with the exception of Captain Ferguson, were in their dressing rooms being rubbed down when Ferguson rushed in and notified his men to get ready to go on the field again, as the umpire, Harry Wright, and himself had decided to play the game out, as there was still time to play several more innings. So the ground was cleared by the 150 policemen present when the teams appeared again and went at it in earnest. At the end of the eleventh inning the Atlantics landed the winning run.

"The army of people present were wild with delight and most of the Atlantic players were carried around the field on the shoulders of their friends. The following are the names and positions of the players who took part in that great game: Cincinnati—Allison, catcher; Brainard, pitcher; Gould, first base; Sweasey, second base; Waterman, third base; George Wright, shortstop; Leonard, left field; Harry Wright, center field; McVey, right field. Atlantic—Ferguson, catcher; Zettlein, pitcher; Stark, first base; Pike, second base; Smith, third base; Pierce, short-stop; Chapman, left field; Hall, center field; McDonald, right field.

The Atlantic team was composed of local players, all born in Brooklyn. The Cincinnati team was a picked one of play-ers from different parts of the country, and really the first big paid professional team. After the game the Atlantic play-ers and their friends gathered at their headquarters down town next to the cor-ner of Boerum place and Fulton street, where the Hall of Records now stands. The mass of people that filled the streets in the vicinity of headquarters that even-ing was great. The cars of the different lines running up Fulton street were blocked until a large number of policemen were sent from the Washington street station house to clear the tracks.

"It seemed more like a political mass meeting. Speeches were made from the windows of the clubhouse by John J. Jacobs, Thomas Faron, Judges Buckley, Hornwell and Walsh, and other noted speakers of that time. The vicinity of the headquarters and the City Hall was ablaze with all kinds of colored fire until a very late hour. The papers announced the next day that Brooklyn was illum-inated that night and Cincinnati was in mourning. The following evening the At-lantics were entertained at a banquet by a number of their friends and each play-er received a handsome present of money in gold for his good work.

"In 1870 the Atlantics defeated the Cin-cinnatis two out of three games played, and it proved the downfall of that great Red Stocking team, which was organized and managed by Harry Wright, one of the most honorable gentlemen ever connected with the game and who had as much to do as any one with building up profes-sional baseball.

"The Capitoline grounds were among the largest in this country and it is very doubtful if any of the present day ball parks are nearly as large. They were bounded by Nostrand, Marcy and Putnam avenues and Halsey street, now one of the finest residential parts of Brooklyn. The blocks from Nostrand to Marcy ave-nue are unusually long. Hancock street and Jefferson avenue now run through that section between Putnam and Halsey.

"The papers generally in those early days of the game gave an account of the attendance much below the actual figures.

There was no padding. Such an attend-ance as that of June 14, 1870, on the Capi-toline grounds probably would be adver-tised to 30,000. The arranging of games and all business, financial and otherwise, was transacted by Ferguson and Chap-man, they acting as managers. The divi-sion of receipts was only among players. The team was captained at different times by Richard Pearce, Charley Smith and Robert Ferguson. Mike Henry, who was an honest, jolly good fellow, looked after the 'gate' and was well remembered by the players for his work. Previous to 1868 the club elected officers every year. William V. Babcock, Fred K. Boughton, Thomas Fassie and others were presidents of the old organization, and it was com-posed of some of Brooklyn's best citi-zens.

"Some of the players of the present day will think it was much easier to play the game in the early days. If anything, it was far more difficult. There was more hard hitting and much more running to do. It is true there is a change in the pitching, but it must be remembered that there is a big difference in the pitching distance. For several years the distance was only 45 feet, while at the present time it is 60 feet 6 inches, a difference of 15 feet 6 inches, which is more favor-able to the present batter, as it gives him a better chance to time the ball pitched or thrown. The ball played with in those days had much life, as it con-tained two and one-half ounces of lively rubber, while at present but one ounce is used. The players used little or no har-ness outside of their flannel suits; now they are well protected with lots of pad-ding, gloves, etc.

"The first big team of the Atlantic Club of Brooklyn prior to 1862 was composed of Boerum, catcher; M. O'Brien, pitcher; John Price, first base; John Oliver, sec-ond base; Smith, third base; Pearce, shortstop; P. O'Brien, left field; Hamil-ton, center field; McMahon and Joe Oliver right field. They played many games in and around Brooklyn and New York and were at the top of the list for several seasons. They are all dead now, with the exception of John Price. Dickey Pearce was the last to go. He died in Brooklyn on September 1, 1909.

"It is my sincere wish," said Mr. Chap-man in conclusion, "that the game will be kept clean and long continue to be the national game of America."

THE NATIONAL GAME.

THE NATIONALS OF WASHINGTON.

A TEAM FROM WHICH AWAY BACK IN THE SIXTIES WAS GRADUATED SEVERAL OF THE MOST WIDELY KNOWN PROFESSIONAL PLAYERS IN AMERICA.

The Nationals of Washington were one of the first really great baseball teams.

From their ranks were graduated many players who afterwards became famous in the professional field.

Amateur baseball rose to a very proud pisition in Washington about 1867, chiefly through the efforts of a certain young Mr. Gorman, who turns out, on investigation, to be none other than the late Arthur Pue Gorman.

By his energy and guidance the old Nationals, that were organized in 1859, rose to be justly styled the "champions of the South." All baseball was amateur, or was supposed to be until the Cincinnati Red Stockings appeared as the first team of regular salaried players in 1869. For that reason, and because the game had been greatly disturbed by the civil war, the year 1867 may be taken as a starting point in an account of the development of the game in Washington.

The leading teams of 1867 were the Nationals, organized in 1859, and the Olympics, who organized in 1865. Beside these there were many junior teams, such as the Jeffersons that date from 1864; Capitals, Continentals, Empires, Gymnastics, Interiors, Potomacs, Unions, Actives of Capitol Hill, Creightons of the Second Ward, Junior Nationals of North Washington, Eagles of the West End, Trinity of Georgetown and Aloysius of the Northeast.

In the earliest days the great battlefield for opposing teams was the White Lot, where for several years, through the indulgence of the president, spectators often crowded to see a match game.

And this might have gone on for many years longer but for the vociferous demonstrations of the rooters at a famous game between the Actives and the Eagles in 1867 when the din of cowbells so exasperated Col. William G. Moore, secretary of President Andrew Johnson, that the privilege was withdrawn at the end of the season.

The ground down there went by the name of the Union grounds; but early in 1867 the Nationals had supplied new grounds for their games at Fifteenth and S streets northwest, and it was here that the big games were played.

It was in 1867, too, that the Nationals undertook their great tour of the West,

and came back with a record of having beaten every team that they played against, excepting only one. They bore all the expenses personally, some $3,000, as no gate receipts were taken at any of their games. But the great measure of the value of their trip was the impetus that their superior playing gave to the game in the towns that they visited for from that day there was a great revival of baseball and a study of improved methods all through that section.

It is not too much to claim as one of the direct results of the Nationals' trip that the great Red Stockings of Cincinnati, that almost immediately became the first club in the country, owed very much of their development to the visit of the Washington team.

The Nationals in that year were composed of W. F. Williams, pitcher, law student; F. P. Norton, catcher, treasury clerk; G. A. E. Fletcher, first base, clerk in third auditor's office; N. C. McLean, outfielder, clerk, third auditor's office; E. A. Parker, left field, Internal Revenue Department; E. G. Smith, shortstop, clerk, fourth auditor's office; S. L. Studley, right field, clerk, treasury; H. W. Berthrong, center field, clerk, comptroller of currency; George Wright, second base, clerk, 238 Pennsylvania avenue; A. V. Robinson, clerk; George H. Fox, third base, Georgetown College.

The trip took the greater part of July, 1867. At Columbus, Ohio, they met the Capitols, and the score was: Nationals, 90; Capitols, 10. At Cincinnati they played the Buckeyes, the best team in Southern Ohio, and the score was Nationals, 88; Buckeyes, 12. They met the Louisville Club and the score was, Nationals, 83; Louisville, 21. At Indianapolis they played the Western with a score of Nationals, 106; Western, 21. At St. Louis they played the Unions of that town and the score was Nationals, 106; Unions, 26. Here, too, they met the Empires, the crack St. Louis team, and the score read, Nationals, 53; Empires, 26. Then on to Chicago, where, in a great game on July 25, they met their only defeat at the hands of the Forest City Club of Rockford, Ill., where the score was: Forest City, 29; Nationals, 23. But two days after they met the Excelsiors of Chicago, that was conceded to be the greatest team in all that region, and the score was: Nationals, 49; Excelsiors, 4.

THE BASEBALL BLUE BOOK.

IT IS A VOLUME SPLENDIDLY GOTTEN UP BY LOUIS HEILBRONER, WELL KNOWN IN THE BASEBALL WORLD, AND IT CONTAINS INFORMATION SUCH AS NO ONE INTERESTED IN BASEBALL SHOULD BE WITHOUT.

There is no book published of more value to baseball officials and players than the Baseball Blue Book of 1911, gotten out by Louis Heilbroner of Fort Wayne, Indiana.

The book, in fact, is invaluable to any one connected with the game.

It contains among other things: Directory of all Leagues, Directory of all Clubs, Directory of League Cities, Directory of Colleges, Official Schedules of all Leagues, Classification of Leagues, Opening and Closing Dates of all Leagues, The National Agreement, National Commission Rules,

National Association Rules, National Association Board Rules, Major League Purchasing and Drafting Rules, Minor League Purchasing and Drafting Rules, Salary Limit Rules of Leagues, Waiver Rules of Leagues, Population of League Cities, Officers and Members of the Baseball Writers' Association of America and other specific information.

It is a book that no president, manager or baseball player should be without.

THE FIRST BASEBALL GAMES IN ST. LOUIS.

A GENTLEMAN FROM HIGHWOOD NEW JERSEY, SHEDS SOME LIGHT ON THAT SORT OF THING.

After the first copies of The National Game reached the East there was much comment on its contents and many a controversy took place as to the real merit of the book.

These resulted in the writing of many letters, some praising the book and others abusing it. One of the most interesting of these letters was the following which sheds renewed light on the early days of the game in St. Louis:

Highwood, New Jersey,
June 5, 1911.

Alfred H. Spink,
    Author The National Game,
    St. Louis, Mo.,

Dear Sir—One of the reporters of "The Standard Union" of Brooklyn, N. Y., showed me a few days ago a book written by you entitled the history of baseball.

To start at the commencement of the game in its first introduction into Missouri I would refer you to the files of "The Missouri Democrat" for the Winter of 1859 and 1860, wherein you will find published "the rules of the game," also a diagram showing the field and the position of each player made from a rough sketch I gave to Mr. McKee and Fishback, the publishers, or to Mr. Houser, at that time their bookkeeper, cashier and confidential office man (and, by the way, a mighty fine young man).

At this same time I was organizing the first baseball club, "The Cyclone," which name was suggested by one of its members, Mr. Whitney, of the Boatmen's Savings Bank.

Other members of "The Cyclone" were John Riggin, Wm. Charles and Orvill Mathews (the latter the late Commodore Mathews of the U. S. Navy), John Prather, Fred Benton, (later a captain under Gen. Custer), Mr. Fullerton, (later a General, U. S. A.), Mr. Alfred Berenda and his brother, Mr. Ferd Garesche, Mr. Charles Kearney, (son of Gen. Kearney), Mr. Edward Bredell, Jr., and a number of other young men of St. Louis.

Soon after the organization of "The Cyclone" several others were started, viz: "Morning Stars," "The Empire," "The Commercial" and later on several others.

The first match game played between the Mississippi River and the Rocky Mountains, (if not to the Pacific Coast), was between "The Cyclone" and "The Morning Stars" and was played in 1860,

just back of the Old Fair Grounds in North St. Louis, "The Morning Stars" winning the game," the score of the game I now have. It is 50 years old, and the ball used in that first match game was for years used as the championship trophy, it going from one club to the other, and the last the writer ever heard of it, it was in possession of the Empire Club. I personally sent to New York for the ball to be used in this first match, and after the game it was gilded in gold and lettered with the score of the game.

"The Morning Star Club" was a "town ball" club and played from 5 a. m. to 6 a. m. on Tuesday and Friday mornings in "Carr's Park," but after considerable urging and coaxing on my part they passed a resolution at one of their meetings that they would try the national rules for one morning if I would coach them, or more properly, teach them, which I consented to do if they would agree to stick to it for the full hour without "kicking," for as I told them they would not like it until after playing it for a sufficient length of time to become familiar with some of its fine points, all of which they agreed to and kept their word like good fellows as they were, but in ten minutes I could see most of them were disgusted, yet they would not go back on their word and stuck to it for their hour's play. At the breaking up of the game to go home they asked me if I would coach them one more morning as they began to "kindy like it." I was on hand their next play day, or rather play morning at 5. Result they never played "town ball" after that second inning and in their first match, as stated above, "waxed" my own club. I could give you many incidents up to the breaking out of the civil war and the disbanding of "The Cyclone" by its members taking part on one side or the other.

Hoping you will excuse my intruding with these little facts in regard to early ball playing in St. Louis, I am,

Yours Respectfully
Merritt W. Griswold.

P. S.—Although I am now in my 77th year, I take just as much interest in that splendid game as when a kid at school in old Chautauqua Co., New York, or when a member of the "Putnams" of Brooklyn, in 1857 and the "Hiawathas" of the same place in 1858-59 in which latter year I went to St. Louis.

INDEX

A page number in bold indicates that the page contains a photograph. A page number in italics indicates that the page contains a biographical sketch of a player, manager, club president or owner, league president, or baseball writer.

Many names of individuals were misspelled or incorrect in the text. The correct name is used in the index, with the incorrect version following in brackets. Nicknames and identifying information are in parentheses.

This index was prepared by Skip McAfee of the Bibliography Committee, Society for American Baseball Research.

Names

Abbaticchio [Abbatichio], Ed, *191*, 203
Abell (Brooklyn NL co-owner), 293
Abstein, Bill, 172, *172*, 243
Adams, Babe, *119–20*, **121**, 142, 242, 293
Adams, D. L., 58
Addy, Bob, **7**
Ade, George, 331
Akers, Tom, *325*
Albee, E. F., 294
Alexander, Nin, *94*, **113**
Allen (Detroit pitcher), 138
Allen, Frederick, *94*
Allen, Ned, 152
Allison, Andy, 170
Allison, Douglas, 6
Altrock, Nick, *120*
Ames, Leon (Red), *120*
Anderson, John, 111
Andrews, Tom, *325*

Anson, Adrian (Cap), **xxiii**, 19, 23–24, 66, 70, *172–73*, 177–78, 206, 294, 300–301, 306, 322–23, 387–88, 398
Archer, Jimmy, 94, *94–95*, **117**, 323
Arellanes, Frank, *120*
Armour, Bill, **xxxviii**, 32, 271, *380–81*
Aschenbach, Charles, *191*
Atkins, Frank (Tommy), *120*
Austin, Jimmy, 112, *208*
Austin, Sam, *325*

Babcock, William V., 404
Backman [Bachman], Lester, *120*
Bader, Art, 238, *258*, *260*, **273**
Bader, Herman, **225**, 238, 260
Bailey, Bill, *120*, *122*, 222
Baker, Frank (Home Run), *208*, 285, 302, 323
Baker, George, 25, **25**, 95

Subjects